The Art of Poetry:

A Treasury of Contemporary Verse

**Edited, with introduction, index
and biographical sketches**

By

JOHN FROST

And the staff of the American Poetry Association

THE AMERICAN POETRY ASSOCIATION
Santa Cruz, California
1985

INTRODUCTION

When we first conceived **The Art of Poetry**, we hoped for an outpouring of poetry which would fill this volume with as great a variety of themes and topics as contemporary writers of verse are exploring. I am pleased to say that our hopes were realized. In this book, I have had the privilege of reading, selecting, and editing a dramatic range of contemporary poetry.

We were impressed not only with the diversity of work we received, but also with the way poets from different backgrounds and different parts of the world all joined together to contribute to this effort. We received the work of poets from literally every corner of the globe.

I speak for all the editors when I say that reading and reviewing the work we received was a rare privilege. This is our first edition of **The Art of Poetry** and, as with all new projects, we weren't sure what to expect. However, all of our editors commented on how impressed they were with the work received. We feel both honored and humbled by the trust and confidence poets have placed in us to review what are often very personal statements. We have done our best to fulfill that trust.

I believe the success of this book shows even more than ever that poetry today is healthy and vibrant. People from all over the world and from all walks of life are creating verse and sharing it with each other.

I am extremely pleased to present to you **The Art of Poetry: A Treasury of Contemporary Verse**. We of the American Poetry Association trust you will enjoy reading it as much as we enjoyed reading and producing it.

John Frost

John Frost
Chief Editor
Santa Cruz, California
August 2, 1985

A Note on the Illustrations

In this volume we are featuring famous prints by great artists of the world. Included are Albrecht Dürer, 1471-1528; Rembrandt Harmensz van Rijn, 1606-1669; William Hogarth, 1697-1764; William Blake, 1757-1827; Katsushika Hokusai, 1760-1849; James Abbott McNeill Whistler, 1834-1903; Winslow Homer, 1836-1910; and Paul Gauguin, 1848-1903.

We hope these illustrations will enhance the reader's enjoyment of this volume of poetry.

Index of Prize Winners

A TALK WITH MR. D.

Slipping through my hands like sand,
The granules of love turned into the emptiness of a memory.
The pain was so intense, I thought I could never love again,
And life was only full of unhappiness and the destitution of loneliness.
With bitterness and a pessimistic attitude, I learned to play the game like a professional,
Refusing to release any emotion, in fear of further torture to an already existing wound.
Time went by and unknown to myself, I started collecting granules of love,
Until love was conceived within my heart once again.
A tragic awakening, only to find out the game was over,
And the fact that I had lost renewed the pain I had known for so long.
Razor blades, an abundance of drugs, a loaded pistol and a rope that fit snug,
Followed me dancing around my existence.
In my deepest depression, I needed a friend,
And there appeared, in what I thought was a dream,
A stranger in the form of a man.
He told me he loved me, that he would never let me down,
He said, he was forever, as his compassion persuaded me to take a few more pills.
Seems we've met before and he replied,
"I've been with you since the day you were born."
Then I asked, "What is your name?"
He said, "They call me Mr. D."
What does the "D" stand for?
Laughing in a haunting manner, he began to fade,
Uttering death, dea-th, d-eath.
Please Don't Leave Me!
                    Please Don't Leave Me!
                             Please.

   Rondall Lawrence Smith

I *AM* MY BROTHER'S KEEPER

For those starving in Ethiopia, this, is for you. For those in America who sent money to pay their heavenly dues — what is life? What is truth?

The lies get deeper — yet, I *am* my brother's keeper.

For those in Poland, this, is for you. Communism and unemployment *both* embrace you. You wonder where the ideals are — at the point of a gun. I thought with Communism, the people are number one?

The lies get deeper — yet, I *am* my brother's keeper.

For those in Ireland, this, is for you. You hate the British — yes, that is true. They are only there to protect, guide and save you from yourselves. They have no interest in dominating or restraining you — is *this*, not true?

The lies get deeper — yet, I *am* my brother's keeper.

For those in South America, this, is for you. You receive guns, instead of food; and yet, each day there is a new coup — will the red flag show the truth? On your knees to pray; more children will die today. Yet, their *souls* will be saved — at least that is what the missionary said.

The lies get deeper — yet, I *am* my brother's keeper.

For those of this world, this, is for you.
How long can we last, if we choose to blast and kill, to gain our "skill." To bomb and maim — where do we put the sick and lame?
One day the lies will get too deep,
then there will be no more brothers to keep.
   Tony Bethel

THE VISITOR

I asked Him if He'd come and sit beside me on my bed.
I asked Him if He'd hold my hand and gently stroke my head.
When I arose to ask Him if He'd stay and have some lunch;
I had not much to offer, just a slice of bread, and punch.
And then we talked until He made my troubles melt like snow,
And when He left, I cried, because I found I loved Him so.
I could not say who'd been here, for they'd laugh and think me odd;
But I'd spent my entire day just visiting with God.
   Evelyn Wallace

I SHED MOISTURE

Singing in the northern lands,
Commercials for outstretched hands;
People prone on sand.

T.V. reporters get woesome smiles,
No water for thousands of miles.
No milk for nursing lips.

Hoarse cries through parched lips;
One teaspoon of stale water
Wets a tongue thick with hunger.

Volunteers break under strain;
Ship terminals with no grain
Like the round stomach

The child displays on camera,
Sucking his thumb for saliva;
People choking on sand.

No future for a starving land.
I weep for thirsty man.
   Tim Moorman

THE STARS AND OUR LOVE

On a warm summer night
I sit beneath the stars
thinking of you.
I look up
and what do I see?
I see you and me
holding each other
as if we never wanted to let go.
I tried to tell you
how much I love you.
But I couldn't,
because my love for you
is beyond words.
Then I closed my eyes tightly
and opened them again.
the vision disappeared.
But I still felt two very special
things left that I knew would
last forever,
they were,
the stars and our love.
   Tracey Novak

THE WORLD OF A PUPPET

Puppet on a string only
   I can work your life.
A gentle tug brings you to life.
   Your legs and arms
   Work just like mine,
   but only to be bound
   by a mere thread.
The strings that I hold
   Are your only life
   line into my world.
Your heart has been carefully
   carved through my
   hands, only to teach
   you love and kindness.
   To never show hatred
   or anger like I the
   imperfect human.
Through you unknown world
   of wood and strings
   maybe you can
   teach me and hold
   my strings as I
   walk the path of life.
   Julie Burch-Landers

HOPE

we bear the stale, strung-out days
dry
thirsting for events
not bitter resolutions

to calculate boredom
and measure its vacuity
is part of unliving a life
wound back to a fresh potential
before wrong turnings

now we are lost
not in woods or mazes
but under street lights
casting obvious patterns
from old decisions
our masks hiding the confusion —
a summer's thirst
to love
again

Mary Wren Small

HUGGABLE, LOVEABLE TEDDY BEAR

Little Teddy Bear round and fluffy,
All that cotton to make you stuffy.
Twinkling eyes made of glass,
Quite a look of first class,
Make you number one care,
MY LOVEABLE, HUGGABLE TEDDY BEAR.

When the nights get dark and scary,
I hug my huggable, loveable teddy bear.
Try to tell my troubles to him,
But I know, that he really can't listen.
It's just that it seems to help,
to talk to my teddy by myself,
My LOVEABLE, HUGGABLE TEDDY BEAR.

When I am angry and upset,
He seems to smile without fret
Hasn't got a worry, or a care
With all the toys to compare,
I pick my HUGGABLE, LOVEABLE TEDDY BEAR.

Jeanne McGuinness

RUNNING IN THE WIND

Outdoors! Playing kickball
All day long
Singing,
Singing a song
. . . having fun
All of a sudden
There's no sun
The wind
Blows hard:
There's no fog to blind
Us on the way, Lord:
We've learned so thankfully, sir
It's going to rain . . .
Finishly finir, fullishly malaisy;
Not of vainglory
And idiosyncrasy:
God bless our salvaged sane story

Of renaissanced saluted minds
Running in the wind.

Beverly Ann Hightower

THE LOVE AND UNDERSTANDING

I saw the battered body of a child in the street.
He was undernourished — He couldn't even eat.
I knew he'd never known what it felt like to be loved.
I wondered what this tiny child had done.

He didn't say a word — He couldn't even speak.
The boy was dressed in tattered clothes; his eyes, too tired to sleep.
He looked around the alley to see he was alone,
And wondered if he'd ever find his home.

The troubled little boy of, maybe, four-odd years,
Was taken in an ambulance; his eyes were filled with tears.
Arriving at the hospital, an inch within his life,
He only hoped his mom would be all right.

Children find it in their hearts to understand bad days.
It's funny how they love their parents, anyway.
It's that love and understanding of a child that's been abused
That's enough to really tear my heart in two.

Too many kids are beaten. Too many children cry.
Too many are misunderstood. And far too many die.
But children should be happy. Or don't they have the right
For a chance to live a long and happy life?

Doreen Campbell

THE CROSS IS MANY THINGS —

It stands as the highest pinnacle of hope
    And the lowest point in man's inhumanity to man,
    It involves a love so great that it overshadowed
    The humiliating mockery of a taunting angry crowd.

You must accept the Cross or reject it —
    It speaks a universal language and is understood by all nations.
    You can grope in its shadow or walk in its light,
    It is death in all its horror, it is life in all its splendor —

It is a tragedy glorified to a living symbol.
    Whatever happens, the Cross is indestructible —
    If every Cross in the world were burned
    The Cross would still live in the hearts of men.

You must see it in all its ugliness,
    You must see it in all its beauty,
    You must feel it shake your very soul,
    You must emerge emotionally drained and atomically powered.

The Cross, in its final message, leads one into the unknown,
    It transcends time and space — It is life after life.
    The Way is open . . . are you able to hang on that Cross with Jesus
    And say, "Father, into Thy hands I commend my spirit?"

Naomi Burnett McGhee

MOM REMEMBERED

She sat beside the window, wistfully alone,
this caring, giving woman loved by all she's known.
She saw two kittens playing across a neighbor's lawn.
Their frolicking brought laughter; her spirit wasn't gone.
I watched, my heart grew heavy, gripped by numbing fear.
The shocking news re-echoed; she won't live out the year.
Her mind still keen and cheerful, her body languished there
warmed by rays of sunlight while dozing in her chair.
My thoughts returned to childhood, where home meant warmth and love,
her stamina and courage emanated from above.
Her talents were astounding, her limitations few.
The virtue in her conduct consistently showed through.
Our home was built on kindness, and nurtured with great pride.
Thoughts of self or malice were quickly put aside.
Her legacy was wisdom, tolerance and wit.
No one ever heard her gripe; no one saw her quit.
She's gone, but not forgotten. Someday I'll see her there,
skipping through the meadows; a garland in her hair.

Edith M. Chandler

GOD'S GIFTS

One of God's gifts is the heavenly lights
One shines at day one beams at night
God also shows me that He cares
When I need Him He's always there
Another is His great gift of life
He helps me with my pain and strife
His greatest gift of all is love
That showers down from the heavens above.

Barbara Ann Cyrier

CURTAIN CALL

Another day
a sky brand-new
sunrise dawning later
yes, winter time is due
darkness soon gives way to gray
touching horizon's view
as God draws up His curtain
sheers of pink and lavender hue

Jaclyn Templeton Marvin

FAREWELL OLD YEAR

Farewell, old year, we'll say goodbye
Twelve months ago, you were so bright.
You're dimmer now 'neath a misty sky
Farewell old year, we'll say goodbye.
I'll watch you as you fade and die
While the new year comes in to night.
Farewell, old year, we'll say goodbye
Twelve months ago you were so bright.

Anna Reeves Hoyer

LITTLE SLEEPING VILLAGE

Little sleeping village,
Ignore the thunderstorm,
Let the rain water your gardens,
Let the wind sweep the sky,
Keep your lights glowing,
Keep a warm fire burning,
For in the morning it will be over,
And you can speak of peaceful dreams.

Denise Fronko

DESIRE

A sunset hot, hot like fire,
Aroused passions filled with desire.

Lips parted, nectar sweet,
A touch so tender, eyes that meet.

The pulse quickens, bodies entwined,
Then fulfillment, like sweet sweet wine.

Lee Lashbrook

A RAINBOW'S . . .

A rainbow's a myriad
Of God's precious jewels,
Kissed by the sun's dancing rays:
Reflecting hope for this moment,
The promise of tomorrow,
And blest yesterdays.

Brenda Irene Helling

LANGUAGE
THE SECRET =

Music is based on whole tones, semitones and quavers.
A tone and a half, half tone, and a quaver is not a rarity.
The same applies to semi quavers, which can be divided more and more.
The smaller the piece, more difficult to play, more difficult to understand.

We call it virtuoso, perfection or art = Mozart, Toys Symphony
41 Concerto in D Major, why not a genius, perfection, the best?
Who can define perfection in a changing universe? Woolfi? Gang?

Mozart Ama + Deus. God loving (Latin) animal. You like the meaning?
Or this: Moza in Hebrew language = Origin of Art, Don Giovanni, or
Figaro's Marriage by the French Molière (Softman).
Can we afford to be soft and singing when we have to work?

Art? What exactly is art? Artisan = working human being
Music an art? Maybe. The sound. The speech everybody speaks.
The only difference between a man and an animal = language.
                                                    ida
Prokofiev = Pro + Kof (Monkey in Hebrew) monkey-minded man.

Ida Fawers

THANK GOD
BIRDS AREN'T IN POLITICS

The lovely trill of a bird is a thrill to start your day aright.
Its lilting song fills all the world with melody — out of sight!
Nothing will interrupt its day or stop its happy message,
Full-throated melody to pray, giving thanks for all its blessings.

Thank God birds aren't in politics, beset by smiles and frowns,
Every day a guessing day of how to please the town — .
No free moment the candidate finds to "whistle a happy tune,"
Give speeches here — shake hands there, launching his shot to the moon!

So I'm "for the birds." If demeaning that sounds,
It won't bother me at all,
So long as I hear their songs in my ear
Overriding the world's noisy call.

I must confess, it relieves all stress from problems that often worry.
That happy trill, the day's greatest thrill wipes them away in a hurry.
Stay free, little bird, completely, stay free and sing on melodiously.
And if you ever need a vote — YOU CAN DEPEND ON *ME!*

Cee Cee

THE LONELY OLD MAN
Dedicated: To My Father, Henry Floyd Tarver

The old man sat at the window,
Of his little house upon the hill,
He thought of the years that had passed,
And brushed the dust from the window sill,
He listened to the sound of the cars passing, on the road below,
Wishing he was young again and had some place to go,
He'd raised a big family, with the help of his wife,
Only to end up here, leading this lonely life,
The kids had all grown up, some moved away,
He wished they'd come to visit today,
His wife had died and left him, a few years ago,
Oh, how it hurt him, he still misses her so,
His mind drifted as he remembered, the good things they'd shared,
If only once again, he could tell her, how much he'd cared,
His sad blue eyes watched the birds darting, in the magnolia tree,
He watched his old dog scratching at a flea,
His world consisted of the house and his dog in the yard,
Loneliness sure has a way of making, an old man tired,
As he drifted off to sleep, his heart filled with sorrow,
His only thoughts were, maybe someone will visit tomorrow.

Cissy Rucker Long

ALL TEA TASTES THE SAME

From the televison chair, I move
    To make tea — and I think of her.
    Channel 4 — A remake of
A remake of a glass menagerie.

The kettle whistle shrieks.

    I've no photos of her — yes I have;
    A vision that I play with in my memory.
    I can't blow out my candles —
    Let alone hers.

I reach for the crying tea bag.

    What's on television?
    A rape? A romance?

    What's at the theatre?
    Absurd? Farce?

    I know and write them all —
    Another item for my resumé.
    I can't blow out my candles —
    Let alone hers.

    I reach for the tea cup.
        All tea tastes the same.

Robert A. Southern

A MOTHER'S NINE MONTHS

A mother knows,
A mother shows,
Her love, her forgiveness
Sometimes a little shyness

A mother thinks,
A mother winks,
When she knows you've made a mistake,
But knows you're all right and gives you a break.

A mother cares,
A mother bears,
Her child for nine months,
Hard and long nine months.

But when you make a mistake
She'll know, show forgive and forget.
She'll care, bear those hard nine months.
just to show you she loves you,
And needs you.

A mother knows,
A mother thinks,
A mother shows,
A mother winks,

All for that same child, she bore for nine months,
A hard and long nine months.

Nathalie Morin

I PRAY FOR YOU

I pray for you when the day is new,
And I pray for you when the day is through.
I pray for you when we talk on the phone,
I pray for you when I'm all alone.
I pray for your safety during a long trip,
I pray for you when you let things slip.
I pray for you to heaven above,
But mostly, I pray for you because you're the
    one I love.

Andrea Lawrence

SINGER

His failing body is positioned for him
against the brick building
like some Fisher stereo system.

Over a soiled T-shirt, an oil-darkened
grey suit with padding adds substance.
A leaning white stick rests against bricks.

Sitting or standing, pick-like fingers
blend steel strings, echoing sounds.
A guitar case lies open inviting criticisms.

Two floors up his husky voice leads
a fixed stare from a shrinking room
as he booms about "The Road to Sham Ba La."

Philip Mancini

THE APPENDECTOMY

Agonizing pain sears the right side
Skilled hands say surgery must be quick
The hospital bed then count to ten backwards
Wheeled no longer awake
Into the surgery room
Mask and gloves and bright light
The surgeon says it will be a right lateral incision
There is a flash of steel
Clamps are applied
The much scarred distorted appendix is removed
Now sutures quickly made
Back to the hospital bed
An awakening and no pain
A nourishing meal
A walk to the bathroom
Three days and home

Rita Maria Brown

THE FLOW

The past was strewn with unexpected rocks
And with the wheels I often wrecked on them.
The future was an empty river bed
In which a mighty flood rolled down on me.
It lifted and tumbled me,
Gasping and struggling,
Into a land I could not have imagined,
Dropping me into a field that is mine to tend.
My goals are now defined, my mission clear,
My tasks imposed, my powers all assigned,
And through it all one truth is clear to see:
One cannot know the shape that life will be.

Bea Liu

A FAIRY TALE

Once upon a time there was a little girl,
She loved the forest and claimed the trees,
The leaves on the trees were her fantasies,
Each leaf hung like a shiny, bright pearl,
The leaves never fell, the girl was ill, years passed . . .
Slowly one by one the leaves began to descend,
The girl was older and could no longer pretend,
In the girl's place was a lady and she cried at last,
Feverishly her fantasy leaves she tried to reattach,
The leaves turned to dust and blew away — free,
The lady was left with a silent naked tree,
Together they stood alone . . . a match,
Slowly a smile, a thought, Spring, new leaves, mother earth,
Start over, this time the leaves will be reality,
They will change with the seasons, sameness, serenity,
Growth is taking place, the lady will be well . . . rebirth!

Mary Ann Gilliam

TWO-YEAR OLD GRANDDAUGHTER

She has hair as soft as the down of a baby duck
She loves to ride with her Daddy in his pick-up
Her hair is the color of sunbeams on a summer day,
and with the dogs and cats and all animals she loves to
play.
Her cheeks are the color of a pink rose and she has a
little button of a nose.

She runs and hops and skips and she hugs me, and
kisses me with her tiny lips
She touches my face with her tiny fingertips
She dances around with glee and tells me, she loves
Grammy.
She often asks me for a treat and looks up at me with
her big blue eyes and smiles so sweet.
I know God sent her from up above to teach me more
about real love.
I love this tiny pearl and love to hear her say she's
Grammy's girl.

Margaret Whitsell Moen

MONUMENTS

Inscribed within a stony brook, enduring, characterized as
Having some certain achievements, like role models for
Future generations.
Although I may be gone, *my* river will remain as a monument
To my life; intensity, as the flow of a current; that all
Reality is objective, and, that knowledge is based on events.
What is done!
It wasn't *easy:* Progressing to master craftsman; Child
Development graduate, having it *all* go down the tubes —
Because of poor health.
I have known accomplishments, smooth movement; having very
Special meanings, deeply felt emotions; functional and —
Purposeful.
I listen — now — to my calling of immediate short-term goals;
Elevating human qualities: needs. Mine!
Now — comes "poetry," aesthetically moving. Beautiful!
Bodacious — instead of a lonely nook; not washed out, or,
Simply — passed by.
I *will* remain — uncompromisingly — me . . .

James Hilton

HERITAGE

A cold mist rolls out from whither amidst,
The desolate, barren trees.
Surrounded, unseen, in the center of this
Rests a house, whose memories weep.
The wind howls through the tattered old frame
As it shakily stands alone.
Forgotten through years, and the passage of time,
Had it really been somebody's home?
Once, there was laughter, and love, all within.
Once, it stood tall with pride.
It housed generations, of the man who had built it,
But too soon, was forgotten aside.
And all that remain are the memories,
Of people, who once lived within.
This ragged old house, has a story, it longs to relive.
But people pass by,
With unseeing eyes,
And don't know where heritage lies.
A lonely old house, is left, to crumble and die.

J. A. Sanderson

GREENER PASTURES

There is a tale often told
Of a foolish man and his quest for gold.
He left his pastures bright and green,
For him life's riches lay in other pastures unseen.

He wandered far about the land
Seeking buried treasures and honors grand.
But what he found was not what he sought.
His search proved fruitless and was for naught.

Tired and wearied he returned to claim
Those pastures green he once disclaimed.
And older, wiser man he had become.
Peace and happiness were now his welcome.

If a moral to the story be,
It should be plain for all to see.
Look not for greener pastures on a distant shore,
For life's riches can be found at our own back door.

H. Hampton Bell

THE BACKBONE OF TIME

I search the drift of desert land
for a fossil embedded ten thousand years,
recognize the found face in the shape of a skull
as my own; my cautious hands wipe the sands
from corrupted teeth and a twisted jaw.
Skilled and scientific, they clean the cranium
of lesser stones with print-perfect centipedes,
small artifacts in yellowed eye sockets.

Except the skull stares now above its ribs
with no subtle call for silent mirrors,
its trace of strangeness entering
the thin bones of my hands.
Whispers echo through angles of the skeleton,
a distant, dry correspondence
elusive as wind on brown grass, on bone,
shadows dusting stirred, vacant emblems,
the quiet transcription of a giant scroll
impressed like a backbone on all time.

Cody Caudron

FENCES

A lady I know has a fence 'round her yard
    to keep corner-cutters, trespassers, out.
I have one, too;
    to lean on.

A couple I know has a fence 'round the yard
    to keep the dog, the children, in.
I have one, too;
    to chat over.

A neighbor I know has a fence 'round his yard
    to keep the dogs, the children, OUT.
I have one, too;
    to stack wood by.

Some folks I *don't* know have a fence 'round their yard
    to keep people out, to block the view, IN.
I have one, too;
    to grow flowers along.

Lois F. Askren

MY GARDEN

At the dawn, the garden's walls surround me.
Everywhere I look — north,.south, east, west,
The luscious green towers before me
Blocking the sights and sounds of beyond.
All I see is the placid, peaceful garden
Full of flowers, color and sweet innocence.

As the day wears on, the feeling of content I once felt
For my garden fades.
It is overcome by a stronger feeling,
One intense longing for
The sights and sounds of the unseen.

Towards dusk, I venture, carefully,
Out of my garden.
I see blurs of color, hear loud noises,
Frightened, I turn to run
Back to the placid, sweetness I'd left.
But, as I whirl around, I see,
The gate is closed.

Cynthia Miller

JESUS MY BEST FRIEND

Jesus is the Lord of my life,
Unto no other will I bow down,
Only Jesus who is one with God
Can reward me with my jeweled crown,
He sits on His throne at the right hand of God,
Receiving constant praise from the angels above,
Exalted above all others
For His faithful unselfish love;
Accused of evil under Pontius Pilate,
Our Lord suffered and was crucified,
"I am King of the Jews" was written
On the cross where Jesus died;
But death is only for the flesh
And life a reward to the righteous,
As Jesus Christ ascended into heaven
He took God's spiritual likeness;
He is Wonderful, Counselor and Prince of Peace,
He is the Alpha and the Omega, the beginning and the end,
He is the Bright and Morning Star,
He is Jesus my best friend.

Lisa DiStacio

DAYS OF SPLENDOR

The days were clad in splendor . . .
          Those days we spent together!
The star-filled nights of ecstasy . . .
          Seemed just made for you and me!
Your touch was like the breath of spring . . .
          Awakening my very being!
But now you're gone, sweet love of mine . . .
          Beyond all reach of future time,
Yet gratitude fills my heart and mind . . .
          For I was blessed, and you were mine!
Bitterness? 'Tis not for me . . .
          For I hold dear your memory!
I know that I shall love again . . .
          Another good and wonderful man.
He'll make his own place in my heart . . .
          And life anew, within, will start.·
New dawns will be all clad in splendor . . .
          Just as those we spent together,
With star-filled nights of ecstasy . . .
          As those when you awakened me!

Joy Hayes Christian

GYPSY SILVER

Floating, weightless in the stillness of the
Morning sunlight . . . fleeing from the puff of
Silken slivers of silver . . . a gypsy . . .
No need to hurry . . . with no place to go . . .
Coming from nowhere . . . expelled from the womb
Of the mother milkweed pod which had formed
Its umbilical cord ever since the
First tiny seedling had emerged from its
Underground haven. No longer did it
Need the succulent milk of the milkweed's
Breast! No moisture in its dry pod to hold
It fast . . . Freedom at last to sail in the
Current of a summer breeze . . . or to be
Blown by a happy youngster's lips! Perhaps
It would ascend into heaven itself,
As its Creator had done two thousand
Years ago! Or would it be best to rest
First in the warm earth . . . and be born again?

Fern Johnson

YOUR FACE VALUE

The soul of a man is a secret place
that contains his hopes and fears.
But it cries out when his face expresses a thought
and causes small lines to appear.

Be the cries sweet or sour they occur by the hour
by the man's and not God's will.
And soon the day comes when a value appears
on a face where time had stood still.

When sour, it's a frown that's been turned down
and that's all that needs to be said.
But when sweet it's a smile, in any language it's styled
an invitation to chat for awhile.

And soon with some luck it will grow and burst
into laughter, the joy of all men.
Then pierce the heart of an old or new friend
and back into a soul again.

So smile darn you smile when you're sad or in doubt
or when worried what life's all about.
And your face will adorn your heart rarely mourn
and your soul only sweetly cry out.

Dr. J. Henry Hoffman

WAVE ON THE WALL

     In a soothing gingerbread hotel
Somewhere under tangling moonshadows
I surrender my phoenix for love's bizarre sweet
Like a thirsty lion lapping at the sea —

     Laughing under silk, yielding, passion stings
Time wings love into a liberation of tears, caress;
There's a wave on the wall . . . memories, but not mine.

     I think of a tangible paradise home,
Where whirling misty blue water somersaults
Backwards like a dance, until the alchemy of tides
Roars into a dragon's bellowing scream —

     Waves . . . liquid mystery rippling from darkness
Where comfort can be water twisting around feet,
While two dry bone voyagers seek love all yes.

     Days pass, suddenly I am in a picture of waves
Running down the beach celebrating dawn
With no distance between us
Until tangling moonshadows
Are just waves
Waves . . .

Arthur T. Wilson

DEAR DADDY

Dear Daddy you're so far away
            but yet you are so near.
As I bend down beside your grave
            you're whispering in my ear.

When I was just a little girl
            Daddy you were so near.
You taught me things for me to keep
            within my soul so dear.

As I grew older the distance grew
            we seemed to drift apart.
We kept our feelings deep inside
            instead of sharing our heart.

Too soon the time did slip away
            and you were gone from me.
To see the distance we grew apart
            "DEATH . . . IT HAD TO BE."

Bonnie Lee

COME FOLLOW ME

To Peter and Andrew
And John by the sea
And to James, John's brother,
He said, "Come follow me"

No place to lay my head
No tent to live in
Sojourner on this earth
He is my living

Move when the trumpet sounds
Go when the cloud lifts
Fire by night before me
When he says, "Come follow me"

Come follow me
Come follow me
No place to call my own
But come follow me

Sally Nickerson

FACING DEATH

Sixteen hollow steps
He walks his life away
He steps into the room
Is this his final day?

Thoughts of murder
Have faded from his head
He sits in grim silence
Today he'll be dead

The clock ticks away
An empty silence fills the air
He offers no resistance
As they strap him to the chair

No reflections of days long gone
Ahead he stares and begins to wait
Lightning Strikes — A phone rings
The call is much too late

Robert Anthony Wilde

SEED OF INTENSITY

You have become a brook to me,
Gently melting toward the sea.
I feel the beauty of depth and height,
In you, the pure; simplicity of life.
Obstacles to stumble, to search the way,
To accept to smile, in gentle sway.
I hear you speak in wordless strife,
Your message of love, the color of life.
You are a spirit so true and free,
To show the way, the blind to see.
Brought but once to the mountaintop,
I felt your breath, then it stopped.
To die so many deaths anew,
To be reborn; yet so few.
In sorrow I was brought,
Through love I was taught,
Then once again I am born
To meaning and purpose through a storm.
As a tree in its seasons,
A seed is planted for passion and reason.

Carole April Binette

BINETTE, CAROLE APRIL. Born: Ipswich, Massachusetts, December 11; Raised Hamilton, Massachusetts and Seabrook Beach, New Hampshire; Living in Maui for the last ten years; Single; Education: Courses at University of New Hampshire and Maui Community College; Occupation: Self-employed, stock market and other investments; Poetry: 'Remain Open,' *American Poetry Anthology,* November 1984; 'Love Song,' *Hearts On Fire, Volume II,* February 1985; 'Child of Love,' 'A Plea for Humanity,' and 'Man Creates,' *American Poetry Showcase,* June 1985; all published by American Poetry Association; Comments: *I love to write what I think and feel about nature — a higher power — in a living relationship with man.*

PIGEONS
HONORABLE MENTION

I like pigeons
Because they don't fly South
For the Winter
Pigeons wear red shoes
But I've never seen two
With the same coat

Scott Hirtenstein

LEARNING
Dedicated to my grandson, Derek Jackson

"What is that grandma?"
My small grandson asked.
At first I did not see why . . .
He had asked that of me.

"That."
He pointed to a fluttering
White butterfly.
"It's a little white piece of paper!"
I heard him cry.

"No . . . it moves so fast,
And lightly in the air."
"Look!
It stopped on that yellow flower there."

Clinging like a feather.
white as a new fallen snowflake.
Resting with its wings quivering.
What miracles of miracles God does make.

A streak of white drifting in the wind.
Purity . . . passing by.
Yes, he discovered
One of God's small miracles . . .
A white butterfly.

Jane Luciene Nowak

WHEN JESUS DIED

When Jesus died upon the cross
The world looked on in awe,
They didn't know He'd live again
His pain was all they saw.

They didn't know He died for them
To rescue them from sin
They only saw His nail-pierced hands
His mother weeps for Him.

They only saw the darkness fall
upon the gathered throng,
They only heard the Savior's
            voice
when He cried "It is done."

They only saw Him laid to rest
In Joseph's brand-new tomb.
They didn't know His bonds would
            burst
To push away the gloom.

They only saw the empty tomb
The graveclothes lying there.
They didn't know that He had
            risen
Victorious o'er sin and death.

Marcia R. Morris

TAFT POINT, ELEVATION 7,503

Swan dive down
through fissures steep
a human body hurtling, like
an arrow loosed from a bow,
is all I can think of at the edge
of cliff sides swooping upward to,
and then creating a platform
diving board of stone
no springboard, but if
a foot should slip — whoosh
down to Yosemite Valley floor.

Joyce B. Eggleston

SEEING CHILDREN PLAY

It was not a good day to be playing outside,
the weather was blustery and cold.
But children seem to have the knack of
enjoying any day.
So there they were, playing in the park
on the swings and a circular slide,
with lots of room to race around, side by side.

There was also a hill, somewhat of a climb,
so they tumbled down and laughed aloud
each time they rolled into another,
and then just sat and talked.
I watched from my window as they played,
then dreamed for awhile of days gone by
when, that same kind of life was mine.

Elizabeth Long

THROUGH THE VEIL

Someday the day will come
When you will see the truth.
Darkness will end for you and
Peace will come to your troubled soul.
Death is not an end but a beginning,
Passing through the veil beyond the bars,
Escaping from the prison called your mind.
You've undertaken the journey to the heartland,
The journey with no destination.
Backwards, forwards, in and out.
The road is narrow and leads to unknown vistas.
Arise, the time is here.
Arise and fly away, o bird in the bamboo cage.

The Master calls you.

Stevan Edward Grant

DELUSION

The sweet smell of her early spring flowers,
sail through the breeze like music.
Her house stands tall and gallantry strong,
it holds all the beauty within it.
Days pass as easy as a sailing ship,
with no winds to tear her sails.
Her life seems to flow like a well-written book,
no hidden stories untold.
She retires at night with her man at her side,
they share all the love that's within them.
He tells her she need not ever worry,
as life will always be easy.

Then the lights come on as you're sitting there,
and you realize you're just at the movies.

Nancy A. Hughes

HAND IN HAND FALL

A wine-chilled mist drifts
its ice-laced fingers
through our clothes against our skin,
against the patent-leather leaves
of curled pastel,
all wind shivered
Autumn downed.

And the while,
above this cast-off gown
of wet beauty pressing on softly bent grasses,
our thoughts enticed
get tease-tangled
sodden down,
the leaves too chill to oblige.

A. L. Fuger

TIME, TIME, TIME
BARS, BARS, BARS!

O, it's time, time, time
To a harsh, echoic rhyme
To the grinding captivation
And the binding condemnation
     Of the bars —
To the banging and the clanging of the bars!

O, it's time, time, time
In a paranoiac clime
In an awful agitation
And a crowded crimination
     Of the bars —
To the bumping and the thumping of the bars!

O, it's time, time, time
For the doing of the crime
O the bitter rumination
From the men's incarceration
     By the bars —
By the slamming and the damning of the bars,
     bars, bars, bars! bars!

James C. Robison

LAVENDER HORSES AT DUSK
(In Memory of a Childhood)

8TH PLACE

Daddy came in from the fields
leading the two gray horses.
Collin and I waited at the well while
Daddy led the tired old grays
to the water trough.
He hugged us close then drank long from
the dipper. He smelled of sweat, of love.
Cricket voices filled the thickening,
mauve-powdered dusk.
The purring cat, with a kitten still hanging
to a teat, rubbed against Daddy's legs.
A stillness, louder than the cat's mew or
the cricket sounds, caressed the air.
Mama called from the kitchen door that
supper was on the table,
and Daddy led the horses into the lot then
washed up on the back porch.
For one magic moment longer, Collin and I
stayed behind to watch the soft dusk polish
the old plow horses with lavender.

Rosa Nelle Anderson

GOT TO WORK

9TH PLACE

Man, this has got to work.
You get all strung-out on the everyday
Until all those cats
Get on your nerves
And your brain don't function right.
You got to find a way out,
But the walls give you nowhere to go.
Man, I hope this works.

Then when it all seems to be closin' down,
You get this idea
Like a freight train come rollin'
Down a track
Poundin' in your brain.
Then all these cats come crawlin' around
Talkin' that same old trash and you ain't listenin'.
You've placed it on the line, bet is down,
And you say, "Man I got to go."
There's no road back.
Man, I hope this works.

Evan Blakely

WIND

Introverted secret keeper
Blowing where you will,
Caressing gently, with
Impersonal intimacies,
Innuendos of excitement.

Inscrutable and fickle
Feminine entity,
Do you understand yourself
Smelling of both
Spring and Death?

Are you angry when you rage,
Or in love with the passion of power?
Searching intuitively
In innocent ignorance of any effect
Except, relief of repressed forces.

Unfeeling cause of pain and awe,
Creator of vastnesses
On soil and within soul,
I experience the truth of powerlessness
In your wake.

Mary Hugh McGowen, OSB

THE BALLOON MAN

He sells them all
the bright, the blue
and colors of a pastel hue.

The little round
and jolly guy
with childlike gleam in his eyes.

The young and old alike will stare,
their faces wrapped in
delight so rare,
at his antics as he blows
and blows
    and blows
        and blows
until he stops, before it goes
    POW!

He keeps them all
in a big tight crowd.
You can see them any windy day,
when like a rainbow-colored cloud
the fat balloon man floats away.

Sandy Gecs

MY CLOUDS

I know not
    What I'm looking at,
Except it suddenly
    Takes on form.

My mind's eye says
    a galloping cat
Chasing a horde
    That doesn't conform;

Of miscellaneous things,
    Maybe fish and fowl,
That smile me wide
    With nary a scowl.

This respite brief
    Unwinds with ease —
Is there for all
    Just, if you please.

Zachary Sosis

MY CREED

When I awake in the morning,
I thank God for the gift of a day,
And ask that I might be guided,
In knowing His will, to obey.
His kindness and great understanding
Have helped me to grow as I should,
To treat others as I'd like to be treated,
To be kind and to seek others' good.
This is a design for contentment.
I don't always achieve that estate,
But I do try to avoid blind resentment,
And that ugly affliction called Hate.
For life is too short and too precious
To allow those limiting thoughts,
We must see broad horizons
For with Christ's blood we are bought.

Jewel Holbert

RAINBOWS

The rainbow has disappeared
    and gone
    as broken promises
    lie in a
    lonely grave

The rain has passed
    the sun shines
    once more
    but the rainbows
    are no more

Josephine Copenhaver Thomas

ADMIRATION

As I sit across the room
I look up and admire you from afar
You move with grace and style
You look just like a star
A glow penetrates around you
Touching everything within its reach
You speak with such knowledge
And sometimes even teach
Sometimes you act like a child,
teasing and laughing with glee
Your face lights up with pleasure
For everyone to see
Because you're unique I love you
Because you're special we share
Because you're my mom I adore you
Because you're my friend I care

Jody D. Davis

YOU ARE . . .

I wanted to know you for so long.
Seeking you in ideas, as the sum of
ideas, I lost my way.

I wanted to hear your voice, know
your word. Thinking of you as final
conclusion, caused my delay.

You are not that which can be thought.
You are not grasped as this or that nor
one object or another.

But in some unexplainable way, without
needing to ask how, I know that you are
the holy, wholly "other"!

Theresa M. Falgiatore

PROCRASTINATION

When you're feeling simply guilty
And your hope has lost its way,
You'll find the word 'procrastination'
Has a thing or two to say

If everyone would stop avoiding
Things they ought to do,
There would be much less confusion
And much more accomplished too

For example: Doing household chores
Can really be some fun,
If you put your heart into it
Soon the work will all be done

Try whistling while you work
Or turn your hi-fi up full blast,
Learn to tango with your broomstick
Time will pass by much too fast

So keep in mind this message
And the word 'procrastination,'
You'll find life is much worth living
By this wondrous fascination

Ellen L. Joaquin

TODAY'S HEARTACHES ARE TOMORROW'S PASSIONS

To feel the feelings
of loneliness,
of sorrow,
the bittersweet remembrance,
the fear of each tomorrow.
To fight
the world,
the worries, the pain,
To hold your head high,
and to know that sooner or later,
it is you, for all you lose,
that will in the end gain,
the strength,
the courage,
all the determination you need,
to survive,
to stay alive,
and most of all succeed.

Emily Neiland

HE DID IT FOR ME

We were just friends,
Like any two friends you've seen.
Little did I know that someday
He would die for me.

It started under an oak;
We were drinking iced tea,
When a young man came along,
And threatened my friend and me.

My friend attacked the man,
Not knowing of his gun,
And before the man shot my friend,
My friend told me to run.

Frightened and very shocked,
I did as he had said,
And I feared when the shot went off,
That my friend would be dead.

If we'd been more than friends,
As he wanted us to be,
We may have been somewhere else,
Instead of under that oak tree.

Reneé Weidert

TIME MUST GO ON

I

Time after time I miss you, you have been gone,
    At times it seems that I'm all alone.
My heart is like a memory,
    Until the time you will be here with me.

II

If I should lose you! I wonder if I could go on.
    I've got to be brave and so strong.
I've got to face what may come my way,
    We will be together some day.

III

It will not be too bad for me,
    With my son's company.
As for the future, I've got to see,
    And not to worry about things that will be.

IV

My heart will find a way to sing,
    Bringing the sunshine of spring.
Listen to the whisper of love,
    And feel the rain drops from above.

Florence Irene Kelly

BROTHER
HONORABLE MENTION

His black eyes shine. Grease and Ball-bearings.
He tucks a wad of tobacco under his lip and spits.
A glob of juice lingers.

I remember my hands lifted his wriggling body
from its crib, the white sleeper, laced at the hem,
beat its violent pulse.

We hike by the creek. Between us the wide years,
like summer cornfields, flutter. He kicks
at clumps of dirt, declares tomorrow he'll be first
to see the checkered flag.

He grumbles, his motorcycle breaks down just
when he's leading. Pride huskies his voice;
he has fractured his collarbone three times.

I squint at bruised and cut fingers, that huge
adolescent hand, and wonder, what if I touched him?

The dark sky heaves. A raindrop startles my cheek.
We sprint past rows of mobile homes. Aluminum walls loom.
Lightning magnifies the trees.

He grabs my hand, "Don't want you to get wet,"
he laughs, "This way's faster."

Rhonda Harris

THE MILL

The old mill is still and silent and white,
A snowfall covered it during the night.
Its ancient boards and once busy wheel
Are contained in pure white blanketed seal.

Its windows look out on a fairy tale scene,
A vision so lovely — it must be a dream.
For overnight scraggly tree limbs changed shape
Into white-clothed gracefulness with rhinestone drape.

Kathryn S. Dance

WILL YOU BE MY VALENTINE?

After two months of marriage together,
Keeping me steady through very rocky weather,
After all the things that have happened to us,
We've managed to stay sane without a lot of fuss.
I want you to know how much I love you dear,
I want you to feel it, I want you to hear
These words I am saying that are coming from my heart,
With every breath I breathe, from every part.
What was it that our vows did say?
When we said them to each other on our wedding day?
To love each other 'til death do us part.
Together with these words our life did start.
And now we share our first Valentine's Day,
And I find I have a lot to say.
Will you hold me and will you show me, love
Tell me you'll stay by me, love.
This is our beginning, a start of a new life.
I can happily say, I'm proud to be your wife.
So without further ado, I'm asking you at this time,
If you love me darling, will you be my valentine?

Laurel D. Smith

I LOVE YOU, SON

My eyes filled with tears of joy
    yesterday —
God blessed me with a baby boy.
The precious time I spent with you
    yesterday —
was a real dream come true.

I do miss watching you grow
    today —
and all the love I have to show.
Even though we are miles apart
    today —
a part of you lives in my heart.

Trust in me that my love for you will last
    tomorrow —
and not to be a forgotten memory of my past.
I hope you share the same happiness I've known
    tomorrow —
when you have a son of your own.

Warren L. Bjelkevig

ON THE WAY TO O.A.
HONORABLE MENTION

she walks down the street
and laughter daintily follows her,
dashing in and out of
hydrants and evergreens.

when she turns there are people
who are minding their business
as if she is to them, no
nuisance or bother.

when she begins to walk
once again the laughter follows her,
creeping upon her to skim 300 pounds of
lumps and crevices.

she turns but no minds are upon her,
so when she walks, she scoops
the laughter from her body, dumping it in the
trashcan or gutter.

Cynthia D. Green

FOR PAUL . . .
THIS DREAMER'S HEART

I had to say goodbye again,
Here I sit with my old guitar,
Trying to make this tune sound right,
And wondering where you are.

I said, I love you very much,
But you don't believe it's true,
Life doesn't mean as much anymore,
. . . It's so empty without you.

I tried in every way I could,
To try to make you see,
How much I care about you,
and how much you mean to me.

I still have all the memories,
and I'll never let them go,
The time we've shared together,
Means more than you'll ever know.

Although we are from different worlds,
. . . A universe apart,
You'll always be the only man,
to have this dreamer's heart.

Linda Miller

I WANNA CATCH THE WIND

I wanna catch the wind
Catch the wind, catch the wind
To see just where it goes

I wanna catch the wind
Catch the wind, catch the wind
To see just where it blows

I wanna catch the wind
I wanna hold it in my hand
Can the wind blow to a new land

I wanna catch the wind
I wanna hold on to its wings
Can the wind blow through invisible things

I wanna catch the wind
Catch the wind, catch the wind
To see just where it goes

I wanna catch the wind
Catch the wind, catch the wind
To see just where it blows

I wanna catch the wind
I wanna catch the wind

Lucian Martin

WAITING FOR YOU

You have gone away, but I still feel
The love, the coming together of hearts
And the warm whispers as we part
The sadness and happiness all in one
As each day drifted into night.

And so here I sit remembering
All that was and hope to be
Listening to the peaceful breeze
swirling through the trees
Waiting, hoping, and remembering
For the day to come when we shall be one.

Marilee R. Bateman

THE ROAD

Lonely, I drive down the road
and meet a car, now and again
it's raining, but the man on the radio,
he says, it's going to stop
but at my age, I don't really care
I drive alone
now in the big city
although there are many cars.
No one here knows how to drive
Just look at this mess.
look at all the soft drink trucks
lined up in a row.
again, I'm alone on the highway
out on the lone prairie, green
look at all the fences lining the road
they keep me from the green
I wish I were a race car driver
driving a test car
over a rough terrain
with no destination.

Bruce L. Ostman

AMERICAN POETS

This is to all the American
poets

We are all dreamers and we
know it.

If you do not have hope, you
have nothing
We're all full of imaginary
stuffing
Give thanks to the things that
give inspiration
A bubbling brook or even inflation
We write about the words of depression,
love and joy
using the words as a toy
They're the key to making our dreams
come true
But my inspiration comes straight
from you

Clara Faye Verkler

TIME

Flowing back upon itself
  like a neverending river
    emptying into an infinite sea
  where waves break
    e n d l e s s l y
  on an eternal shore
Time passes through the eons
  hidden in the mists
    of past
      and future.
Our presence is but a speck of foam
  upon the sand
    of that immortal shore
Yet without our lives
  to create that foam
All our futures
  would cease to exist
And thus in insignificance
  we control
    the destiny of time.

Lynn Cawthra

MAN'S LAST JOURNEY

If man could somehow find a way
to journey light years far
clear across the universe
to reach most distant stars

and having reached out farther
than he's ever gone before
would his journey find a purpose
in the things he's looking for

If he could reach the outer limits
where he had never been
would he make a great discovery
as his journey neared the end

and having crossed the universe
a million years from home
would all the light years traveled
still find him all alone

If this were man's last journey
to discover all he can
would the stars, he hoped to conquer
lead him back, where he began

Bruce Luedeman

EMPTY HOPES IN SIGHT

Love cries throughout the air,
the hope of life is drawing near.
I stagger along and there
I see your gentle eyes looking
down on me. I don't think
twice to capture the light, to
feel your presence in the
tunnel of life. I anxiously
give my heart and my soul.
But only to await, as your
heart turns cold. I blindly
ignore the facts as they come,
I excuse your mistakes for
we all make some. Mine
is the biggest for others to
see . . .
    . . . For I am in love with
only memories.

Tammy Paulk

FROM MY WINDOW

I stared out from my window
I watched the stillness of the night

I saw a lantern flicker on
It helped provide the evening light

I watched the trees sway back and forth
To the rhythm of the wind

I saw the people come and go
As the night chills chased them in

I watched the raindrops while they fell
Forming puddles on the ground

I saw the moon when it came out
Casting shadows all around

I stared out from my window
I watched till the morning rolled in

I saw how day overtook the dark
And filled the space where night had been

Ruth Ann Harris

SUPERFLUOUS FLIGHT

Technology's tail,
A gray-line cloud
Dividing the crystal sky
The split forcing nature to sigh.
The center that disjoins
By intended plans or causes that are fortuitous
Should never separate us from the whole
For all of us make it one
It's within our soul.

Boundless beauty to infinity on either side
The division's function is an awareness
We must cogitate
Before the aggregate is severed to die.

The jet continues to soar
Tears flow to my chin,
The tail grows all the more!

Carmine R. Sauchelli

SAUCHELLI, CARMINE R. Born: Newark, New Jersey, 2-6-58; Happily Single; Education: Seton Hall University, B.A., 1980; Occupations: Pit Sorter for U.P.S., and full-time ambition for writing; Comments: *I'm a gavone for eating my thoughts and excreting them onto paper, expressing the simple to complex, reality to fantasy.*

O MASTERS! LET ME BE SEEN FOR MILES!

Theme: Beautification — De Cordova Bend
Speaking to its population

O Masters! Why have you stopped?
My face is an awful sight.
  In the past you've kept me all but clean;
  Hardly a scrap of rubble seen.
Outsiders claimed I'd been scrubbed and mopped.

Won't you take a closer look?
Note how papers lie about.
  One could blame it on new construction;
  Perhaps no one meant destruction.
Far too many liberties you took.

Don't I compliment your dress?
I beam at your pretty things.
  Plant your flowers in my tender skin;
  Sit back and watch them bloom again.
My roadways must not be such a mess.

Tomorrow? Fill it with smiles?
You betcha I'll do my part.
  But first you must throw away my trash;
  Place it so it'll burn to an ash.
O Masters! Let me be seen for miles.

H. R. Krauss

CHILDREN OF A FIGHTING LAND

Tears pour out from every child's eyes,
No more freedom, peace, nor love.
"Help me, please," is one of their sad cries,
Their only help can come from above.

All their parents and these strangers fight
For reasons that are unknown.
The day has turned into the darkest night,
And all chances of peace and freedom are blown.

Their playground has become the dirty street,
and no safe toys have they.
No clothes have they, no shoes to cove their bare feet.
No bed have they upon which to lay.

No food to eat, no shelter in which to stay,
Contaminated water is all they've to drink,
All the love and freedom they had yesterday,
And all of their peace the fighting did sink.

Whether or not tomorrow comes, they do not know.
Come one, let's lend a helping hand,
And happiness for them let's show.
The poor CHILDREN of a FIGHTING LAND.

Ruth E. Roseman

A POET'S DREAM

A poet's dream is to grow a garden
Of beautiful flowers in her audience's minds;
Or to paint an impressive scene
That portrays what's in her heart.

A poet's dream is to share
Her feelings with her audience;
So, they, too, would feel
The sensation of her thrills.

A poet's dream is to lead
Her audience to her avenue,
So, they, too, would view
The beauty out of her window.

A poet's dream is to dream
Of compassion, patience, or love;
A poet's dream is to keep dreaming
And make these dreams become alive.

A poet keeps on dreaming
Of simple or complicated things,
That would serve as inspiration
For her to write lines or verses.

Melecia L. Casabal

DOWNTOWN
HONORABLE MENTION

The lights just came on
The marquee is all lit up.
Cars are passing at
About three per thirty seconds.

It's pretty quiet in here.
The lights are buzzing
Not much other sound
Excepting the ruffling of papers.

I'll probably get into the refrigerator later.
"Let's see is there anything in it?"
(Not much except pop and celery.)

I don't mind working late.
There's less traffic then.

Cecialia Petrea

LOVE

The way birds fly,
And the wind breezes through the trees,
Is the way I wish our sweet love to be,
Undoubtful in our trust,
But yet unknown in our everlasting destiny.

From day to day I think of you countless times,
Thinking how sweet and gentle you are,
And wishing you were by my side,
And wanting to love you in the rain,
While the sun is in full shine,
Just like nature where at first nested time.

Dreams of you I have from daybreak that continue
        at nightfall,
Realizing soon one day we both will have it all,
Joy, love, togetherness and yes nature,
The one which best expresses,
The way we feel for each other,
For GOD only knows I don't ever want another!

Jose Suarez

THE RED BRICK WALLS

The mile long line, of red brick mills,
Standing quietly and abandoned along the river.
Their water wheels silenced long ago.
No plume of smoke from tall chimneys.
Looms and shuttles forever silenced.

The network of canals silently flows,
Passing through the flume, no work to do.
Older persons recall their labors,
In these old red mills of dust and noise.
Young generations cannot imagine,
The sweat and toil of their parents.
A mill comes down to vacate its place,
For a building with a different face.
Another burns and must be razed.
Adding to the dejected look through the haze.
An era is gone from this town.
But, many remember when it was renown.
As the birthplace of what now is known,
The beginning of the Industrial Revolution.

Walter L. Peterson

PLAY WITH ME

As I was doing my work one day,
My son came running to me from his play.
"Mommy, can you stop for a while,
and play with me?" he said with a smile.
With a hug I said, "I'm sorry son.
I can't play now, there's work to be done."

With a sad little frown, he walked away,
And by himself, he began to play.
With a feeling of shame, and a heart full of guilt,
And tears in my eyes I began to wilt.
What chore could be so important today,
That I cannot join my child in his play?

For he's growing so fast, he soon will be grown,
Then me and my chores will be left here alone.
I think today I can forget some tasks,
And play the game that my son asks.
For I too, get pleasure and joy,
Out of the happiness of this little boy!

Frances Lewis

UNREQUITED LOVE

A blossom that briefly bloomed.
A blaze too quickly consumed.

Your love and mine, (mostly mine)
Unripened grapes on the vine,
Given more time,
Could have been sweet, luscious wine.

But now that you're gone,
I'm more than alone.
Not even myself,
Can I call my own.

Without you near, I'm incomplete.
I'm missing a vital part.
When you turned and walked down the street,
Along with you went my heart.

Gary E. Sabbag

SABBAG, GARY EDWARD. Pen name: Gary E. Sabbag; Born: Brookline, Massachusetts, 1-25-52; Married: 1970 to Betsey; 1971 to Cecilia; 1973 to Cammie; 1976 to Karen; 1979 to Lolly; Education: University of New Hampshire, B.S., Business Administration; Occupations: Carni, Cook, Chef, Truck Driver, Citrus Picker, Model, Painter, General Manager; Memberships: Tucson Athletic Club, Dade County Library Cardholder, Poetry: 'Oasis,' *American Poetry Anthology,* 1979; Other Writings: "Stormy Weather," full-length play, 1983; "Myrtle and Chuck," story for children of all ages in verse, 1982; "One Uncreative Night," short story, 1984; "Life Sentence," one-act play, 1982; Themes: *Love is the most common theme in my writing; love and understanding, love and misunderstanding, love in all its varied forms . . .* Comments: *I want to entertain and enlighten; evoke and emote emotion . . . Writing is one way I can contribute to our world; it is one of the noblest occupations of my time and effort . . .*

THE CAT'S MEOW

There's something warm and pleasing in a purr
Emitted either by a him or her
But, fearing fleas, one orders: "Pussy, beat it!"
And kit's response, alas, must be deleted.

Colette Burns

BARRIERS AND DITCHES; DOORS AND BRIDGES

Barriers like mountains are hard to overcome,
But, we have to keep at it or it will never be done.
Barriers are made of our own emotional fears,
We are as scared of them as we are of bears.

I wonder if he noticed the door in the wall,
The one through the barrier that is easy to open.
His heart holds the key, all he needs is three words,
And the door won't swing open without those words.

He's building a ditch; oh, so deep!
He's on that side, and I'm on this side.
This ditch that he's dug has a problem you see,
This ditch has no bridge to get across with you see.

I've built a bridge and he's opened the door,
Those three little words were spoken ashore.
He decided that the barriers and ditches were all man-made,
I decided to teach him that all barriers and ditches have
        doors and bridges.

                 I LOVE YOU!!!

Dianne K. Barth

MOTHER

A mother is a mother only by chance
    but a mother is a friend by choice
Someone who can heal a wound with a kiss
    or be a comfort with the sound of her voice
With her you can talk and laugh and joke
    or dream your wildest dreams
She assures you life won't pass you by
    or come apart at the seams
My mother has been all these things to me
    and more, oh so much more
Not only do I love and respect her
    but she's someone that I adore
Through the years we have grown to be
    alike in so many ways
From the clothes we wear and the thoughts we think
    to the little sayings that we say
I've had friends that have come and gone
    and I've had friends that stay
But my mother will always be my friend
    in a most unique and special way

            I love you with all my heart,
                    Rikki Sue

Rikki Renfro

THE REPENTANT ONE

Striding the length of life's treacherous lane
Seeking a goal of that higher plane

Being careful not to offend or deny
The authority of one who sits on high

Piously I worship on a Sunday morn
Although my attention might be a bit torn

By the pressures of the day, rather than His word
Even though my entry to His kingdom seems assured

How can one so pious ever be denied
Compared to a contrite sinner who knelt and cried

God in His wisdom may forsake my petition
As he did in the biblical rendition

For one who repents is never too late
If the good Lord chooses to elevate

Stanley S. Reyburn

SEASIDE GOOD-BYE!

A burst of yellow rays, warm the sea below,
As I watch from the shore, the serene winds blow,
Sailboats are drifting endlessly in time,
While we share memories over a glass of wine.

The sun sets where the water meets the sky,
We sit on the sand together, you and I,
The moon is shining, it is in full glow,
It will be hard to leave you, but I must go.

We walked on the rocks, as we did in years past,
Both of us realized this was to be our last,
Descending the rocks to the shore,
I looked in your eyes and said, "I love you!" once more.

Michele Pfeffer

OUT THERE ON THE RANGE

There once was a cowboy who wandered the range,
    who kept to himself, folks thought he was strange.
He roamed through the mountains, prairies and plains,
    and could occasionally be seen cussing out the trains.
For they brought in the people, with their families and home,
    to lessen the area he could now roam.
He kept moving on like a calf gone astray,
    ahead of progress he was trying to stay.
Finally one day it caught up with this man,
    everywhere he went they had fenced in the land.
He gave up his riding, his horse and his saddle,
    just to sit on a porch and fight a lonely battle.
So if you see this old cowboy don't think he's strange,
    he's just longing to be out there on the range.

Raleigh E. Green II

ARS POETICA ACCORDING TO THE SAGE

Epic or dithyramb as great or small
having simply to be, at a poem's end
seeming to contemplate before it all
the art of the lyre in springtime's *anwachsend:*
sensing a swelling song in the vibrant strings
of dew's phenomenon: lucent pearls that hung
broidered on fences when the ardent winds
blew in the face of May at break of sun.
Color, voice, rhythm, harmony
just as sages ordered, magnitude
to dramatize and orate tragedy.
Better still a meter understood:
and what is simple diction or iamb
without the fervor of a dithyramb?

Edna Brigham Harrison

A DAY MAY COME

Some day perhaps when woods are bright
And autumn casts her spell upon the land
I shall no longer think of you
Or try to understand.

Nor, when the rain drives o'er the hills
And batters at my doors and heart
Shall I relive with tears and bitter pain
The hour we had to part.

The day may come when winter's snow
Or breath of spring will bring no thought of you
That day may come, but when it does
I know my days of living will be through.

Lucille Dyer

HOMER, Waiting

The gentle breeze of spring
  Touches the leaves
  Swirls my hair
Of all the places we could be
  I'm thankful it is here
The breath of life stirs once again
  In each new budding leaf
The rolling waves come softly
  As they touch against the reef
The season of death is over
Young calves in fields of clover
  Winter snow now ends
It's time for love and laughter
  Running through the grass
Following the dreams we're after
  Hoping it will last
I give to you this season
  Whatever it may bring
Nature gives us her reason
  For loving in the spring.
                Kay Odom

MY REVERIE

Do you remember when you said,
"You fit just like a glove"
The first time that I danced with you,
That's when I fell in love.

The smile and glow upon my face
Showed happiness supreme,
But then you up and went away —
Now it all seems like a dream.

Today, you say you love me
And I do believe it's true;
But the meaning is not quite the same
If I say, "I love you, too."

My feelings now are guarded
To protect me from the pain;
On my heart there is a lock and key
So it will not be hurt again.

What the future holds in store
I really couldn't say;
I only wish it could have been
Like my dreams of yesterday.
                Rosemary Mitchell

THE TIGER LILY

It grew by the side of a garden walk
  in the roots of a cedar tree.
How it came to be in that unique place
  was a mystery to me.

I tried to get the bulb, but
  in safety and secure
It seemed to say, "This is my home
  and here I will endure."

I admired its courage. Though encamped
  beneath the roots in sod,
It pushed its way to the light of day.
  Praises be to God.

Every spring it bloomed anew
  with lovely speckled beauty.
It was a joy of life itself —
  never called a duty.

Like the lily, do your best,
  wherever you may be.
It lived its long and beautiful life
  in the roots of a cedar tree.
                Lillian Hugh Lawson

IN RETROSPECT

I was my Mother's pride and joy
With golden curls and dimples,

But all too soon I grew to be
Tomboy in jeans — no pimples!

I learned to be Dad's right hand man
At cutting wood and haying.
Our homestead chores left little time
For goofing off or playing.

The war years came, we did our best
To feed and clothe the nation.
Two boys were raised, but left the farm
For cities' population.

The years have passed so swiftly by
That I hardly knew they went,
But they have left behind them now
This oldtimer's sad lament.

Although life has been good to me
I've come to this decision,
The things I miss most at this age
Are *memory* and *vision.*
                Louise Freese

ARMENIA'S CRIMSON CROWNS

Drops of morning dew
upon their crimson crowns
make them sparkle
under the warm blue sky.

Their robes of emerald green
caress the earth
and as they rise
silver droplets fall.

Gracefully they dance
among the grass and buttercup,
between blue waters
and snow-capped caravans.

Sweeping their silken robes
past hand-carved stones,
they pause to bow
as ancient bells resound.

The crimson crowns never die.
Though when the season ends
they seem no more,
the flowers soon return
to dance upon the rugged land.
                Knarik O. Meneshian

WORTHY STEPS

He took small steps up a lonely hill
no hesitation was seen by the crowd.
His face set as a flint.
He was paying a price for you and I.
The crowd jeered at him.
His eyes on the distant cross.
Calvary will have its mark on our lives.
Love, forgiveness, eternal life.
Jesus, Our Savior, did not stop climbing.
He was determined to fulfill his promise.
We must take steady small steps
and live in that eternal sacrifice.
Love paid it all.
His worthy steps told for endless time.
                Naomi C. Ricci

ELEGY TO A WANING MOON

It was winter last night
I was cold, with broken voice
Throwing questions to the wind
To silent fields of wheat and barley;
The green motionless crowd
Raised heads, dusted eyes
Pricked up ears
To catch mumbled words
Whirling in the air

It was winter last night
I was alone, under the starry vault
Turning my straw hat over in my hands
Feeling pangs in my veins
Wondering why
A waning moon had walked you away
At dawn of a distant Friday
Through foreign tongues and towns
Miles and miles of highways.

                Silvano Zamaro

LITTLE SOLDIERS

Little soldiers off to war
Not knowing what they're fighting for
Do they know that they may die
Before the sun has reached the sky?

Are they really yet aware
Too many people just don't care
— So many soldiers off to die
— So many mothers yet to cry.

Little soldiers off to war
Stop awhile. Think, "What for?"
It only takes you, every one,
To stop the fight. And peace is won.

Decide today you want to live
Decide to keep life — not to "give"
Little soldiers say, "No more!"
"No more will I go off to war!"

                Rose Hodges

WHY?

Why do things happen to me?
Yes, it happened to me this time;
I cannot eat or sleep
For I was a victim of crime.

More terrible than the sting of death
When a dearly beloved one departs,
Is being a victim of crime;
Created by those who have no heart.

Yet they say crime is on the decrease,
This I cannot believe;
I was a victim of crime
And was not deceived.

Thank God for the blessings
That He bestowed on to me
In a time like this,
Because it could have been worse you see.

                Mrs. Frank J. Dohm

TO PAULA,

This universe inside emptied out by . . .
   . . . the pain, the hurt
    This emptiness filled by you
      Your touch, embrace
        You could fill a thousand Universes
The love and warmth
  Exploding inside
    To fill the void
      Emptiness and despair are exiled
Only tender feelings remain
  for you
    I am complete.

Fred Mastrogiovanni

MASTROGIOVANNI, FRED RICHARD. Born: Vineland, New Jersey, 2-5-65; Education: Attended Rider College, Lawrenceville, New Jersey; Memberships: Volunteer member of the Vineland Fire Department, Board of Directors for the Vineland Jaycees; Awards: untitled poem published in *American Poetry Anthology,* Spring 1983.

YOUR MEMORIES

I am reading your poetry . . .

  Your memories are joyful,
  they brighten your day, you say,
  and germinate the kernels of your mind.

I am learning of your sweetness . . .

  You recall your encounters
  with a God who helped you feel Him All.
  His love you radiate when you smile.

I am learning of your suffering . . .

  The memories of days
  when you begged for an answer
  are recorded in a corner of your mind.

I am admiring the words on your lines . . .

  The terms you use to express your recollections,
  the inflection of your grammar
  transform my unhappy state.

I am conquering myself . . .

  As I understand your feelings
  I overcome my fears . . .

    Someday I'll gain memories of my own!

Ruby M. Shelton

IN MY OLD ST. BERNARD

Sitting by a fireplace in my old St. Bernard
It is a modern one I know
But it reminds me of the real one
We sat before a long time ago.

I can see my mom and dad
Sitting in their place
all the kids on the floor
in front of the old fireplace.

We popped corn and roasted yams
And toasted marshmallows, too
It was a simple way of life
But were things we liked to do.

So, when I speak of the good old days
What I really mean —
I miss that real old fireplace
Where I learned to love and dream
In my old St. Bernard.

Wilson J. Molero

DREAMING

I dream away the day thinking of you
The perfect being to fill my empty spaces
I dream of you, just you
You take me to paradise
You never let me down
You take me wherever I want to go
When I'm dreaming of you

Limitless is my imagination when I'm dreaming of you
I take everyday doings and things and place you among them
Your eyes sparkle and laugh at the people who cannot see you
The one who fills my empty spaces
The one I dream about
The dream I've lost my heart to
Reality does not compare to my dreams of you

But, you don't live in reality, only in my dreams
I look for you every day, but you haven't been found
I'm still looking for the man that has sparkling and laughing
                      eyes, just for me

Eve Boye

*(Two young souls touched, though worlds apart.
    Forsaking not their wanderlust.)*

Far across the universe, he holds my heart
    within his gentle hands.
A warm embrace that draws me ever close to
    sweet memories I once believed were mine.
        But after all was said
        And after all was done
I felt no sad regrets, for love means having
    wisdom to let go.

At night I watch the clear Opiri skies
    for just a fleeting glimpse of
        some familiar battered ship.
Each shooting star reminds me he is gone
    and never coming home, as it dips
        into the inky void below.
        But after all is said
        And after all is done
I give no wistful thoughts to changing any
    moment of the love we shared long past.

Penny J. Taylor

BLOCK ISLAND MORNING

Early in the morning twilight
coffee from the night before wakes me.

Oh, I am home again on Block Island's
fair shore after traveling abroad.

The breeze through the window carries caressing
warmth dampened by scents.

The lone bird starts the morning serenade
which heralds forth a growing pink.

Ocean waves break in the background as yet
another bird begins to sing.

A dark blue sky is silhouetting the town
which I can see from my bed.

My one regret is the light I need to guide
this early morning pen which blots the natural realm.

How easily I call myself the fool to leave this
paradise where mornings are sweet.

No heaven could be fairer than the lush thick sights
and scents of Block Island.

The geese are honking off along the beach and join
my other pretty fellows in welcoming the dawn.

Brett McCabe

FOR ALL THINGS

Thank You for elephants with big floppy ears
For butterflies, chipmunks and dreamy-eyed deers

For whiskery kittens and puppies that wiggle
For circus clowns, monkeys and children that giggle!

Thanks for the sunshine that brightens the day
And night that brings rest from work and play

For rain and snow that replenish the earth
For the promise of spring and its constant rebirth

For babies whose lives have just begun
And for the old folks from whom those lives sprung

Thank You for oak trees and redwoods that tower
For tropical tree-fern and desert wildflower

From deep roaring ocean to high mountain range
From still valley meadow to vast desert plain

You created all things . . . now God, teach us please
To live together in friendship and peace

To care for your world and each creature thereon
As You cared for us, when You sent your Son

A tiny babe from Heaven above
To give us HOPE, and show us LOVE

P. J. Gripon Waldron

THE JUNCTION

I am confronted by this newborn day;
This second chance at life to freely spend —
To waste or wisely use in my own way,
Not knowing what the future may portend.
Oh life, the game of blind man's bluff you play!
Providing us with circumstance to fend;
To keep our heads or lose them as we may,
While always looking for the magic blend
Of worldly knowledge and the higher road
That sympathetic avatars have shown,
Who've personally known the Cosmic Code.
And we, the blind, in faith must journey home.
The morning's forking intersection waits
While Life attends the traps and sets the baits.

Margo Koller

THE LAKE OF DECISION

We, as two, walk down a path of life,
straight and narrow, full of obstacles,
hard to come aft,
yet keeping us close.
As that path approaches
the lake of decision,
each of us takes a separate path.
Both of us share points of doubt.
But that lake is surrounded
by the strength of the earth
on which travels that path of life.
It is up to us to meet
on the other side where the path becomes one —
wide, open, and full of love.

b.e. hargest

BOYISH YOUTH

The sins of youth still daily haunt me.
For when I was a budding boyish youth,
I'd rouse and play the games
That beckoned to me,
Never contemplating how they would come out.
But now I tremble at their final foment
Ever knowing of their solemn wanton grasp.
Alas, asunder in the sins
That I have lived through,
With not a flicker of redemption left
Within my soul.
I now await the hands of that Grim Reaper,
Who comes to harvest
One more of his wayward fruit.

Robert Weetman

REMEMBER WHEN

Time fleetingly escapes our grasp,
Life is passing us much too fast —
Leaving only memories lingering behind,
Perhaps it is only a sign of the times.
As I watched my children playing today
I prayed I'd be here to guide their way.
To warm their hearts, or take their hand,
Our love not lost as time sweeps the sands.
Our gift to our children, love from our hearts.
And if we live it, it will remain once we depart.
For, a gentle hand erases a small child's tears,
As our arms encompass that child, erasing his fears.
GOD please protect them once we no longer can
And help them to always remember when . . .

Sue Ann Myers

AUNT KASSY BABYSITS
for Jamie

I rock you and pink dolly,
sing nighty-night songs,
tuck flannel-covered
diapers in bed.
And
    if just for this night . . .

I give birth
to paper babies
nine months of labor,
one night of pain.
My own creations
may live lifetimes,
die in my time.
I kiss their foreheads,
fold and tuck them
in manilla beds.

Why tonight
do I rock you,
Sing lullabies,
    Sing lullabies . . .

Kathleen A. Wilson

BEYOND THE CLOUD

What is this emptiness,
this longing, this sadness
that comes down like a cloud?

It is a nothingness,
a searching, a yearning
for what I once had been.

From centuries past,
the memory lives
to haunt the striving spirit.

The memory of goals unrealized,
of dreams shattered,
of paths diverted.

What then shall I do
to bring peace to my Soul?
Yes, there's always tomorrow.

A tomorrow with hidden beauty,
with attained goals,
the promise of a rainbow.

Georgia Fox Smith

MYSTERY SURROUNDS ME

Enter the maze of social interaction,
Intertwine personality forces,
Envelop the spirits with doubts,
Encase the minds in steel.

Eagerly we attempt communication;
Encourage each other's hostilities,
Invite malicious barbs,
Ennervate our drive,
Incapacitate mutual yearnings,
Involve destructive oppositions,
Enshrine hearts in pain,
Entertain notions of comraderie.

Mine is not the gift of speech:
Mention my attempts with compassion;
Maintain my equanimity,
Mimic me not.
Mystery surrounds me.

Lisa Ackerman Weyland

ONE LAST FAVOR

When I die I want a casket of pine,
with some extra nails if ya gottem.
'Cause I heard with delight a story last night,
of a man who fell through the bottom.
Well I guess there his body lay,
under a bright and sunny day.
His spirit watched it all from above.
Men standing 'round in tuxedos, women in black dresses and gloves.
When the shock wore off some men coughed,
and others did faint they say.
Then the men looked around, picked him up off the ground,
and continued on their way.
There was a laugh from above at the ones that he loved,
he could truly appreciate their problem.
So when I die I want a casket of pine,
and some extra nails if ya gottem.

Mike Taylor

SEASONS THROUGH MY OAKEN TREE

Oh, seasonally etched window and massive oaken tree, you are my
refuge when I need an escape.
You are my solitude and inspiration, you are my ever-listening ear.
In the frosted window of winter you are quiet stillness and the
burden of mother nature's heavy snow.
In the spring you are bright rays of sunshine the buds promising
heat.
But in the autumn you are my castle of orange and golds, oh, during
this time it is so hard to let you go.
If it wasn't for my seasonal window and my beautiful silent elder,
my mind could not expand to the heights I need to escape the earthly
cares.
So always stay by me oh, mighty tree and always be my strength,
for when my despair becomes too much, let me gaze out my seasonal
window and escape through the carefree arms of my oaken tree.

Shirley Hillhouse

A REVELATION

I wish I were an atheist
But that is not possible, for I see a God,
A perverse and sadistic God;
A God that delights in the suffering of His creations,
A God that holds by a tenuous thread the nuclear Damoclean sword
And wickedly displays not only the sword,
But also the weakness of the thread from which it hangs,
A God that rewards consummate Evil with the pleasures of the world
Paid for with the death and misery of the meek and helpless,
A God that has given us hope for tomorrow
So that we shall be blinded by it,
A God so thoroughly low that to be and do good in spite of Him;
To deny Him and His ways,
Is the ultimate affirmation of, and honor in, existence.

T. A. Lanthier

REMINISCENCE

Light shimmers through the white wine in my glass.
It runs in rivulets down the side, as I swirl the stem in thought.
My mind wanders back to another time . . . Remember?

The fire . . . the wine . . . the sharing of us.
Sitting with you; wrapped so tightly in your arms . . . my head
on your shoulder.
Watching the fire die slowly . . . the flames dancing through the embers.
The smell of the burning juniper . . . your cologne.
Feeling the warmth of our embrace and the glow from the wine.
Time stood still for us in that moment.
I felt safe and content . . . as if the world outside couldn't touch us.
The sweet memory of that moment lingers with me and comes back at times
when the world overwhelms me a little . . .
Like now . . . I miss you . . .

Karen S. Lewis

SOUL-FLIGHT

When your body ceases
and the soul takes flight;
your life's just begun
'cause
you're in the presence
of the One who made
heaven and earth

Then you know
where you fit
in His master plan
and how valuable
you are to the one
who made heaven
and earth

Mark A. Kelchner

FILED UNDER "Y"

Deep within memory's halls confined
Are cobwebbed files stored in my mind
Of dusty scenes where time in repose
Lies catalogued in rows and rows
Of those past moments, noted page by page,
So within each moment we may engage
On any random thought we choose
To conjure up for interviews.

It's here on cloudy afternoons,
I ramble through my memory's rooms
And linger in that mystic maze
Seeking out past sunny days;
Where today's problems fade away —
There is no now; in yesterday.

Delores Hendricks

DENIAL

I sought my fill
    of love and life
Young blood ran full
    and hot
When out of the silence
    in the dark of night
A whisper came "I am"
    I cried out, "You are not!"
Too many loves
    and too much joy
When dying became
    my lot
A voice thundered through
    that final dark
"I am" but you — are not.

M. Mary

MUTUALITY

The hummingbird hovers nearby.
The flower awaits what it will do.
Each has needs the other provides,
Two in need of mutuality.
For one it is the nectar of life;
To the other it will create new life.
The hummingbird moves toward the flower;
It will drink its fill of life.
The inward thrust of its searching beak
Gently disturbing the stamen within,
Causing pollen to loosen and fall
To the pistil waiting below.
An old life has been extended;
A new life has been started.
Mutuality — the key to existence.

Arthur W. Brown

CHANGELESSNESS

Transfixed
into the quietness of the night
comes the harsh wintry air

For a moment
    a shock of freshness

Then

Silence

Wing Hong Loke

I searched for a straight
    and narrow path to tread.
I thought it went up a hill
    so I climbed
but coming down the other side
    I faltered and fled.

There never was a straight
    and narrow path
nor a pointed way
    to where it led.
ILLUSION!

Roni Bell

DESPERATE LADY

Into the land of broken dreams.
Awakened by fears from horrible screams.
Oh, desperate lady, why do you run
Farther away where there's no one?
Your cry for help is so far away.
It's like a shadow in the night,
Which slowly fades away.
Oh, desperate lady, leave the
Darkness behind.
Forget that you had known it,
For oh, sometime.

Barbara Wirkowski

INSPIRATION

I — Imaginitive
N — Nondescriptive
S — Special creative
P — Place
I — In the heart of
R — Reality
A — At the enjoyment
T — To achieve
I — In our souls
O — On which we live, a
N — Notable acknowledgment

Debbie Lee Waite

NONPAREIL

The luminous light
    shimmered
        as the citron
            candle burned.
            The brilliant glow
                was splendorous.
            Red-Orange fire
            against pale wax.
            Blue-tipped flame
            against white wick.
A perfect paragon.

Dixie M. Turner

IF THERE IS A TIME

Alone, I wait.
The time that isn't real passes.
And the distance since our last meeting
Grows longer and longer.

July to December? January?
The two points on my lifetime
Are closer and closer.
Alone, I wait.
And time passes — if there is a time.

Life interferes with my aloneness.
If I could but sit —
Still like a statue.
And think of us.
Or write lines on parchment-thin paper.
If I could but reach down
And pick the two of us out of this living
And place us close together upon a shelf.
But time is time.
And I wait alone.

Joyce Green Sells

SELLS, JOYCE GREEN. Born: Pensacola, Florida, 1-7-46; Married: 2-7-76 to Haskell Lee Sells, II; Education: University of Alabama, Respiratory Therapy Certificate, 1973; Wake Technical Junior College, Associate Degree in Nursing, 1981; North Carolina State University, Raleigh, North Carolina, selected courses; Jefferson State Junior College, Birmingham, Alabama, selected courses; Occupation: Registered Nurse with specialty in Respiratory Therapy; Memberships: American Association for Respiratory Therapy, North Carolina Association for Respiratory Therapy, National Organization for Women; Awards: *Who's Who in the South and Southwest,* 1985; Poetry: 'Feelings,' Sample Press, Garner, North Carolina, 1981; 'The Iconoclast,' Sample Press, Garner, North Carolina, 1981; 'Summer Song,' American Poetry Association, 1983; 'Reason or Chance,' American Poetry Association, 1985; Comments: *My poems are introverted. They focus on and substantiate my feelings and observations.*

REFLECTIONS

Reflections of reflections
mirrored back and forth,
childlike images
receding into the past.
What grandparent possessed
the same brow
and twinkling eye?
Whose tone of voice
echoes when you cry?
Whose humor shows
when you laugh?
Whose style of walk
strides down the path?
Link from the past
into the veiled future,
reflecting and reflecting
Nature's chain of life.

Bernice Lear

CAT NAP

Sugar, sleeping on the chair,
Are you dreaming dreams I share?
Are you in a summer day
With a little girl at play?
flying feet and lilting laughter . . .
Crafty kitten quickly after . . .
Do you hear her call once more?
Are you running as before?

Faster yet have run the years.
Joyous laughter turned to tears.
Silence muffles summer's song.
Endless time can be so long.
Empty echoes in my heart
Warn we're more than miles apart.
Could I, would I, bridge that gap
In dreams like you, if I cat nap?

Claudia Hall

SHANNON'S BIRTH

What secret silence
and depth of dark
brought you
to this form of flesh?
Birthed by what mystery?
Thrust by what force
that changed you
from a piece of star
swimming through
eternal waters
to a pebble
placed on the path of life?
Shell-pink and shining,
you blossomed
into bone and blood:
a songbird singing
the joy of Being.

Shirley Linden Morrison

THE CLOWN

Has won his round,
And now is free to be
Himself — and simply make the
World happy just behind
His make-up — that silken
Painted iron mask.
Don't ask . . .
Don't pry . . .
There's so much more, and yet no more.
Don't ask . . . the why . . .

M. Regina Auzins

THE SAD AFFAIR OF
LIVIA OF ANDOVER AND SIR BAINBRIDGE

Cool and lovely, Livia sat, astride her sable-colored mare —
Maids all around, a proper escort through green and rolling England fair.
   Now hoofbeats raced this stately band, a rare and valiant steed;
and eyes of grey its rider bore, to pierce poor Livia to the soul.

   A falcon sat upon his glove, a plumed hat on his head. He touched
its brim and bowed, "Good day," then merrily followed where they led.
   Later on, and lovely still, our Livia wondered at his spell — and tried,
but calmly, *calmly* please, to ready herself for the castle ball.

   'He' was there, prepared to coax, and as Livia gazed
at his cool grey eyes, she hadn't a chance; nay, her fate was cast —
   Sir Bainbridge had wittily caught his prize.
Through marriage songs, through feast and wine, fair Livia danced,
   by love entwined; in hopeful fancy, now a wife, forever Lady Bainbridge.

   But ah, love is fickle; alas, fate is cruel. And the whole
of the land bore witness, to the childless home and the loveless bed,
   and the promise of life grown dim.

   Now, later more and lovely once, sad Livia pines in wedded bliss;
and living not, she wanders still, through darkened moors
   and the English mist, upon her sable-colored mare.

Dana Rae Pugh

BORN TO BE A PRINCESS AND HERE I AM STRUGGLING AWAY

I am a Princess and the world is mine for the asking
But now my senses continue their masking
Of rubied reminiscences of thoughts nontaxing
So that emerald efforts can direct the casting
Of the next diamond dream to complete this tasking
So the struggle to continue struggling will not have been in vain.

It's hard at times — the struggle, not being the Princess
And I must chuckle to keep from thinking senseless
the guilty angry self-hating helpless and hopeless
Actions of those running around denseless
Struggling for no struggle but only for vainness
And energy to continue depressing their depression.

For it's only the artist's sensibilities
That allows her the totality
To convey the poet's responsibility
In painting the Princess' vitality.

So the Princess sits here undepressed by depression
That the world is hers is not even the question
But they are in it and still running in succession
From learning even their own self-taught lesson
And here I am shining emerald efforts with determination
So the struggle to continue struggling will not have been in vain.

Sharlyne B. Seabron

LET THEM EAT KETCHUP

"Let them eat ketchup." said a Blockhead Secretary of Agriculture.
But he didn't know that someone else was taking notes.
Reagan agreed, "Let them eat ketchup."
But he didn't know that someone else was taking notes.
The people raged, "At least Marie Antoinette gave us cake."
"Oh why, Mr. Reagan, oh why must our subsidized lunches have
   ketchup substituted as a vegetable," cried the little children,
   "You gave Bonzo bananas. Aren't we worth as much as Bonzo?"
"God save the children, god save the children." prayed both young
   and old.
Well, the Blockhead and the cowboy got together and decided
   that substituting ketchup for a vegetable wasn't such a
   good idea after all.
The little children wept with joy.
And both young and old prayed, "God save the children, god
   save the children."

Josephine Aurelia Graham

GOIN' HOME

Honey get your travel togs together,
While I go rustle up the family grip
Had a message from a little Birdie,
That we're a'goin' to take ourselves a trip.
Be ready for a bright and early risin'
B'gosh we're startin' by the break o' day,
For them wide open spaces 'way out west,
And Honey we're a'goin' back to stay.
Honey, can't you almost hear them raindrops
Come patterin' so gentle on the roof,
Smell the new-mown hay hear the cattle low,
And hear again the clatter of their hoof,
I wonder if my pal will be there waitin'
It seems as though I can't forget his neigh,
We're headed for the wild and woolly west,
And Honey we're a'goin' back to stay.
Back to dear Old Oregon, where the
Katydids and Larks,
Will sing to us all night and day
And the Dogwood trees have barks,
Where the mighty old Columbia
Keeps rollin' on its way,
Goin' home, and Honey, goin' home
to stay.

Mary E. Pitney

PITNEY, MARY ELEANOR. Born; Junction City, Oregon, 9-24-91; Single; Education: Oregon State University, B.S. degree, 1918; Post-graduate work from five different universities and colleges; Occupations: Instructor in high schools of Oregon, Wisconsin and Montana; H.O. Supervisor; Travelled and sold for the Goodwill Drug Co. of Omaha, Nebraska; Travelled and sold for the Investors Syndicate of Minneapolis, Minnesota; Personnel Department of the U.S. Portland, Oregon shipyards during last world war; Institutional Management for the U.S. government in Portland, Oregon for years; Retired in 1955; Writings: International anthology about "Dad" International Poetry Association, published about 12 years ago; 'Lost One,' American Poetry Association; Writings in 25 different magazines, papers, high school annual, university annual, etc. *Yesterdays Todays and Smiles,* containing poems of years ago — old-fashioned: 1) Declaration Day celebrations, hoop skirts, etc.; 2)Today — about planets, UFO's and the like; 3)Smiles — comic poems of kids, animals, spoonerism, etc.; Themes: *The wonders of nature, thanks to God for them, flowers, animals, birds, etc.;* Comments: *I write because I enjoy sitting and making up poetry about things I see in everyday life — love animals and flowers of all kinds. Also I love to paint and have sold several thousand dollars of my paintings — still paint.*

WHO KNOWS?

There is a magic formula, that I would like to know.
What is it makes a smile so sweet, and smiling eyes to glow?
I don't know what makes up a smile, or why it is so sweet;
But faces that don't wear a smile are somehow incomplete

We really think we know a lot, of formulas, and such;
In fact, with atom bombs and things, I think we know too much!
We know a lot of useless things, and lots of things worthwhile;
But who can give the formula, that makes a sunny smile?

There are a few wee odds and ends, we haven't found out yet;
Though life is revolutionized with gadgets that we get.
They take no end of money, but we still get all for free,
This fleeting bit of magic, that completely baffles me!

An atom bomb has power that is magic in its might;
No doubt a great explosion, is a most impressive sight;
But 'tis a puny power, when compared to just a smile,
Whose tenderness is magic, that makes living more worthwhile!

Let's analyze a smile a bit, and see just what we find;
It sparkles from a loving heart, and flashes to the mind;
It lights the world around about, with love's transforming glow;
God holds the magic formula — it's best to leave it so!

Elma Helgason

NIGHT SONG

"I'm old, so old," sighed the Wind to the treetops,
As he cradled them up in his fleeting arms.
The dark Night whispered, as he swirled around them,
"The Moon has been watching but has dimmed all his charms."

The Night sang on with the Wind in the branches,
A composer's melody mighty and great.
The bow strings of Heaven vibrated with music.
The world cared not that the hour was late.

Wind tossed, and fleeting the storm clouds crossed Heaven.
The sky and the stars all faded from sight.
The dark churning mass of the distance above them
Gave mortals a glimpse of the wild stormy night.

"I'm old, so old," sang the Wind to the treetops,
As he flurried the snow in great fluffs to the ground.
"I was here before mortals, and before time was measured;
For centuries and eons I've been blowing around."

The night passed on; the new day was dawning.
Now the Wind only whispered, for the storm had been long,
"Listen at night on the edge of the forest,
When the wind is rising you will hear the night song."

Louise Donahue

TO THE UNKNOWN VIETNAM SOLDIER

They wave the flag and drape your bier,
Cannons salute, the bugles sound;
But where were the bombs you needed
When wounded on the ground?
Did your tired eyes scan the skies
For planes to bring destruction
To a hidden enemy just over the rise?
Were you tall or short, slim or stout?
Did you wonder at the last what the war was about?
Did you save a buddy the last shot you fired?
Were you alone and bleeding, covered with jungle mire?
Soldier Boy, we loved you but did not feel your pain,
Or bring you back smiling at all the fuss we made.
Now hear this, Unknown Soldier, your buddies have rallied 'round
That high wall telling people of all the sacrifices they found!
Sleep sweetly, Unknown Husband, Sweetheart, Friend,
America has found you at last and promises
It will not happen thus again!

Louise Butts Hendrix

OH WICKED ONE

Oh wicked one
Your disgust and pain transmitted
Through the air
Oh, how you have never cared.

Your wealth of sin and bloody pain
Touching those with innocence
And leaving them lame.
Oh wicked one
You will not escape
The one I worship
With his colorful cape.

Let not the wrath of defeat bother you
Oh wicked one, for it was you damned to flame.
Pardon my majestic power of endurance
But, the power of love shall always remain the same.

You in flame
Burdened with constant death
Oh, why do you cry?
For it was you, who had the choice
The precious choice to live, or to die.

Kimberly Faye Contrascere

THROW IT AWAY

It's too short, too long, too old.
I don't like it . . . THROW IT AWAY.
What happened to "Waste not — want not?"
Why do we throw so much away?

In a small house by a river
Lives a family of four today;
A conceived child made it five,
Unwanted 'twas aborted away.

When time ages us all, why must
"OLD FOLKS" be put out of the way,
While the "YOUNG FOLKS" do their own thing,
Precious years are thrown away.

IF GOD would come to us today,
Viewing our earth — our wasteful way,
Would HE too shake HIS head and say,
"I DON'T LIKE IT . . . THROW IT AWAY!"

Antoinette Capek

MY LEGACY

It wasn't lands, silver or gold.
No, it is memories which I hold
Of a white cottage, nestled in a grove of trees
    Along a country road.

Memories of a yellow shepherd dog
    With which I played;
Baby kittens on new-mown hay
    by their mother laid;
Winter nights, Mom's homemade fudge, Dad's checker game.
    After all chores are done.

And the lessons taught by word and deed
    Within that cottage small
Of loyalty to family's ties,
    And hope and love to all;
Of helpfulness and trust and faith
    Which make life worthwhile.

If my inheritance had been lands, silver or gold
It could have been lost, or hard-pressed, sold.
But my legacy is now even more valuable and also will be
    To those who follow me.

Lela Shine

ONE FOR MOTHER'S DAY
5TH PLACE

She brims with joy at my small victories
goes darkeyed at the stupid world's neglect
gives Dad black looks and snorts
that he wants me on time for work
— they should be so lucky I go there at all — !

So here's one for you, Mom,
classiest of bag ladies in my old, holey tennis shoes,
the orange stretch pants and that fleece-lined, purple shirt.

Here's one for you
because we look around, look around
out of the same, wide eyes
and because you have to hear through your skin, now,
flapping a hand at pain to get out of the way,
you're busy.

And because we are both so full of stifled song.

You could do better, any day
on a church program or grocery list
or at a wedding, whispering.

D. Meeks

THE SILVER CORD

Moonlight mingles through
    Diaphanous webs
        Tied to the corners of my soul.
Carefully, it beams down
    Dark corridors of stillness
To focus onto the retina of my understanding.

    Restless fingers of my brain and body
Swirl and toss memories,
    Impulses,
        Of a reckless day,
            and cat-eyed night.

Finally, they've pressed me, weary,
    Into sleep, with and without dreams.

Now, the morning walks to me,
    Cool, coral, serene,
        A Goddess leaning
To shuffle and describe all into order.
    Fragile, yet sterling,
        I lie still,
            and consider.

Edith Scott Johnson

GRANDMA

Grandma was a sweet ole gal;
She fed the chickens and milked the cow,
Planted a garden and watered the seed
and took care of grandpa's every need.

She darned his socks, and cut his hair,
Washed his clothes with very much care.
Shod the horses and plowed the fields
Churned the butter and cooked the meals.

She fixed the fence and cleaned the barn,
Cut the wheat and shucked the corn.
Baled the hay and baked a pie,
Watered the cattle and sowed the rye.

She drove to town to buy some thread,
Came back home and made the bed.
While sitting and rocking, she hummed a tune,
Happy she had finished her chores by noon.

John T. Hudelson

CANDLE GLOW

Candle glow jumps at my heart, snatches at my soul,
thumps out the part of the beautiful, but treacherous thing called love
which can as easily be doused by water, drowned in tears to slaughter the pain
and purge the misery.

Flames leap high, jump at my heart,
lick the insides of my thighs
tease my soul lest I fall into the pit of flaming snakes
lecherous fakes who sing their tune of
"Come to me, baby love . . . "

I cannot let that candle glow too bright anymore
Cannot risk my feelings, can say no more.
Cannot believe words I'm told, "Je t'adore . . . "
The glow is much too dim from a distant shore,
the hurts, much too filled with blood and gore,
the relief hardly comes anymore.

Janet Castiel

CASTIEL, JANET ELLEN. Pen Name: Janet Castiel; Born: New York, New York, 4-16-54; Education: Vassar College, 1976; University of Madrid, 1978; Occupations: Free Lance Writer, Television and Film Editor and Producer; Memberships: International Radio and Television Society, American Film Institute; Awards: 'Secrets,' *Hearts on Fire,* contest, 1984; "Sewing It Up," (Television Script), International Film and TV Festival, New York, 1983; Poetry: 'Secrets,' *Hearts on Fire,* 1984; 'Love Poem,' *Hearts on Fire,* 1984; 'Grandma,' *Up Against the Wall,* 1983; Other Writings: "Sewing It Up," TV Show, Tradewinds Productions, 1983; "Twice A Woman," TV Show, ITI, 1981.

A FORGOTTEN DREAM

I dream of you — once long ago.
And you were tall, and had the smell of earth and sky about you.
You held your hand to me, said "Come —
Come climb this mountain, you and I."
You helped me over rock-strewn paths and showed me God's green earth
So beautiful, that lay beneath my feet.
"I'll find this man someday" I cried.
"I'll find my Love who is the color of earth, the color of sky."
The years passed by, and I began to doubt my dream!
"Foolish girl, 'twas but a dream — signifying nothing;
There is no Love for you!" my head would say. My heart would cry.
One day you came, and you were tall, and strong, and like a mountain.
But, alas, my dream had been forgot.
Then on a day, when shadows come to join with night
You held me close, and kissed me.
Your searching lips went deep into my soul —
And woke my long forgotten dream.
My only Love, how strange I knew you not.

P. A. Percival

THE WINDMILL

I watched the breeze turning
An aged windmill,
That has stood many years
On the side of a hill;
"Though the village may burn,
While the breezes are blowing,
The windmill will turn."

There may be no tomorrow
Left for you and I;
But the windmill will turn,
When a breeze wanders by.
Though we laugh or though we cry,
Though we live or we die;
The windmill will turn when
A breeze wanders by.

Marjorie Kingston Skusa

NEBRASKA

Out West in Nebraska —
There's waiting for me —
A heap of good fortune —
In old cow-country —

Now I have no time
To spare on my hands
I'm heading on back
Just as fast as I can

At night the red moon
Lights the prairies aflame
Somewhere a guitar's playing
"Home on the Range"
Believe it or not
Sure my heaven will be
When I get back to Nebraska
In old cow-country

Where a stranger's no stranger
A friend is a friend
I'm a settling on down
With my kind of kin
Nebraska I'm a'coming
Start counting me in

Phyllis Joy Catuska Wallace

IMAGES

Though the distance between us
is measured in miles
often you are here with me
I can hear your infectious laughter
when I say my silly nothings
I can see your come-easy smile
as you take my hand in yours
I again feel the warmth
being held in your arms
I imagine your gentle caress
and know your tender kisses
I see your intense-telling gaze
giving away your inner thoughts

As my memory creates your image,
you are suddenly transported here
I'm lost in thoughts of you
and the miles between us are gone
I'm in your arms once again
cherishing the closeness we share

And as I slowly return to reality,
along with it, comes sadness
as you fade out of my arms
and I am alone, missing you

Debi Buettner

IF I WERE

If I were a lyricist,
  I would write you a love song.
If I were a poet,
  I would write a beautiful poem about you.
If I were a sculptor,
  I would carve your unforgettable image.
But I am only a dreamer,
  And I can only dream of you.

Teresa M. Polverini

THE COMFORTER

From my insides a quake of fear I felt,
The painful fright gripped the core of me.
My sounds proclaimed, "I'm scared."
Another voice secure and calm replied,
"No harm will come to you as long as I'm near."
A human stated the words, but no, not really —
They were only spoken by a mortal,
God was the source!

Carole Whittacre

NATURE'S CREATION

I am the sun who beats thy rays upon Earth.
The moon who smiles down at glistening oceans,
The stars that light the blackness of night.
Clouds that dance in the softness of blue.
Sand; the grains of time upon the distant shoreline.
Needles on evergreen trees, blossoming for years on end.
I am the rain, snow and the frost of a bitter wind.
I am nature's creation.

Susan Leff

MY LOVE

As the days go by I grow more lonesome inside,
for you are forever on my mind.
It took me so long, even years after you'd gone,
to realize how much you meant to me.
At times I can't hide these crazy feelings of mine
and I have to break down 'n cry.
Oh please tell me "why *my* love" has survived through
all these long long years since you've died.

Gina M. Moore

SKETCH

Ageless elf,
Wide-eyed, wondering, laughing Thing,
Feather-lovely, flower-souled,
A trouble knits your brow and darks your eye,
Then light as thistle-down it floats away
As shadows flee before a merry sun.

Arline Spaeth Vanasdal

AT SUNSET'S BRIDGE

Sitting hunched over in a wheelchair,
By a sunny window.
Looking out through time-dimmed eyes,
At the world beyond vacantly seeing little.
Forsaken by friends,
Ignored by family.
Large-print Bible resting on lap,
Awaiting God's angels.

Virgil Bakken

LOVE TAKES COMMAND

The angry hand raised in haste,
  God's love intervenes with grace,
    Anger recedes, love is renewed when;
      Love takes command!

The broken spirit, bowed in sorrow,
  God's love intervenes and on the morrow,
    The spirit is filled with healing peace when;
      Love takes command!

The tear-filled eyes are raised in fear,
  With compassion God wipes away each tear.
    Love's seed is planted when;
      Love takes command!

When hearts are open to receive,
  The "Word" made flesh, and we believe,
    We become one in the Spirit when;
      Love takes command!

When we learn to love our fellow man,
  When in praise we lift our hands,
    Burdens are lifted, peace is assured when;
      Love takes command!

Mary E. Filby

SYMPHONY OF THE BROOK

Only a rivulet, a little stream,
Cascading over rocks and rills:
For years it's been my fondest dream
To return to those enchanting hills.

At a bend in the brook where wild ferns adorn,
I would sit spellbound on a golden day,
Secluded in rapture on a given morn
To hear the brook's symphony trickle its way.

A musical tinkle so crystal clear!
What a sound and joy that thrilled my soul,
Sweet harmony and color tones filled my ear
As I sat in a trance 'til the day grew old.

In a world of confusion, fear, and unrest
We are caught in a web of hate and despair,
And a Heaven of joy seems an idle quest
As time and burdens silver our hair.

Come to the brook: God's there it seems.
In His still, small voice He will speak to us there.
We'll find peace and joy beyond wildest dreams
As we list to the symphony in His beauty so rare.

W. W. Arnold

JUST PERFECT

Beginning of the world. From a mountain's top,
Looking over the forests, that never really stop,
A brand-new place, where no man stands,
Vast blue oceans, and untouched lands,
Eagles that soar, with pride and grace,
No fears as he glides, in the sky's open space,
Water that runs, from pure crystal springs,
And air so clean, to create all of these things,
Rain in the darkness, and sunshine at dawn,
Animals run freely, like a deer and her fawn,
Winds without force, time without measure,
All joined together, and all live in pleasure,
Snow at the poles, of this great new earth,
Always so peaceful, yet giving new birth,
The waves and tides, splash free on the shores,
And the outlands above, have stars by the scores,
Life in its beauty, that shall never cease,
For they all live together, and all live in peace.

Randy G. Randall

FRIENDSHIP

When solitude becomes winged and flies from you . . .
   Sing for me . . . Call my name

When alone leaves you cold and lonely . . .
   Sing for me . . . Call my name.

When the poison-tip barbs of reality pierce you . . .
   Sing for me . . . Call my name.

When friends and family back you to the wall . . .
   Sing for me . . . Call my name.

Your words will be borne by the gentle breeze . . .
   I will hear your song — My heart will always
     Answer — Share your burdens . . .
      Make your troubles lighter.

When the first flowers of Spring greet your eye . . .
   Sing for me . . . Call my name.

When a day — So lovely your heart sighs . . .
   Sing for me . . . Call my name.

Your song will reach me on rays of Spring sun . . .
   We will share joy and double it.

   Sharon Joyce Hoffman

BLACK PAN

Black Pan, you sit on careful lawns,
Your old melody silently fluting away,
Here at least the old, nod sleepy
     in the sun,
Your temptations near all undone —
I hear your tender trills,
     look the other way,
My sunsets taken up with the mysteries
     of you and I.

You will again hold sway, leading
     our carefree young
To shining pools, quiet forest glens, offering
Wings to soar with eagles, chariots
     of fire,
They, blood of our blood will follow, nay
Racy gay, to merry tunes
     we heard a day.

I see your knowing grin, the pipe
     held high.
Oft at night I hear your cry of glee,
You in impish effigy, with Bacchus
     and the other three
Holding court in some mountain fast
Drunk with power over them and me!

   C. H. Fletcher

ON ETERNITY

Please tell me, are we part of some great joke,
Too blind to see the fire for the smoke?
When this poor life is through is it the end
Or is there something just around the bend?
We half-believe today's glib rhetoric
Yet still pursue some carrot-on-a-stick.
We claw and climb to savor each desire;
We gather years and burn them with our fire.
And though we squander every shining day
Oblivion's a bitter price to pay!
I want to feel — to know — that there must be
Somewhere a valid gilt-edged guarantee
   That when I've shuffled down that darkest hall,
   I'll find a new beginning after all!

   Floyd S. Knight

SONNET TO THE HONEY BEE

When I consider how the busy bee
So "wondrously improves each shining hour" —
Distilling liquid sunshine from each flower,
And thus enriching both herself and me;
And ponder, too, the order to be seen
In all the busy hive's activity —
The field bees, nurse bees, and Her Majesty,
   the Queen —
Each with her task, yet all in harmony;
Consider, too, the golden bounty stored
In each six-sided waxen chamber sealed
For winter use; and know this golden hoard
Was gathered in many a flight to woods and field;
When I consider all of this, I say:
God's hand is in it — sure as night follows day!

   Harold Hendrickson

HENDRICKSON, HAROLD CLIFFORD. Born: Rock Creek, Minnesota, 1-16-20; Occupations: Farming, Bee-keeping; Poetry: 'On Your Fortieth,' 1984; 'A Christmas Candle,' 1937; 'God Bless Our Land,' *Evening Beacon*, 1976; 'Thanksgiving Prayer,' 1974; Comments: *Coming from a large family, I have written several poems celebrating anniversaries. Other subjects: Love of God and country.*

LAMENT OF LEO THE STUFFED LION

Time was — When excited young children
Came eagerly to stay overnight at Gramma's.
"Where's Leo the Lion" they'd gleefully shout,
Then I'd be tucked in and cuddled all night.

I felt so important when all of them came.
Each one would bicker, "He's mine," "No he's mine."

They pulled both my ears, tweaked my poor nose,
And one little rascal twisted my toes to
Where they still are today — but
I loved them all dearly anyway.

Where have they all gone — it's so quiet now!

I see Gran's sad eyes so full of dreams
Of children who gaily romped through the house.
I try to say wait — please don't despair,
Soon other young ones will surely be here —

Their children will come to take their place.

The house will again ring with joyful laughter,
And I'll once again be important thereafter,
Just as I used to be, Oh so long,
Long ago, when — Time was.

   Faye Cohen Levy

SONNET

I am completely unaware of time,
Oblivion will overtake my fear.
The sounds of life become a pantomime,
I know the point of no return is here.
Unable to react, my senses hard,
My rosy face is nothing but a mask,
My worries, with my hopes, I must discard;
Performance seems a vaguely distant task.
Beside my pending needs the world is naught,
The celebration of the day is night.
Here is the great result my work has brought:
The dark in no way differs from the light.
   I care not for the better or the worse;
   An hour asleep destroys the universe.

   Dana Kirchman

A PHEASANT IN SEPTEMBER

A walk along the Kansas byways brings
Quick contact with a handsome immigrant.
From undercover there's a sound of wings,
My step has flushed the wheat field habitat.
He steeply climbs, soars into graceful glide,
A blur of color, lands and crouches low.
The jewel of the Kansas countryside
Is safe, concealed and hid from hunting foe.
Head feathers' iridescent purple gleam
Metallic green, red wattle, yellow beak,
He struts in open fields, or drinks from stream,
A game bird, prized for beauty, strength — unique.
   To see the ring-neck pheasant in his flight,
   Or watch his mating dance . . . is pure delight.

   Betty Jane Simpson

SONG OF QUIETUS

Death yields its path to the lonely stranger,
   Leaving behind unheard soliloquys
   and unsowed dreams
As breath is arrested from life's unknown granger.

Remember that mourners weep, but as many have
   Droned — it is never for eternal keep.

And as bands of gold unfold new hope,
   Harpers emerge in play with such
Grandiose display,
   To summon life's message — Now found;
Now lost, as they waken the rods of solitude
   To discover new meaning.

   Marlene Gutierrez

MISSING YOU

The fire lighted by your charm,
The comfort found in your arms,
The memories of these things in my heart
Have kept me together, since we've been apart.

Maybe when the months turn into years
I can begin to control my tears;
Tears because I miss you so very much,
Tears from the hurt of longing for your touch.

As you travel across the miles,
You may be away for quite awhile;
I know if it's God's will, by His grace
You'll return to kiss the tears off my face.

   Mary C. Brittian

INSPIRATION

I remember writing with such a fury —
              A waterfall of words, cascading
From my mind, down my arm, into the pen, onto the paper.
        Fast and oh so deafening,
Taking me to a world where words
              Tumble, but never stumble,
           Towards finished thoughts.
I forget the here and now
            With an urgency, such as to be
            In command of a holy war.
After the final word has been written,
        A mystical situation occurs and the rush
           Fills me with
           Amazement, tears, and a wonderful joy.

       A poem completed.
          A voice heard.
             Thoughts fully connected.

   Mary A. Sadowski

SO MANY SPACES TO FILL

When a seam is sown, the material is finished.
When a heart, mind, or soul is damaged — what can the
thread be?
Perhaps the sun, the warmth and the glow of a child
in the wonderment of life renewed?
How can one person with so many spaces to fill find
the answer?
We are each to one another a thread; finer than the web
of a small puppy with eager eyes for love.
Music — a staff of notes long forgotten, will this fill
the spaces to comfort?
Words, songs, dance, wine, the clinging to the last
of all that brings happiness?
Slowly my spaces to fill will be done: for I have the
way — for looking up into the eyes of Father Sky will
ease the gaps.
HE smiles and I smile back — HE is ready to fill the many
spaces I have to fill; with very special words.
Thank you for the language — Father Sky!

   Charlotte Bell

TWO FOOLS IN THE RAIN

The longest forever you've spent
Perpetuating around us unnoticed
Until mutual meditation causes realizations about
How long we've actually known each other.
Eight weeks? Eight years?
How long must it take two to
Become as close as we? (eight hours?)
Stars and moon observe the
Tides passing under our bridge:
Your smiling eyes tickling my laughter while
My massages kiss your shoulders and neck.
Elated dance and rejoicing under (magical?)
Sky water accentuate contentedness.
We are the play — and the life — that we are:
Two fools in the rain . . . But
We know the mist shall clear and time will pass.
Do not let the mists invade your eyes, however,
For we know they remain —
Waiting where time is no longer a concept.

   Emilie W. Storrs

The warmth of her love
is like the morning sun
bringing life from above
to the sleeping rose

Bart A. Tinsley

THE PARASOL

Your hair was wet from the summer rain:
Your face like a China doll.
When first we met there in the park,
To share one parasol.

Your wet clothes showed your lovely form;
And the rise of your heaving breast:
My stricken heart beat madly,
Like a river at full crest.

We stood there laughing in the rain;
While the world rushed madly by.
And while that world was drowning,
I drowned in your lovely eye.

And when the rain was over, Love,
And the sky an azure blue;
I laid aside the parasol —
But never, never you.

Now thirty lovely summers, Dear,
Have faded into fall.
With you beneath my parasol,
I've loved them, one and all.

Carl Freeman

FREEMAN, CARL FLOYD. Born: Red Oak, Georgia; Education: North Clayton High School; Ten years off-campus study at Emory University; Three years vocational study in Electronics and Communications; Occupations: TV Repair, Security work, raised on farm; Memberships: VWG, Unknowns, Dixie Council of Authors and Journalists; Awards: Book of poetry, *Time in a Bottle,* poems, 'The Iron Horse,' and 'Stone Mountain's Reflecting Pool,' Poetry: 'Stone Mountain's Reflecting Pool,' historical, *The Blue and the Gray;* 'Ballad of the Bicentennial;' 'Lot of Things a Dummy Can't Do;' 'The Old Man of the Mountain,' Epic Ballad; 'The Oldest Rat in the Barn;' all in book, *Time in a Bottle;* currently writing a novel; Comments: *My poem, 'Tutankhamun,' elicited a letter of commendation from late Egyptian leader, Anwar Sadat. 'The Iron Horse' I consider to be my best poem. I try to express life as it is; and was. Man is above the animals — And just a little below the angels. I try to remind him of that. My writing has been successful, to a degree. And I ran for President a couple of times. I think my name and signature are in the Smithsonian — but without any doubt, the crowning glory of my life was finding Keron Blissit. In comparison, everything else pales.*

CLOUD SCULPTURE

Sometimes
the wind makes quite a show
convolving clouds.

One day three clouds
became three giant birds
limned against the western sky.
With pointed beaks
and outstretched wings
they flew to greet the sun —
    grace in angled flight.

To the north
a swirling cloud
became a fighting cock
suspended in the air
with archèd neck,
and talons curved
to strike his foe.
But clouds below
obscured the drama's end.

Paulyne Downing Tompkins

CONTEMPORARY LOVE

It is not the twinkle in your eye
that says "Dare or Die"

It is not my sudden smile
that has held you all the while

It is not the meeting of our eyes
with our emotions undisguised

It is not the fun and laughter
that we often share together

It is something from a long and
distant past

Where once we loved and when?
We can only guess

It is the blending of our spirits
and our souls alone, at last.

Margie Roemele

UZZIAH

*". . . for he was marvelously
helped, till he was strong."*
2 Chronicles 26:15

I was weak, but faithful
before my strength arrived.
When weak I once
built a siege tower
higher than a fortress wall
and climbed it to look
down at my enemies.
I, the able, perfect prince,
allowed so near You yet
exempt from close scrutiny,
never looked up in envy.
At my strongest You denied me!
Weakest when strong,
corrupted, just briefly faithless
I raged.
Where is our faith
when we are strong?

Steven G. Prusky

LIFE-LOCKED

I looked at you and I saw through
The rainbow mask which hid your face;
Satin dress lined with silver lace;
Golden curls slipped out of place;
A custom, costume, colored zoo
Overrunning restless blue

Your latent look — clothed covered book —
Facial smile sealing soul frown?
Begging body guarding gown?
Proud will forcing feelings down?
Or shield of one whose spirit's shaken
And former life has been forsaken?

Memories past a looking glass —
Forever forgotten — remain
Mistress of mime, slayer of sane;
Covering cuts, preserving pain;
Adding armor as abuses amass:
Building cold body cast.

Rick A. Diemert

SEARCHING

There are how's and why's
to war and peace . . .
To life and death,
but where are the answers?
Comprehending . . . yet not.
Through war comes peace
By living I see death,
But why so many questions?

Our mainstream of existence
comes through daily encounters.
the only answers I've found
tug within me . . .
So many mangled thoughts
Countless entwined questions;
All forcing me to see
that one's real enemy is himself,
or by being born I started to die.
I'd far rather risk gradual death
than sacrifice my one true gift . . .
        EXPERIENCE!

Mary Ann Steis

MY BROTHER'S GUN

When I was twelve,
You gave me a gun;
You knew the reason,
And the purpose.

You gave me strength,
To carry and kill;
My first deer,
With a little fear.

On the hill,
Where I'm at;
You gave me a gun,
To protect and kill;
From my window sill.

With my gun in hand,
And God by my side;
I know, you'll bring,
Me, home again.

Deborah James

WORDS, WONDERFUL WORDS

Volumes of books with millions of words;
Like a tree nourished unceasingly
from underground streams . . .
Yield fruit and foliage ever green.
Even though some disappear from sight;
They may still exist, giving light.
Dictionaries, Commentaries and
Reference books as guides:
Men write all types of literature
with the greatest pride.
Sometimes the grammar may be atrocious,
And some ideas rather specific,
But . . . give my heart words for Poetry . . .
To me they are most terrific!

Eleanor S. Follmer

OUR SPECIAL FLAG

Our American Flag is a special one
It stands for Freedom, Faith, and Fun
We can write, or speak our thoughts aloud
Stay alone, or gather with a crowd

We can worship God, each in our own way
Use the talents He gave us to work or play
Our flag gives us faith, and helps us be tough
Fills us with courage when living gets rough

It represents freedom to laugh and have fun
However we wish, if not hurting someone
Our flag stands for everything America has got
And it's mighty special, for we've got a lot.

Fatima S. Atchley

CREATURE

She lives in the park.
When it rains, she crouches under benches.
When it snows, she hides in subway corners.
She is small and dark like a mouse's shadow.
She carries a feather pillow and an oriental parasol,
And wears cloaks in layers,
And does not speak the language well;
She knows "help" and "money."
Even the bums have stopped bothering her.
Only yesterday I wondered
If problems were a human creation —
Meaningless beside infinity.
She is blind.
But there is a world behind those eyes.

Kathryn A. Brown

SONGS IN THE NIGHT
(Job 35:10)

When sleep flees from my eyes because of pain
That leaves me twisting on a restless bed
The haunting sweetness of some old refrain
Will sing itself again and yet again
Persistently inside my aching head.
"Kentucky Babe," "Killarney," "Sweet and Low."
Songs of my childhood, and the things they said.
Remembered love songs add a silver thread.
"My Sunshine." "Souvenirs." "For All We Know."
And comfort. "Rock of Ages." "Let us Sow."
"He Lives." "Praise God from Whom All Blessings Flow."
That silent singing brings my soul release
And joy in spite of pain that will not cease.

Helen Bradford

ITEMS AND TASKS

Once I wrote a letter that I wish
all people could see. It was of
items like Respect, Peaceful Relations,
Economic Equality and more. I encountered
some human beings with this letter
and they did not know of the topics.
They were all foreign to them, as if they were
learning those words for the first time.
It would be a large and difficult task
indeed to instruct all people on these items.
Yet, it was of paramount importance, so
I began the long, arduous search for
those who *were* well-informed, so we
could cover the earth and instruct the
universe about the ideals that no one
seems to have heard of.

Karen Tiegs

TIEGS, KAREN. Born: 7-20-60; Education: Nicolet College and Technical Institute, Rhinelander, Wisconsin, Merchandising Diploma, 1978-80; University of Wisconsin, Green Bay, one semester, 1984; Memberships: Wisconsin Regional Writers Association; Poetry: 'Song in My Heart,' March 1982; 'Fog,' May 1982; 'Contrast,' September 1982; 'Winterland,' December 1982; 'A Moment with Music,' July 1984; all published in *Green Bay Press-Gazette;* Comments: *Since about age 12, I've been writing. I write because it's a joy and over the years I've received good encouragement. Whenever I see a piece of my work published, it's always an accomplishment. In some I give a different way of looking at things. Other pieces of my work are about nature and the outdoors; still others are philosophical works. The Rhinelander School of the Arts workshops are a good source of learning. Writing seems to come natural to me.*

SERENITY

Within myself an inner serenity grows,
through quiet reflection upon a soft night's embrace.
Its strength creating a warmth of love, a peaceful aura
upon an approaching storm.
Orange and yellow hues form upon a glowing surface,
show images of a more peaceful time not felt much now.
That ebb through my consciousness numbing the pain.
Within myself an inner serenity grows, through quiet
reflection upon a soft night's embrace.
I can go on now.

Kathryn Saunders

HOKUSAI, Crossing Stream

CALVARY

Suffering in Man's sight —
"Eli, Eli, lama sabachthani," you cry.
Mary Magdalene filled with fright.
Those below you are the ones that die.

Natalie Newton Pepis

EMOTION

It wells up within me
as waves in the sea
Sometimes it is bottled up,
other times, flowing
freely as the breeze.
I try, but it is not
always easy to express
what lies within me —
the very core of my spirit
wanting to soar as an
eagle in flight.
Yet, at times,
it is in bondage, as a
man in a cold, dark cell.
If I do not learn
to control it,
this very thing has the power
to control, even destroy me.
It can . . . but I will be in control.

Linda Davis

HE WAITS FOR YOU AND ME

(John 14: 1-3)

Have you ever dreamt of Heaven
   The place of perfect rest,
Free of strife and turmoil,
   The home of all the blessed;
and longed for the day when you'll be free
   Of all besetting sin,
To reach Heaven's portal of Peace and Joy
and forever be with Him?

Do you have Jesus as your Savior,
   who came to earth to die,
That your sins might be forgiven
   So you can reach your home on high?
Someday earthly fetters will be cut
   and we will then be free,
To take our flight to the realms above
   Where "He waits for you and me."

Raymond M. Hering

OFF ALIEN SHORES

(From Island Series*)*

. . . There are those hours
closed in with myself
enwrapped in showers
of thoughts
of sensuous trade winds
off alien shores
where exotic birds fly . . .

. . . Though now but memory,
Those tree-fringed shores
— once so real —
still live stored
as legacy

in the secure vault
of my heart
where time does not exist . . .

V. Mony Snyder

ODE TO A FRIEND

Like the breathing rose
cascading satin gentleness
As a groping branch
clothed in leaves of green

A soft summer rain
massaging the powdered soil
Sunlight's silent beams
creeping through the clouds

The awesome snow-frosted mountains
casting unmoving shadows
The seemingly infinite sea
rippling in serene ecstasy

      And Friend
Such as these you are to me
A wondrous gift of God

Share with me the sorrows
Come to me in joy
Seek me out this day
tomorrow and evermore

Darla Dawn Lukac

LUKAC, DARLA DAWN. Pen Names: Dew-Kissed, Ghost Fox; Born: Lethbridge, Alberta, 2-27-63; Married: 6-18-83 to Karel James S. Lukac; Education: Lethbridge Community College for Watershed Environmental Science, 1980-82; Occupations: Freelancer for farm newspaper, Freelance Photographer, Librarian; Awards: High School English Scholarship, minor poetry contests; Poetry: 'Child's Magical World,' free verse, *Taber Times,* Alberta, 1980; 'The Blood of the Lamb,' free verse, *Western Producer,* Saskatchewan, 1981; Other Writings: "Ballads by the Clouds," short story, *Western Producer,* Saskatchewan, "These Canine Characters," article, "Garskis' Gold," article, *Farm Week,* Alberta, 1985; Comments: *I got my first thrill at fourteen when a ditty I had written about Elvis was published in* The Western Producer, *a Saskatchewan newspaper. From then on it was production city. Verbal communication is not beyond me, yet I feel more at ease with a stylus and some paper. The English language has always amazed me with its myriad of color. It gives me a powerful feeling when I can magically fill up a blank page with meaning. Life is an inspiration and I write poetry to share the deep emotional side of it with others. Poems upon war and triumph, gentle love and anguished heart, living nature and its bosom are all part of my collection. Poetry is a means of combining fantasy and reality into a wonderful and memorable concoction. Expertly weaved verse releases inhibitions and makes way for inner strength.*

LITTLE GIRL/WOMAN

Sometimes I wish I were
a little girl again
free from all the worries
of the woman that I am.

The little girl would sleep and play,
be happy with her friends.
She'd smile and laugh and seldom cry —
and all the while she'd sing.
She'd help her mom whenever she could,
and her mother would think
"I hope she grows up to be like me."

But the woman has to sleep and work
and worry about meeting ends.
She frowns and cries, and loses her temper
at even the slightest thing.
She has to do things on her own —
for now, she's independent . . .
just like she's always wanted to be.

HiDee Silverwood

WALK BACK WITH ME

Old love of mine
To whom the past
Is but an occurrence;
Walk back with me!
To where eyes did shine.
What happened then
That killed the hope,
The happiness to be
Walk back and let's see
If there is a way
To ease the pain
Fill the void
Still the fear.
Is there something to say?
To repair the torn
Quiet the shame?
Out of an old love
Create a new day
Set me free
To love again.

Nita Jamison

PRESENT PAST

I just saw you in Graul's parking lot,
And my heart nearly stopped.
It hurt so much
to see you within reach
And, yet, not be able
To touch you, your face, your hands,
Your hair so soft and white . . .
It brought back the memories
Of bygone days
That you *now* want in the past
I know not why,
But that *I* cannot forget,
For you brought me so much
Joy, as well as pain,
That you are an unforgettable
Part of my life,
Always present in the past
Even though not in the present,
My everpresent past,
My beloved past, forever present

Frédérique Marcy Roberge

WITH OPEN EYES

In pastel blossoms of infant spring,
In dewy April showers,
In the brilliant summer sun,
Omnipotence is ours.

In amber leaves of showy guilt,
Stained-glass trees and autumn wilt,
When winter blows its frosty breath,
Nature goes from life to death.

The sphere of life goes 'round and 'round,
Spring to life; death to ground,
We push on relentlessly
To endless time, eternity.

When stars peek down in evening skies,
When gleaming rays uncover our eyes,
Discover Eden in this day.
If only . . . God, I humbly pray.

Barbara Stewart

DANDELION, OH FRIEND OF MINE

Dandelion, oh friend of mine,
For you there is no need,
To dig a hole in the ground,
To plant a little seed.

Dandelion, oh friend of mine,
You grow of your own free will,
I'm sorry there's no place for you,
On my window sill.

Dandelion, oh friend of mine,
I do acknowledge thee,
For you come to brighten up my lawn,
For everyone to see.

Dandelion, oh friend of mine,
I doubt that you'll succeed,
For society sees you as,
Nothing but a weed!

Cheryl Lynn Piskule

LIFE IS LIKE A SEASON

Life is like a season,
There is no reason,
It just comes and goes.
Passes like the breeze
Goes with the sun
Fills the world.

Life is like the spring,
Blooming, beginning again.
Like the summer,
Sunshine and laughter.
Like the fall,
Full of color, but with gloom.
Like the winter,
Full of coldness,
Full of long days,
Passing slowly like falling snow.
Life is like a season
There is no reason.

Donna Jones

POSEIDON'S CALL

I stand on the sandy shore,
and look out to the deep sea.
The beautiful blue sea that I love,
and fear more than anything I know,
and yet . . .
I would welcome her depths to me,
for I hear a call from King Poseidon.
He calls and beckons me to his lady,
the sea . . .
I will stand looking out to the sea,
and Poseidon shall call to my soul,
but alas . . .
once more I shall have to deny him,
for I am a mere mortal, land bound,
from his world of immortality.

Patricia A. Nickle

FIXTURE

The years she watched the people come
With shining eyes, and go,
Life after life,
Whispers in the semi-darkness,
Fingers on fingers, lips, eye upon eye,
And eyes into eyes, winking, asking,
Saying, telling;
And she — tallying,
measuring schemes as yardsticks
unnoticed on the balconies of time
Before her, never letting on,
The talk and plans in meteored time;
Until they say she fell
from her frame
Upon the wall.

Robert D. Nagle

MIDNIGHT EYES

Midnight black eyes staring
straight ahead,
Now looking left, now looking
right, taking in the sights
and wonders of the world.

Watching, watching, always
seeing.

A mysterious purple veil
covers the earth,
only the man with the
midnight black eyes can
see through the purple
mist.

Sadie Kempker

CARE

The pain was so intense,
It was so hard to bear.
The words, Love and Dedication,
Has placed the pain and tension there.
Deep in the hollow of God's creation,
Bore a secret love for the tall,
    tanned lanky human,
Who believed in saying,
    I care.
No one understood but,
What do the people know.
Of a burning desire,
Between two dedicated individuals,
Who just had the courage to say.
    I care.

Debra J. Jackson

SONG OF STAR WARRIORS

Nearer to Thee we come,
Nearer we come.

Not in spirit
But with "star wars."
To do in heaven
As it is on earth.

Nearer, nearer
To Thee we come
With "star wars."

Rinkart Eze Okorie

ODE TO A LEMON

Sweet of sight with sunshine skin
But to a death she grew akin
And through earth's loss the heavens win
And now she withers brown to lie
And so I laid her down to die
Her only tears no more to cry
I cry for thee my lemon tart
I cry, for you and I must part
I feel a bitter broken heart
My life survives but without you
And knowing what I felt for you
No other lemon now will do

Renée Varak

TAGGING HATS

Hat brims flap like shirts
Upon the prairie clothesline
And finally explode like rockets,
The jet into the wind
And people chase them,
In games of tag to win.

Patricia A. Newgaard

HAIKU

The acorn is small,
An off'ring of a giant
To the cup of earth.

The tree is not free
To roam on a zephyr trail —
But the tree is firm.

The pigeon is not
As timid as the blue jay —
But beauty is rare.

Harold D. Miller

ONE TOO MANY

Once green with breezes flowing,
    now fallen leaves and bareness showing.
Perched, nestled high and alone,
    winter's beginning,
        I go alone.

Clouds of snow make their way,
    they hide at night and dare by day.
Frosted mornings, cold felt nights,
    one too many,
        I wake to white.

Jane D. Bennett

SPRINGTIME AND HARVEST

White wings of clouds. Pollen is scattered.
The science of yesteryears hears the drums
of change
Pounding far away as an old tree resonates
Bow strings taut with the grief of joy
Extended beyond the realm of desire.

Was it mind
Or heartache we listened to when great word
slipped
Like the whisper of a ghost into silence
As ages shot up walls and clanged gates
shut
And nearness evaporated the golden ring
of promise
In hidden sound that was once superlative?

Is the face of memory no longer a mnemosyne
Grown to branch over daylight cut off
With lisp of word like gold on the tongue
Translating the hour of its own infant child?

No. Under the veil, a symphonic chord stirs.

E. Manuel Huber

COVENANT WITH EUTERPE

O Spirit of Music, Euterpe, thee
I ever praise, who biddest me
To yield my all, O hear my plea:

If to Love Divine thy power submit;
If Truth through song shall benefit;
If thy chords of harmony mortals knit;

If in thy discipline thou canst fuse
My will to God's great purpose and use,
Then this I promise to thee, dear Muse:

A chapel in my heart for thee I'll build,
Where I'll pray thee refine my talent till skilled,
Where the metronome's chime can ne'er be stilled,

Where we compose new praise to the King,
Where thou art the loveliest expressive string
My heart can play in thanksgiving,

Where Joy is thy tonic tone,
And Love thy dominant like God's throne,
And the mediant — Beauty — Euterpe, thine own.

Helen Sims Smaw

THIS WIDE HOUSE
HONORABLE MENTION

This wide house has room for him,
Rooms in rooms that smell of sunshine
And discovery.
I am virgin soil hidden here for him to come upon,
Perhaps in soft surprise.
Juniper and moonlight kiss my firehair
To light him on his way
To rooms behind rooms,
Where the sky tumbles in
Through windows that reverse the stars
And float them gently to my bed;
Delivered in velvet,
These wishes find me dreaming lightly,
Lightly of mosaics underneath my feet,
Ringed with succulents and violets
That are breathing with me,
Our exhalations ladening the air
With waiting.

Laurie B. Maynard

PROMISES

yes, i want you to smile
                    little one
        though the nights are long
    and the days never quite long enough
no — our work is never done
            and we just can't seem to find the time
    we promised one another . . .

but the hard part is past
                    i think
        and little faces ease the pain
            of the struggle we endure
                    because we know   after all
        we wouldn't have it any other way . . .

so wipe your tears
                my love
        and hold me till the dawn
        of longer days and shorter nights —
                    and yes, we'll find the time . . .
        i promise   i love you
                    . . . now smile!

Stan Yockey

PERENNIALS

We are Love's late bloomers.

The thirsts of spring
The toils of Life's summer
Turned to winter before we knew
The waiting buds within us.

We are two roses, blood-red in the snow.
Tender green leaves of wisdom
Have broken all thorns away.
We bloom in this crystal, pristine place
Too remote for the world to know.

We are late bloomers, but taught
By the turning seasons we
Fade not with the coming of spring.
When ardent new seeds begin their tortuous grope
Through the stony, cold earth
We are already here, full-blown.

We are the early bloomers.

Marie Ferneau, Msc.D.

MY ALLERGY BLUES

My Nose it looks like a big red balloon.
    Black circles are under my eyes.
I couldn't sleep a wink last night.
    I look like I've been in a terrible fight.
I cough and I wheeze, and as if that's not
    enough, I sneeze half of the night.

I ask myself "How in the world can I survive?"
    My vision is all blurred,
And my speech is all slurred,
    I scratch and I itch here and there.
I spend most of my time sitting inside
    I find pollen everywhere.

What I wouldn't give for a breath of fresh air.
    Oh, my poor, poor, drippy nose.
I've wiped it until I can't touch it anymore.
    I moan and I groan it's so sore.
I'm ready to scream,
    If you know what I mean.
From all my allergies.

Ida Rasch

33

DEIDRE
(based on the old Irish legend of Deidre of the Sorrows)
HONORABLE MENTION

Warmth and laughter
Knew you little
Lady of sorrows;
And the dream that
    sang to you,
the wild keen of your
Irish princess' blood —
was it worth
    the pain —
your stolen love?

Cyndi Straub

RENEWAL

The branches were bleak and bare,
Then a bud appeared there.
Spring came almost overnight
In profusion came blossom bright.

A thrush sang gaily in a tree,
It brought such joy to me.
The days that had been cold,
Felt springtime's youth unfold.

The world is so full of trouble,
Man's sorrows seem to daily double.
Give us in our hearts, Lord, Spring,
That man may learn again to sing.

Susie Katherine Smith

BRIGHT LIGHTS IN THE DARK

Bright lights in the dark
    Are the closest to you
Headlights, stoplights, the light of
    The train coming around the bend,
The light of the soul,
    And the light of
        Souls touching,
The light from above,
Lights from the moon and stars and
        Rising planets,
Light from within
Light from within windows
Bright lights in the dark
    Are the closest to you

Nacy B. Williams

FOR KERRY —

You stilled my restless heart
You soothed my troubled mind
You touched my life with tenderness
I thought I'd left behind

I lay beside you gentle
You kissed my tears away
You took my soul to Heaven
Now I want to stay

Wrap your love around me
Protect me from tomorrow
Find a way to ease the pain
And free me from my sorrow

Dena G. Dunn

HEARTSTRING DUET

Love and life with
Imagination in her
Nicely nurtured one
Done dancing two
Alike above both
Joyous joy coming
Awakened attenuated
Needing needing
Each ending

Loving lovely she
Imagined invincible she
Needed nonetheless she
Designed delighted she
Afloat annexed he
Joining jasmined he
Anchored allysumed she
Nested nascent she
Ecstatic essenced she

William K. Bottorff

THE GREAT PERFORMANCE

Lord, grant me the grace
        to accept old age
as just another performance
        on a brand-new stage.

Keep my mind clear;
        give me sight enough to see;
give me the ease of movement
        to make a grand entry.

Help me play the part
        with great finesse;
like the moving of a king
        in the game of Chess.

When the performance is over
        and I take my final bow,
give me all the applause
        that time will allow.

Frances Norton Russell

FREEDOM FOR ALL

America; the land of the free,
And the home of lady liberty.
The place where everyone is free,
To do and be what they want to be.

If only we truly had the choice,
To govern ourselves and express a voice.
But laws are slowly closing in,
And bringing freedom to an end.

We no longer have the right to reject,
The laws that are made to protect.
Laws are even invading our homes,
The one place that should be left alone.

We have even lost the right,
To refuse to die in a needless fight.
But we are living in a democracy,
America; the land of the free.

Darryl Griffin

BUT FOR ME

Without me never soared the lark,
    To greet the early morn;
Nor whirring partridge flew across
    The green and rustling corn;
Nor kingly eagle sailed above
    The lightning and the storm;
Nor in the golden sunshine shone
    The princely peacock's form.

I deck the helmet of the brave,
    The headdress flowing free;
And Shakespeare's page might now have been
    Unwritten, but for me.

The rainbow's brightest tints are mine,
    The whiteness of the snow,
And even midnight's ebon hue.
    A rival I can show

La Verne Jackson

COLLEEN

At first glance
it appears only to be a blue stone
that she wears on her finger.
A closer look reveals the spectrum
of its color,
she is more than just a girl.
Its color changes subtly
but unexpectedly,
unpredictable and impulsive.
Its brilliance attractive
and use versatile,
intelligent and fun.
The stone is shallow
for its size must be finite
but its depth unfathomable,
just as she.
Both are prisoners.
One of a cold metal
and the other of a cold world.

Patricia A. Clina

THE WALL

A wall, is a wall, is a wall . . .

Peaceful stone
stained with tears
and blood.
Standing today
modest, simple, old.
Strong as yesterday
though a remnant of what was.
Filled with prayers, hope, love.
Peaceful stone
living through battle after battle.
Syrians, Greeks, Romans, Crusaders . . .
History has played on you, against you,
Peaceful stone;
but history has passed.
Peaceful stone,
perch for a dove,
old cracks filled with firm new roots.

D. C. Herman

THOUGHTS OF YOU

As the ocean's tide enters and leaves,
with each rising and setting of the sun;
Each day I think at least once about you,
and realize my life's just begun.

Like the green cut grass of a summer's day,
and the scent of springtime flowers;
My heart is filled with the radiant
sunshine with each passing hour.

Like the butterflies that fly free in
peace and content,
I think of you and all the happy moments
we've spent.

But most of all like a silent miracle
performed without a clue,
You can never imagine how much I
love you.

Camille Williams

THE OLEANDER

A fraud, as the oleander,
this evergreen shrub so lovely to see,
But once consumed
how very poisonous it can be.

This camouflage that never fails
to take the strong and make them weak.
I can tell you many tales
of the new orphan men who walk the streets.

Like the greed that takes over,
that selfish desire beyond reason.
Like the oleander needs its water
to keep it growing through all seasons.

The roots grow deep
As it spreads across the land.
And always there's the inept men
Ready to water and give their hand.

Shelley L. Coombs

THE GRANDSON

To: Fannie

Nearby, where I fished
Our neighbor's grandson, tossed
By the same mysterious moment,
Drowned in our mutual lake:
I have a confession to make,
I pinch the crickets' heads off,
Before I bait my hook and while
Cheating myself of their invisible, yummy torture,
I catch less fish, or none.
The oily lake was clear
That day, below the spillway,
The fishers laughed, uncommanded, as yet,
By God, on which side to cast their hooks.
It wasn't hot that day, summer dying,
I remember, the wind scattered
The bream away, or made them wise,
I sat with my dead cricket,
Who I am sure, was grateful.

Dorie LaRue

the sigh

the taste of spring is always in my mouth —

barefoot days and naked nights,
green and gold, blue and yellow,
bright and burnished.

no winter chill can kill the thrill of spring —

aromas stabbing deep, like
honeysuckle's sweet perfume
and stinkweed, too.

but spring seems far away —

barefoot days and naked nights have fled;
bright days no longer barefoot,
nights ablaze but not now naked.

so when I sense a tiny hesitant hush —

a flickering sigh almost unheard,
dim in the morning suns,
trembling in diffusing dusks —

my hopes leap high; reality must come —

but is it **SPRING?**

James R. Newton

A GREAT TEACHER

A child, born to free us from sin;
A great teacher, He grew up to be.
Great rules He laid down for you and me,
To shape and perfect in everyone's mind,
The law and knowledge, He left behind.
Now, with His doctine we are faced
To instruct our human race.
His rules to plant within their heart —
There to grow and bloom forever into eternity.

Antonetta Knowles

TALK OF A PARTY

The sun melted into a fire truck.
The stars were green and many said,
"Let's give God a birthday party!"

"We can't do that!" one man declared.
"Nobody knows where He is."

"God is dead! God is dead!" many yelled.
"It's not true!" another said.
"I saw Him on the streets of another world!"

"How did you feel?" they wanted to know.

"The roads were fire under my feet
And I was no longer me.
I was a wave upon the sea."

"But if you saw Him?"

"The birds will tell you!
If they will not say,
Find some real people!
My eyes fester, my flesh is sore."

He said no more.
They watched him go beyond the gate.
Then turned to each other with askance.

Alta Adcock

NUBIAN TEARS

HONORABLE MENTION

Ahmed served tea, Christy listened as I told again
    Of Isaac, Ishmael, Moses — and Noah.

At the last name, Ahmed frowned and said, "Noah — a man, but no,
    For the Nubians, Noah means tears.
    Our fathers say it happened this way:
        While crossing the desert,
        A traveling man met
        A one-eyed dog.

    The journeying man stopped, stared,
        Then laughed.

    The misshapen dog, surprised and saddened,
        Inquired of the passing stranger,
    (For in Nubia, animals could speak)
        Are you laughing at me,
        Or at the God who created me?

The one-eyed dog wept in such sorrow his tears covered the earth.' "

Ahmed paused, then addressed me softly, "Madame, we
    Nubians, black sons of the desert, understand such tears."

O gentle remnant of Egyptian glory,
    I no longer laugh at one-eyed dogs.

    Doris M. Compton

COMPTON, DORIS MARTHA. Born: Eudora, Kansas, 7-9-27; Married: 6-8-54 to Dale K. Compton; Education: Fort Hays Kansas State College, Hays, Kansas, A.B., 1949; University of Arkansas, Fayetteville, Arkansas, M.A., English, 1951; Occupations: Professor of Speech, Composition, and Literature; Memberships: American Association of University Women; TESOL — Teacher of English to Students of Other Languages; Poetry: *Whisper in the Pines,* collection of poetry, self-published, Cairo, Egypt, 1972; 'My Son, My Son,' Religious — Mother of Judas, *Inner Visions,* Caribbean Consolidated Schools, 1981; 'Lament,' Questions about handicapped child, *Inner Visions,* Caribbean Consolidated Schools, 1982; 'Student Safety,' Philosophical statement of values, *Rocky Pride,* Rocky Mountain College, Billings, Montana, 1984; 'Allegro,' Tone poem to Christy about growing up, being set to music for Soprano and oboe, San Juan Conservatory of Music, San Juan, Puerto Rico; Comments: *Dale, Christy, and I spent thirteen years living overseas where we became more than tourists. We became a part of the so-called "Third World." I have written* Whisper in the Pines *and a work just completed,* Gigli and the Santos. *All are reflections of the images I have met, and the effect of that world upon me.*

CHASEN

Snow poured chaste
    cloud bushels:
Quilted shawl
    many trees.
Froze river
    into hushles.
It is winter
    please.

Now pine bough
    trinket dazzle
Icicles enow
    wrought soon
Or North Pole
    worn by frazzle
Spins east west
    ice chase moon.

    Orien Todd

TODD, ORIEN WINSLOW III. Pen Name: Orien Todd; Born: San Diego, California, 5-18-23; Education: San Diego State College, Sophomore; Occupation: Veteran; Comments: *Natural contours tend to abstraction.*

TOMORROW?

A mother holds her child
Closely to her breast.
She's walked for many miles
Denied of food or rest.

We see the look upon her face
As her precious child dies,
And as we sit and watch
We hear the mother's cries.

We watch as naked children
Laid out side by side,
The life drained from their bodies,
Are starved and crucified.

And yet we make excuses
And ignore the pain and sorrow.
We go on with our lives
And say we'll help tomorrow.

Another child cries in pain.
Another mother weeps.
Another baby fades away
Slowly as he sleeps.

We can't wait until tomorrow
To show them someone cares.
Now's the time to help
With the power of our prayers.

    Susan Jean Bell

A LETTER TO MARY BETH

Dear Mary Beth, my heart's delight
Your love makes everything so right.
I'm writing you this little letter
To try to help your day go better.
I know it's hard when we're apart
But when we're not, you fill my heart
No one could ever take your place
And when I see your smiling face
Or call you on the telephone.
I know I'm never quite alone.
Because in fair or gloomy weather
I know that soon we'll be together
I love you more each passing minute
And my future's brighter because you're in it,
So remember this when I am gone
And our love will help you carry on

                Very much love,
                Ralph

Ralph Bruce Ames

LOVE'S REFLECTIONS

If you can look into my eyes
And see the "me" that's hidden there
Behind the changes in myself,
'Mid life's confusion laid so bare;

If you can look beyond my face
And see the "me" you loved before,
In spite of imperfections great
And life's frustrations by the score;

If you can look into my heart
You'll find it's full of you, so free
Of imperfections that you shine
Like mirrors, reflecting back at me.

If you can feel the arms of my heart
Reach out and love the "you" I see,
You'll find *you're* beautiful, strong and free,
Just like you patiently see in me.

Ann Ruble Bieberich

THE BAG LADY WAITS
IN THE LONG SLOW DAY.

Of monsters there are many on the moors
and in the crystal forest under trees,
and skulking in the caves by ocean shores
where they whimper in the sea's coldest breeze,

but unworldlier far is that haggard ragged hag
rummaging the refuse of our city
like a rat, till GOD'S benign moneybag
spills out the sun, human truths, and pity.

That garbage she collects becomes her food
and cloth and lamplit daily amusement,
and she prates and she animates her good
night's pickings, in adequate tenement:

she maunders to flowers found last night, a stone,
an image of a pert maid, or a son.

D. Castleman

OKLAHOMA PRAIRIE SKY

Celia, my small black pony, and I
raced across the prairie
toward a setting sun.
A light fragrance of green grass and scrub oak
combined to make perfume — almost intoxicating.
The wind in my hair spelled freedom.

I lifted the reins; Celia slowed
to a leisurely gallop.
It was easy for me to settle into
the same smooth rhythm.
The monotonous beat of Celia's hooves
could lull me into daydreams anytime.

And so it was that the sky was no longer just a sky.
It was a huge, round, blue bowl turned upside down
and decorated on the inside with a sunset.
Tumbled clouds, deep pink, blended into baby pink,
interspersed with dazzling silver
radiating from a hidden sun.

The sunset wasn't far away —
or so it seemed.
Celia and I would be there soon,
where we would become
a visible part
of that glorious burst of color and light.

Leota Cooke Hall

HALL, EMMA LEOTA. Pen Name: Leota Cooke Hall; Born: Torre de Cillas, Texas; Married: 1949 to Donald Clarence Hall; Education: University of Oklahoma at Norman, Oklahoma, B.A., English major, foreign language minor: French, Spanish, and German; Occupation: High School Teacher: I taught English, French and Spanish; Comments: *I love reading poetry and I enjoy writing it. There is no common theme. For example, my poem in the 1983 American Poetry Anthology is about war. My poem in the 1985 anthology gets its theme from the Bible. And this poem, written for* The Art of Poetry *is a true story about myself. It all happened a long long time ago, but it seems like yesterday.*

KATIE

Swing up high o missy fair —
feel the breeze
blow your hair . . .
Mommy's pushing you with delight
Still a baby but oh so bright.

Winter will come
and the snow will fall —
Your cheeks rosy red
A snowman for all.

When spring will come
a little girl will arise
pumping herself
with great surprise!

Jessica

COLLOQUY

In halcyon
water flows:
tumbling over rocks
gurgling and purling
finding crevices
gathering in pockets
lapping against the shore
stealing slowly the earth.
In anger
water roars,
pounding the rocks
relentlessly
beating, splashing
tearing at the shore
cutting it away.

Christa Payne

FIRST LOVE

My first love
Was no different than
Any other first love.
When I met him,
I was sure
That he would be
My one and only.
But after awhile,
We lost touch
With each other.
No matter
What changes,
I will always
Care for him
With all my heart.

Dawn Clark

IS THIS REAL

I am in a state of illusion
A feeling tickling me deep within
Magnifying a weakness so foreign to me
Such a new experience
I almost fear the feeling.

Whispers of a voice, vision of a smile
Lingers within my mind,
Warm embrace still so real.

A relationship so intense
So magnified
So fulfilling
Could I be in love?
Or is this an illness of fantasy.

Judy G. McCormack

THE LAST ILLUSION

Oh the singing and piping
Marching and leaping
Are futile . . . you see
. . . in the last review.

Because

The pine soughs a lesson true
and long I listen 'mid
Dusty meadow rue. — That
Life's final illusion is you.

Sandra Thomas

JUSTICE

Is it the judge who judges you,
or you
Who judge the judge?

Harshly nor too lenient
let the pointing arrows twain
though in fairness seek
to strive I — and both in time again

In awe both edges cut
Balanced into time
Why the fold upon my head
the reason I am blind

John Massaro

AVALANCHE!

My desk
is a disaster area!
Loose streams of
calculator tape
winding carelessly
over tops of journals.
Vouchers buried
between pages of
ledger books.
Pencils sprawled
between open cracks
of desk.

Franklin Delano Gesswein

TO BE IN LOVE

I cannot express in words or deeds
How you have filled my deepest needs.
the day has arrived in all its glory
To celebrate, to unfurl this story
Of another year that you are here
To bless me with joy and good cheer.

Humbly I bow to all you say
With hope that the vote is ever Yea!
I bless the time that you appeared
For I was then smitten and seared.
But to know you is to be in love
And so I am, by the One above.

Jack Tusin

SEE THE SUN

See the sun rising so brilliantly
Golden orb rising majestically
Warm the earth and flame the skies
Ball of fire burning eternally

Rising sun lay hold the earth
Spinning morn to evening in your light
Your planets held in their orbital paths
Galaxy's heart God's good light

Turn your eyes to eastern skies
Receive the glow and drink full the sight
New the day O cosmic Christ
God's own son we rise to greet you

Richard Edward Morris

FLY HIGH

Fly high, let your thoughts fly high.
Up to the heights of wonderment.
To the brilliance of the shining stars.
To a place of unknown bewilderment.

Fly high, let your thoughts fly high.
Up to the bellowing clouds above.
To a spiritual shining light.
To the unseen flame of love.

Fly high, let your thoughts fly high.
Up to the Resurrected One.
To a place of peace and joy.
To the love of God's own Son.

Theresa Heiman

LOVE IS

Love is like the flowers
That bloom early in the spring.
Bonds of love are forever,
Like the circle of a ring.

Love is all around you,
Everywhere you go.
And when you find that someone,
Feelings of love will grow.

Love is very special,
And someday you will find,
That someone you will love,
With all your heart and mind.

Linda Ann Berry

INCOMPLETE

Leave me something to dwell upon,
Or joy of life would then be gone,
Don't let me think that I have done,
Enough that life is fully won;

For there is always more to learn,
The right to life I want to earn.
Please never let me feel complete,
For that would be my worst defeat.

Don't let me fail to question why,
The miracle of sun and sky.
The day I think I am fulfilled,
My mind and body will be stilled.

Joseph M. Byron

REMINISCE

Days of shorts and sun-streaked hair
And lazy pool-side bliss.
As we'd walk by, we'd catch a glimpse
Of boys that were sun-kissed.

The meetings at MacDonald's
The backyard pool parties.
Staying out late and cruising the town
In our comraderies.

The drive-in and the cycle races.
We were just having fun.
The summer just got started,
And our lives had just begun.

It was almost a California summer;
With everything but the seashore.
But we made the most of what we had,
And it was more than we had hoped for.

Now smoke from chimneys fill the sky,
And summer is three months past.
Autumn comes falling in;
Summer never lasts . . .

Miki Rankin

GOODBYE

We said goodbye a long time ago,
knowing that we'd never part in
our hearts.
     But goodbyes are not forever.
Forever is being apart.
     We wait and we wait, for one
hello, but silence is what we hear.
     The phone doesn't ring, the mail
doesn't come. I sit in my chair
counting the minutes that seem
like years.
     The time we've been apart
has broken my heart. I've turned
to stone.
     I await your return with an
angry soul and anxious heart.
     But you never will say hello again.
It will always remain goodbye.

Nancy E. Ansley

A PROMISE OF LOVE

I'd love to open wide my arms
And gather you close within.
Close to me so I can feel
Your sweetness and devotion.

I'd love to look upon your face
And see my love reflected.
To show you how I feel inside
And know I'll be respected.

I'd love to hold your hand in mine
Knowing it will guide me
Along the same paths you will walk.
Strong and always steady.

I'd love to feel your lips touch mine
Trading our mutual love.
Tenderly we breathe our sighs;
Parting never dreamt of.

I'd love to feel your heart beat fast
Pulsing love within you.
Your promise you have given me
My promise yours now too.

Margie Frey

IMPATIENT PATIENT

Nothing to do,
Nothing to say,
Nothing but lie here
Day after day.

Nothing to drink,
Nothing to eat,
Nothing but needles
When I crave meat.

Nothing but nurses,
Nothing but blues,
Nothing to wear,
Not even my shoes.

Nothing but doctors
With scissors and knife.
Nothing but bills
For the rest of my life.

Gertrude Payne Lewis

WISH

Sing a song of pain and sorrow.
Or sing a song of love and light.
I just live to hear you sing,
Wish I may or wish I might.

If we bid farewell for a short while —
If the rainbow's dark and lost its hue,
Burn the candle high at midnight
And I will find my way to you.

Lie upon a bed of feather;
I'll tell you stories of what could be.
Or lie upon a bed of brass and
I'll play you any melody.

If you feel as if you're losing,
And there's nothing left to choose,
Rest your weary eyes a moment
And I will build a new world for you.

Laura C. Antonio

SORROW'S WORST

So deep a wound it was to see
     Those tears upon her face;
Like thoughtless words, they fell so free
     And took Joy's rightful place.

Her world was crushed by sobbing blows —
     Deep wounds I could not heal!
And Sorrow's worst I came to know,
     That here, I could but feel.

In helpless arms I held her tight,
     As if to leech her pain;
But only Time, with fingers light,
     Was blessed to lift that stain.

How dear we hold our future names
     On Life's eternal Wheel:
For though our greatest joy they claim,
     Their pain, we too must feel.

D. C. Doede

A PRISONER OF THE SEA

Just where the blue skies meet the land
And the gentle seas caress the sand;
There, I'll spend eternity,
For I'm a prisoner of the sea.
I'm imprisoned in a lonely Hell,
Upon the sea with rise and swell;
Like a ship afloat on some strange sea,
You made a prisoner out of me.
I know that there is no release;
Yet, someday I hope to find peace,
When My ship sails beyond that shore;
There will be peace forevermore.
I love the sea I don't deny;
My ship beneath a starry sky,
But why make a prisoner out of ME?
Release your hold and set Me free.

ENVOI

When I die please cremate me;
Spread my ashes o'er the sea.
Spread them where the four winds blow,
So the sea can recall my soul.

Le Roy F. Oates

THE CALLING

To feel my soul's heart
And touch the Glory of God
I am like the shadow
Which exists only in light
An image which does
Not exist in the darkness
For in darkness all things
Are shadows and nondistinguishable
It takes the sharp contrast of
Light to bring out from reality
The subtle and the unsure.

Victor Darnel Hadnot

HADNOT, VICTOR DARNEL. Born: West Los Angeles, California, 8-17-54; Single; Education: Associate Degree; Pharmacy Technician Diploma, 1980 and 1982; Occupations: Pharmacy Technician; Musician; Poetry: 'Honor and Majesty,' 'The Moon and the Earth,' 'The Morning Walk,' and 'Departure,' all published by American Poetry Association; Comments: *My firm belief that Lord Jesus Christ is the Son of God is what "calls" me to write. Talent like all gifts of God should be used to serve Him. Hope, charity, and faith can be expressed in different ways for different reasons.*

INDULGE ME PLEASE
(I'm new)

I try to write verse every day but sometimes
get in my own way, with thoughts and
words that just won't say — my feeling.
I fumble this and jumble that and never
wind up where I'm at, the ears doth ring
the head goes flat — and reeling.
Well that's when I just pull up short, pour
some coffee have a snort and light a cig
so I don't court — the ceiling.
Hot dog at last I'm back in thought, the words
start coming like they ought and flow forth
fast like they've been caught — concealing.
Now all that's left for me to do is get it all
across to you, in words, a bunch or just a few — appealing!

Dorothy Barton Benson

LET NOT MY WORDS

Let not my words be thongs that bind you mute,
That make me tyrant to your way and will.
I would not have your ardent courage still,
Your dreaming heart be empty, destitute.
Let not my words be bars that shut you in;
I would not have your questing spirit lie
With folded wings because you love strange sky.
Far hills and vales are where your dreams begin.

But let my words be an oasis where
You come at last across the desert waste,
Weary from battle, burned with the mind's own fire.
And when you stop to slake your thirst, may there
Be words enough to stay your restless haste
And may they last as long as your desire.

Merle Price

THE SUN

When the sun falls down
It leaves us alone in this town
When the sun falls down
Tomorrow I'll be fighting off one more round
I failed as a clown
My woman waits for me in a golden gown
Her hair matches the sparkles in her eyes
When the sun falls down
It leaves us alone in this town
Practice makes perfect
Love destroys freedom
Practice makes perfect
Love destroys memories
When the sun falls down
It leaves us alone in this town

Hugh J. Ehlers

OLD JEFF

"You know, I never knew his name," so many people say,
But many a time he stopped to talk and pass the time of day.
All remember well his craggy, laugh-lined face
And the hearty, ringing laughter that echoed through the place.
Each day the streets of town he'd walk
He'd take the time to stop and talk
Of simple things, that make our lives from day to day.
He'd joke a bit and then go on his way.
He's gone now and the legacy he left behind
Is one of pleasant memories that will often come to mind.
Like most of us, he had no claim to fame
But in days to come, at mention of his name
What better monument when life is at an end
Than to have the people say, "Remember Jeff?
Of course! He was a friend!"

Evelyn Horn Welch

REACH OUT AND BE A FRIEND

Reach out and be a friend,
    Be a friend to those who feel
discouraged,
    Be a friend to those who feel
defeated,
    Be a friend to those who feel lonely,
    Yes, reach out and be a friend.

Reach out and be a friend,
    Be a friend to those who feel
afraid of life,
    Be a friend to those who are not
sure of their value in life,
    Be a friend to those who feel like
copping out,
    Yes, reach out and be a friend.

Reach out!
    Yes, I said reach out and be a friend,
    Reach out and take somebody's hand,
    Reach out and give something of yourselves,
    Yes, reach out and love somebody.

Reach out and be a friend,
    Be a friend who helps,
    Be a friend who advises,
    Be a friend who understands,
    Be a friend who cares,
    Yes, reach out and just be a friend.

Lois Nicholson

SCARLET TANAGER'S GIFT

When I sat by hearth's fire
My thoughts were inspired
As my gaze would fall fondly
On her — and 'cause I loved
Her too dearly —
I just tweeted too clearly
Having learned how to tweet
In her own special way

I still recall how she scuttled
When acting macho and subtle
I would hustle and bustle to —
Tweet out my love to her every day.

Then, like a storm without warning
I awoke one morning, and found that —
My tweetie was not in her bed —
I squawked and I muttered at not seeing —
Her flutter and my tweets were unlike
The ones that I squawked in happier days

Lots of courage I mustered as I stepped then
Much closer to look at my sweet little scarlet
Tanager's bed.

I was startled by tweetings
My thoughts gently fleeting
It was then when I noticed
That my tweetie — gave me a bird!

Judy Palmieri

HAPPINESS IS . . .

Each new day God gives to you . . .
Knowing that God is ever true . . .
Going through life with someone you love . . .
The silver lining in clouds above . . .
Hoping each day brings something splendid and new . . .
Watching the children as they play . . .
Being with someone special today.

Mrs. A. Mullet

THE REFLECTION

Each tiny line tells a story,
    Each crease upon the brow;
Each strand of hair changed colors,
    Earned the right to be somehow!

The eyes look tired and weary,
    Yet the twinkle still remains;
A cough; A breath; A wrinkled smile
    slowly quivers with the strain!

Outside she's old and tattered;
    Forgotten by all her kin,
But the memories life has left her,
    Keeps the flame spurred within!

No time to tell the story.
    No one to lend an ear.
Just the looking-glass reflection,
    Of the woman in the mirror!

Colleen Doyle

PARTING AND REUNION

There comes a time when we must leave
Our loved ones in God's keeping,
For there is nothing to be gained
With all our tears and weeping.

The hurt may linger for a while
As you recall your sorrows
But God is watching over you
With brightly filled tomorrows.

While comfort sweet drawn from His Word
And stronger faith He's giving,
Just keep on trusting in the Lord
In all your daily living.

The saints in heaven and those on earth
with souls joined in communion
Are waiting for the Lord to come.
Oh, blessed sweet reunion.

Meta Rucks

THE UNBORN SOLDIERS

Who will cry for the unborn soldier?
Who didn't have a chance for the
Outside world.
Soldiers of many colors, boys and
girls.

There didn't have a chance, to cry for
Food, or anything.
They would have been better off if
They was just a song to sing.

At least then they could have been
heard. But they didn't get to say,
Just one word.

Who will cry for the unborn soldiers?
I will and so will many others.
But most of all the unborn soldiers'
Fathers and their mothers.

Mary Brown

REMEMBER

My life's ok,
My feelings tender,
What happened to the times
I love to remember?

When we were one,
Till the days were done,
What happened to those times?

And remember when,
Our love was strong,
And we'd be together
On the days that grew long?

And then we'd sing our songs of gladness,
Even in the times of sadness.

But even now,
With feelings tender,
Don't ever think
I won't remember.

Chris Paulk

FOR JOHN LENNON (d. 1980)

Starting over —
the Great Wheel
turning
once more.

A clear light
falling upon
the world
once more.

A toy world
of peace,
imagine . . .

Imagine!

Out of the
rising mists
on strawberry fields,
lifts the light,
shines the light.

Bruce Ross

I'm all alone — but there you are
Close to me — you're not far

The bond I sense carries through
It's unbreakable — yet fragile too

As with you, treated with care
tenderness and much more shared

And much of 'other' is so far away
because to you, my heart does stray

This bond is a most outrageous thing
So much so it brings a sting

People know the way I talk of you
and it sounds as if I really do

I LOVE YOU

If these are similar to other lines
It's because you fill my time

Jacqueline Corso

THE DRAGON'S FLIGHT

Perilous is the dragon's flight,
haunting where he will or might.
Lurching in and out of sight,
he cheats the moon and steals the night.

His rabid path of to and fro
commands the embered midnight glow
to taunt an ashen world below
with when he'll be and when he'll go.

Snarls maraud cherubic sleep
and penetrate within so deep —
to where dragons ever keep —
the timeless halls of memories weep.

Scream silent, child; no motion sway
for either lures him by your way
and thrusts you into dragon's play
'til he succumbs to light of day.

Robin J. Gauthier

AN OBVIOUS EXPLANATION

I care so much about you
just because
I care so much about you.

Martha A. Hirsch

HONORABLE MENTION

From this desk
I create new worlds
carved from old habits
finally laid to rest
in a labyrinth of bones,
those rituals I gave lip service to
all the days of my youth
when doggedly I made my way
to sacred steps of sterile Saint Francis,
and stubbornly, as in rehearsal,
filed to the altar:
lamb to the chopping block,
puppet made to dance,
mind made to follow,
heart to praise
what I do not, cannot,
will not see hidden
in a dried piece of bread
raised high above my humble head
where I dream of new worlds.

Joan A. Ledoux

LITTLE THINGS

Now that you're gone
I think of little things
Like fishing rods
You left in my basement
Your straggling mail
That still comes to my house
I think about
The funny way you snore
And how your eyes
Crinkle up when you laugh
And look too blue
To be real eyes at all
And how quiet
You are when you're afraid
Did I mention
I wish you were still here
It's little things
I turn around to tell you
Now that you're gone

Donna Upton

AULD LANG SYNE

The old goes out, the new comes in,
        The year is past.
We celebrate with noise and fun,
        We have a blast.

But time goes marching, leaping on.
        And we go, too.
Day in, day out, and year by year,
        Each one is new.

We can't recall the time we've spent
        In days of old.
So we must live each day we have
        As though it's gold.

No sadness in this Auld Lang Syne;
        Instead, rejoice!
And live life to its full degree
        By conscious choice.

Francine Morrow Keehnel

A STAR

A star came down from Heaven tonight
        And whispered in my ear,
"Ralph loves you even more today,
        More than when he was here!"

A star came down from Heaven tonight
        And softly kissed my cheek
As tenderly as he kissed mine
        That day by the winding creek.

A star came down from Heaven tonight
        And gently held my hand,
"We'll comfort you till you can join
        Him in that Fairer Land."

Oh, star tonight take this embrace,
        This tender, loving kiss
And give them all to him till I
        Join him in Heaven's bliss!

Thelma Van Scoik

THE NAMELESS ME

My trunk does not carry clothes
But curls, gently touches
And slurps up liquid flow
That cleans and cools my thirst.

My tail is nothing to prize,
But a gadget ready to spot
And flip off stubborn flies
That use my skin encamp.

My tusks are ivory rich,
For which man seeks my life.
For want of jewel enrich,
Man seeks my clan to blank.

My size and strength a team,
Can strip acacia bare and flat
To munch for life and wait
For man to trace my track.

Kaakyire Akosomo Nyantakyi (Sam)

MY ROCKING CHAIR

My old dilapidated rocker
Is the only friend I need
        I don't have any money
And my yard's just one big weed

        But me and my patched-up rocker
We get along just fine
        We just sit a-rockin' and a-hummin'
It's the only thing that's mine

        You know — that crazy rocker
Has got so used to me
        It even rocks when I ain't in it
How close can two friends be

        I wouldn't give my rocker up
When there's nails and paint around
        I'll even put a headboard on it
And use it six feet underground

        Then I'll rock my way to Heaven
And find a cloud up there
        And spend all my time a-singin'
On my faithful rocking chair

Lee Mason

It was a shooting star
In the dead of night
Not one but three

Some say accursed is that star
For it sets ablaze the earth

Others say blessed is that star
So make a wish

I say God has wept a tear
and it has traversed the universe
for you; reach out for it,
Let it smolder in your eyes
Let the years of memorabilia come to you
Let the longing and aching increase

The star will soothe you
Grasp it — for God may never weep again.

Mrs. Ismet Abdulla

THE OLD HOMEPLACE

"Here you can no longer stay —
        Sell the place and move away!"
Those are the very words today
        That my son to me did say.

Sell the place that's been my home,
        Since my footsteps ceased to roam?
Sell the place that is a part —
        Of every dream that's in my heart?

Sell the place — oh nay, oh nay,
        Let me linger one more day!
Let me gather all my souvenirs
        Of these many happy years!

The peace, the happiness and content
        Of the many hours here spent.
Now you want me "just to go"
        But my rebellious heart says no.

I know you think it's for the best,
        That from my busy life I rest.
But given my choice, I will say —
        Just let me stay here one more day.

Mary Sachs Zello

IMMIGRANTS

Though they may have neither discovered
        nor explored,
They gave up ancestral countries to make
        America home
Bringing with them customs, traditions,
        and skills,
And all the moral values with which they
        had grown.

Willing to work hard in pursuit of their
        many dreams,
They overcame poverty, misery, ignorance,
        and indignity,
And while striving to make life better
        for themselves,
They have taught their descendants true
        meaning of liberty.

Eva Marie Ippolito

BOUQUET OF LOVE

Kittens hiding by the steps, in among the
flowers,
When I was just a little girl, I whiled
away the hours,
Playing with the kittens and watching
far-off towers.

I would sit in the garden in the warm
glow of the sun,
And play and dream all afternoon until
the day was done,
Then I'd pick some bleeding hearts and
make a bouquet,
I'd hurry home with my prize to hear
my mother say, "Thank you, dear, they're
beautiful," and that would make my
day.

J.D. MacLellan

THE CLOUD

I weep the world over,
heavy, leaden with sorrow,
and angry thunderbolts leap from my side.
In winter I bury mountain and valley alike
        under snow.
I dissolve myself so
when I can no longer bear earth's gravity;
        some say I die.
But sun shining through my tears
        makes the rainbow;
and it is the same sun
calling my spirit back from earth,
the sun toward whom I rise invisible
to be reborn, high
        in cold thin air,
                                light,
wearing a blue fringe of sky.
Pamela Mausner

MY WHOLE LORD

My whole Lord is in that drawer,
Pictures of everyone I've ever known
And every place I've ever been:
Mementos from times totally or absolutely
Otherwise forgotten.
If the contents of that drawer
Were to disappear,
I would be gone;
Because my whole Lord
Is in that drawer.

Betty Jane Yadede

A SPECIAL FLOWER

The winter rains have left our soil,
    So mellow — rich and brown.
Spring is here and little flowers
    are blooming all around.
God knows this is the year,
    that the seed He must sow,
Will be a "Special Flower,"
    to make the others grow.
A flower with petals of purest white,
    to dance in the wind with sheer delight.
She'll flutter softly in the breeze,
    and cast her spell on all the trees.
She'll smile and wave her tiny hand,
    and leave her fragrance on the land.
As we walk down the path of Memory Lane,
We'll see a "Special Flower"
    "Princess Paula" will be her name.

Kathlyn Marie Kilgore

MY FATHER'S DAUGHTER

Before the morning light crept through his window,
my Father would sit on the edge of his bed
waiting for the alarm to scream.
His cigarette lit, intruding into darkness
with its red eye floating, glowing.
My Father, in silence,
waking long before the birds would sing
to stare somewhere upon the floor.
Smoking   pondering,
maybe he was thinking, perhaps
thinking about me.
I cannot know.
the dwindling red-eye-glow
is all that I can see
as I sit on the edge of my bed,
Smoking
Pondering

Andrea M. Tait

LIFE IS A DRAG

Life is a drag, an ersatz masquerade . . .
Sometimes it's a Halloween party unmasked;
At other times it's almost funereal,
Desperately sad, a tearful wake . . .
A fox, a chicken, a slippery snake!

People impersonating people,
Acting, reacting, giving and taking,
Sniveling and shaking, never themselves . . .
Monsters, gargoyles, weak little elves!

The only time you are truly you
Is when you're lying abed, awake, alone,
Thinking about it all, counting sheep,
Awaiting the call to peaceful sleep.
Life is a drag!

Theodore V. Kundrat

SEARCHING FOR YOU

Walking down the street I'm searching for you
The one that will take away all my blues
When you're in sight
I'll know you're right
'Cause in my ear there will be a jingle
And in my body there will be a tingle
Of hope and joy that you will be
The man I'm soon to marry
'Cause I have so much confidence in my heart
That will keep us bound together and never apart.

Sandra Riggins

PARTING SMILE AND TEAR

When you arrive — write up just a few lines,
I'll get quiet receiving them
And doesn't matter if many full stops . . .
Beyond them I see your face,
And doesn't matter if many full stops . . .
Beyond them I see your face.

No full stops they are, they are your hands,
That's your lips and your eyes,
I memorize all of your words
And the hope of love flamed up,
But more than any words clear told me —
Your parting smile and tear,
But more than any words then told me —
Parting smile and tear.

I memorize all of your words
And the hope of love flamed up,
But more than any words clear told me —
Your parting smile and tear,
But more than any words told me —
Your parting smile and tear.

N. Far

FAR, NET. Pen Name: N. Far; Born: Ukraine, 5-28-23; Education: Law Degree, 1948; Mechanic University, Engineer, 1960; Occupation: Mechanical Designer; Poetry: 'Melting Hope of Love (Cranes),' 'Love — C'est La Vie,' 'I Love You With Your Blind Eyes,' 'When You Could Know,' 'Velvet Night,' 'Where,' 'Your Words, Flowers, Love,' 'Do You Recall?' 'You — My Closest,' 'White Narcissus,' 'Farewell Schoolmate Woltz'; Other Writings: "Insulted and Undeservedly Beaten Baby," scenario, "Tranquilizers for . . . Crying Guards (That's Amore)," "Baby Accepts His Divorced Father"; Comments: *I write for the same reason for which one writes: because he can't not write, and, in addition, it's one of the ways of ego manifestation, a 'sin' which many, if not all, of us more or less possess.*

LOVE'S ROSE

The rose of love, each petal holds the memories
of the times spent with you.
The thorns are a reminder of the hurts we caused each
other.
And the fragrance is like the beauty that I see
in you.

Richard Browne

THE AUCTION SALE

Buying things you do not need
Like an old bird cage made from reed.

A comfortable chair used when models posed
The surprise, when the auctioneer said, "Sold"

Objects that have a heart appeal
Such as the old spinning wheel —

An old garden gate too small to use
A box of jewels your friends would not refuse —

A one-seated car, you always wanted
By now your thoughts, the cash should be counted

The last you bought was an old trunk, too heavy to carry.
But no thoughts of doubt or worry.

Anxious to open the trunk with care
We found treasures and the motor for the car —

Ella A. Buck

MYTH OF A GHOST TOWN

Tall they were and silent
amid the ruins.
And as the noise of the sea
tumbled up to them, they
remembered the storm, the floundering houses,
as winds and wild rains whipped the streets,
and people fled, claiming nothing
but the struggle to stay alive.

Never would they return, they had cried,
unanimously.
But having reached the calm of sheltered ground,
the storm-tossed lives could only accept
what the heart told them was so.

Too gentle were the calm, the rippled creek
and corn growing green in strange fields.
Instinct pulled.
And from restless calm, to the ever-restless rocking
of the sea,
two who are brothers have come home.

Ruth Summers

RE BIRDS

Sea birds must know the secret of peace.
Pelicans on piers are serene, undisturbed.
Wild geese speed across the sky in V-formation,
Honking in unison. Herons and egrets share food.
Sea gulls space themselves on wires silently.
Sandpipers play beach games, uninterrupted;
And when the games are done, they scamper along
The water's edge together, then lift off and
Fly away without argument.

But I have watched robins fight like gladiators,
Reel drunkenly after eating pyracantha berries,
And a returning pair of swallows disagree on
Where to build a new nest, then separate forever.
Crows, woodpeckers and mockingbirds are vicious;
They wage territorial wars, I am told.
Placid old hens in the chicken yard do battle
If the pecking order is violated, and then
The rooster becomes the police at once.

Land birds know war. Sea birds know peace.

Grace Patrick Madigan

TWILIGHT PEOPLE

My people are the twilight people . . . Ex-
factory horses and garbage rats . . .

Early in the morning when the . . . shape
and stench of left-overs line the street . . .

Early in the morning when the pickers
come to pray . . .

Early in the morning . . .

My people are the twilight people

Leonard M. Kuras

IMAGINATION

Have you ever tasted a wild strawberry?
Its taste is unique, inimitable and
Far sweeter than anything cultivated by man,
Who is at best, a protegé of the divine mother.
She was sowing and reaping ere man
Held a seed in the palm of his hand.
The same is true of poets,
For while some thoughts may be cultivated
Through toil, their taste remains bitter
In comparison to the sweet, spontaneous,
Wild imaginings of a poet,
Through whose eyes we are permitted a glimpse,
Into the immortal.

Jeffrey W. Jensen

THE AFFAIR

Like a splash of perfume
A memorable zigzag of lightning awakening our respect
Fireflies in darkness
The celestial blaze of a comet in a starry sky.

  It was. It was hot.
  Then forever gone with an end but no ending.
  Without beginning.

    Just a perpetual vacuous ache from the crispness
    And depth of it all.

    It lingers . . .

Charlotte A. Bowlds

MEMORIES

MEMORIES are visions that never fade.

I wonder if they are just a charade.

There are good MEMORIES and bad MEMORIES,
  but they all seem to come together quite well.

Some may get you in trouble and others will make you happy.

Remember no one can take your MEMORIES away, good or bad.

MEMORIES are forever!

April Evonne Powell

REMBRANDT, Great Jewish Bride

SOUL MATES

What is a Soul Mate
But one which you've looked for,
To share with you, your life
And eternity as no one before.

They come together
Dressed as most men and women,
Speaking the same language
Warm, honest, trusting and human.

Taking time to be friends
Before being lovers so dear,
With a romance that lasts
Year after changing year.

The gift they offer
Is the gift of love,
They encourage, coax and inspire
The other to reach above.

This love drenched in color
As they found each other,
And their lives were transformed
As Soul Mates touched one another.

William E. Poe

Loving you
was easy
never any hesitation
only emotions
spilling from my heart
should I have held back
it's too late now
I'm lost in your world
and it's tearing me apart
I need you
want to hold you again
but I am only
clinging to empty promises
searching for an answer
waiting for the end
it never comes
only disillusions
love me now
end my fears
or let me go

Christine Durbin Beelitz

THE BUILDER

Looking out my window,
I see a strong, good-looking man,
Measuring off the footage,
Laying out his plans.

His face shows pleasure,
As he does the work at hand.
Using saw and hammer,
Building forms upon the land.

His strength is overwhelming,
He's absorbed in his work;
As he pours the foundation,
To this huge lakeside resort.

The hammers, saws and machinery,
Bring pleasure to the mind.
As the hum in perfect rhythm,
Aiding men of day and time.

The building is completed.
He stands with hat in hand.
He's proud of his creation,
As he shakes the owner's hand.

Von L. Decker

THE HAND OF GOD

A crystal mist of ocean spray,
The chimes of golden bells,
A scent of Jasmine in the air
That lingers as it dwells
Amid the pine and cedar trees,
Where green grass decks the sod;
Some think it all a happenstance —
I know it comes from God.

A haze of smoke in summertime,
That lingers in the sky;
The honking of the great snow goose,
A-winging south on high
The charms of lowland split rail fence,
the sight of Golden Rod,
Some think it all an accident —
I know it comes from God.

A thunder in the ocean tide,
A surging, roaring swell,
A foghorn on a misty coast,
Where rocks and buoys dwell;
Oh a sense of endless beauty,
In fields where oxen plod;
Some think it evolution —
I know it comes from God.

James A. Hanf

THE CRYSTAL OF ABSENT LOVE

I dreamed of shadows beyond the horizon,
While moonbeams danced a step —
I saw the figures of lovers once lived;
They were laughing, they were left.

Out of the woods I saw a rainbow,
It spoke of how the sun passed away,
And how, along with life,
Did all our memories turn to decay.

I heard some music soft to hear,
I felt some anger fill its calm,
And then, I realized it was too late,
For all the kingdoms had fallen to fear.

James Wesley Duren

THE ONE WE LOVED

The one we loved,
Was the one who cared,
And dared
To do it his way.
Sometimes the wrong way;
But always his way.

Slightly naive,
A prankster,
Always full of fun,
Looking out for number one.

A man-child,
Wavering,
Between the innocence of youth,
And the maturity of man.
Ever-growing ever-changing.

Man-child into eternity,
The loved ones left behind,
To catch up later.
He waits;
To lead them to a better life.

Some day all will be reunited.

Deanna Decker

GOD IS THERE

There are so many roles in life,
Roles we're asked to play.
We make such hard work of them;
There is an easier way.

When you're called upon to teach,
Think, there's your peer.
When you're called upon to be a nurse,
The Physician will be there.
When you're called upon to be a rock,
A pillar to lean on soon appears.
When sadness and grief overcomes us,
He's there to dry the tears.

Why do we doubt His presence
When emotions tear us apart?
God is always close to us,
Just look within your heart.

There will be trials in all our lives
that we'll be asked to bear.
But truly we will never be alone,
Remember — Always — God is there.

Sharon Powell

A SWEET SYMPHONY

When the Lord brings together,
Two people in love,
United as one, and blest from above,
When a man leaves his mother,
A woman her home,
Together forever, the two become one.

Two lives that will travel,
Through laughter, through tears,
They'll count all their blessings,
Throughout precious years.

May laughter and sunshine,
Brighten their life,
As together they journey,
As husband and wife.

They'll walk hand in hand,
Down an aisle of their own,
Never again, to be all alone,
May their lives hold together,
In sweet harmony,
A musical opera or a sweet symphony.

Shirley Ostapowich

LIFE

Life goes on and on
As the days and years go by.
Time never stands still;
It makes you want to cry.

You must live life to its fullest,
And not let others in your way;
For life is short, time so fast —
It won't last forever — they say.

There are many things in life
That's part of our growing;
Greed, love, hate, and endurance —
And everywhere it's showing.

You must endure a lot in life,
If not, you will perish.
A person has to understand,
Then many things he'll cherish.

Carol Vidrine

MY GRANDMA DIED
May 25, 1984 — Minnie Shaw Died

I will not forget you,
For you were like a mother.
I cried a million tears,
For you were gone.
We shared a very precious thing, love.
Oh love, how true it is,
And hurts so bad,
And I felt so sad,
For you were gone.

Iris Shaw Cardenas

LOVE

Your love I treasure
You fill me with pleasure
Your love cannot be measured
It is like a dove
Sent from above
A love that will endure
A love that is kind and pure
True love is hard to find
Yours is loyal, faithful, loving, and kind
Yours will last to the end of time
Love is made by God divine

Geneva Perry

STANDING ROCK MONUMENT

Stone Woman,
From holy travois treasured
Now pedestaled for all to see.
Look not back in anger
Your heart is a part of me.
Ask not for more to be
Or to have been.
Your life repeats itself in men
Of every tribe.
Stone Woman,
Pedestaled, be their guide.

Marcia L. Nesset

RAGE OF WINTER

Dumped pounds of snow
around my house
locked me in
to grieve for summer's joys
and loathe the time of January
until I see my windows
patterned in crystal tinsel
the wood beyond
alive with locust shadows slanted
among the avalanche.

Jane Seip

PRECIOUS JESUS, LEAD ME HOME

    Upon a cross He was crucified.
He had to die, to give me life.
He rose up into Heaven,
So that sins may be forgiven.
For all who glory in His name,
Life will never be the same.
Through your faith, you will grow.
He will protect you always and never
leave you alone.
One day as He promised, Jesus will come
to take you Home.

Mary Flanigan

IN FULL BLOOM

Hanging in front of my
daughter's glass entrance
is a Julia Horton Fuchsia.
The flowers hang down
in deep pink bloom
With sharp-edged petals
lying across the top of
each upside-down live basket.
From its lower edges
hang tiny feet in dancing shoes.
They like to grow in groups
of three or four.
Yesterday a hummingbird
came in, adding to the picture.

If a woman with
Jehovah's help can produce
such a scene
why does anyone doubt
a God of love?

Sarah Fountain

FOUNTAIN, SARAH MAE. Pen Name: Sarah Fountain; Born: Battle Creek, Nebraska, 1893; Married: to Emray B. Fountain; Education: Nebraska Wesleyan; Occupation: Taught High School for two years; Memberships: YWCA, Secretary for teenagers; Poetry: 'His Magic Hands,' God's ability to paint, 1982; 'Who You?' rhyming work, *On Wings of Thought;* 'A Happy Old Age,' 'In Full Bloom,' sent to a contest, 1984; 'What Will it Be,' the disappearance of a ranch life; Comments: *I write because I love to write poems. I wrote most of my poems because an idea just hit me.*

Unconfined

Thought

upward, onward,

soaring free

loosed from this concept

called me

finds its own reality.

Christine Simoncsics

AGE

I used to be so happy
Full of joy and full of glee,
But now I'm only lonely
   As they say old men should be.
I used to run about,
   Used to sing and used to dance
Yet now they say I sit
   As if in a state of trance.

Alas, my life is growing short
   and I dance only in my mind.
But, I refuse to shrivel up,
   Or leave this world behind!
A man once told me long ago,
   and I quote it in this stance,
He said a man can return to his youth,
   Well, I'm just waiting for my chance!

Tatjana Shepperd

SILENCE

Silence — I know your voice.
I hear you through the roar
          of any sound;
Above the cataract's fall,
The screeching call of machine
        up and down the thoroughfare;
Above the empty babblings
     of human speech;
Through the millenniums of
     recurrent memories,
I hear you speak.

Eleanor C. Hamel

ENIGMA

The mysterious girl moves silently;
Her raven eyes pierce the night.
Her long white gown whispers in the breeze
Moments later, she disappears.

Only a haunting memory of her presence —
They call her name Enigma.
Their search for her is in vain;
Still her magnetism makes them return.

Again she embarks in the dusk,
Her beauty lingers in the shadow.
The mysterious Enigma
Reaches out her small ivory hands.

Only to fade again in the darkness.

Elizabeth Powell Tafoya

COLD FISH

Your words return to me
unexpectedly.
Dark night and a damp breeze
recall you by degrees.

The cold sand is beneath me again
the warmth of you above;
your whisper haunts my memory,
your promises of love.

A bright moon hanging in the night,
a shine painted on the sea.

A cold fish in a warm wave
presses his gills to me.

Cheryl Reich

OF SEEDTIME AND HARVEST

The sheaths are fallen
    to the ground,
    their greenest green
    now turned
    to amber.

Even the gleaner's hand
    will not touch
    what remains.

Silence, the mute, non-sound
    of rotting squash
    signals the start
    of winter.

But Spring will come
    again, 'tis such
    a promise sung,
    in great chorus,
    low, but vibrant,
    from the earth.

Belinda Pruett

LIQUID SUNSHINE

See how the wind blows
the white caps 'cross the water
See how every wave
Has its own place in time
Look how the raindrops
Splash off the sidewalk
See how the clouds have their
Own place in time
Living here
Here in this world of sunshine
Can't help but think
everything is fine
People here are
the waves and raindrops
And every wave and drop here
are sublime
Oh see how the wind blows
White caps 'cross the water
And look how the raindrops
Splash off the sidewalks
See how everything has its
Own place in time

Kenneth James Hale

FRUIT OF THE GARDEN

Proud beasts bound excruciatingly tight
by black white conformity habit
she obeys in silence,
flesh and soul controlled
by vowed life cross —
dedicated to perfection.
Generations in penury hooded her penances.

Eight years harboring Vatican II pass
darkest light emerging, brightening
to confused, resolved decision.
Bodily perfection, sensuous musky curves
between birdlike appendages,
plucked quickly
a virgin plum at thirty
cast amidst rotten and ordinary apples.

Her long-limbed daughter grows
like the chirping fledgling robin
hopping among tangles of cherries
having freedom of choice —
to sow or spare each encased seed.

Paul C. Williams

THE UNWARRANTED

Words of expression said hastily
Thoughts creating feelings of mistrust
Emotions inflamed by jealousy
Self-control should be a must

Such is human nature
Can we learn from our mistakes?
Let's analyze our human substance
Do we have the things it takes?

Filled with humiliation
Foolhardy is what we've been
As much as we apologize
We'll revert to foolishness again

Plagued by anger and bad judgment
We react in ways we shouldn't
We wanted to do things differently
But somehow we just couldn't

So paying the price is our consequence
For not controlling our response
The thorn of anguish haunts us
Quite often for many months

Because our souls are mixtures
Of joy, of love, of hate
The times will come again
We'll make the same mistakes

Keith L. White

YOU CAN DREAM ON A WINTER'S DAY

We had a snow last night
Not too much, but enough to
Cover things nice.

The signs are out when
It snows you know, rabbit, mouse
Deer they passed right through here.

It's fun to follow their trail.
I do it sometimes wondering
Where it may lead to sheltered
Brush or wood.

There's some familiar tracks
Shelly's and Marcy's
They've left for school

I guess I'll follow them a ways
Which way will they go?
Maybe a teacher, maybe a nurse

They took the lower path, down
By the lane, it's the best way
To school. I'll turn back now.

I hope they're happy on their
Way. I'll pass back by the
Brook, there may be some signs.

Mahlon Gallup

Red and black dots of color
stop to visit awhile,
brightening up my world,
making me laugh and smile.

Ladybug, harmless ladybug,
you may fly away.
More than tiny dots,
you're my freedom for the day.

Pamela Barton Carpenter

LADY IN THE HARBOR

There's a Lady in the harbor
Greeting all that come her way
With her promises of freedom
For the ones who want to stay

Wear your crown of glory proudly
You have earned the right to be
In the hearts of all who've found you
And a homeless soul like me

Oh, grand lady in the harbor
You hold freedom in your hand
And the hope for new tomorrows
For those who come from distant lands

As the harbor fog surrounds you
Even on the darkest night
You bring joy to homeless wanderers
When they see your welcome light

Oh my Lady in the harbor
In our hearts you'll always be
With your torch raised to the Heavens
There for all the world to see

J. K. Forrest

SNOW

The snow, the snow, the beautiful snow,
    Comes so softly down,
Covers the earth with a beautiful gown,
    And forms a carpet on the ground.

It trims up all the trees in white
    Just in a single night.
Makes me think some fairy grand
    Had touched it with her hand.

It covers all the death of the freeze,
    It hides the fallen leaves;
The withered grass we do not see,
    But just a pure white canopy.

Someday when we have been laid to rest,
    And by all folks are forgotten;
Still yet the little flakes will fall
    And spread its sheet of cotton.

The snow is beautiful and white
    It comes falling down so polite;
But I love the flowers of spring,
And the chirping birds that sing.

Opal Marie Hayes

AND LIFE GOES ON

I was standing on the shore of life
Admiring the view
When a troubled sea appeared and
Caught me before I knew
This happening.
The undertow was all-possessing
Forcing me to yield
All that was in me.
Only the sand I had to grip,
Hard in my hands, then turned to
    nothingness.
In one unguarded moment of this
    dark beauty gone mad
I pulled myself from its salty jaw
With all that was in me
And now I stand on the shore of life
Awaiting a calmer sea,
Awareness my company.

Joan Paparella

TIME STANDS STILL

I feel the joy and wonder yet sadness overbears.
Tempering the now and the what's been lost, I stop and compare.
Precious time passed while I yet watched, wishing the years so
quickly away.

Reflecting I listen to life's signals calling memories to me.
I see the richness now, yet I did not linger to hold her beauty.
Will there be that promise of tomorrow to guard and enjoy?

Life surrounds me at times I feel alone yet a peace awakens me
and I walk ever-so-softly, carefully not to lose the sunlight
drifting through the trees.
Playing tag with time my heart beats a secret music.

I sense a presence and my mind recalls a higher consciousness.
An endless love that brings space and time together.
In silence I focus on the present, a flowing warmth enfolds me.
Memory hangs as if in perfect balance, a verse leaps out from
my subconsciousness, "Be still and know that I am God."

To my heart it is a whisper, to my soul it is a new fragrance.
In my darkest moments He reaches out and touches me and I am still.
Seasons may come and go but His wisdom He will always bestow.
Life's dying is really but birth and this in silence I resolve.

Ronnette Ward

MAKING YOU HAPPY

It will be my lifelong obligation to make you happy,
If only you'll tell me.
I can't read your secret thoughts,
It will be Christmas every day with you,
My present to you is one of a kind.
There's no buying it with money.
It's something that can be used year 'round.
It can fill lonely nights when I may not be there.
It can fill up spaces if we have a fight and there's silence for a while.
It'll share all moments, good or bad.
It will take time to erode away my present.
Go ahead and open it,
It's only my love.
It can't be much of a surprise,
You should have known it was there.
Please help me make the dreams a reality —
If there's no you,
Then there is to be nothing.

C. H. Danion

TWO FACES OF A COIN

I found a coin from afar, a strange beauty, struck in gold!
On one side was a leaden face, eyes molten, stare so cold;
They tell of seeing Life's bare truth — of Light sad prey to Dark;
Of Nature's deadly storms' rampage — land ravaged — trees so stark.

They know the freezing ache of Snow that numbs when Death is nigh,
They've felt the searing burn of Sun that makes Life shrivel, die:
They've seen wild winds and furious rains — the violent oceans rage;
They've watched young Beauty wither, fade — a parody in old age.

The other face — a rampant lion — his fearless eyes gaze wide,
They see the truth with different eyes — life's bounty at high tide!
They know the flashing thunderstorms bring Rainbow's brilliant hue,
That rains will bring a fruitful land — all buds will burst anew.

They've felt the sun's caressing warmth that nurtures life from birth,
Her sunset splendor tossed across the sky, to light up earth.
Sun cedes her throne to velvet Night, with moon and stars aglow,
Bare trees stand proudly shielding their bronze carpet's dazzling show.

They've felt the power of snow, so pure, uplift, exhilarate;
They've known God's hand on oceans deep, to awe, inspire, elate!
Restless Youth in search of Self, seeks love and truth — finds strife —
But peace, insight and vision — gifts of Age — fulfill Man's life!

Alex Stewart

BIRTHDAY SONG — TO PEGGY

How,
in the starflight of this earth
just twenty-three full cycles
'round the sun,
has such a miracle been done?

Here,
in this present time, you are
full-blown and rich with beauty
like a flower,
and full of mystery and power!

Yet,
just a score of sun-swung flights
ago you were a seedling
crying red
and squalling helpless in your bed.

God!
That the passage of so small
a sample of transforming,
plastic Time
could work this miracle sublime!

Hal Barrett

COMMUNICATION

Soundless minds,
    trying to communicate
    with incessant thoughts.

Projecting unreal images
    to other minds,
    blemishing relationships.

Innumerable hearts,
    not beating as one,
    unable to hear other throbs.

Soundless minds,
    too sensitive to enter
    other soundless worlds.

Like a violin string
    wound too tight,
    breaks when bowed,

Hearts break asunder
    their minds unforgiving,
    left soundless forever.

Ruth Calkins

MENTOR

Slightly bent
hair laced with gray
face creviced by age's hint
eyes recessed by the long days.

First gaze renders bland
and elsewhere thoughts turn
as youth relinquishes its stand
and experience's wisdom comes to term.

And from behind stern eyes
wisdom's thoughts brandish youth's impulse
as youth quivers fearing demise
trying to control rampaging pulse.

Aware, sternness relegates to compassion
as youth airs its innocence
and time's hesitation tempers
the mentor's hint at thought's essence.

Victor A. Brewer

THE SILENT BATTLE

Thoreau once said we each live lives
Of "quiet desperation."
We each have inner wars that rage;
Wars we hide with proud determination.
I thought so long it was only I
Who vainly battled alone with fears,
Until you opened your heart to me;
Until you let me see your tears.
Oh, let me help you carry your burden
On through this long, long day,
Then tomorrow you'll help me
As we climb together life's rocky way.
Our loads will be lighter when they're shared;
Our cares won't dismay and overwhelm
Because we've exposed our vulnerable hearts,
And that is more than most dare to do
On this earthly realm.

Ava J. Sailors

TRAVELING THROUGH PALOUSE COUNTRY

Clouds, like cotton balls, float across the sky,
some black, white, gray, some low and high.
Separating themselves, falling to the ground,
floating so quietly, not making a sound.
Rainbows appear, as we drive along the road,
all around the rain clouds with colors so bold.
There, the end of the rainbow, what do we see?
Golden wheat fields, what else could it be.
In miles and miles of nothing but land
Washington's Palouse Country is oh, so grand.

James A. Morey

IN MEMORIAM OF THEA

Above me the sky flies by
Under the ground my dear one lies
I am here and she is there
So mystically we two seem to glide
Here and there side by side
Memories come alive speaking to my heart
Soothingly offering relief for my grief
Though I know in Eternity she has made her start
Yet an aloneness seems to have a grip
That chokes in my throat and leaves tears that smart

My Thea left me riches no money could buy
She didn't ever want me to cry and sigh
Put your hand to the plow and never look back
She said when I would get slack
Look to the Lord and He'll guide you through
For life everlasting will I have and so will you

Richard D. Cagg

A WARRIOR GONE HOME

In Memoriam to:
Rev. C. L. Franklin
New Bethel Baptist Church

Though Fate silenced your eloquence,
You now dwell in the Mansions of Eternity.
Though your mortal cry is heard no more,
You live in the Memory of Men.
What you did for others,
Will span the Wings of Time.
Sometimes we saddened and bruised you with our ways,
Yet in your Pathos, you endured . . .
You've gone home, now, to your Father,
A warrior among warriors, . . . a Prince among Preachers.
You too "belong to the Ages."
"Good night, Sweet Prince."

Mary Frances Lawson

A DEEPLY HIDDEN AND DISGUISED HURT

You cannot hear the hurt that I cry
It is a deeply hidden and well-disguised hurt
Buried deep, deep, deep down in my heart
And cleverly disguised by a fake smile
Invisible, not to be seen by anyone
Silent, not to be heard by anyone
Untouchable, not to be felt by anyone
I am expected to smile, always
I am expected to entertain, always
I am expected to be happy, always
Hurting . . . never, never, never
For I have to tell the jokes
Articulate the obnoxious, and
Make it eloquently and acceptably funny
It is a hurt never to be seen, heard or felt
That is why I have it hidden
Deep, deep, deep down inside of me
Never, ever, ever to be known

Alonzo Davis

THINK AGAIN

Try and catch me if you can,
But what led you to believe you can touch a shadow?
Or perhaps you think you understand,
The transparent movement of the wind across the meadow.

Your eyes are closed and yet insist,
They see the unfolding of a morning-glory,
And why do you try to lasso a tornado's twist,
When we all know that's a fairy tale story.

You sincerely believe all you see is apparent,
Never striving to look beyond the cloud,
Doesn't mystery surround all we inherit?
Are you the wisest of our earthly crowd?

So I say to you, my foolish one,
You whose belief lies in disillusion;
Walk in the brightness of the noonday sun,
Be alert to the new moon of confusion.

Remember, a bird of paradise does not a bat make,
Throw your net but please stay aware,
Now in warning I say for your own sake;
Try and catch me if you dare!

Janet Lee Kontur

FREEDOM

Love of Country is Freedom,
A freedom to be cherished by all,
Standing up for what is right,
Protecting your country's freedom.

Loving your fellow man is a cherished freedom,
Not much love is shown in our world today,
But only in the United States,
Do we know the true meaning of brotherly love.

Respecting one's right to learn,
Is a knowledgeable freedom,
Learning about the unknown,
Is the beginning of wisdom.

Protecting our wildlife is a rewarding freedom,
The beauty of its right for life,
Can make you sense a beauty,
As only wildlife can bring.

Show more love for your own country,
And be more considerate of your fellow man,
Make yourself more knowledgeable about learning,
And take more pride in your wildlife.

Vincent T. Vinciquerra

THE PLEASURE OF YOU!!!

Ahhh, the pleasure of you!
You create your own special occasions any time, any day
You bring real satisfaction in every way.

I experience good comfortable feelings
When I enter your welcoming arms.
You're ingeniously superb
With incredible charms.

I feel outrageously secure . . .
'Cause honey, you know what to do!
Whatever I look for, I find in you!

Ann D. Little

ABOUT THE DEATH OF THORWALD

That Leif's brother died in the New Found Land
There are two different reports at hand.

One story tells how Vikings explored
Along a New Found Land fjord
Until they came upon three skin-covered canoes.
Three Skraelings were hiding under each with views.
The Vikings decided to battle the Skraeling crews
Before they were able to spread the news.

Vikings began to battle Skraelings without plea.
Eight Skraelings were killed — one did flee.
He sounded the alarm to a host they could see
Of wild men who descended on the Vikings for pain.
In retreating, a Thorwald and others were slain
By arrow that rapidly came.
But THORWALD is a common Viking name.
Thus it is not our aim
To assume this one was the same
As Leif's younger brother of fame.

Cleveland C. Matchett

MATCHETT, CLEVELAND CALVIN. Born: Palatka (Putnam County) Florida, 12-28-27; Education: Hiwassee Junior College, Madisonville, Tennessee; East Tennessee State, Johnson City, B.S. in Social Studies, (Secondary Education), 1953; Graduate work at University of Chattanooga, Middle Tennessee State University, Murfreesboro; Occupations: Teacher, Clerical Worker in Y.M.C.A.'s in Chattanooga and Portsmouth, Virginia, Teacher in Portsmouth, Virginia and Oneida Baptist Institute, Kentucky, Signal Mountain and Athens, Tennessee; Writings: Series of 18 epic (story-telling) poems published in a dozen anthologies. These deal with historical themes, except one which is about my home town in Tennessee; Comments: *In most of my poems there is a thread that might be summarized by a riddle: How far from Brattahlid to Gardar? These two places represent different life cultures that are worlds apart yet collide head-on. There is love and tenderness that tempers the violence and hatred. There is a strong religious theme in most of these writings. I am trying to make history come alive with real people who faced real conflict in relationships and over great difficulties.*

THE TOUCH OF A HAND

When your way grows dark and dreary
You tire long before it's night,
Just reach your hand high;
You'll feel by and by
A touch that will make all things right.

A calmness will settle upon your soul —
A calm you may not understand;
Your load grows lighter,
The day grows brighter —
The touch was your dear Master's hand.

There'll be times you can help a companion,
Just as God helped your way to clear,
When a gentle touch
To them will mean much
If they know you care and are near.

Try to console a friend in grief —
You just can't find words to explain;
The love that you've stored
Can then be outpoured —
The touch of your hand will speak plain.

Iola Bashline Dovenspike

INVINCERE

Be not ashamed if you weep from
pains endured,
It does not mean that you are
any less mature.

Let not your head hang after the
battle is done,
If your heart and soul were put forth
then your effort was not in vain.

When the final gun sounds and you
retire, body aching and bruised,
Walk with pride and dignity as you
depart from the arena, unashamed.

Forget not what has taken place,
Learn from your mistakes as well as
those of your companions.

For you have left your mark with
a quiet grace,
And no number will disprove that
you are a champion.

Hanswurst

WHY DADDY?

When did you get old — and why?
Remember when I used to cry
In the middle of the night?
You'd come, pick me up and hold me tight.

As that little girl got older,
Someone told her,
"Big girls don't cry!"
No one ever told me why.

Now that I'm older, I wonder why and
Who picks you up and holds you when you cry,
"Help me make it through the night,
Or just until things seem all right."

Maybe before I'm too old,
The secret will be told.
Then I'll finally know why,
Big girls and daddies don't cry . . .

Cheryl L. Reich

HARMONY

The streaming rays of moonlight shimmer.
Upon the river which beckons its glimmer.
The mountains tower toward the light.
Capped in snow glistening all through the night.

The lonely owl calls out its warning.
Beware, beware, the day is dawning.
When all out of slumber will then come out.
To scurry around and run about.

The moon descends to give rise to the morning.
The sun breaks through to begin its adorning.
The flowers stretch their petals out quietly.
To embrace the warmth alighting ever so slightly.

The birds their chirping do begin.
As they frolic in and through the glen.
And the bears for slumbering do get ready.
While squirrels gather nuts ever so steady.

And every creature knowing its place.
Fulfills its purpose in this race.
To begin and end their calling each.
To reach and learn, to seek and teach.

Christine Schwartz

PROMISE ME SMILES

You are entering my thoughts
more often every day.
Even as I believe my love is for another,
your image breaks through.

How can it be that someone, you,
can possibly pull me out of the rut
my last love left me in?
Can it be true?

Months have passed me by
with only sorrow to share my hours.
Is it really possible that
you can bring long lost happiness into my life?

How I long to live again,
love again; I think.
Only, my heart has shattered so often,
it cannot break again.

Promise me smiles,
promise me happiness and good times.
Promise me love and promise me
a happy ending.

Lisa Jacobson

It is now —
    walking along the beach,
    that I see your spirit in the sunrise,
        its colors washing the walls of the dawn with light.

It is now —
    in the call of the birds welcoming the morning,
    that I hear your voice,
        so long silent.

It is now —
    with the warm wind blowing through my hair,
    that I feel your touch,
            calming the storm that is my soul.

It is now —
    kneeling at the edge of the endless sea,
    that I see you,
        in me.

April Killingback

IF JESUS CAME TO VISIT YOU
(Rev. 3:20)

If Jesus came . . . To visit you
To give you a . . . needed helping hand
And show you . . . The Way of Truth
I am certain that . . . You will understand
        — Jer. 33:3 —

If Jesus came . . . To visit you
According to God and . . . life's destiny
It happened that way . . . in my Christian life
For . . . Jesus came to visit me.
        — Num. 12:6 —

If Jesus came . . . to visit you
To help you in time . . . of human need
The Almighty God . . . who created you
Search the Scriptures . . . you will see.
        — John 5:39 —

If Jesus came . . . to visit you
How wonderful . . . life would really be
To have a Blessed . . . Heavenly Visitor
As when . . . Jesus came to visit me.
        — Job 27:11 —

If Jesus came . . . To visit you
Your most precious . . . Christian Friend
Who has promised . . . To always help you
From the cradle until . . . The end!
        — Matt. 28:18, 19, 20 —

Leopold C. Martinez

MARTINEZ, LEOPOLD CINTRON. Pen Name: The Christian Friend; Born: Puerto Rico, West Indies, 12-31-12; Married: 3-17-42 to Evelyn E. (James) Martinez; Education; Fifth grade; I have no school education, but I do read history books and the Bible; Occupations: Farmer, of U.S. Military Service, Truck Driver, Prize Fighter; Poetry: 'Introducing — Leopold C. Martinez,' If Jesus Came to Visit You,' 'My Vision-Dream of Heavens,' 'My Promised to the Almighty,' 'The Epitaph of a Christian Minister'; Christian poems, some published in *The American Poetry Anthology;* Comments: *The turning point of my life happened in my deathbed at the age of 21, because of unusual punishment while in the U.S. Military Service. I pray to the Almighty God for help of thus. 'My Vision-Dream of Heavens,' of thus all their wonderful Christian poems were inspired upon me of especially 'If Jesus Came to Visit You.'*

THE THOUGHT OF MARRIAGE

If loving you is where I'll be
And you beside me, loving me
And you and I will be as we . . .
Then I will think of marrying.

And if beside you I'll lie
And wait the hours drifting by
And feel your warm and sleepy sigh . . .
Then I will think of marrying.

If you should wake before I do
And you're with me and I'm with you
And you're content with all we do . . .
Then I will think of marrying.

And if I vow to love you true,
Include you in the things I do
And spend life gently touching you . . .
Then will you think of marrying?

Howard E. Johnston

BLACKBERRY WINE

Ahh! Secrets that are mine
Sipping on Blackberry wine,
Slowly your hand steals in mine —
While sipping on Blackberry wine.

Idle chatter fills the air
Sipping on Blackberry wine.
Wondering — wondering, would I dare?
As I'm sipping Blackberry wine.

Then I'm looking right at you
Can I, will I briefly be thine?
So then, what do I do,
But sip on your Blackberry wine.

When in a small space of time —
I was really, really thine.
Ahh! Secrets that are mine,
Because of your Blackberry wine.

Alma Jean McKinstrey

COMPASSION

I walked inside the rain today
and spilled my inner treasures,
upon the earth in hopes to bring
the world unending pleasures.

But they were crushed by rushing feet,
fooled by man's desires,
locked in cold hearts' freezing beat
and cast in Satan's fire.

Picking up my scattered thoughts,
the ones they left behind,
now are spinning visions
placing songs inside my mind.

And though the world with evil plots
still lingers in the air,
God has placed His hands on me —
through Him, I know He cares.

Carla Boroff

OH, WHY DO WE LOVE KENTUCKY?

It is our home with grass so blue it looks like the sky has fallen.
We have beautiful horses. We have horses that run like the wind.
We have two State Capitols, one old and one new. Anyone who comes
to Kentucky hates to leave it, for everyone is so friendly and you
never meet a stranger. For you shall always return to her. The
river runs right in the middle of town. Sometimes she gets angry,
and will overflow, but we love her. Oh! I forgot we have the
Kentucky Derby where people of all walks of life come. Don't you
see why we love Kentucky. With its hills and caves, it's like
heaven off to itself. We may leave, but we shall return to it.

Oh! Kentucky, I love you, we all do!

Martha Guthue

REFLECTIONS ON THE SEASONS

SPRING,

A time for meditation on what the year will bring,
A time for revelation as life is ushered in,
A time for eager planning and happy, fruitful thoughts,
A time for expectation of dreams that aren't for naught.

SUMMER,

A time of tranquil days laced in a work- and pleasure-mingled maze,
A time of realizing dreams, and planning many future schemes,
A time for us to ponder life, and hope that we can bypass strife,
A time to plan for Winter's cold, looking forward to Fall unfold.

FALL,

A time to see our tapestry unfold, with colored hues of blue and gold,
A time to hope success and strife are, somehow, equal in our lives,
A time to measure life to find that we are creatures undefined,
A time to hope for warmth and glow to ready us for Winter's snow.

WINTER,

A time of year to glean the fruits of all our past truths, and yet
A time, in Winter, to reflect and wait for Spring to come anew, and, yes,
A time to plan and dream, and scheme, and strive for more new hues for
A TAPESTRY OF LIFE SUPREME.

Betty G. Small

TWO YEARS ONE LESSON

One thousand and ninety-five
    Days ago the telephone rang in the city.
She answered and agreed to meet.

She came clad in a yellow, flowered dress,
    Her blonde hair stopping somewhere between her hips and knees.
I asked, she accepted in early spring.

Holidays, Anniversaries, Birthdays, Summers.

We saw the seasons change eight times
    Together, always seeing the joy they brought us.

Hard to eat, harder to sleep. Thinnest I was in years.

She eventually hooked on with a football star from an East coast school.
    As is often the case our separation was bitter.

While she married, I carried
    On, but barely.

I must admit, however that those two years, those moments
    Are still remembered and will be . . .

My present wife and I met on a Tuesday afternoon in the rain.

Patrick J. Westlake

MOTHER

We've heard it said before, it's true,
God can't be everywhere,
So He created Mothers
He knows that when a baby's born,
So helpless and so small,
That Mother will take over,
That she will give her all.
He knows that through those helpless years
She'll guide those tiny feet,
She'll kiss away the hurts and tears
And make the childhood sweet.
He knows, too, that as time goes on
She'll lead in paths of truth,
And guide and counsel hearts and minds
Through turbulent days of youth.
He also knows her love goes on,
Her prayers she'll still employ,
For, whether six or sixty,
It's still her girl or boy.
No wonder, then, that poets say
God can't be everywhere
So He created Mothers
And depends upon their care.
He knows the depth of Mother love
Did He not it impart?
Thank you God for Mother
And her understanding heart.

Mary Unwin

BIRTHDAY RAINBOW

I got a rainbow for my birthday!

I want to store it in a nice, safe spot,
So easy to get to, I can visit it a lot.

I could keep it in my pocket,
Or, in a cupboard lock it.

Should I make a deposit?
Maybe, put it in the closet.

How about the little drawer,
Or, slide it just behind the door?

No, none of these seems right,
A rainbow needs lots of light.

It likes it where it's light and airy,
So pleasant that it makes you tarry.

Oh, now I know just the place,
I think I know the perfect space.

It's way up high, above the crowds.
I'll keep my rainbow in the clouds.

Barb Nolley

GROWN-UP MAKE-BELIEVE

The peace that is sought
may be found
look hard enough,
and rejoice in the newly found.
Is God the answer?
Perhaps not to it all.
He is the adult escape
from the childhood fantasy lost
Playing pretend?
It could be.
But no one said that being an adult
would be easy.

Carmen J. Villanueva

LOVE

On clouds so high above,
Sweet air flows of love,
On wings it cometh nigh,
Making dreams weep and sigh,
And gives a heart fair raiment,
Like warm rain on two lovers.

Tony Luczak

GOD REIGNS

God reigns, eternal,
    Through countless ages.
God reigns, eternal,
    Your God and mine.

Though all earth crumbles
    And heaven opens,
God reigns, eternal,
    Your God and mine.

Geraldine Costanzo

COSTANZO, GERALDINE CRISPEL. Born: Noxen, Pennsylvania; Married: 3-21-42; Education: Wyoming Seminary, 1935-37; Marywood College, B.A. in Music, 1937-40; additional work at Syracuse University and Cornell, 1940-42; Marywood College, M.S., 1963; Occupations: Teaching — piano, organ, voice, violin; Counseling; Memberships: (formerly) NEA, various music organizations in Pennsylvania and New York, Publishers Commitee for Moral Majority (more recently); Awards: World's Fair Anthology 1940 for 'Recompense (to a Sand Sculptor)'; The Poetic Voice of America for 'A Eulogy (to a Sandpiper)'; Other Writings: 'God's Rainbow,' song, 'Hail to Thee, Fair Marywood,' song; Comments: *Probably I write because this desire (or talent) was inborn. My father (Rev. F.S. Crispel) who went to his reward on Sept. 24, 1984, has written volumes of poetry — beautiful, humorous, and true to life. I believe he had inherited much from his mother, Lydia Crispel. Also, my sisters write, and their children.*

THE GOLDEN KEY

He, at heart's door stood knocking
    I bade Him to come in
Repenting and believing
    He cleansed my every sin.

He gave unto me God's word
    To feed my hungry soul,
And I shall thirst no more — while
    The living waters roll.

I'm trusting in His promises
    And keeping His command
And I shall rest assured
    I'll reach the promised land.

I'm holding to His garment
    I've surrendered to His will
And by His very stripes
    He cures my every ill.

And He knows my every need
    His angels are ministering
I'm an heir of salvation
    And Jesus is my King.

I once did grope in darkness
    But now I see the light
I once did faint in weakness
    But now in prayer, there's might.

Mina Huffman

HUFFMAN, MINA HUDGENS. Pen Name: Anne Onymous; Born: Newburg, Missouri, Phelps County, 6-28-08; Married: 12-25-26 to J. Millard Huffman, (Deceased); Education: Business College, St. Louis, Missouri; Teacher's College, Warrensburg, Missouri; B.S. in Education, University of Missouri, Columbia, Missouri; Bob Jones University, Greenville, South Carolina; Occupation: Elementary Teacher for the gifted; Memberships: NRTA, AARP, OES, University of Missouri Alumni Association; Awards: Four Award of Merit Certificates, three Honorable Mentions, and one Special Mention, World of Poetry; Poetry: 'From My Hotel Window,' published in Istanbul, 1979; 'Room Twenty-one,' and 'Meeting Her God,' written at Bob Jones University, published by American Poetry Association, 1984; 'Waiting,' 'Taken for Granted'; Comments: *This is a paragraph from a letter a girlfriend wrote: "Have you done any writing of any kind, your book or poems? You should pursue this, Mina, you have talent and, as I mentioned before, whatever happens I might incite you to begin. Your poems are beautiful because they reveal what's inside you, and your deepest feelings." I have now completed 44 poems under the title, Wise to Love, and 68 others.*

GOD'S POWERS

In the bed, her eyes closed,
lies the lady, she looks composed.
But inside her head a tumor pounds,
inside her mind the terror mounts.

She has a small child to raise,
her thoughts in a whirl she prays and prays . . .
Surgery is set for tomorrow,
she feels a growing horror.

She has one thought, no other:
"If I die, who will love my daughter?"
Who would love her child like she?
So she confided her fears to me.

The fateful day arrived,
and God let her survive!
She got a chance to live again,
to raise her girl, feel joy and pain!

I noticed though, her values changed,
like her life got re-arranged.
She takes time to admire sunsets and flowers
and greatly respects GOD'S POWERS!

Heidelore I. Perry

GRANDMA'S TOYS

I love to go to Grandma's house,
And play with Grandma's toys.
To run and jump and touch her things,
And make a lot of noise.

Grandma says it's okay,
With no sounds in the house it's too quiet.
Daddy says to settle down,
Or at least would we try it.

Grandma's toys are old and torn,
From years of kids' rough use.
But each new child thinks they're the best,
And doesn't notice past abuse.

Grandma kept the toys she had
When she was a wee tot.
She says that we should try to do
The same with what we've got.

It's hard to keep the toys we've got,
It seems they just won't last.
But we all love Grandma's toys
She kept from in her past.

Dottie P. Schuster

UNHOLY EMANATION

Now I plunge my pen against the page
and scribble toward a purpose unperceived,
for now, in breathful, placid frame,
I am no more a poet than a rose;

but images I view, although receptive
to my bid (my muse is busied elsewhere,
nursing other selves), and I desire
exercise, enveloped by pleasant melancholy.

Enabled to imbue with silhouette of life
a bit of pesty matter, from so faint
a state as this, I would label it as mine
(ostensibly): mine to brag of, mine to burn;

but when I feature feeling from the dream
it flies from me, like writing on a pond.

Hugo Whither

MOONSHADOWS

The moon cast many shadows in her room
Frightening shadows that brought memories of the past
Shadows full of sorrow
Then many shadows melted into two
They came together like strangers in the night
Softly, sadly as if a waltz were playing
Enfolding them as they swayed back and forth
She a feather in his arms
Looked up at him
His smile beckoned
He laughed and his laughter was like wind
Whispering through the trees.
She knew somehow she was in love
Would that the evening never end!
But then the waltz wafted them apart
And there were many shadows in her room.

Ginny Wilder

JUSTIN WILLIAM RICHARDS

The nurse smiled and told me I'm the lucky one,
I just gave birth to a healthy son,
Justin William's life has just begun.
     You were conceived through love,
a gift from God above.
     God chose to place in my womb an embryo,
to care for and nurture, so it would grow.
     When you were born, I felt I had gained the whole world,
and retained my soul, for to God's family, I've added to
the birth toll.
     Your father and I feel so rich in love, a millionaire,
we're so lucky to have a son who'll always be there.
     A child's birth is a miracle, involving us three,
God, your daddy and me.
     Miracles can come true, on July 17, 1984,
we witnessed one, with the birth of you!

Dino Serventi

A NAME

A name I know; has come to be,
The ruler forever; in eternity,
This name had died for you and me,
A name that will last through eternity —
A name so true; it has endured,
To seek out life that will endure,
This name it searches for you and me,
Waiting to take us to where it'll be —
A name that turns all fears away,
Brings joy to you each day that comes your way,
A faith so deep; you can endure,
Life's adversities that loom and lure —
A name that came and will come again,
Will take his church and will rule till there's no end,
I heard a name called Jesus Christ,
I read of this name in the book of life —

Benjamin E. Thompkins Jr.

WHAT MIGHT HAVE BEEN

Where is the child that ran & played
& fell past heaven's door, headlong
into manhood; unaware of losing
the bright spirit, the telling eye?

Tell me, did I turn from you, there when your
lips yet smiled? Say I didn't push on by
(eagerly hoping to lose you from sight,
ragamuffin, as though 'twere right)!
& when my heart fell, knew murder, maim,
all breathing stopped, did I not know why?

Helen Howard

THE GOOD LIFE

Awaken! A new day is born,
A new beginning is here this very morn.
Yesterday is but a memory, tucked away.
So live this moment, this hour, this day!

Make new friends, do good deeds,
Sow some kindness, plant the seeds.
Forget yourself, love your brother,
Have faith in mankind, trust another.

Share with those who are without
Give and forget, but never doubt
Your reward will come if you try,
The Accountant is perfect, up in the sky.

Praise those most who trouble you.
You confound them when you do.
There is gold buried in every heart,
Not always found at the very start.

To like yourself; never stumble, never fall
Over self-gratifications, most of all.
Live out your life in peaceful contentment
By giving of yourself, without resentment.

Epps Adams

DREAMS — A BRAND-NEW START

I look into the bright, blue sky
And wonder what I'll see and why.
That sky has so many things for me
Yet I dream of what its wonders might be.

The fleecy clouds roll softly by
Skipping and lolling throughout the blue sky.
Leaving me thinking of shapes and scenes
Made only in my vivid dreams.

Lots of pictures flash quickly along
With each silver-lined cloud giving a new song.
Melodies of love overflow from my heart
Giving my feelings a brand-new start.

My dream of dreams is always aglow
To let the love within me grow.
Then the sunbeams take that love
Letting it fit the finder like a glove.

Those dreams become so sure and real
When I see my love in hands that feel.
A smile from the finder assures the heart
That a dream CAN be a brand-new start.

Lou Bodden Buxton

'round the bend, on a winding path lies —
    a blanket upon the ground. a warm sun
sparkles through towering trees; a waterfall
against stone wall — dances and sings —

together upon that blanket; ignorant to
    scattered twigs and leaves — two hearts
savor a great surge of emotion, spontaneously
they sense the same taste of affection where
both inevitably to love — do yield.

come visit again this place with me, cast
    this new friend from your mind —
return with me to the water's edge, turn
and face me — face to face and as
twilight falls upon the day, in its glow
will find again — two silhouettes —
flesh to flesh, upon a blanket
'round the bend —

Marcy Zerhusen

BOLBEC STANDARDS
*Dedicated to Deborah Bolger and her quest for
"Champion Bolbec Standard Poodles," Godspeed!*

Distant dreams are calling me.
The dreams are a vision the reality precedes.
The reality will fashion the dream that I see,
For the dream is my heart, my reason to be!

And follow it I will, with heart on true course.
For the heart is the guideline that proves its
    full worth.
And if I should strive for more than its birth,
Perhaps all its meanings aren't worth the full purse.

So follow what you think are right, precious ways —
For inside is my reason that brings light of day!
And maybe I'm wrong — but maybe I'm right,
I just never quit 'til my heart's got full flight!

S. A. Dombrowski

TRIBUTE TO A GOLDEN GIRL

Gold was the color of her
    hair
When she was very young,
Gold was the color of her speech
    a kindly tongue.
Gold was the color of the gown
    I saw her wear
Gold was the color from which she got her name.
Golden was her nature, she was the same.
White was the color of her hair, while she
    was ill.
Serious was her condition as she lay white,
    and still.
White were the sheets covering her alabaster
    skin,
Battling for her life, I hope that she will win
Bring gold back, hold her standards high,
Bring back the golden girl to live,
    not die!

Edith English

HIDDEN DREAMS
For Zahna Lynn

As I look into the deepness of a powerful sky
Wondering of its hidden dangers
Feeling somehow protected by
the warm green growing grass,
underneath and around me.
Still looking up into the deep spaces of the sky,
Thinking of the gift I was given
On a dark and lonely night.
As I saw a bird of snowy wings
Waver and swoop above me
taking swift dives to earth
and then fluttering into the depths of a
somehow warm, yet cold iced sky.
But yet as I lie here now
with green grass and the wavering trees
I know the sky is just hiding
and sheltering my peaceful dreams.

Dawn L. Sparks

CEMETERY, SAINT LAURENT

You see the creases shining in the sun,
Above the beach sleep those who paid the price.
Scarce all the words of all the tongues of man
Could honored homage pay the sacrifice.

You ask, what manner woman bore such men,
The courage and the crushing back of fear;
The unborn centuries will not forget
And generations will pay tribute here.

Rann Newcomb

ELUDING

A lone bird flips high above on lavish wings,
stirring the air,
of marshmallow clouds,
cobblestone sky etched in pink and lavender.
Pregnant hills cascading to the ground below.
Heavenly white wisps of snow withering the empty streets,
echoing a vibrance of sound,
with cushiony pastures beyond.
a silent mist happens to lift, over all, over me.

Sharon Duprey

WINGS OF LOVE

Beneath the tall pine tree,
A child dreams in play,
Billows of time escaping,
Spiralling, nonchalantly in air.

Listen, a discourse, softly, like whispering,
A child grown,
Wearily reaches up to gather those dreams,
Beneath the tall pine tree.

Barbara L. Hackett

MASQUERADE

Farewell to arms, my spurious friend —
Self-pity. Oh, what fool
To heed my cry
With shrouding eye
In predatory rule . . .
To feast upon my wounds a banquet of despair!
For what you scent as victory's ebb
Is but a frail and crimsoned web
Upon which sunlight's sceptre burns away your masquerade.

Hazel Anne Coffman

THE TEAR

Into my heart
I drop a tear
freshly plucked from that sensitive reservoir
in my swollen eye.
So gently does it fall
that to no one else's knowing
is it recognizable
as one begotten
from your parting kiss.

Michael Hooven

SHAME IN MY HEART

White fluttered as burden had to be carried.
Thorns forced upon head to be crowned.
Cries echoed with each step of worn leather.

No shame was pressed on his heart.

Burden carried called for two.
One for ignorance, one for JEW.
Arms reached to engulf the world,
Feet together, crowd still there.

Still, no shame was pressed upon heart.

Eyes were cast, mouths were open.
Unkind words, blasphemy spoken.
There he rested, cried out loud
Forgive them please
They know not what they allow.

Up came hard earth soaring through air.
Landing on flesh that for people did care.
Eyes on crowd, tear did fall.
He spoke with his heart . . .
Forgive them, Father, forgive them all,

Shame shall be pressed on their hearts.

Howard Murphy

OPENING NIGHT

Fifty strangers sleep alone
Homesick hearts beat on creaky green cots
The sergeant's voice lingers
like pool room smoke in a low-budget western
Fantasies of guzzling pink champagne
on some icy moon

I'm hot as August glass
Dry as a widow's gin
Feel nailed to a laundromat wall
Want to be mopped away
like tears of train station tile

David J. Weber

TODAY

Timidly you peered from around the birch tree
    scanning the sun-bathed swamp with gentle eyes,

Then gracefully you sauntered to the water's edge
    and lowered your majestic head to drink from
    the quiet pond reflecting the gold and scarlet
    hues of the early autumn morning.

The sentinel trees lining the hillside were struggling
    for a last glimpse of themselves in the blue waters
    lapping at your feet before the ice formed,
    and amid the woodland beauty, you WERE BEAUTY.

You gave me a moment touched by God. You were one of
    His beloved creatures — a stately deer.

But this afternoon, a hunter saw you with different eyes.
    You were a trophy to be sought and captured.

And now you are a bloody, eviscerated carcass slung
    carelessly and triumphantly on the roof-top of
    an automobile.

All that is left of you is the imprint of your hooves
    on the lakeside sand
        and in my heart!

Rosemary Baker

NOW

To think of days that I have rued
For cloudy sky and chirpless bush,
While unnoticed by such as I,
Time flew by in a mighty rush.

To catch the day whether cloudy or fair
Is the essence of life itself,
For life was never tinsel-wrapped
And cloudless lies upon the shelf.

Tarry not in wordless days
Overcast by doubt or fear
For *now* is all we ever have,
And *now* makes future yesteryears.

Rejoice in love, in tears, in clouds,
The blemishes that we all see,
For *now* is the word that lifts the shrouds
And snatches us back from eternity.

Lydia Zola

TRANSITING OWL

You had flown that road many times before
and were too self-confident of survival.
But a blinding light came out of nowhere
and your once certain flight
shattered into death.

Your body was still warm when I found you
beside a gravel road so little travelled
that I was astonished at how you were hit.

I hope it was not wrong of me to take
your claws, feathers and one undamaged wing.
For it was with love that I kept them
and buried you next to my house,
an arrowpoint in your beak
as an offering to your Master
flying on your one wing
into the domain of Spirit.

I would have your eyes
to see clearly the shapes of darkness.
Yet I would keep my own
to recognize the light.

Francis P. Broussard

THE HEART OF A CHILD

As I grow older
Watch me play.
Listen to the things I say.

As I grow older
Wipe my tears.
Help me overlook my fears.

As I grow older
Shelter me,
But give me the freedom to be me.

As I grow older
Show you care.
Too soon you'll look, I'll not be there.

For when I am older
Apart from you
I'll need fond memories to remember of you.

So, as I grow older
In your rush
Please, make time to watch me grow older.

Julie Meador

SEA SPIRIT

I am One with the Sea Spray and Mist,
And the Cry of the Gull is my Heartbeat.

The Cool salty Air and the overcast Sky,
With its Silver-grey Light is my Soul.

Take me away from the Gentle white Fog,
And from the Sound of the Whispering Tide,

It's then You'll divide my Heart from my Soul,
And I'll Cease to exist in this Life.

Shannon Murphy

THE PEOPLE

Ovid wrote of Rome, I write of the U.S.A.
After driving taxicab for thirty years
There is so much I might say

The People were my Patrons, each a precious fare
The ones who kept my economy up
And I enjoyed them being there

Today I am disabled, unable to labor any more
But all of those people I have met
Gave me much to put in my store

H. G. Scholl

A STORM

The dark clouds form fast in the west,
    Like thundering stallions at their best . . .
Then ride across the massive skies,
    Stampede and swerve before our eyes;
And suddenly — there is no day;
    No light escapes those streaks of gray.
A dancin', anglin' cloud drops down,
    As wind and hailstones beat the ground . . .
As God's creations, big and small,
    Are twisted, torn — they rise then fall.
It seems so endless year by year,
    When winter's gone and spring is near.

Marjorie E. Jones

THE MARRIAGE OF THE SOUL

The yearning starts deep in the soul for love to enter gladly,
The expectant heart is free . . . gallant . . . beating madly.
To have a unison of heart and soul is rare to see indeed,
The mind accepts, the body craves, the soul absorbs the seed.
For purest love's unselfish, giving, one's ultimate goal,
It's priceless . . . exquisite . . . this marriage of the soul.

Margaret E. Mandeville

THE TRUCE

Liquid dog-eyes gaze upward at the speaker,
sneering lips shape loose disapproval.
The student mocks still-warm words
with studied blankness of face.
There is past warfare in the silence,
bloody battles in the open spaces
between the teacher
and the taught.
They have fought forever
in shadow-filled rooms.
Each waits for the other to break
the tenuous truce.

Maude Lewis

THE SPIRIT OF LOVE

A newborn babe clings close to mother,
Perhaps because it knows no other.
Inquisitive eyes are open wide,
With spirit of love locked deep inside.

Now the child of youth is more aware,
Seeking new beauty, dresses with care.
Making new friendships, being so kind,
The spirit of love rests in her mind.

Alas, the teens seem always to phone.
A full-time job so never alone.
To talk with friends is their desire,
The spirit of love is sent by wire.

Some day to marry and settle down
And with her spouse travels 'cross the town.
Soft words and whispers seem to be said.
The spirit of love rests in our bed.

Life seems so fleeting, ages have run.
Death takes its toll and stops all this fun.
We seem to float so far from the sun.
The spirit of love has made us one.

Rich Gelatt

ESCAPE

We all seek handy ways to get release,
    Diminish momentary states of strain,
Shelter our minds from stress, find bits of peace —
    Avoiding duty, boredom, fret, or pain.

To save our health, or keep harm to its least,
    We have a snack, a cigarette, a drink;
We take a holiday, attend a feast —
    Getting away, if even to death's brink.

Recourses, therapeutic at the start
    Become adaptive ills. We loaf and swill,
Carouse and chain-smoke to content our heart —
    And sink in drugged and drunken twilight chill.

Escape — meant to save us from getting worse —
Overused to counter sadness, is a curse.

Robert C. Wysong

ON MATTERS OF SUSPENSE

HONORABLE MENTION

Da Vinci knew. He said that man could fly,
With no one there to doubt, it could be done,
For had he not? How many times — alone . . .
He could not show the wings he had been shown
And cursed himself because the doubters won.

We beat our way through air to meet its lack
In answer to the daystar's siren call;
With metal stage and man himself as cast
We space ourselves but tie him to the mast
For freedom means that he is free to fall.

While falling free the god-like myths emerge,
The sky becomes a tightly fastened door.
Man's time and orbit match; we realize
That if this is not so we say he dies
Repeating curses Leonardo swore.

But man and metal fly. This we have done.
Da Vinci knew but could not say the word
To build sufficient rhythms for escape,
The circles widen while we stand agape
Afraid that Mother Earth will cut the cord.

Marilyn A. Francis

SWEET PEACE —
GOD'S PEACE

Sweet peace that comes with rested mind,
And body that is at ease;
Sweet peace that comes when I can find
Those moments of surcease.
When all is still, when calmness settles
Over body, mind and heart;
Sweet peace that comes when eyes are closed,
And all life's troubles depart.

Sweet peace that comes when I kneel down
To commune with God on High;
Sweet peace that comes, as in Bethlehem town,
When angels sang there in the sky.
Waiting and listening in peaceful calm,
This body, mind and heart
Takes on the peace of Eternity:
Lord God, never let me from peace depart!

Hilbert S. Collins

BLACKIE

High on the back of a big easy chair
    From her lookout, perch and lair
Half asleep as she scans all around
    Watching for any who would invade her ground

Stretched out on her side, asleep on the lounge
    At peace with the world, and those around
With amnesty for the day's deeds and poise
    Yet instantly awake to any intruding noise

Content in the car for miles and miles
    If surrounded by love and smiles
But at stops for toll, gas or directions
    Only the door glass prevents altercations

Some dogs are disturbing, troublesome and a bore
    Some are tiresome, irksome and more
But some are delightful, pleasant and wacky
    Like our dog Blackie . . .

Leon H. Nunn

BIG APPLE PIT

I listen to the sounds of the moving mobs
Carelessly groping their ways on
One another's feet and stepping over
The stumbling bodies that fall in their path.

Iron doors that open, then shut, receive
Most of the mangled mass of bodies
Into the crowded, careening cars
That fly downtown toward Wall Street station.

Until the morning rush is ended,
The sound of myriad scrambling feet
Fills the caverns beneath the street with music
Of harsh pitch, uneven beat, painful notes.

Then the noise dies, the crowds disappear,
And peace comes to that hole beneath the ground.
A train silently roams the empty black —
But at five the noise will be back.

Arnold Sinclair Mohnblatt

HOGARTH, The Rake's Progress: In Bedlam

HE

He prances in illusions of
Tempting array,
Bright lights of beauty,
Its sickening sway.

He promises in gold, of
Greed he reaps,
Diamonds of glass and
A hopeless seed.

He perceives the future of
Blossoming flowers,
Unleashes the elements,
Then hides in their power.

He is the shadow of
Inexorable time,
Piercing the heart
With dreams of decline.

He is the author of
Death in our young,
Who think there is peace
In his Abyss of Dung.

Marian Pruiett

MASKS

The masks people wear
Can hide and deceive
Trying to see behind it
Is difficult I believe.

Some of the happy faces
Mask sadness and despair
Who would seek to probe
Who would even dare?

Loneliness and sadness
Often walk hand in hand
Cheerful faces mask these
All across the land.

In privacy alone
True expressions are revealed
With only thoughts as company
Most people can only feel.

People should be more open
Others want to help
And by revealing your troubles
You'll only help yourself.

Jean M. Porter

PHILE'MON

Picturesque love knots — locked
betwixt cadet and paternity; ease the
Sonneteer's jeer.

Sincere love feasts chaste and planned
— Perchance Partisans ungloved
parentage unveil Courtesan shame above
the Couvade's trade acclaim.

And artisans love-making enshrine
mysticism anodyne.

Yet mignon love aerograms — in tram;
Plea to pater familias's balderdash.

And within a flash — Cadet return to
thee caché

Michael Williams

HEED ME O ANCIENT SPIRITS

Heed me, O ancient spirits,
For I have come to remember you
In your yesterday.

I have come to reawaken you
From your stagnant slumber,
And to remind you of your glorious deeds.

I have returned to hear
Your chants and lamentations;
To drink from your wine goblet,
And to dance amongst you
In your merry-making.

Lo, young spirit;
Shy not away from me,
Your true companion.
For I have traversed the eons
To be alongside of you,
Here, in the scarlet meadow
Of your sacred age.

George Malouf

MALOUF, GEORGE. Pen Name: Ghassan; Born: Jerusalem, Palestine, of Lebanese descent, 8-31-46; Married: 1-3-71 to Yiota; Education: University of Texas Tech at Lubbock, Texas, B.A., Major in French, Minor in Italian; Occupation: Store Owner of the Range Western Wear; Memberships: American Lyceum Association; Awards: Critique Litteraire, L'Esprit Français, 1968; 'How Beautiful You Are,' bicentennial edition of *The Hereford Brand*, 1975; Poetry: *The Pebbles of Time*, book, 1985; *The Lovely Blue*, book, Carlton Press of New York, 1972; *Ethereal Moments of Truth*, book, Vantage Press, New York, 1984; 'An Ode to Lebanon,' American Poetry Association, 1982; 'Steer That Ship O Seaman,' *World Treasury of Great Poems*, 1980; 'The Cry of a Soul,' *Our World's Best Loved Poems*, World of Poetry Press, 1984; Comments: *I write in order to relax; I enjoy bringing out those simple moments of beauty, simplicity, and of humbleness of man before nature and God; moments, which otherwise, are lost to a non-heeding world.*

GLIMPSES

Everywhere I look
I see you.
I catch the sunlight
reflected by your hair,
the sparkle of your eyes,
the sweet pout of your lips
the essence of you
taking me back to a comfortable time.

I turn around
expecting your face,
only it isn't you
   it's a memory.

Gigi Goren

THE ART OF LIFE

The art of life is the art of love
For neighbors near and far away.
This is the greatest art of all
Reach out for this, today.
Through the harmony of great pictures
That hang upon the gallery wall,
Through the music of great symphonies
Which the soul of men enthrall,
From these great interpretations
Of love and life as they should be
We will evolve to understanding
In love with God's reality.

Phyllis Hill

SIDE TRIP

tumbling
down the
wishing well
all dreamy
and soft-sided:
its bottom
trampolined
for bouncing
among
the rainbow colors
of
crystal thought

Susan R. Fagan

EDUCATION

Quote:
"Must you learn to read and write
   To be so well-informed,
No one can make a fool of you,
   Or keep you misinformed?
Well! I guess! makes good sense:
   Unless, of course to begin with,
A feller lacks intelligence;
   Ain't got the gumption God gave a goose!
In which case he is so dense,
   He's just plain ignorant . . .
And he don't know the difference!"

Luke Nathaniel Baxter

RESIGNATION

As I unstrap my buckled sword
And let it fall without a word;
Hang it not on trophied wall,
For I have found I whimper tall
When forced to quit the battlefield,
And courage drains when age must yield
To Time's relentless sword and shield.

John P. Clark

WINTER PSALMS

The white calm
Of a winter afternoon,
A certain slant of light.

The eerie balm
Of a daytime moon,
Up well before the night.

Snowflake psalms
Fall — lacy, rattling tunes
Played until Spring ignites.

Linda Kellogg

THE PREMONITION

I lifted the 3-shaped roof off the telephone
House, listened in to the downstairs kitchen
Buzzer, going off on the oven through the chimney
Wire. "Imagine if my home's flue curled like that!"
I spiraled my lips in a smile to myself,
As I poked my *numero uno* index
Finger in an O-pen window,
Pushed upon its lucky plastic
Sill, till the flower of all the dormers spun
In a left-to-right circle. "Imagine if sashed spaces
In walls of this anthracite residence moved . . ."

Like a cat, I dialed in every groove
I needed in that funeral-dark cottage of speech.
My paws at the end, when the feline screech
Of the 'I don't work!' signal shrieked, clawed the lawn,
Green desk, which my dwelling with bell ring sat on.

Scratching tabby phalanges then tiptoed up
The sidewalk of papers and stoop of the buck,
That I'd left at receiver's foundation to play
The lottery. O-one-three won that day.
Ted Yund, M.D.

YOU'RE THE MEANING IN MY LIFE

"You are what no one else could be, a creation
of God, which he has bestowed upon me;
You are the meaning for which I live, and
for this, my love I shall give;
You are the meaning in my life and my
inspiration."

"You are what dwells in my heart and I
thank the Lord for this I can be a part, and
the feeling I have had, has always been from
the start;
You are the meaning in my life, who stands me
up and tells me to fight when I am weak and
begin to lose sight;
So I stand with you because our love is so
true, and I thank God for each minute I am
with you."

"You are what I have been looking for, always
giving of yourself and so much more;
You are my inspiration and by far all of
my expectations."
Joseph Geralis

PASSION

Passion touched me with glistening lights,
with songs of joy, who cares if I'm right?
Deep thoughts of you keep running
through my mind,
I do think about you from time to time.
Remembering the touch of sadness,
apologizing all the same turned it to
gladness.
I thought about that special kiss, oh
was it sweet!
It was like Romeo and Juliet,
remember how they had met?
birds were singing from the trees up above,
Now, no one could not tell me that I was not
in love.
Sweaty palms trying to hold on, for I
knew that it would not be long,
Until the love we had would soon be gone.
No one ever said that love was here
to stay,
but why didn't someone tell me that
Love would hurt this way!
Roxann Harris

NOT SO FREE VERSE

Genius minds of olden times
shaped the sounds of language — exquisitely.

There was the Ballad, Blank Verse and the Couplet,
The Sonnet, The Ode,
The Pantoum, The Quintet,
The Rondeau, Sestet and Sestina,
The Shakespearian Stanza,
The Tercet and Terza Rima,
the Triplet and Triolet
and last of all The Villanelle
the Shepherd's Song
that graced the dell.

I thrill to the Bible
The Psalms, Book of Job
Solomon's Lyrics
Paeon and Ode.

My Poetry of Choice
Free Verse with its cadence
Strophe of Greek Chorus
circle completed.
Marie Zaharias Daughters

SENSATION

The superannuation of the rocks
That craggy rise around the lucent waves
Bespeak an ancient ocean. Is a sleep
The succedaneum of such a sea?
Unutterable winds upon the surf
Uplift it into vapor on the sand.
And all that I can hear is what I dream;
And all that I can sense is what I feel.
The sky is like the surface of the sea,
All littered with the beds of little clouds.
And the ocean, like a warm and living hand
Writes its perfect poetry upon the shore.
And there is no contradiction
In the presence of the sea.
And that sense should think of paradox
Is paradox to me.
Since all of earth is novel
And all of life is new,
How can there be paradox
Or anything seem strange?
And the gentle oxymoron
Of the whisper of the sea
Leaves mercy in the infant,
And leaves evening to me.
Joseph Hart

FUNNY CLOWN

One day I felt so lonely
I thought that I might cry,
Then I met a funny clown —
And began to laugh, oh my!

His face was painted like spots of cherries,
His hair a blazen red,
His clothes were loose and baggy,
A floppy hat upon his head.

He ambled slowly down the street
Tripping along on two long feet,
Smiling and laughing with all he met;
A nice funny clown, the happiest yet.

Now, I forgot to be lonely,
I also forgot to cry.
So, I want to thank you, Funny Clown
For brightening my day — That's why!
Frances P. Brown

TAKE ME OUT OF THE WAY

Dear Father, please take me out of the way.
Work in my life, dear Father, every day.
Please show me the words, that you would have me say.
Please take me out of the way, I pray.

I know that I can do it, if you will help me.
Yet when I try, I get in the way, and I cannot see.
I want to do Thy will, dear Father, and I do try,
But I keep messing it up; and that I can't buy.

How can they see Thy face, when I get in the way?
How can they hear Thy words when I don't know what to say?
How will they know Thy will or what to do?
How do I fit the bill? How can I best help you?

So, please, dear Father, take me out of the way?
And work Thy will in me, dear Father, I pray.
Show me just what you would have me to say.
Let them see you, not me, in my life today.

I am all tied in knots and I don't know what to do.
Won't you please take control of me; my whole body through?
Help others to see thy matchless love in me.
Take me out of the way, dear Father; show them Calvary.

Alice May Shutt

JUST EXPERIENCE

It tickles me down to the heel of my shoe
the way folks will say when things worry you,
No matter if marbles or living expense:
"Just count it, my dear, as experience."

It tickles me too, when I'm down and I'm out,
No friends, no money and no Run-a-bout,
Someone will say, though lacking suspense:
"Count it, my dear, just experience."

So when you feel blue, your bills are all due,
Your friends all forsake you, health is passoo,
Just laugh at collectors and friends who are dense,
And say, "Count it, kind sirs, just experience."

If you are hard-up, need food, clothing, cash,
Don't tear your hair, or do anything rash,
Sit down and laugh as if you'd lost all your sense,
And count it your income — just experience.

So when I'm through with this old Earth so dear,
I'll laugh at you people who still stay on here,
And I'll say to you as I shall fly hence:
"Count it, dear people, just experience."

Ruth G. McAlley

A SILHOUETTE SUBLIME
Dedicated to Patricia Loomis,
"Someone very special to me . . ."

My darkened eyes perceived, upon a moment's glance;
A silhouette sublime, encaptured by romance.
Awakened from a dream, perhaps a lullaby;
To wist a glimpse pursued, a twinkle in my eye.

Of pondering bereft, a spectre to behold;
Entranced by her beauty, a captive to a mould,
Of silken auburn tresses, and bodice genteel;
To coiffured elegance, of lace and florappeal.

My heart began to thrive, upon this livid sight;
Memory could not erase, her visionary light.
And as those eyes beheld, the longing in my soul;
Her gentleness caressed, my thoughts without console.

Glen Patrick Young

IMMORTALITY

I strive and endeavor to create with simplicity and grace,
Each word with care, so that it shall tenderly embrace;
The heart of each soul whose eyes shall weep to read
These words of love, passion and tears for the heart that bleeds.

With pen in hand and paper in place, this is my immortality,
With dreamy muse, the goddesses of music and poetry;
I write of ecstatic love that is cleansed with bitter tears
The rare pleasure and the constant strive through the years.

The emptiness that shadows the prayers I've prayed,
I wonder if God hears, and if He knows I'm afraid;
To laugh, to breathe supreme thoughts of endless love
So I am sad, and lament for the secrets lie above.

In death and life my soul shall forever be
A melody of sadness, of love and mystery;
I exist, I do not live
But only in your heart;
For I shall never die
We shall never part.

Naomi Draughn

I COULD

I know I could be a lover to Stareyes.

For I could be a poet to write poems for
    you/me and the friends we know.

Only peace was strong in God's world. There could
    be so many wonderful things to have.

Can't understand why I am so blue so much
    Stareyes.

I try to be happy when I think about
    hunger it turns me sad/blue.

So I guess I have to bring it up higher with God's blessing.

So I wouldn't have to be blue, don't know
    I'll never be sad again about home.

So I just got to bring it to the limit, Stareyes.

Felix Louis Wicks

NEW YORK SUBWAY TRAGEDY
(An illustration and a lesson)

The tragedy on a New York subway train
That occurred not many days ago,
Was an illustration and a lesson
As to what might and will happen
In a great American civilization,
On which we pride as being
The greatest in the universe.
Then, why must human protection
Appear insurmountable?

Harassment can be highly provocative.
Not all human beings react alike when attacked;
Whether anger is concealed or revealed,
The equation is all the same,
Violence begets violence
When the victim fires a gun
Forcing the aggressor to cower and run.

    'Tis a pity for what happened
    In New York City.

Johnye Boyd

HOW FAR SHALL YOU TRAVEL MY LADY IN BLUE?

You stand there in tiny black patent
shoes,
    with black satin bows adorning your
toes,
    Wearing angel-white socks edged in
tiny delicate lace,
    while your soft brown hair forms
ringlets upon your cherub face.
    Your large brown eyes are gleaming
with brand-new emotion,
    as your very first step gives you
new freedom of motion.
    How far shall you travel my little
"Lady in Blue?"
    Will you just take one step — or will
you take two?
    Please, don't travel too far or too
fast,
    for these moments to me are precious,
I want them to last!

Joyce Maloney

TEACHER

    Teacher, Teacher teach us
of love, Teach us of how Christ
came from above.

    Teach us of how he came
and bled, and how God raised
him from the dead.

    Teach us of how when Lazarus
did die, sweet Jesus' eyes couldn't
help but cry.

    Teacher, Teacher feed your
flock well, so that your words
might save them from hell.

    Teacher, Teacher love your
flock, so that at the end of your life
clock, when you are judged in
heaven above, your soul will be
found like that of a dove.

Jimmy R. Stitz

WHEN THE SWEAT MEETS THE RAIN

Divorce.
Rent.
Bills.
Child-support.
Pressure.

Hunger.
Bicycle.
Cold.
Cloudy.
Sale at store on crock pots.

Rain.

Sweat.
Pedal.
Home.
Shower.
Food.

Rest.

Wm. David Franklin

A WRITER'S ENCUMBRANCE

Rambled thoughts encased in bone
    eager for permeation
        from mind to seasoned pulp
    Lay in wait

Seconds pass, and minutes linger
All uncertainty clouds the unseen trail
    from newborn mind, to aging hand

Lifeless lines which bare no use
    are closed between the hand which writes
        and one which bares no haste
            to easily discard

Hours pass and toils its weight
    upon the tiring mind
One sitting's work
    is now contained in crumpled heaps
        inside a battered grave of tin

For want of worth
    a slumber brain
        takes respite from what was lost

Robert T. Thies

THE CHANGELING

Who is this stranger, so still in death?
It cannot my brother be.
It is not his brow,
as he wore it raised in easy wit,
not his smile, wild and free.
What face lies cold and still in the dark?
Not my brother's face,
his lively and expressionistic,
a dimple here, a crinkled eye.
This cannot my brother be.
'Tis a changeling,
swathed in my brother's clothes,
donning my brother's features,
but not his warm, warm heart.
'Tis a chameleon, with
the hue of my brother's skin,
the fullness of my brother's form,
but not his live vitality.
This cannot my brother be.
Death has taken my brother away from me.

Shirley Montgomery

SPRING

The moisture-laden wind
is from the East,
slowly fingering on
from the fog-wrapped Bay.
All Nature is in deep silence
as in abandonment of quiet sleep.
Only the far distant cry
of returning geese flight
reaches down into the
ever-spreading stillness of
this precious mystic dawn,
as morning unfolds
to display her precious
array of endless beauties.
The welcome loud croak
of the early frog
accompanies the soft lyric note
of morning's joyous sparrow,
in unison with the far, far cry
of the sea-roving kildeer —
assures a most warm return
to the welcoming debut of
yet another joyous Spring!

Ansel B. Sterling

INDIAN WAR DANCE

The smoke from the teepee goes to the sky,
The buffalo pass by,
The moon is covered by the cloud
Indians dance to drums loud,
Teepee tom tom teepee, teepee tom.

Headdress feathers in the wind blow.
From the campfire glow,
Indian warriors painted in red,
Dance to honor the dead,
Teepee tom tom teepee, teepee tom.

Indian chief of the land,
We follow you as a band,
The raid is at sunrise,
White man we will surprise,
Teepee tom tom teepee, teepee tom.

The smoke from the teepee goes to the sky,
The buffalo pass by,
The moon is covered by the cloud,
Indians dance to drums loud,
Teepee tom tom teepee, teepee tom.

Ralph R. Payton

NOTHING SO DARK

Look not into the darkness
    where the cold air creeps,
but into the light
    where in love He keeps
us warm and strong in
    the midst of a storm.

In darkness we are blind
    not seeing the holes
which make us stumble;
    not avoiding the branches
which get in our way.

In His omniscient light,
    He shows us where to make
our bridge over the miry depths.
    He shines his light
across our paths to keep us
    from falling off the rugged steep.

In His radiant light, there is nothing
    so dark we cannot see
God's purpose for being there.

Tandra V. Heiser

THE MASTER'S HANDS

The plans we've made together
our hearts will never sever.
He's made our own special plans'
only drawn by Master's hands.

Did I say we made them?
They were made in heaven.
They are our special plans
drawn by the Master's hands.

Still, He has plans for you.
Special things you could do.
He'd make your special plans
and draw them with His hands.

He always plans for us.
He plans no matter what.
We choose to use our plans
drawn by the Master's hands.

Veanna Hansen

TO VENUS A BRIGHT STAR

Heavenly Shepherd whose eternal radiance
Penetrates the silent gloom of night,
Illuminate the unknown! Thy glimmering brilliance
Keeps a faithful watch upon the flight
Of centuries, majestic and splendid still,
That find their way to God because of thee —
Thy clear, cold flame ascends the towering hill
Of destiny, whose rugged pinnacles, free
And unfathomable, breathe an air apart;
Where beyond our power to comprehend,
Thy shimmering diadem, pale counterpart
Of truth, beholds infinity; legend
And prophecy proclaim thy distant mystery
Impervious; thou fragment of eternity.

Bernice Anita Reed

REED, BERNICE ANITA. Education: Bachelor of Arts Degree with a Major in English and Dramatics; Master of Arts Degree in Sociology and Counseling; Three years of intensive training in Psychotherapy at Duke Hospital (University), Durham, North Carolina; Occupations: Psychotherapist and Counselor; Awards: Certificate of Merit and Honorable Mention, Poetry Contest for Tall Men Of State, World of Poetry; Comments: *I am writing a series of Anti-War Poems, poems with psychological significance. I write poems to augment my treatment of patients' emotional problems. I write to express beauty, to address universal phenomena, to utilize time in a meaningful manner, and sometimes because subjects haunt me, pursue me until I express them in poetic form.*

WAR OR WARS

Nations in War much blood they spill
Retreating from battle or charging a Hill
Some will die, some lives are spared
The beginning of War comes undeclared.
Many will answer when duty call
Some finish unhurt, many will fall.
Prepare for the Aggressor, we swear to defend
A Historic beginning, a pledge to the end.
Nations come together, lift the Pen and sign
Regrets for the sadden dividing line.
Coming out from the mud, wind, and rain
Those that were lost we pray in vain
When all Men open their eyes will they see
War or Wars should never be.
Man and War long before my Birth
Let love and peace conquer Earth.

Ed Lewis

WHO? ME?

God balances nature by a thought that man almost forgot
He is the God with patient love between the cold and hot.
Our temperatures we read as normal; our weather we like it clear
Capacity is the outer limits, His love is always near.

God is the creator of the worlds, the moon and hovering stars
He has a mystery we cannot know what He permits or bars.
Ecology is not just a word to which we should relate
But the balance of natural processes before it is too late.

Our streams are swollen from the fires we burn so thoughtlessly
The smoke ascends to outer space with deep intensity.
The CO_2 we put in space while CO_1 is worse
Our cars and traffic patterns foiled while riding in a hearse.

Oh man who spurned the universe and fixed his joy in time
What pleasure-seekers we have found to help this world to rhyme.
We gamble in the lottery and curse the earth God gave
We manufacture all the goods to waste rather than save.

Our clock in time is running down unless we heed the sign
That God who cares for one and all has little thoughts like mine.
He is concerned how we behave upon this ball called earth
Humanity is all we have to know the Divine worth.

Bernard N. Morris

POETIC IMAGE

Aleph princess bathed in light,
come into the wonderstruck world
farrowed fawn.

Raven queen,
daughter of darkness;
sable bishop helpless as an alabaster pawn.

Consort of sun and stars,
burgundy luxury;
strange drifting tide bearing love.

If there were a gold star
vanishing in the ink-purple gallery,
captured by myself, mine to give;
the golden passion in waxen tallow is yours
for all of time.

Richard J. Serrano

THE RAINBOW

So wetly and so utterly wetly the wet rain wanders
in a crevice and colors it wet. Nowhere's a dry device
can stop the wet from going wetly anywhere it likes.

One butterfly flutters by insanely and flounders
and plummets to the vast wet below, singularly unamused,
by chance a wet beast on this wet earth,
by chance elsewhere, otherly.

After struggles that span centuries
the beast is bitten by the hungry dark, slips kicking
into a patient blank from this miserable fool's parade
unasked, unmasked at last.

Wet are the rocks of this earth, wet
the stark ribs of windmills not camouflaged in foliage
as if trees, and wet that mortal fellow our sad sun
(resembling an eye of blemished light
dissembling a mind's true pitch).

Wetly the soil is wet and wetly it wettens yet wetter.
The fabric of the butterfly's beautiful sails
lies tattered wetly on these waters
of our human winter.

Brodrene Castleman

LOVE'S TEARS
(For Bryan)

Love has its sweet words and smiles,
Its soft caresses and kisses —
But love, too,
Has its tears,
Which slip through
To slide down my cheeks
When you are gone.
I cup my hand to catch
Not tears —
But bits and pieces of my heart
As they shatter-splash
To the floor.
But love, too,
Has its tears
of happiness —
Which flow endlessly onto you
Upon your return.
And you being the gentleman that you are,
Offer my heart back to me
Along with your own.

Monique Simek

FINISHED SYMPHONY

Ranging in dynamics,
my shallow body
was capable
of great flexibility.
My music, sweet, sensuous
and soul-awakening,
subsided suddenly
with a crescendo
to a mournful melancholy,
pensive and elegiac.

Now, echoes of haunting melodies,
undying memorable tunes,
play on my heart strings
a tribute
to your love.
There is no real music
without you,
no encores
I am a violin
Without a maestro.

Dorothy Wilder Halleran

I KNOW YOU

I know you
You're into loyalty
Leos are like that.
I'm just a Virgo
with a lifetime of love
and a heart
that stays broken.

I know you
You can't be drawn away
from dreams that
glide effortlessly
on a wingspan
of confidence and glory
and a spirit that soars on summer air
above everything
Leos are like that.
I'm just a Virgo
my wings are like a baby sparrow's
falling from the nest
unable to fly.

Marie Mitchell

JUST TAKE A MOMENT

Just take a moment and try to be
  happy, try to smile the whole
day through,
  Try as hard as you can to break
down the burdens and cares
that may always surround you.
  Just take a moment and lift
your heart and mind to the
  beautiful heavens above and
see all that God has to offer
  with all his lasting love,
He has a lot to share with
  Us, more precious than Silver
  And Gold,
    He can give us peace of mind
  With happiness and joy to behold.
  He can change our lonely
feelings, fill them with a great
delight, so just take a moment
  And think of this, before you
give in to the battle of life.
Inez Pulliam

REACHING OUT

If I could
But touch you,
Would it help?
If I could
But reach you,
Would it heal?
So very much
I want to hold
your body to mine,
To let my soul
Intertwine
with yours, and heal.
But would it be
Enough?
Am I just too
Late —
To soothe the hurt,
Heal the scars,
This world caused you?
May I try?
May I try?
At least, you'll know
Someone cared.
Sally A. Barrows

THE KING

He was the best,
The king of the streets,
To our neighbors,
He was no pest,
He was the protector,
The king of the streets.
He was mean and tough to intruders,
Put them in their place,
He was nice and gentle to everyone
else,
No matter their race.
The king had his harem,
And a family to love,
He was greater than any tom,
He was way above,
But now the king is gone,
Went to that place,
The "Great Unknown,"
He is happy there,
Resting in peace,
I love my sweet Bear,
And I miss him,
That beautiful beast.
Lani Watanabe

IN THIS GENERATION

The last ship leaves her mother behind
in darkness
where love and peace exist no more
to sing their song in protest
to the wind

The last survivors of mother depart
looking slowly behind to see the dark
and fear they can't return home anymore

I say it's time, an age again
when we breathe freedom in the sunshine
and realize now we must save our home
from the bombs of two toy soldiers

Are you with me?
Yes! They cried.
We want to see our future,
and we turned the ship around.

Tegan

BUTTERFLY

Butterfly, butterfly
why not soar into deep blue
and kiss the stars
as the skylarks do?

You prefer the earth to flirt,
from flower to flower to fly.

Each year you appear in May
teasingly with tots to play.

Thy multicolor robe
is as rainbow,
fragile are you as snow
naive like doe.

As a boy in my native "Golden Horn"
with your beauty I decorated my room.

You have myriad admirers
among men, fauna and flowers
for you scorn not the ground,
my butterfly!

Peter Ionesco

WAITING

Mountains here
rise above the timber line
and tease me
with fears for you,
my love.

You are there
amid slide rock
where piñons
do not have your courage
and dare not defy the
natural law.

I am here
wondering
with tasks that
take new importance
to divert and
warn against worry.

Yet when day ends
I miss you,
my love.

Elaine Baker

66

COMING HOME

Leaving you after our
                  togetherness!
I think of you and our
                  special times together!
Your smiles
                  make me smile!
Your arms around me so
                  I feel your embrace!
Your eyes so warm
                  I see warmth of great depth!
Your kisses so playful
                  I feel your lips
                  urging mine closer!
You . . . Lying close by my side
                  I feel contentment within you!
I think of you
                  our special times to come
                  as I miss you . . . Indolently
                  During the hours we spend apart.

Kathryn Ann Hohn

A VIRTUOUS WOMAN

A virtuous woman is hard to find and when a man is
blessed by a virtuous woman from the Lord he should thank the
Lord Jesus every day for her because a virtuous woman is
Far more precious than all of the rubies, gold, diamonds
in the whole world, a virtuous woman is a big blessing
to a man and the man should love her with all of his
heart and should respect and honor her all of his life
through and cherish her all of his days on earth a
virtuous woman will uplift her husband when he is down
and she will praise him and never tear him down and she
has a lot of wisdom when she speaks and her husband should
listen to her when he does not know which way to turn a virtuous
woman will be a blessing to everybody that she meets she
will extend her helping hand to the poor and needy and
ask for nothing in return a virtuous woman will raise up
in the night to look after the children and see that everything
is all right, she watches over the ways of her household and at
the end her children will call her blessed. And her husband
will praise her with an everlasting praise

Gary Espinosa

I reach to you, Rebekka, with outstretched hand.
  You reach to me with your heart.
Your love I cannot command,
  Yet you withheld it not from the start.

I look into your eyes and see the sky's beautiful hue.
  And I realize I can't express the deep love I have for you.

Yet somehow you know that my hand is my outstretched heart,
  And as we love the heavens above we shall chart.

I will teach you what I have learned of beauty and truth.
  Yet you see so much in the dawn of youth.

As you look to the heavens I know now what you see,
  Do you see the angels as they look upon thee?

In your mother's eyes I first saw the skies.
  Now your part of the love will never die.

Benjamin Pressley

BUSINESS GIRL

Oft in the quick'ning light of the city hour —
Stern morn by the surge of a driving power
And the clock's grave face and a thousand restive,
And things forgot that so late were festive —
Oft in the morning's dutiful hour
I saw her going with eyes that were knowing.

And oft in the hearty lull of the city hour,
Hale noon by the sheen of the waxen flower
And the clock's still hands and a thousand swinging,
And earthen dishes their chatter bringing —
Oft in the noon's impartial hour
I saw her pass in my window glass.

And oft in the bustling drone of the city hour,
Man's own by the clock's drooped face in the tower
And the drowsing purr of the city dragon,
Stooped with the draught of his human flagon —
Oft in the young eve's thoughtful hour
I saw her move toward night's wide groove.

Eugene J. Devlin, J.D.

DEVLIN, EUGENE JOSEPH. Born: Bay Ridge, Brooklyn, New York, 11-29-02; Education: University of Detroit, A.B., 1924; LL.B., 1927; LL.M. and J.D., 1931; Awards: Class Poet, University of Detroit High School, 1920; Occupation: Lawyer, private practice; Professional Memberships: State Bar of Michigan, American Bar Association, Macomb County and St. Clair Shores Bar Associations, Catholic Lawyers Society, Irish-American Bar Association.; Poetry: 'The Poet Laureate of Christ,' 'As to a Mother's Sweet Soliloquy,' 'Remember December,' 'The Holy Rosary and the Divine Computer,' 'Ave Atque Vale,' and 200 other poems published by *Parishes, The American Legion Magazine of Michigan, Michigan Disabled Veteran, etc.;* Themes: *The Creator of the Universe, Holy Trinity, individual and world peace, the immortality of the soul; I wrote of Thomas A. Edison's great gifts to the world out of the West, etc.;* Comments: *I have always been single (lived with my mother until her death).*

SUNSET FIELD

The old pond glistens the last hint of light.
The moon slowly rises as day turns to night.
Gold shines through the trees as the sun starts to yield,
And the sunset reflects off the old western field.

Laura Quick

PARALLEL SCREAMS

In some dark room where very few go
An infant screams, as if near death
Parents listen, but they have screams of their own
And yet the infant's cries are ignored

Mother sighs, she'll be there shortly
As Dad just wishes the noise would cease
What the baby needs may only take a moment or two
But they're much too busy to even bother

Baby gasps for air and chokes instantly
One last scream erupts from the tiny throat
Parents find the silence most reassuring

For little do they know
They've sacrificed a newborn's life
For an uncontrollable passion
In the heat of a summer night
And now they scream at each other!

Eric Knight

B! a type A?

What am I to do on this day
                    of collapsed stance?

For I am far too sunken down
                    to go about and prance

My motive powers have lapsed
                    and have but a shrunken chance

I cannot pull myself
                    out of this languid trance . . .

Even though
        I know
            I should be
                    up!
                        and away —
I didn't want to be a **type A**
                    anyway!

Randy Ruff

YESTERDAY AND TOMORROW

The past has a way of silencing one,
Keeping one from saying what's true;
Like it's done for me
When I want to say how I feel about you.

At times I come so close to saying
What's really on my mind,
But then I think of a love gone wrong
And what's left, but dreams we couldn't find.

You walked into my life unexpectedly
And swept me off my feet.
You taught me how to smile again,
And to know a love that's sweet.

Each day I learn something new about life,
And living and knowing the score;
About you and me and the feeling I have,
And learning to care even more.

Jamie (Jenkins) Harrison

A PRECIOUS PROMISE

For each long search for understanding,
A light twinkles up above,
For every unkind act or word that is spoken,
God sends us His great Love.

Faith is the light that guides us
Even though the way be long,
It is God's warmth and wisdom
That makes us well and strong.

Margaret Rebrinsky

QUICK BE OUR HANDS TO HELP

Though mighty, whining turbines the torrent's power steal,
                    send searing forces pulsing through the night
        Yet fearsome power, flashing vibrant from the lab'ring wheel
                    must seek a lamp to give its gift of light

So God, who made the world and love, its moving force
                    must work in hearts with holy zeal alight
        To send love's power coursing, though omnipotent the source
                    through willing hands to set the world aright.

Ruby Bode

A FLOCK OF GULLS

A flock of gulls I saw this morn,
They flew overhead with exquisite form,
With undersides aflame and heads held high,
They moved across the winter sky.

From the sunrise crest to the ashen moon,
I listened carefully to their haunting tune,
And I felt a sense of joy within,
For the gulls and I are truly akin.

Alvin Robert Cunningham

UNTITLED

It is easy to let a moment open up
the heart's lacy gates.
It is easy to let the world go away
in instants of glory, wonderment and surprise.
And then because of devouring rays,
open wide and receive and give
questions unanswered and dreams of tomorrow
on the wings of a fading past.
For today is the gift.

Monique Adam

SEEKER

I, walked along on byways and sought:
The Painter of roses on a dew-swept morn.
Nomad of love songs on a sand caravan.
Vagabond of sorrow on a highway of dreams.
Clown of three-rings in a realities world.
A drifter in forests where wind touched the bough.
Weaver of thoughts by a wild stormy sea.
In lonely places, I walked, has come peace;
and God, where the wind has found rest.

Mystery Alires

MY LOVE

James has a touch
that heals me;
he has a smile
that pleases me;
there's something about him,
the kindness he shows,
the courteous ways he bestows to me and to others.
He has a way about him that's very beautiful!
One time he asked me: "Shall I call you my
little Rosebud?!"
Because I blushed a lot, and still do.
I shall always remember him saying that sweet
sentence to me.
James is very special to me.
And to me, in my eyes — No other man can hold
a candle to him.

Sonda Penner

9/29/83

Why is it always, when you realize it is too late,
there are so many things yet to be said and done?

I LOVE YOU GRANDMA!

But I never told you that often enough.

It came so easy to me when I was a little girl,
then I grew up and away from you.
I took you for granted, assuming you would know
what I could not put into words.

Trying to be an adult, I was instead childish.

Putting it down on paper now, I know cannot make
up what is now lost to me forever.

My hope is that although you are gone, God has allowed
you to retain the eyes of your heart, and it is really
not too late to tell you what a central part of my
life you were and will remain.

I miss you Grandma,
and I Love You!

Teri Kalisz

TO PLEASE THE LIKES OF YOU

It isn't an isle in the Caribbean,
Where they play Cole Porter's Begin The Beguinne,
Nor is it in the South Pacific
Where the climate is so terrific,
But what it has will last
The peaceful country and the city blast.

The honky tonk of Coney Island
The ghetto of Bedford Stuyvesant,
The tennis scene of Forest Hills,
The social set of the Hamptons
The motels due East at Montauk.
The East River on the West
Long Island Sound on the North,
The gigantic Atlantic on the South
Converges the lip of the Eastern tip,
Where Sound and Ocean are joined
At a Point better known as Montauk.

Astoria, Jackson Heights and Flushing,
Jamaica, Garden City and Huntington,
Airport to airport, ballpark to ballpark,
From Riverhead to the sailboats of beauteous Orient Point,
This glacial deposit from the Ice Age came through
To please even the likes of you.

Brad Lee

ET TU, F. SCOTT?

We sailed, we dined, we danced till dawn
In Sydney, Singapore, Dar es Salaam, Beirut and Istanbul
(You weren't the only one, F. Scott)
But now those gay expatriate days are gone

Many islands beckon from out there:
Mykonos, Santorini, and the Island of Roses
There's Malta, Sicily, Sardinia, the embers of Stromboli

Ancient walled Dubrovnik rates a line by itself
(Were you there, F. Scott?)

I've been back to Cairo, Alexandria, Vienna and Athens
Lisbon and London, too — all the capitals over there
(You knew Paris well, F. Scott)

Like your Gatsby, I found my green light.
I'm drunk with love for the enticing, intriguing
whole damn world

But, oh, F. Scott, I wouldn't want to go mad like Zelda
Or Ophelia. There's too much of the world inside my head
So I'll grab it all, put it down on paper
And relive it all again

Helen O. Perrin

PERRIN, HELEN VIRGINIA. Pen name: Helen O. Perrin; Born: Spirit Lake, Iowa; Married: 1939 to Frank W. Perrin; Education: Fullerton Junior College, A.A.; University of Denver, 1953; Merced College, Los Banos Campus, 1980-81; Memberships: Dos Palos Literary Guild, Dos Palos Women's Improvement Club, Los Banos Writers Workshop, The National Writers Club; Poetry: 'Winter Stars,' Lit. Art Magazine, Merced College, 1982; 'Wondering,' Lit. Art Magazine, Merced College, 1982; 'Rural Childhood,' Fine Arts Press, 1984; 'Without You,' *Hearts on Fire, Vol. II,* 1985; Other Writings: "A Dust Free Room," short story, Lit. Art Magazine, Merced College, 1982; Themes: *Varied, with a foreign flavor.* Comments: *I have a compulsion to write. I try to express feeling, beauty, in my poetry. My short stories are personal adventures experienced in many years of living around the world, from the Stone Age Island of New Guinea in the '50's , to sophisticated capitals around the globe. Was recently graduated from Writers Digest School, where I made the dean's list.*

SMALL THINGS

I've watched You guide the sun across the sky,
and at Your hand, I've seen the moon comply.
I've witnessed how the trees bend with the breeze
As wind and rain bow down by your decrees.
I've seen how oceans stretch from land to land,
And watched all nature follow Your command.
I can believe You'll cause the sun to rise
And calm the storm — in this I know You're wise,
But in small things You ask me now to trust —
Remember, Lord, You made me but from dust!

Carol M. Balogh

ALPHA

The night dawns upon us . . .
Sitting on the greyhound bus . . .
Day closing its eyes . . .
Night's eyes starting to open . . .
Now is when the stars start to show . . .
Unmasking the bright sky . . .
Daylight night known by the moon . . .
A shiny bright circle hovers . . .
Uncovering earth's dark secrets . . .
Awaiting birth within the womb . . .
A child's room of dreams . . .
Sleep seems to grow brighter at night . . .
A sight to behold . . .
Untold stories awakened . . .
Taken for real . . .
The bad cannot steal . . .
The wheel of fortune rolls on . . .
And so goes the night dawns . . .
    Omega

 Gerald Frederick Mlodoch II

NATURE DANCES

A striped cat prances in the shadows of the night,
 Nature dances in perfect timing and oh, what a sight!
Branches move, branches sway,
 Having such fun on a breezy autumn day.
 And in city alleyways the winds waltz without a care.
Golden wheat dances from side to side,
 Rhythm consistent, steps smooth, then glide.
The old mill slowly grinds away,
 The rushing waters tumble so happy and gay.
Snowflakes glisten as they drift to the ground,
 A swan swims gracefully with fluffy feathers, soft down.
In Africa a gazelle shifts into full speed,
 Stealing the show, taking the lead.
An eagle soars so proud, so bold,
 While a fawn struggling to walk is a miracle to behold.
Colorful leaves twirl and tap-dance down the street,
 'Cause nature possesses such talented feet.
What a performance, what a ballet!
 Let's applaud nature every day!

 Linda C. Grazulis

LATE TWO

To speak of love, all forgiving, what have I done
Your gracious heart, yearning to trust, I meant to hurt none
 My novice understanding, of your growing
  lead me away, not knowing
You held me above all, like precious stones
Telling all the beauty which you held
 Struggling, I freed myself, of your trance
   a fool was I, not to see
The glory that you held in me,
 How deaf not to perceive, your plea
   I was so confused
No one will ever, match your beauty
The sunshine of your smile, warming all
 How I long for a glance
Innocent eyes, believing, confidence implied
 But you could not hear me, crying
   the pain, of loneliness
 Wasn't the weary, showing
As you circumvented

 Charles W. Livingston

RAINBOW MEMORIES

If I could find days of following rainbows
And raindrops on my skin,
I would go to those days back yonder
And never come back here again.
Days of smiles and no umbrella, not caring
For the rain, for it fell so sweet and tender
in those days that I lived back then.
Pigtails and butterflies, wild clovers blossomed
And little calf newborn, sweet life all around
bright shining dew covered morn, air as sweet
As fresh-churned butter, everyone shared a
Smile. All my memories of pigtails and rainbows
Sweet life of an innocent child.
Mama calls us to supper young-uns it's getting
late. Out to the yard to pump our water
Mama she'll patiently wait.
Say our prayers Daddy goodnight.
life is so sweet to me, I close my eyes
A small country girl in my rainbow memory.

 Yvonne Ferguson

THE SPRUCE GOOSE

The Flying White Horse, or, is it a bird?
We've seen it arrive, like an omen of peace.
Our eagles look great on the emblem of the state
But, oh, you should see the Spruce Goose,
 flying bird of them all!

Wingspread 320 feet — so wide, it equals the tide!
Eight engines so high you could fly through the sky
At a speed 200 miles per hour that equals the fastest
 of wings.

The Wright Brothers started what Howard Hughes brings.
It's a giant, 750 people it'll hold *or* two Sherman tanks,
 six sabre jets *or* eight helicopters from the Army
 are stored in its tail.
The officers sit forward and room for them all.
Go down to Long Beach and watch it swim in 70 feet of
 Pacific Ocean under its dome!

 Frances Oglevee White Percival

GOD'S MESSENGER

 A little bird perched on the porch rail
one bright and sunny day.
 I opened the door just a crack so he
wouldn't fly away.
 When out of his throat burst a beautiful
song which somehow gave me peace
 I knew he sang at a command from
God, would his wonders ever cease.
 So do not covet riches that you have
Yet never may.
 It's the little things in life that bring
happiness our way.
 At times when I awake and fear the day
may go wrong, I open the door and listen
for that little bird's song.
 Then if I hear it there is only one
thing to say.
 "Thank you God for sending your
messenger to sing my blues away."

 Velna Jordan

YOUNG FRIEND

On yesterday I found a one
I'd met so long a time ago.

Intent we were in thought and talk;
As time passed on, we did not know.

The beauty and the beast, it seemed,
Were in rapport and harmony.

The hour stood still — for two or three —
She gave her heart and mind to me.

In years gone past I'd lust for her;
But now, today, it's not the same.

A greater love I have of now.
Lasciviousness I've learned to tame.

The youthful beauty of her stride
Revives the agèd beast in me.

On yesterday I found a one;
I've a feeling — She'll always be.

Thomas Gallant

WIND GAMES

When evening breezes beckon me
To join them in their games,
We romp and play above our world
Where nothing is the same.

Soar high o'er lofty mountaintops
Through valleys deep and green,
And play with frothy ocean waves,
And see most wondrous scenes.

On moonbeams spun of molten gold
I'll drift in sheer delight,
And dance among a thousand stars,
My diamonds of the night.

Then hasten toward a blushing dawn
To greet the morning sun,
Fast rising in the eastern sky,
Proclaiming, "Day's begun!"

On fleecy clouds I'll float to earth,
To the winds I'll say, "Goodbye,"
Until again they beckon me
To play with them on high.

Mary Patricia Peralta

Beyond the pool
Where the monster lives
In the form of a humpbacked shark
Lie the crystal springs
Where the bubbling brings
Silver wings
To refresh the snow-white bird.

Crystal circles expand
In the willow land
And the widening pure white light
Softens the wavering pines
Reflected lines
In waves of crystal light.

Images on wings
And earthly things
Appear and disappear
In the wavering light.

Virginia M. Weber

M E M O R I E S

I went to mother's house one day.
She was glad I'd come that way.
Her house wore a lovely smile;
I stood and gazed a little while.
Of food she bade me partake,
And thus she cured a deep heartache.
I recalled the many ways
That she had helped in former days.
It was there I had knelt and prayed
In trousers that were torn and frayed.
She brushed my hair a little while,
And I began to wear a smile.
And to heal a deeper hurt
She wiped my tears on her skirt.
Today I'm a man that's fully grown
With a family of my own.
I stand and look at the house again,
And my heart is filled with pain.
Yesterday, my darling mother died,
And the tears I cannot hide.
From the house the smile has left,
And my heart is most bereft.
I shall remember the smile in her eyes,
And plan to meet her in the skies.

Ralph Futrell

HER LAST GIFT

She left in chilled night,
leaving behind earthly limitations
where long days faded
into gray tomorrows
tainted by suffering.

Winter stays long.
In my tangled grief,
remnant leaves whirl 'round and 'round.
I go alone and weep,
bury my sorrow under the snow.

She arrived there
in bright morning,
arrayed in celestial beauty,
finding loved ones in luminous robes.
fruits and flowers of Eden.

She left her lamp to shine
in the eyes of posterity.
I write of the peace of death,
touched by memories, echoes,
like butterflies celebrating in air.

Marie Fuhriman Olsen

PRAELUDIUM

O give to me my pheasant quill
And let me drain my mental still,
But first within this crimson urn
Crush from grapes the wine I yearn.
I'll quaff this drink of minstrel muse
And in my heart 'twill warmth infuse
And fix upon my humble quill
Erato's flame, Euterpe's skill.
O come, ye angels of my soul;
Accost the vellum of this scroll
And in man's heart make bold appeal
To resurrect youth's lost ideal.

Ah, finished now for thee to read
This music which the grape did bleed!
Unsheathe for me the lyric lyre
Once quivered by Homeric fire;
And once again for thee I'll sing
And trill with care Mnemosne's string.

Joseph H. Killelea, M. D.

POOR POET

Oh a poet's life is a lonely one
regardless of what some might say
he must write and rewrite his thoughts
day after day after day
he must change the words so often
to try and say what he would like to say
and through it all he must do it all
with little or no pay

Walter Gauntt, Jr.

A LOVE SONG TO THE SEA

Oh, great sea of azure hue
And endless edge surrounding,
With raging wave and silent calm
And white-winged ships abounding.

Wretched sea of treachery,
Your lure is sore demanding:
Into your open arms I sail,
My lovelorn heart remanding.

Extant sea of ecstasy
Your siren song entreating:
How many souls, how many souls
Your influence defeating?

Oh, great sea of azure hue,
I fear demise befalling,
Yet, in my heart and soul I find
Ascendancy enthralling.

So, great sea, capricious sea,
My white wings not enduring,
I cast my lot with all the souls
Who found your call alluring.

Ronald Paul Laramie

LARAMIE, RONALD PAUL. Born: Claremont, New Hampshire, 10-17-33; Married: 4-25-58 to Barbara Joan Olsen; Education: Los Angeles Valley College, Coastline Community College; Occupation: Senior Manufacturing Engineer; Memberships: Westminster Lions Club, Society of Manufacturing Engineers, American Institute of Industrial Engineers; Poetry: 'The Hill Behind My Father's House,' American Poetry Association, November 1985; Comments: *My work is an effort to express my feelings and attitude toward life in general and, more specifically, mankind.*

I REMEMBER YOU

And you touched me
    and I was warmed by the
    knowledge of you.
an old line, a new line
a stanza, a phrase.
music only the lonely can hear.
a promise, a taste, a touch
    a poem.
a lingering near;
    so very near my soul.
like the wind you tousled my hair,
joined me for awhile — then blew
    on by.
forever to go, to see, to remember,
    me.

Jeanne Marie Bailey Duren

LITTLE LOST DOG

There was a little dog
That got lost in a fog
And didn't know which way to turn.
Was it this way
Or was it that way,
Or was it straight ahead?
Oh how I wish I were home in my bed!
I'm hungry and cold
With sniffles in my nose.
I must find a place
That's warm to my toes.
Now what's that that I hear?
My master's real near!
What fun to get home
And chomp on a bone!

Clara Downing

SELDOM IN JUNE

Apologies seldom come true in June.
There is no need
When Life is young
And first stands steady
On its feet,
With roses at its knees
And warm nights
Full of song to hear
And stars to watch.
Then it is best
Not to pause in the rush
Of green and golden days
But to run ahead
With untipped hat
Through clouds of butterflies.

James Pecquet

TODAY!

I have watched hordes of
Flesh driven
By some unseen force
Under Heaven!

I have seen the ignorant
Male and female
Forced by evil ones who knew
Ignorance knew no vail!

But then, I knew inside
ME
Someone wonderful stood
A force, not semen . . .
No Idol of stone or wood!

K. Langley

DARK CLOUD

You think your road to making's empty
when you stand there looking
at a covered electronic tool
that helped your making of unpublished
    W a n d e r e r   S t r u g g l e s
In the heat of youthful years;

but now the 60's & the 70's
are over & barely escaped
an incredible blow of destiny
             in the crotch

& plunged into the fast-crossing new
two-mile-shy to the edge
           of the next century:

f a t i g u e d   &   d u s t y —
intermittently working
with your head on your shoulder

expecting never again to be found
under this d a r k   c l o u d.

Alfonso Plaza

HUMAN HOROSCOPY

All movements are caught
By those attentive eyes
Which seem to be like
The lens of the special cameras.
Beware when you wouldn't like
To show what you are doing.
Those attentive eyes
Scrutinize the horizon
And their scrutiny doesn't
Even miss what's going on
In the surroundings.
Sometimes, those attentive eyes
Are behind the spy-glasses
And many a time they are
Behind the tinted glasses.
Slow and rapid movements
Are rolled by those attentive eyes
Like the reels of the cameras.
It's surely in the affirmative
That nothing will escape
That human horoscopy.

Victor Marroun

NO ONE BUT YOU
*Dedicated to Raymond Brake,
The One I Love*

There is so much I have to tell you,
For it's all bottled up inside.
So many feelings I want to share with you,
So many things I wish not to hide.

A mystery in itself,
A dream that seems so far away.
Held so deeply within myself,
Just holding onto each and every day.

Time goes on,
Slowly passing us by.
Still I have not gone,
Wanting to be by your side.

Show me the way,
Help me make my dream come true.
Try to understand what I have to say,
For no one means as much to me, as you.

Diane Marden

SENIOR PARTNER

He fired me on a cold, gusty day.
I remember how gray rain rattled
At his office windows,
And how I sat down suddenly
In a client chair of phony leather
That wheezed like a rich, old man.
He was saying, "I've been getting static,
So you'll have to go. I'm sorry,
But that's the way the cookie . . ."
I noticed that his desk was veneer,
Just plastic imitating walnut,
Not the real, righteous thing
I'd always thought it was.
"That's it, then," I said and stood,
Dizzy, knees shaking, mouth dry.
He got up and stuck out his hand,
But I didn't take it.
Turning to go, I saw that his smile
Was of the same stuff as the cracked
Plastic armchairs and the desk

Harry E. Beebe

STORING MEMORIES

There is no past, only a memory,
There is no future, only a dream,
Just this instant, here and now
The sound of a plane droning overhead
    A cricket, chirping his chirp —
    Cars speeding to places unknown

Shall we store sounds of the moment?
Was life made for this instant?
No one, rich or poor may call on more
How foolish to barter with God for
    A day, a month or a year —
When one has all his time at hand

Poor foolish souls, asking for time
    To store more memories
Memories of pain, hunger and cold
When all the while the chirp of a
    Cricket should be enough
        To store — for the moment.

Verna Lee O'Brien Clark

IMAGES

Gaily painted streamers
Tossing wild in the wind
Reflecting springtime.

Tiny bits of wild things
Fanciful earth flight
Against an emerald field.

Arrow-pointed aspens
Rustling leaves in the wind
Pressed against the sky.

Small gray rabbit
Bounding joyfully in the grass
Skips alive and free.

I watch silently
Innocence of the wild
Penetrating my soul.

Sally Kay Emerich

THE PROMISE

God never promised me a life
Of contentment every day;
Neither did He promise sunshine
All the time along the way.
He never planned a "bed of roses"
For the life He gave to me,
Nor did He send forth His blessings
To be hoarded selfishly.

God never told me I would find
A pot of gold at rainbow's end,
Nor did He say there's happiness
Around each curve or bend.
But He did promise me His love
And life in eternity,
If I would merely believe on Him
In all sincerity.

Naomi Sullivan Rhoades

RHOADES, NAOMI SULLIVAN. Pen Names: Naomi Bagley Rhoades, Naomi E. Sullivan; Born: Ware County, Georgia, 3-13-23; Married: 9-18-71 to Samuel S. Rhoades; Education: Dundalk Community College, Baltimore, Maryland, Freshman Writing, 1974-75; Famous Writer's School, Westport, Connecticut, 1969-71; Habersham College, Georgia, 1941; Occupations: Medical Secretary, Paralegal, Freelance Writer; Poetry: 'The Prince of Peace,' *Watersedge* Church Program Brochure, 1980; *God's Gifts of Kindness,* poetry album, selected poems published in *Church Beacons,* 1983; 'To Help Us Through Gloomy Days,' *The American Poetry Anthology, Vol. II, Spring/Summer,* 1983; Other writings: "Prayers for the Pastor," short story, *Adventure Magazine,* 1974; *Bagley Family Genealogy,* history book, 2 volumes, to be published in 1985; Comments: *Most of my poetry verses are religious and inspirational, but I've written on many other themes, including nature's beauties, patrriotism, history and human character. I write because God has chosen to give me the blessed gift of penning the words He consigns. With His guidance, I try to see inside the heart of the reader and convey to him thoughts and ideas so he can enjoyably digest the reflections of the written word. I am also an avid genealogical historian, a pastime which has afforded many hours of satisfaction in freedom of expression.*

POLLUTION

Plans of folly
We exhort
When nature's way
We abort

Max Sheffield

My love; I've sailed
the empty sea and touched the
sky. I've seen eternity and life
immortal, everything I've known my
love was there, my love is everything
and in solitude she is
there, my love is the light of day
for whom without there would
be darkness my love is my life
when I flirt with damnation she
is a goddess she taught me how
to live, how to love, and how to
laugh, she is my love my only
love

Debbie Bailey

WHAT A DAY FOR WEATHER

Big black billowy clouds
like thunder shrouds
enveloping me

Crying out in silence
with bits of rain
whispering to the earth

Of nature's strength
and sometimes crying
with tears of pouring rain

Showing nature's mending ways
for below the shroud
an inch of space

The winds aloft do blow
sparkling with pure light
are the colors of her show

Blue skies and golden sun
are peaking from below
showing promise

Of a tomorrow
For whatever life will hold

Sharon Olivia

WINGS IN THE WIND

When night relinquished its hold;
the dawn of time begins to unfold:
As I hear the fluttering of wings in the wind
I watch a flight of doves towards the heavens ascend.
Peace has sole reign upon the earth;
In this time before mankind's birth.

Though the day has taken its hold;
The sun can't warm hearts that have turned cold:
For I hear wing engines sputtering in the wind
As I watch fighter planes first ascend, then descend.
Peace shares its reign upon the earth;
As war closely follows mankind's birth.

When night moves to reclaim its hold;
The end of time begins to unfold:
As I hear the fluttering of wings in the wind
I watch a band of angels from heaven descend.
Peace has sole reign upon the earth;
As if mankind never had its birth.

Faye Gordon

ANYONE'S COOKIE

He's a sweet Cookie.
a sexy Cookie.
Vanilla and Chocolate
Rolled into one.
He has flashing brown eyes,
Curly brown hair.

His body is firm and strong,
Yet sometimes gentle.
He is a real sweet Cookie
From head to toe.

A lover, a lover,
God how he can love!
He just don't give a damn What Persuasion!
He knows he's a Right on Man.
Getting his kicks and his
Satisfaction.
He's anybody's Cookie.
You dig!

Vivien Merriam Sterling

SILENT THOUGHTS

The elderly gent,
Quietly thinking,
Musing as he walked
Wherever he went,
It always seemed,
News was always sad.

As he climbed the slope
He saw what must be done:
'Quell the fears and hates
Of those who like to mope
And teach them love instead;
Hell shall be no more!'

He gazed across the chasm,
Breathed the fresh clean air,
'Taste but once of love,
Of hope, enthusiasm
And one can live without
Haste, and learn to live.'

Margaret Houben

THE UNICORN

A wise old sage
As human as you and I
Watches; he can't change the world.

A wise old sage
As human as you and I
Contemplates; time the prison cell.

A wise old sage
As human as you and I
Waits; for someone to set him free

A wise old sage
As human as you and I
Sits; stunned by life

A wise old sage
As human as you and I
Helpless; looked to God.

Carol Horton

I WOULD LIKE TO BE A HOBO

I would like to be a hobo and sail the wintry seas
I'd set my sails for far-off ports and do just as I please.
I would sleep late in the morning and stay up late at night
Then I could watch the stars and moon as they vanished from my sight.

If I could be a hobo I'd walk the dusty roads
I'd speak to everyone I met and help them with their loads.
No one would be a burden for there still are those who'll share
With other needy hobos for we all have special cares.

I'd really like to be a hobo, that's been my heart's desire,
To roam the plains and woodlands and sleep under starry skies.
I would feed the wildlife from my pack with no thought of tomorrow
And wondering if I'd have a snack, or if I would have to beg or borrow.

But I realize I cannot be a hobo strong and bold
And tramp the dusty roads at night, and sleep out in the cold,
So I'll satisfy my inner self by staying close to home
But in my dreams I'll always be a hobo on the roam.

Clair Parker

MY DEAR OLD DAD and ME

I used to walk along this lane, when I was just a kid.
I'd walk up tall, my head held high, just like my father did.
Then, I would stop and rest beside — the river clear and cool,
I'd think on things my dad had said — things never learned in school.

My daddy was a wise old man, or so he seemed to me.
He taught me many things of life — of what there is to see.
"Son," he would say, "to be a man, there's much you have to learn;
No matter what you do you'll find — the hands of time still turn.

When you're not sure, just what it is, that's right for you to do,
Just think back o'er the years, my son, of things I've said to you.
The world is filled with foolish talk, so please don't take its part,
But listen to the little voice, that speaks within your heart."

The clouds so high, so soft and white, drift slowly 'cross the sky,
Past the graceful, gentle glide of — an eagle as she flies.
I've learned that beauty can be found, in everything we see,
Like beauty in the love between, My Dear Old Dad and Me.

Michael E. Schultz

THE TEACHER

A dark stranger is what I see opposite myself.
Dominating and cool, he sits oblivious of my thoughts of him.
Commanding is his way of life, dark and mysterious are his
words and thoughts that I find myself wondering about them.
His strength is in his manner as well as his being.
Though the day is old, he appears as fresh as the morning air.
To find myself alone with him is hard to fathom.
His gentleness, at times, surprises me to the point of standing
in awe of him.
Totally complete is his every thought, thinking already the
consequences of every move.
In total control of every situation
I find myself envious of his wisdom.
As a pupil in his school of life, I've begun to learn much
about life with a hint of ever so much more to learn and discover.
I find myself waiting impatiently for the next lesson to be
taught.
Finding myself the eager student awaiting the teacher's next
lesson.

Cynthia A. Neeley

THE MERMAID ON THE REEF

Let others worry time away;
I played by night and danced by day,
And wove my thoughts in daily lines
By candlelights and German wines.

But darker thoughts discarded those
Like needles over Alpine snows —
Until you came with April words,
With ilex leaves and morning birds.

We bent love like a beam of light;
It echoed on the folding night,
The weary footsteps of a sage
Who wanders down this kindless age.

You and I know time's candle burns,
And from that hall no light returns —
But we let others turn that leaf;
We've seen the mermaid on the reef,

The scattered petals on the slope,
The Persian sultan's standing rope;
The magic lovers understand
That makes their world seem wonderland.

Richard Chandler

FACES OF LOVE

Love has a face of kindness,
and one of great compassion.
A face of understanding,
blended with tender wisdom.
A face of sincere concern,
mixed with genuine emotion.
A face of giving,
without thought of taking.
A face of knowing,
without words being said.
A face of trying,
no matter what the adversity.
A face of belief,
with no evidence,
A face of sharing,
with no reward expected.
The faces of love are infinite
and its rewards are endless.

A. M. Zaccarino

THE HARLEQUIN

Masked in diamond patterns
Of the night
What do you call your lost abode
A masquerader of lost dreams
The lost stranger at a Beaux Arts Ball.

A myth of mime and romance songs
Searching for someone called Cymbelline
A ghost of an illusion seeking love
Someone captioned Harlequin.

On a sleeve of silk
He wears a heart of gold
On stage he can recite bold rhymes
This lad of sequined love
That moves about the incognito
Clock of time.

A masquerader of lost dreams
Strumming, to each one romance songs
This Bal Masque dancer of lost dreams
This poet of a thousand moods and masks
Costumed in myth and fantasy,
I call him Harlequin.

Joan Giltner Canfield

BLAKE, Dante's Inferno: The Circle of the Falsifiers

DAWNING OF A CHILD

Dawning of a child —
A being of **vulnerability**
                    versus
                         Measureless **capablility**.

Innocent and **tender** —
A life fashioned
  by someone else's agenda.

Dawning of a child —
A major concern
Because of what
  some of the children
  of the past have learned.

Discord has been **declared** on your **abuse** —
  so the abusers will
  no longer have an excuse.

Dawning of a child —
Our leaders of tomorrow
The time is here
  to free you from your sorrow.

Mankind's indispensable need
  hoping this — the human race — will heed.

Dawning of a child —
Man **must** reserve your place
  so there will be a **future**
  for you to face.

Omar Ashaka

SPRING SATURDAY

A robin chirps in a nearby yard on a beautiful spring
    afternoon.

A lawn mower snarls around a stone driveway.

I hear the shrill squeals of children playing jump-rope in
    the neighbor's yard.

Mother whistles happily from the kitchen as she bakes
    chocolate chip cookies.

Yet the television tells me that all is not well.

It tries to convince me that the threat of nuclear war is
    growing.

It tells me that famine is raging in Ethiopia.

I sit at my desk without firsthand knowledge.

And I ask myself whether or not it is true or whether or
    not it matters.

Why are they telling me about something I have no control
    over?

Can I return to my world without feeling like a criminal?

Can I just turn it off?

Alex Goldsmith

THE WILLOW TREE CRADLE

Rock me to sleep in my Willow tree cradle
Let the troubles of the world pass me by,
I can sway to and fro with a slow swinging motion
While the wind sets the rhythm with a sigh.
Through the long supple branches, an azure sky above
Filled with cotton candy clouds drifting high,
Is the last thing I can see, as my eyes begin to close
From the soothing song of Nature's lullaby.
Far below verdant grasses, and a ribbon of a stream
Makes a home for many creatures of the wild,
The air is pure and sweet, and the water crystal clear,
For here, the hand of man is not defiled.
So take me back home to my Willow tree cradle,
Lift me high above the world and all its harm,
For I'm sad and oh, so weary, and the only place to rest,
Is within the cradle of her loving arms.

Emma Lee Stocum

OUR HOPES AND DREAMS

Hoping and dreaming are part of most lives,
Like sunshine and rain, they help folks survive.
For hoping and dreaming can brighten the day,
When problems are foremost, and dreams far away.
For dreams are desires, for something ideal,
And with fulfillment, the dreams become real.
Some dream of success, others dream of a home,
While some search for wealth, and others to roam.
All dreams are different, to each person or pair,
Sometimes there's a group, and one dream they share.
But if you have a dream, there is much you can do,
For hard work, not just hoping, can make it come true.

Hazel Adelman

MIND

People press on my mind,
Flitting in and out like slippery ghosts.
Some stay longer than others.
I can't make them go away.
Their words are contorted in my silent maze:
Some for anger;
Some for love;
Some for pity;
All heavy.
The noisy voices kiss and praise and argue.
Weak corners come alive.
My wisdom ripples unchallenged,
And I always win.
My head is hot with transaction.

I think I'll rest now.

Jenny Wright

JUSTICE

When the pendulum swings and someone sings
  the mighty axe will fall.
Someone will pay along the way
  with death's beckoning call.
Many a man has been caught
  in the web of innocence
And died for a crime he didn't commit
  and logic makes no sense.
The guilty go on with their evil deeds
  another poor wretch they find
To cover their ways, someone else pays
  enough to blow one's mind.
No more justice in this world
  for the poor and the meek
For those in power, often crime is their tower
  there is no justice to seek.

Lawrence G. Price

I THOUGHT OF YOU

Last night I was with someone else
and what did I do,
The whole time I was with him I thought of you.

I could have had so much fun
and not be blue.
It would have been perfect but,
I thought of you

Why do I still love you now
I know we're through?
I woke up happy but then
I thought of you.

Last night he told me he loved me,
that he'd be true.
I tried to love him but then
I thought of you.

I started all over and tried to forget
all the love we knew
It was working, oh so well until,
I thought of you.

Sheryl Semmel

THE TRANSFUSION

My weakened body sinks
Deeper into mortal infirmities
Holding my soul prisoner in imaginary dreams;
The twilight where my heart reposes.

As I lie helpless and afraid,
I find false friends and foes alike
Disperse in winsome fun and folly
And reach not with helping hand
Nor speak soft words of comfort.

There are those who wish to share
My burden, but cannot
For I am the lone knight; the worn soldier
Surviving yesterday's abortments.

My soul turns to its beginning . . .
And in His sweet commune,
I have no need for human voice, nor touch.
My soul fills with soothing warmth of faith
And as I pray the loneliness recedes.
My all too human fear crumbles before
The tender eye of the keeper of our souls.

Dr. Clayton Bell, Jr.

THE LIGHT

As a flash of light,
Memories only faint reflection;
Shining bright like sun reflection on mirror.

Body soft and sleek;
Mind young and vibrant;
Lips move not, message clear.

Open heart,
Searching soul,
Eyes see,
Strength, wisdom and love flow within bodies.
The lost found;
The missing return;
Need not search further.

Image fades from eyes;
Presence remains in soul;
Spirits together go on as one.

Susan M. Puetz

CHANGE OF HABIT

For reasons not quite clear to me . . . my life must
undergo a change.
There are things I will have to rearrange.
nature has dealt an unkind hand . . . and I wonder for
what purpose it is to serve.
At times, I ask myself if this is what I deserve.
So many decisions only I can make . . . Oh Lord, I
pray I do not make a mistake.
It is my life . . . for sure I have only one.
So much to do . . . so much yet to see.
Yet I know whatever I decide it will be the right
choice for me.

Shirley Hutcherson

COUNTRY IS RIGHT

Listen to the sound on the juke box,
it's singing a love song to us.
Telling of the stars in the heavens,
and the winds that blow softly across.
A place where lovers can also be friends,
and a chance for people to survive.
It's far from the city, where dreams can come true,
it's country, and country is right.
But, little does that juke box realize,
the pain that lies deep in my heart.
"Oh babe," let's not give up on our life,
let's try that country life.

Candy Lee Koolhaas

OF PEARS AND PICKLES

I picked a pear, it turned out to be a pickle.
The pickle was supposed to be sour, it was sweet.
I went back to the pear.
I wanted the pear to explain. It would not.
What the pear said made sense though.
It said, "What is supposed to be, is not always.
Love is one of those things. You can't explain it,
but it is. You try to communicate it with words.
You can not. Similar to myself and the pickle."
Maybe the next time I pick a pear, I'll try an apple.
At least I can't pick love or I don't think I can.
Can you?

David Spaulding

TABERNACLE CHOIR INAUGURAL HYMN

Three hundred choir members rang out loud and clear
In Washington's 25 degree night air,
Ten million visitors stood in awe,
Ready for the 40th inaugural ball.
A huge float with a replica organ,
Made especially for this occasion,
Range out with the "Battle Hymn of the Republic"
A request from Lady Nancy Reagan,
With colorful sparks and cannons booming,
The U.S. Army band helped out with the tuning,
And the choirs of angels from heavens above,
Through cheers and tears send Reagans their love

Aurelia Beddes

HOPE

The hope is for the future.
    The children can see deep inside.
    They bother not to stop and look upon the color.
The hope is for the future.
    The children know that we are equal.
    They bother not to judge.
The hope is for the future.

Judith Ann Marsh

BEFALLEN FATE

We smile in our September years and live to reminisce
On all the times we savor most — those filled with happiness.
The times we laughed, the times we loved, and even those we cried;
Though great success eluded us, throughout our lives we tried
To grab the ring of life and run — a brass one, I'm told —
And all our lives it seems we tried to turn it into gold.

The obstacles so obvious now emerged unseen back then.
To analyze reactions, though, would go to no good end.
We ask ourselves if we should try to justify our acts . . .
Or should we just accept decisions made and face the facts?
Those choices made so long ago cannot be made again;
But oft we think, in error, yet, by doing so we'd win

The game of life that all must play with hopes of victory,
And all, I fear, would say that they would do things differently.
But we should never let ourselves regret befallen fate
And never should we think that happiness will come too late;
For life is what we make it now, the past best left alone . . .
The love of friends and family being all we need to own.

Patricia A. Roark

HOME

The house was beautiful with a porch across the front
The orchard, gorgeous when in bloom.
Family life bustling with garden, cooking, rabbits to hunt,
Days filled with activity were gone too soon.
A brother carved useful things from the wood of the land.
A pony cart, a piano for a playhouse under a tree (not a baby-grand);
All children in the family did well according to strength and Destiny.
One daughter, never well, had to be given up.
She left a lesson in loving, caring, not always willingly.
Giving in to God's Will and a taste from life's "Bitter Cup."
It was a family of too many burdens, not enough money
Unbearable illnesses — often lonely,
No training or instruction in family life.
They had strong Faith in God's guidance in strife.
Neither parent gave up and left children with the other
Nor gave them to an orphanage nor foster father and mother
Now — the orchard is gone, buildings worn out, family left.
A legend is there of a family tree put to a test
The roots and branches are growing still
For all to see the strength from obeying God's Will.

Thelma M. Warning

DISSOLUTE MAN!

She was slenderly fashioned, fair, and so young!
Please lift her with care, take her up tenderly.
She who was so pure and womanly, is that all that remains of her.
Think of it — picture it, if you can, dissolute man!
The crowd through muddly impurity, dreadfully staring.
Everyone could see only the beautiful nature had left on her.
Her dark auburn hair was wet wonderment spread over her lovely shoulders.
On that stygian night winter's bleak wind had made her shiver and tremble.
But not the black flowing river, or the darkness of night.
Glad to death's mystery and made mad from life's history.
She hurled herself so swiftly — anywhere out of the world.
No matter how cold, boldly she had plunged into the deep darkness.
Over the brink of the cleft the rough river ran cold and cruel.
Think of it, picture it, if you still can dissolute man!
Drink of it, lave in it, then, of the young beauty you once loved.
Please lift her up tenderly, take her up with care.
She who was slenderly fashioned, fair, and so young.
See the one you had loved from afar, her limbs stiffen frigidly and too rigidly.
You help the men on the rescue boat kindly, decently, compose, and smooth them.
The one you had once loved is staring now so blindly — her eyes, close them.

Glenn Edward Waters III

When my innards wild are roiling,
And my temper's close to boiling,
It's way past time I allow God's grace
To put my life-plan back in place.

For while my values may be right,
They never should that much upset me.
I must more wisely use love's might,
And not let things unduly fret me.

Seth A. Parker

CARPENTER SQUARE

While I sit with pencil in my fingers
March winds drift the swirling snow.
The blues are mine as winter lingers
For work is getting kind of slow.

Here I am . . . past middle age,
amazed at all the time I've spent,
Just working for a meager wage
And being broke . . . or badly bent.

If I could do some worthy thing
Like putt a golf ball in a hole,
Knock someone silly in the ring,
Or run and jump like hell or bowl;

If I could write a dirty book
Of sex and blood and gore,
Be some kind of low-down crook,
Or own a liquor store;

If I could play and sing some rock,
With loony tunes and lyrics,
I'd soon have money in the sock,
And people in hysterics.

If I were not the square I am
I'd catch up with the times . . .
For driving nails ain't worth a damn . . .
and ditto that for making rhymes.

Shadrack Nosnibor

FRESHWATER OCEANS
(composed December 6, 1984)

Slip in . . . slip out,
With your lacy fringe,
Slip in over the sands.

Tell us, whisper softly,
About far-off times —
Mountains that once stood here.

How you wore them away
With that lacy fringe
Over millions of years.

Tell us about icebergs
That sank continents,
About continents that

Rose and tilted, colliding,
Rising endlessly.
Tell us about the first

Man — how his eyes
Could not contain the
Immensity of the sea,

How you stared at this man,
At his perfection,
Before She strolled by.

Sarah Cameron

BECOMING SPRING DUSK
For: L. D.

Dusk draws a sketch in charcoal
    when gold and scarlet die . . .
A spray of pregnant branches
    are shadows on the sky . . .
The tardy sea gull calling
    to one who waits at home . . .
becomes a silver bullet
    above the floating foam . . .
You become my cover
    when warmth faints into night . . .
while I become your lover
    the stars absorb sunlight . . .
Come and lie beside me
    beneath the rising moon . . .
Spring dusk can't last forever
    and morning comes too soon . . .

Carolie Poe

POE, CAROLIE LYNN. Pen Names: Caroly
Poe, Carol Lynn Ropos, Carol-Lynn Del; Born:
Cleveland, Ohio, September 24; Occupation:
Writer of column in Cleveland paper; Member-
ships: 10 years in Barber Shop Singing and
Dancing, Choreography also; Awards: Certifi-
cates of Merit for 'Bring Me Your Tears,' 'Bor-
rowed Babe,' and 'Blue Rose,' 1982-84; Poetry:
'Blind Alley,' World of Poetry, 1978; 'Coleen,'
New Worlds, 1980; 'Never, Angel,' Poetry
Press, 1982; 'My Morning Child,' New Worlds,
1982; 'The Intruder,' Poetry Press, 1985; Com-
ments: *I write to reach out to people — most of
whom I will never meet, except in and through
the mental images I create. I hope to bring a
smile; a remembrance; a lost or forgotten "feel-
ing" to the reader.*

SOMEONE REALLY CARES

I know someone really cares
When things go wrong,
Someone really loves us dearly
Watches over from His throne above;
Jesus cares about you and me.
He will never leave us all alone,
Let's all take courage
In Him have faith, hope, and love
Someone really watches us,
Down this earth below.

Hazel A. Gould

FAMOUS MEN UNDER MY WINDOW
HONORABLE MENTION

The first was Robert Penn Warren
Through the campus fog
Out of the net of dead bracken
The lush Kentuckian came —
He in a wool hat and raincoat,
He with prized red beak up
Listened. It was early.

Allen Ginsberg came at night
And raised the dead from
Residential sleep —
He beat the leg of his lecture pants
With the hand of experience
and I lost his explanation
Of the beat, to the dark.

These men did less than my father
Who was first
And who came in.
Far more they did —
They walked under my window
And passed on.

Jennifer Smith

ARLINGTON NATIONAL CEMETERY

I stood upon the gentle brow
And gazed across Virginia's hills
In perfect lines the crosses stand,
A solemn sight — the heart does thrill.

Beneath each cross a marker stands
To name the one that rests beneath
The shadow of that snow-white cross,
A memorial to the one beneath.

Across each rolling studded hill
The rows of stately crosses stand.
In silence guard each sacred spot
Where rest the heroes of our land.

Rest on you heroes bold and true.
You served your country long and well.
To you all fame and honor due.
Emotions cause the heart to swell.

In somber silence then I paused
And breathed a prayer for those who rest
Beneath the shadows of the crosses.
A sinking sun fades in the West.

Joe B. Cox

POETRY ART

The art of poetry
The creation of rhyme,
So many have tried
Though none could define!

Well you need not find
The sun, to shine;
So, savor the time
Fruit of the vine.
Oh don't try to make
A pear of a grape,
Just give and take
Art for Art's sake!

Yes, creators of rhythm, wit and reason,
As autumn leaves, pass with the season.
Yet, the poet eternal, never departs,
For the Poem is Spirit — Poetry, Art!

William F. Scolavino

WARM WINTER AFTERNOON

The trees are brown
and the air is crisp while
the sky is a hazy blue, it's
all part of God's great plan
on a warm winter afternoon.

The gulls are screeching
and the water is clear
the buds on the bushes are
beginning to fear that the
midwinter heat will soon disappear.

Night is falling and the air
is cooling old man winter has
only been fooling but we're
grateful and happy for our brief
reprieve on a warm winter afternoon.

John J. McDonnell

ROSE OF ARLOV

Reviewing in symmetry line, datelining
Date lines and triangle figures of 1915.
Heaving our thoughts to the highness of
        clouds in the sun!
Reckoning the H.M.S. Britannic, the
S.S. Queen Elizabeth, S.S. Carinthia,
Seashores of Nassau, Bahamas —
Leaves of the rose of Tasmia, red clover
        Of St. Moritz Bell Square.
Shedding dust grain: shabby destiny!
Alas Aloma of the great sea,
    Oh! High palace tower attending
        Aloft where death reign in the
        Underworld perish hope.
        Written in the wind:
            Look toward immortality
            To destiny "Uranus"
The stars high above mark time
        through the ages of time.
    Cross in the book, life in the stars!
Allaying through space sacred wings
Pearls, dust sun rain and other things.
    Magnetizing the antheral petals of
    Every flower till finding the
        Solitary Rose of Arlov.
    Allan De Fiori

CLOUD COVER

O! Saucer! Unidentified!
Whence came you to my sight?
From East to West thou roarest on
As earth wraps up in night.

And night is not enough for you.
Elusive, sneaky thing!
You wait 'til clouds befog our sight.
Knowest thou what troubles they bring?

Or hast thou figured some of this,
With calculations fine,
To pounce upon our atmosphere
So Earth shall be all thine?

Would'st escape in silent mystery
And leave us never knowing
If heat is not, or cold is not
Wherever thou art going?

Skip the sky! Sky-skipper!
For space is vast and dotted.
A planet's here. A star glows there.
The Milky Way's all knotted.

Eleanore Lindsey

MIKE

You came along and stole my heart and made me care for you.
You gave to me a special hope, a dream to reach out to.
I never thought I'd meet someone who made me feel this way.
I think about you all the time, and love you more each day.

You've given me a reason now to show you that I care.
You've given me a special hope, a dream for us to share.
The time we spend together now is less than when apart,
But all the love I feel for you, I feel with all my heart.

The loving way you show you care, the faith you have in me.
Are just a couple reasons why our love was meant to be.
I need the love you give to me, the closeness that we share.
These precious moments help me through, the times you can't be there.

I wish that I could have you here instead of only dreams.
But if I close my eyes awhile, you're here with me it seems.
In every day that passes by, in all I say and do.
The memories that I treasure most, were made since I met you.

I think ahead to one day soon, how different things will be.
When we don't have to be apart and you can be with me.
I want to spend my life with you and share the years to come.
Already we have more than most, and we have just begun.

I've never felt this way before except with you and me.
Together we can build a life, and raise our family.
Each day that passes slowly by, I thank the Lord above,
For giving me a special man. The man I dearly love.
                    I LOVE YOU
                    SANDY

Sandy Ambrosek

DARE I DREAM

She looked for him a thousand years, a thousand years it seemed.
She'd looked for him in every face, in all the dreams she'd dreamed.

Where had he been this prince of hers, this knight all dressed in white?
Had he been looking too this long had he dreamed of her each night?

In disbelief she touched his face with trembling lips they kissed.
And all at once their souls entwined and they knew what they had missed.

He loves her, dare she dream this dream, a dream of dreams come true?
A dream so real, when he touches her, it's like he always knew.

He looks at her with eyes so full of love, it breaks her heart,
To know that he was there always and he felt it from the start.

How deep inside, this love of hers, connected to her soul.
How sweetly now her spirit soars, to reach out for her goal.

To keep him tight within her arms is all that she can know.
She is frightened deep inside her now to think that he could go.

To lose him now would break her heart, and surely she would die,
A darker death she would never know, if he did say goodbye.

The fire, she sees it in his eyes and feels it in her veins,
His love for her, her love for him, is life and it sustains.

She held her heart for him to love, her soul for him to touch,
But never in her wildest dreams, did she think he'd love this much.

Kay Jones Whitlock

RAINBOWS OF HAWAII

Beautiful rainbows
Colors of Hawaii,
Beautiful rainbows
Caress our distant shores

Fragrances of flowers
Sprinkled in the dew,
Sending you a scent of love
Whispering, "I Love You."

Trust in me
Cries the colors of the rainbows,
Can't you see
I am so in love with you

Beautiful rainbows
Colors of Hawaii,
Treasure of these Islands
Upon our silvery sea, made for you and me

Marian L. Santiago

FIREFLIES

Fireflies, Fireflies
Lanterns all aglow
When the night is over,
Where do you go?

What do you search for?
Flying all about
Where do you go
When your lanterns go out?

I can see you glowing
Coming from the grass
When the twilight deepens
See you flying past.

Sometimes children catch you
And put you in a jar.
Fireflies, Fireflies,
Better fly far.

Ann R. Yarbrough

GETHESEMANE

I wander in this lonely place
Of darkening sky and swirling mist
And marvel that my heart still beats
And I exist.

My small endeavors of the day
Are meaningless and empty things
Like birds attempting flight in space
With broken wings.

The hour I saw you laid to rest
Suspended Time within my soul
And left me to my memories
Without a goal.

Yet every twilight turns to dawn
And winter bows to mellow spring
Reminding me that clouds must lift
And solace bring.

Marie Lundgren

RAINBOWS IN THE SUN

You've been so special through my years
    not just for things you've done.
You've managed to see through my fears.
and showed me rainbows in the sun.

I love you Gram, take care you hear
    'cause I'm so far away.
But not too far to feel your tears,
they touch me every day.

The love you gave is part of me
    to share with my kids now.
You'll always be that certain key,
    that unlocks pain somehow.

Deborah Preble Leone

LEONE, DEBORAH JO. Pen Name: Deborah Preble Leone; Born: Trenton, New Jersey, 9-21-57; Occupations: Mother of three, Writer of poetry and songs; Memberships: Songwriters of America; Poetry: 'Precious Moments,' *American Poetry Anthology,* 11-84; 'What We Have Is Rare,' *American Poetry Anthology,* Spring '85; Other Writings: 'Yesterday (Was Lost), Today (Has Just Been Found),' Tin Pan Alley records, 12-84; Comments: *I try to express my feelings of love and friendships. For me it's always been easier than saying them.*

SPELLBOUND

    The sparkle of your eyes whispering
Softly into my ears, hearing the delicate
Sound of your voice touching the bottom
Of my heart.
    You reach out to me with a
Powerful hand, holding me safe in
Your arms until we've fallen under a
Magic spell.
    The night sky swells beneath
the warm breeze cuddling between us.
    Sand so soft, flowing freely through
graceful entwined bodies.
    Together we grow sleepy as the
Morning star blankets our bare souls,
While the purrs of the tides, and
The birds in the skies, fill the morning
in
    Perfect
        Harmony.

Janice Grevesen

DARK ORBS OF TENDER FIRE

Dark orbs of tender fire
Heats the flames of my desire.
Solar visage in the sky
Lights the glimmerings in your eyes.
O woman, my love, my heart's delight
Let me keep you near and tight
Upon this breast of aching flesh
That leaps with joy to be
Confirmed by your being there
Ever so close to me.
Illusive web of love we spin
While music plays we can begin
To cast a shadow upon the wall
Substantive flesh so that we call
Our light to dark in opposites merged
We joyful dance upon an urge
Guiding sweet with painful need
O love, my love, we can succeed
To make our dreams reality
So long as you are here with me.

Andrew Chavez

CHINOOK PRAYER

Great Spirit in the mountain
Hear our voices raised.
White men come and take our land,
They marry our women
And push our tents close together.
They bring sickness to our people
And the feel of pain and death.
They teach old men to cheat,
And give fire water to braves
To make them mad like hornets
And their blood weak like water.
Great Spirit in the mountain
Come out and shake your wings;
Rattle the sky like drums
Drop your vengeance and power
On the white man marauder.
Great Spirit in the mountain
This is thy people talking
We listen for the thunder
And the whiteness of thy coming.

Irene M. Ryder

THE HILL CHRIST DIED ON

Christ uttered this great cry:
"Eli, Eli, Lama Sabachthani,"
The heavens, the earth, and
time stood still,
When Christ died upon a
special hill,
Upon this hill you will find,
Mixed with dirt and sand
combined,
The blood that dropped from
Jesus' head,
The many tears that Mary shed,
The sweat from his body
when he died,
The water which flowed
from his side,
The promise made to man
he did fulfill,
When Christ died upon a
special hill.

Angela Hines

EXPECTING ABSOLUTION

Stampeding across the eminent tract
Prostituting the firma
Butchering the beasts
Expecting absolution

Frequenting the oasis
Exurient without thirst
Glutting without clemency
Voiding without empathy
Expecting absolution

Seeking warmth from an emberless vortex
Hoarding the harvest
Appurtenant to atrocity
Violating modest justice
Expecting absolution

Pressing the courser to the solstice
Blinded by self-inclination
Wanton toward any aspect
Drifting without penitence
Expecting absolution

Kate Smith

LEGEND

Guitar slinger,
sensuous grin.
Rowdy rhythm,
newborn sound.

I was yours when first you rode
that strange, upbeat track.
And long after the train
was no longer a mystery
you wore idolatry with everyman air,
robed in spangled stage wear,
musical karate punctuating each beat.

I'll treasure always ardent embraces,
taste forever passionate lips —
though we never touched,
never kissed.

Even now as I walk lonely street
your flame sparks air waves,
perpetuated by fire of voice,
an eternal light to keep me.

Sandy Bedlovies

FAREWELL CHIEF COCHISE

I met him many years ago,
Shaking his hand, to say hello.
Nino had deeply touched my heart,
His stories could make me laugh,
Or tear me apart.

The Lord has called him home today,
Those of us, honored to meet him,
Will remember him, each in our own way.

We will miss our precious friend,
Till we meet him at our journey's end.

The sunset tonight
Is an artist's delight.

I know the chief is in the arms
Of "Golden Bird," his beautiful bride.
Forever he will be a part of us,
He will live within the heart of us.

Klara Farnum

MOONLIGHT

Where is God? I asked one day,
The answer came in a surprising way,
I was lonely that night, and feeling blue,
So took a walk to a lake I knew.

The moon was lovely and a beautiful sight,
Round and full and very bright.
I sat on a log and looked and thought,
There came to me then, the answer I sought.

The moon's reflection was on the water,
That night down at the lake.
Its beams sent a light flowing softly around,
From the tips of the trees to the grass on the ground.

All was touched with shimmering silver,
'Twas a bit of Heaven come down.
No sound was heard save the Cricket's song,
And a lonely frog's hoarse call.

As the beauty-filled night cast its spell over all,
I felt God's presence around.

Mary Louise Brooks

WORDSMITH:

He is called the wordsmith, his tools — the pencil and pen;
he forges the thoughts, emotions, and actions of all
feeling men.

He is called the wordsmith, his room is his workshop —
where words of steel are set aglow in the fiery furnace
which gives the flow, the flow of ideas; the flow
of punctuation; the flow of concepts; the flow of
enunciation.

Yes, the mind is a furnace where ideas are smelted,
touching others' hearts until they are melted,
I hear him forging words in the distance,
hammering with delight, trying to come up with
the phrase that fits just right.

Wordsmith! Wordsmith! Hammer your words well,
give us the inspiration to save us from hell,
Hammer your mighty pen upon your iron pad, and
let the sparks of ideas flow from out your head.
Lift us and take us to your level of delight, let
your work live forever, let your craft give us sight.

Tony Bethel

PURE GOLD
Golden Wedding Anniversary

In 1933 I was blue, felt left in the lurch
Then, "bang!" I saw Peggy, I saw her at Church.
My eyes blinked hard, felt my heart's palpitation.
"Is she a real person, or a darling apparition?"
My tongue stuck in my cheek. I was speechless; I was mute.
"You can't tell me there is anything that cute!
She's built just right, she's absolutely perfect!"
I knew I must reach her; but how to go about it?
After a few weeks I learned her name,
Found out where she lived then started the game.
Two years went by. Two years of pure bliss.
Our love was consummated via many a kiss.
We were married at night as the rain came down.
What matters the rain when love so abounds.
True love that withstands the *rigors & rents,*
Voiding the *fury* that a *stormy* life vents.
Only the Heart of our Father above
Can create & bless a pair with such love!
So Peggy is mine! She's still mine today!
She'll never grow old. She's mine for Aye!

Theodore Andrews

MY MOTHER — MY FRIEND

You taught me how to love and share,
And no matter what, you were there.
My life got rough — you helped me through,
And I hope you know that I love you.

We had our laughs — we had our cries.
We had our lows — we had our highs.
But through it all, we became friends.
My mother, I pray it never ends.

You always gave me good advice,
And sometimes your hug was suffice.
Through my falls, you took care of me.
You're my friend — the best there could be!

Now I feel strong — you showed me how
To get through my life alone now.
But if you need me, I'll be around.
Since I value the friendship we have found.

Cindy Schnuriger

BY THE WAYSIDE

She sits and stares through windowpanes
With eyes of faded hue,
Her skin a pale translucent veil
with veining showing through.

Her circle of old friends and neighbors
Has thinned as they've died one by one,
And the sounds of the voices and laughter
Have diminished as faces have gone.

There's not much to hold her attention,
Just a grandchild or two once a year.
She's outlived the people who knew her,
Left alone by the ones she holds dear.

Jesus, reach down your hand to these children,
Who sit by the wayside alone;
Be their Hope and their constant companion,
As they wait to be taken on Home!

P. Ann Nikolaisen

TO MY FATHER (I NEVER HAD)

When I was being beaten up
You didn't have a care
Just so long as you went bowling
Life was more than fair

And when I had holes
In my shoes
You were in a bar
Drinking up my soul

I never understood why you got chops
While I got macaroni
Why was my milk dry
And your milk Vitamin A & D whole
I would have given you
All my peanut butter
For one thin slice of hard salami

Should I still love you because you're my father?

M. L. Norus

I BESEECH THEE

Good morning friend and brother,
where hides your heart today?
Did you lose it in the cellar?
Have you wasted it away?

Does Satan always taunt you,
about your worn and sorry life?
Can you tear from his clutches?
There's no ending to your strife.

If you're looking for the answer,
strong mercy flows from Jesus.
Our Savior conquered Satan.
Christ will never leave us.

Cast your eyes beyond yourself,
and search your wayward heart.
Pull "Old Adam" off your back,
and make a brand-new start.

Ask the Lord for mercy,
as you bend your knees in prayer.
Pledge your life to service,
and Christ will keep you in His care.

Wayne C. Roisen

THE ROSE

Scarlet, so sweet, as wine —
Creation of beauty, sublime:
The rose of Sharon.
Awakening, thy roses of dawn —
Enjoyed of springtime,
Enthrall'd, the mighty throng.
Thy rose persistently glows,
A state of arrogance:
Bloody array of velvety folds.
Reborn so freshly young,
Oh, so glorious —
The rose of Sharon.
Erst, but last to fall —
All its beauty surrendered,
The answer to God's call.
For love is as strong as death,
Amidst the folds of the rose —
Amongst the still of wrath.

John E. Behringer

EMPTY WALLS

Your castle walls are too imposing
I can never feel at home
Love can't live where trust has perished
All the hope I had is gone.

The costly drapes there at your windows
Seem like prison bars to me
The chandeliers are casting shadows
That make your face too dark to see.

Inside these walls I feel a coldness
Not the warmth I'd like to know
Your hearth is dreary, dark and lonely
The embers there died long ago.

I'd rather have your arms around me
Than a mink or ermine stole
And I'd rather have your kisses
than your diamonds or your gold.

I'd rather have one tiny rosebud
Given with a word of love,
Than empty promises and riches
And a lifetime without love.

Elsie Marie Phelps

UNEXPECTED ENCOUNTER

Ironically, you struggle up
the rock-strewn slopes against
tremendous odds and battle
the urge to accept the comfort
of more peaceful plateaus
only to find the winds at the
top, a more fierce adversary
than any you've ever known,
determined to blow you back
to a level of secure mediocrity
and to intimidate you
into remaining there.
But, somehow, more determined
than they to succeed at what
you do best, you must conclude:
That you would rather brave
the winds at the top of the
mountain than endure the
calm of the valley below.

Ann Alice Wilmer

OBLIVION

Dark is the night,
That carries us away.

Into a peaceful sleep,
Where only good is portrayed.

There, light comes from darkness,
With brightness abounding.

And dreams can become real,
So true, it's astounding.

Then the glory of Beauty
Silently becomes the bride of the light.

And slowly they ascend,
Consumed by their flight.

Karen Lee Jones

IN CLOUDS

Floating in clouds,
Enveloped by stillness,
Abandonment,
Unseen turmoil.
My heart races,
Spins,
And grasps at emptiness.
All is here
Yet nothing.
I am gone,
Torn apart,
And cast away;
Like a dying flower,
A broken vase.
Left alone,
On my own,
To wander
In the clouds
Of my mind.

Leigh Earls Lenz

SORROW

*"Sorrow is parent
to discipline and joy"*

Oh, sweet sorrow
In rapture bend.
Lead us to heaven's stead!
What life is ours
To bring us dread?
The blossom of our
Parents' stead.
What clock will take
Us from our bed,
In thoughts written
For posterity's shed.
The book of life is
All that remains,
Written in posterity's shed.
But lead us not
In life to dread the joy
Of posterity's bed!

David Anderson Coon

THE TORMENT

I heard your voice
But couldn't decide
Where it came from, the
Heaven or the Hell inside.
I've never met an angel.
I've had some breathings with one, though.
Are you a mystical extension
Of my filmy soul?
Or does your cackle reveal
A spell you plan to cast
Upon me, sensually
Tangled in your grasp?
As to the moth's obsession for the flame,
To you I'm drawn, as Icarus to the Sun.
Will I dance in ethereal flight
Or end in circumvented run?
With arms pressed around my head
I cannot escape your taunting strain.
Are you sublime imagination
Or madness in my brain?

Nancy Ander Rutschmann

CLOCK EXCHANGE

Time didn't stop when the aged clock
was lifted down and hauled away.
Softly it chimed its lofty last time
before going to salvage today.
Its ancient face is being replaced
as memory hides it from display.

O, such a calm face and hands aplace
Well-worn by the duties of time.
Chimes stilled, to the longago willed
in a silence of forever's resign,
Left ample tear-haze of yesterdays
to throngs mourning its recline.

In view's claim a new clock-face came
accurate with neat simplicity.
We are aware of a new clock-face there
the time and temperature to see.
Time in lieu will raze this clock too,
now flashing time so dependably.

Myrtle Willoughby

MY LITTLE STAR

One night I glanced at a very tall tree
And a brilliant little star winked at me,
Attracting my attention, there and then
So I kept going back to look again.
I could only look from a certain angle
In order to see my little star spangle,
When I looked again the following night
There it was, still sparkling bright!
I had never seen a little star at night
Reflecting such beautiful streams of light,
I looked again as I had before
But to my surprise, it wasn't there anymore;
Then suddenly in the heavens, a flash from afar
Caused me to wonder, "Was that my little star?"

Virginia L. Wilson

WILSON, VIRGINIA L. Born: Petersburg, Virginia, 2-8-22; Education: Attended Virginia State College, now University; Occupation: Clerk- Typist, retired from Virginia State University after 20 years service; Awards: Merit Certificates/Honorable Mention, World of Poetry Press, 'Sadly Touched,' 1983; 'The Sycamore Tree,' 1984, with words of praise; Poetry: 'Little Lena,' *The Progress-Index*, 9-82; 'Fifty Years Late,' *The Progress-Index*, 9-82; 'With Love, to My Sons,' American Poetry Association, *Hearts on Fire*, 1985; *God's Touch*, booklet of poems, Virginia State University (50 copies given to ROTC Department for troops overseas), 1983; Comments: *When I made a commitment to Christ, at age sixty, He graciously bestowed this talent upon me. Therefore, as I experience the reality of God's love, and the fulfillment of His promises, it is my ardent desire to reflect the same through poetry. My work is predominantly religious in nature.*

NEPHEW

little hugs, little hugs, little hugs
— and a trick!

            . . . peeping grin.
Now run, run, run
and hide behind the giggling curtains with feet.

Where's the boy?
(giggle)

Mitchell D. Piper

GOODBYES

People are the tall ships that sail the seas of my life.
They dock at my port and bring me visions of another
        world, sharing feelings that sustain my growth.
How precious are these tall ships!
They come. They go.
They share their cargo in moments of time.
Yet time takes them from me.
The cry of the seas calling the sailors home.
They leave my heart breaking — tearing the fibers of my
        soul like a storm ravages a sail from its mast.
Yet ships were built for sailing, not docking.
Shall I linger so long on the ship's shadow in the
        sunset that I miss the greeting of the
        rocking rowboat at my side?
Goodbyes can mean hellos.
The small craft, too, have valuable cargo to share.
Cargo that can nourish me 'til another tall ship touches
        my port with visions of a deeper friendship
        and love beyond the seas of my understanding.

Sandra L. Beese

NEWBORN BABIES

There's a joy around, when another is born
no peace and quiet, but they are so warm

Not a moment's rest, since the baby's birth
but all of the world, can't be more than he's worth

A lot is said, for a newborn baby
especially a girl, who'll grow into a lady

As for the boy, it's rough & tumble
but when he's a man, he's so ever humble

Enough for the future, let's get to the present
they're powdery slick, and a wonderful fragrance

Not enough can be said, when it comes to their lives
what they mean to us, and a joy to our eyes.

C. K. Naholowaa

I AM

Borne from the depths of a fire without a flame.
Soothed by the waters from the ocean's deep
I stretched forth. Reached out. For I am.
I am the void of endless space.
The silent music of the universe.
The love that falls from heavenly grace.
I am hope, faith and despair.
I am the thunder, lightning and rain
that fill men's feeble hearts with fear.
I am the snow on a cold winter's day.
I am music in the air.
For I am.
I am the storm that sinks a helpless ship.
The quake that rents the Earth to weep.
Yet I am also the fragrance of a spring morn.
The sound of new life being born.
I am the sun that gently warms the sail.
I am the sky, moon and stars.
I am free. For I am everything and nothing at all.

Anne I. Bent

MANIFESTO

When the world around us becomes complicated and confused
and difficult to figure out:
When the systems of government, business and the family unit
no longer work for and with each other:
When the deterioration is observed in lower forms of life,
environment, atmosphere and in the minds of human beings:
When the logic behind peace, harmony, brotherhood, and
sharing are no longer with us:
When we resort to the unconscious acts of greed, lust,
irresponsibility, terrorism, murder and utter war:
Then we have waited too long and it is time to change.
The system is not working toward the best interest and
benefit of everything in it.
Change will take place no matter what.
Be it through destruction, desolation, dictatorship and
exploitation or by the intelligent illation of facing
up to the truth.
We must change or we will be changed!
Let us strive to work with each other in harmony
with the universe, with mother nature, on planet earth,
in the grace of God.

Erika L. Corette

THE BUZZ

*The Bahnoff Zoo is a German book
about drug addicts in Berlin.*

Once upon a time when I had nothing to do
I saw a young girl reading the "Bahnoff Zoo."

I looked at the pictures of death and destruction
all in relation to life and construction.

The children asked, "Dad?" He said, "Shut up and eat!"
He was real smart. Drove his kids into the street.

The children are searching for the answers to life
their parents don't know them, they've been through their strife.

But the answers to their questions died on a cross.
Their dad doesn't care, he thinks he's the boss!

Eat, burp, and sleep, and work at the factory
The answer for dad is quite satisfactory.

Bruce Christman

THE ANGUISH OF AN ANCIENT RHYMER

O, dear, sweet, Jesus, Cathleen,
My fair, blue-eyed colleen,
Why does life mainly demean?
Why can't I be
A lad of 23,
And you desiring me?
My love, come with me now! Let's fly to Tahiti
Where I'll treat you royally — like Nefertiti.
We'll make searing love in a cool lagoon
Providing, of course, there isn't a monsoon,
But even if there is, we'll be immune,
For I'll hold you tight in wind and rain
And never let you feel a drop of pain.

The ancient one stands alone now by the sea,
Despising any return to reality.
O, dear God, Cathleen,
My lovely colleen,
Why is life so mean?
As the tide rises the wind seems to shout,
The old poet has gone to help God out.

Colin Clift

IN MEMORY OF ROBERT LEE WILLIAMS

Robert Lee Williams, you're one in a million
Your heart was worth more than silver or gold
You lived a good life, you fought a good fight
The story remains untold

One of your qualities I loved so much
You brought me lots of cheer
With laughs and tears, down through the years
Most of all a son on New Year

A daughter so tall and linger with pride
and two more of your flesh and blood
I cherish our love, I still have that love
I thank God in heaven above

We did things together, in any kind of weather
We were in love I agree
You taught me things I didn't know, you cared ecstatically
With our ups and downs and all around
Was how our love was meant to be

Vivian D. Crawford

LOST FRIEND

Today I lost a friend, through no fault of my own
My body, mind and heart, feel as if they've turned to stone
No more to see, to touch or talk, as we did so before
My life will now become stale, a real drag, and a bore.
Where does one turn, when crying brings you no relief?
Can you trust again after all the hurt and disbelief?
My thoughts now turn to self-destruction and as such
Only consolation is the family who love you very much
But after everyone has gone home, left you all by yourself
You make a solemn vow, to put yourself upon a shelf
But what about all the time that looms ahead each day
How will you fill it, when you have nothing left to say?
You would like to crawl like an animal and just plain hide
Go out nowhere, see no one, have everything sent inside
But you know this is not the way, simply can't be done
'Cause life goes on like the moon, rain, even the sun
No one can take the place of the friend you have lost
As their loving memory in your mind is forever embossed
You take the time, evaluate, plan just what to attend
Then go out in search of and find yourself another friend.

Jeanne Aintablian

SONG OF MELANCHOLIA

Memories taunt as thoughts reach back
to part the silken folds of past.
Heartaches haunt as scenes review
the years gone by, from first to last . . .

Must our hearts be broken
at every turn on the highway of life?
Must our mingling tears
pave the road to future happiness?
Must every joyful moment be gone —
swept away by the breath of our sighs . . .
Must love like ours pass on
devoid of peaceful contentment . . .
Dream fragments, and shattered hopes,
Must these be our lot?

Memories taunt as thoughts reach back
to part the silken folds of past.
Heartaches haunt as scenes review
the years gone by, from first to last . . .

Corinne Lillian Egerton

THE WHITE TRIBE

My roots eat the fruits of the Africa Sun
my parents are white, invented Apartheid
my future — my past — and my right to exist
my people, my country — are on a black list

And just because Colonialism has paved the way for Communism
but what of me — my tribe is white
don't I have the right to my tribal rites?

Has the white man in Africa no human rights
has the white man in Africa started the fight
who is throwing the bombs who is starving the child
should we fell all the trees and switch off the lights?

And just because Colonialism has paved the way for Communism . . .

Elli Meckler

MECKLER, ELLI. Born: Peisern, formerly Germany, now Poland. Childhood in Communist East Germany. Now citizen of the world. Last ten years living in Africa. Married: to Alexandre; Occupations: Catering, Journalism, Guitar and Singing; Memberships: Amstel Play of the Year Awards, SA Scriptwriters Association; Writings: "Divorce is Such an Ugly Word," play; 'The Atomic Rape,' do; 'Love Escape,' do; *Der Brennende Kaktus,* Comments: *Poems say in a couple of words — in shorthand — what the soul needs to sing about.*

NATHAN

a working man — six days a week he labored feverishly
        his family so high on a pedestal
        he laid gifts at their feet
                providing was his salvation

a giving man — all things in their own time
        just as oceans forever swell and subside, his coffer never
        emptied for the more he gave the more he had to give
                giving was his salvation

a quiet man — he walked the earth in cat-paw steps
        sheltered by unbending manliness he protected his fragile beauty
        that could be shattered only by thoughtlessness
                silence was his salvation

a dying man — everything in its own time
        just as summer trees sense the wintertime sleep
        just as the setting sun knows it will rise once again
        his house could only weather so many storms
        the walls were ripped open once too often
        and as the moon and sun danced their dusky ballet
        the house crumbled slowly to dust and
                death was his salvation

Stu Greenberg

GOSSIP

Gossip on my evil friend —
you have so much to tell,
like the spider, a web you spin,
to engulf the fly that fell.
Evil thoughts, like evil deeds —
are causing so much pain —
if your wagging tongue succeeds,
you'll hurt someone again.
You have the fly within your web —
now inject your poison slow —
the squirming fly may soon be dead,
but your turn will come you know!
Gossip on you silly fool —
go spread your tales of woe,
gossip is the devil's tool —
and he reaps the seeds you sow!
Dorothy I. Gary

AN ETCHING

Your profile,
then made manifest by the grace
of a New England sunrise through
    window glass,
was not especially pretty, nor
giving of
    warmth.
Yet time has revealed
its etching on leaves
that now fall gently
through the changing colors
    of my mind.
David Goble

CLOSE FRIENDS

We share special closeness
    which no one else includes.
It's always just the two of us
    and no one can intrude.
We have the sweetest memories
    and time is on our side.
We always stick together,
    our love, it will abide.
Your eyes, they show your caring,
    and everything you feel.
And when you're hurt I know it,
    to me you do reveal.
Your friendship means so much to me,
    two dreamers of the same.
We'll forever be the closest
    and our love, it will remain.
Stacy Zolman

I'M SORRY

You felt so hurt
and humiliated.
And I
could only hold you
for an instant and
say, "I'm sorry."
The things I wanted
to say,
about how much I cared,
felt hurt for you,
and how important
you were to me,
stayed trapped inside
and you went away
to be
alone.

John W. Moore

FROSTWORK

Finest crystals of awesome symmetry,
Silently wafted by wintry whispers,
Make festivities of sparkling traceries
    to adorn all nature
        in delicate bridal array.
Flaky gems so fragile,
    graceful,
        tender,
Yet, like the meekness of the Lord,
"Strong enough to be gentle."

Barbara Schlautmann

LET IT BURN

Stand apart from the crowd
But they laugh and call you a freak,
Even though where you are
Is where they'd like to be.

Wear a shade of brown
In between the green,
Watch the hate in their eyes,
As you march right on by
Completely free;
Or just to me?

Have we really passed the mark
Never to return,
To the ranks of the programmed monarchy.
Zombies of society.

Don't laugh at me,
Criticizer of my little group,
Until you have tried
To shake the hold of your noose
Is it loose?

Are you the people who have
Passed the mark, never to return.
What was it you said about
Individuality — let it burn!
Let it burn!

Michael Chaly

GIVE ME THIS DAY

Give me this day love,
to try and seal my
love in your heart
to be with you alone
even in the crowds,

Give me this day love,
it's all I ask
time to enter your heart
touching it with love

Give me this day love
and silently I'll wish
to lengthen it for all
love brings us to share

Give me this day love,
to show you my love is boundless,
and love
after spending this day with just you
the touch and nearness of you
and being into this day together,

you'll know
there's no other feeling
giving so much
as love.

Ruth Perry

WALK A WELL-TRAVELED ROAD

You see wild grapes growing upon a tattered vine.
Their flesh grows older,
Some will perish,
Others remain for a time.

The bridge you once knew as a child is now food for the current,
Swiftly flowing water sends your dreams swirling to places never gone.

Softly spoken words echo the land,
Whispers never heard,
By unknown ears,
Remind you that you are nothing more than a man.

Wes Mossburg

Why so many angry thoughts, and why must I not see
What moves this world I'm standing on around Eternity?
How can eyes which see so well stare so vacantly
When viewing all that's happening in Heaven's majesty?
Why must peaceful truths defy an honest question asked;
Inquiries so demanded of a long-forgotten past?

My honesty has much to learn; my blinded eyes must grow
To cherish all I'm given and all I long to know.
For Truth is offered freely, and Love prefers to share
Togetherness and All in One with those who choose to care.
Step softly through your endless days, that outstretched hands might one day hold.
An understanding, giving heart may lovingly unfold.

Lynne A. Thrul

SEVEN SEALS

Seven seals on a cryptic scroll which no man may breach,
the Word has opened for man to know his beginning from his end.
    Deceived we feel our vision's clear and seek the paths of foreign love,
but war shall raze our haughty minds, the whore shall come to see our shame.
    Victuals rare and waters foul a thin man stares with glazy eyes,
but soon the pestilence draws his card and chokes the breath from his feeble life.
    Those hearts which served the heaven sent their blood is spilled by vengeful law;
but then the earth shall sorely shake as sun and moon conceal their form.
    Let the world search out the sky while men run screaming to rocky caves;
a beast ascends the water's depth, its many heads wage angry war.
    Yet one who holds true peace and joy shall turn the ruinous winds away;
a King shall come with splendid throne to confound the haze of bloodied eyes.

Robert Ernest Empson

A REAL FRIEND

A real friend is a person who shares whatever comes their way, who helps
by thoughtful works and words to brighten our days.

Who knows the little worries that lie heavy on our minds and tries to ease
the pain of each, by being kind.

A real friend helps to bring the sun and chases away the rain, who clearly
convinces us our dreams are not in vain.

And if we travel many miles to where the rainbow ends, we'd find no
greater delight than the love of a real true friend.

Linda M. Barron

NEVER TOMORROW

Never tomorrow, for time is fleeting and tomorrow too distant.
Live for the moment, life offers no guarantees, no second chances.
Cherish each memory for they are the scripts of our lifetime and
Each special to us.
Love every minute, for love is the elixir of life and is as fleeting
As time.

Joe Fiorillo

As a servant of love I run
And join with all the rivers that have ever been wept.

I run with the tall pines
That stretch their fragrances toward heaven
With arched backs and needle-laden fingers.

I run where crimson flows
There many hearts have travelled.

I run where silent grasses sleep
Dark, dewy, and damp.

I run where streams grow fresh
I know the rocks
This human weary flesh.

I run where the silent raindrop
Brushes the faintest wisp of air
And touch the stars.

Anne R. Fawcett

FAWCETT, ANNE R. Born: Champaign, Illinois; Education: UCLA, B.A., Elementary Education Teaching Credential; Occupations: Customer Service Operator, Teacher; Poetry: *Sounds of Morning Silence, Poems of Anne R. Fawcett I,* collection of original poems, 1984; *Poems of Anne R. Fawcett, Book II,* collection of original poems, 1985; Comments: *My poems deal with God, life, love, family. I write because it gives me joy. I try to put the thoughts down on paper when they come to me creatively. I try to express hope and the ability to accept challenges and overcome difficulties.*

PLAYTIME FOR THE WIND

You can see where she's been as she hurries past,
As she whirls, she swirls, as she goes so fast.
She's the wind as she searches her playground vast.

While she looks for some mischievous prank to play,
She picks up the sticks and hurls them away,
And she huffs, she puffs at the boats in the bay.

    She whips up girls' dresses,
    And stirs up their tresses.
    "What fun," she confesses.

      "I could do this all day."
      You know what they say,
      "It's the wind at her play."

Mary Alice Rich

IN PASSING

where I used to live is not a place anymore
a dusty road that once held a treasure
setting courses by attaining goals of inspiring grade
multiplication tables, fractions, common
denominators that presented a challenge
in a prosperous town that possessed a feeling
beautiful in every aspect reflecting
younger days, school bus #17
tire tracks fading from view
coming home in the afternoon was little else

where street names didn't exist
and numbers were easily forgotten
syllables that never held a meaning
expectations shattered
of the corner dime store
fragments seemingly out of proportion
to ties that linked a family together
combining promises and hope
where I once used to live
in a place that soon came to pass.

Glenn O. Kirms

ALL OVER THE WORLD

Peaceful slumber is not something seen
In a world of hunger undreamed
Of, by our mind's blinded eye
It ravages, even though they try
No rain falls, the land is parched and dry
Even if you can give no money
There is much you can do
Light a candle in their name
And say a prayer or two.

The children suffer when we fight, not me and you
And with the wars come famine
There is nothing they can do
All their lives are spent in huts
Under a burning sun of gold
And though they are only children
They too, have grown old
And when Hunger claims them
Mothers and Fathers, they cry
There was no food last morning eve
So they watched their little child die.

Virgie M. Tabaco

REPLY TO A NAUTICAL FRIEND

With that tenuous string dangling
between earth and sky
we are driven back and forth
slipping and sliding across the ship's deck
while buffeting winds whip the ropes
to and fro, just beyond our reach.
The familiar creaking of the wooden mast
and the spray in faces grown worn
from endless storms
does not, cannot comfort our
sea-cold hands or lips.
While we struggle relentlessly
just to maintain our stance in the constant
fury, the ship on which we stand
begins to founder — do we pull together
or apart
or go down like men, with the ship,
But ships
like men, have been known to recover their
balance, and there are always lifeboats
for those who believe in tomorrow's calm sea.

Chris L. Hudgens

FOR EVA WITH LOVE

You became my new decision,
You outweigh all competition,
Now you're in this composition,
    For Eva with love.

We have lived love in the future,
That is why we are so close here,
Now I started out this new year,
    For Eva with love.

You reminded me of lost love,
We feel comfort in our soft touch,
And you hear what I am thinking of,
    For Eva, with love.

Michael J. Finn

FINN, MICHAEL JEFFREY. Pen name: Pentel; Born: Oak Park, Illinois, 1-26-54; Occupation: Disc Jockey; Poetry: 'Sharon,' emotional, self- published, 1983; 'Judith,' hopeful, self-published, 1982; 'Believe in Me,' trust, self-published, 1981; 'We'll Go On,' faith, self-published, 1978; 'Happy To Be Free,' joy, *Berwyn Life News,* 1975; Themes: *The result of sincere relations that are unspeakably lost;* Comments: *My satisfaction of completed and printed products are the rewards of personal content.*

CAMOUFLAGE

HONORABLE MENTION

I would not show the pain that
Would turn the walls
Yellow curious colors.

And my crimson face
Would not allow my friends
To analyze my misery.
It was my emotion.

For if I should reveal
    a vulnerable soul . . .
A river of lost affection
Trickles from their mouths.
It sounds blue
And streams onto the shaggy
Woolen carpet.
For all of us to walk on
And sweep under the rug.

Mary E. McMahon

HIS PRESENCE SHALL GO WITH THEE

I sensed an inner longing
    nothing could satisfy;
I felt the Great Eternal God
    had suddenly passed me by.
My soul was stunned and silent,
    My life was bleak and bare . . .
Until I gave my heart to Him . . .
    Now He is everywhere!

My daily tasks are all a part
    of His wondrous plan for me,
No shadow mars His Presence
    He is with me constantly.
I crave a closer walk with God
    that leads me to His Home
Where I shall worship eternally
    around the Great White Throne.
        Tressa C. Terry

TO A BABY DEAR

A baby, Dear, is like a flower.
It grows more lovely each hour.
A baby, Dear, like a flower
Is a gift from God above
And needs: constant tender care, love,
Food, sunshine, water, air,
Vitamins, plus clothes to wear.
Not excessive heat or cold
To conform to human mold
And be a joy to behold.

A baby, Dear, like a flower
Is more precious than pure gold.
And, is loved by folks young and old.
So, grow like a flower in your bower
And throughout your life bring cheer
To all you know every year.
        Mollie E. Miller

OF ITS OWN ACCORD

Lifeless,
    the branch clung by a sinew
to its existence,
    a useless, nonproductive entity.
It should be snapped off quickly,
    and thrown aside
or gently laid down.

New life does not stem
    from old veins
So it lingers, waiting,
    perhaps hoping.
No one moves it,
    fearful of the fatal touch.
We let it be,
    waiting for it to fall
of its own accord.
        Melody Raney

MIND

Brow dripped with sweat
Thy body is numb
There's no sanity left
in this brain.
Skeleton of flesh
The mind is stripped
from its soul
What nectar of poison
Gives this human
form breath!
        Myra Abbott Keef

DEAR VALENTINE

If all the world were
    Just my own,
If I possessed it
    All alone . . .
My path would be
    Just one of thorns,
With darkened skies
    And dewless morns;
No lilting songs
    Would reach me, dear,
No laughing brooks
    With roses near,
For all that I
    Could ever own
Would be an empty heart,
    Alone . . .
Then all the world
    Won't mean a thing,
An empty heart
    Can't feel the Spring!

Ruth M. Lommatzsch

MEMORIES

Puppy dogs and pollywogs,
    kittens playing with a string.
They all bring back the memories
    of pleasant childhood things.

It now seems so long ago,
    those days will come no more.
Only in my dreams,
    can I capture the days of yore.

The dress-up days
    of childhood ways,
bring laughter to my heart,
    and rekindle the childishness
        I'm willing to impart.

Out on the meadow
    flying kites in the wind,
        it swoops and it sails
            but it doesn't bend.

Telebree

THE STORY

I have notes and clippings galore.
They're scattered all over the floor.
(I've seen this mess here before).

I have scraps of fiction I started,
facts that to me were imparted,
all kinds of things that I started.

I pick out what tickles my fancy.
I can't afford to be "chancy."
The product must have necromancy.

I work through all hours of the night.
This story's become dynamite.
Now I must get copyright.

To the market my story's been sold.
Fame and fortune unfold.
The writer's story's been told.

Georgette Crifasi

DÜRER, The Riders on the Four Horses

Horse-type creature —
coat pure white;
one single horn
which shines so bright.
Deep brown eyes —
all seeing and knowing;
taut muscles ripple,
their strength showing.
Unicorn, long past is
your time of leaving;
but in you I know,
there is magic in believing!

Christine Raye Tannis

TANNIS, CHRISTINE RAYE. Born: Waukesha, Wisconsin 8-17-67; Education: Currently a student at Memorial Senior High School, graduating class of 1986; Occupations: Student, Babysitter; Memberships: AWANA; Poetry: 'Reawakening,' Christian Board of Publication, May 1984; untitled poem, American Poetry Association, Fall/Winter 1983; Comments: *I began writing poetry seriously when I was 14 years old. I've written on various themes from love to religion. The Lord has been a major influence on my writing since I became a born again believer at age 15.*

When you left our side,
Our eyes filled with sorrow,
The Lord began to guide,
Us to a brighter tomorrow,

As I watch you lay,
In your garden of eden,
All I can say,
Is our love will never weaken,

Our fears ran wild,
Because you weren't there,
Then there came a child,
That had no fear,

We will see you again,
On the coming day,
But until then,
We have one thing left to say,

We will always miss you,
You were a true friend,
You were one of few,
Whose love will never end.

Michelle W. Riley

GRAVE OF A RETARDED GIRL

For lack of title, will Margaret, do?
    She called her doll that name;
And pacing in the morning dew,
    Twice to our cottage came.

Though all alone, she loved this place;
    Did she not often stroll,
And muse with many a happy glance,
    Upon this very knoll?

Her father never wends this way;
    Her mother turns aside;
I was her only friend the day
    This child of Nature, died.

Faery Harper

THE ROSE

As I was looking at my rose bush,
And saw the little buds therein.
I thought how beautiful the rose,
And how the thorns could prick your skin.

My mind went back to the Bible,
And the scriptures I had read.
How my Savior hung upon the cross,
A crown of thorns upon his head.

A rose to me is a symbol,
Of beauty and of love.
And Jesus Christ our Savior,
Who guides us from above.

Polly Pennington

OLD PHOTOGRAPH

I see a little girl
Her dress is long and white
Her arms are folded across her chest
Her hair is pulled back trim and tight

I see a little boy
His pants are short and baggy
His socks peek out from run-down shoes
His hair is wheaten and shaggy

Two little children in one photograph
Two little faces without a laugh
Deep in their eyes a sadness comes through
I wonder what became of the two

Sue B. Brock

THE FOG

Lost in the fog, too thick to see,
Its icy fingers beckon me.
Farther into the depths of its hold,
Until my very soul grows cold.
Everything grows deathly still,
To run away I've lost all will.
Everything lost from lack of care,
My world has gone beyond repair.
My mind refuses to take anymore,
When I come upon an open door.
Behind it is another world,
In front of my eyes it does unfurl.
Until I simply fade away,
And cease to live another day.

Rhonda Folmer

THE SEASONS OF MY LIFE

It was springtime when I came to be
how sweet and simple life was to me
Just watching the birds fly swift and free
To land in their nest, high in a tree

Too soon the summer moved in on me
And who can stop the powers that be
I was a woman; no longer free
I soon had my own nest, high in a tree

The long summer days are dead and gone
I shiver with cold at early dawn
The bitter cold seeps into my bones
My hands and feet are as cold as stones

I greet the cold dawn with a low moan
I get out of bed with a deep groan
I most certainly have to agree
That old age has me trapped in my tree

Marciana Garma

DINNER FOR TWO

Table lace and heartfelt grace;
    We love to nibble and chew.
Can one find a greater place
    Then near baked duck for two?

What care we took to select
    The rib cage of this fowl,
And now we find we must protect
    From little eyes and growl.

Our dog and cat perceive
    Just what we have to eat.
They nip at busy sleeves
    And like the choice of meat.

So by our chair rest two
    For they have had their fill.
And now it's time; dessert is due
    And we are hungry still.

Barbara Carver

LOVE'S END

I sit and think,
and across the room
she has a drink . . .
quiet as a tomb.

How did it go?
Where could love have flown?
I've sunk so low;
I feel so alone.

Love made life bright,
with her at my side.
Blow out the light
on two hearts that lied.

I've heard it said
that life will go on:
my heart is dead,
and I won't last long.

David R. Cook

91

THE POET: A PAINTER OF LITERATURE

A poet is a world shaker,
His pen makes life brighter,
Or darker, in many poems.
A poet is a sort of disciple,
A man or woman of courage,
Often working late at night,
Until the words are right.
A poet wears blue jeans or his best tuxedo,
To feel like one of his heroes.
A poet tries to remember his name,
And works at keeping his fame.
But a poet is often lame,
Uncovering the feelings of his mind.
Until he remembers: he's one of a kind!

Josephine Pouliot

THE END OF A DREAM

Green are the woodlands and fields I once knew,
Greener still are the dreams of the place I grew,
A wild mountain stream is running swift and strong,
And once again I yearn to hear its song.

But never again will I darken the doors of home,
Nor walk again the paths I used to roam.
For all of these are shadowed in the past,
And, like my youth, have faded much too fast.

Yet, left for me are dreams of other days,
Of bluebirds, mountain streams and other ways,
With the memories in my heart again I roam
But the saddest dream of all, I can't go home.

Blaine W. Bittinger

WHY SHOULD I DOUBT

Why should I doubt the strength of Him on high,
and limit with my finite, trifling thought
His power, Who formed the earth and sea and sky,
And signs and wonders through the ages wrought?
The future, can I not entrust to Him
Who sees and knows the tiny sparrow's fall?
Can I, with mortal eyesight weak and dim,
Envision the outreach of One so tall?
He moves in storms and gives the thunders voice;
He holds the planets in their rightful course.
Should I then fail to make His will my choice,
Or let Him move my mountains with His force?
   No, I but make myself more weak and frail
      To doubt the strength of Him Who shall not fail.

Hazel C. Sack

MEADOWBROOK CASTLE

Gazing across the bare tundra
beyond the great stone wall,
there peeps an ole castle tower
where Meadowbrook once stood tall.

The Spanish moss hung teasingly
dipping playfully at the seething moat,
her ancient drawbridge creeking horridly
straining each rusty chain, pulley and belt.

The elements of time have been unkind
only in memory does she remain,
a sightly figure to dream on then
now merely ruins spread upon the plain.

Monica Silver

THE ESCAPE

I watch the psychedelic disk spin swiftly
   as the metallic pinpoint absorbs the collection
      of banded threads.
   I sit in silence,
   my receiving ears devouring every pitch,
Every note striking me as lightning may.
            Until suddenly
I slip into a comforting trance,
               All worries float miles away.
Flying through my dream world,
                  I reach eternal bliss.
      Then my eyes sadly open
         as the tune fades to a quiet hush.
      I awaken, discovering

            reality . . .
   Sharon G. Smith

THE PLIGHT OF THE SCHOONER GHOST

Out of a foggy haze sails a ghostly
      apparition;
Frozen riggin' dripping wet hides her
      recognition.

At water level aft *Schooner Ghost* appears;
A windjammer lost in a storm off Algiers.

Thirteen men met their fate that day;
She either broke up or capsized they say.

One thing's for sure — as the old woman knows;
The ocean she keeps never giving up her souls.

So lend me your ear on a chill misty night;
A whistle she sounds, the *Schooner Ghost Plight!*

   John L. Emory

LIFE'S PATHWAY

As along life's pathway we trod
Ofttimes we fail to see our God
With eyes downcast we fail to see
God's bountiful blessings for you and me.
When days are dreary and rough is the way
God will hear if we will only pray.
Sometimes sadness overwhelms us
And troubles seem so strong, but
God will hold your hand and
Help you along.
Life's pathway can be strewn with woes
With lots of thorns, but also the rose
We need only to remember we are not alone
The rough spots then become stepping stones.
When we do press on toward our goal
Soon we forget the thorns and remember the rose.

   Thelma H. Sherrill

PEACE

Today as I knelt and prayed to Thee
I felt Thy presence so tenderly,
I knew that Thou wast very near
Stilling my doubts and all my fears,
And as I unloaded my burden on Thee
Peace crept in and my heart felt free.
Peace like a field of waving flowers
Calm and washed clean by the summer showers,
Peace like the ocean on a summer day
Lapping the shore in a gentle way.
Let me forever experience this peace,
Let my faith grow and never to cease.

   Mary E. Smith

EBONY PEARL

First love, plain and true
Is it lasting for me and for you?

Though we go through heartaches and pains
The love we share will always remain!

Now this doesn't mean the path will always
be smooth.
It just means our love will withstand all
the wounds.

So when it seems as though our love is no more
Think again and then some more!

Nothing comes easily
Not money
Not fame
Nor eternity
And certainly not an ebony pearl like me!

So try and try hard for that true love
Fight to hold on to the one you love
Believe it or not we are all ebony pearls!

Phyllis A. Baker

FRIENDS

When your world is turned upside-down
And there's no one to lend a helping hand,
Don't walk away — let me be a friend to you —
I promise I will try to understand

I can't make your problems disappear,
But we can try to find some answers
To the questions going through your mind
So you can live without foolish chances

Though you have fears, you are not alone
You have a friend who really cares for you
One day at a time you make your future —
You need some help to make your dreams come true

We can work things out whatever happens
That's what good friends should always do
No matter what each tomorrow brings,
Together, we'll always see it through

Marcile A. Bergen

W O R D S

Words wrestling 'twixt tongue and teeth,
rising on inflection, describing the poignant
sorrows and disappointments of mankind.
Words passing for thoughts that come,
stumbling into the silence that surrounds concentrated effort,
and then fades into eternity.

Words telling of the beauties of nature,
extolling virtues, deriding puny efforts of mankind,
to find everlasting peace.
Words twisted from mouths turned awry with suffering,
words giving forth light to give emphasis to basic emotions,
laughing and singing at the dawn of life.

Words that are still in the throat of the mute,
seeking to ever express the joys of life,
vivid in portrayal, telling that which lies
beyond the ken of man.

Words sung, that makes the emotions soar above the blue,
buoyant and carefree, lilting and musical.
Words that tell of the trials and successes.
Words everlasting, and that will ever end with Amen.

Hugo J. Forde

POET'S SONG

Who knows what words my pen shall say?
The power of which my feelings convey.
My innermost thoughts now made clear.
Awaken your senses to what you hear.

In reading my poems, perhaps you might,
Grasp of my vision, or follow my light.
Your emotions now I shall try to reach,
As the pain and pleasures of life I teach.

Shall I touch your heart, make it cry?
Or instead, cause your soul to soar on high.
Who knows what words my pen shall say?
The power of which my feelings convey.

Louvenious Apperson

A HALF MOON

Hanging low in the southern sky,
A silvery half moon sidles by,
It's effulgent beams caress the earth,
Inspiring all lovers of romantic verse.

The stars will soon be peeping out,
Like giant sparklers in the south,
How pleasant is this summer night,
Yes, everything seems so right.

The birds are chirping their goodnight song,
Asleep in their treetop nests ere long,
This bright illumination from above,
Is just God's way of showing His love.

Bernard Jacob

HIDE-N-SEEK
HONORABLE MENTION

Lost mind, tired, unthinking, blind.
I like to be lost sometimes. Blank.
Never a thought about who thought what of me,
What I should wear tomorrow, or
What will I do with my life.
In my own grayness, mist, I am resting, dreaming, playing.

Reality will come roaring at me
With its one million machine guns aimed at my mind
And I will be found.
Forced back into what they are saying, thinking, living.
An unkind invitation to join their world.
I don't have to accept it.

Ellen L. Barber

HAVE YOU EVER

Have you ever been lost at sea, friend,
when the weather hasn't done what it should?

The wind is getting stronger
and the ship's not looking too good.

You don't even know where north is
and you doubt that you ever knew.

The waves are washing the deck off
and there's not much left of the crew.

Have you ever been lost at sea, friend . . . ?

Lennie Fuerst

REPOSE

My lips are
Sealed
My soul is
Silent
As I repent

Of wasted time
Without reality
Seeking to pursue
What was not mine

To stand a moment
And contemplate
If my words
Were in time

Doralene Blakeney

IMAGES

*Dedicated to you and I in complete
simplicity
and Ingmar Bergman, my favorite
Director/Producer*

Shapeless Impression
Just a fading desire
Pierceless images
Faces of the façade
Mirrors of the shadows
Misty rains come forth
Ballets of priceless memories
Play behind the faceless
Images thought of and desired
Glistening sights of expression
Blades of sadness pierce the
heart
Focus inception of thoughts
Shadows of deceit infiltrate
the mind
Images of imagination

Bhatkin Devi

DEVI, BHATKIN. Pen Name: B. Devi; Born: Jackson, Mississippi, 1-8-51; Single; Education: Northeastern Illinois University; Northwestern Evening Divisions School; NIA Writing School, received M.S.,1983; Eastland College, England; Occupation: Currently Sales, poetry writing, short story, essay, Domestic, Waitress, Surveyor, Cook, Advertiser, Songwriter; Songs: 'Love Lost,' 'Springtime Love,' and 'A Long Way to Sacramento,' recorded with Columbine Records; 'As I Think of You,' and 'Tell Me Why,' recorded with MSR; Awards: Honorable Mention for 'Thought Wonder,' World of Poetry Press, 1983; Special Mention for 'Life's Undisputed Truths,' World of Poetry Press, 1984; Other Poetry: 'Writing,' 1982; 'I,' 1982; 'Life Moving Along,' 1983; all published by World of Poetry Press; 'Life,' and 'My Soul Sings of Your Love,' published by American Poetry Association; Comments: *I write because I like to express ideas, philosophies, nature, love, joy, sadness and realism, to give and share in common bond with the readers their reflections and mine of the true existence of life to humanity.*

WINTER SCENES

Sunshine is on the decline.
Frost; leaves dying grass behind.
Brisk winds rip leaves from oaks.
Cold waves wrap man in cloaks.

Frigid weather call birds to flock.
Apathetic stand the livestock.
Snow-covered countryside looks,
God White Painted! Meadows and brooks.

Wild ducks and geese on wing.
Leader breaking the wind.
Resting and feeding nights,
Sustaining flock their flight.

Livestock letting farmers know,
Feeding time nears, they must go,
Hay, Alfalfa, Grain, and Oats;
To feed and grow thick coats.

Supper most Folks rather,
Nothing more than family gather.
Share bounty from land and Lord Divine,
Blessing the food on which they Dine.

Lewis En E'Crit

MARCEAUX, LOUIS. Pen Name: Lewis En E'crit; Born: Kaplan, Louisiana, 8-20-38; Married: 12-26-62 to Hazel M. Schexnider; Education: Kaplan High School Graduate Class of 1957; Occupation: Louisiana Department of Transportation and Development since 10-1-57; Memberships: Louisiana Engineers Aide Association & Public Affairs Research Council; Awards: World of Poetry, several Honorable and Special Mention awards; list of top poems by various publishers; Poetry: 'Autumn,' *Wide Open,* poetry magazine, 9-84; 'Wheat Field,' Poetry Press, 12-84; 'America's Freedom of Press,' APA, 3-85; 'Christmas,' *Pot Pourri,* 3-85; and 'Natural Day Dream,' Yes Press, 3-85; Themes: *God, Nature, Life, Death. Relaxation, Release Vexation, Mollification. God's role in all things.* Comments: *I plan to freelance full-time after retiring (from Louisiana Department of Transportation and Development) with at least 30 years of service, maybe 35 years of service. Writing will consist of historical ancestry and poetry.*

MOTHER

Gentle woman
    mother of the universe
        giving birth to all of life

Gentle woman
    walking silently among mankind
        ever giving of yourself

Gentle woman
    strong of heart and mind
        fragile as a blade of grass

Gentle woman
    loving and caring
        for each person that you touch

Gentle woman
    bathing my wounds
        cooling my fevered head

Gentle woman
    come touch my hand
        let me feel your strength
            and drink from your cup.

Jackie L. Booker

BOOKER, JACKIE LOUISE. Born: Portland, Oregon, 8-1-38; Single; Education: Two years of college; Occupation: Private Investigator; Memberships: International Association of Intelligence and Organized Crime Investigators, American Police Academy, CAAR; Poetry: Untitled, American Poetry Association, 1984; Comments: *I dare to enter the sanctum sanctorum of the mind and attempt to perceive the world through another's eyes. Were I to title a collection of my works, it would be "Observations of a Foolish Mind," always with the question: Do I know or do I think I know?*

TO MY CAT

A mischievous paw flirts with
a lock of brown hair.
A piercing meow precedes a
"tell me what you're doing today" stare.
Humans leave in haughty confusion
when you embrace me like a hairy sweater;
then your gray-green eyes seem to mock
"Michi, I understand you better."

Michelle A. Lovin

ROSAMOND

Across a satin ribbon,
   Written in words of gold;
is the name of my beloved,
   Rosamond — my Rosamond.

Like the light of a star shining,
   Her love for me — up there;
As beautiful as any angel,
   That walks the Golden Stair.

The pain of parting is so hard;
   I'll miss you, Rosamond,
You are my own true love —
   To you, my heart belonged.

Life must go on, my darling,
   Somehow I'll carry on,
You are my key to Heaven
        Rosamond — My Rosamond

Meva Cooper

COOPER, MEVA M. Pen name: Cricket; Born: Colorado City, Texas; 5-9-08; Widowed; Occupation: Retired Nurse, Song Lyricist; Other writings: 'Little Mother of Mine,' Poetry and Song, Nordtke Pub., 1945; 'Winter Moon,' Poetry and Song, Sta Pub. Co., 1946; 'Showers and Broken Sunshine,' Poetry and Song, Sta Pub. Co., 1946; 'Heartbeats,' Poetry and Song, unpublished; 'Sailboat in the Blue,' Poetry and Song, unpublished; Comments: *I am now writing two novels and a book of poetry. I write from the heart and memory. I have to feel what I'm writing.*

SPIDERMONKEY

You swing and laugh at gravity
Scooping up jungle
With excellent knowledge.
A pulsing pinwheel
Living a lazy confusion,
You gaze violently in your sleep
Seeking your friends in shadowless cities
Whose judgment has been taken
By tempered steel bars.
They peer back towards you
Only to see statues
Crying at the graffiti
On their sleeves.

William Costanza

MY CREATURE

He's made from a lump of clay.
He was here for only a day.

He was smashed by some
     people's hands,
Now he sings in an angel band.

They say he went away
    but I'll see him again
    some day.

When he's tired of walking on
    that golden strand,
He'll wait for me in
    that lovely land.

Glinda Young

YOUNG, GLINDA GAIL. Born: Munich, Bavaria, Germany, 1-22-65; Education: I am a freshman at Ohio State University, Marion. I want to get a Bachelor's degree in business with an emphasis in accounting. Awards: Award of Merit Certificates for 'My Hippo,' 1984; 'I Love You Because . . . ' 1985; 'On My Twelfth Grade English Teacher,' 1985; Comments: *I write for the sheer joy of it. I like having the words flow onto the paper right before my eyes. Sometimes, the words run through my mind and I just have to get up and write them down. Most of all I like it because it gives me a feeling of achievement.* Common Themes: *love, friends.*

MISSING YOU

A stolen kiss,
One last embrace.
Those do I miss,
Those, still do I taste.

It is said,
   Parting is such sweet sorrow;
I find it not.

It rings in my head,
   Piercing my heart to the marrow.
For it I seek not.

Elizabeth Waldrip

THE ROBIN

On this quiet winter morning,
   Long before the spring,
The ground with snow is covered;
   But, I heard a robin sing!
His faith is sure and steadfast
   That summer winds will blow
And he lifts his voice to heaven
   His thankfulness to show.

Give us, oh God, the courage
   These feathered friends can bring
So we, too know that surely —
   After snow — comes spring;
After trials comes peace of mind,
   Joy comes after pain;
Unwavering faith in Jesus
   Makes our lives good again.
                Louise W. Beers

AUTUMN RITUAL

The sighs of Summer
   Utter a silent cry
As the verdant foliage of hot days
   Turns a burnished bronze.
The vitality of life
   Slowly prepares itself for
      its annual ritualistic
         Death of Winter.
The warmth of the earth
   is transmogrified
      Into a cold, clay crypt,
Burying the remnants
      Of a former life,
Lying in a period of slumber,
   Resting and awaiting
      its resurrection
         Of a new season.
                Kenneth G. Geisert

NO LOVE TO GIVE

While everyone's asleep at night
I cry my silent tears
my dreams they keep me awake.
Until the early morning dawn.
Wondering about a newborn day
While as a child no love I had
growing up I had few friends
my fears they were many
But no one to share them with
No one to kiss my tears away
or take away my loneliness
no tender kiss upon my face
no gentle hands to guide me with
In the world that was to face me
The love I was given was like a
faded flower.
that dies and doesn't return.
                Martha Mullins

GOD'S JEWELS

God cast diamonds
   from the Heavens.
Each one a perfect
   tear-shape gem.

At night He placed
pearls against black velvet.
   During the day He set
A yellow diamond in the sky.
   jewels: rain, sun, stars and moon.
                Mary Streblow

HARBORLIGHTS

            . . . Swaying gently
by the glow
         of a mutual Moon,
our thoughts are anchored, buoyed
               in the harbor
      of Love . . .
                     . . . Closing
      my eyes, I cradle seashell ear
            near, so near — hearing
the echoes of a trembling heart . . .
            . . . gazing into eyes of
indigo-blue fathomless depths conceal
                  eternal mysteries . . .
. . . Kissing waiting lips,
            eagerly drink the waves
   of emotion wafting upon
               this thirsty shore . . .

. . . God . . . let us remain
                  anchored here . . .
      . . . forevermore . . .

      Sheldon Young

MY LOVE

*(Dedicated to Richard Coatney, with love,
Tammy)*

What more can i say
      Than i love you,
For what you mean to me,
For what you have given me,
For what you have shown me.

As every day passes
      The more i see you,
The more i admire you
For what, and who you are.

You have shown me
      More love and caring
With your silence
   Than a thousand words
      ever could . . . .

   Tammy Kipker

KIPKER, TAMMY. Born: Fairfield, California, 5-28-59; Occupation: Licensed Emergency Receiving Home for Foster Children; Poetry: 'Memories,' APA, Spring 1985; Themes: *Poems of Love;* Comments: *To help express my inner feelings I always have someone special in mind to inspire me. I feel that with today's society, everybody takes Love for granted, not taking the time to tell someone how special they are!*

TWO GIRLS

Two girls
Walking hand in hand

Looking at the rain
Playing in the park

Fingers entwined on hair
Gold, like a bee's honeycomb.

Two girls, looking at the rain
Bees buzzing sounds
Like gold silken thread rustling

Swinging on swings
Made of Ariel's web

And hair, silken hair,
Fine like a bee's buzzing

Two girls swinging arm in arm
Down some imaginary lane
Where there is place

For two girls
Happy

   Libby Bryant

LAMPS OF FRIENDSHIP

The little lamps of friendship
      We light along the way
Go shining on far down the years
      And brighten every day.
It's love that keeps them burning
      In sympathy and trust
God help us that no lamp goes out
      Because we let it rust.

Yes, every road is rougher
      Without good friends to cheer it;
The longest trip is shorter
      When friendships true endear it.
So measure then your riches
      In true friends and in old
More lasting, they, than silver
      More precious than pure gold.

While traveling through life's journey
      Let us pause along the way,
And make friends for a lifetime
      No, not for just the day.
Of music and of friendship,
      Time is the truest test,
For old friends, like our old songs,
      Are always loved the best.

   Florence M. Craven

Empty space
in the center of my being
engulfing my all
Not capable of being filled
by any human

Longing
in the center of my being
for something not comprehensible
to the human intellect

Filling
of the empty space
in the center of my being
by the spirit of God
bringing peace and love and joy

   Linda Comte

ONE MORE CHANCE

Last night I dreamed I died,
I awakened to my resounding sigh.
My God, I hadn't had the chance to pray,
or given any chance to say . . .

I want to cleanse and be forgiven,
now that the second chance is given.
To apologize for the hurt feelings,
in the wake of some sad dealings.

I want to rescind any unkind thought,
restore lost hope, which can't be bought.
A chance to show my love for him,
although at times, the view grows dim.

I want to kiss the child's cheek,
before too soon a mate she'll seek.
I want to touch an old friend's hand,
maybe walk together in the sand.

I want to smell the earth's fresh air,
with goals achieved to make it fair,
for my last wish, after all was said,
to never hear, "she's finally dead."

Marlene C. Cossette

TO BARBARA

A noble culture gilds
The fringes of your speech
And the candent curve
Of your loving lips

Golden light limns
Dimpled contours
Every curve and swell
Of your lovely form

A magnificent alchemy
Created living perfection
Of body and soul
And all that is you

Centuries of music
Cannot ease your absence
Nor lights of galaxies equal
The sparkle of your ardent eyes

The East's fabled perfumes
Cannot match your sweetness
Nor resplendent fall colors
The glowing sun of your smile

Donald J. Venturini

THE WEB

I want to avoid the web,
Yet I am intrigued by its design.
I decide to examine it closely.
I lazily hover above the web,
admiring the beauty of a task well-done.
I touch down upon the web,
my feet sink into the soft silk
    I am trapped!
I struggle to free myself.
I become further entangled, as
the proprietor of the web bounds
down upon me.
I feel her embrace,
her fangs sink into my flesh.
My mind whirls, my vision clouds,
my lifeblood is drained from me.
    I die!

Lewis Fram

ONE AND ONLY

You are the only one for me. There is so much that I want to
express to you, but the words I cannot find. My feelings for you
are so powerful inside my mind. Deep within my heart, I seek all
my dreams that I know want to come alive. In my dreams, it's you
that will arrive.
You are the one and only that so gently touches my emotions. They
move in such stimulated motions. The game of love is what we play.
Please don't lead me astray 'cause then all my love will live so
lonely inside my bones. I love you so strongly that my love is
burning red-hot. Do you feel the same way too?
You are the one and only that puts animation to all my impossible
thoughts. My one and only 'Oh' how I love you. You're my angel
from heaven. Into my arms you fell. I finally found my own glowing
star. You are my one and only by far!

Susan Hatker

HATKER, SUSAN LYNETTE. Born: Catskill, New York, 3-2-69; Education: 10th grade; Awards: Honorable Mention for 'Being With You,' 10-31-84; 'Pictures in My Mind,' 12-31-84; 'Deep-Hearted Love,' 2-28-85; Poetry: 'Being With You,' John Campbell, 10-31-84; 'All My Time,' 'If Only . . .' 12-12-84; 'Heartbeats,' 10-4-84; 'Without You . . .' 2-27-85; Comments: *My common theme is on love and the ups and downs of it. I write poems (mostly) to express my feelings that I have for a special person. I usually keep my feelings and emotions to myself and writing poems just lets me express them somehow.*

How can I know inside myself, what's inside of you?
To penetrate your inner mind, your thoughts to plainly see,
To look within your private house, the walls see clearly through,
And hear your secret meditations, spoken plain to me?

How to peer into your heart, see the person hid within.
Come to know your private self, a shrouded mystery kept so well,
Be priveleged with your confidence, know the things you're holding in.
Pierce the veil that's cloaking you, and penetrate your private shell?

I'm asking you to open up, your quiet self reveal.
I want to listen to your words, your free communication.
Just be yourself and talk to me, in honesty for real,
And show me who's inside of you, and give me revelation.

Just be at ease and let me see the person that you are.
Without your help I cannot know, you're really not an open book.
As much as you will let me see, by all means go that far.
Present the inner hidden you, and let me take a look . . .

Believe me when I tell you this, I count your words a sacred trust.
I'll set a guard upon my lips, the things you share I won't betray.
I'll shield your confidence in me, I'm friendship bound, by honor must,
Protect the things you give to me, and guard the private words you say.

Brandon McIntosh

SOMETHING HAPPENED THAT NIGHT

Something happened that night
Out by the water
Under the moon
And stars
And shadows of the night
Something wonderful happened
As I gazed into your eyes
And held you close in the coolness of the air
I was overcome by the gravity of your
        deep dark mysterious eyes
            and the warmth of your touch
Your smile led a path to my heart
        and I was overwhelmed by your sincerity
Something happened that night
That I care always to remember
For out by the water
Under the moon
And stars
And shadows
We started a beautiful relationship.

David Elsasser

3RD PLACE

A dark day, again and again;
things I touch
not seeing my own hands —
I am not afraid, I am only careful;
not to go too far from the sunset hills.

In the morning I drink a cup of strong tea,
a milky-gray day — good for lonesome fishing,
the resonance of boat, smooth and glossy air,
I boat along the bank, then left, towards a slight stream.

I scan the stream, seek the side of the spring,
turn my eyes towards the tops of the silent hills,
in the course of years whipped by raging winds
they show west — the way storms draw away.

A fresh track, in thickets of shore grass,
I get out of the boat, pacify my blood,
describe a circle; and though the wind roars
I hear a song, behind hills, an opening pass.

Zbigniew Konofalski

ONE METHOD OF FLIGHT

Flying is forever on my brain.
I am a child.
Wishing I could sprout wings and fly like a bird.
Looking at a picture of angels with wings.
Flying here and there; their method of transportation.
I would love to fly.
I tie a part of a bedspread around my neck and wrist.
By the sweat of my brow, I prepare to descend
From the barn window to the hay below.
I hold my breath and close my eyes.
I quickly jump.
I am flying, soaring like an eagle.
I move my arms to stay in flight.
Lower and lower I soar.
Gliding without care.
I drift as the wind touches my face and restyles my hair.
I am joined by flying things from the ground,
Bees, flies, dust and leaves.
I softly land on the hay.
But the desire to fly is there to stay.

Ann Lewis

ROAD OF LIFE

I'm walking down the road of life.
That was paved for by my Christ.
When they hung Him on the cross of Calvary

How they struck Him with the sword,
Blood and water flowed in the road
And the water and the blood did make us free.

How they wrapped Him in a linen sheet,
Rolled the stone and trapped Him neat,
Yet He arose to make our very life complete.

Yes the blood it sets us free,
To a life of eternity,
If we keep walking in the footsteps of our Lord.

So take up the cross of life,
Take the road that leads to the right,
And the Christ who saved your life is waiting for you there.

He will put His hand in thine,
Help you walk the narrow line,
Holding you close for His love of all mankind.

Delores Ballinger

AWARENESS,

feeling the warmth of the sun upon my arms
        I write the meaning of my emotions.

tears are now falling from my eyes as I
        discover the beauty of being alive.

the sounds of birds and cars sing with rhythm
        as they carry on.

suddenly an awareness of freedom flows through
        the air.

with a smile from my heart I consider the
        future with hope and confidence.

reality has become a sense of its own.

the past seems so far away, while the future
may never come.

aware of your presence, I'll allow my
        feelings to speak.

Liz Peralez

MY VISION

I dreamed I was a shepherd,
Near Bethlehem one quiet night.
I heard an angel chorus,
And saw His star shine bright.

It seemed I could see through the swaddling,
Scars on the hands and feet.
Of the Babe I saw in a manger,
So beautiful, tender and sweet.

I saw the marks on His tiny brow,
Foretelling the crown of thorns He'd wear.
On the way to a hill called Calvary,
And the cross He had come to bear.

I cried so hard my pillow was wet,
When I saw Him nailed to a tree.
Through my tears I saw no greater love,
He gave His life for a sinner like me.

Clara G. Stinson

HOW DO I TELL YOU?

I've spoken the words a thousand times before
Yet I feel the need to say them just once more.

How do I tell you of the joys I've saved; the
laughter and delight?

How do I tell you that you've been my morning
and my light?

How do I tell you of the loving times spent in
a hundred special ways?

Of candy-apple autumns, catfish summers and
dogwood days?

How do I speak to you in that fragile moment
when we must part?

How do I tell you? In the silence I can only
tell you with my heart.

Betty Allen

SISTERS

(For Evelyn and "Teddi")

Twins — Sisters — Humans Rare.
Compassionate, warm, loving — sincere
Close to truth and full of knowledge,
Long in years — and truly held dear.

Letters — Writings — Poetry
With loving concern and grace.
Offering heartfelt commiserations,
and unbounded sympathy.

Sweetness, kindness, caring thoughts;
Warmth, gentleness, hospitality.
Qualities of humanity rarely found today;
Residing in one's mind like the sun's warm rays.

Hearts so soft — as lilting music,
As the comforting touch of God's Holy Spirit.
Two souls in perfect harmony;
A veritable human symphony.

Paula jean Courtemarche

MICHELLE

Without a friend as sweet as you, what in the world, would I do?
You came to my rescue, when I was down and out
Now, how could a person just sit and pout?

There aren't many people, that care like you do.
But, you know, I care as much for you, too.
We haven't known each other too very long;
You've made me feel that I belong.

I think that Glen's pretty special too;
You make a good couple, the two of you.
You both made the kids enjoy Christmas this year,
Watch out you guys I just might shed a tear.

If ever there's a time when you need my help,
Just holler and scream and I'll be there myself.
So here's a hug and a kiss — be sure you don't miss;
To my new big brother and little sis . . .

Friends . . .

Cathy Blackman

She aged . . .
like burning candles that flicker out,
like smiles that come and go,
coaxing cares from those whose hearts had skipped a beat.

Time, rolling on with the waves
takes us as far as we want to go.
Do not let your dreams drown, though harsher
hands than hers may drag you down.

You'll resurface and float awhile
And be carried to the shore if you cannot swim
Either way, you'll know the tender touch of survival
The touch that makes the heartbeat faster,

Desire building, we mount her breakwater
and ride upon the body of the sea.

. . . and at the water's edge, dismounting,
and walking through the sand
We turn and see her graceful rise and fall . . .

Contentedly, she aged.

Susan L. Howerth

GOD'S GREATNESS

God's greatness shows us
He always gave His people the hope to endure the many problems
that may arise
He always gave His people the extra strength to find a
solution to their many problems
God's greatness shows us
He has never deliberately let His people down
He always had a reason for letting us suffer at our mistakes.

God's greatness shows us
He is able to bring His people together in a moment of crisis
God's greatness shows us
Many centuries ago He gave us His Son
He gave us Jesus Christ,
who was born under the great star
Jesus was put on this earth for a purpose,
just as we also were put on this earth for a purpose.

Jesus was nailed to the cross
He died for our sins
When we come to a point we cannot bear
Let us climb the mountaintop where He suffered.

Julie E. Crowder

FOREVER

Although years pass, allowing the escape of time,
The changing phases of the moon
Forever cast a golden glow
Upon your hair.
For you were mine
And eternally fair.

My eyes painted you
When love created a timeless spirit for a portrait,
Its aura becoming our chamber.
Candlelight of the soul
Burns beyond the grave —
Suspended are you in time
And eternally young.

Forever warmed by the rushing of passion's waves
We embraced and joined together,
Rocking, united, wet and weeping —
Bonded by the gift of one another.
We belonged to youth with tender grace
When you were mine and I yours —
And love seemed immortal.

Priscilla Taylor Cawley

THE LONE MADRONE

Gazing at the portly stance
I felt the soul of the
handsome tree with a
primordial sense.

Dark lustrous leaves
borne on slender smooth arms
overcast the secret of the
bark that sheds, showing a
wood already polished.

White bud flowers erect
hail the visitor to share the
sweet nectar and find the
lone Madrone to
consummate the cycle.

Naedeen McWalters

McWALTERS, NAEDEEN L. Pen Name:
Lenore; Born: San Jose, California, 1934; Education: Lane Community College, 1970; West
Coast College of Astrology, 1981; Occupations:
Licensed Practical Nurse; Computer Astrologer; Memberships: National Wildlife Association; Awards: Award of Merit, 'In Touch,'
1984; 'Inamorata,' 1984; Comments:
*Eventually I would like to provoke thought
where there wasn't any.*

WEDDINGS AND FUNERALS

Not much difference between the two,
All pomp and circumstance — a public
acknowledgment of a joining —
   or a leaving

The bride is fiftyish, in ecru lace.
Third time around for her
Twice with this same man

The groom is sixtyish in grey silk suit.
He pushes his wheelchair aside
So he can stand for the ceremony.
Chemotherapy has robbed him of
his hair, his strength and
one hundred pounds of his flesh —
but not, Oh God, his courage.

After the ceremony, champagne is served
to sad-happy guests who lift their glasses
to a joining —
     and a leaving.

Lorraine Standish

RETURN OF A LEGEND

Beauty come for Beast is calling
Young and sweet it is the dawning
Of a long forgotten lore

Hero stands with Lady nearing
Hand in hand, we be peering
To a small and distant shore

Doeskin black and safe with iron
But no shielding from the sirens
On their hidden homeland coast

Harp in hand, ice-fired eyes
Silken locks and flute-like sighs
The very gods shall be thoughtful hosts

Douglas D. Conklin

I'M GLAD I'M NOT A FLY

In the lily pads sits
   a bull frog
balancing upon the
    water.
Waiting for flies and
    whatever other
     insects that fly
      by.
What a simple life
   our frog has.
I'd rather let him
   eat the insects
   than I.
I think I'll just keep
   watching them
    fly by.

Julie Kirkendall

THE ARTIST

Frost painted the leaves
Green, brown, gold and red.
Early in the fall,
Before they were shed.
This array of color,
Is unmatched by man
The artist God painted,
As only He can.
He paints the rainbow —
He paints the sky
He paints the leaves —
Better than you or I.
He paints the roses
And the flowers in summer.
Then along comes winter
With His gleaming snow cover.

Hazel Nelson

A MIRACLE

Amongst the human rubble,
the trash of centuries,
I found
a salmon-colored marble.
I picked it up and held it high
into the morning sun.
I asked in wonderment
who then am I and suddenly
I felt
tears of uncertainty:
My gesture — of archaic priests
or of a child at play?

Andreas

I HATE IT WHEN THE DANDELIONS KILL THE FLOWERS!

*To Rena with love,
who grieves the loss
of seven family members
in an accident
caused by a drunk driver.*

The instrument of death
Four wheels and no more breath
Seven flowers upon a throne
are softly laid to rest.

Intoxicating power
Strew the little flowers
And escaped
With their last hour.

I hate it when the dandelions
Kill the flowers!

In seven little boxes
The precious ones displayed
As vivid memories live
Where the little flowers played.

God of mercy keep my bouquet
In heaven's sweet retreat
Where little flowers live
And at your feet we meet.

I hate it when the dandelions
Kill the flowers!

Dar Hartwig

FOR STEPHEN J., . . . BECAUSE I LOVE YOU

A cold November night it was
As the wind howled across the sky
The mission over, it was time to go
He made his final goodbyes

He packed his gear and made his plans
One last fling before he left.
He and his buddy had planned it all
Make the most of this night they said

On that cold November night she came
A stranger passing through
She'd done her part, it was time to leave
She had other things to do

He stared at her . . . she smiled at him
All other things forgotten
Yes Fate had played its hand that night
And set the wheels in motion

The morning light caressed the sky
When he left for parts unknown
A stranger . . . she had on her mind
As she drove the long road home

Not caring for the obstacles
Which life had put in their way
Everything works out for the best
The howling wind seemed to say

That's the way it was my friend
What will be will be
When least expected, Fate steps in
With all its glory and might
And that's how their love was born
On a cold November night

Gabrielle Mansfield

MEMORY: GOD'S "MASTERPIECE"

Somewhere deep within the heart
God forms a masterpiece
Mem'ry paints a precious part
Each picture bringing peace.

Bright the sunshine of a smile
Driving shadows away
Sharing heartaches all the while
Trusting for each new day.

Love painted skies true blue
Joy reached a mountain peak
Ling'ring dreams of rainbow hue
As memories we seek.

If the picture holds some rain
God paints it o'er with care
Mem'ry casts away the pain
Leaves love and faith to share.

From your tears He forms each gem
Makes them the picture's frame.
Blest the image held within
Then signs the "Artist's" Name.

Sara E. Page Smith

SMITH, SARA ELIZABETH. Sara E. (Page) Smith; Born: Logan County, Illinois, 9-4-15; Married: 6-11-32 to Russell H. Smith; Education: Returned to school, received High School diploma the same school and year with my five grandsons graduating. Have three college credits and would like to finish the course.; Occupations: 30 years Business Office, Credit Managing, Senior Citizen Activities Director; Memberships: Church of the Nazarene, National Society Daughters of the American Revolution, Logan County Genealogical Society, Lincoln, Illinois; Poetry: 'Ancestors,' *Central Illinois Genealogical Quarterly, Vol. IX, No. 1,* 2-73; 'Across State Line,' Book & Records of Clark County, Illinois and Vigo Co., Ind. NSDAR, 1976; 'Swift Wing, My Love,' *American Poetry Anthology Vol. III, No. 1-2,* 1984; Other Writings: *Family and Church History* — Articles in "History of Logan Co., Ill." Taylor Publ., Dallas, Tex, 1982; *My Heart Reached a High Hill,* Poetic Devotions, Book of 75 poems; Contributed to book, *The Loving Family in America,* Harp and Thistle, Warner Robbins, Georgia, 1981; Comments: I believe God inspires my poetry. Most words I say or letters written are inadequate. Only through a poem can I express myself. Then I feel complete and content. I write for self-satisfaction and to share with others. I write of relationships, love, heartbreak, dreams, ideals, grief, nature, animals, etc., also devotional and patriotic.

DESIRE IS THE EYE OF THE BEAST.

With my hand I trace your hand, unweaponed babe, and with human lip
embrace fragrance of your skin, unsullied, without scent of mortality
yet encrusted. We accept easily you know nothing, although you assume
and witness enormity with a frightening clarity and with a purity
relinquished by ourselves. Much paused with a falling seed.

You've distinguished lone fowl wing pilgrimage on heavenly avenue, so
intensely desirous of roost in one ampler world by them sedulously gathered,
once in time's lighter mood. Abusers of the vision of innocence, we
acknowledge all absence of twilight, and the confusion of beast and infant.

Pensively the sails bend from the harbor unheralded, wreathlessly,
requesting waters to lend balance. Beneath our waters' humbling urge
moves maelstrom, yet the sea forgives a floating existence, submits.

The grapes winnow up the field, are burst by females brutal and fantastic,
by males too accusative of less than you, (mild child,) and lascivious lips
unzip to incur the sweet juice and it plunged madly within seamy tissues
unctuously and limps in stale rivulets animal maws and animal bellies
earthward, bloodily to burnish costumes with a martial vehemence.

Alas, my babe, I am no better and no worse, for so gratefully I pull
the luscious blood and grovel unminded and maudlin, and, the damp nightmare
you suck so thickly channels your challenging streams and kills you.

D. Castleman

HER NAME WAS DORIS

When she was a young girl full of dreams
(That day wasn't really so long ago)
Just to hear her name spoken out loud
Would fill her with a trembling presence of what that name would someday mean.

He came into her life flying banners of glory
After her name and she had reached their shining pinnacle
Then they began to drift on a lonely downward arc
He vowed his love would change that course and bring her back to joy.

But she thinks forevers don't last that long these days
Though she believed it all when he gave her his name
She still cries when the white light of his passioned promise
Sputtered and went out so soon.

Oh it's still true people, she still has his name
But hers ceased to be so long ago
She hasn't heard it spoken out loud in a thousand days
No one really knows if the girl or her name are still alive.

See the fool and her folly waiting in limbo hoping he will remember who she is
Hoping he will notice there were two of them on the pathway to today
Tell the fool to waken and emerge from her tunnel of dead things
Throw a three-sided dice and go away where she can hope or dream or live once again.

Doris I. Warren

COME FLY WITH ME

"Come live with me and be my love." Ah me, if only it could be, dear one.
The words are beautiful, they thrill my soul, tug my heart and excite my dreams,
And I have waited long to hear these very words from you. But still, I feel
It cannot be, nor could it work; for though it's true that you are still your
Same dear self, that dearest heart I loved so well, I am not the same; for
I have changed and grown, my feet don't touch the earth, and truth to tell
My mind and heart are one with God and all His Universe. I've learned to
Stretch my soul and take wings. Shall I become earth-bound?
Can I forsake my destiny? If only you would let your mind expand, let loose
Your soul, open your heart and stretch your wings along with me.
Imagine the worlds we'd find unbound by mundane eyes, the galaxies we could
Explore beyond our farthest fantasies. Stranger things and seeming
Inconsistencies have happened oft before, have blended well together,
Perchance the gods could make it happen just once more?
Could you unwrap a portion of your soul, the part that's hidden from your eye,
We might traverse this Cosmos, you and I.
Oh, dearest one, come fly with me . . .
Let's fly!

Isolde V. Czukor

A MEMORY OF LOVE

I remember New York City
in April. When the lilacs bloomed
at the Cloisters.
Enchanting Spring —
In some forgotten year.

In my memory is an apartment
shared by two
And sounds of love and laughter
are filling the rooms.

We never belonged there —
as some people do.
Our stay was brief . . .
Even before Spring ended
            we parted.

I traveled to distant worlds —
Living in strange places . . .
But I lived with the memory
of sharing your love
in an apartment in New York City
            Many times . . .
Years ago.
            Marie Geile

RUSHING WATERS

Down rush the waters
Of the mountain high.
Down rush the waters
In a gushing sigh.

There by bubbling stones
She spends her day.
There by the bubbling stones
The child goes to play.

Above the roaring waters
Hangs a pale blue sky.
Above the sing waters
The girl's day goes by.

By the babbling waters
She lies all alone.
By the whispering waters
The woman's day is done.

Above the gushing stream
Stand the stately pine.
Above the chatting stream
Wind begins to whine.
            Carolyn S. Crawford

INTIMATE LONGINGS

You stared at me; I at you
A chanced meeting
At a moment when both
Were weathering desolation and despair
We shared the same thoughts
Much more the same dreams
Of finding our own places
In this universe
A brief encounter but nevertheless
Had made our lives richer and meaningful
Such a twist of fate
To find love with so little time
You need to go; wish you luck
And hope we find each other again
Possibly another time
In another place
In the world
Which we could call our very own!
            Evelyn B. Bergonio

REFLECTIONS

I used to know a reflection
So beautiful and bright
With eyes so very shiny
They lit up like a light
The reflection seemed so happy
And it always wore a smile
Its face was always bright
Just like a little child's
What happened to the reflection
Is to some a mystery
The reflection that replaced it
Is a sad sight to see
Its eyes are misty from crying
Its face is streaked with tears
This is the reflection I see now
As I look into the mirror
            Karen Edwards

falling in love
again
no
this is different
somehow
this feels light
        with hope
this feels bright
        with color
this feels warm
        with peace
this feels gentle
        with love
this feels strong
        with power
        to carry me
        away
        from my fears
            Jan Miller

SPRING IS ON ITS WAY

The wild geese are flying North,
In a beautiful, perfect "V".
Spring is on its way,
What a thrilling sight to see.
Their long necks stretched out in flight,
With a constant conversation,
As they wing their way Northward,
In search of their destination.
But how do they know where to go —
Where their nesting place will be?
I find a lump rising in my throat,
They are so beautiful and free.
Yes, spring is on its way.
The wild geese are now in flight.
What a wonderful symbol of freedom,
As they disappear out of sight.
            Romie Clouse

HEAVENLY FLIGHT

As my spirit soars to heights unknown
I feel God's warm embrace.
I touch the clouds as they pass by
And yield within their grace.
I'm carried oh so softly
To a star that's shining bright;
It glistens so, with a saintly glow
I can't believe the sight.
Then suddenly I feel a pull,
I know I must return
To a body that lies sleeping
So lessons can be learned.
            Lori Thienel

(FOR THE) LOVE OF A ROSE
Dedicated to Grandma with Love

Lasting
    but
a brief instant
in the infinity
        of time;
Yet
    possessing
splendor beyond
the elegant magnitude
        of space;
        conceived
only
        to begin to end
and,
    with silent
demur
enduring the pace.
So passes
the love
of a rose.
        So passes life.
        Christine M. Hansen

THE LONG WAIT

HONORABLE MENTION

Brisk young woman in white,
please look past lined brow,
canvassed chair with chrome wheels,
sterile green walls lonely
To smooth beauty of youth,
vibrant dancing vitality,
home filled with laughter,
children, friends, old loves,
And see me as I really am.

Frown not on my pitiful pleas
for simple pleasures needed now
for my survival — for my worth
As I sit trapped within
strange body, unfamiliar halls —
antiseptic, frightening, bare,
watching others like myself,
waiting, waiting, waiting
for only a kind word,
            understanding,
                death.
        C. Lynn Bennett

MISSING YOU

why did you say you loved me
and that you cared
If you weren't really going to
be there?
why did you make me feel so
warm inside your arms
And then just let go?
I believed there was really
an us!
It is hard to realize it's over
but I must
And I have something you
will never take away.
That is the memories we had
together — and now again I'm in
a daze.
All I ever wanted in life is just
to have someone to care.
And when I needed that special
hug they were there!
I miss you so much and long
for your soft touch.
            Karen A. Robare

WINTERTIME REFLECTION

Dear Lord when it comes my time to go,
Please don't call me away in the snow.
Give me the call some day in spring,
When the first flowers bloom and the robins sing.

Let me depart on a gentle breeze,
When spring first kisses the mountain trees.
I'll greet these things along the way,
And tell them I'm sorry that I can't stay.

Give me this last memory to keep
Before forever I fall asleep,
Grant it so when I leave this earth,
I may witness the promise of thy rebirth.

Minnie Fargo

STILL WATER

I gaze upon still waters —
Each motionless wave, tranquility —
Basin in my soul brimming,
No wind, no rain.

Reflections veneer the water —
Storms of days old —
Wrath of the wave unruffling;
I will nap upon the vessel.

Vex me not you gust of wind;
Allow one weary soul to drift.
Ventures through deserts have brought me thus far,
To gaze upon still waters.

Zel Carr

Today let me awake to the chirping of the birds.
Watch the butterflies flutter from flower to flower.
Today let me smell the sweet fragrance of the rose.
and the honeysuckle blossoms beside the road.
    For there will be no tomorrow!
Today let me smile at a friend and shake their
hand and tell them how much I value their friendship.
Today let me do well the things my hands find to do
and leave nothing undone for tomorrow.
    For there will be no tomorrow!
We lay our head upon our pillow at night and drift
off into dreamland. Sometime in the wee hours of
the night tomorrow drifts away in the mist of the
darkness.
We awake in the morning and it is today.
    For tomorrow never comes.

Dora Joseph

MY SENTIMENTAL HEART

To whom does my heart belong?
It's unfair that I have to die when my heart
lives on.
It can stop and it will stop in its own time.
I listen to my heartbeat
and it chases after affection and yet
it does no harm.
My heart is bold, anxious, strong but weak.
Whatever? A feeling is always there.
Why do I love when it's time to love?
My heart loves to love love and still
it does very little for me.
Until it's in the right place, my heart will
run on like an escaped prisoner.

Jennie Elizabeth McLean

CIRCUMSPECT LOVE

A message for you drifts my love
Immediate and constant to my mind
From the depths where I've buried deep
The bond that burns and never sleeps

Two lives we are with souls as one
We searched our hearts and found the sun
Which glows brightly in aura rare
Few find the secret garden there

But we have known of the silent waters
That stir as we draw close
To gaze into the pool inviting
Ne'er to touch our lips that thirst

For there are those who know so well
When drawing nigh the heart that tells
Silently, pleadingly of kindred desire
Fantasy alone to feed the fire

Brushing flesh tender ecstasy
For wandering hearts like you and me
Content in myriad reveries
Of what might have been . . . yet never to be

Elaine Feazell Szemkus

A POEM ON PRIDE

Traveling is fun to do,
But you always compare it to home.
When you go and see the world,
Appreciation for *your* land is shown!

America is where I'm from,
Home of the free and the brave.
I wouldn't trade it for anything else,
Better than the rest so we rave!

The melting pot of every country,
Looking for a good way of life.
People from all over flock to the States,
Away from their troubles and strife.

Although we're still young, we're clever and bright,
Competing and beating the rest.
I'm so damn glad to be a small part,
A resident, not just a guest.

Pride in a place as deserving as ours,
A *true* American has,
A chance to accomplish your wildest dreams,
Remember, we don't finish last!

Anne Maul

TO LOSE HEART

To lose heart
When rough winds fly
When wild storms encounter your eye
Be calm my heart
Soon you will see the heavens blue

To lose heart
When dark clouds beckon the sky
When God gives us a sign through harsh weather
He is straining the sinner's heart
And awaken him from his lust and powers wild
But don't be disturbed, he won't hurt his child

To lose heart, when people hate you in this world
And throw stones your way
Believe you cannot change their way of life
God relieves you from abundant strife

Maria Leber

DISAPPEARING

The dismal sky, it sheds its tears
And whispers words of hope that aren't sincere.
The lonely people, clutching for golden cups,
Don't realize that they aren't loved —
Just forgotten by Time.

Deanna Lynne Schrier

McCORMICK, DEANNA LYNNE. Pen Name: Deanna Lynne Schrier. Born: San Antonio, Texas, 9-3-63; Married: 9-3-83 to Douglas L. McCormick; Occupations: United States Navy Personnelman/Yeoman; Awards: Elizabeth Dorrance Award, June 1981; Poetry: 'Desert Anger,' American Poetry Association; *A Chance Encounter*, poetry book, copyright; 'I Love You,' Oxford VA; Comments: *I have been writing poetry and short stories ever since I can remember. Most of my poems are either personal experiences or observations.*

ONLY ONE MAN

Who am I to take on your pain?

How can I give you the strength to fight —
    fight for the health and life you so rightly deserve?

How can I make you see the good in yourself
    I so easily perceive?

When you cry, when you feel the anguish of your
    existence, I too cry.

As you die unto yourself, a part of me dies with you
    I am not a god — I am only one man.

I say lean on me, I am strong enough to accept your
    fears, your doubts.

I can support you as you strive to make sense of your life.

I can challenge you to discover the truth
    But I cannot take away the pain.

I cannot make the discovery of who you are any easier.

I cannot give you peace of mind, only the means to
    understand what peace is.

But I can care — care deeply for the person you are

    yesterday, today and tomorrow.

Janice C. Jordan

MY FLOWER, I LOVE YOU

You are the flower that blooms within my heart,
    so beautiful, so honest, so true;
    It's like the voice of a meadowlark
    when my arms reach out for you.
I opened my heart and let love come in,
    knowing how sweet it would be;
    love was meant to have wings of joy
    that will keep you so near to me.
You are the flower that blooms within my heart,
    that's where you will always be.
I will guard this precious possession,
    today and through eternity.
    If my flower fails to bloom,
    my life would end, I know.
    I could not live without you.
    My flower, I love you so.
Now the years have passed on by
    and God took you away.
My eyes are growing dimmer
    and my hair is lined with grey.
I've replaced my flower for a star
    that shines so bright above;
    it tells me you are waiting,
    just waiting for me, my love.

Betty Butler

"Suppose we saw that the poem is an organism. Then it has a physiology. We will figure its organs, and to me it seems satisfactory if we say they are three: the head, the heart, the feet." — John Crowe Ransom

This poem runs fast as a pony headed
for the fenced grey barn. Give the poem
its head; the heart will be reflected
in a daisied pond near the pasture.
You must image a child, cooling
the pony after the run; there is a hose
with a curve of water in sparklets.
In the grey barn, an incense of hay
and warm honeysuckle. The child leads
the pony there, stroking the wet mane
with a hand, fat and tan as the pony.
If you have done as asked, you have made
a poem while the daisies did nothing
but nod in a breeze that ripples
the pond.

Charlotte Gafford

CLIMB A TALL MOUNTAIN

His hair was like gold,
Shining in the sun.
He shouted, Hey; Everybody watch me,
See how fast I run,
I can fly like a bird, climb to the sky,
Run like the wind, and do you know why?

It's all the love that I get, day after day.
For me, my dear mother prays,
That God will keep me happy and strong.
That's why I can do these things all day long.

I can sail a big ship,
Fly a big plane,
Climb a tall mountain,
Play in the rain.
I can swim like a fish, jump far and wide,
His eyes are all bright, and sparkling with pride.

Dear God, please keep him happy and strong,
Fill him with faith, keep him from wrong.
Give him courage, wisdom, and good health,
And all of the things, that mean more than wealth.

Faye Randell

BLAKE, Dante's Inferno: The Whirlwind of Lovers

DAUGHTER'S WEDDING DAY

What a lovely time for you, my pet,
I know it must be true
For soon those lovely wedding bells
Will be ringing just for you.
I've watched you grow; the time seems short
From a baby to a girl
And your precious face, so fair to all
Has always been my world.
I hope I've helped you through the times
When it hurt so much to grow.
Having you to fill my life
Means more than you can know.
You mean so very much to me;
You are life's dearest treasure
And I wish the very best for you
Beyond what life can measure.
May your wedding day, my love,
Be the brightest you have known
And may God truly bless this union
With a love-filled, happy home.

Mary Kay Reynolds

TODAY

Wondering through life, counting clouds
which run as fast as the hours which I live.
Wandering, I amble through that narrow path
which will take me to that place I call home.
I whistle with the thrush and
pull what impedes my passage.
Twilight dies and the lights of the nocturnal sky
kindle one by one with each thought of mine.
I proceed and with my eyes,
I am master of the horizon
and the sun that sets.
En route towards my slumber,
thoughts of the light which I
forgot to kindle provoke me to run.
The moon laughs while tears of horror
dim my windows to the world.
In the distance I see
the blackness which I know is my sojourn.
Almost, almost reach it but . . .
One breath and all is dust and tomorrow.

Lydia Rijos

YESTERDAY

Yesterday, they took my neighbor's son to jail,
And his parents kept asking "Where did we fail?"
He'd been a good soldier for Uncle Sam
And fought bravely in Viet Nam.
Though he tried to get back in the game,
He knew things could never be the same.
Those faces kept coming back at night,
And he'd relive some horrible sight.
We grew up on the same block,
And he and I could always talk,
But now I didn't know what to do
He was very quiet, and the gap between us grew.
I had one day thought I'd be his wife;
Now I just wanted to erase it all, and give him back his life.
He left us for people who understood,
In a way none of us ever could
They were there too, and so they felt his pain
With them, he didn't have to explain.
I hope someday he'll let me in,
Because no matter what, I'm still his friend.

Peggy Pierson

THE WOLVES OF TIME

Racing across Heaven's dome
In an eternally set course,
The fiery, horsed vehicle blazes.
Even the spheres are set in their dance.

The child cries out to the lesser beauty
That passes in a lower state.
Holding the reins of his golden coursers,
He stretches out a free hand to his silver sister,

And goes on his way. The nine spheres
Chime in their heavenly laces,
And angels cry out as the hungry wolves
Pursue their fleeing prey.

The skies tremble as armies march
In giant strides towards the arching bridge,
And the old gods fight, lest darkness fall,
All the legions of Hell.

For the wolves of Time devour the Sun,
Who stretches out a despairing arm,
And drags his sister into his fiery embrace
To take her down into eternal night.

Lynn McCrary

LIKE FATHER, LIKE SON
or
Boys Will Be Boys

Two little boys were playing one day
While the fathers were branding,
     some distance away.
The boys decided that they, too,
Would find themselves some branding to do.

They looked around
To see what could be found
To take the place of cattle to brand.
They finally decided it would be grand
To do a job on the fowls at hand.

So each, a pair of scissors found
And went to work with busy hands;
And when their mothers looked for them
They were clipping the wings of the family's hens.

It never was told what the mothers said
But I would guess that they took the shears
And back to the house the boys were led
And given a lesson they'd remember for years.

Charlotte M. Lewis

ODE TO A REDEMPTION

A shadow of mythology
A prayer for humanity
Encompassed by a darkened sky, eternal night
Existence is a sense of being, a mystery

A brotherhood will take control
of futile attempts to win a war
Consistent are man's tendencies
to violate the natural state
A traitor to his own creator

To his world, an amnesty
Among the stars a sun will beam
and resurrect the will of man

As now he is meant to coexist,
in time, as one, with the monolith

Brenda Kloiber

LOST DREAMS

Dreams are lost to those of us who remain indifferent,
  never lending themselves to go beyond their own limitations.
Even if we fail in our attempts in reaching those goals,
  it is not important. For if the cause is just,
  others will carry on, and the cause will triumph.
And if the cause is not just, that too is not important,
  for to put forth every last ounce of personal effort
  will be all that is needed. And in the end of all of this,
  if we still have lost our dreams to our indifference,
  we will have only ourselves to blame.

Those dreams that we lost due to our indifference,
  shall always come back to us in one form or another.
In whatever we do, or do not do, in those things which
  we cannot control, or understand. And all our tomorrows,
  will be an attempt to recapture past glories, and lost dreams.
And after all we do is over, if we are left without any dreams,
  this will be our personal punishment in which we all must
  learn to live with, due to our own lost dreams.

Randall Tom

SOUTHERN SUNSET

How the sky overwhelms me,
From the North to the East and back over to the West.
The part I love best
Is the South sky where I gaze,
As it's set all ablaze.

In Carolina the dusk loves its part.
As any great artist could, it warms the heart.
Creatively preparing a master's surprise,
A fabulous feast for worn and weary eyes.

Accessories almost none,
A few cumulus clouds and one vast and inflammable sun.
Mix and match and mingle
They set the sky afire.
Brightening your darkest dreams and highlighting your
innermost desire.

But oh, darkness fills the sky as the opening act ends
and the curtain falls.
The "real stars" come on the floor,
Leaving me here applauding.
I do believe a "Southern Sunset" deserves an encore!

Colleen Marie Zygmund

DIALOGUE . . . IN SEARCH OF WORK

Lord Jesus, where?
Where do You want me to go!
Day and night I search — hopefully, tirelessly, unrelentlessly
Pleading, seeking
But where Lord?
Where should I go now?

Possess me
Assure me
Connect me,
Comfort and
Secure me Lord.

Yes! "Your Kingdom come
Your Will be done."
Again I search streets, cities, towns —
Search for work.

He looked gently on me — "Rise faithful child, rise.
Courage, perseverance, conquer all
Put your hand in My nail-print Hand
Together We go
Armed secure . . . in search of work."

Sister Caritas Martinez

MEMORIES

You have given me a rare gift you know.
Allowed me to be free, allowed me to grow.
To know who I am, and what I will be.
You have allowed me to be me.

You have shown me the beauty of the world it seems.
Encouraged me to follow my dreams,
To seek and fulfill the wonders of life,
And to know the beauty of being your wife.

We have built memories you and I,
We have soared high into the sky,
Above the clouds, above the sea,
Building memories for you and me.

Our children are like all dreams complete,
Which God has entrusted in us to keep.
He has given us the power and wisdom to know —
When to set free to grow.

Tommia (Luttrell) Asher

IN SECRET

In secret places in my heart
  I let your memory grow;
Then in dreams you are so near
  your children do not know.

They think it does not matter now
  So many years have gone,
I pretend it's that way too
  no need to prove them wrong.

Yet it's only when I see your dear sweet face
  my heart is filled with song!
It's knowing you shall greet me there
  though it takes forever long.

So in the sunset of my years
  I let your memory hide!
You chased away those salty tears
  and filled my life with pride.

Belva C. Call

THE TRUE ARTIST

To see a glorious new sunrise,
And the beautiful colors of butterflies;
  When I smell fresh flowers in spring,
I know God thought of everything.

When I hear birds singing in the trees,
Or the wind whispering through the leaves;
  I find the beauty of His touch,
In these things I cherish very much.

Who else could know our every need,
Except Thee Who brings life from a seed?
  With showers of His loving grace,
He makes this world a better place.

God is the true artist in every way,
To love Him more each day I pray;
  And joyfully now my heart I give,
And just for Thee I will live.

Cheryle Dawn Hart

MY DIARY

My diary is a little book that my dad left for me.
I knew that after he passed on, that book was still empty.
He bought that book for who knows what he planned that book to be.
Only now that book is full as it can be. I do not write every day,
It is too much for me, but when I do some special thing
Like writing poetry, attending weddings, writing
Folks who tell me what they do, what I cook and
When I bake that pizza pie or great big cake,
About the cookies I'm asked to take to potluck
Dinners at church or club
I could never remember the time or date as
The days pass by; it is my fate to think about
What the future holds and forget the past as
Time goes by so very fast. The little ones are
Big ones now. I can return to those precious
Days of long ago and read about their childhood
Ways from crawling to riding a trike
And then a bike; after awhile they will drive a
Car and travel the roads to places far.

Eva Cook

DON'T TELL SUMMER

On a freshly covered valley; with a crispness in the air
I stand and feel the snow-laden land; with its blanket everywhere

It's moments like these I cherish, when my eyes tear up from chill
And the quietness that abounds here; seems like it always will

It's so different from the springtime, when the newness breaks the ground
And there's a freshness with the flowers as each one opens with a sound

And the summer meadows linger; a sultry haze that heats the air
Not a time to gaze in silence; when I walk in stillness there

And the leaves that swirl past me, crash and break on autumn's ground
There's no escaping to the oneness; there's no silence to this sound

Until it's back to winter's stillness, and its darkness closes in
And I feel God's warmth around me; even though it's always been

So, crisp night, in a hallowed winter; I scorn your days but love your night
Don't tell summer about these feelings; let each feeling be what's right

So take my breath and cover your beauty; break my words as they hit the air
Wrap me in your embrace of twilight, in the winter — love's found there

Lucky Rimpila

RIMPILA, LUCKY DEAN. Born: Wadena, Minnesota, 7-3-50; Education: High School, Hastings High School, Hastings, Minnesota; Occupation: Sales Manager, Medical Supply Co.; Poetry: 'Into Me (Echoes of Winter),' 1985; 'Canyons of Echoes,' 1985; 'Side By Side,' 1985; all published in *New Voices in American Poetry*, Vantage Press; Themes: *Life and death, the ups and downs of.*

THE EVERPRESENT GOD

The Lord God's at my right hand
And tells me not to fear.
Whatever things may happen,
With me He will be here.
He is forever with me
Throughout my life each day,
And He does always listen
To me when I do pray.

I am abandoned never
By the great Lord on high,
Though others may deride me
And make me want to cry.
And when my life is ended,
To heaven I shall come
To dwell with my great Father
In His holy kingdom.

Suzanne Clement

MOTHER'S LOVE

I live in a very private world,
    Within my mother's womb,
Protected, loved and cherished,
    In this very safe cocoon.

Never in want, never in need,
    Free from all knowledge of fear,
I am fulfilled no matter the creed,
    Because mother is always there.

A day will come when I must meet her,
    I must leave this world I've known,
I'll yell and cry when I greet her,
    But the love she has always shown,
Will comfort me in my new world,
    No matter how old I've grown.

Jacinta B. Phang

UNREQUITED LOVE

Slowly she walked down the aisle
Of the dimly lighted church
Looking for him. He was there
In the same pew; the same gray coat
That knew of her love for him, but could
Not tell, and he would never know.

She knelt behind him, moved up close;
So close, her fingers touched his coat;
So close, her blushing face did brush
Against his dark brown hair.
A soul did stir; a heart, it leaped!
He did not move, absorbed in prayer.

He did not know a heart had cried . . .
That heart had now been satisfied.

Vander Smith

FOR THE SAKE OF LOVE

As the wind and I know,
Regardless of what the night brings;
It shall not bar, a new tomorrow.
The coming of another day,
A chance to start again;
For the sake of life
For the sake of love
For the sake of you
I care,
I really find I do.

Kathryn Tracy Allen

THE ICEBERG AND THE TORCH

I touched it once,
  and it was warm.
When I was young,
  and in all her charm.
It grew hot,
  as a torch.
I pulled away,
  before it scorched.

And grew into,
  an icy cold.
The blueing flesh,
  for me to hold.
Colder and colder,
  year upon year.
A heated cold,
  tear by tear.

You can change,
  my iceberg, nay.
You a torch,
  melt me away.

  changing face.
You are no match.
  you are here to stay.
    Francis Stroeder

SUMMER

11TH PLACE

in the slumbrous blue
cupped over the world
we stroll down our street
with freer limbs in
virgin night

clustered hydrangea
    plumped lilac grapes
against
heated stucco

home, I bathe in ash darkness
musk dissolving
from my skin

gingered
Ivory foam
in rivulets slithering
between my feet

in the bare window
in the fluorescent beacon of a church:
lemon crucifix without
the hanging flesh and bones
    Susan Penberthy

DEPARTURE

When I leave
As I must go
My children free
Left to hold
A memory
As the final knock
Comes to the door
And winter's ghost
Lies near ahead
May sleep take me
From my bed
I'll go joyously
To ever tread
Eternity.

    Linda Lyness Wright

DAWNING

A gentle breath of coolness blows
  Across the fairways green.
The rippling water hazard shows
  Flags flutt'ring, so serene.
How peaceful and relaxing, this
  Time early in the day,
When rays of sun reach out to kiss
  The clouds of night away.
The grass is moist with early dew;
  It glistens in the sun.
And wisps of mist rise up anew;
  Another day's begun.
    Andree C. Peters

OUR PLACE

Our place was meant to be.
It was meant for us
it's all we have left;
us and our place.
Nothing else matters
until the time comes.
No one else knows,
and ever will.
We leave slowly
as time passes.
We leave everything else behind,
as the future passes.
    Karen M. Lane

LIMBO

Here am I
        suspended
in time and space
The past too painfully sweet
    to dwell on
The future too insecure
    to contemplate
Like a puppet on a string
        waiting
for an unknown force
to propel me forward —
    to what?
    Creta Stickney

MOTHER MENTOR

You cradled me in your arms
  in the beginning
Taught me how to view the world
  in perspective
Through the years, I would falter;
Your patience was my crutch
Which I would lean on often.
Your love — my secret medicine
To heal the wounds of growing up
While I grew older, you grew wiser
Then passed that wisdom on to me
What I have is yours.

    Gordon A. Salway

FOOTPRINTS

Our footprints melt in the snow
and wash from the sand.
Few are the footprints
that time will see
and even fewer are they
that history will remember.

    Jacqueline A. Thompson

I SPEAK
— for me

I speak
in recognition of my greater me
my higher me.
I take a pen in hand
and create.
The words,
sometimes fast
sometimes slow,
spill onto the page
and obeyingly take their positions.

I speak
of the moon
the sky
God and man.
Me and you.
I speak
in full appreciation
of my greater me
my higher me.

    Lewis P. Bell

CLOSED TO THE WORLD

The beautiful words
Are written by fools
Whose eyes are of visions
And hearts made of jewels

The music and sorrow
Can bring laughter and tears
And the one who is lonely
Only he who hears

Closed to the world
Are those wonderful things
That people can't reach
And very few who can see
And the many who wonder
Are the ones who seek me

Yes, I am the fool
Who can write you this vision
But they're closed to the world
As to be only misgiven

    Cary Robinson

LINES

HONORABLE MENTION

She calls me on the phone —
the wire wrapping around me,
strapping me to her voice.

Months apart dissolve.
We were never strangers,
just dangerous to each other.

She pokes the fireplace that is my mind.
The good times sparkle and snap,
the flames throwing a glowing warmth.

I sliced these ties that bind.
She spliced them.
Once again power trickles away from me,
dripping into the cup she holds.

Her voice gives me rebirth
all the while she is killing me.
She wants all my lives.

    Charles E. Ambrosia

KINDRED FRIENDS

Part of yourself, every day you do give
To strangers, to friends, each day that you live.
Yet certain "secret parts" that are mostly unknown
Are kept for specially chosen people alone.
Those "secret parts" which you hold with tight reign
Will take a special person, those secrets to gain.
A person of greater understanding and
            deeper appreciation
Will be the type of person to receive that revelation.
Most people are not of that type,
            they don't even come near it
For it takes a person of kindred mind and
            kindred spirit.
To that person, Goodbye is a word you will never say
For the part that you've given, he'll take away.
Yet you feel no sense of loss, just a gain in the end
For he's more than a kindred soul,
            he's a kindred friend.

Volten Corley

TWO WORLDS

Our science fiction tells about another world,
      A universe that parallels our own:
A world we see, another world we cannot glimpse;
      Of matter one, to matter one unknown.

Could it, in truth, be that the universe we see
      Is one projected from that other clime;
Our thought and feeling, mind and heart somehow derived
      From that far world around us all the time?

When we behold the sunlit, snow-crowned mountain heights;
      The foothills' miracle of spring's appeal;
The summer ocean rolling ageless, blue and free,
      Beyond all these, unseen is something real.

This world beyond, with our world somewhat parallel,
      A spirit-world, like spirits this unseen,
Influences our lives as far-off sun and moon
Make earth a vibrant, ever-pleasing scene.

Lord Jesus to disciples said: Thy will be done
      On earth, as it is done in Heaven high.
We are of two worlds born. In this world hear
      For that bright world your own heart's secret sigh!

Everett Francis Briggs

ONE'S ON THE WINDOW GLASS

Right now as I glance I see millions, perchance,
Yet, it's a warm day and they'd rather away stay.
Sometimes they make a haze that on no one can I gaze,
As each so closely flows and none itself singly shows.

One's on the windowpane, strung with many a vein,
For I count twenty and four, yet there are many more.
As it sits helplessly none of it soon I'll see,
But as it ends its race another will take its place.

A man is not his brother, for one is unlike the other;
So are they in feet and wings, feelers and such things.
Thus on the living stage strut they, their parts to wage,
And like man they pass by and very soon quail and die.

There's a monstrous graveyard as they fall and pile hard,
With the last players upon the first firm layers.
Like man they recycle, though some become Icicle
Who stays in beauty, before comes her watery duty.

Upon a man a mere snowflake can an impact make,
For I ponder on it as on the glass it does sit.
So man, think how you do to the One higher than you,
For 'tis only once you pass o'er earth's window glass.

Felix Jenkins Archer

THE MIRACLE

The joy in your eyes reflects the love in your heart,
You give it to others as you help them become a part,
Of the miracles you work with your gentle way,
And the love you bring to others each day.
You help others rise above,
As you give the miracle of your love.

Radiating love to the people you touch,
You never stop giving so much.
It's life's love and laughter you're sharing,
Because you never stop caring,
As you help others rise above,
As you give the miracle of your love.

Someone came near searching in vain,
Looking for answers and still in pain.
You touched their life as no one else would,
You gave the miracle as no one else could.
You helped me rise above,
As you gave the miracle of your love.

Penny Pigman

MY FRIEND

Do you remember when — we so casually met?
Two strangers — not knowing each other yet.
We walked for a while — then went our ways.
We met and talked — on some other days.
Time went by — with friendship to form,
Good times and bad — we shared our storms.
Our friendship strengthened — lose or win,
With letters and visits — every now and then.
Once again when together — we could forget,
Time and distance — with talk and no regret . . .
Our opinions "yes" — but judgments "no."
Each doing our things — fast or slow.
Our thoughts expressed — what we both share,
Time has proved to us — that we still care.
When exploring — as we went on our walks,
Friendship was forming — from small talks.
As then, I now — still hold you so dear
Within my heart — it gives me great cheer.
Many miles and much time — separates us not,
Just as you have not — I have not forgot.

F. K. Whaley

MY LITTLE GIRL

My little girl is only four years old
With long blonde curls and eyes of blue.
Let her out to play and she'll put
            on a party.
Out in her Daddy's back yard.
From mud and water she makes her cookies.
Bakes them in her make-believe oven.
After all my little girl is only four years
            old.

With long blonde curls and eyes of blue.
She calls her friends on her make-believe
            phone.
And gives them all a party.
Oh dear you should have seen her.
When the party was over.
She comes in all covered in mud.
She looks just like walking mud cake.
With long blonde curls and eyes of blue.
After all my little girl is only four years old.

Flossie Ritchie

DISCOVERY

I did not try to look deep in your heart,
Or realize you laughed to hide your grief.
If I had known I would have been more kind
And tolerant when your long loneliness
Began to chill you and you called my name.
Then, I knew sorrow, and I found it made
Much easier to bear because of you.
Now eagerly we lean toward life with hope
Since we learned every hour moves too fast.
I realize I need you as a friend
As you need me, before it is too late.
        Colleen Barton

I see your eyes, they gleam with pride
        that you have me by your side.
Your eyes seem to say just how much you care;
        but only, your mouth doesn't utter anything more
than the deep depth of dark silence that fills your mind.
        You seem so near, but you act so far away.
Where is the comfort of your words that I rely on day by day?
If I should say what is on my mind, would you see me cry
        alone, or would you tell me to cry for happiness
because your feelings are the same as mine; and I am not alone?
        Let me feel your soft warm lips against mine, for
                gentle reassurance that you care.
Just let me say what is on my mind; and then you can leave.
        Pamela Lawrence

HEART OF HEARTS

Ribbon and hearts embellish a valentine bonnet.
If I could write a sonnet about a pretty valentine,
I would wish for what is in your heart.
You could wish for what is in mine,
that is, if both are feeling fine
and hearts are filled with love.
Today I will autograph for you a
pretty lacy valentine and wish upon a
shining star and say, Happy Valentine's Day.
Even though we are near or far apart
love lies deep within my heart.
        Edna Dewberry

LIKE A BUTTERFLY

I awake from my cocoon hungry for life.
Uncertain as to what will lie ahead, but
I keep trying, striving, for the struggle
is in me. Though I am plain and raw to
the eyes of man. It doesn't matter for I
know one day I will peel the plainness, the
rawness of my life, leaving a skeleton
behind. Then I will spread my wings and show
the world my beautiful colors. How proud
I'll be at the amazement they'll see. The
butterfly no one knows that was deep down
inside of me.
        Katrina Hooten

THIS AND THAT

The slight shimmering is the light pittering
    Of the rain.
The frightful darkness of the spiteful hearkens
    To the unworthy.
The breaking clouds highlight the streaking shrouds
    Of misty rain.
The bright sun calls to it the right ones
    Of this day.
The rain and darkness flee in the reign of greatness seen
    In the Son.
        Donna Weyd

UNTITLED

With the shining light that shines within
In a place I've never been
Looking for what?
I don't know
Maybe the magic I lost long ago

My son, believe that all things pass
All things grow; the trees the grass
And as things grow the whole world is changed
Born anew
Just for you

Well I've found something it's called faith
Something I hope we share
And with it *I* will grow and change
Born anew
Just for you
        Martin Nothstein

DOES ANYBODY HAVE THE TIME?

A question heard a lot;
But what is its plot?
Is time as so stated; irrelevant?
No; it's the only thing truly prevalent.
From the seconds of a sexual climax,
To the minutes it takes to melt wax,
To the hours of a good night's sleep,
To the days when our love was once steep,
To the weeks of a summer's bore;
To the months of winter's gore;
To the years of protection out of the womb;
To the decades of frustration to get to the tomb!
So I ask you, do you have the time?
Just listen to the bells chime,
To conquer time, you must find love.
The two of you working like hand and glove.
When discovered don't let that love go,
Or your race against time will be all too slow.
        Philip J. Ward

THE TIDAL WAVE RUN-OFF CHANNEL

All of California was a tidal wave run-off channel,
a thousand or so years ago,
with interior borderline mountain sentinels,
capped with icy snow.
Then came the little ants,
in a hundred and fifty years of flow,
to topple the sentinels for progress,
leaving one dangerously unguarded hole.
Earthquakes warn of danger,
for the tidal waves remain unbotched.
The disaster is now forthcoming,
the waters are upon the shore,
although not one ant seems worried,
by the strange knocking at the door.
Mommy look out the window,
and tell us what you see,
she answers nothing's there but the sea,
and how it got to Idaho's border, is a mystery to me.
        Ronald L. Miller

LONGEVITY

Longevity — Is that what we fear?
Or is that the hope that we harbor in here?
Our emotions are mixed and not at all clear.
We've lived out all of our three score and more,
And question what the future may still hold in store.
Is it worth all the struggle that's gone on before?
Do we dread or cherish another full score?
        Myrtle Misch

LOVE

Today my love is a raging storm
The emptiness surrounds me, and I am torn
Realizing I'm not there and you're not here
I sometimes shed a sorrowful tear

To think that for sometimes to come
I'll be without the one I love
Promises and thoughts of you will come to pass
But! I'll never be satisfied 'til you're mine at last

Like a fine wine that's oh so fine
Our love affair was hard to define
It's said a person's worth is only as good as their word
I stand behind all my promises you've heard

As for our love there was no time and no cure
For love we shared was surely pure
Loving you is like a bright shiny day
While being without you leaves me nothing to say

I really love you, lady, but my time is up
Moving on to bigger, and better stuff
Things between us has gotten too rough
You know my feelings, but enough is enough

William C. Glenn

THE ANIMALS

I have watched many animals at work and at play
And I wait to see one go out of his way
To harm another or to do some misdeed
Unless there's a reason, unless there's a need
But we as a people, made in image of GOD
Will harm one another, yes even applaud
Another man's failure, poke fun at his race
We'll steal from him, and spit in his face
We'll cause him dishonor, douse him with shame
Cause untold agony, abuse his name
We'll deny him this or refuse him that
Pretend we're a friend then leave him flat
We'll curse and betray him for little or naught
Walk away from his wreckage without second thought
Of the grief, the torture, the endless pain
We might cause thoughtlessly or in vain
Oh! if only we did as the animals do
This world could be good for me and for you.

Don Dixon

IS THAT YOU, REBECCA?

Is that you, Rebecca,
you who never saw through impossible eyes
and dreamed dreams not in black and white
but blazing Technicolor?

Is it really you
whose feet stood firmly in the sand
while the tide carried the rest of the world
out to sea?

And what of the Eagle
who would soar above it all
and the leopard
whose spots would remain unchanged?

Has the explorer who sought the mountain's peak
been felled by too much cragged rock
or did your feet simply grow tired
of the uphill climb?

Poor Rebecca, it IS you —
but a mere reflection of the Eagle
whose wings were clipped
when you fell-in-step with the rest of the world.

Jean Cantrell

SEPARATION

Once, two little "drops of water,"
Held hands on the "Great Divide,"
And cheek to cheek, on their "mountain peak,"
"Flowed" close to each other's side.
Though rains came down, they held their ground,
But, then one day they parted.
Towards the "western sea," away ran she;
Down the east slope, he had started.

Racing on in a quickening clip
Astride pride's gallant steed,
Forever gone, the companionship
That once filled common need!
So now, a mutual friendship ends,
Each towards their separate "sea";
Too far apart to make amends,
But, too close to be free!

Willard Silvey

WINTER SONNET

The grass by winter's snow is covered deep;
And yet, the snow in flakes does downward fall.
The wind that blows from frigid North does heap
Already fallen snow in drifts so tall,
That thus a bright white blanket covers all.

The raw winds rage and roar their frozen gale
(Forever gone seems now the summer breeze),
Each tree does wear an icy coat of mail,
The mercury falls below zero degrees,
And on each pane is formed a frosty frieze.

The grass by winter's snow is covered deep;
And yet, by winter's cold it's laid not dead,
For spring will come, the grass will raise its head,
And, snow then gone, it shall with rain be fed.

Duane Wilson

A SOLDIER

The night is as quiet as a baby sleeping.
You can hear every sound from the woods.

This war is a multiple choice test.
You don't know who your enemies are.
You have to walk looking in all directions.

How can you fight when you're not sure what
                the cause is?
We are as foolish as little children.
Trying to help people who won't help
                themselves.

Here comes another bomb.
If I had my way I'd be home watching a
                baseball game.

Ann Costanzo

PASSING

         The silence of the black void oozed into the room.
Onward it crept, gobbling light as if starved.
         Passing it noticed several objects strewn upon the floor.
Apathetically it moved on toward greater light.
         Passing by remaining unnoticed a small manuscript.
It read: Man has reached his end.
         Space flight is denied, for he cannot take the stress.
And he has ruined his world.
         Now he has no place to rest his weary head.
Except in the next plane of existence.

Richard A. First

MOTHERS KNOW

Joy and pain when giving birth —
        Mothers know.
As children grow, problems get tougher —
        Mothers know.
Soon they'll be gone —
        Mothers cry.
Thorny flowers grow along the way —
        Mothers' mothers know.

Roswitha Petretschek

THE BIOGRAPHY OF A STRAWBERRY

It's May;
   I'm growing each day.

It's June;
   I'm in bloom.

It's July;
   I'm in a pie! Yum!

Eleanor M. Trnka

FOR BRIDGET

With memories bittersweet
Jealousy and anger compete
The legacy of a broken heart
When angels made us part
Now my dreams lie broken
A crucifix, a token
Always to remind me
My tears have yet to set me free

Kevin Brooks Coughan

SHOWERS

April showers bring May flowers,
But love was falling on my heart.

April showers brought May flowers,
Love had bade us never part.

Let it thunder, let it storm,
We have flowers each month long.

O. Eldo Armstrong

THE ROSE

The rose, its fragrance oh so sweet
Is introduced when two hearts meet,
A symbol of each one who cares
And gifted when their love they share,
But thorns adorn this beauteous flower
And hurts . . . as on that saddened hour,
When those two hearts, each now apart,
Walk bleeding as their love departs.

Jean H. McDavid

To you . . .
  . . . I am who you think I am!

To another . . .
  . . . I am someone else!

To me . . .
  . . . I am everything possible!

Kristin A. Smiley

THE EDELSTEIN SANDWICH

To Vice-President Patton
Citibank

He needed an eye-opener,
The Vox Populi Patton
When his contempt of Deity,
Reversing God's activity,
Had made him the Son
of the Vox Dei.

His all-knowing Mind,
Sole reflection of Edelstein
And based on human will
Forgot that, standing still,
And never in a hurry,
Our Father would pave the Way
And lead me, without anger,
To a Georgian leader
Known as: Jimmy Carter!

Gisèle Guerre

GUERRE, GISELE RENEE. Born: France; Occupation: Legal Secretary; Awards: 'Dearee,' American Poetry Association, 1983; 'Easter Dream,' *Hearts On Fire*, American Poetry Association, 1985; Other Writings: "Pre-Rebellion Student Memoirs" Educational Human Rights Denial, 1969; "The Bushes," Housing Human Rights Denial, 1981; "The Edelstein Sandwich," Pursuit of Happiness Denial, 1984; Themes: *All that which is related to human rights, law practice, New York City and New York State.* Comments: *I write about the denial of human rights, civic and civil rights as a cover-up for denials of educational rights and subsequent intervention to delay their process, combined with New York City government, New York State under Hugh Carey, Columbia University Housing office persecution, involving now the State Division of Human Rights under Governor Mario Cuomo.*

Breeze of the Summer
If only it could paint
The flight of a butterfly!

Rekha Shah

A GENTLE BUT DESPISED KING

He wore a crown of ugly thorns
He was dragged to prison
Despised and mocked
He bore insults and transgressions.
Yet no hatred or rage
Was in his heart.

Though they jeered him
And spat upon him
He gently extended his arms
As they fastened him with nails
To the Cross.

They raised him on high
As the earth shook!
He opened his arms to love
While the heavens darkened
And thundered above.

Yet he uttered not a sound.
The elements spoke for him,
This gentle King of the Jews!
This King of Love!

Sister Marie Scaletty, CSJ

AS LOVE ENDS

Will love ever end
or must we pretend,
to hate the one;
who gave us the sun?

Who can replace,
that loved one's space,
that's inside your heart
after you're apart?

Why did love come,
only to turn and run,
and leaving behind,
nothing left to find?

Will it ever be the same
and who's the one to blame,
that there's no one to care
and nothing left to share.

Does the end —
come with a friend
or does it just end?

Veronica F. Tripoli

NEW LIFE

As the tonic of water
To the roots of a tree,
As a spring in the desert —
Providence is to me.

I had labored so very long.
I was careworn and sore.
Still I kept on trying;
I labored all the more.

My helpers were torn away —
I was hedged in by the thorn.
I pulled on in single harness —
For Utopia's cause was I born.

Now I have new co-workers.
You can surely believe me —
It is water to my desert;
It is sap to my tree.

Lyle D. Smalldridge

AMERICA'S RAT RACE

Inspired at high altitude on my way to California

My friend, there are many races,
But have you heard about "Rat Race"
In America is number one at high places.
Getting up early with eyelids out of place.

Taking wives to work while dozing off,
Before we awake, children to school,
Driving safely, keeping alert, staying up,
Being careful at all stops, keeping cool.

This is a race in America, no mistake.
Without this test we could not build,
Our roads of strength that will not fade.
Let's call it rat race, of struggle's quilt.

Alfonso Te Rodriguez (Chief)

MY CROWN

Your love is a crown of jewels
    I wear with head held high
Its radiance reflected in my smile
    And in the gaze that lights my eye
Each gem a symbol of your way
    The diamond your deep trust
The emerald your deft, healing touch
    For lending joy to every day
The fiery opal your playful wit
    That teases every drear to shine
The amethyst rare your keen perception
    Of the roles in life we're meant to play
The ruby red your urge divine
    To intertwine your heart with mine
In rapture of the souls so sweet
    To crown my life — whole and complete

Dee Deverell

MESSAGE TO MOM — FROM CHERIE

Dear Mom, I got your message where I am up above
I read it over and over and was filled with so much love
I know I'm not forgotten, although for a year I've been gone
I know we'll be reunited, then we'll sing our joyous song,
We'll laugh and sing and hug and kiss,
And know in heaven, together we'll have eternal bliss.
I know you've been unhappy ever since I went away,
But please look to the future, to a happier, brighter day.
The day for laughing, no more tears,
We'll lie together through all the years.
I love you, Mom, with all my heart,
Please don't let my leaving tear you apart
For in God's time and with His grace,
We'll meet again with love and be face to face,
Our hearts will swell with joy and love,
When God unites us up above.

Rose Long

ISLAND CONTRASTS

The moon made a path of silvery light
across the rippling waters of the bay
that sparkled in the moonlight
as they swept onward toward the shore.
The light wind filled the white sails
as a boat glided gently across the waves
In contrast the small boats
at anchor bobbed gently on the water.
On shore the pine trees stood tall and straight
dark against the shore's rugged rockbound coast
all presenting a picture of serenity
on a Maine night of quiet beauty.

A. Jane Adams

MOTHER

I longed for warmth
just a touch
but her power had taken her away, away from me
her daughter who reached for her hand and all
that was felt was a cold wind
All I enquired was another problem, another illness
I glanced for a response,
when I huddled close to her drained, exhausted body;
but she was so far away,
dead from her own daughter . . .

Laurie Lynn Kamar

EVEN AS I READ THIS

    Even as I read this another mother sighs,
Another baby cries, another body dies.
And, even as I read this, another oath is sworn,
A bugler blows his horn, a child has just been
born.

    Even as I read this a cloud is giving rain,
A patient is in pain, a mind has gone insane.
Yet, even as I read this, another thought is
formed,
A baby's bottle warmed, a spirit is transformed.

    Even as I read this a dew becomes a frost,
Another soul is lost, we near a holocaust.
Yes, even as I read this, a joke provokes a grin,
Another race we win, the Earth maintains its spin.

Steve Boone

TO PATRICK

Patrick and his wife own my beauty salon.
They make a good team — he answers the phone

And takes care of the money while his wife makes
    people pretty.
He's always bright and cheerful, and even some-
    times witty.

He does a good job and we all admire him so.
He loves his coffee and can make it although

He has one problem, but he doesn't seem to mind.
You see his problem is that he is blind.

He's an inspiration to all who know him,
So I take this opportunity to show him.

Frances Hough

MAKING A STAND

In a field somewhere there's a beautiful flower
    and a child safe at play
But they can destroy it, in less than an hour
    if we don't put a stop to it today
So I'm making a stand for you little boy
    So your playground don't become a mine field
I'm making a stand before it's destroyed
    And everyone rests in peace

In a field somewhere there's a fully armed soldier
    and a child behind a gun
They can destroy it all just like I told ya
    so listen to me little one
I'm making a stand for peace little boy
    so you don't have to grow up to fight
I'm making a stand little boy — little boy
    it's gonna be all right.

Mike Schleimer

GHOST TOWN

Gusting winds sigh and whisper
Through window frames without glass
As sun and rain work together
To erase evidence of the past.

A door creaks on rusty hinges
Left open to the weather.
Tumbleweeds gather against worn walls and fences
And aging porch rails stagger.

Dust devils race through the town
Covering everything with a gritty grey veil,
While a chipmunk plays the clown
With a sweep of his bushy tail.

Woodpeckers work on what is left
Of a once strong and sturdy barn,
Even the mice are now bereft
For it's no longer safe or warm.

The river still meanders by
As it did many years ago,
While breezes through tilted headstones sigh
The story, long told by the winds that blow.

Ruby Seegmiller

SPRINGTIME

O, to breathe the breath of Spring,
See the sky azure blue, hear the birds sing,
The trees arrayed in shades of green,
A more beautiful sight can never be seen.

I watch the sun rise in the East,
Dew glittering like diamonds in the trees,
Smell the sweet aroma that fills the air,
It just seems to come from everywhere.

The beautiful flowers no human plants,
Springs forth with blooms that enchant,
God had spoken; the seeds were there,
Their beauty of Spring in love He shares.

The creatures and animals who survive
The Winter's cold, seems to come alive,
I watch the baby calves frolic and play,
Just over the hill at the close of day.

As the sun sinks slowly in the West,
One shade more, one ray less,
Lining the clouds with silver and gold,
Leaving us beauty to behold.

Annabel Franks

A VALENTINE

I'm thinking of a love of mine,
The sweetest little valentine.
'Tis very darling, oh, indeed,
And one I like to see and read.
There is no store where it is found,
However hard you look around.
'Tis not of paper, strange to say,
All sweet with lace and verses gay,
And dainty hearts, red ribbon, too,
And Cupid's merry form in view.
It's not like this, it's better still,
Its smile like music, gives a thrill.
Its hair is silken, smooth and bright,
Its pretty face is pink and white.
But hidden is its heart so true,
Where precious thoughts go skipping through.
The answer's this, there is no other.
Sweetest lady, she's my best friend's mother.

Bertha M. Wilcox

THREE GHOST RIDERS IN THE SKY

Very late one afternoon I looked up in the sky,
There were several ghost riders they all
were flying high,
They all were on horses; With swords slung
at their sides,
I began to have some fear, And so I tried to hide,
One was on a black horse; He gave a clear loud yell,
Another on a white horse tried to bid them
fare thee well,
Another on a grey mare was charging very fast,
Then they all came together; I could hear
their swords begin to clash,
The rider on the white horse; Very much in control,
He seemed to be a great man; And his sword
looked made of gold,
He touched the other riders. They seemed to disappear,
He had the look of victory. And then he
came real near,
He gave me a gentle smile as he raised his hand,
He was saying goodby; I knew he was a gentleman,
I felt I would see him again; And he would
never die,
The man on the white horse, the ghost rider
in the sky.

Lavern S. Walker

BLOODY MOONS HATCH IN AN INNOCENCE OF MIND

Splashing 'round our edge of understanding
those angel-plumed mists so coil about us,
deepening as into one holy ring
surrounded by holy rings past notice.

Beyond are unknown clouds of dwellingplace
beasts invest with a divine mythology,
as contemporary bias and race
decides who'll be dwelling there, who'll not be.

No human land or time lacked a favorite
picturesque absolute to be honored:
with gods abhorred, and gods of cleanest light
whose eyes awakened worlds and wept and bled.

To each his fellow is the lesser martyr
vaguely preliminary as was Christ,
and each man is Judas, born to barter
substance too real for a substance of mist.

D. Castleman

WHAT AM I?

What am I but a butterfly caught on a wisp of air,
Gliding along, feeling strong, not a worry or a care —
Then the breeze stops and down I flop.

The kids are yelling,
The dogs are bellowing —
The dinner's burning in the pan.

The door's a knocking,
The noise not stopping —
I wish I were in a far-off land.

The phone keeps ringing,
The radio's singing —
The house is in a terrible mess.

The dishes are piling,
My flowers are dying —
I'm going to go crazy I guess.

I'm going to quit my job,
Turn into a frog —
Burst and blow away.

Ruth C. Jaworsky

MY CHILDHOOD LAKE

Come friend, and share with me the lake of my childhood days
Come walk with me along the paths I often trodded
With youthful steps so filled with dreams not yet come true

The swaying sun-kissed palms still stand like stately guards
beside my lake
The wind-caressed waters still tremble with rippling laughter
The blades of grass still grow in silence with dewdrop freshness
While waterlilies softly whisper, opening their rainbow petals
to the morning star
From a distance, the cooing dove and the graceful swan
unruffle their snow-white feathers to a newborn day

Come friend, share with me the lake of my childhood days
Walk down the old familiar paths with me
Share in its reflective waters my bygone carefree youth
My present days of turmoil and perhaps a distant dream come true

Come friend, and bathe your image in the crystalline waters of my
childhood lake
Listen to its endless song of gladness and of sorrow
A song of laughter today . . . and tears tomorrow

And if you listen closely friend, so very closely, in the silence
of a dark velvet night or in the brightness of a sunlit day
Her humming waters yield forth, an eternal song of Love.

Alma Leonor Beltran

BELTRAN, ALMA LEONOR. Born: Sonora, Mexico, under the sun sign of Leo; Widow of Emmanuel N. Arvanitis; Education: Los Angeles City College, Theatre Arts; Famous Writers School; Lee Strasburg Academy of Acting; Occupation: Character Actress (Theatre, Films, Radio, T.V., 35 years); Memberships: Screen Actors Guild, American Federation of T.V. and Radio Artists, Equity (Theatre) Guild, American Film Institute, Nosotros (Latin American Actors Association); Awards: Poetry Merit Awards for: 'Velvet Eyes,' World of Poetry Press, *Our World's Most Beloved Poems,* Summer, 1984; 'Comforting Friend,' *Our World's Most Beautiful Poems,* Winter, 1984; Poetry: 'Friend, Lover or Fantasy?', romantic, 'Revelation,' 'Unfoldment,' inspirational, American Poetry Association, *Showcase,* 1985; 'Solitude,' 'Today's Song,' World of Poetry Press, *Our World's Most Beloved Poems,* Fall, 1984; Comments: *Poetry, to me, is the most fulfilling expression of our innermost thoughts and feelings on life, and our experiences. Life is truly a school of wondrous learning and through poetry I hope to share what I have observed and hopefully learned along the way on this Earthly journey. There are many fine forms of poetry, but I prefer the verse that rhymes, it is like a melody running through the spoken word, enhancing it. My preferred themes are: inspirational, romantic and philosophical. Most challenging. I can only say I strive — and dare to try.*

FOUR SEASONS IN NEW ENGLAND

Winter:
The icy wind whips, whirling the chanticleer vane;
Sleet patters, peppering the windowpane.
Moaning above the ocean's roar,
The foghorn warns the mariner off the craggy shore.

Spring:
The cat uncurls; rolls in the warm shaft of sun,
Craftily eyeing the robin, whose song has begun.
New warmth seeps into the dormant beds
Of the daffodils and they lift their cowering heads.

Summer:
Sprawled in the shade with a popsicle treat;
Trying in vain to escape the heat.
The sun beats down from the cloudless sky
To the buzz of the bee and the drone of the fly.

Autumn:
There's a tingling chill in the brisk autumn air
From the top of a wind-swept hill; and from there,
The splendor of the countryside — a multicolored sea,
Sent a warm glow upward and it encompassed me.

Ann C. Church

WHAT TREES DOTH REVEAL

It is daylight
And it's Fall out
The leaves on the trees have been turning . . .

And it's real,
Yet Illusion
For the scenes that we gaze can't be brought home . . .

'Til the vision is held in our minds
Inspiration doth lead us to reason . . .
Simply seek from each tree all the beauty and strength
in its growing . . .

It is peaceful
And it's love here
The bark on each branch speaks of promise . . .
And it's fruitful and glowing
The seeds of new life have been sown here . . .

Yet the wonder within still remains
Though the vision has captured the soul's search . . .
Like trees in the sun
Each ray has unfolded life's riches . . .

Valerie Augustyn

48

And in her forty-eighth year she determined
to take a trip. "You," the fierce maenads
screamed, "forty-eight," and and they danced
and chanted, "forty-eight."

She lingered for a while trying to comprehend.
Soon she whispered, "and in the night when he
comes to you straight from the bath with
protection — to keep you unsullied — what then?"

The screams reached a new high, above them she
heard, "Beware bitterness, bitterness beware."
"Yes," she replied, as she sank beneath the mire,
at last reached solid ground, pushed and pulled.

Found a creek and swam.
Yet, she walked always
with the smell of love
on her.

Patricia de Belloy Williams

ST. ANTHONY'S ON A STORMY DAY

Solidly it stands there by the clamorous highway,
a colossal, new hotel; walls built of gripping red bricks.
St. Anthony's spreads itself widely, multi-storied,
straining itself to reach and pierce the driven clouds.

Inside St. Anthony's it's cosy, calm, contented.
Narrow glass-walled elevators ride their sole rails
at the back of walls, riders filled, rising planes;
Within confining black walls, people ride the escalator.

Sapling-dotted, wide parking lots lie in front.
Glossy cars stand within the white lines waiting,
mobile luxury. On the carports limousines stop;
weary people exit; they're greeted properly.

Bored counter clerks in blue striped suits, muted silk ties
stand behind the curving counter, faultlessly correct.
Overcoat-wearing travelers lamely stand, luggage-laden.
Decorously they wait while the storm strikes mercilessly.

On that paper-pale day, mauled by the wild wind,
hounded by the riding raindrops, the inhospitable cold,
they have arrived, fleeing the filled highway,
the storm in tooth and claw. The hotel is a calm port.

John Mathew

THE ROPE

Sometimes it's hard to hang on a rope,
Wondering if you can reach the top,
Or if you will fall . . .
Sometimes it's hard to think good thoughts
And sometimes it's hard to smile to a friend,
When you feel like a wilted rose.
It brings fear to be on the rope.
The Rope of Life it is said . . .
It hurts when one slips slowly down,
Burning their hands along the way.
It sometimes hurts to look above,
When you slip low;
But suddenly you find
That the rope you're on has no more length.
If you fall, you will still be at the rope's end.
And there's nowhere to go but up;
And sometimes it may hurt to climb,
But once you do you will survive.

Katherine Brumley

THE LURE OF GOLD

He was only a burro, a long-eared jack
With a heavy load lashed to his back
The man with the burrow was withered and old
Trudging the desert in search of gold

Gold is elusive and so hard to find
But the lonely prospector sticks to the grind
As the sun was setting in the western sky
He made his camp so lonely and dry

Kicking around in the desert draw
Looking for snakes but none he saw
He pokes the fire with a crackling sound
And pauses a moment to look around

Off in the yonder a coyote wails
And he thinks again of the lonely trails
There in the coals as the campfire dies
He sees a face with hurt in her eyes

Once he was handsome, young and so bold
Now he was gnarled, withered and old
Gold was the lure that led him astray
But search he would, to his dying day

John C. Curtis

LOVE'S ENOUGH TO MAKE A GROWN MAN CRY

I've always heard, "that a man ain't supposed
to cry." Men have muscles of steel
and nerves of iron. Let me tell ya. "In
this day and time," love's enough to make
a grown man cry. Man, dry your weeping
eyes. Stop feeling sorry inside. Somewhere,
in this big wide world, there's a good woman
to walk by your side. Looking for
the perfect man or woman? There is none.
There's some good and bad in everyone.
No one's perfect under the sun. Life, is
what you make it and some. Looking for
true love keeps you on the run.

Catherine Jones

LOVE

Love is a teardrop
Shed for a deed of kindness done.
Love is strolling through autumn leaves,
Linked arm in arm in the noonday sun.
Love is a warm kiss under Yuletide mistletoe;
Love is doing things together,
In summer sunshine, or in winter snow.
Love is a warm feeling of deep contentment;
Love is a quiet peace within,
Though a storm rages without.
Love is a power to achieve one's goal.
Love is a strong belief, deep within the soul.

James W. Payne

TO GIVE TO YOU

I'd like to give to you the stars in the sky,
And a fleecy cloud that's floating by.
I'd like to give to you a rose of red,
And a violet from its soft sweet bed.
I'd like to give to you the sun of Summer's day,
And a moonbeam's long and pretty ray.
I'd like to give to you a kiss of love,
And hand to you a pure white dove.
But you can't look into my heart,
You'd only turn and just depart.
So I will only wish you well the while,
And greet you with a friendly smile.

Margaret Adams

MY CHILD

So young and impish, cowlicks twirling uncontrollably in his
dark hair, black eyes shining with happiness.
My child . . .
Wants only little boy things, but gives his all and expects
the same in nature
My child . . .
Will grow into a kind and gentle man, finding good in people
that others never thought to look for.
My child . . .
Will grow up and leave me, yet will return, bringing back more
of himself to love.
His child . . .

Aline Farthing Wilson

He didn't go to Princeton.
But he was a great preacher.

He never drove a Trans Am.
He did a lot of walking.

He didn't live in a big house.
He was happy in a very small one.

He didn't shop at Macy's.
Nor did he dress for style.

He didn't dine in fancy restaurants.
He was satisfied with cheese and bread
    at times.

He never went on drugs.
He never drank for fun.

He loved his fellow man.

No, he was never married.

Do you know his name?

It's . . . . Jesus Christ.

Ann Costanzo

LIVING

I saw the clouds beneath the sun
I knew that God and nature were one
I felt the moisture-ridden sand
And walked the green-flowered land
I smelt the aroma of new-mown hay
As the sun peaked at midday
I heard the cries of a newborn babe
Of exquisite beauty whom God had made
I watched the joy of a learning child
And plucked the stems of flowers growing wild
Whose fragrance dazzled me
Setting my sense afire and free
To all these ends I did fend
To enjoy what God had made to be.

Sanford L. Glassman

To Keepataw Lalka

Blue-eyed faithful feline friend,
I miss your greetings of joy each day!
Empty silence now prevails!

When entering the Pearly Gates
Were you greeted and given a Sapphire Crown
For being most elegant?
Did you offer your paw in gratitude?

Whose throne did you choose to hide
And claw with your slender paws?
The velvet blue or gold embroidered lace?

When you become frightened and run away —
The Angels will return you
In a Golden Chariot!

Are you more aristocratic now,
When you put your teeth
On the strings of a harp and violin?

St. Agnes and Francis of Assisi
Sing the Hummingbird song
To my lovely Siamese —
Love and tuck her in at night!

Elynor A. Baran

I THOUGHT

I thought if I locked up the love you left behind you, dear.
In deep recesses of my heart and left it for a year
I could at last traverse the road with calm serenity
that we two traveled long ago
When days were light and free.

I thought by now our love would be like flowers pressed in books,
A slight aroma dimly sweet recalling smiles and looks.
I meant to live in memory the happy days gone by
When soft enchantment first I knew
And bright-hued was the sky.

But love like ours will never die, the kind of love we knew,
Its iridescent threads just glow no matter what I do.
the months will not erase the touch of fingers on my hair,
Nor still the pain that haunts my soul
Since God took you up there.

I yearn to see you once again, to hold your curly head,
But dreams like these have gone astray, and tossing on my bed
I smile at the vain foolishness when once I thought it true
that reminiscing could be sweet
And time would banish you!

Denny Moore

IN A PLACE WHERE IT IS ALL PINK

A cubical; pink taffeta walls;
Sheeny reflections, moiré ceiling,
Beribboned nosegays,
Carpet, plush as a crimson-etched cloud
Graceful ballet movements, "A Sweet Sixteen"
A sheer flounced dressing table, mirrors,
Revealing blush in her girlish cheeks;
Silk boudoir shades, filtered light
Veiling of dewy complexion, a pleasant smile;
Radiance — a hot pink Tu Tu,
Chimes of a Victorian clock,
A Strawberry Sundae,
Cooling shower droplets,
A soft lace-trimmed nightie;
Misty illusion,
Faint fragrance of sweetheart roses;
Lotioned body of a real live fairy,
A canopied bed, "In the pink and airy,"
A downy pillow, tints in Satin;
Soft musical strains soothe her sleepy,
Floating amid pleasant dreams,
Her castle "In Precious Pink,"
Serenity, confidence, anticipation
   for a rosy, rosy future.
Margaret Kerr

LIBERATED WOMAN

We ladies decided to speak out what was on our mind,
Just tell the world what has been there all the time,
Times are different and the world has changed a lot,
Now is the time for us ladies to give it all we've got!

Liberated only means there's many things we'd like to do,
They are just as important to us as yours are to you,
We want to go out there and show the whole wide world,
That there's a whole lot of brains in all of us girls.

There are some of us ladies that rather stay at home,
If we have our choice, then it's certainly not wrong,
Fellows, it doesn't mean we no longer care for you,
We can be a loving wife and a good Mother too.

Most of us ladies know how to cook, clean and sew,
But for some of us, there are higher places we'd like to go,
We ladies are just saying that we want a chance too,
To make our own decisions, as to what we want to do.

Mrs. Willard Lee Skelton

A SPECIAL PLACE

Living in a world all to myself.
No one can enter.
It is a place where my dreams come true.

There is only one place where I
can go to escape all my troubles.
I love going here.

I share this world with *NO ONE*
It is my world.
I have no friends in this world
of mine.
It is like reality
It's like they all leave me one by one
What is a person to do in a time
of need when there is no one.

Go to my world and dream
and ask for the guidance of
GOD.

Dawn H. Johnson

JOHNSON, DAWN HOPE. Born: Blooming-ton, Illinois, 1-23-67; Education: Currently a Senior at Urbana High School; Comments: *I write poetry in my spare time, to express my feelings that I keep inside. They are the words that I cannot say out loud. My inspiration I owe to Timothy and Michael, two people who keep me going.*

THE INDIAN CENSUS

"We have come," the white man said,
"to take a census of the Indians
living upon the reservation
and I would like to speak to
the head man. Who is in charge here?"
And the old white-haired man with
countenance stern answered,
"The Lord is in charge here,
and how would you go about
measuring grains of sand upon the desert?
And how would you go about
measuring whole grains
and half grains and quarter grains?
And where does the blood
of the red man stop
and the blood of the white man begin?
Since for eons our blood has mingled
and there are not many of us left
who can claim the purity
of the original red race."

Virginia Lemperle

FLYING ON THE WIND

When I die
   no lonely grave
     for me —

Rather, cremate me
   and on a
     windy day

Climb to the
   highest point
     around

And fling my
   ashes far
     and wide.

Think of me
   as flying on
     the wind.

(I always wanted
   to travel
     unencumbered.)

The wind and I
   will whisper
     to you

Caress your cheek
   and ruffle
     your hair

While singing
   sweet love songs
     to you.

Remember, when I die
   no lonely grave
     for me —

Karen Elaine Drager

TURN TO ME

Turn to me
For a good time —
I'm the friend called fun.

Turn to me
For shedding tears —
I'm the friend called strong.

Turn to me
For free advice —
I'm the friend called wise.

Turn to me
For spilling anger —
I'm the friend called patient.

Turn to me
For a lending hand —
I'm the friend called kind.

Turn to me
For easing pain —
I'm the friend called gentle.

Turn to me
For open thoughts —
I'm the friend called honest.

Turn to me
For I won't go —
I'm the friend called true.

H. Kristina Hightower

OH ROSIE DEAR

Oh Rosie Dear,
the days are long
but not as long
as the night . . .

The thoughts that run
through your head
crowd every empty space.

You wonder how you
function, in your
time of dismay.

By the grace of GOD
you plunder through
life as HE has
planned you to . . .

Our program varies
from Day to Day,

But *HIS* Love always
stays.

Mary Wilson

GRAND RIVER

We walk on path by river
As sun comes rising high.
Everything looks so vibrant;
Grand River flows on by.

Maple leaves now are turning
As are the birch and oak.
We walk path by Grand River;
We stop and tell a joke.

I miss dear old Grand River
For now we live by the sea.
With all its charms Grand River
Now flows so silently.

Like clouds a vapor passes
Over river now in Fall.
In homeland I remember
Grand River most of all.

Merle Ray Beckwith

HOLD A CANDLE

Hold a candle with its light,
Lift it high glowing bright
   To guide the wanderer
Through shadows in the night.

Hold a candle let it glow,
Its spark is animating you know,
   If one is fearful in the dark,
A need of faith to embark,
   A star it is to quench the night,
And lift his spirit to greater height.

Hold a candle would you care
If someone's need might be there,
   Reveal a friend — reach out to him,
A sign of love, a kindness now or then.

Hold a candle its flickering ray,
Guides steps through darkness as of day,
   The right — of — way it calls,
A light and lift to all.
   A friend who understands,
Is a breath of God in man.

Virgie McCoy Sammons

A TREE FOR THEE

Oh tree of beauty
  tree of light
what has happened on
  this Holy night?

A man was born
  in days gone by
who promises of
  life up in the sky

"The Everlasting Life"
  its labeled name
has left us here
  still mostly sane.

So what is it
  shall tomorrow bring?
The carolers sing
  and church bells ring.

The coming of the Lord
  they say
and they'll wait
  and wait another day.

Sig Reckline

AUTUMN LEAF

Autumn
    Leaves blow and scatter on the wind
Time
    You said it's a lie but it kept moving
Dreams
    When we were young we shared so many
        But the seasons changed
    And autumn came
        The leaves left the trees
    And drifted away
        Leaving only the one
    The last leaf
        The last dream
    Our last hope
        Clinging true
    Remaining strong
        For us then for us now
    We are one

Steve Bedney

A DAY IN YOU

Dawn's multi-color rays expand
Ignite horizon 'round the land
Propelling color beams to fly,
Brilliant, 'gainst Thy winter sky.

Morning's hazy fingers grope
Into dreams of ours unspoke,
Pleasure dared and gladly risked
December winds caress our kiss.

Noon sun climbs, and rises,
Ecstasy, released surprises!
Hot flesh, reflect warm fire's glow
Scorch silhouette onto virgin snow.

Winter dusk absorbs our lust
As soft loins join and thrust.
Midnight, cloak our lovers' gleam
New Moon, brighten, spoken dream.

Love battles at the glacial cliffs
Of polar ice spears frozen stiff,
Tremble walls built 'round our hearts.
Melt false fears when we're apart.

Carol A. Reed

THE HEART

The heart is a gentle place
So let no hatred dwell in there,
For it will show upon your face
And follow you just everywhere.

And when bereft of "Joie de Vivre"
Which very often happens, too,
Try filling it with love and see
How it will help the rest of you.

Marie McDonald

BEAUTY

Beautiful are trees, green with splendor,
Budding with life, regal and bright.
Beautiful are flowers on parade,
Shimmering in the sunlight.

Beauty is all around us,
Surrounded with beauty are we.
Look, then you will see.
Beauty is you, it's me.

Sonia McIntosh

RIB OF MY LIFE

Let there be light.
Let there be perfection.
And there was a bright and perfect you.
Rib of my body,
Light of my life.
You are the sun defeating all darkness.
You are the power plant of my existence,
  and the joy of my soul.
PRAISE GOD FOR YOU . . .

Carl D. Johnston

A KITCHEN CLOCK

The reflection was vivid
In the glass china door
Of the old pine clock
That stares only at floors.

I could hear the ticking,
And then I could see
That time was sweeping
My life from me.

Sheremy Rowe

A A

When you've hung one on and feel low
There is nothing like juice of tomato
Course a swig of a Bloody's good too
To cure morning after ills that plague you
If you're one who cares not for the fruit
And have no restraint from a toot
One can cure those weaknesses fast
Have both elbows put in a cast.

Russell T. Gratner

A SMILE

Let's consider the value of a smile
For it surely is worthwhile,
Smiling is contagious
And its effect outrageous,
Smiling does a Blessing bring
Changing thoughts and everything;

A smile will cheer a weary Heart
Giving friendship a new start,
Strangers can be made to be
Friends that never used to be;
Give a smile! It's worth so much
To the weary ones and such;

A smile, one easily can afford
If the thoughts are in concord,
Smiling fills the Heart with cheer
Pleasantness does then appear,
Happiness can then be had,
Smiling is what makes one glad.

Urban Steidinger

HEARTS NEVER LISTEN

On and on my heart beats
and Round.

"Stop!" I say
But hearts never listen.

Tomorrow is the same

On and on my heart beats
And Round.

"See, I can live without you,"
I cry.

But on and on my love grows
And full.

"Stop!" I say
But hearts never listen.

Joi Mealer

XMAS — '84

The divorcée, a teacher, sat,
  Watching buses pass with a
Rhythm that led her to
  Realize she wasn't so
Alone as she'd believed.
  A jet passed; she thought of
Its pilot, then, the police,
  Firemen, hospitals, gasoline
Stations, convenience stores,
  — untold laborers.
Meanwhile, "The Messiah" was
  Choraling on the television, and
A Spanish family was bidding their
  Newly wedded daughter
"Feliz Navidad," outside her apartment.
  As they had the night before,
With her, and a friend, seven children
  Fested the Nativity with
Their dad and step-mom.
  This was Xmas — '84.

Carole Leinberger

THE POET'S WORLD

It is a place where only *one* can go;
    A time and space where only *one* can know
What underlies and penetrates all things:
    The forces mortals feel; why some have wings
To fly the heights, while others may succumb
    To pressures all around them — are struck dumb.

It is a world where Nature plays her part
    To open up to every eager heart
That seeks to know her secrets — turns the key.
    Then Beauty bares her hidden meanings. We
Will not be satisfied with what is less
    Than Truth about it all — joy, or distress.

Oh, depths will not be plumbed, nor heights be scaled
    Until the traveler, stumbling on, has failed
Time after time to make his cherished goals;
    Though there are times he scales the heights — deep holes
Keep yawning at his feet, and with strength spent,
    In mind he clambers up — he'll *not* relent!
At last, the dawn — he travels on —
    The poet helps all others know it . . .

Katharine Braun

BRAUN, KATHARINE MARIE. Born: Baltimore, Maryland, 12-26-09; Married: 1-23-53 to Charles William Braun, Sr.; Education: Business High, Eastern High School, Washington, D.C., received sufficient credits to complete, 1924-25; Occupations: Secretary; Chief Supervisor of Border Patrol, Washington, D.C.; Deputy Probation Officer, Redding, Ca; Ranch Clerk, Bureau of Land Management, Redding, Ca.; Memberships: Daughters American Revolution, North American Bluebird Society, American Academy of Poets; Poetry: 'Saga of the Bluebird,' Exposition Press, Inc., New York, 1982; 'The Ardent Bluebird,' North American Bluebird Society, Maryland, 1981; 'Sue,' World of Poetry, 1981; 'Stand and Sing,' Poetry Press, 1982; 'At Cana's Wedding Feast,' Poetry Press, 1982; Themes: *The wonder and beauty of nature, and of its birds — especially the Bluebird.* Comments: *I have donated my poetry, and vignettes, to the North American Bluebird Society, Silver Spring, Maryland, which they published in their quarterly journal, Sialia (which means Bluebirds), to help them make possible the return of the endangered species, the Bluebird, to their original large numbers. They are a non- profit organization. I also write for the honor and glory of the Creator — God — and for the benefit of my fellow man.*

DANCE FEVER

My twinkling toes will never stop to rest.
I swing my way through ragtime, rock and jazz.
Terpsichore my limber legs has blest,
Though jealous jerks may rant and rave and razz.

I twist and twirl her chassis 'round the floor,
Then tightly clasp my pigeon bust to chest.
With giggles, grunts and groans she squeals for more.
She'll never fly back to her dreary nest.

The lights grow soft; the music goes bebop.
A twelve-piece band blasts rhythms hot but sweet.
No tango, twist nor trot nor bunny hop
Can tangle, maim or still these pounding feet.

String tickle and toot for a dancing fool,
A red hot potato who is hard to cool!

Leon A. Doughty

DOUGHTY, LEON ABBETT. Pen name: LAD; Born: Atlantic City, New Jersey, 4-11-12; Education: Princeton University, A.B. *cum laude,* 1934; Georgetown University, 1930; American University, 1947-50; University of Virginia, 1979; Brevard Community College, 1983-85; Occupation: Attorney at Law; Memberships: Federal Bar Association, Phi Theta Kappa.

OPTIMISM'S VICTORY

Our humane quality is tested
        When negative thoughts arise

Beneath the clouds of resentment . . .
        Dark'ning the bluer skies.

With a measure of faith and fortitude
        Dare to embrace the sun . . .

Enjoy the hope of tomorrow . . .
        Adversity's battles are won.

Let positive rays of sunshine
        Eliminate clouds of despair . . .

Like the wings of an eagle, keep lifting
        Our spirits beyond earthly care.

'Tis the mark of a genuine Christian . . .
        Because of his source of hope . . .

In spite of suff'ring and hardship . . .
        To find the strength to cope.

Phyllis Wallin

THE STORM

There is a chaste and carven beauty
In the tumbling clouds that fill the sky,
The strange fragrance of the coming storm
Rolls in on the west wind's beating wings.

A wall of deep purple foreboding
Billows eastward until it covers
The firmament. The insistent wind
Releases fire from its lashing tail,
Thunder fills the earth with crashing sound.

Creatures huddle in groups. They crouch by
Shifting leaves, by trees, or in shadow
In whatever offers as if darkness
Could hide them from the wrath of the wind:

People close doors and slam down windows
Hoping that wood and brick will shield them
From the loosed armaments of the sky,
The earth bows down, and living creatures
Cower from whom there can be no hiding.

Genieva B. Pawling

MY "LITTLE WAR CLOUD"

Quite a brave soldier
That Little War Cloud
Surviving through war
And shrapnel wounds.

Those memories are haunting
My "Little War Cloud."
When he talks of Vietnam, water wells up in his eyes
And beads of sweat stream down his face.
  If you ask him
    Where he'll go when he dies,
  He replies, "I'll go to heaven,
    'Cause I've spent my time in hell."

But Little War Cloud has fought
For the American Indians
The American People
For peace, for freedom
And served his country well.
Sitting Bull would be so proud
If now he could see
My "Little War Cloud."

Susan G. Morrison

SNOWMOBILING

TODAY

I gazed out across the wind-swept fields
Covered with huge drifts —
Waves frozen in mid-swell
Sparkling
As if strewn with millions of tiny diamonds.

TONIGHT

The wind howls around the eaves
Adding fresh snow
To the billowing waves
Obliterating
Yesterday's paths.

TOMORROW

I will go out again
To sail my ship
Over the waves.

Helen Standing

God's Representative
defunct
          to the world he claims
          infallibly rules the faithful
                    with his princes in holy
                    alas loveless celibacy
robed in fourfivesixseven luxurious outfits
                    unequaled colors and riches
                              Jesus
that extravagant man disregards his poverty vow

how will this Powerful Hypocrite
          living in the greatest palace on earth
                    go with his limousine past the starving
                    through the needle's eye into heaven
God of Justice.
                              End.

Elisabeth Locke Ellis

LOCKE ELLIS, ELISABETH. Pen Name: Hedda Rektare; Born: Silesia, Germany; Married: 10-2-76 to Dr. Martin Locke Ellis; Education: Grammar school in Germany; English as a Second Language, 1956; Secretarial College, 1960; Extramural course in English Literature, London University, 1968; Occupations: Clerk/Typist, Psychiatric Nurse, Receptionist, Housewife; Awards: Third Place, Religion, American Poetry Association Annual Contest, 1983-84; Poetry: 'My Body,' APA, 11-15-84; Other Writings: "Banana Delights," cookery recipes, 5-27-76, and "Delicious Four-Legged Game," 10-15-81, *The Lady Magazine;* "On Your Feet, Pain-free," 11-77, and "What to do if you're tired of fatigue," 4-83, *Here's Health Magazine;* Comments:*I like to depict human relationships, religion, environment, nature, culture, and challenge limitations into personal and social assets, showing how to make life happier, more beautiful, healthier, richer and peaceful. I like to write poetry, articles, and books to provoke unthinking men and women to analyze different points of view.*

TO KNOW

She wants to know,
  Can I forgive her
    Can I forget the things that cause such pain and start again.
She's a passionate woman . . . if she kept her passions in check
  I would feel the loss.
She wants me to believe in her, to have faith in her, to resign
  myself that everything she tells me from this day forward
  will be true.
She wants to know she can count on me, as I did her.
She wants our future, our children, our twilight together.

She wants to know,
  Can I forgive her
    Can I forget the things that cause such pain and start again.

She wants to . . .

No.

Richard Leegan

FISHING

My fishing rod bobs idly;
Oars grate at intervals in rusted oarlocks.
The darkling forest silhouettes tallest trees
Against the aureole radiance of a full moon;
Leaves rustling their song,
The murmuring crispness of a blaze.
Through the darkening haze a loon,
Deoxygenated, appears above surface,
Flaps saturated wings in panicky flight
Lamenting shrilly to the night.

My fishing rod bobs idly;
The supple catlike breeze purrs
And ripples the water with soft paws.
As waves creep by, I gaze at prismatic sparks
As they shimmer and dart into the liquid.
Thoughts of self evaporate
In celestial assurance of immortality.
The bow creaks rhythmically
As I reminisce my nonage,
The warmth of a mother's embryo.

Ralph E. Martin

REVOLUTION

Some loves were better unconceived
some hearts best unawakened
some lives are best left undisturbed
this heat, unleashed, can sear the soul
consume the mind, grow unimaginable
interference.

Listening between the lines, I strain my ears
to hear all the myriad things
you are not saying.

When so much of you feels so much like myself
is it possible we're not
speaking the same language.

Seized with reckless urgency
I scatter seeds
which will germinate their thousand branches
ever growing, reaching
spreading, changing forever
the course of our lives
the very souls of us.

Sue Rauch

POTENTIAL

HONORABLE MENTION

A swift impulse, an impetus,
That quivers in the nerves
Generates an image
That need but grow, be nurtured, shaped, and formed
To give a kind of immortality.

The image stays curled there,
A clump of thought, not patterned yet,
With time would come a growth;
Delineated, articulated,
It could stand forth and
Move with ease and grace across the page.

Yes, with time. But I have other things to do.
I cannot care; it interferes, annoys, demands.
It clings among my cells
And will not leave.
I could give it substance, and
Labor to give it proper birth.
But I must pluck it out, wondering why
I spawn these things of little worth.

Delta S. Sanderson

DESERT WIND

The wind is dry, and there is no rain,
And across the wide and dusty plain,
No wild horses trod the vast expansion,
Nor humans walk in quiet expression,
Nor man of redskin: nor man of night;
Where only buzzard glides in flight,
To tell there's life at any cost
Across the sand and cacti waste,
A holocaust of dunes, and furrows;
One silent hovel in glaring light;
A lodge pole corral of gray, still burrows;
And red, red rock, like a Devil's tongue,
To mock the bleached and sandy ground
Where dancing dust devils swirl across the adobe flats,
Stretching, infinitely, to distant mountain heights,
Capped in snow in deep blue sky,
And silence deep . . . Oh, silence deep . . .
In reverence this desert keep,
For the voice of the wind has a tongue of sword,
And the rain is never . . . Oh, never more!

Jean Bernice Miller

HENRY'S LAKE

Last night Henry called, and wanted me to play
I went to the lake, sat by the tree,
And dreamed my life away.

Upon a hill the bison pranced
In the meadow two fawns played,
While the squirrels danced.

In the woods I heard a bluebird sing
A camp-robber came to steal my lunch;
A robin sang it's spring.

Above my head the sky was blue
Clouds floated by, the earth was free;
Like Eden bright and new.

Last night Henry called, so I went to see
The animals came, the birds set free,
The tree was grown from me.

Kris Hamby

SHA'-MAN

There are two of me in one soul
Part of me seeks freedom with the eagle,
The other watches . . . as I soar.
The eagle cries and so do I
Then vanishes into mist of mountains,
Carrying my soul's partner, carrying me.
How I long to fly free, to reach the Heavens
In one breath . . . as he.
I am flying with the other
Though my feet are firmly on the ground.

Two of me exist in one soul,
There is room enough for freedom.
I watch as that freedom ascends to the skies,
My soul cries and so do I.
We vanish into mist of mountains,
I can fly, I can reach the Heavens
In one breath . . . as the eagle.
I will never fly with the other
With feet firmly on the ground.

Florence Roll

124

THE LOONS

They cannot be seen, in the dawn's grey day-night,
As together they summon the sun to appear.
Only their call in the fog-shrouded light
Predicts once again that daybreak is near.

Forever they were, this melancholy pair,
Guarding the passage from darkness to day.
Their plea is the same, as it floats on the air,
Their call to return to some much simpler way.

Soon many mixed voices, awakened, ere long
Will add to the chorus as morning stands tall.
But none can compare with that primeval song,
That stirs up some long lost response in us all.

We listen, but briefly, then turn to our own
Cacophonous jumble of life out of tune.
We dare not give in to our fear — We're alone,
Save the wind and the water, and the song of the loon.

Ronald Przybyla

PUPPY LOVE

I hear a familiar footstep:
A key in the lock at the door.
I know who's in the hallway,
And I bound across the floor.

It's you that I've been waiting for;
The sound of your voice calls my name.
I wish that I could speak to you,
And let you know I feel the same.

You pat my head with gentleness,
I lick the fingers of your hand.
I'm surprised sometimes by your love for me,
That you accept my "57" brand.

Wagging my tail I follow you;
We go into the den;
And if I could I'd tell you so;
I'll always be your friend.

Nan Maddox

COPING WITH LIFE'S MANY SURPRISES

Many are the surprises that one in life finds,
Some pleasant, some not, but all to be confronted,
For not even the sharpest or wisest of minds
Can always make things turn out quite as expected.

Furthermore, most anytime and anywhere
Have life's surprises been known to suddenly strike.
Thus, we each should come to expect a fair share
Of these surprises, both good and bad alike.

Yet, with thought of the real discomfort that follows
Occurrence of many an unwelcome surprise,
It might seem best if we all could be spared the flows
Of life's surprises, pleasant or otherwise.

Still, perhaps surprises do play a needed role
Somewhere in the course of daily activity,
For, whether they be pleasant or disdainful,
Surprises help offer life more variety.

Ernest Chang

THE UPPER ROOM

Thank you God for the upper room,
Where the twelve and the Master gathered
To eat the passover, to wash the feet,
To break the bread and pass the cup;
To chart the course between God and man,
Known to us as the Christian plan.

Thank you God for the upper room
Where centuries later wise men gathered,
Cloistered through days of summer heat,
Sorting their dreams, and daring to choose
To chart the course of a youthful nation,
To write the law that became its foundation.

Lord, at this time of confusion and gloom,
Please guide our steps to an upper room.

Martha Bell Hays

SHE

She cannot see
But she images the mosaic
of shades, molds and splices
in life's design.

She cannot speak
but she owns a tendril touch and silken smile
that beacon a charming mystique.

She cannot walk
but she wears the shoes of a shepherd
and travels far to protect her flock.

But she can hear —
thumps and crashes, shouts and sneers, shrieks and groans.
She wishes she did not.

Barbara Joan Grabowy

WANDERED TOO FAR!

Wandered too far from our beginnings,
trusting it all to luck.
She's as fickle as the rest of her gender,
the lady we learned to call luck!

Her smiles are a siren's calling, forever
luring us on, to the rocks and shoals of our ruin.
For we wandered too far, going back, is believing
it's not so.

Wandered too far we did! Left her waiting,
back on the road somewhere?
Smilingly awaiting the day, we'll surely
come to our senses.
For even the Queen of luck's reluctant,
to travel the distance full!

William R. Raike, Jr.

small, soft child, whose face stirs such love,
his leg draped over your arm,
and you, sir,
slowly drifting into a peaceful sleep . . .
      content — pleased — gentled —
by my munchkin's obvious love for you.
this i see before me, sir — more . . .
      this scene i *feel* within me.
maybe it is but a dream —
                              who knows?
and maybe i will never wake —
      but sleep this feeling forever.

Nadja Hunt

ALONE WITH YOU

The sun is going down.
No soul to be found.
The water moves rapidly;
As it falls down beneath me.
The traffic goes by.
Over across the sky.
I gather my thoughts and say them out loud;
For no one is here, just you in a cloud.
Looking out to the faraway sky.
Asking myself the question "Why?"
I want to be so right but yet some people condemn me.
Are they jealous because now I live for you eternally?
Father, you have been showing me the way.
Now I want to include you in every day.
My feelings I have inside I cannot explain.
Though living for you I have so much more to gain.
I will leave this place in which I came to be alone
with you.
And will do my best in every way to never neglect
you.

Angela Detwiler

ESSENCE OF THE MIND

Sunsets of marble, waters of stone,
In this land the blue moon shone
Over the ice of a waterfall,
Over the tree stumps that grew so tall.
And on still further 'til the night becomes day:
A silent cry at the sun's first ray.
And then with the second, the blue floats by,
Only remaining where the land was dry.
The green of the sun has too left a trace,
Like tears running down Saturday's face.
the stars in the sky are joined as a flower;
Leaving the essence of some mystical power:
The mind learns to listen
To each word as command;
The world is resting in a
Small child's hand,
With only the hope that she'll
Never let go,
Else the whole world would
Again become snow.

Jill Anne Douglas

MAN'S INGRATITUDE

Oh! This world we swing and catch
A hoop of broken pledges,
As faithlessness reign and galore.
Hatred I get for my smile;
The divinity of man dots n' dashes my consciousness,
Wickedness, they sing and ring.

Yesterday, my fret made the blind to see
Today, my face they hate to see.
The day before, my vigil made the deaf to hear.
Today, my voice they hate to hear.
The other day, my faith made the cripple to walk
Today, they kick me with their newfound feet.

To weep at man's ingratitude, I refuse
The shortness of man's shrive, I nail
Kindness to my fellow man, I oil
Learned to love not hate
Smiling amidst rain or storm
Cheering the needy and the last, I wed.

Jude Murphy Uba

MY LOVE/MY LIFE

My love for you is most profound
Your touch spins my heart 'round and 'round
The pride and smile within your eyes
Causes the best of my life to magnify.

When I'm so sickly, even down and out
Nursing me back to health without a doubt
You massage, you cater, you even retrieve
Giving me the best of care I could receive.

Your thoughtfulness is so very spectacular
But washing whites with duds is a bit peculiar
The idea you really tried is most heartwarming
Everything you say and do is so, so loving.

You have a unique understanding of me
Of my depth that before you, no one could see
The magic of the love in your every caress
Keeps me so alive, my life so full of bliss.

Karie Philomena

THOUGHTS TO PONDER

Lord, let me this moment remember
    As I quite relaxed seem to be.
The toils of the day are behind me,
    An evening from work I am free.

And when the morrow dawns with its pressures
    May the lessons I learned from this day
Guide me, sustain me, uphold me,
    Help me each step of the way.

Little things seem to upset me!
    But now for the moment I'm free!
Oh, let me, dear Lord, just remember
    That trusting in You is the key!

Then the days of my life will be peaceful,
    The hours will be pleasure indeed,
The shadows will flee like the lightning
    Because this day's lesson I'll heed.

Pearl Sandahl

ONE LAST GOODBYE

As my timing slows down, and I can't keep a beat,
And my footsteps are halfsteps, to walk is a treat,
I rise in the morning and nap around noon,
And hope in the evening a friend comes by soon.

If only a phone call or a knock at the door,
If a stranger stopped by I wouldn't feel so poor.
I look out the window and watch for the mail.
It is hard to be ninety, all wrinkled and pale.

My mind seems to wander, my thoughts are not clear,
And I say a few words knowing no one will hear
The hurt in my voice or the fear in my heart,
Can I care for myself, can I still do my part.

Alive but not living as I try not to feel
The tears on my cheek, I know they are real.
And I try not to think that God passed me by.
I have waited so long just for one last goodbye.

Lynda B. Barnett

LOVE
A FRIEND

Life cannot be lived at peak experience
It's too much tension for the soul.
The ultimate high of being in love
Needs always to see its valley below
It seems a natural law:

> Steadiness of friendship
> Is safer for the soul

The irony is, when later feeling's fire cools
The most intimate in sharing hopes and dreams
Are never more to be seen.
That intense ephemeral spark
Absorbs the meaningless void when:

> Caution and fear consumes the flame,
> Then time blows away what ashes remain

Instead, we fill our lives with routine,
Pursue pleasant pastimes with people we like
And exist without power or pain of great passion.
The gentle warmth and common bond
Of mellow friendship seems:

> The Golden Mean
> Of soul survival

Carol Tebbs, M.A.

TEBBS, CAROL A. Born: Columbus, Ohio, 9-9-39; Education: Whittier College, B.A., 1963, M.Ed., 1971, M.A., 1973, English; Occupations: Teacher (Honors English), Wilson High School, Cycles Study, Researcher and Lecturer; Memberships: Delta Kappa Gamma — Honorary Women, Teachers' International, NEA, CTA, HLPTA, President of ISAR International; Poetry: *Reflections in Verse,* ACS, San Diego, California, 1985; Other Writings: "Cycles" and other articles, *KOSMOS Journal,* ISAR, Los Angeles, California, 1983, 1984, 1985; Comments: *Faith in universal order and fundamental meaning to all that is life — tragic to heroic — pervades my work. I believe every thought and action translates to meaning at some level of being. Awareness of patterns in nature as reflected in human nature gives us some measure of self-understanding and courage to grow.*

EXPECTATION

When a light is seen in the darkness
Daybreak is almost here,
With the first blushing streaks of morning light
Night shades will disappear.
With each new ray there is hope
That fills our very hearts,
Because the coming of dawn of each new day
Is likened to a brand new start.
When darkness gives way and the sun comes up
To the beginning of another day
We look around and we will see
God's world is on display.
There is something about the early morn
When the earth has been bathed in dew.
The light that has been born from the dark
Will stir our emotions anew.
To look for each chance that may come
As night gives way to day,
Means a fresh new start, a fresh new time,
To live a better way.

Rosalind Branch Gwin

FATHER WAS BEST

Father Littell was strong
     With authority and power.
We felt he could do no wrong,
     From the highest church tower.

Toiling from dawn to dust,
     Assuring fertile soil no crust,
Cleaning, oiling, preventing machine rust,
     Not to falter among the disgusting lust.

True and loyal father he must,
     His word to be his lasting trust,
Spotless examples thrust,
     Upon his precious children most.

Father was best for his tender
     Love and understanding . . .
Problems too big alone to render,
     Taught us not to hinder,
Rely on God's Love, guidance sender.

Bertha Felder Littell

LIFE

Life on earth as we know it
     is such a fleeting thing.
The years pass by so quickly
     mingled with joy and pain.
But there's peace amidst the turmoil
     and strength that floods the soul
When we trust the Blessed Savior
     to cleanse and make us whole.
No trial in life will defeat us —
     no burden's too heavy to bear
If in faith we look to the Savior
     and spend much time in prayer.
As the years pass by and we come to the end
     of our time on this earth below.
Our bodies may die, but the Spirit takes flight
     and the glories of Heaven we'll know.
We'll walk and talk with the master,
     We'll have life that will never end —
And the joy that we'll know will be unspeakable
When we meet our Savior and Friend.

June Shoemaker Leibhart

UNTIL TOMORROW

Here we are just you and I, all alone.
You looking at me, me looking at you.
An hour ago, the day was a deep blue,
Now, dancing shadows of coming darkness
Anxiously await your disappearance.
We sit, enjoying the quiet of evening.
From you a soft yellow and orange glow
Halos the glistening sky's pale blueness.
From me a regret of the natural end
Of a glorious peaceful forlorn scene.
We must rest, for the intruding darkness
Has come to take over remains of today.
The scene as painted by you is all gone
At least till dawn — so until tomorrow!

Ron Melson

RIVER FISH SWIM DEEP

How gradually the clear stream
In the meadow of my youth,
Wound to a darkened river,
Away from the meadow's truth.

Silver minnows glinting
Over the bottom sand,
Were quick truths I captured
In my swiftly reaching hand.

Now the twisting river's
Muddy waters keep
Complex truths away from me;
The river fish swim deep.

Marjory Steel

WHAT USE AM I IN ALL THE WORLD?

What use am I in all the world
Amid the rich, the great, the learned?
I have not fought with flag unfurled,
Nor tutored men with wisdom earned.
The mind of man soars to the heights
Unlocking secrets only by God known
And wrestles like a Jacob in the night
To gain the blessing for mankind alone.
Creatures great and creatures small —
Each quite intricate in design;
Precision-made, as Redwoods tall,
Coming from the Master's mind.
Amazing truth — to which I must attest —
That God made me exquisite like the rest!

Mary Joyce Reynolds

HARVEST

We planted the garden together
My Dad and I
Seeds and sprouts
for nature to grow
Tomatoes and peas
kohlrabi and corn

Now all that is left
in October's sun
is a bare fresh-turned patch
of deepest brown
one sack of potatoes
a few frozen peas
and a carrot or two.

Beverly Horacek

PARIS

I'll laugh with you now
as I know that is what
you want.
And
since our time together
will soon be
gone.
And the music and laughter
will be so hard to find
where I'm going
I'll laugh now.

But
deep inside there is something
beginning to ache
just knowing
that the tears must come

As they always do
whenever I have to leave you.

Patricia L. Burkhart

God is great
You can't mess with Him
He is my friend
Call to tell the beauty of His praise
He is slow to anger
He gives   He calms the sea
He knows where you are
He is living bread
He is one with assurer
God loves all
God is successful
You can be a believer
He died for me
His love lives on and on
Wealth gotten   Vanity shall
Be diminished
But He gathers by labour shall increase
Store going out of business
My God is near
City light is out city near gone
My life growing with God — in view
Consider me old young

Roslynn Hatchett

GNARLED

Like her gnarled hands
      The apple tree
Was old and gnarled
Its limbs and hers
Had borne the weight
      Of fruitful years.

One more season —
      Another spring —
The leaves pushed forth
      In wisps of green
But blossoms were scarce.
She looked and sighed.

      Her cane in hand
She leaned thereon and sighed again
      "We live too long
      Too long, too long
      The tree and I
      We've lived too long."

Dorothy Howard Adler

THE PEACE OF GOD

The peace of God
comes in a softness
      a quietness
      a wholeness.
It comes to lift the spirit
      calm the mind
      and soothe the soul.
It knows no limit
   sees no bounds
   and has no end
filtering through the darkness
giving life where there seems no hope.

Glen Abel

MAGPIE

A splash
of black and white
spraying into trees
flashes once
in the sun
whispering
shiny blues and greens

Michelle Stone

THEY CALL US CIVILIZED

   Normal people in a crowd
Kill a man
      and then act proud
Kill a woman
      — no alibis
Kill a child
      because it cries

Who are these people acting queer?
I must confess . . .
      It's you I fear

Carl A. Sernoskie

IMPRUDENCE

I built myself a house of cards
Their price was very high
But firm and truly did they stand
I could not pass them by.
My house was fashioned all of hearts
(I threw the spades away)
I took my love to live with me
And settled down to stay.
My house of cards soon tumbled down
And never will build it back
For I'd ignored that well-known truth:
A joker lies in every pack.

Katherine Y. Boegehold

BROKENNESS

From broken egg, a bird is freed,
From broken soil, a sprouting seed.

The broken bread feeds young and old,
And broken rock reveals rich gold.

Through broken clouds, a new sunrise,
From oyster shells, a pearl, rare prize.

Through broken heart, upon a tree,
Christ gave His life for you and me.

Evelyn Barnes

THERE'S SOMETHING I MUST SAY

There's someone I appreciate, that's made my world new.
She's someone very special, she happens to be you.
I'm proud that you're my girl, you help me feel alive.
These are my true feelings, that I express from deep inside.
You've given me many things, things only you can give.
They're very special feelings, that help my will to live.
I feel that I'm becoming a man, I say with pride and joy.
But I know within your heart, I'm still your baby boy.
I've let you down in many ways, we both know this is true.
But now I've planned a worthy future, and this I'll show you soon.
Yes, I know I hurt you many times, and I know I caused you pain.
But even though, it's in the past, I'll remember this with shame.
I have these special feelings, they come from deep inside,
It's knowing you're my Joanne, and it's filling me with pride.
These things that I have said, please believe they're true.
I would like you to remember, and believe that I love you.

Victor Rochall

ROCHALL, VICTOR HENRY. Born: Los Angeles, California, 1-20-66; Single; Education: High School graduate, 4-29-85; Occupation: Writer (Full-time Student); Awards: Martin Luther King poetry contest, first place trophy, Paso De Robles High School, 1984; Poetry: 'Joanne,' 'My Wonderful Love,' and 'The Girl of My Dreams,' all love poems; 'There's More to a Poet,' understanding a poet, 'Happy Birthday, Carmen,' birthday poem; Comments: *I write poetry to help me better understand myself and my world. My poetry is of the earth, of the barrio, of the streets. I dedicate my life of poetry to Joanne Murillo. I haven't the words to express to Carmen Murillo for giving me strength to carry on, and for being a mother to me when I most needed her.*

SEPTEMBER DAY BY THE SEA

Lazy, lazy, summer day.
    The sun was warm and bright,
The sea was calm and peaceful,
    Not a cloud was in the sky.
Overheads the sea gulls were gracefully flying.
    The children's laughter was heard near by.
Tranquility was felt through the air,
    As one laid upon the sand of time.
A thousand memories run through the mind,
    Wondering what became of those friends you held so dear.
Who claimed their loyal love for you would never cease.
    In their time of need you helped and guided them in the right path.
And now they have forgotten to remember, even to say "Hello!"
    Then, with a sudden jerk, without warning,
The yellow jackets stung you with all their might.
    Spoiling what seemed a perfect day, and feeling sorry for yourself,
Reminding one, you can't have everything in life.
    We are all like the rolling waves just passing by,
Just to spread good deeds and greetings to mankind.

Marie V. Spadaro

MY CORNER OF THE WORLD

There is a time for all of us
to find a place not to fuss.

It may be in the city,
or else in the countryside.
A place of relaxation.
A place to unwind.

It is a small place
upon this troubled land.
A small corner of the world
is found sometimes in the sand.

My favorite corner of the world
is a place where I find peace serene.
A quiet little corner,
beside a floating stream.

Rose Milburn

AN UNDYING LOVE

I thought about the man I loved
But my heart was filled with pain,
I thought about the memories
As I watched the falling rain.

I thought about the summer beach
With me close by his side,
And I thought about the snowball fight
Where we laughed until we cried.

But my love then turned to obsession
As my wants went on and on,
And as I turned to touch the man I loved
I found that he was gone.

Now the man I love has gone away
Just like the shifting sands,
I had it once, some love and joy
And it slipped right through my hands.

So here I sit and reminisce
Over all these lonely years,
And those drops that fell to earth as rain
Were actually my tears.

Barbara Lane Wells

MOONS AND STARS

For me, he made the moon and stars
That hung in the bright blue sky
Then held me close when shadows chased
The clouds across the sky.

In his arms I felt so safe
Nothing my life could dim
Then all at once the skies grew dark
For I was losing him.

Oh, God, don't take him away from me
I prayed as tears fell fast
I need him so, I cannot live
My moon and stars slipped past.

I know that God hears our prayers
I vow it must be so
A voice seemed to say to me
"My child, I need for him to go."

Today another moon shines bright
The stars twinkle up above
But my moon fell long ago
When I lost my love.

Nell Handley

DETERMINATION

From moments of deluge . . . to
    minutes wrought with strain
The fiber of my poetic zeal
    adhere to human pain.

I flinch at cumbersome tones
    commune with moral purge
And yet my vision of the world
    convinced of social surge.

Indeed, there must exist a myth
    of which the world evolves
But not until I find relief
    in me the world resolves.

Jay

WATSON, GERALD JAY SR. Pen name: Jay;
Born: New Orleans, Louisiana, 10-18-46; Married: 10-28-78, to Theodora; Education: Southern University, Baton Rouge, Louisiana, B.S., English Ed., 1970; Occupations: University Instructor and Assistant Director for curriculum studies, Greater New Orleans Urban League; Advertising Director, Black Collegian Magazine; Business Executive; International Consultant; Poet; Memberships: Former member: New Orleans Chamber of Commerce, Tourist Commission and Minority Business Association; Themes: *Themes and ideas in my poetry are usually abstractional. My aim is to teach through my poetry.* Comments: *I try to express a deeper meaning to our existence — our realities. I vent my emotions through creative expressions.*

TRUNK

There it stands,
thick and mossy.
His bark is peeled,
although he looks rough
and motionless,
His long hollow passageway
holds warmth and a large heart
thumping slowly inside;
Trunk.

Rima Osornio

AUTUMN AT THE SHORE

White caps glisten, crest of the surf, flowing whiteness upon the sand
    Morning sun sparkles, the azure swirl of the ocean movement, far-off
Storm fences traverse various angles, their slats casting striped shadows
    Gulls undisturbed, perched on jetties, swoop down, snaring fish, rising aloft.

Sand marks rim the edge of debris, washed upon the shore, toll the flowing tide
    Soft wind, a desolate beach, loneliness enjoyed, only by a few,
Sand dunes, their majestic reeds, swaying rhythmically by the offshore breeze
    Anxious anglers, casting their stretched lines, piercing the chilled dark deep blue.

A tranquil time, the faded sun shadows, reflect along the shore
    Walk imprints dot the sand sculpture, washed smooth by the rising tide,
Cool wind, crisp and clear, cast the rainbow glow of the incoming spray
    All this, soon to be missed, relent to the fury of the winter's bide.

Edward F. Price

PATHWAYS THROUGH MEMORY

The pathways of my memory are lined with thoughts of you.
It seems you've been a part of most everything I do.
You've shared, along the way, more shady quiet spots than any other
Since I was placed within your arms and you became my Mother.
You watched me grow and learn each day as I went from toddler years to teen.
We shared so very many things in all the years between.
From the very first day of school to the diploma of the last.
Oh, we had so many happy times along the trailways of the past.
Sometimes I find a not so pleasant time hidden neath a pile of leaves.
Here I tarry only briefly — there's no use to dwell on these.
There are winding narrow trails and some so very wide,
But always somewhere down them I find you by my side.
Tho I married and raised a family as years passed one upon the other,
Still the lengthening memory pathways are mostly shared by you — My Mother.

Eulaliah T. Hooper

. . . A N D . . .

. . . and finally he discovered that all was lost
and he had survived on mere hopes which always betrayed the end;
and truth was always coincidental, spiritless and unfaithful;
perhaps a pattern which contained the vision on the surface
and enslaved it to changing details;
and he never wanted truth,
and insulted all that was self-evident, all that he *had* to trust;
for, trust was no more and deception was all;
and truth which was the aim of hope died in the cradle of faith,
in fact, like a scorpion killing itself.

and after and until the end, with no beginning or end,
and outlasting the end with many many ends
starting other ands and ends . . .

A-H. H. Ozbudun

A FROSTY MORN

It's sunrise on a frosty morn, across the meadow by the way,
I hear the sound of Mourning Dove as he welcomes the new day.
My hound, who's hunted through the night, comes home with tail a'waggin,
And stops a few feet from the porch to rest beneath the wagon.

Jack Frost has played his favorite trick on every windowpane,
He's done a most fantastic job, with icy fingers once again.
While down in meadow, past the pond, the woods, with glamour gleam,
With leaves of yellow, red and brown, shades of orange and still some green.

High on fence, our fiesty cock, sounds a herald to the day,
that is answered by resounding calls from farm half a mile away.
I look around and all is calm, the country is awakening,
It's sunrise on a frosty morn, there's peace here for the taking.

Emily Pyle

FOR THE LOVE OF A ROBIN

Did you ever see a robin, sitting high up in a tree
   Start to choose his mate for summer, and find which one his wife would be?
Well, he doesn't have it easy, as for me I must confess,
   If I had to make the choices, I would only have to guess;
   Maybe she has far more feathers, and he likes her, "O so well."
Soon he sees her sitting calmly, on a swaying limb, below
   So he makes his first advances, she's a little jarred, I know.
Then, he circles 'round, entreating, takes a dive toward earth, and then
   Perches himself bravely by her, there they sit the cock and hen;
But in natural bird-lore language, she informs him he must prove
   That his love for her is greater, than the other lover's love.
So, from some unknown direction, in a ruffled sort of way
   Comes the other lover, scolding, "she is mine, now get away";
But the truer forceful lover, is not easily deterred,
   A fight ensues, he wins it, so he is the one preferred.
A quick kiss, they're off together, and her breast grows redder still
   Airy flights for their enchantment, then a nest, then eggs to fill.
Soon there are some little young ones; don't tell me that they're a pest.
   For of all the birds that fly, dear, I just like the robins best.

Ruby Henry

MOTHER

As co-creator of Our Lord, Mother, you came to earth;
And through your "yes" response to Him you gifted me with birth.

Anointed with maternal powers, you tendered me with love;
And nurtured deep within my being respect for truths above.

Throughout the years, each day and night you kept me ever near;
Assuring me during tempest times — with God, no need to tear.

How soothing is your every smile and look into my eyes;
With gentle, loving touch you kiss away all fears and cries.

I know that God will grace your walk along His Golden Way;
And pray that strength and peace of His be yours each single day.

Mom, you are easily recognized by rare beauty in your face;
God bless you with eternal joy reserved in Heaven's place.

Sister Marie Roccapriorie, M.P.F.

HARD LOVE

I gave birth to a beautiful son,
I had to make a decision I was so young,
I slept with him in my arms in my bed,
With more than 1,000 thoughts in my head,
He was so innocent, so sweet, so nice,
I started to realize I had to pay a big price,
I cried and I prayed, I prayed and I cried,
Time was going so fast, and now I had to decide,
There were the papers, I was going to sign,
Right then I wanted to draw the line,
I held my breath and opened my eyes,
And down on the papers were the tears that I cried,
I looked down at my beautiful son,
and I knew forever he would be gone,
Then I asked for a pencil or pen,
I was glad when that moment came to an end,
I dressed him to send away my 3 day old son,
It was real hard, but the best I have done,
And now I think he's where "Father in Heaven," wanted him to belong . . .

Tammy Dahl

FREE!

How I love it,
When King Neptune
Sends his stallions,
His high white waves
To stomp the shore.

They pound the beach,
I can hear them shout,
"We are free! Free!
King Neptune has given us
This entire day
To dance and prance
Along the shore!"

At nightfall,
He will call us home,
Then, tired and happy,
We shall sleep
In ocean's barns —
Far below the deep!

Georgiana Lieder Lahr

THE COMPOSER

You look at me,
watching me dance to music,
but you are deceived.
Yes, I am the composer,
I write the lyrics,
I create the music,
but I do not play an instrument.
I create,
others control.
The rhythm is in their hands.
They may speed it up,
or slow it down.
My actions must
keep the same pace.
Someday my feet will
be keeping different time.
I will listen as I please,
hearing my own music,
and portraying it
as it is meant to be.

Jayanne Assunto

LAST EVENING

The silkworm
Discontent
Spins dreams
And by desire becomes
A prisoner
Of her own devise.
So silkworms dream
Of butterflies?
I would it were
All wings and things
Like magic carpets
And riding unicorns.
I would I'd never
Heard of ants
And death in metamorphosis.
Now I lay me down.
I pray for butterflies
And gardens
Full of flowers,
And you.

Leona Elizabeth Hay

A NEW BEGINNING

Asleep in His house, I see
in the innermost recesses
of my being, an apparition

Through a mist of fire above the Dead Sea
a beautiful red mare emerges
prances on puffs of steam with each hoofbeat
as droplets of fire explode

Out of the night sky, lightning bolts
fracture the atmosphere, thunderclouds open
a black stallion appears, descends
races to her side
Their time is come. They meet

A kaleidoscope of colors
bursts forth in the Heavens
swirling, pulsating through space

These visions mesmerize, enlighten my soul
I see futures in time
God's white horse is born.

Thomas A. Phelan

PHELAN, THOMAS ANTHONY. Born: New York City, New York, 1-20-28; Married: 8-31-57, to Ann Ward; Education: Bergen Community College, Fairleigh Dickinson, Creative Writing Courses, 1981-82; Occupation: Private Detective and Karate Instructor; Memberships: New York/New Jersey Crime Clinic, Retired Detectives of the City of New York, Academy of American Poets, New York City, Word Shops Poets, New Jersey; Awards: Honorable Mention, "One Act Play," *Byline Magazine,* September, 1984; Poetry: 'My First Recital,' *Byline Magazine,* 10-83; 'Treasure Chest,' *Byline Magazine,* 3-83; 'Our Mortal Enigma,' *Words of Praise,* American Poetry Association, 1984; 'Birth of a Poem,' *The Courier,* 6-28-84; 'Love Dream,' *The Courier,* 8-2-84; Themes: *Psychology, Philosophy, Crime, Love, Fantasy;* Comments: *I enjoy writing because it's very satisfying and gives me a feeling that I've accomplished something worthwhile. In poetry I try to express the feeling that comes over me at that specific time. I'm presently doing two poetry books, titled* One Act Play, *and* Zen Haiku.

NO SYMPATHY

Don't trouble me! what nonsense! worries?
About a miserly few hundred dollars rent?

Really you are a most inconsiderate friend!
Sympathy you — simply have not got!

What matters your silly insignificant lot?
You're incredibly undiscerning! the bitter end!

I just lost out on the sale of a yacht!
A yacht! my heart was so set on, friend!

Alisa Morris

HURTING ME

I hate to see you drink so,
Running around with friends.
You know if you keep it up, your life is going to end.
You say it makes you feel good, but what you cannot see
Is that the more you do it, the more you're hurting me.
I try to tell you nicely. I try to be so kind.
But that doesn't matter. It doesn't seem to help.
You're gonna get addicted and then there is no way out.
You go at night whenever you get mad.
You say "I'll show her," but it only makes me sad.
You find another girl and together you get blasted,
If not for that, we just might have lasted.
Everyone knows our problem, it's very plain to see.
It may not bother you, honey,
But it sure is hurting me.

Lisa Perkins

THE UNIVERSAL FORCE

Creator God of Universal oneness
Consider man created from the mind
Who came to earth to dwell amid the wonder
And beauty of the Brotherhood Divine

When I survey the Earth in all its splendor
And view the mountains rising to the sky
I hear the birds in treetops gladly singing
Their praises of the universal eye

Inspire in me the secrets of the ages
Instill in me the Greatness and the Might
Through endless Love the wisdom of the Sages
Will keep me in the Universal Light

Then teach me now to cherish all the Beauty
In Harmony and Peace on Earth
Then guide me now to seek the Highest Order
Of the Universe, Of the Universe.

Margaret Patterson

PATTERSON, MARGARET J. Born: Bamberg, South Carolina, 6-15-18; Married: 3-15-42 to John H.; Education: Queens College, New York, 1954-55; Queens Borough Community College, New York, 1967-70; Occupations: Retired Supervisor, Hospital Care; Memberships: Investigator, Social Service, Local 371, Bridge Association; Awards: Instructor — Metaphysics, 1984; Poetry: 'Philharmonic Hall,' American Poetry Association, 1983; 'I seek God,' Vantage Press, 1985; Comments: *I believe in sharing my creative works with others. My motto is "I think" and have faith that others will reach their highest level of awareness and will be inspired by my work.*

TO MY LOVE

Take my face in your hands and
    look at me —
If not with love, at least
    with caring;
Touch my lips, gently, with your
    finger tips
And knowing they're yours for the
    sharing.

Kiss me —
Hold my lips with yours,
Until a feeling pours over us
    that we can't ignore.

L. Ann Brown

BROWN, L. ANN. Pen name: L.A.B.; Born: Wichita, Kansas; Education: B.A., 1979, must finish thesis for Masters Degree (MSSA), Masters of Social Service Administration; Occupations: Professional Counselor, Poet; Memberships: YWCA, NAACP, VAADV, Bonneville Business and Professional Women, Weber Community Health Center Advisory Board; Poetry: 'Unusual Friends,' American Poetry Association, 1983; 'The Scent of Lilacs,' 1981; 'Moonrise,' 1982; 'To My Grandson,' 1976; 'Pleasant Reminiscence,' 1976; Themes: *Love, life, general observation, emotion, nature, everything.* Comments: *In poetry I'm able to express things, feelings, I can express in no other way. It's a release for me. It's a necessity.*

YOU HOLD ME LIKE A KITE

You hold me like a kite
close at first
then slowly
I am wheeled out into the sky.
I fear I will get tangled in a tree
or nosedive into cement.
I flap loudly in protest,
I am made of paper and can do little else.

Firmly on the earth,
you pinch the string
between two fingers.

B. C. Best

SEA GULLS AT EVENTIDE

The ocean roars when evening's
Near. Soon the breakers will
Appear. They'll rise up high
Towards a darkening sky, while
Sea gulls float on currents high.
The waves break with a resounding
Splash, spraying white foam on
The green sea grass. Sandpipers
Flit about on the shore, gathering
Food from the ocean's floor. Tiny
Sand crabs hop about on the strand,
Looking for a hole in the sand.
The sky darkens, but here comes
The moon. Silvery shadows it'll
Be casting soon. Calm waves gently
Caress the shore, as up above,
The sea gulls soar.

Lea McGowen

GOODBYE
For Brian Huntzinger

I saw you walking down a dusty road
In a wood.
The sun was setting
And you stopped to watch it.
I remembered how you loved sunsets.
I called to you,
But you couldn't hear me.
You started walking until
You came to the edge of the wood.
I saw Him standing there in a field
You stopped and turned, and waved to me.
I hugged you a thousand times inwardly.
I looked at the Comforter
But He was gone . . .
And so were you.

Debra J. Huntzinger

THE POLKA-DOT PRINTER

The Polka-dot printer,
in Peek-a-Boo town,
took great big words
and squeezed them down.
He took big, fat words
and made them thin,
then tried real hard
to wedge them in.

The Polka-dot printer
was completely arrayed
in an alphabet shirt
with lettered braid.
He wore inky-black pants,
and a bow-tie made
of wonderful pictures
In every shade.

Lavinia Hunton Palmer

OH, MY BEAUTIFUL ICARA!

To royal heights you aspired,
My love, to be the queen,
Defying your rivals,
And blind to us below.
Splendid, glossy wings you bore,
True daughter of Daedalus.
Too close to the sun you flew,
My love: oh, brother of Icarus,
Your shining feathers melted apart
And down you fell into the sea.

W. Edgar Vinacke

THE LOVELINESS OF TODAY

The loveliness of today
I shall long remember;
As I enjoy the quiet
Beauty in nature's
Continuous wonders,
And every sunset brings
The promise of a new dawn.
I live in the beauty of
Today and the surprises
Of tomorrow.
I appreciate the miracle
Of a sunrise,
When yesterday was dark
And dreary.
The past is my heritage.
The present my responsibility.
And the future my challenge.

Carl J. Proia

FRIEND

Through the Best of me
    and the Worst of me.
My Cause you can still defend.

Through the Sunshine years
    and the Vale of Tears,
Staunchly my hopes you befriend.

Through Strength I profess
    or Weakness confess
Always on you I depend.

If on Heights of my pride
    or Depths where I hide
Find you by my side,
Then you are truly my friend.

Veronica O'Hara

AS TIME GOES BY

When I look into the mirror
I see a stranger
Someone older than me
Who could never climb trees.
Time passes by fast
And it shows in my face,
But when I see your eyes,
The look on your face
I feel as young as
When we first met.

Suzanne Youman

JUDAISM — A RACE AND A RELIGION

Like sheep we have wandered
Over hill and plain
Not to know our home or name.
Who then is this "I"
Who has wandered and lost
Reflecting God's love from His High
Majestic Temple in the Sky,
Always struggling, always shy?
Crude and Arrogant I cannot be,
Blessed be God's Grace to shine on me,

I pray . . .

      to be!

        Amen

Phyllis Phillips

SHADOWS

Shadows in purgatory
After the death of Day;
Shadows in repentance
Cease to dance and play.

They lie silently on the wall
Suffering amongst the leaves,
Wailing their "Pilgrim's Progress"
'neath the slender eaves.

According to the Priest's promise
They slip to heaven in the night,
Sad and holy they go
To make room for kindred-shadow sprite.

Shirley Levi

NEVER ENOUGH TIME

No time for all that you must do
and what of it when you are through
    children's toys and golden rings
worked for years to gain these things
much like a twirling carousel
so many things to buy or sell
and all that you give or take
you never know the mistake
until it's too very late
never used the time to wait
and with no more than when you came
you're still looking for one to blame
no time for all that you must do
and what of it when you are through?

Fred Perry

NEVER SUMMER

On the never summer range,
Snow-topped mountains call my name,
Flowers wildly paint the lane,
Of the deep green, grassy plain.

Long and winding, narrow streams,
Subtly suggest a dream,
Sunlit skies are crisp and clean,
Starry nights leave warmth unseen.

Nature lies in balance there,
Never claiming to be fair,
Holding on without a care,
To abundant treasures there.

Sherry Newman Latter

LEAVES OF AUTUMN

I walked among the Autumn Leaves
    In days when I was young,
And learned from them the many songs
    Of Nature left unsung.

Unlike the somber Mockingbird,
    Whose song has made it known,
Gracefully and silently
    The Autumn leaves are blown.

Poets too, in some respect,
    Compare with leaves and birds:
Some reach the ear of all mankind —
    While some remain unheard.

Carlton J. Duncan

SHAYNA'S PRAYER

May my night be quiet
    as I go to bed;

May God grant me comfort
    in the day ahead;

May God protect me
    and keep me from fear;

May God bless me
    and keep me near.

Shirley Irvine Rossin

THE ECHOING LAMP

One foot in the jungle
unbalances mankind
dragging him to primal closures
not to harmony
Unaware he limps
pouncing on dissidence
yet eyeing sovereignty
So the jungle calls to him
echoing his deformity
He goes unchanged
never shedding his fur coat.

Dorothy McLain

JOURNEY OF THE WIND

The wind is rushing,
Down over mountains,
Twisting through the valleys,
Sprinting across the plains,
Breezing through the meadows,
Spinning in the cyclones,
Howling through the forests,
Rustling in the orchards,
Whistling through the canyons,
Blowing back my hair,
And then moving on.

Amy K. McGee

PRISMATIC PASSIONS

The scourge of solitude
Cannot refract prismatic passions.
Imprudently they implode,
Engulfing my soul.
Shadowboxing, I cower before my opponent.
Reluctant to step back into the ring,
I tend to new and old scars.
In the dark your smile beckons me,
Eluding daylight and promises.
So, I stroke your brow in neverland,
Hoping to smooth away boundary lines,
And fueling the fantasies.

Nina LaGrassa

LAMENT

Why do I face yet another Spring
without you, my love?
Lacy young leaves
sprouting in timid green
flutter in the tranquil breeze;
all earth awakens,
but not for you
to whom it would have
brought such joy.

Edith Hertz Smith

LAMENTING A YOUNG GIRL'S UNTIMELY DEATH:

A fresh new seed
The joy of today
All hope for tomorrow
What can I say
The young and the beautiful
For whom we pray
Denied of their lifetimes
They're taken away
I've said it before
I'll say it today
I would go in their place
To allow them to stay
There must be a reason
I need to believe
A cause for the season
In which we must grieve
Can I do more than they?
In my own backward way
Can I stand in the night
And relieve them of fright
Or is it their goodness
That makes them so dear
To the power beyond us?
They're not allowed here

R. J. Cierlitsky

CIERLITSKY, ROBERT JOSEPH. Born: Pennsylvania, 6-15-57; Single; Education: no formal education past high school; Occupations: Construction Worker, who spends the rest of his time, if there is any left, as Poet, Songwriter, and Musician; Writes and performs with a "good-time music" band known as the "Coal County Express," plays Lead Mandolin, and occasional fiddle and violin; Poetry: 'I Thought I'd Try It Anyway,' 1980; 'The Hurtin' Side of a Lie,' 1980; Song Lyrics: 'A Long Lonesome Ride,' 1980; 'There Ain't Enough Beer in Milwaukee,' 1985; 'It Looks Like I Found You,' 1985; all copyrighted RJC; Comments: *'Lamenting a Young Girl's Untimely Death,' and I continuously fail to produce a more concise title, was inspired by a depressing newscast on the evening news. I considered sending the poem to her parents but never remembered her name. It is a pure reflection on "why." I feel I must write my creative thoughts because, not only are my thoughts and feelings fleeting moments that should be preserved, but my points of view should be scrutinized by others who feel the same way.*

COMFORT

I cried.
And the tears
streamed down my face
onto His hands
and
trickled through
the holes there
and
were gone.

Jennifer R. Schrader

HOMER, On the Bluff at Long Branch

BE THANKFUL

The grass is long and papers flutter by;
Against the fence some rusty tin cans lie.
A broken bottle, label badly torn;
A symbol of a dark remorseful morn.
Is this what meets your downcast eye?

It need not be; instead your eyes could raise
To greet the glories of the newborn days.
The morning light could give a hopeful lift
And dawn's clean air could freshen and the drift
Of woolly clouds could meet your wandering gaze.

The birds fly by with many of their kind.
There's much your searching eyes could find
Of glory that could fill your wandering gaze
And fill with warming wonder all your days.
God's blessings are not easily cast aside.

So push aside the sights that make you sad;
Instead accept the sights that make you glad
To be alive, and give your fervid thanks
For blessings that are yours and that
Your burdens are no greater than they are.
Gordon E. Warnke

AWAKENING

To lie awake in a dream, Asleep!
Holding my heart in my hand.
Why is it cold — Do you hear it crying?
I tried to awaken I think, tired!
Why is it so dark — Do you hear me breathing?
Has my body moved into motionlessness, silence!
Only once again to close my eyes in fear.
Why is my sleep so restless — Do you hear me calling?
But with light comes a new dawn, faith!
To let me break these bonds of pain.
Why is the night so long — Do you hear me awakening?
Let go of the taste of stagnation, freedom!
Opening my eyes to growth.
Why is the morning so long in coming — Do you hear me yearning?
Am I tired of being asleep, dead!
Never wanting to be forgotten in a dream.
Why do I burst with excitation — Do you feel me moving?
I want to grow in love, life!
And love in this growth with the sun shining in.
Why have I been so blind — Do you feel me living?
John Mann

HE WILL

He will make you happy, if you'll let him in
Your thoughts and dreams, and all your schemes
Just think of him
He will make you happy, just open your heart
You can't go wrong, he'll make you strong
You'll have a brand-new start
Through every day in every way, He'll help you make a stand, and
When you pray just try to say, you will do the best you can
He will make you happy, with him you can't fail
He'll be your guide, and help you stride
Down lifeway's narrow trail

He will bring you gladness, his strength you'll receive
When things look bleak, and you feel weak
If you'll believe
He will bring you gladness, throughout all your life
He'll show the way, how you each day
Can overcome all strife
He'll fight for you to keep you true, his care and strength abide
His love is there for you to share, he'll be always at your side
He will bring you gladness, so please try to smile
He'll see you through, in all you do
And make your life worthwhile . . .
Jack R. Oakley

DAWN

Full moon darts amongst clouds adrift on an endless sea,
Skipping stones on the tide,
        shattering the moon's reflection effortlessly.
Sand crabs shuffle by curious of their shadow,
        then scurry to their holes to hide.
The moon fully aware, slowly drifts by.

She danced on the shimmering sand;
        arms flowing about her as if caught in the wind.
Her nude form expressed the coming of child,
        then mother of earth she danced; father of time I became.
The moon's brightness slipped into the cloud,
        leaving only darkness before the dawn.

Charles Kelly Giles

TROUBLED WATERS

There are times when I am lonely and I
Just think of you, for there are times when
I think no one loves me, no one loves me
But you. I just look up to heaven and
See your smiling face. I feel your
Love surround me and know I'm not
Alone in this distant place. Your loving hand
Always guides me through, doors that are locked.
With your words each door is opened through
Pathways where I trod. As I feel your presence
Near me, I just smile and say, thanks for
Calming the troubled waters that I walked
Through today.

Carolyn M. Jones

LOVES BLOOMING

Two seeds from different places,
    drifting without a course,
Through inviting winds of time,
    Soaring to new heights,
touching all the bases,
    a carefree life,
The seeds meet at first,
    floating with the winds of time and change,
going freely where nature takes it,
    the seeds appreciate the life they're ending,
Instead of one now there are two,
    for with two the plant has no doom,
for as a flower; love will bloom.

Deborah Ann Seipp-Lilsegren

THE BRAVE PINK DEFIANCE

I often recall that gentle Fall
when the magnolia in our yard
bloomed again off-season
without any calendar reason;
tricked by warmth and sun,
while trees already half-clad for winter
stiffened in shock, like oldies,
at this mad fling of youth.
In truth, that dreamy display of pink wonder
stays with me today, inspiring, consoling,
even though ice and snow had come to plunder.
In a world beset with cruelty, violence and abuse,
Beauty is its own excuse.

Edna L. Hirsch

I've meant to ask you

Though I never have
Maybe I'm afraid your answer
Will be no —

Do you like poetry?

It means so much to me
At least the ones I understand
The ones about love and friendship
Maybe that's because these are the things
of which I'm most aware.

Solitary people are that way you know —
Aware of things —
Deeper things than meet the eye.
We measure thoughts and words
And look for deeper meanings —
Always listening, seeking —
Trying to find a kindred soul.

    Kit Conrad

CONRAD, KITTY KAREN. Pen name: Kit Conrad; Born: Louisiana, Missouri, 5-31-38; Education: St. Mary Hospital School of Nursing, 1960; Occupation: Registered Nurse; Poetry: 'Questions,' American Poetry Association; 'Mirrors,' 10-72; 'Touching,' American Poetry Association, 7-82; Comments: *I write for myself — I am what I write — If anyone can understand and care about my writings they can understand me.*

HUNTING, HOME

*"Aren't lovers forever reaching verges
in each other,
lovers, that looked for space, hunting
home?"*
Rilke

2ND PLACE

I see on your face as you wake an expression other lovers
must have discovered on mine. I don't move.
Your eyes reflect the glare on the corner of the window,
four dead flies on the sill, nothing.

I kiss the dark hollow in your neck. "Forget it."
In the kitchen sunlight laps my ankles, cold and white
as spilled champagne. It is all so ludicrous
and sad. Deftly I break eggs into an old, chipped bowl.

"I don't understand," you say. "What's the occasion?"
Your face is dark, featureless, in the shadow of the door.
"It's Sunday," I murmur. "You've been here before.
You should know by now there are rituals in this house."

    Heather Tosteson

THE GAME OF LIFE

Contemporary life leaves me feeling cold
Why must one so young be forced to be old?
No job to be found, for cash to pay bills,
No friends, now money's gone; no sympathy for ills.
My dad lives down south, my mom in the east,
My husband's in a grave where old crows feast.
I'm here with one child, trying to cope,
But telling the truth, I've run out of hope.
One daughter's married, my son's on a ship;
Claimed by the Navy, "It's time to get hip."
One sister's in Detroit, the other out west;
They both are married and trying their best.
Our daily cares bring an end to love and joy;
Repeated lessons teach us life's no toy.
My mother-in-law's in a nursing home,
My sister-in-law's married and loves to roam.
Their children are three, all girls sad to say;
They're scattered too, in this game we play.

This is a verse that has no ending,
But twenty lines is all I'm sending.

    Ann Ferris

FERRIS, KATHERINE ANN. Pen Names: Leslie Penn, Annabelle Lee; Born: Kankakee, Kankakee County, Illinois, 10-19-39; Married: 11-14-59 to David Whitney Ferrs; Education: University of Miami, Florida, 1957-58; Kankakee Community College, A.A., 5-82; Occupations: Wife, Mother,Homemaker, Community Volunteer (many areas); Memberships: Certified Genealogical Record Searcher for Kankakee County, 1976-80; Awards: Chicago Poets Club, Poets & Patrons Contest, 1982 — tied for First Place Dramatic Monologue, for 'No Burial Place,' and won Second Place Science Theme for 'Winter's Shawl'; Wilory Farm Contest, 1978; Kankakee Women's Club, 1985, for 'Obituary Notice'; Poetry: 'The Nursing Home,' Wilory Farm, Michigan, 1978; 'Regeneration: Blossoms Only for a Time,' *Purpose,* Scottdale, Pennsylvania, 4-82; 'The Tide,' nature, *Great Contemporary Poets,* World of Poetry Press, 1978; 'At Rainbow's End,' *Lyrical Treasures,* Fine Arts Press, 1983; 'Butterfly,' Poetry Press, 1978; Themes: *Primarily a connection between what is visible, in nature, & invisible, felt or thought, by myself.*

CRYSTAL SHIP

Crystal ship, glass figurine
All part of a complete form
With care and time,
Out of molten quartz you unwind,
A thought in someone's mind.
Sails that seem bellowed and filled with air,
Your riggings strain.
Though you are not real
You carry me afar in a land
Of undreamt dreams.

    Buddy L. Russell

FROM THE ASHES OF THE PHOENIX

Ashes, cold and stained with tears
broken dreams and fulfilled fears;

remnants of Devotion's flame
lighted by a lovely name:

Lost among the ashes where it fell
a lifeless, hollow, ever-broken shell.

The fire of Passion's love was dead
though hanging on a glowing thread;

the prayer of resurrected life
devoid of Adoration's strife.

The plea returned on wings of love;
precious gift from realms above:

The ashes shed the name of scorn
to life anew, a name reborn;

once assigned to Love's rejection
born again to rouse new passion;

bright new flower born of Spring;
enchanting song for Love to sing;

a miracle born of embers' death;
a name now loved 'til Time's last breath.

Harvey Alan Sperry

HOLD ON

Visions of curiosity . . .
Wonders of the mind

Perhaps a dream of happiness
that only you will find

You search your heart deep within
as far as you can see

But all you find is confusion
for both you and me

scattered thoughts you toss and turn
hoping the answer will appear

But would your mind deceive you
and leave you with nothing but fear?

Like the shadows of darkness
the light will turn to day

Like a rainbow is to Happiness
as a potter is to clay

Happiness is the present
as you can plainly see

Hold on tight with all your strength
don't ever let go of me!

Debbie Kellems

HERE THEY COME

Orientals now flood our shore,
Buying property more and more.
　　　You can't call it an invasion,
　　　They use Dollars for Persuasion!

Robert Emmett Clarke

A LITTLE GIRL'S DREAMS COME TRUE

When I was a little girl, I loved to make hats for my dolls.
While I was sewing, I would dream of going to New York
To buy hats, and perhaps someday have a shop of my own.
I had no idea where New York was!

Sometimes when I was drawing pictures
I imagined it would be wonderful to become a real artist.
My sketches always seemed to come out mountains or a wigwam by a lake.
As I grew older, I still wished to sell hats, have a shop and be an artist.

When I was ten years old my parents bought me a piano.
I took lessons and music was very easy for me.
In my teens, I was asked to be our church organist, which was a great honor.
And when I was requested to play for "study hall singing" in school, I was thrilled.

Some time later I saw an ad in a magazine — "How to design hats."
I sent for the course — completed it and received my diploma.
In the meantime, I had become Junior Assistant in a Carnegie Library.
I resigned my position — to sell Designer hats in a very elite specialty shop.

About this time, I had a call — would I be interested in taking an art course?
It was a very extensive course, hard work, but I loved every minute.
Now I have many paintings and sketches I have created, hanging on my walls.
A little girl's dreams really did come true!

Mildred A. Martin

MARTIN, MILDRED ALME. Born: North Tonawanda, New York, 6-16; Education: University of Buffalo, 1936; Famous Artists School, 1950; Hat Designing, 1952; Institute of Children's Literature; Occupations: Jr. Library Assistant, Millinery Buyer Assistant, Secretary and Receptionist; Memberships: AARP, Teaching music in church, Council on the Arts in N.T.; Other Writings: Manuscript for children's book with pen and ink sketches, several short stories for children not published to date; Themes: *Joy of travel, making new lasting friendships, beauty of places visited, joy in seeing God's beautiful creation, happiness, sharing love;* Comments: *To share my joys of people, places with many snapshots and slides, work hard to earn money to make dreams come true — to look at mountains such as those in Colorado — have all the cares go away while drinking in the beauty of our beautiful country. Meeting people years later invited to visit as I was (Hawaii).*

A CRICKET IN MY MILK

A cricket is swimming in my glass
I wonder what has been his past
I wonder if he has a mother
Is his gender female, male, or other
I wonder what he thinks of me
I wonder what he hopes to be
I wonder if he can recall
I wonder if he thinks at all
His antennae are waving in the air
Can he hear, smell, see, or care
The cricket is leaping up and down
My milk is splashing all around
The cricket is bellied up for sure
Now I don't wonder anymore
I think that it's such a pretty day
I'll drink my milk and go out to play

Delma Runyan

THE BABY FAWN

A Baby Fawn in a woodland
forest a mystery for all to see.
   The Little Fawn ran across
and brightened the horizon, as
the birds sang with glee. Standing
bravely alone on a hill.

   Sweet and frail one day not
too far away. The Baby Fawn
will grow into a strong grown-
up deer.

Millie Curtis

THE MORNING WAITS

Time is deep,
and goes by fast;
the morning waits,
but never lasts.
Life is full and,
death is still;
the light of morning
is yours until;
you live your life,
don't be useless and die;
until the morning waits
and uses your cry.
To be remembered
to know and feel;
that the morning waits,
but it's never still.

Sharon Hendrickson

AIRBORNE

Peacefully I watch the gulls soaring
towards their Heaven.
Flying far above the tranquil cotton balls
in the sky.
In my solitary kingdom,
I shed the scale of tension.
Alone, I take in a breath of fresh air,
and expel responsibility.
I've released all grief.
I rejoice in my kingdom
knowing it to be aggravation-free
Attached to the wings of the gulls,
my inner being soars with them.
As we go higher, and higher.
I feel the freedom of life in my soul.
Costing me nothing.

Cynthia D. Warn

ST. GEORGE CHRISTMAS

This brief festivity in green and blue
An humble affirmation makes
That sunlight gilds the mighty clock
And garlands wreathe the heart that wakes.

Awakening now the winter tree
Is but a temporary sleeper,
And painted brick is set in stone
For both the giver and the keeper.

The kneeling sky is blue and kind
About the Gothic tower.
The iron hand is lightly placed
On the illuminated hour.

And soaring music mounts to heaven
On carved and sharp extended wings.
The massed and mighty voices carry
The song and him who sings.

The marble finger sets ajar
The door we could not open,
Revealing saints in majesty
Astride a word unspoken.

Marcia Drennen

DRENNEN, MARCIA SIMONTON. Born: Columbus, Ohio; Education: Ohio State University, B.A.; Occupations: Reporter, *Memphis Press-Scimitar, United Press,* NBC TV News, Senior Editor, *Reader's Digest Condensed Books;* Awards: Second prize, Katherine Lyons Clark Prize, 'Summer Sunday,' 1964; Honorable Mentions, Edna Shoemaker Prize, 'Exhortation,' Margaret Deland Memorial Prize, 'Portrait,' 1964, (Pennsylvania Poetry Society); Poetry: 'Rachel,' *The Lyric,* 1972; 'The Sonnet,' *International Poetry Review;* 'Northern Spring,' *International Poetry Review;* 'Prose Poem,' *Scimitar and Song,* 1963; Comments: *For me, poetry is listening intently, as if about to hear music.*

HAIKU

Dawn casts first grey light.
The cranes are silhouetted;
The wind holds its breath.

Kathleen T. Babits

ENDLESS TIME

The endless days go on and
on, now that your love has gone,
And time never seems to end,
There is no joy in anything,
Only endless time.

Each day brings only new
despair,
And days all seem dark
and bare,
As endless time goes on and on.

You look at sky so gray
and dull,
And feel that there is no
joy at all,
You turn to God to find
your peace, and pray
that endless time will cease.

Mildred F. Witte

WHY AM I SO AFRAID?
Dedicated to Gene Traver

Why am I so afraid?
I am afraid that our love
may not meet.
I'm afraid that
what we have so delicately hidden
may not surface until
it's too late.

I long for your arms around me,
the tender, gentle kisses,
the soft embraces.
What's worse,
I long for the love I know is there,
for what we had once,
a long time ago.

Please,
don't let this moment,
this strong and severe love
pass us by.
Let us acknowledge it now,
before it's gone.

Elise Jacobson

THE STAR OF THE KING

The night
God's Son was born
The shepherds saw the star
And heard the angel's words of "Peace
On earth."

With faith
Wise men had come
To bring their gifts to Him
And worship Christ, the newborn King
Of Kings.

Today
Through halls of time
The message we still hear —
In Bethlehem the Holy Child
Was born.

The bells
Of Christmas ring;
Our carols fill the air
To praise the Prince of Peace, God's gift
Of love.

Nettie Johnson Hult

SHARED MEMORIES
For my Mother

Through all the years I kept my memories
Wrapped tenderly in love and tucked away
Inside my heart, like netted potpourri,
To chase away my blues on rainy days.
Then, when I looked around and found you gone,
I took them out and unwrapped every one,
And beheld a strange phenomenon.
Without you looking too, they came undone.
As their smiles reached out to touch my sorrow,
They found my tears and simply turned to rust.
I wrapped them in my hopes for tomorrow
And placed them gently in yesterday's dust.
They will abide inside my veil of tears
Like small thorns beneath blooms of future years.

Connie J. Smith

LOOKING FOR PARADISE IN THE AEGEAN
HONORABLE MENTION

The island is full of windmills and songs
where a soldier forgets his mission
dancing under fig trees wild with poetry
Bouzouki players are sunwashed on the sky's veranda
where life dances with ouzo glasses on bronzed heads
or plays backgammon with time
along the warm waters
a coffee house owner grinning at his espresso machine
etched and brassy
promises feta cheese fresh bread
and a life of black olives
to any musician who can fetch the wind
like a flute untamed
and sing an epic of golden days

Arlene Maass

BIRTHDAY PARTY

I gave him a party, poor as I am
I sent invitations, everyone ran.

Our door was open, nobody entered
Didn't they know that Christ was the center?

I felt they knew as I read the review
They had their fun and their profit too.

I can't believe how small people are
Who ever heard of ignoring the "star"

Sure I am hurt, you would be too
So here's wishing the curse on all of you . . .

Helen McMillan

THE GARDENER

You're more than a lover, more than a friend.
You're more than a beginning, more than an end.

You're more than the strength I lean upon.
You're more than the courage I need to go on.

You're more than the one who calms my fears.
You're more than the one who comforts my tears.

You, you are the keeper of my dreams, and I love you so.
Because you've nurtured them kindly, and helped them grow.

With you as keeper, I know someday there will be;
a reaping of not unripened dreams, but of reality.

Christine A. Frederick

THE LONG WAIT

We met briefly — living across the nation,
 leading very separate lives.
  You in a career and me in college.

I went my way,
 You went yours . . .

Drifting through years of heartaches and lessons.
 Waking in the arms of darkness and realizing you
  Were in my dreams; again.

Now and again our paths met,
 re-creating the inner happiness only you were
  able to stir deep within my soul.

A divorce and a college degree later we found our
 love still blossoming.
  Alas — true love found.

Patricia Faith Miller

AURORA BOREALIS

Your love was so great I am overwhelmed by
your constant generosity and kindness,
but cannot understand why you continually thank me
when I am the one more indebted.
If only I knew how to thank you for
turning my only before dreamed of love
into a reality never again to be grey.
Still I feel undeserving of such greatness,
and inadequate in that I am unable
to remove all your pain as I once hoped.
What I would not give for clairvoyance;
to know the cause of your vague crippling fear,
so I might wrench out that terror.
then you could also live in this world of joy,
borne of our pure love in the joining
of our spirits into one flesh.
In this the greatest love of earthly life,
I give all my love to you forever —
in this life and far beyond.

Rebecca Ruth Whalen

CREATION
HONORABLE MENTION

Not even the Chinese moon-bright Nightingale
enchanting all with his song of lust
over your pillow loves you
as delicately, as exquisitely as I with only
my smiles kissing your breath scaling it
like a treadmill as you sleep through the night
my whispers, dark as my desire, for you
clutching at your shadow — its shad-blow of care
that drops blossoms —
Where attraction leaps and lands
love finds it is waiting there to be filled — like
        flowers who seed and sigh into
         compost
we all gather in what wishes to survive.
Repeat and renew in creation
costs every cell.
The Nightingale's ambrosia!

Sallie McCormick DeBowman Adams

THINKING OF YOU

Such good friends, flow like wine
Bubbling, rich, enhanced by time

Such good friends, free with favors
Never frowning o'er the labors

Such good friends, there in need
Asking not, for praise the deed

Such good friends, not a word
Thoughts atune, all things heard

Such good friends, heads together
Sharing secrets, telling never

Such good friends, meet and part
Weaving ribbons of the heart

Such good friends drawn so sweet
Kindred souls destined to meet

Heartaches, lucky breaks
Two who share the toll life takes

God, I'm glad
We're such good friends!

Linda G. Collins

LEFTOVER WINE (BITTER) SUITE

Leftover wine
Bittersweet of memories.

Leftover wine
Sweet cocaine
Clouds the brain
Numbs the pain.

Wedding bells & dark red wine
White roses & feelin' fine
All gone stale now with time —
Wilted flowers float in leftover wine.

Soft white lace turned yellow with age —
These roses have thorns —
There's a bowl of leftover wine.

Bloodstains on a photograph
and the room smells of gas —
Leftover wine spilled on the table.

Silver rings & broken wings —
Tears & leftover wine.

Dust to dust
Ashes to ashes
And leftover wine.

K. C. Lazzari

A POEM OF LOVE

A heart that beats as one
when it is joined with another.
Of all the good and bad
that goes along the way,
and sees the troubled as well
as happy times of every waking day.
An understanding hand to hold
with eyes that gaze with love,
and seem to talk without words.
Someone loving you . . .
Together growing old.

Josephine Barkhamer

THIS ONE TAKE THE CAKE

I'm a work-a-holic as everybody knows
I just can't seem to break away when all my buddies go
I have to check things over, I'm always working late,
Of all the stupid things I do, this one takes the cake.
I'll give you two fine examples of how work fouls up my days
How Life slips through my fingers, while all my buddies play.
My girl friend called me from the airport and said —
"Honey I just got in."
I told her I would see that she got home, so I called up my best friend.
I asked him if he would go pick her up, 'cause I was working late,
Of all the stupid things I've done, this one takes the cake.
I never saw them again, and on love, I closed the door
Until one day I met my match, and loved her like I've never loved before.
She called me one night when I was working on a deal —
and said, "Honey I need you so."
I told her I couldn't break away, until this deal was closed.
So I called up my old buddy and told him my love was depressed.
I asked him if he would go and cheer her up, you can guess the rest.
When I reached home they were gone, I certainly was irate,
Of all the stupid things I've done, this one took the cake.
When I finally heard from them, this is what they had to say,
We hope that you can make it on our wedding day.
Well this time I made plans to be there, no more of this working late.
I made sure that I was the first in line, and I ate that WHOLE DAMN CAKE!

Nelda Wilson

YOUTH'S COMPANION

I simply called you Cat. Another's name would have diminished you.
I can't conceive what path of Fate had led you here, but I
am grateful. Companion of my awkward youth, you showed me
what I should become. I watched you grow, and marvelled
at your transformation from scrawny kitten to sinuous cat.
Your silken ear alone knew the anguish of my growing up, the fears
in my soul, the loneliness in my heart. I remember the times
I cried with no comfort for my pain except your presence.
Although you could not speak, your calm amber gaze soothed
my suffering more than any words could.

Your temperament inspired me — an admirable mix of diverse constants
making you unique. You taught me pride without vanity, assurance
without conceit. You proved grace to be as much a state of mind
as body. Patience, dignity, gentleness — these and more I saw,
yet greater than these, I learned from you the infinite capacity
I held within myself to love. Your gift to me is one I can't repay.
You were killed by the wheel of a passing car which betrayed
your trusting nature. I mourned alone; no tears were shed for you
save mine. Sleep, sleep friend, in eternal peace beneath the lilacs
on the lawn.

Robin Paine

Am I to be as those I behold?
Wearing mask, adorned with silken cloth, bangles and beads to cover my throat.
Am I to speak as those I hear?
With bellowing voice, gnarled scream, with gnashing teeth, and grinding bone.
Am I to race with knave and knight?
Owning magnificent castle, glittering chariots, with soft plush adornment.
Am I to taste the sweet of this life with deceit?
To cheat, steal, or commit to murder, or to rape.
Am I to follow such as sin?
To teach perverse ways, to covet that which is not mine to covet.

Nay, I say! What, then, am I to be?
What, then, is my course?

I am to teach the words of love and give only what is mine to give.
I am to follow as the Master taught — loving all!
I am to know the bitter field before the taste of honey.
I am to use the stars as my coverlet and the ground as my bed.
I am to speak soft words of comfort and truth!
I am to be as the Master chose, wearing the armor of God.

That is as it should be!
Then that is how I am to be. This is my course.

L. Lee Heckman

A DAY FOR LOU RAE
(afternoon on "Beatlejuice")

I reached out in a scooping gesture,
took in warmth, sun, seabreeze and blue skies.
I put all in my pocket as it was treasure,
tucked in smiles, tender kisses, sealed it with sighs.
That contented soul, the heat of the sun,
and the water's spray are now a part of my sensory.
The beauty of the day and the companionable fun
was imprinted on the canvas of my memory.
And though we won't think or speak of it
nor hearts be stilled by any anticipatable hold,
when the weather changes and we are hit
with clouds and rain, wind and that abominable cold;
like grandfather's cherished time-piece in a locket,
I will pull out this summer's day from my pocket.

Linda M. Hopkins

A FEEL OF SPRING

The feel of spring.
   Winter is fast asleep
Spring is here again.
   And as I traveled the trailways
And up mountain roads
   And back down roads leading to sea.
I see a spring which came to welcome us
   in every flower and breeze.
And as I see the beauty and God's Love
   in every flower, bush, branch, and tree.
And I feel the breath of God upon me in every
   little breeze,
— then it dawns on me — God was watching over me
   I felt God's Love in my heart then.
I felt at ease.

Ilabell D. McMillan

   I want to consume a continent in one enormous bite
and savor all the flavors of life.
   I want to quaff an ocean so that my thirst is quenched
and I never thirst again.
   I want to embrace the earth and hold her close, squeeze
the breath out of her, love her and smother her with kisses.
   I want the fury of a thousand storms, lightning from the
fingertips, thunder from the voice that spoke of love.
   I want to cry the rain, to clear the skies of awesome
clouds of anger, to shower the earth with golden sunshine.
   I want the birds to sing, the flowers to bloom, the deer
to browse in the evening hours after the storm, under my rainbow.
   I want to shower the earth with goodness and fullness and
kindness.

   I want the earth to love me,
      for I love her.

Gary C. Hubbard

BITS AND PIECES

Country colors; rich browns and warm blues
The cities chrome and neon
Childlike hopes mixed with an old woman's grace
Potted flowers and champagne

Blue jeans

   Silk

      Romance

         Mischief

Bits and pieces of a woman

   Kit Knox

RESURGENCE

our roles are mixed; despite our pleasure
we demand a life; of unending leisure

pursue we must; this earthly flight
we ne'er wonder; though well we might

through a life of denial; our faith is revealed
through a life of acquittal; our sins are concealed

who made the promise,
this scurrilous flight

the glove, the rings, the endless night

swimming in madness,
receptive to none, we who are withered,
alive yet so young.

When the vibrant city
shines w/ lost cause

refusal disposes as we draw near

the clouds will part;
the sky will clear

Beneath our hearts true blood remains;

the trends don't change;
the game's still the same.

Daniel Larkin

SIXTEEN

I wish I had written a poem of when I turned
   sixteen;
Recording those memories of long ago, and the
   magic happening then.

Of hopes and dreams and plans and schemes, of
   forever being young;
Of casual laughter, secret loves, or the music
   that was sung.

Of the special supper Mother made . . . of chicken
   dumplings, tapioca pudding and chocolate
      ice cream cake.
Of Dad rearranging the furniture and setting
   out the party plates.

Of an ice chest filled with soda pop, and the
   chips and dips and petit fours, stacked
      on papered dollie trays.
Of the red-eye on the Hi-Fi trembling, as Fats
   Domino sang "Up on Blueberry Hill."

Of my heart leaping to the first knock at the
   door;
Of the friendly smiles and hugs and kisses . . .
   the greatest thrill of all!

I wish I had written a poem of when I turned
   sixteen;
Keeping those memories from fading, and the
   magic happening then.

Faye R. Bonin

TITMOUSE

The tiny tufted titmouse is a charming sight.
He spreads his wings quite boldly when he's ready to alight.
He cares not if I'm watching as he perches in the tree,
But grabs a seed with titmouse speed and stares right back at me.

Judy Lockhart Di Gregorio

CATACLYSM

Every motion sooner or later comes to an end.
Every rhythmic oscillation suffers some loss
    of rate and comes to a stillness.

The planets ride through a lesser orbit.
The sun shines less warmly and brightly.
The blood runs cooler and more slowly
    in our dessicated veins.

We don't hurry anymore.
We dream of the extinction of the self.
Societies disintegrate.
Cities fade into darkness.
The earth is a chaotic theater of decay,
a gloomy drama of energy in irreversible degradation.

Coordination which is life
passes into diffused disorder
which is death.
The cycle
the endless cycle of time
will last.

Michele D'Uva

D'UVA, MICHELE. Born: Italy, 2-26-53; Education: City University of New York, Associate Degree in Liberal Arts, Fall 1984. Presently attending Pre-Law School at City University of New York; Occupation: Translator; Memberships: Co-founder of the Universalist School of Literature; Poetry: *A Journey to Universal Poetry,* co-authored with Eusebio C. Moreno, Universal Publishers, 1984; 'A Joyful Tear,' American Poetry Association, 1985; Comments: *My poetry seeks a universal meaning. It tries to be borderless in its contents. Finally, it reflects the human condition of everyday life as caught by my non- conformist eye. My poetry has been affected by Walt Whitman and Pablo Neruda. Presently, I'm working on a dialogue entitled* Dialogue Between the Abstract and Concrete, *and on a new collection of poems titled* Tessellatum Opus.

BEYOND THE BEGINNING

Readiness beckons beyond the silvered sphere
All intensity sans pre-planning offers inviolate violet
Without while a warmer, wetter color palpitates within
Shattered reflections flash inward — an endless panoply

It had all happened before the third parallel
A wondrous promise of verdant blossoms aching pink
Trolley tracks glistened into the murky distance
As beyond all pain lurked in smoky-grey arms

Yet that embrace, or the promise of it, was seductive
Even though scaled tentacles slithered on raspy shards
O blue sky of Motherhood where was your eager error
An icy touch of tender, infinite warm that scalds and scars

Time to forget, time to remember, vows melt into confusion
Almost as confusing as this apparently pointless poem
That yet exists within and without sans form
Hovering, floating, melting into the final oblivion

Ephrem A. Bell

BELL EPHREM A. Born: Atlanta, Georgia, 9-6-47; Education: Atlanta University, B.A., B.S.; Occupation: Accountant; Comments: *My poems express deep internal turbulence that is a reflection of society's inadequacies to self-direct.*

ANGEL
(from the Art of Children*)*
by a boy, age 10

HONORABLE MENTION

A very large angel is flying like an astronaut
over this country of orange-roofed houses.
With only one wing,
he is filling the sky.

Think of it, the kool-ade blue air parting
in front of him,
Toucan-colored clouds soak the top of this paper.
Half a sun shines.
It's Sunday, painfully white-gowned, the right day
for angels.

One-dimensional flowers bloom in the sky over his head.
Well-bred, he wants to give us as many bouquets
as we'll need.
"Gum-drops," he murmurs,
trying to tell us about his own childhood.

Muddy and mortal, we pretend we don't see him.
"Christmas," he weeps, rising
like a perfect skater over the real ice
of a pond.

Gayle Elen Harvey

There it floats,
At the surface of the lake.
A small inverted body rolling gently with the tide.
Its eyes wide with horror and gills gasping heavily,
It frantically flips a withered tail.
Motionless, it is carried on the murky tide, its fluorescent
Blue and Orange speckled scales sparkling in the evening light.
The grey-white mass emerging from its swollen belly creeps over
Head and tail, gradually enveloping the tiny fish.

T. L. Rothwell

BEGINNING WITH PUPPY LOVE FILLED WITH EMOTION

The heart is a pump. A red lovely feeling inside appears
when there's a love in you. Your mood changes and you
begin to feel "puppy love."

Suddenly all different sizes of hearts come bursting in
the air filled with colorful stars.

In your mind there's a full peace in your life when
hearing the lovely sound of music with your attractive
date or lover in the warm, moist air.

Our dreamy eyes meet and sing a song together. Holding
our glass of champagne in our hands and making a toast.
Then guess what happens? The happiness in our lives
appears to our mind that leads to marriage and having
our positive feelings shared.

Your feelings of trust and sense of humor appear.
when two lovers meet, they use their natural senses
such as listening to music, eyes meeting and smelling
of perfume or after shave.

Appreciate each other with a lovely gift for loving
care. For females wearing various kinds of kissing
potions which leads to a fresher kiss and makes the
male feel sweet in him. For males wearing a lovely
after shave lotion which has a sweet smell appears
good to the woman. These senses are the examples
which are the emotions in you.

Lori Allen

TALENT

We all have hidden talent in some form,
And it's in us, from the day we are born,
To find this art you must search real hard,
For that is the start, and the hardest part.

Once you find the talent you may possess,
Hard work and study, will always be stressed,
Only through continuous effort, can you achieve success,
And your talent will rate high, above the rest.

If you have talent in music, dancing or in poetry,
It must be developed like a singer, reaching high "C,"
For within you, the expressions and feelings must come,
As only in that way, can your accomplishments be done.

Talent is born within you and it is a gift,
That you can further and build on, if you wish,
To strive for perfection, must be your goal,
And it's continuous study no matter how old.

Talent is a precious thing and cannot be learned,
And it's your gift of pleasure, to give in return,
If you have been fortunate with this blessing from "God,"
Then bring out your talent, where it can survive.

And your talent will work if you try hard,
As you must do your share, right from the start,
No one but you can bring out the best,
Of the "talent" given you, and not to the rest.

Louis D. Izzo

ASHES FROM ASHES, DUST FROM DUST

A spark, from birth through life 'til death,
Generates the soul that carries one's breath
Through heights, through depths, through darkened trails
Which lead heaven's youth through aged hells.

Such spark of life each one possesses
To brighten e'en the darkest recesses,
Zealously given, more willingly taken;
Assenting cherubs, heaven forsaken.

At birth that cherubim spark ignites
A warmth, a dream, that lights the nights
Of hearts expectant of one small child:
Engendered love, perfect, undefiled.

Then grows that nymph from one blessed spark,
Carried from Heaven in love's puerile ark,
Unto maturity, then the grave,
There to rejoin its heavenly conclave.

Ashes from ashes, dust from dust,
Life's sole purpose is but a trust
Created of coal from withered stem,
Darkened ashes to glorious gem!

Jerry Lee Sanders

THE FEAR IN ME

Do I want to further my career or enhance my education
I've got to make a decision on this situation
Am I going to fall in love and have a family of my own
Or will I stay out here in the ice and turn to stone

I fear the feeling of rejection from the personal inspection
When you reach out to me I want to know if you see
The fear in me, baby can you be here for me
To handle the fear, it's causing the tears you see

I'm going to round up my horses and set them in the stable
I'm going to give them good care so when I'm ready they're able
We'll go riding in the rain up to the top of the mountain
Maybe I'm insane I've made mistakes but who's counting

I feel the fear in me, I hear my own confession
I get the feeling from you, you've got the wrong impression
You know me inside and out you've seen me ride
But do you know about the other side, the fear . . .

I fear the feeling of affection when you look in my direction
Can you really teach me not to feel or see, the fear . . .
The fear you see is getting to you, and you know it's true
The fear in me has done something to you, and you know it's true

Donna Marie Ivery

I wish I could hold forever in my hands,
all time would then stand still,
my heart would be happy, my eyes wouldn't cry,
we'd be together at will.

We'd watch the sun rise and the sun set
and live without fear or pain,
yes we'd walk so free in paradise
in the soft and gentle rain.

We'd stay together for eternity,
no change would take us apart,
sweet friend I'll love you to the end
for your love is in my heart.

It's there I know, I feel it inside
and soon forever will come,
my heart will be happy, no more will I cry,
no more will I want to run.

D. E. Meritt

BEHOLD THE CHILD

Behold the child
Eagerly waited for
Behold the child
A new spirit added to the world

Behold the child
Extending the chain of man
Behold the child
Part of God's eternal plan

A child not only perpetuates the race
A child renews the charity of God's grace
A new life endures because God's plan
Assures the survival of man

Man is renewed
A new bond is formed
And we see
God, the child and humanity

Behold the child
As we all have been
Welcome and love
For the world endures through him

E. Filchock

FILCHOCK, E. Poetry: 'An Ode to Seventy,'
American Poetry Association, 1985; 'Song of
Joy,' American Poetry Association, 1985; 'A
Unique Mystery,' American Poetry Associa-
tion, 1985; Other Writings: 'Jane is Her Name,'
song lyrics, Nashco Music Co., 1984; Com-
ments: *My poetry is related to life. Each poem
provides a glimpse of the many facets that are
present in an individual lifetime.*

NATURE'S LAND

Villages, parks and monuments
Only the ruins remain
Bring this earth to wildlife
Let nature take its hand

Opaque to idle curiosity
They stand quiet and dumb
Soon surcome by overgrowth
The earth reclaims its land

Now the creatures roam through streets
To find their maker, God
Awed in mother nature's light
To find the spirit was in thy hand

W. White

AN OPTIMISTIC WAY TO LOOK AT LIFE

This will shock you! I'm never lonely here.
For I have four men in my life! Don't tell, my dear.
I get up in the morning with Charlie Horse and that's no lie.
I spend all day with Arthur Itis at my side.
I dine with Will Power but does not pay the bill.
And I go to bed every night with Ben Gay, it's better than a pill.
Everything is further away than it used to be in my day.
It's twice as far to the corner and they added a hill in the way.
And there's no way that I can climb those steep stairs that they make.
Why don't they make stairs like the old days? That way I will not ache.
Have you noticed the smaller print they are using in the newspapers now?
And there is no sense in asking people to read aloud.
Even people are changing. They are much younger these days.
And that's quite a difference from the time when I was their age!
On the other hand, people my age are so much older than I.
I ran into an old classmate the other day. She did not recognize me and quietly said, "Goodbye"
I hardly even recognized her! She had aged so and I do care.
Got to thinking about the poor thing while I was combing my hair.
Glancing at my reflection in the mirror. Thinking of myself as an eager beaver.
You Know!!! . . . They don't even make mirrors like they used to either.

James A. Abrahams

THE YEARS AFTER

It's now a year after, and my girl is in remission.
The Lord did indeed help pull her and me through.
And yet I can't really rejoice and forget
For I know that at anytime the cancer can start anew.
So Lord, I'm still putting her life into Thy hands
As I seek ways of coping with the unknowing
While I wait for the mystical five year point in time
Not knowing, will or won't her cancer again start growing.
I think of my girl and I become anxious rather than secure
Even though the treatments are stopped and we're in a waiting stage.
For we've been robbed of the belief that tomorrow stretches forever
While my little girl plays out the role of life upon her stage.
But we've been granted the vision to see each day is precious
And we must fill our minds with other thoughts than cancer.
While living out the rest of her precious life
Filling it to the brim with fun and generous laughter.
Thank you Lord for all you have done for her.
I shall always be eternally grateful to you.
Even at moments when we feel perched on the edge of a cliff,
I will still be eternally grateful, Lord thank you.

Shirley B. O'Keefe

TWO BECOME ONE

From this day on, I will walk close by your side; attempting always to be your strength and your weakness.

A tear will never fall because of a crack I've made in your heart. I want to erase your fears and chase your enemies.

When cold nights fall, I will be your warm soft blanket. Always I will be no less than your best friend.
All that I possess in this world is yours. May God help me from this day on to keep a smile on your lips.

If ever I fail you, don't let time or words pass by; speak out for mistakes can be corrected.

In the twilight of our years, I will only love you more. When darkness comes and my eyes are closed; I will leave you in love, only to wait for us to come together in another life.

OUR LOVE WILL GO ON ETERNALLY . . .

Apryl Ariane Palen (Castor)

KTJ — 1981

It seems so unfair that the
    death of a piece of my flesh
    should return me to my papers.
That I should be so inspired
    Now — during the unrelenting
    sadness of occasion — when I
    had all those years at my
    grasp —
My mind drifts to you frequently —
    The wonderings of you —
    — of who you were — of who you
are now forever destined to be.
    I only care that you are happy
Now — that you made the right
    decision.
    My only wish — a selfish wish
    that will haunt me for
my own eternity — gnaws at my being —
    I wish I had simply told you
        I love you.

Kim Fitz Randolph

THE SEA AT SOUTHAMPTON

On our way through Southampton we
        Stopped to see the ocean
Ever a joy to look upon glorious
        Perpetual motion
Enchanting sight colored by sky
Always interesting to see and hear
        Delightful to mind soul and eye
Pleasurable to be near the sea, it
        Was livelier this day
Making an ominous roar, a serious
        Aspect deeper than play
Nature sends this alarm a hurricane
        In two days will be here
The sea begins to portend fear
Wind and waves threatening might
A beginning fierceness bringing light
Mighty ocean starting to display
A hurricane telling it is on its way
A sample of a force coming to be
Endless fascination of the sea.

Wallace Nelson Miller

HALLOWEEN NIGHT

I see upon the hill beyond
A shadow in the night;
Jumping, swirling here and yon;
Oh! 'Tis a gruesome sight.
The pale moon shines upon this thing,
Creates a ghostly glow.
The thing which casts the shadow is
Something I do not know!
Is it a ghost, ghoul, witch or man?
Its shape I cannot tell.
But rest assured the shape does not,
Upon our earth now dwell.
It jumps, it leaps, in swirling bounds;
It sways and floats in air.
To move in closer to this thing,
Is something I do not dare!
A cloud then passes o'er the moon;
The thing is gone from sight.
Don't worry though because this form
Is seen each Halloween night!

D. L. Moss

MEMOIRS OF A CHAMPION

He won the round and won the game,
But that is not the half of it;
He had himself and life to tame
And won because he would not quit.
He failed, and then he failed again;
Fell down, and down, but never out;
Embraced toil and sweat and strain,
And won because he would not doubt.

P. R. Wilson

POETRY AND ART

Poetry is like the whispering
of the wind . . .
a messenger of centuries past.

Poetry is like river streams . . .
nature's journey that has inspired me.

I'll be up there . . .
painting among the stars,
with brilliance of colors . . .
gleaming real bright.

I'll be up there . . .
heaven knows why,
'cause a painter's self-portrait . . .
will never die.

Joseph A. Burgos, Jr.

BURGOS, JOSEPH AGNER. Born: Hato Rey, Puerto Rico, 5-6-45; Education: Haaren H. S. Aviation, graduated June 1964; New York City Community College, Liberal Arts, June 1975; Occupations: Professional Artist, Writer, Photographer, Museum of the City of New York: Exhibition, June 23, 1985, sponsored by Peter Bloch; Memberships: El Museo del Barrio, A.H.A. of New York, Association for Puerto Rican-Hispanic Culture, Inc.; International Biographical Centre, England; Awards: Certificate of Merit, Men of Achievement, Eleventh, 1985; Poetry: 'The Space Theme,' lyric, *Songwriter's Review,* December 1973, Volume 28, No. 10; *Poems for the Hidden Truth,* 4 poems, *Cornucopia,* Contemporary Literature Press, San Francisco, California, 1978; 'Pure Ancient Knowledge,' *New Earth Review,* November 1982, Volume 8, No. 1, Murfreesboro, North Carolina; 'Creative Imagination,' *The American Muse,* Fine Arts Press, Knoxville, Tennessee, 1984; 'The Cosmic Ball,' *Voices of the Majestic Sage,* New Worlds Unlimited, Saddle Brook, New Jersey, 1984; Comments: *Poetry is in our family roots and there are messages that will rise the soul to new frontiers. Like my father, José F. Burgos, brother to the late Julia De Burgos one of the greatest women poets in Latin American Literature. I plan to publish my first book of poetry.*

WHY DO I ALWAYS SMILE?

I smile when I look around
At the wondrous sights to see
Because I know they were created
To be seen by you and me.

I smile when I look down
And see my own sweet child
To know at least when he is sleeping
He's oh, so meek and mild.

And then I look and I can see
My son's pretty little sister
For me, that's plenty to smile about
I don't know about you, mister.

I smile when I look beside me
And see my loving wife
It's comforting to know she'll be there
All the rest of my life.

I also feel the need to smile
When I think of my father and mother
The love that there is between us all
Could never belong to another.

Art Harris

A FAREWELL

The glow of the fire formed silent shadows
    At the close of a Winter's day,
And darkness consumed my Soul
    When the Ghost took Ann away.

Not even a word — not even goodbye.
    Just nothing, and she was gone.
The silent shadows upon the walls,
    They too, went away at dawn.

Time cooled the embers of the fire
    That seemed so far apart,
From the enchanting fire that glowed there
    When Ann first found my heart.

Maybe, the glow in the fire might
    Bring back the shadows that went away,
And the one who took my Ann
    Would bring her home to stay.

In my heart, I face the truth,
    My Ann is gone from me.
Somewhere, someday, we will meet again
    In the other Life that will be.

Eileen Bates

BEGINNINGS

I would catch you looking,
    we would smile
I would glance at you and wonder

You would talk to me,
    we would smile
The ambition in your voice
    stayed on my mind

I believed in you,
    we were young
We talked, we laughed, we loved,
    we would smile

That was long ago,
    the beginning
And still we smile.

Patricia Lynn Higgins

PROVERBIAL REALITIES

The mind — a vacuum or a fruitful gourd?
Well-worn passages or empty hallways lead
to and from the source.
Who is this source, this guide from heaven?
Do you know him? Can you call his name?
He who cupped the wind in his hands and
bound up the waters in a cloak. A magician?
Perhaps, to some, but for those who understand
He is all. You, me, life.
A mirror of images with sameness, yet different
shadows beckoning our love to join hands.

Linda Spring Andrews

BLOODROOT VALLEY IN FOG

The hills step off into silence —
My white breath hovers like a cloud.

In such soft morning light
A forest's emerald moss shines, even flowers.

No sound but the moony call
Of a morning dove to its half-hearted lover:

A plume in the path
From the ghost of a pheasant

Lends what life it can to their barren affair.
While under her hood of bone

The papery sun
Masquerades as a face white as china

Through a glowing blue mist:
A poor caricature.

But you and I have come to find solace:
Two tumbling wolf cubs

At play in the clear, piercing eyes
Of their carnivorous mother.

Henry Lawrence

LOOKING OUT MY WINDOWS LIKE AN IMPRISONED BIRD!
*Written on February 12, 1985 after a three inch snow
that followed a ten day ice storm that paralyzed North Alabama.*

Which state this is, I think I know
But my house is covered deep with snow.
Some may see me dazed, peering out
To pray that this unwelcomed white will go.

Some of my friends must think me strange
To want this cold white out of my range
That covers my world and all about
My yard and street. Oh, I'm about insane!

I look out the window and give myself a shake
To see if I am dreaming or is it a mistake.
The only other sounds that I hear
Are stalled cars on the street. Oh, I am awake!

Sure the scenes are lovely if you forget
But finishing a school year one can't omit!
For those graduating, new dates must be set
And for all the others, your days must be met.

So please dear snow, won't you go away.
We want to return to school and finish the days.
Chicago just loves you. Blow all snows their way.
They are equipped to handle you and still have their plays.

Bobby G. Adams

MY DEAR ROSE

I have a sweet lady that's come to my life
Who makes me forget life's troubles and strife.
The sound of her voice is a delight to my heart,
For I miss her so much when we are apart.

Her pretty eyes are like the sky above,
When she looks at me with the look of love.
The beauty and radiance of her skin and hair,
Reminds me when we're apart how much I care.

She puts up with my moods, my ups and downs,
But hardly ever complains or frowns.
I tend to forget about life's rat race,
Whenever I see her smiling face.

My faults are many, heaven knows up above!
And I forget often to tell her of my great love.
Deep in my heart I believe she knows,
Because, you see, she's my Dear Rose.

Joseph S. Dylik

THE IMPORTANCE OF DECEMBER

Ask many people the importance of December —
You will find most don't even remember.
They think of the presents and good food and fun
But forget about Jesus, God's only son.

At Christmas in Bethlehem, Jesus was born
The hope for us sinners was sent here that morn.
Jesus was born for you and for me.
Why isn't He as important as the Christmas tree?

We seem to forget the real meaning of the day —
Our wonderful Savior who was born in the hay.
To show He has come for one and for all —
The rich and the poor; the large and the small.

Remember the reason behind all the fun
And celebrate the day with God's only son.
Christ IS Christmas — It's His birthday, you see.
How thoughtful of Jesus to share it with me.

Brenda Janish

TEA AT FOUR

Tea at four o'clock in the morning . . .
    thoughts swirling around much too fast —
        time ticks by . . .
        people sleep.

Tea at four o'clock in the morning . . .
    work to go to, so very soon —
        drink some tea . . .
        write those thoughts.

Tea at four o'clock in the morning . . .
    thoughts and emotions flowing past —
        they demand
        attention!

Tea at four o'clock in the morning . . .
    thoughts and emotions compromised —
        tea cup clean . . .
        now to sleep!

Dale Behrens

FRUIT SALAD

Peaches,
teeth bite into plushes of fuzz
and rub,
porcelain against velvet.

Nectarines,
leather with pictures of sunsets
on their skin.

Oranges,
styrofoams peel
slices are draped with
interfacing,
underneath the
soft cushion pillows
lay shredded
satin tears.

Apples,
spheres of cotton dressed with taffeta.

Audrey Najor

MOUNTAIN AND SUMMIT

one way to the top
or many different routes?
decision to climb
preparation essential
conditions a consideration
lower altitudes are easy
as climb progresses
trail winds ever steeper
sheer cliffs scaled
danger of falling
air thins
temperature colder
determination one glove
faith, the other
darkness, snow, wind
the summit reached
joy seeing others
climbing other ways
sharing victory together
viewing the world in new perspective

Rosemary Napier

ADDISON'S MAGIC

Remembering
Chubby cheeks
And drooping diapers
Words, smiles
And always laughter,
Books, music
And long rides.
Kindergarten
Intruded upon
Our private world.
You adapted,
I never will.
Life continues
On the run.
Years
Race by
Leaving happy memories
Of all
The boys you
Used to be.

Kim S. Wakefield

DESERT RAIN

Well me and my friend were
Driving over the plain, into the
Desert when it began to rain, my
Wipers were going we were headed
Back North — into the Desert rain.
    You know there's nothing like
Breathing the air after a desert
Rain, open those windows and you
Begin to live again.
    Believe me when you open your
windows you begin to live again!
Well, we were searching for the answer?
But this was not to be.
And through the heat of the desert
we made it back home, tired and
exhausted we couldn't complain because
we experienced the pleasure
After a desert rain.
    So my friends if by chance you're
driving through a desert one day,
I hope you breathe some magic
after a desert rain!
            Mike Meslin

THE COLD ZOO

Battling winds,
The glitter of cold eyes
Peering from shadowed harbors.
Black bear sitting in a recess,
Laps at her water dish,
And with insomniac eyes
Wishes for sleep.
Wolves gathering in the snow
Pace the walls,
Heavy paw prints trailing behind.
In their confined series
Eagle's nest, shunning the air;
Cages thwart their soaring wings,
While vultures tear their meat.
Here the hungry cats
Prowl freely in their cages,
And here the hyena laughs,
Believing it can escape at will,
Yet preferring to remain
At the cold zoo
Where the meat is free
And the time is easy.
            Joseph M. Olonia

THE SIXTIES

I'm sick of the Sixties,
Between the Seventies
And Fifties,
They were heavenly
With Aquarius,
But deadly
And nefarious
In Vietnam.

The music was great,
It really did rate,
There was the dirty movie,
And Sunday was groovy,
It was the best of times,
And the worst of times,
When people still begged for dimes,
and hippie poets wrote rebel rhymes.

I'm sick of the Sixties,
Sometimes,
But they were also nifty,
And I miss those times.
            Alfred Elkins

YET I TOUCH YOU

I cannot hold you now

yet I touch you

You are so many miles away
I cannot reach these weary
arms far enough
to bring you
close to my starving body

yet I touch you

softly
with these words
that sing within me
& now are shared
for you to feel

oh I do love you

            Michael C. Mack

INFINITY

Time flows on endlessly
Like a river to sea
Into an empty void
That's called eternity.
The cycle is a span
The life of beast or man.

But an endless cycle
We do run from littlest
Star to the brightest sun.
Pain and suffering all
Time will erase and we
Ourselves are soon replaced.

A few years does consist
Of a living span and
We strive to do the best
We can as we exist
On this green world of ours
Beneath sun, moon and stars.

            Elspeth Crebassa

APHRODITE ON THE BEACH

    the sea's laboring tongue
pulls cadences in deeper
        and speaks treading ashore

    hands gather together
the likeness of a female form
        scooping out the wet coast

    he dug moist breasts
from pebbles and took crushed shells
        to form non-existent bones

    she lay complete
like a soft continent
        wedged in the waist

        underwater into the wave's lips
she vanished from the place
        where he carved her

            Philip Algosino

ME AND THE TERMINAL HEART

Beneath the yellow rising fear,
like Arabian oil the arteries hum.
Souls flash by like telephone poles,
and business booms in the subsequent slum.
A war with awareness that only can start
between every beat of the terminal heart.

The skid row Romeo and Suicide Sam
play Russian roulette with Pandora's Box.
The fountain of youth is eighty-six proof,
and history ticks like sizzling clocks.
Yeah the boys nailed Jesus and fried Joan of Arc,
and made the world safe for the terminal heart.

And still they get born in the eye of the storm
with no way to know their senses are dull.
But baby remember the axe needed Abel,
and Chicken Little's got a fractured skull.
Three monkeys just sitting and cursing the dark,
and the candle and me and the terminal heart.

Phillip Tongue

I CAN SEE YOUR FACE

As I sit here with memories of this place
                    I can see your face,
There's a spark flashing in your eyes
                    Telling me where yonder lies,
Beyond the deepest part of the sea
                    Like kinship you and me,
Is that a smile I see on your face?
                    Or a teardrop for the human race?
No, your sisters and brothers can't hear you speak
                    Telling them of love to seek,
They only see the silver in your hair
                    Lines in your face aren't there,
But I see a glow on your brand-new face
                    Just a reflection of your resting place,
My question — Are you happy about time past?
                    For there are no tears at last,
With clear tender loving eyes you stare
                    In wonder of fulfillment there,
The courageous love you left fills this empty place
                    So I'm proud I can see your face.

N. Marguerite Echols

THE BYSTANDER

You read about it every day
How a child was abused
Some have died — how many more?
How many more must die!
Because of some parent that has a problem
You hear them scream, you hear them die,
And you turn your back.
Afraid to get involved, are you wrong?
You are just as guilty!
Have you looked into the eyes of an abused child?
Their stare makes you shiver.
It's hard and cold, so full of hate.
They are so young to learn of hate so soon
Think about it, you could have prevented it and
saved a life.
Because if the child didn't die, their spirit did!
How many more must suffer,
How many more must die!
Before someone stops it,
Can you look at an abused child and not cry?

Mark A. Jorgenson

UNTO THESE HILLS

Spring does not enter softly in these hills —
No misty veils of gently falling rain,
With sun between the diamond-jeweled showers
That drop caressingly on budding flowers,
And stir to life some cool and cloistered rills.

These clouds rise swiftly, rolling full and dark,
With drops that dash the dust and plash the pane,
With thunder's cannonade down echoing crest,
And cowering trees by furious winds possessed,
And skies that splinter with the lightning's spark.

Spring crashes in with tears of stormy wrath,
And lusty Summer presses on her path.

Dorothy Vaughn

THE REALM OF DREAMERS

Our trouble is
We're dreamers in a realistic world
Or maybe it's the magic
That we have caught in moments spent
That most of the rest of the world
Denies the existence of
But once this magic in presence is sensed
We fall into the realm of dreamers
Though these dreams are in destiny only to awaken
And that is the tragedy
For, we expect to know its air as it is in our dreams
When in reality
It can never truly be that way

Renée Varak

A FADING LOVE

When I look into your eyes, I still see —
A special twinkle left for me.
Though we have drifted further apart,
I know you will always remain in my heart.

You know you were very special to me;
At least I have memories to cherish.
My love for you's strong and will always be;
Too bad it's not *you* I can share with.

Although we were parted much too fast,
My love is the kind that lasts and lasts.
You don't know that I still care
Or that my love will forever be there.

Rebecca R. Fisanick

SEPARATED LOVE

When you're gone and all alone
And you've left the ones you love at home
Your memory takes you to the past
The days seem long the nights a task
You're happy and sad as your mind wanders
There are the good times shared and the bad reminders
You wonder if you could have been wiser
You wonder if you've done good by her
You'll do better or will you, you query
There are surely some changes necessary
One thing for sure is as solid as rock
As steady and consistent as the tick of the clock
I'm deeply in love with that woman of mine
We'll be together as one it's just a matter of time

H. W. Hannah, Jr.

REMNANT CONQUEST

A due I do without relent
In earnest haste and condescent
To complete the task before life has spent
The substance of my being.

To gain the contents of promises foretold
To collect the balance youth is owed:
I will not surrender to obstacles placed in my road
No matter how hopeless success may seem.

But in peaceful sleep, I often dream
Of faraway places and coquetry ravines, though
You may not find me there, there my heart clings;
Wry, rococo, and in need.

You may wonder or you may know
Things others doubt or even deny are so
But if you believe in your convictions, don't let go;
You are the strength that you seek.

A due I do without relent
To fulfill promises made me, for the youth I sent —
To faraway places to help others accent
To a happiness I could only dream.

Kenneth B. Thomas

GRANDMOTHER

I thank the Lord for a grandmother like you;
you gave me love so sincere, and true.
You took me in, and gave me a home.
you held me high like a queen on a throne.

You shared your life with an orphan like me;
a greater love there could never be.
You gave me guidance so straight, and strong.
you taught me the difference between right, and wrong.

You lost your love real early in life;
you were left alone to face trouble, and strife.
Yet in your heart you had room for me,
and in my heart you will always be.

Though many years have come, and gone;
in my heart there is a song.
A song of praise grandmother to thee,
for taking me in, and taking care of me.

Now you are gone from this life here below;
you are in heaven with grandfather I know.
So I thank the Lord for a grandmother like you,
and I thank the Lord for grandfather too.

Nona A. Pendleton.

ODE TO UNCLE JOHN

He was a strong man, he didn't talk very much,
But you knew he was there,
He worked, he worked hard,
As a matter of fact that's all he did
was work,
He was a quiet somber man,
His jokes could scare you half to death,
But he was gentle, fair, and kind,
He could not hurt anything or anybody.
Even so I was deathly scared of him,
not so much scared, just
in awe and respect.
I loved him, I loved him very much,
and I never told him.
When he was sick, I never
went to see him;
Now it's too late;
I Love you Grandfather

Robyn Carter

OLD AGE

Looking down at my useless sagging breasts,
That long ago were welling with milk,
I see again the downy head that rests
Upon my arm, and touched his hair, like silk.
My thighs that strained with love so fierce and strong
Are sagging too; all signs of passing time.
Only my mind stays young remembering
The love we had; of bearing children
And suckling them with joy.
Let this old body wither with the years,
There are more joys remembered than the tears.

Mabel R. Bennett

NEVER AGAIN

I pulled a chair up to the fire, and took a book down from
The shelf
The time was only ten o'clock, I'd read and relax
Myself
The cover open, I soon was engrossed in a tale filled with
Murder and gore.
When suddenly, a quiet step, heard from behind, another, then
Nothing more.
Chills, hot and cold, traversed my spine and I inwardly
Shook with fear,
What could I do, should I call for help, or was death
Too near?
Then I felt something soft prod my elbow, my spirit began
To sink,
But wait, what was this, a voice soft and low, saying,
"Mama, I want a drink"
Faint with relief, but now, quite bold, I gathered my child
To my breast,
Too shaky to talk, all I could do, was nod to her
Request.
But, you can guess, that since that night, I had my
Awful scare,
My shelf's still full, but you won't find, a murder mystery
There!

Ann Murrell

MURRELL, ANN. Born: Indianapolis, Indiana, August 6; Married: 12-19-64 to John H. Murrell; Education: Post Graduate, English, Social Sciences; Occupations: Telephone Surveys, Import/Export; Memberships: NAMP, C.O.M.B., Import of the Month Club; Awards: Award of Merit, three Honorable Mentions and three Special Mentions; Poetry: 'Do You Know You,' John Campbell, 8-6-84; 'Love Hate, Relations,' John Campbell, 11-26-84; Themes: *Relationships with God, fellow man, life in general are my themes.* Comments: *I write to relieve tension and gratify inner longings and emotions; self-therapy. I simply love to compose.*

BEACHES OF HAWAII

How beautiful Hawaiian beaches lie —
White coral strands, crushed black volcanic rocks —
Wide curves, long stretches, under tropic sky.

Far echo-calls of peahens and peacocks.
*Iiwi** birds, red blossoms where they fly —
How beautiful Hawaiian beaches lie.

The sounds of life in shore trees mystify —
Surf music of wind tunes and interlocks
Wide curves, long stretches, under tropic sky.

Bright wonder for man's unbelieving eye . . .
Noon lift and fall of dolphins gleaming clocks —
How beautiful Hawaiian beaches lie.

Here rainbow colors shape and unify
Footprints of man, toeprints of feathered flocks . . .
Wide curves, long stretches, under tropic sky.

Do not question creation, nor ask why
All footprints disappear — a paradox —
How beautiful Hawaiian beaches lie —
Wide curves, long stretches, under tropic sky.

*Iiwi (small Hawaiian bird) pronounced: ee — ee — vee

Gertrude May Lutz

I AM . . . THOUGHTS

I am the poet's mistress —
A source of pleasure —
The cause of distress.

I am the alcohol that overrides reason —
The rich woman who sports her fur coat
During the wintry season.

I am blind eyes trying to discern the faintest light —
A lone candle shining during the stormy night.

    I am insanity that breeds sanity
    An ego that indulges in vanity.

I am a suicidal maniac contemplating
The world of silence —
Corrupted justice that incites violence.

I am a lame man who somehow
Knows that he can walk —
A deaf mute who can somehow hear and talk.

    I am the thoughts that transcend
    This time — this place —
    Thoughts that like a deadly disease
    Plague the human race.

Carolyn Williams Maxwell

IN HOPE

I've watched the sunbeams dance upon the wall,
And thought how joyful life could be,
If all the love you have for me, could be expressed,
In more than words, to show you love me best.

I've watched the children play, with carefree air,
And hoped your love for me, you'd sometimes bare.
How oft I've prayed, you'd let yourself be free,
And somehow show, you really do love me.

I'd be like sunbeams, dancing in the air,
And just like little children, living without care.

Jean McDavid

CLAYTON

In Tribute to Joel Clayton
For the Clayton Historical Museum

In 1856, Joel came here to settle down —
And to build a little town!

He was a rancher, a farmer and worked in the mines —
His life was during the hard grueling times!

So Joel gave Clayton his name —
The town was wild, but it slowly tamed!

Wagon trains came from all around —
To settle in Joel's new found town!

The settlers built vineyards and laid out plans —
To cultivate and farm the land!

The coal mines were going strong —
The sweat rolled down and the work was long!

But soon it was a bustling town —
With farmers and settlers all around!

As the years passed by through and through —
The towns around the valley grew!

And now the farmers and vineyards are no longer around —
The settlers and miners have long left the town!

The train that used to take you about —
And the taverns are gone, and the gambling is out!

New generations were born —
And a new way of life was formed!

Joel and all his friends are gone —
But Clayton's past will forever live on!

Diana Kierce

A PRAYER OF THANKSGIVING

This prayer was written especially for the
Indian Festival of Arts Thanksgiving Feast
held in 1962 in La Grande, Oregon and has
been used many times since by popular request.

Great Spirit or Heavenly Father; We stand before Thee
and give thanks for all Blessings given unto us.

We feel Thy presence as we stand before the candle-lit
altar or sit around the campfire at twilight, and
again as we listen to the divine music from man-made
instruments or the song of birds as they greet the dawn.

We see Thy handiwork as we gaze at the beautiful stained
glass windows in our houses of worship, the delicate
tracery of color in a butterfly's wing, the great
paintings of man, or the gorgeous hues of sunset on the
clouds in the western sky.

We hear Thy voice in the beautiful hymns sung by choirs
of singers, the gentle murmur of the brook or pounding
of surf on the shores of the sea.

Guide us each day in all that we do and lead us along life's
pathway, even though we do not all travel the same path,
we will all reach the same eternal land where we will stand
before Thee and be judged on that final day and if we be
worthy let us enter for all eternity.

Earl Van Blokland

SOUTHERN MEMORIES

My barefoot days were over and time to say goodby.
  Braids in my hair, tears in my eyes, I left my Southern Skies.

The grasshoppers, the butterflies, the yellow jackets too.
  The rainbow-colored morning-glories, the early morning dew.

The many walks down dirt roads, the hills I had to climb.
  The hot sun beaming down on me, all memories of the time.

The old folks peering over glasses, old wise tales to share.
  The love, the feelings, the warmth we felt, nothing to compare.

The Proud Carolina Mountains so beautiful all around.
  Whenever I called out to you, you echoed back a sound.

Those special memories of the south shall remain until I die.
  I miss the Carolina Mountains, I love YOU Southern Skies.

  Wilma McDonald

DOODLE POODLE

This started as a doodle but turned into a poodle —
A little black poodle named Babette.
I wonder what goes on in the noodle of a poodle?
She surprised me with her answer, "Don't you fret."

Her cocky tam-o-shanter and her poodle-talking banter
From her Scotch or French ancestors did she get?
What is more entrancing than her French-heeled slippers dancing,

And her dainty feet a-prancing in their mincing flirting
With her powder puff tail a-wiggling (which is a poodle's way of giggling)

She looks around for new adventures gay.
Then the dogs came by oodles,

The dogs were all a-barking, "Hurrah!"
As she sat there perusing whom she would be choosing,
I distinctly heard a poodle, "Oo la la!"

  Rosemary L. Kintzinger

THE KING IS GONE

It was August 1977 that Elvis went to heaven to join his brother, mother.
His wife and daughter feel his presence near. Rock and roll was his game,
and fame was his name. Forget him not, his name will carry on for life, and
he will always remember his wife. Lisa is now grown and Elvis will remain
known. The King is gone may he rest in peace.

  Richard A. Pelvin

WORLD WAR II YEARS

Of these long years I don't like to remember,
But the memories come back each 7th of December.

We were sitting around the fire that December Sunday morning,
Ready for church time when the radio gave us the warning.

They said the Japanese were bombing Pearl Harbor,
Killed people and tore up those buildings just like they were arbors.

Very soon our dear friends and loved ones signed up to go.
They wanted to defend our dear country and their love to it show.

I have many dear loved ones who fought in that awful fight.
Some didn't come back, others are still buried in a faraway country tonight.

I pray they are resting and ready for the day
To hear God say "Come into heaven. This is the way."

  Oleta Cox Garrard

A PLACE IN THE SUN

Baby I am a Rich Man
Baby I am not clutching at the sun
I want a place in it
I'm not shooting at the Moon
The moon shines on me
The stars they sparkle on me
I don't want to Rule the land
God does it for me
There is a place in the sun
For those who seek it
I will find it
The one who puts her trust in me
Won't be let down
And together we will find our place

  Billy Woillard

WOILLARD, WILLIAM EUGENE. Pen Name: Billy Woillard; Born: Slaton, Texas, 3-7-46; Divorced; Education: Texas Tech University, 1964-68; Occupation: former Silk Screen Artist, Austin, Texas; Memberships: Writers Club; Poetry: 'Game of Marriage,' American Poetry Association, 1984; 'I Was Taken for Granted,' unpublished; Other writings: *From Good to What,* book, unpublished; "The Return the Year 2011," play, unpublished; *The Diary of From Love to Lust to Dust,* book, copyright 1981; Comments: *I like to express my views of history, love and philosophy of life.*

If I had just once to tell
you this
I'd tell you in a story

The obstacles, adversities
and seemingly catastrophies
are nothing
but a giggle
hidden sweetly
in the puzzle
on this subliminal journey
through cyclic time
and dimensional space
interrupted
only
momentarily
by your mind's

Beliefs

  Jill E. Holden

YOU ARE SO SWEET

When I at first knew you,
My darling dear, to greet,
I looked in your blue eyes
and said, you are so sweet.

When in your arms I'm held,
Oh, how my heart does beat.
Oh, how I love you dear
Sweetheart, you are so sweet.

To press your lips to mine
Again, I do entreat.
I'll tell the world once more
My dear, you are so sweet.

And now my darling dear
My joy is so complete.
You've told me you love me,
My dear, you are so sweet.

Theodore Sparks

IMPERFECTIONS

Some people think we all should be
like this and not like that.
It's okay if you are skinny
but it's not if you are fat.

Come Sunday, and you're not in church
your soul will surely burn.
It's you who'll have to answer
the day it comes your turn.

"Her legs are much too short," they say,
"His hair; it is too long."
The perfect people play the judge,
and they are never wrong.

Let's tell them to come down to earth,
'cause they're just people too.
They all have imperfections,
just like me and you.

Rhonda B. Huff

MIRRORED EYES

When I woke up this morning,
And looked into mirrored eyes;
Saw at once who I really am
Without make-up or disguise.

Feeling like a diamond in the rough,
Where beauty lies dormant there
Then to polish for a gleam and glow
Means that I really care.

Caring also about this world today;
About how it's politically run,
About the environment, starvation, wars;
and pestilences to overcome.

The beauty to find is the peace we bring,
When changing focus on mirrored eyes,
Trying to polish the rough crude world,
Brings out the brilliance which underlies.

Gladys I. Swanson

TOGETHER

Right from the start
You came to me
Your eyes sought mine
It had to be
The heat of Summer now is gone
Will you stay with me?
Although Autumn is cold and brisk
Stay here with me and take the risk
All through Winter, wet and white
I'll keep you warm each and every night
And when Spring comes you'll agree
That from the start you've needed me
And if ever we should become
Two of us instead of one
We'll know our love is forever strong
All is right and nothing's wrong
And at last when death is near
We'll know for sure we have no fear.

Patsy Collins and Johnny Spears

THE WORLD

This world is a cesspool
(we're as maggots in slime)
What we do with our lives
is a matter of time.

It once was a paradise
blessed and pure
(Although at the time
it was quite immature).

We've grown much in wisdom
in all the wrong ways
which we shall regret
for the rest of our days.

Unless there's a change
'mongst us creatures of sod
to turn ourselves back
to the teachings of God.

God weeps as we falter
yet it still could be
we could come to His altar
and could all be set free.

Felicia Nauck

MY FIRST-BORN

Twenty years ago today
    A gift from Heaven sent
Close to my breast you lay
    My first-born.

So gently cradled in my arms
    So sweet, so dear, so warm
I gazed upon your baby charm,
    My first-born.

I held the world tight to my heart
    Though other joys have come
No other could fill quite the part
    Of my first-born.

'Tis then I felt God's purpose true
    And felt akin with her
Who loved as I, but mankind slew
    Her first-born.

So may this thrill be yours someday
    When close within your arms
Completest love will come to stay
    With your first-born.

Hazel Smith

WINDOWS, WORDS

Silent words
    scream at me
    from pages yellowed gray:
stately lines
    of print on page
    and words of many kinds.

Silent sounds
    of ghosts of thought
    reflected before our eyes:
whirling words
    transcending minds
    of print on papered time.

Colin A. Sachs

PUBESCENCE

Blooming in the dead of winter,

Bumps and curves show
through the girly gown.

Eyes shine a knowing sheen
of pending change.

Golden daughter, flower girl,
wears her crimson badge,

All blossomed out in the dead of winter.

Malikah Abdus-Salaam

MY ROSE

Early summer bloom lifting
    Yearning toward the sky
Hungrily nourishing
    At sweet mother earth
Thirsting for the raindrops
    Breathing fresh clear essence

So soft, so delicate
    So vulnerable
So easily bruised
    So quickly crushed

So like my fragile Self

Annie O'Dunlaing

A PART OF THE UNIVERSE

Gazing into the universe in awe,
    marvel that it should be
And to me it draws
    to something of wonder

Something of wonder I see,
    meant to be just for me
For I marvel that one
    is like the glitter of the universe

Yes, though he has passed on
    that glitter remains
Oh philosopher, father mine.

Phyllis Smith Sanderson

TAILOR-MADE

Farewell despair, sorrow, endless longing
  another page of history slowly curls;
Turning softly away are grief and heart loss
  Barren, yet soon to be forgotten;
Just replaced by feelings too intense to mention.
  Most gently may I thank you, tender dear heart,
I'm grateful for your presence lingering, mellow.
  You've given me a new day radiant, gleaming.
My heart was breaking severely, 'til you brought me
  Quiet rest in the warmth of your compassion.
I'll follow you closely, and trust you each crossing
  of old roads over new, we'll face the challenge.
We've come a long way now, let us not falter;
  Our hearts are soldered closer with time's passing.
If only we had met years before to give
  All the dreams, heartaches, pleasures time to grow
and repeatedly kept each cherished moment undisturbed.
  Yet, here we are in this our day of splendor,
Held in love's tight grasp, until it seems
  Our lives, our very heartbeats were tailor-made.

Sharon Rasmussen

INEVITABLE EDIBLES

Each eats of something delectable, peculiar to its taste;
the raven, in its rookery, digests the rodent of the race,
and fan quail quiver in delight on grained fair; all mornings,
munchings start the day, in hay lands, shore and hill,
God's creatures stalk and search their inherited edibles,
breads upon the waters, insects in dank pools,
seeds fallen to the soil, fish and fowl, the human kinds,
and coiled beings, nibble, sip and masticate, in daily turns,
lace ferns drink of moistures fallen in the night,
while worms wend their ways in the silent, undulating earth,
digesting gobs of grained soils, bacteria, tasting green mildews
amid soft humus, molds and clays, wriggling nutrients
in their tunneled stay; the hawk, his glare spied down
upon the unsuspecting mouse, scurried from his house,
winged down, torn asunder, immortalized the velvet-footed wonder;
and the dragonfly, from beneath his water bedding,
strained up to gulp a skittering strider, dead;
while in the Everglades, the macaws call
and gnash on larvaed things, above the closing jaws
of spiny, warted, voracious crocodiles.

John Francis Speight

SEASONS OF THE COTTONWOOD

  Gnarled bare fingers grasping space
Dark gray bark against light gray sky
Drifts of snow piled around your base
Shuddering at the wind's harsh cry
Dread winter has you deep within its hold.
  Supple boughs nodding in the breeze
Dark red florets hang adorning
Nestled amid your light green frieze
Eagerly you greet the morning
As fellow denizens of spring unfold.
  Young couples seek your cooling shade
Dark green bowers invite romances
You delight in each man and maid
Boys swing again from your branches
Just as they have done since summers of old.
  Golden crown regally held high
Your beauty displayed with disdain
Flaunted against a bright blue sky
Prepared to meet winter again
Gathering resources to fight the cold.

LaVaughn Linnens

WE ARE JUST GETTING BETTER

Loving you is like a fine wine;
It's gettin' better and better with time.
There's snow on the rooftop,
But there's fire down below.
We're not growin' old,
We're just gettin' better.
The kids are at home on holidays,
And you know that we're kinda set in our ways.
Folks say that we should act our age,
and we should stop our runnin' around;
But they're just jealous, don't you know;
We're still in love and we let it show.
Times have changed but not so much;
'Cause we still remember our first touch.
Folks may gossip but that don't bother us;
We're happy and it shows.
God only knows;
The time we have together;
It keeps gettin' better, better and better;
'Cause we're just gettin' better.

Bernice Morrissey

MORRISSEY, BERNICE LAWS. Pen Names: Bernice Lineberry, Dixie Bryson; Born: Bryson City, North Carolina, 10-20-49; Married: 1966 to James Lineberry; 1982 to R. E. Morrissey; widowed, 1982; Education: Rowan Technical College, GED, 1979; Walla Walla Community College, C.N.A., Medical Secretary, 1981-82; South Central College, Photography and Journalism, 1983; Davidson County Community College, Human Relations Development, 1984; Occupations: Nursing, State DOT truck driver, Free Lance Photography; Memberships: Women's International Bowling Congress, Civil Air Patrol, Disabled American Veterans Auxiliary, Coast Guard Auxiliary; Poetry: *Through My Window,* book of poetry, 1982; Other Writings: 'Roses Don't Last Forever,' song, 1978; "A Time for Kids," short story, 1984; Comments: *My writing is an emotional show of senses, reaching out and letting go, sharing a caring, existing in time, written with reason and sprinkled with rhyme. Writing is an enjoyable pastime when I have a break from the everyday hustle and bustle world and yet it's a down to earth feeling that I love sharing with you.*

YEAR OF THE BIG TREE

February, 1985
Oregon's lifting up her skirt for me
Playing fast and loose with my emotions
Like a drunk at an office Christmas party

Me
This man of California
Once removed from Chicago
That me

Getting easier to surrender, harder to say no
To a new zip code, a new FM station
Perhaps my last great move
Oregon would do that to a man in early 1985

John Shaberg

SPECTRAL GROUND

A journey homeward; after many years
Over spectral ground; houses, streets,
Empty; save for fleeting ghosts, weaving in and out,
Everpresent to an intangent sense
Welcoming us home with memories of days forever gone.
The schoolyard, strangely quiet,
The stadium echoing memoried cheers of football's heady drone.
The well-hid trysting place, known to every swain,
Appears exposed in tattered clothes for everyone to see.
A generation long dispersed to winds of cold and balm
When meeting for few minutes fleet, act like strangers in a dream.
Youth is gone, high hopes have died, and routine sets in aspic.
Only in mind's eye are we allowed to see what was
Only in a dream can we again repose in bygone's blurry buzz.
Walk slowly over sacred ground;
Close your eyes as shades of mists try in vain to reappear in mirrored
shapes of days remembered when —
Stand your ground without a sound,
Only shadows of the mind, know the way o'er spectral ground.

Earl F. Pasbach

WHAT IS IT?

It is the cry of a little boy who is finding his life to be a bore.
It is the studious activities of a pupil who hopes that his schooling
will not be a trial.
It is the cry of a newborn infant that will find the world that
he has just entered to be different.
It is the hard work of a mother who keeps her painful feelings
smothered.
It is the entrance of a man into his household to find that his
life savings is stolen.

What Is It?
It is the dreaming of a student who hopes that one day his educational
achievements will be beaming.
It is the writings of a scholar in the hope that they will earn him
at least a dollar.
It is the singing of a songstress although some songs may cause her
some duress.
It is the dancing of a couple that sometimes creates a ruffle.

Michael Leroy Porter

COLD GRAY BUTTERFLY

4TH PLACE

His winter coats were always gray. His eyes distant, cold,
wandering as does a stray dog.

I can't remember as he did much. I remember him fishing most.

I still see him walking, stalking, always searching for something
that didn't exist.

Vivid in my mind is the way he loved me. He was the only one who
knew how. He chose me.

He always left me to burn rubber on highways, always returning after
weeks, or months, even years.

He comes back from time to time. I guess he never found anything
funny out there.

Connie Wentworth

GRAMPIE

Grampie of my childhood
Working with the pine wood.
Building boats, dollhouses, chairs,
and climbing up the cellar stairs
To leave his sawdust on the floors
When we ran in from out of doors.
Grampie of my adult years
Slowing step and weakened frame,
But the smile for us was the same.
No more working with the wood
But our long talks were just as good.
Grampie of your last few days
Even in your final phase
You greeted us with a smile
And wanted us to stay and talk for awhile.
Grampie, now you are gone
But, somehow, your smile lingers on.

Storm Ann Grogan

FOG HORNS

Lonely,
Disquieted,
Restless!

She watched at the window
As darkness approached,

Damp, eerie, ominous.

The fog settled in, and

Sounding akin to a mother cow
Bereft of her calf,

Fog horns began moaning,
Repeating their mournful cry

Over and over,
Again and again,

As if remembering the many times
Their warning had gone
Unheeded.

Viola Vomhof

JAR, SITUATED ON TABLETOP

7TH PLACE

Sit there, then: complacent,
impervious to worldly currents,
fancying yourself a house

for butter-bright daisies, scorning
our sad offers of poinsettia cuttings.

We have apologized for our fingerprints.
We have bathed you in water
of holy flouride.

We have given you a kingdom
of paisley tablecloth.

We have fed you
grains of gravy-coated rice.

Now you are melting in our memory,
relic of an almost-perfect childhood,
collector of angry dinner-argument stares,

serene, dulled glass,
a vision of yourself.

Thomas Glave, Jr.

In the middle of the journey of my life I confronted myself in
the dark woods. And there I stood as a shimmering ray of sun
squeezed through the dense foliage of towering trees. It was as
if that beam of light came to rest upon my soul, splitting me
like a laser, allowing my stored-up decades to diffuse into the
atmosphere. Part of me escaped to indiscriminately touch the
world. Ahead there is a clearing where sparsely swaying trees
fail to encumber the warm light of day. A clearing which allows
me to be more perceptive of others and more keenly aware of myself.
The forest has been my hiding place for years but now I've come
from behind the trees ready to face a new tomorrow. While some
will find favor with my new release, others may not. But it's
too late to turn back now.

Robert J. Goodstein

TAPESTRY OF WORSHIP
*(Dedicated to those whose Music Ministry spins Threads of Gold
for Worship "Tapestries.")*

I come early to the Chapel to listen and to pray.
Sacred hymns of Love and Praising to our Father as of old
Pour out worship as piano and organ softly play,
And I feel that they are spinning Love to threads of Lustrous Gold.

And Love is *there* as church-bells ring and as the Chapel fills,
As brethren add their prayers and praise and joyful — sing along
Thanking God and weaving — led by Pastor's loving skills —
A Tapestry of Worship with threads of Gold from sacred song.

Then with Tapestry presented for The Father's waiting Eye,
Though part, as mortal artifact, could fall short of Heaven's Plan
We trust in His Abiding Grace to accept our earnest try,
And hope our Tapestry will please — *aglow* with Love from Man!

Douglas M. Jones

THE AFTER CHRISTMAS BLUES

When my children were growing up, especially when they were small,
They drew pictures on the windowpane and left muddy footprints in the hall.
And it seemed that there was a lot of noise from morning until night.
And on those certain days, it seems, there was sure to be a fight.
But somehow, along the way, they learned to be quite good.
And learned to be more thoughtful, as normal children should.
But now my children are grown and gone, and I miss them, one and all.
There's no picture on the windowpane, or footprints in the hall.
And all about the place right now, it's quiet as can be.
For now it seems so lonesome, for there is only me.
Now those children who were so boisterous, have children of their own,
Who even now have children: Oh my, how time has flown.
But then again, on Christmas Eve, they all come flooding back
And it seems that they are Santa Claus, with presents in a pack.
They stay awhile and then all leave, and I miss them one and all.
They leave no pictures on the windowpane, only footprints in the hall.

Katherine Oberg

FOOD FOR THOUGHT: WHY DIET?

Almost everybody talks about his or her new diet:
When at a party, it's impossible to keep folks quiet.
Someone suggests the giraffe steak sandwich, a triple decker,
For the goofy lover who wishes to be a long necker.
A sly wag says the rabbit stew diet is simply terrific;
But beware! It's only for women who wish to be prolific.
If you're keyed up, under terrific pressure and wish to slow down,
Be sure to take terrapin soup; it's guaranteed for people of renown.
Some diet fanatics suggest that if you wish to look as thin as a rail,
Hike a mile, eat a small hush puppy and nibble on a lobster tail.
Timid party folks might think of eating apple sauce, the Eden fruit,
But such a diet might tempt you to run around in your birthday suit.
If you strive to be a social pariah or a renegade outcast,
No doubt a big serving of parboiled skunk liver is unsurpassed.
Thousands and thousands are looking around for a fat-free diet;
But I am a three-dessert man! Why don't you join me and try it?

J. Fay Anderson, Esq.

GRAND ALASKA

Alaska hold your majesty high
Where God's fingertips touch the sky.
One can breathe only cool crisp air
And tramp in the snow without care.
See in the mountaintops freedom flowing
As past you the clouds are blowing.
There is no state as grand as she
Just as the Sequoia is to the tree.
Although Kentucky is my home
My heart in Alaska will always roam.

Patsy Collins

THE HUNTER

Eyes of the hawk,
Tall and sinewy
Like a tree
Stands the Hunter.

Alert to every movement,
Every breath;
He listens for prey.

Branches breaking —
Fear!
Quicksilver dashing through the trees,
White tail flashing as he flees;
The stag falls to the ground
Dropped by the sure arrow
Of the Hunter.

T. L. Hutcheson

THE COIN

Seek a perfect round shape
coin of shining silver, and let
it rest on your thumb.

Flip the coin in the air see
how it turns 'round, and 'round.
Call it for goodness' sake before
it stops.

It strikes the surface very
hard it bounces up, and down
how it lands I do not care.

Heads I win, Tails you lose
for this little coin will tell
me so.

Jesse Ceuteno

PONDERING!

Reminiscing — Meditating!
        Of a time,
    A kindly touch
            Was mine!

Seemingly,
        A shield from harm!
An assurance of security,
        Faith, hope, belief.
A motivation to carry on!

The sensation lingers
    Steadfast —
                constant —
                    True!
    Missing you!

Nina W. Kurkamp

157

ESSENCE OF FRIENDSHIP

Petals from our favorite the yellow rose
lily-of-the-valley blooming fair
peonies plus daffodils
babies' breath and more
bits of lemon rind and orange
cinnamon stick with cloves
all blended and dried with care.
Perched atop this potpourri jar
a glass bird, immobile, sings eternally.
When the lid is lifted gently
soft essence of Nebraska floats
from my flower garden to you.
Dear friend, each time you open it
picture us here on the rolling plains
the joys of childhood and youth, as we romped,
together tending our friendship until it grew
beyond the realms of time or place.
This wee jar brings a rare gift of remembrance
though far apart we are forever near
space never parts two souls so together in mind and heart.

Velva Arlyne Urwiler

THE SEASON WITH A REASON

The crocus are poking up through the ground —
Trees are all budding all over town —
The sap is running from the old maple tree —
Out on the lawn a robin I see —

The river is cresting around the Ox bow —
Soon it will get higher and then overflow —
The meadows are changing from white to green —
Signs of spring are easily seen —
The bluebird is singing a sweet refrain —
As he seeks out a worm in the falling rain —

Many a fancy will turn into love —
As old man winter gives spring a shove —
It's a beautiful sight for all to see —
That will find your heart with ecstasy —

Put some springtime in your heart —
Enjoy mother nature's work of art —
Then you'll be entitled to a new start —

Ella L. Plourd

ANGST

HONORABLE MENTION

My outré fascination, who ne'er had eyes for me,
But in whose eyes a misanthrope of solitude I see;
   And such angelic face
   Did not da Vinci's canvas grace.
My guru, my Yoko, my yin . . .
She lifts me up and brings me down again.
   Sheer white hose
   And soft-hued clothes:
That linen would I fain see o'er
The rod above my shower door,
And play her body like a lyre —
To strum it softly by the fire.
   A glance askance will hold me fast
    And take away my breath;
   Such is to trepidation life,
    And to all courage, death.

Am I ready for the conflict? Is my armor all in place?
God, grant me a strong beard, for weak is my face.

Richard W. Bolson

BORROWED PEN

A minute, infinitesimal part of the poetic world
A borrower of, "The Poetry Masters," thoughts and pearls
A guider of the unprecedented quill
I cannot seem to get my poetic fill.

Do the, "Masters," mind; the small part
That I am playing to get my start?
Are they enthused with my daily "Thanks?"
For the prepared way, they did enhance.

Are these guardians of the "Mighty Pen"
Transferring thoughts to me, and other men?
They appear to have entered my very being
And pressed the pen into all I am seeing.

The "Masters" have given me more than planned for
By introducing me to a world of grandeur
Though I am penning all that I feel
I cannot express the elation, with a zeal.

It would take all the poetic expertise
To describe my feeling and still be brief
For I am awed and totally astounded
By "The Poetry Kingdom" that they have founded.

T. Steven Watkins

LAND OF THE GOLDEN MOON

Passing by, these night creatures
   once startled, gaze upon your golden features.
"Let it begin!" announces the owl.
   And all attend — animal, fish and fowl.

"Do not pass us by," the owl gently cries,
   "before we get our fill.
We look to you for guidance —
   without you we have no chance."

The creatures are weary yet become very still,
   for the night-lance is present and is ready for the kill.
The moment is there the chosen one knows . . .
   magically, the image wanes, then suddenly goes.

Your rising light
   once again protects those creatures of the night
the night-lance vows to select.
   With shadows, you shield them from sight.

Amidst the fury from claws empty and bare
   there is no need to worry.
The night-lance looks up and stares,
   "You never play fair!"

Dennis A. Spoonhour

THE NEW VAMPIRES

They creep about in their orange and white,
Obtusely stalking the town day and night,
Yearning the blood of unwitting victims,
Fained by the flow of the precious fluid,
Pained by the lack of its presence.

The curse of those who toil in pain,
Not by choice but the need of the time,
The suffering of others becomes a need,
The joy of blood becomes a want,
Caught in the flow of everpresent gore.

Fangs whet to sip the precious blood,
The more they taste the more they want,
Beaten by the bug infesting the time,
Abound by the world at hand,
The thirst and lust for the blood ever grows.

LeRoy Vickerstaff, Jr.

DAWN

Gray, silent, mystic hour
  When dawn and dark contend.
Suddenly over yonder tower,
  Sol's first rays do bend.
How still! And yet this silence warns
  Of life that's yet to come.
How still! When day is newly born
  And peace and I are one.

Now the veil lifts rapidly
  And piercing lights invade
The corners that were, formerly,
  The kingdom of the shade.
Where night's protective blanket lay
  o'er a sleeping fen,
Now Phoebus, with his powerful rays,
  Rides triumphant o'er the glen.

Carey Tenen

EL GRECO'S HOUSE

I have walked in
El Greco's garden
my shoes powdered
with timeless
summer dust.
Winding ivy columns
once brushed past
hands and now mine.
Have feasted on paintings
in soul communion within,
a heart of dreamer's magic
lit with lantern roses.
In his studio my eyes
have met the canvas tears
of Saint Peter.
While twentieth century
curtains danced with
clinging confessional beads
in combined love of Toledo.

Doreen Breheney Robles

the guitarist

he weaves fingers among musical warps
twining harmonies into rich fabric
embellished by the fibre of his voice —
delicate rhythmic vapors blended with
subtle three-strand chords hypnotically
bind us to the strum of the tapestry.

k. i. mcdaniel

DUCKS ON CRISP LAKE

HONORABLE MENTION

Toward evening the air is thick
with summer as ducks ballerina
the blue surface of Crisp Lake.

Time is winding down these days —
even sparrows seem blessed
in the blue bowl of sky sweeping
up and down in evening air.

The trees beside the lake are oak
and briar, willow and spire ringing
the mass huddled in their houses:
the hand shakes, the sleeper drowses
and the ducks on Crisp Lake
are never aware of darkening themes;
but only swim and breathe the cavendish
of oak and spinning dreams.

Glen Enloe

THE ROCK

I found it lying on the beach,
half-buried in the sand.
Battered by time,
wind,
and rain.
What tales could its worn surface tell
of times past?
How long did it lie there
in the sand,
waiting to be found?
What was it made of?
What could it tell me
about the Earth?
but silent and smooth,
it would not answer my questions.
So I let it drop,
returned it to where it had been found.
Back to where it had been
before I arrived
and disturbed it.

Michael P. Dunn

EDUCATION

Under the fluorescent glow
Posters of pedagogy gaze
Upon the neatly, occupied
Desks of learning.
Scribbles on paper discuss
Halls of ancient myths and events during
Centuries spoken long ago.

The podium stands erect
Reigning with pride and distinction
Abaft, a voice calls
Upon its audience
To listen, feel and display
The knowledge of another day.

The world perceives a lifestyle
Thoughts expand and flourish
A new dawn approaches
Discarding the obsolete
Possessed in search of the truth.

Karla Korff

I'LL SEE YOU SOON

Dearest daughter,
I'll see you soon.
It has been quite some time
Since you and Mommy left — together.
It was not my fault;
It was not Mommy's fault;
It surely was not yours.
Someone needed you both more than I.
I was unhappy then —
I tried to understand.
I knew you both were happy.
I said before, "I'll see you soon,"
But something always intervened.
This time I'm sure;
All preparations have been made
I know it will be a one-way trip.
I learned of it today.
The doctor said, "Jack, it's terminal
you have a week to go"
I'll see you soon — Love, Dad.

Edward J. McDermott

ROSEBUD SHELL

Each tiny rosebud is a shell
Tossed by the waves upon the shore:
A creature within used to dwell;
In the ocean's ceaseless roar.

Each expired and left behind,
The shell to beautify and use:
A touch of magic, you will find
A bouquet anyone might choose.

When life for us is through,
Pray what we leave not be in vain:
May all the good we sought to do,
Be reclaimed and used again.

Una Marzie

TIME

I behold a photo from years before.
It has the power to open the door
And let that time live once again
When I was but a child of ten.
I see a girl with eyes so wide
And round cheeks dimpled on each side.
That little girl I used to be
Has changed into the present me.
It seems that I have changed so fast,
The present blending with the past.
I think I need to understand
That time is always in command.
I should not wish for it to go,
because it shall before I know.

Deborah J. Dion

TO MY WIFE ON VALENTINE'S DAY

Valentine's Day was set aside
  For a girl like you
Who is by my side
  For the love you have given
    Has made my life
Seem like living in heaven
  For our years together
    Has molded us into one
Which sure was plenty of fun
    And as the years go by
Our foundation will survive
And so to you my dear
I cherish our love year after year
  Which I hold so close and dear

Edward Gottesman

EXCHANGING HEARTS

What profit a man to conquer?
The world at his feet lay
But, if he is not so loved
He uses cupid to capture
And, wins hearts by valentines
Expressing love through poems
Persuading with love notes
Used by men of modern times
With lace and words bold
A tale in love sonnet told
Spreading a message of self
Combining with motivation
The exchange of love wealth
Sending a pattern heart melt.

Louise Helene Bros

The wind blows away
we look around
at who we are

Derek Ray

CREATION

My father often told me
When I was very small,
There was a time when
No one had to work at all!

God made the whole big world,
The animals and the birds,
Trees, then flowers and fruit —
Even taxes were unheard!

It took Him six long days
So His world would not fade —
The seventh was for rest, and
God liked what He had made!

He got busy making a man
To enjoy and live here, too
But man was very lonesome, so
God brought a woman into view —

Everyone was happy, but
When all the birds had nested,
Ever since that glorious day,
Neither God nor man has rested!

Edna M. Parker

PARKER, EDNA MAE. Born: Near Leith, North Dakota, 3-17-10; Widow; Education: High School Graduate; Occupations: Bookkeeper, Private Secretary, Postmaster for twenty years; Memberships: Newspaper Institute of America (Graduate), Sierra Club (national), Cedarville Area Historical Society; Poetry: *Every Memory Precious,* book of original poems, Monroe Publishing Co., 1984; 'My Daughter,' *American Poetry Anthology,* 1983; 'Has A Nice Day,' *American Poetry Anthology,* 1984; 'Creation,' *Art of Poetry,* 1985; Comments: *My goal: to portray the happiness of a Christian Life to encourage and help people in every walk of life, regardless of color, race, or creed, with special emphasis on the children.*

I'M SORRY

Harsh words leave my lips
Quickly.
So quickly
That I can't catch them.
I'm sorry.
I didn't want to say
What I said.
But Anger brought the
Hurting words out.
Please come back to me.
Don't leave me
Standing alone.
Wounds heal faster
When treated right away.
I didn't want to hurt you.
I love you.
I feel so alone.
Come back to me
Please.

Tina Jo Race

HAUNTING MEMORIES

Within the corners of my mind;
    remembering,
Reliving memories
    through stirring emotions —
Some good, others horrid
    They cut deep within
    my soul.
Still, some unexplained fears
    never-to-be solved —
There's no purpose now
    in dwelling upon them.
Time scurries past
    leaving unanswered questions.
Wondering, doubting,
    soon-to-be erased
Permanently blissful feelings
    to take their place.
Kneeling, silently sobbing,
    I am forgiven.

Rose Marie Augustine

MY SOUL

my soul has been
pulled to the ground
        secured
by weights
of hostility

Monica Page

WELL BEINGS

Do we become WELL BEINGS with medical
    treatment from physicians?

Can we self-mend our body and soul;
    are we the magicians?

Or is it our faith in the Savior that
    radiates the healing powers?

May it be the strength given by family
    and friends; our depending towers?

Is it according to individualistic beliefs
    that contributes to a WELL BEING?

For these reasons I would base my decision
    whether one would go WELL, on living?

Gloriann McLin

COMPASSIONS

I presented footprints
to a lonely pasture
It showed me unending flowers and trees

I gave to a beggar
A peace of mind
He shared insight with me

I provided food for a squirrel
When winter was harsh
He showed me the beauty of nature

I gave to a child
Warmth of heart
Shared with me was the emotion of life

I doubt I should ever see
A granted gift to forever be
Greater than living, for life is the key

James Toal

TOAL, JAMES EDWARD. Pen name: The Sangamon Valley Poet; Born: Newport, Kentucky, 3-13-47; Single; Education: Northwestern High, Palmyra, Illinois; Occupations: Poet and Writer; Memberships: Disabled American Veterans, Van Meter Lodge #762 AF & AM, Athens, Illinois; Poetry: 'Essential,' American Poetry Association, 1984; 'Ole Muddy,' *Hoosier Challenger,* 1984; 'Ole Oak,' *Illinois State Journal Register,* 1984; 'Ole Sangamon,' *Menard Magazine,* 1985; Other Writings: "The Day a Hog Was Judge," short story, *Menard Magazine,* 1985; Comments: *I enjoy writing and express feelings relating to places and people past and present which have influenced me to the degree that I feel a part of.*

the
TWINkleTWINkle
lights on my christmas tree
are flashing PEACEonEARTHgoodWILLtoMEN
in
MORSE
code

Cathleen G. Cuppett

BURNING SHIPS

Slip sliding embraces of love
Kisses tasting deliciously fine
Loving you this dark, cold night
Allows me to savor your sweetness like a fine wine.

Heavenly clouds crowd my head
Saturating an already stimulated brain
Looking forward to our destined rendezvous
Your scent drives me totally insane.

Sizzling emotions stand perked and ready
Holding undercover feelings on track
Imagining your body entwined with mine
Forces blood to rush to my heart and back

One little kiss would make my day
PLEASE! . . . surrender to THESE awaiting arms
Snuggle atop my muscular chest
Share with me all your wonderful charms

Collect each heartbeat as a token of love
Help cool intense heated lips
I pray this evening lasts forever
as we sail, as one, . . . embracing . . . BURNING SHIPS.

Jerome Sheldon Silverberg

LITTLE ANGEL

It was many and many seasons ago,
In the beauty of June's warm days,
God sent to earth a blessing of love,
A symbol of His wonderful grace.

The blessing of love, cheeks pink as a rose,
Eyes bright as gems in the night,
Was none but an angel, come down to earth,
To shed His heavenly light.

And this angel dwelled for nine sweet years,
Among mortals like you and me,
Then by some mystery received her wings,
Flew far beyond the sea.

I've longed to gaze upon her smile,
Hear her soft voice now and then,
A dear little angel, come down to earth,
Whose name was Kimberly Lynn.

But memory has seen her lovely face,
Heard her voice ringing gentle still,
Beyond the fading rainbow trail,
Blue waters and green rolling hills.

Jean Manning

YOU ARE MY WORLD

You are the peace I feel within.
The dawn that starts my day.
The sunset that puts my mind to rest.
The moonlight that shows the way.
You are the stars that twinkle in my eyes.
The twilight of an eternal flame
That burns with love every day.
You are the mountain that I lean on.
The river that flows with happiness.
You are all seasons
Bringing us together as one,
Flying through the universe
On the wings of the unknown.
Our lifetime together is like a burning star,
An eternity of shining lights.
You are my world
And I will love you
'Til the sun is no more.

Gladys L. Leturgey

KARMA

One rat, one mouse, one cat. The rat's eyes were always filled with red. The mouse seemed unsure of the amount of freedom to allow himself. At times the hate gleamed in the eyes of the mouse. The cat spent a great deal of time fast asleep in his basket. The three lived in that way, each and every day, one against the other.

One night the mouse sat at one end of the house without a grandfather's clock. The mouse escaped death more than once from the cat, whose interest was more in the size of the rat. The mouse lost all his luck that very same night.

The rat and the cat got in a fight. The cat gave the rat a good thrashing, after using all his might. The cat so very proud for the deeds that he had done, got killed by a dog for no reason except fun.

The dog with a grin started for his house. The dog got hit by a car driven by a drunk, who was mad at his wife.

When the drunk hit the dog, he lost control, and rolled off the bank. In those same minutes that seemed like hours he lost his life.

The owners of the cat searched in vain. The owners of the dog found his end, and felt the pain. The wife of the dead man collected insurance money. Her secret lover thought it was funny.

The crippled rat still with his breath, the others involved were locked for a short time in their deaths.

Robin Williams

WHY THE LITTLE THINGS MEAN SO MUCH

People wonder why the little
things mean so much;
why I often cry over such. Is it
that my heart is too easily touched?
Or am I just sensitive that much?
Like a person with a fractured leg depending
on a crutch; the little things to me mean
that much. Why is this? I may never know;
people wonder why as days come and go.

Changing my attitude about the little things
might help; but I'll never forget the
pain I felt. I put my heart above my head;
that's why I live in darkness like those
that are dead. My heart keeps saying it's
just not fair; for me to live forever in despair.
I'm continuing to search for something that will
last, but time keeps going by so fast,
just like a car running out of gas; hoping
this all will soon pass. My heart is
beating faster than the speed of sound.
Wondering where I am bound? Maybe
it's just a heart too easily touched;
because the little things mean so much.

Regina Cooke

THE FORGOTTEN CHILD OF IRAN

I am the forgotten child of Iran
Crying out loud as the earth hollows beneath me
The hand is all that's seen I grope for the sky
As the walls close I shout
   Wait I'm here
The forgotten child of Iran

Life turns dark I think my bones crack
Pain rushes in and controls my being
My throat is clogged with blood flowing to my mouth
I try to scream I probably manage a garbled
wait it's me the forgotten child of iran

No one listens nobody cares I possibly die believing
My blood is drawn through hate though I spell love
Nothing will remain whole except perhaps my soul
It may leave my diary safe in the dust

Please toast a coke for the child of Iran
Francis Antho Govia

CHRISTOPHER

It was a night in early September
  before the moon was shining bright.
That the stork came o'er the mountains
  to pick a Jackson landing site.

He was glad to drop his burden
  and thankful it wasn't two,
As he took off for the next delivery
  before the night was halfway through.

The directions with the package read;
  "If the baby is wont to cry,
Keep one end stuffed and happy
  and the other end clean and dry."

Before seven in the morning
  he was bathed and tucked in bed
With a very happy mother
  that was glad she had wed.

So he came to "Old Wyoming"
  to a home upon the hill,
And Mike has applied for the Stork's
    assistant
  to help settle up the bill.

Charles F. Spencer

LOVE

One fine day
I made a Valentine gay,
  With red foil bright
  And fluted lace so white.

I carefully tucked it in
An envelope thin.
Soon it was on its way
To my friend far away.

Have no fear,
My message was clear,
Though many miles apart,
I LOVE you with all my heart.

Sr. Cecilia Reising, S.S.S.F.

FUN-CITY KID

My rats; my bed!

Fun city: where the action is,
  where it Happens; an
one-time, all-Time Hit city!

Junkie on the roof top,
  pusher on the corner,
  rats on the fire
escape (rusty, useless),
  rats in my bed!

Take me away from here!
I can't!
Give me what YOU've got!
I won't!

You WILL!

I AM the action, (exploding?)
I AM what's happening NOW!
Oh, Hell!
I'll give you my grass,
  my rats, my bed —
I'm FREE! that day IS

Grant La Farge

WE NEED THEE LORD

We need thee Lord to help us
This we always knew
We're living in a mad world rush
We don't know what to do

Please give us your tender love
We are very sad today
Send us your love from above
And guide us on our way

We need thee Lord thou knowest
It's rough in this world
Of gleaning in the rows
We've become so hurt

But no matter what comes
Our way, we love Thee
The bird sings the bee hums
We'll look around and see

We need Thee Lord and always will
Until the time thou callest
us to Thy home or yonder hill
Keep us from all pitfalls.

Dorothy H. Harvey

MEN

Men are always hanging
    around
Some are out to put us
    down
Men come in black and white
Many young men are outta
    sight
Some men are hard to hold
they'll take over our body
    and soul
Men work hard each and
    every day
When they come home we
    take their pay
Men are hipped and men
    have soul
But some men you just
    can't control.

Nora A. Squash

WALK WITH ME

Walk awhile with me
Through the cool forest and you will see
Time is ageless; nature endless
Life's secret lies plain to see.

The babbling brook that twists and turns
Knows why our paths do cross
Can you not read the leaves on the trees?
They tell of the dreams we have lost

Walk awhile with me
Across the vast beaches and you will see
Eons have passed; hopes have gone
Life's sorrows and joys go ever on

The rolling waves that swirl and swell
know of once great plans
Can you not see the script written there?
It tells of the life of man

Look to the sunrise sparkling with dew
Gently caressing our souls
It speaks softly of promises new
It tells you all you should know.

Rose Brandon

NIGHT

Moon shadows
slide across the bare wood floor.

Night sounds
  the chirrup of crickets
  breep of tree frogs
  howl of a moonstruck god.

This late world rustles with
  whispering wind
As faraway points of light
  chase across distant galaxies.

Valerie A. Smith

ALONE WITH ME

Silence screams and
I can't sleep.

Sadness chokes me and
I can't weep.

Loneliness knocks and
Friends bustle in.

The smile on my face is
Replaced by a grin.

My lover calls and
I'm not home.

My television answers the phone.

My father died and
My mother is dead.

I'm not the only one
Inside my head.

I'm alone with all my fear.
It's time to move; it's crowded here.

Evelyn Wood

SUNDAY AFTERNOON

Two hours since you've gone and still
I can feel your arm across my back,
your breath against my neck.

The breeze billows the curtains
as it sweeps through the window
  and curls up beside me.

It discovers that the sheet is still warm.

The linen lies bunched to the slopes
of your hips and shoulders, and the pillow
pretends that you haven't left.

Your perfume haunts the room
  and tantalizes my nose,
    which instinctively probes
      for the back of your ear.

The noonday sky threatens rain,
but the clouds crawl past
in reverence to the glow
of your lasting presence.

I close my eyes and dream
  of your return.

David Schrader

FRIEND

Someone you can count on
Who's always by your side
With trust and understanding
To always be your guide
Someone who accepts you
Without question or a doubt
No matter what your needs be
Who always helps you out
Someone that you care for
In a very special way
Who feels the same about you
From whom you'll never stray
Someone whose inner beauty
Is wholesome, rich and rare
Who makes you feel you're special
You've much you want to share
Someone who'll always be there
Until the very end
Who never fails to show you
The meaning of a friend.

Helene Cohen

ABOUT AN HOUR

There's a gray barnboard plank
Across our stream.
I remember when we splashed
Barefooted through the rill.
Now, I cross gingerly
With my leather shoes,
And linger on the far bank alone.
I look out on the fields
And think of those times, with you.
Then back I go to the edge
Of that weathered board,
And I notice the moss in the cracks.
I peer down at the pebbles
That once appeared pearled.
Now they are just ugly rocks
In a reflective pool.
The plank is a sponge
With a backbone of strength,
Left over and waiting
For time to descend; like us.

Linda J. Bartlett

MUSES

Loneliness,
a struggle deep within
a war you lose or win.

Conscience,
reflection of the soul
mirror of the mind.

Love,
the utmost fulfillment
a woman's deepest woe.

Desertion,
ravishment of the spirit
scar imbedded forever.

Survival,
turning stumbling blocks
into stepping stones.

Ann Moutray

ENTRUST

Meadows tell their
secrets to the mountains
but who can the mountains
          turn to . . .

The valley perhaps?
Not a wise choice,
for the valley echoes
          all it knows . . .

Marianne Andrest

ANDREST, MARIANNE JANE. Born: Gloversville, New York, 7-21-65; Single; Education: Mayfield Central School, graduated 1983; currently attending Fulton-Montgomery Community College with a major in counseling, 1983-85; Occupation: Part-Time Clerk, Nichols Department Store, Gloversville, New York; Poetry: 'Side by Side,' love poem, John Campbell, publisher, 1984; Comments: *Through my writings, I express love and kindness. I revolve my poetry around the following concept: before you can be a friend to others, first you must be a friend to yourself. Also, I feel that a lot of couples suffer needless pain because of a lack of communication between them. Individuals have a difficult time expressing themselves, as I do. In return, I complement my setbacks in life by expressing myself through poetry.*

SPARROW

Just you,
          inside me.
The pain
          of death
near.
          We plunge,
and then . . .
          the birth cry.
And I
     behold you,
my
  hungry sparrow.

T. M. Townsend

INDIAN SONG

He has a rich heritage,
Filled with war and peace.
He is filled with pride.
The last of a dying breed.
But in the days of ancient
          lore . . .
He would be a great
     warrior, defender of
his tribe, a great chief.
He would be honored
     instead of unemployed,
needing only a medicine
     man instead of liquor to
          ease his pains.
the last of a dying breed;
     the song dies as an echo
          through the mountains.
His ancient tongue lost,
breeding a moody silence.

Ann Nelson

TO LOUISE, MY WIFE

If I a millionaire could be
I would shower you with jewelry
Sparkling diamonds, pretty pearls
You would be the envy of the girls
Latest fashion, fur and mink
Hats and dresses, blue and pink
There would be candlelight, champagne
Traveling the pleasure train
And we would go to every land
The very best at our command
And all the pleasures life could bring
You would be the queen and I the king.
But if my dreams do not come true
I always will be loving you
And as the years go fleeting by
We together, you and I
Are as blessed as we can be
An inspiration for my poetry.

Nils Rahmberg

RAHMBERG, NILS YNGVE. Born: 8-10-03; Married: to Louise; Education: High School in Sweden, College of Hard Knocks in U.S.A.; Occupation: Dining Room Maitre'D; Memberships: Scottish Rite; Awards: 'The Finger in the Vinegar'; Poetry: 'By the Sea,' *The Tower News*, 1972; 'A Dream,' *The Tower News*, 1968; 'The Seventh Day,' *The Tower News*, 1967; 'The Advent,' *The Tower News*, 1980; 'En Jul-Tanke,' Sweden, 1982.

WHAT IS A DAUGHTER?

A daughter is a beautiful person
Who worries about your health
And has no interest in your lack of wealth
She will only see the shining sun

She is the one who will care
And the one to make you aware
Although she is grown
With a life of her own

She never forgets you
She is forever true
Although her days of leisure are rare
She is always willing to share

That sweet little girl you raised
Is the one to be praised
Her heart is made of gold
Her hand you want to hold

Sharing love with your daughter
Is like walking on water
When God put her on this earth
You had no idea of her worth

Elizabeth C. Holden

LET THERE BE NO WAR

To see
    and not be seen.
To hear thoughts
    and know them as true.

To guess
    and guess correctly.
To see
    the past, present, and future.

I saw what's to come
    and was afraid.
I heard cries
    and was uneasy.

I guessed what happened
    war had come.
There will be no future
    the present is gone.

Our past is dead
    as is the future.
There's no one left
    to carry on.

Ruth Bressette

THE FRIGHTENING SEA

Hear the whispering
Of the wind,
See the colorful rainbow
Wandering through the clouds,
Moving like a whirlwind over
The mountaintop.
Know that there are no deserted
Stars in the sky.
The brightness shines in
My bedroom window,
Sometimes you hear the roaring
Of the angry sea.
Flowing furious in the night.
It's frightening for awhile,
Sounding like the bottom
Of the sea walls are caving in,
This is Mother Nature doing her
Work.

Jimmy McKay

THE POSSIBLE DREAM

From The Impossible Dream
Came The Possible Dream
For I took The I,M off and stated!
I'm Possible, For That May Be
As I make things happen
The magnitude of thinking never ends
For it is of the mind
Our great world began
which makes it possible
All from a plan
So why settle for negative
It's nowhere to stand —
Just one straight line
When positive gives us two,
Leading all directions —
It's All Up To You
So quote the word clearly
And make it your scene
Just say — I'm possible!

Paulie

DOOM, ARSELLA PAULLETTE (JOHN-SON). Pen Name: Paulie; Born: St. Charles, Kentucky, 2-9-51; Divorced; One Daughter, Reo; Occupations: Home Interior Consultant, Writer; Poetry: 'Hand Out A Smile,' *Ashes to Ashes,* anthology, Poetry Press, Pittsburg, Texas, November 1984; Comments: *I have just now started publishing my work. I am putting a volume together titled:* Life & Love As One, *and I am also writing a novel titled:* In Search for Love, *to be finished in September 1985. My common themes revolve around life in general. Although I write with double meaning, love is the emotion most generally expressed. I love my writing because it fulfills my purpose within myself.*

MY SISTER

Enjoying
Life while
Indoors and outdoors
Zipping through time
As if life lasted forever
Becoming more mature and
Enriching her talents
Thus it seems the past
Has finally paid off

Elsa Ramos

ON FREEMAN HILL

Up, on Freeman Hill;
The Trumpet summons us.
In gleeful haste we race,
To view majorettes dancing fair.

Far, on Freeman Hill;
Sweet Golden Plum falls.
'Tis the treasure of the land,
An ardent search can gain.

Yonder, on Freeman Hill;
The wind goes skipping.
As birds and squirrels,
Sing and cheer.

High, on Freeman Hill;
The sun squat so low.
Oh, we wish for the night,
Just to snatch a star.

There, on Freeman Hill;
Where little girls dread to tread,
We quietly watch this world go by,
And dream of more to come.

Walter C. Savage

PURPOSE

Friends are made
(If "made" is the word)
To be a bridge across
The abyss of loneliness:
The gaping breach that
Consumes all.

They are brief sparks in night,
Golden stars in ebony,
That sear the darkness, then that which
Fades into mist:
Cold, ended, concluded.

It seems that we all fear being alone,
And we want someone to walk through
Life's turmoil with:
Never being truly alone nor truly free.

Karen Gensiorek

SPLINTERS AND SHARDS

We built our love
    out of fragile glass,
neither tempered nor tested
    by a storm's pass.

We built our love
    to glisten and shine,
dedicated to each other
    the reflection so fine.

When the time for testing did approach
    it all came tumbling down,
splinters and shards of our love
    were all that could be found.

Each one sharp, double-edged, blind —
    and muddied now with fear,
I stopped and said, "We can rebuild,"
    then turned, and you weren't there.

Looking back, I can see
    it just wasn't in the cards,
your love wasn't even strong enough
    to help pick up the shards.

Judith Broadhead

PICTURE PERFECT

A camera buff I'd like to be . . .
    To capture the beauty and serenity
Of the world, awakening this early morn —
    Depicting the softness of an endless dawn.

Sleep was broken by this awesome sight . . .
    Bringing to an end, this restless night.
The honking of geese pierced the air —
    Making my senses much more aware!

The sun came up in all its glory . . .
    Revealing another timeless story.
As I watched this overzealous otter —
    Making circles upon the water.

A fishing boat cut through like a knife . . .
    Bringing the glassy waters back to life.
The ripples splashed against the banks —
    And waves thundered like roaring tanks!

No wonder folks call this "God's" country . . .
    No one else could render such a bounty.
The sun on the water and birds in the trees —
    Swaying gracefully in the gentle breeze.
        Clara E. Schauman

THE FIRE OF LOVE

The fire of love you kindled in my heart
Gives me assurance we will never part.
As far as the winds of earth are blowing,
I dissolve in laughter just by knowing
My love for you is strong enough to beat
The wind's speed and might by miles of white heat.
In wondrously beautiful month of May,
When all the buds burst open, I will say
None is so miraculous as our love,
Having choirs of nightingales to sing love.
The flowers, the doves, the sun, and the moon
I love, but none rivals yours through me strewn.
Changing seasons shift me on rapidly
As I breathlessly care for them dearly
Because of their wonders, yet I point out
My love for you is supreme beyond doubt.
So burn, fire of love, fill me with red coals.
Hail, my Lover! Touch me! Feel my red coals!
        Camella B. Schreyer

TIMELESS EXPECTATIONS

    A baby cries and longs for mother.
An old man dies and searches for God.
    The fruit in Winter fall asunder.
The flowers in Spring leap to the sun.

    So our world is ever balanced.
Hanging even on a golden thread.
    Nothing new can be enhanced,
Till something old has reached the dead.

    A cycle born in ages past.
Equal extremes come together as one.
    We count our days to the very last.
Keeping check by each new sun.

    Within this span we try to find
The answer to this cycle's way.
    Of picking those who are to be blind,
And helping others to reach peak grey.

    Sometimes we assume the way is cold,
Though some may find a door to dreams.
    But always it appears, death faces the old,
To make way for the newborn screams.
        Curtis Chappell

SUICIDE NOTE

So you cried out in your desperation on life, no
one answered you; leaving those numerous notes of
questioning suicide, she just didn't think you'd
really go that far. You see, many of us have felt
as you did, we have cried quite similar tears.

So you put the barrel to your head and pulled the
trigger, blasting your brains out — you went away
and left us. The mess you left behind scorched the
lives of those who loved you. May we learn from your
experience? Don't you see, you're dead forever now.

I'm sorry your desperation was so strong; we heard
your cries and we tried to show love to you, we tried
to reach you. We couldn't touch the pain you held
within, we didn't have the right tools to work with.
I still feel anger for what you did to yourself.

I'm so tired of the ugliness, trash and greed in life;
I often wish I could join you but something inside of
me keeps me from going through with it. Can't quite
understand it — I'm still here and you're gone. Why?
Hey hun, we were never promised an easy life.
        Sharon Hemker

MOTHER AT 511 GRANT STREET
6TH PLACE

Her jars are all over the place. She has them everywhere.
Beautiful daughter who grew up in the back bedroom
kneeling by the bed, counting beads on her knuckles.
The prayers hit the painted-shut window
and flattened.

She's got jars of plums, tomatoes, pears, great heads
of cabbages waiting. She's got onions up attic and peaches
down cellar. For months on end she cans.
Thumbs swollen with slipping off skins.
The house sweats with her effort.

At night she dreams cabbages, peas and beans.
Again she gets up and begins.
Sweet syrup and pickling brine. Steaming bath.
So carefully she carries them down to the cellar.
So quietly she lies down with her bad back to wait.
The garden won't quit.
        Mary Antonia Koral

EASTER

Christ died on the cross our souls to save.
On Easter Day he arose from the grave.
Will you in His service be brave.

He ascended into heaven high.
We'll be there forever by and by
Someday we will be in the sky.

The price for our sins he did pay.
Let us praise Him every day.
In everything we do and say.

Will you lead people who are in sin
To Him for their hearts to win?
Let new life in you begin.

If we walk or ride
Let us keep Him by our side
And in our hearts abide.

Let us with all our might
Try to do what is right.
So we will be pleasing in His sight.
        Ella H. Hollander

COLOR IT GRAY

How red is a rose?
It's not red at all
If it blooms on the yellow bush
That grows by the wall.

How green is the grass?
It's not green at all
When summer is over,
And we're well into fall.

How black is the night?
It's not black at all
When the sun floods the morning,
And the mockingbirds call.

How blue is the sky?
It's not blue at all
If my true love has left me,
and the shadows are tall.

James A. Bowman

TREASURE FROM GOD

Her home is very humble,
And one might say she is poor,
But the treasure of the love she has,
Is inside her heart's door.

She has the love of Jesus Christ,
And as she humbly kneels to pray
Tears of joy flow from her eyes,
'Cause she was born again one day.

The grace that comes from God,
Is truly freely given,
And until you get it friend,
You're not really living.

She has personal salvation,
Which comes from Jesus Christ,
And nobody can buy this,
No not at any price.

Irene Downey

MORNING-GLORY TIME

Oh morning-glory time of love
With heart so young and true
Your vine entwines around my heart
And keeps my life anew.

You circled me beneath your wings
In precious barefoot days
Your power to heal the bruise and sting
Gives comfort in your ways.

Your embedded vines of yesterday
Grew honey-cups of gold
The pipe-dreams that you lent me
Overflow the brim fourfold.

The greatness of your silvery touch
Above the lofty archway bloom
Portrays a trust within my life
And sheds away the gloom.

Jenny Ruth Lewis

ALL I'D ASK OF YOU

Just to care and be there with each other,
In all that we say and do.
Is all I'd ask of you, my Dear,
I'd hope you'd feel the same way too.
Oh, to have you near to hold me close
When I feel so sad and all alone,
To dry my tears and calm my fears
From the storms of life I have known.
To hear you say, I love you,
Just every now and then.
To see a smile and feel a tender touch,
Would mean so much at the day's end.
When the nights are long and dark
And rest I cannot find.
To reach and find you, oh so near,
Then to know your love so warm and kind.
Oh, to care and to share with you,
When life seems so hard to bear,
Now and forevermore
And for each other always care.

Joan Lee

psyche

rumbling,
tumbling,
thoughts,
afraid to
        think about
thoughts,
all my thoughts;
over
and
over, again.
keep on,
            keeping on
takes
all I have.
the result
is the same,
there is no
        way out,
but,
    through.

Lois C. Cavanagh-Daley

THERE IS SOMETHING DEEP

I want to write
But my mind went blank
And I can't think what to say.
I sort of feel like the
World went dry;
Or like I am far away.

There is something deep
I wish to express
But it will not surface now.
My mind tries to guide
My wandering pen,
But the thoughts ring empty somehow.

There's a deep-down urge,
And I want to expound
'Til it rings on the far-off hills;
But it will hold back and
Confuse my thoughts,
And refuse to obey my will.

Rhoda E. Torsak

EYES

The stars are eyes
belonging to one who
walked the way you now do
They are watching
They are saying out of love,
"Wish upon my eyes
I see if you are deserving,
if you are sincere.
I will take it to the master,
whose face hides in the vastness
I will wish while I watch,
mine eyes follow you as you move
I was once a part of you,
now all I lend are these eyes
There's an eternity of blackness
In life . . .
Yet, you're never alone for as long
as you search the evening sky
For as long as you still believe
In the wishes these eyes have seen."

Roxanne Monteleone

THE CALL

Table for two, soft music,
    and candlelight,
wine and hors d'oeuvres,
a few flowers, . . . all to set the mood.
Run to the bedroom
    to look in the mirror,
check the dress, the hair . . .
    . . . listen for the bell.
Instead comes a call.
. . . "sorry dear," the dinner
        can't be had.
Dinner and dishes are put away.
The candles are blown out.
. . . with the wine I toast the night,
    and the music softly spins on
        to blur with salty tears.
I fool myself and say
it's hunger that keeps me awake,
    not thinking about
        him . . .

Mary Pat Crewse

SAMANTHA

Samantha, your name sets
my phantasy on fire.
Like Pythia's in Delphian Oracle,
my perceptions go awry,
and I visualize you as princess
of rare and astonishing beauty,
of mystic strength that makes you akin
to bionic or wonderwoman.
I see you living in a palace
of white, green and pink marble,
surrounded by exotic gardens
that keep guard on outside intrusions,
while inside the scents of
luscious flowers everyone there
lulls into sweet oblivion.
Samantha, with your head on my lap,
your long, silky ears in touch
with the world of reality,
let us our voyage begin
to the world of phantasy.

Lidija Murmanis

JUST STANDING BY

Mother's job is a busy one.
Full of patience, love and joy.
'Tis one that requires a watchful eye,
But her hardest task is "just standing by."

When she knows so well, what would be best,
Yet she dare not advise nor guide,
For each of her flock must meet life's test
And by the laws of life abide.

For there comes to all a time in life,
When we think we know the way,
We need no hand to guide
In this our modern day.

Yet Mother knows the pathway well,
The trials, the doubts and fears,
Of griefs and sorrows she could tell,
Disappointments, pain and tears.

But she is always there,
Though we climb the mountain high.
If we need a prayer, a song, or smile,
She'll be ever standing by.

Ruby Bratton

BRATTON, RUBY F. Born: Forest, Indiana, 8-31-02; Married: 11-8-24 to Howard D. Bratton, (deceased); Education: Clinton County School, Lebanon High School; Correspondence Course in Literature; Memberships: P.T.A., P.T.A. City Council, Methodist Church, Business and Professional Women, Public Relations for Business Women Club, Work with United Methodist Women District; Poetry: 'The Horizon,' American Poetry Co., 1982; 'A Friend,' Church Magazine; 'Love Is My Refuge,' American Poetry Association; Themes: *Inspirational, for family and friends, food for thought, fun, love, religious.*

Dear God
Before it is too late,
        In humble prayer
        Answer this my question.
What mighty bell tolls for me?

Thank you God
        Let the majestic bell toll once more,
        Allow me to repent, and once more to hear
        The bell's graceful tolling
Tolling for my soul's freedom in paradise.

SALVATION

Ralph B. Williams

MY HEART CRIES OUT FOR YOU

My love for you will never die.
        Oh why, oh why has yours?
I ask myself the question why?
        Over and over, until the thoughts run dry.

And my heart cries out for you
        but no one answers.
The pain races through my heart,
        as if on feet of tiny dancers.

And now I sit alone in my tiny room.
        I sit where there once were two.
It seems as if I'm doomed in gloom.
        I don't know what to do.

But alas I find one way to speak.
        It makes me shiver; It makes me weak.
A tear runs down my colorless cheek.
        Tears of sorrow, but tears that are sweet.

And my heart cries out for you
        but no one answers.
The pain races through my heart,
        as if on feet of tiny dancers.

Barbara Albee

ALBEE, BARBARA JEAN. Born: Detroit, Michigan, 1957; Education: Central Michigan University, Oakland Community College, Schoolcraft College; Occupations: Salesperson, Nursery School Teacher, Songwriter; Memberships: Audobon Society; Poetry: 'O Light Your Way,' American Poetry Association, Fall/Winter 1983; 'The Bird Who Was Afraid To Fly,' Little's People Press, 1985; 'His Eyes Behold Me,' American Poetry Association, Winter 1985; Other Writings: 'Don't Hide Your Heart,' Song/Album, Columbine Records, 1984; Comments: *I write poetry or songs when the thoughts flow from my mind onto paper like a vigorous mountain stream. I hope through my words that I make people either think or feel, hopefully about something that is of significance.*

THE POET'S MUSE ELUDES ME

I want to write a poem,
But words are hard to find,
The vivid scenes I would portray
Just do not come to mind.
The good Muse has evaded
My pleas and my commands.
Could lack of inspiration
Be caused by life's demands?
I think not. For all others
Have burdens, I agree.
A subject for a poem
Just does not come to me.
A contest is a challenge.
I've tried with all my heart
To write a proper entrance
Of twenty lines of art.
But, the poet's Muse eludes me,
So, please accept these lines
In place of inspiration's
More intricate designs.

Edna Powell Weegmann

FOR THIS WE VOWED

Those sacred words of wisdom,
Have often been said in vain.
But there is a pure and clearer vision
As we walk down Memory Lane.

Love was made in heaven
And descended onto earth.
Where it will always reign forever
From the very date of birth.

We vowed to love each other
Till death do us part.
We'd never take another
For we knew it from the start.

Yet so many things could turn you around
Temptation confronts our paths.
Then look to God where hearts are bound
And forever your love will last.

Wiley Hamilton, Jr.

WILL YOU DANCE?

Flashing eyes, sparkling castanets —
Toes arching upward,
Hair whorling —

Graceful fingers tracing the air
With symbols
And cymbals.
Flowing,
Yielding body
In perfect harmony
With the Grand Beat,
Swelling
And ebbing
Passion
And Pain.

Worlds whirl,
Lights leap
Through the cosmos
For Siva.

Bobbi Hannon

THE DREAM HAS AWAKENED

The mysteries of God surround me.
    Every breath I take, fills
Me with life.

        It flows through my body
    Like the blood in my veins.
        I walk quietly, feeling the
Wind as it whispers by my
        Ear.

        Singing the songs of laughter,
Knowing within the time is here.
        Love has captured me,
Feeling the essence in my Heart
        Like raindrops, as they fall
From the sky, dancing with joy
        It has yet to bare a
Rainbow with surprise.

        The Beauty of the Dream
has awakened.

        We are all one. Man, animal,
Nature, the universe, the raindrops
    That fall. The rainbow with
The wind whispering through it.
        Feeling the essence of Love.
We are all immersed from Beauty.
        Beauty another vision of God!

CoCo Saltzgiver

I REMEMBER
In Memory Of
MR. ARISH ALEXANDER DAVIS
(1909-1982)

I remember a smile that warmed my day
Even in the coldest winter;
I remember strong, brown hands
That's what I remember.

I remember a slow, steady gait
That I could tell a mile away;
I remember a voice that made me feel safe
With the simple words he'd say.

I remember years and years of strife
Sprinkled with happiness and some tears;
I remember a hearty, boyish laugh
That dispelled all my silly fears.

I remember a man whose life
Has affected me so very much;
I can't imagine a part of my life
That his life hasn't touched.

I remember a smile that warmed my day
Even in the coldest winter;
I remember strong, brown hands
That's what I remember . . .

Regina Davis

QUANDARY

Back in the whispering dark of time
I drift in silent wonder —
Staring at familiar faces
of people I've never known,
while foreign sounds of deeds —
            long past,
engulf my troubled mind.

Alma I. Powell

TO THE CELLAR CREATURES

Down in a cellar on earth
tunes are being played
Creatures out of this world
enter the kingdom of feeling
in isolation from universe
Shankar with his magic strings
brings hope on a ball point pen
Bach on celestial tunes
cries out the symphony of time
All is dark
only the odors
of an essence, of feeling
surrounding moods
trumpets, flutes
ball point pen
and the Cellar Creatures
taken their place.

Rosa Maria Munoz

A KISS

It can be loving,
    Or painful.

It can be caressing,
    Or brutal.

It can be perfunctory,
    Or ardent.

It can be friendly,
    Or cold.

It can be rewarding,
    Or disillusioning.

It can be peaceful . . .
    Sherrilyn Polf

ONE-MAN SHOW

Brushes of Spring spread the silvery light
over the landscape.
My canvas, stretched and waiting, while I
prepare my palette
With colors for the lacy tips of leaves,
New formed, in palest green.
Yellow daffodils bend beneath the trees
in the growing light.
With awe I take my brush in hand
to copy these.
Before my eyes the landscape changes,
Nature's brush, more swift than mine,
Full leaves had formed and
tinged a darker green.
Watching her technique I see
A new masterpiece,
Waiting to be forged by me . . .

E. Sue Sturgis

RUNNING TIME

The ticking of the clock
Its sound is haunting
There is fear
Time passes swiftly
Before me
With a feeble hand
I grasp at life
All I get are
Fragments of life
That time allows

Lillie Zable

SACRIFICE

I am proud of you and proud of me
Proud indeed that we
Though living in these selfish times
Have thought it right to sacrifice
Our God-given love
For other life

God is proud of you and proud of me
Proud indeed that we
While trusting Him, would give this cup
Of sweet communion up
So no one would hurt —
But we

Penelope E. Cates

FRIENDSHIP

I am so lonesome
for the friendship we used to know
the chats we had,
the dreams we shared
seems so long ago.
Your friendly touch
your gentle voice
your endless faith
in me, that I needed so much
but God had other plans
it's so comforting to know
that someday, we'll meet again
in God's own Holy Land

Edith Law

STATE OF FALL
HONORABLE MENTION

I will pack unspoken rancors
tight in their skin
like ripe cucumbers;
push them down well
burst all bubbles with a sharp knife
or perhaps
the wrong end of a wooden spoon.

When canning season is passed
I will face the hill
and snake wood down
for wintertime fires.

Marie-Noelle Chris Long

BE REAL

You got to be real
I said myself to me
Why? He answered back to me.
Because you do.
And myself answered back to me
You have to be you
And I have to be me.
But, I said myself to me
We're the same,
Isn't that plain?
And myself
Answered back to me
Are we?

Franklin H. Swan

FRIENDS

A friend is one to turn to
When all the world looks blue,
Who knows the pain you're suffering
Without a word from you.

A friend can lift your burden
By simply being there
To offer words of comfort
Expressed with loving care.

A friend is like a mirror,
A reflection of your soul,
The image of two hearts and minds
Combined to form a whole.

A friend can look into your heart
And loves you just the same
Despite the foibles hiding there,
Too numerous to name.

So, thank you, friend, for giving me
A love that's pure and true
That I can share with others
And then send back to you.

Sharon Terry Winn

WINN, SHARON TERRY. Born: Merkel, Texas, 8-17-38; Education: North Texas State University, B.A. (Magna Cum Laude), 1961; Sul Ross State University, M.Ed., 1973; Occupation: High School Librarian; Memberships: Delta Kappa Gamma Society International, Sigma Tau Delta, Alpha Lambda Delta, Beta Sigma Phi, Association of Texas Professional Educators, Texas State Teachers Association; Awards: Second Place, Beta Sigma Phi international song contest, 1981; Poetry: 'Forbidden Love,' free verse, American Poetry Association, 1983; 'The 'Perfect' Pair,' humorous, 1984; 'We Are the Builders,' free verse, 1984; 'I Like Chemistry,' lyric, 1980; Comments: *Writing is a catharsis, both for joy and for sorrow. My best poems seem to flow effortlessly from heart to head to pen. Common themes concern human relationships — love, friendship, altruism. I write to evoke an emotional response and to share a thought with which I hope others can identify although most of my poems are intensely personal in nature.*

GOD'S GLORIOUS GARDEN

God's garden is crowded with glory untold
  Fantastic throughout its design
With color proclaiming each wonderful flower
  As efforts unending combine.

Some flowers are as tender and precious as love,
  As charming as spiritual care,
Exquisite in symmetry, patterned in plan
  And fragrances vie in the air.

Some flowers are a riot of color expressed
  Surrounding a tall slender stem
Profuse in abundance as blossoms explode,
  A gloriously built diadem.

While others are clusters far out on a stalk
  With leaves as a curtain below
To give them a verve over all of the rest,
  A marvelous fortissimo.

Such beauty could only be found so profuse
  In wonderfully perfect design,
God's glorious garden beside the trail
  Extolling His power divine.

    Larry Wells

THE PICTURE SHOW

One cold and snowy night last November,
We sat before the fire
And watched the flames flicker against the walls.
We held out our hands,
Then let our imaginations run wild.

You were the king, so handsome and tall,
And I was your queen, forever at your side.
We ruled together, you and I,
Conquering the evil enemies,
But loving the people and the animals.

We roamed the countryside,
Searching for the answers to the questions of love.
But at first all we saw
Were rabbits, horses, and dogs.

In time, the flames turned to embers
As our search was drawing to a close.
We watched the rabbits, horses, and the dogs
Fade into shadows on the walls.

And then we knew the truth was real;
Not hidden in the picture show made by the flames on the logs.

    Jan Maxwell

AS SUN APPROACHES . . .

As sun approaches in earliest morning,
  She sends forth foraging fingers,
    Lighting her path.
Her bashful beams promise a glorious day,
  One filled with unspeakable bliss.

Sun's colors, when seen upon rising,
  Are multi-hued, golden yellowish,
    Unforgettable pink.
Should you give or take one tint or two,
  Similar indeed to vine-ripened fruit.

Quickly she is the darkness dispelling,
  Brightening every nook and cranny,
    Scattering darkness —
Leaving from nighttime, elongated shadows;
  Whispering, "Time to be up and about!"

    Sarah A. Janes

TOP O' THE MORNING

Out of the silent home I wandered
Early to view the vernal dawn.
"Top o' the Morning" I cried
To the tiptoed sun reaching high.

And I spied the little night caps
peeking through the dewy mold
coloring fields in turquoise and gold,
And the lambkins gazing on
Frolicked in the pastoral fold.

"Top o' the Morning," I sang
And a madrigal through forests rang.
And feathery folk in lilting trance
Echoed the song in necromance.

As my dreams went riding
Ablaze with beauty diving
My thoughts wove into an anodyne
Where flesh and fleece, flower and feather
All joyfully gathered together
And in a roundelay sweet and low
Paid homage to "Top o' the Morning's" glow.

    Clarence F. Dickopf

He sat there alone in his pinstripe suit
silently thinking, "now isn't she cute?"

Her hair the color of his mare "Bess"
but she is the one, he would like to caress.

Her eyes match those violets by the creek.
he surely would like to "plant one" on her cheek!

She gazes into the distance — awaiting someone?
her father? her brother? surely not her son —

He must finish lunch and go on his way,
for he had not come to this area to stay.

He was seeking — always seeking, his only son,
wondering in silence, "Could she be the one?"

Upon realizing their family resemblance,
lead him to his long lost son? Perhaps!

    Fern Roche

SCARF OF THE DESERT

Ubiquitous denizens of the desert,
Those lonely, dancing dust devils
That form a weird, wind phenomenon.
On a clear day when the sun
Overheats the surface of the earth,
They arise from the dry and dusty ground
To form a desert whirlwind of convective plumes.

Like a Venetian scarf across the desert,
Blown by the wind they come . . . . ·
In pairs but sometimes in groups of five or six.

Where will they go? Do they have a home?
Mayhap they'll return to the Ventana Cave,
The home of the dust devils
As related in Papago Indian folklore.
Or, will they seek refuge in a local habitat
Only to dwindle into dust and die.

But perhaps as a last recourse,
They might lift majestically from the ground
And disappear in diffused phantom shapes
Into the searing desert sunlight.

    Carolyn M. Kurth

FROM YOUR DARLING

Feel so warm, safe and cozy in my mommy's bag —
    am anxious to see my Dad
just wallowing in a jet lag.

All snugged and safe from the big wide world
soon going to be my first glance
Wow! A big cry — Sis will see that I'm dry.

Felt your hugs, soft pats — kind words of love
    longing to sit on your lap —
sure you know happiness, nothing like when you see me
I'm your little honey bee
    you wait and see.

Been just three in the family
thought there would be no more
    surprise! there will soon be four.

Coyett H. Gray

TWO WORLDS

Two different kinds of people meet, love and
Accept the others' ways and change just a little
Love brings an understanding experience and an
Awareness of having hope and finding a world of serenity.

An underground discovery knowing each world and
Finding what makes their unity and relationship
In the back of their minds is that fear and
An unknowing sense of belonging together.

There are mixed thoughts of laughter, tears and
Emotions high, hold and join these two to one world
To an everlasting life of tranquility, sharing and
A soul experience of sensitivity in their dreams.

The world of signs, symbols, meanings, peace and
The moon's position holding answers in the stars
Turning on an imaginative escape from reality and
Having peace of mind lingering on altered illusions.

Into another world leaving for a moment and
Being alone together holding on in their world
Two worlds apart yet two who believe and
These two worlds unite making it one.

Susan Murton

PAINTING THE HOUSE

The walls are badly smudged
With assorted stains, character dirt,
Imprints, unintentional Picasso
Fingerprints of no legal use.
The walls need a new suit.

Should we get a suit that peels?
Or would skin tight as bones show better?
Strange how we think the interior needs it more.
The exterior takes abuse from sun and snow;
Kinder hands are more harmful, I suppose.

Before the paints, words hit a cul-de-sac.
Remove the paint; silence dominates.
Communication dirty walls improve;
Inanimates have trustworthy ears.
Blue and green loosen tongues.

Peelable prints grate the nerves;
Painting fun is in changing minds.
Paint the walls white and one color more;
Our life we can paint all black.

We are colorblind to the walls of our lives.

Al Palomar

CRYSTAL PASSAGE CONTINUUM

Sweet darkness descended, kissed me
  God's envoys stood silent, in neutrality
    Through templed stillness — etched crystal mold
      Within bevelled refractions — my soul rolled
        Lovely Mallory: Earth's glorious seduction
        Human creation could — be — massive perfection?
      My tumbling heart — oh no — I could not hold
    Within bevelled refractions — my soul rolled
  Disharmonious sonnets sung: she, remembered
Endlessly, I tasted, thirsted — despaired

    Warryn Syde

MY LOVE

My lover is oh so sweet
I like to kiss and hug him whenever we meet
He is handsome gentle and so fine
With ebony eyes that blow my mind
Our time together is all that I need
Because with him my passions are freed
No one else makes me feel this way
That's why I tell him I love him every day
Our love together is just so right
This is why we never fight
Building a relationship with love and care
Our hearts shall never feel the throes of despair
With these feelings our love can go anywhere
He is often the clown but through the ups and downs
I know his love is true
When he tells me those favorite words
Baby I love you

    Edith D. Johnson

THE WINGS OF A DOVE
Dedicated to Mrs. Nevovia Thomas

Wings of a dove spread far and wide
Gracing the skies with its beauty and pride

So were the wings of the dove I was blessed with
Gracing my life with her love and her strength

Her wing span of love could spread to all boundaries of life
With courage and grace she'd swoop through perils and strife

Her beauty and gentleness from God would erase all fears
With a brush from her wing of love she'd wipe away tears

Though absent from my eyes is the dove so precious to me
Full is my heart with the love and grace I no longer see.

    Gwendolyn Y. Rose

NIGHT SOUNDS

Outside,
  the scruff of crickets scrapes the dark
  two bluejays quarrel in their wakefulness
  on asphalt trails tires hum and spark
  while town clocks count aloud the hours
  planes thrust their bodies into time and space
  relentless in their need to conquer both.

Inside
  sharp tappings join to breach the hush
  a faucet drips in tempo with my heart
  one keening violin rules the radio
  walls settle with vague crackings here and there.
  Sounds such as these are portions of my joy

  at having you beside me through the night.

    Ellen V. M. Carden

TRYING TO MEDITATE IN GOD'S HOUSE!

I sit here and I try to meditate. I try to tune out all the surrounding
  voices, sounds and whispers. It's not always easy, because of
  the many negative thoughts being expressed by others around me!

But somehow, I just let go and let God, be still and turn within and
  thank God for everything. I thank him for my life, health, my
  children's life, health, intelligence, my mother, and for all the
  good things he has done for me, is doing for me, and will do for me!

And very shortly afterward, it's time to listen to a dynamic service.
  I like the feeling I get from attending. I enjoy the many talented
  voices I listen to. And, I am in God's house and he welcomes,
  everyone.

He loves us all, because we are all his children! But, the best part
  about God is when you leave his house, He goes with you. Because,
  WHEREVER WE ARE, GOD IS!!!!

Janice D. Hanley

THIS OLD SHANTY

The sun breaks up the morning casting shadows into dawn.
I look around — realizing you're gone.
The kitchen smells of bacon. There's coffee on the stove.
Sea birds take early flight above the cove.

This old shanty's lonely whenever you're not around.
I wish you were on a Greyhound homeward bound.
There's laughter in my heart when I look into your eyes;
and Heaven reveals love in sunny skies.

Daylight shines through the window tracing shutters on the shades.
I sit and sip my coffee while the mist gives up its haze.
I read the morning paper while sea gulls scream at play.
The month is December but I wish it were May.

I stroll the hills along the beach going barefoot in the sand.
Somewhere in a harbor sails a ship for distant land.
I check the noontime mail. There's no letter in the box.
My heart frustrates in anger, tormented by a fox.

This old shanty's lonely whenever you're not around.
At evening time a Greyhound comes to town.
If you're not on that bus I may forget about us;
and my loneliness and I will settle down.

Raymond E. Witte

DEAREST ELVIS

Dearest Elvis, it's been seven years today, since you died,
    Each year, I try pulling myself together after I've cried.
You have always held a special place, in my heart,
    Half of me dies too, when we had to part.

You came a long way baby, after some rough years,
    I still see your face clearly, even through these tears.
But you and I had faith, in The Man Upstairs,
    And we knew, He would be answering all our prayers.

I have always been very close to you, you know
    But couldn't tell you, while you were on the go.
In the whole wide world, you are still "The King."
    And the most loved and admired, of any human being.

You, your songs, and your movies, will be remembered forever,
    Do you think everything you've stood for, will be forgotten, never?!
All ages loved you whether they were young or old,
    After you, God threw away the pattern, from your mold.

Remember to reserve a seat for me, next to yours,
    So we can go together, when you're on your tours.
It comes without saying that I still love you so,
    And it broke my heart, when you had to go.

Sandy McDole

TORCHLIGHT

You asked for my heart
  And stole my love
You begged for affection
  And found my weakness
You laughed at my fears
  And healed the scars
You cried at my sorrow
  And melted the pain
You smiled at my dreams
  And created new ones
You listened to my wishes
  And then you became them
    Jackie Rubin

MY REFUGE

When the morning sun awakens me,
I go to God in prayer,
I know that I can lean on Him,
And each problem He will bear,
My burdens are much lighter,
When God lifts them all away,
I never need to fear the worst,
For He is my hope and stay,
God listens to my humble words,
And directs my every path,
We always need to serve Him,
And fear His mighty wrath,
But though the path is crooked,
And the soul within me cries,
I just look up to God above,
For that's where my strength now lies.
    Kathy A. Freeman

TELL ME ABOUT LOVE

Tell me about love I said.
He smiled and showed me instead.
I've seen trees touching the skies,
People with laughter and sighs,
Majestic mountains, flowers,
People praying by the hours,
Skies giving new life to seas
Then giving itself to trees,
Valleys, lakes and all of earth,
His children fed and childbirth,
Birds free and singing their song,
People searching to belong,
Loving another, caring,
Trusting, forgiving, sharing,
Lover's nights, families and friends.
In truth, His love never ends!
    Paul W. Tomkins

I'LL NEVER FORGET HIM

I could still hear the words as I sat
down to cry,
the words that hurt so much as he held
my hand and said goodbye.
When I think of the times he said he
loved me,
and the feel of his warm lips on mine,
when I think of the feel of his strong
arms around me
and how his lips tasted of wine,
the tears stream down my face,
my heart is a big hollow empty space.
My eyes are so full of tears I could
hardly see,
I hope he will remember me,
I know I'll never forget him.
    Michelle Shahan

COME

Come into my soul feel my sorrow.
Come into my heart feel my love.
Come into my body feel my pain.
Come into my mind sense my intelligence.
Come into my own eyes look at yourself.
Come into my ears hear what I cannot.
Come unto me listen to my cry —
OF LIFE.

Angel M. Toll

CLOUDS

Clouds drifting endlessly
Over the horizon never
having anywhere special
to go sometimes moving
swiftly, have they
passed this way before
I guess we'll never
really know.

Joseph Reed

TO AN ODE

An ode to an ode,
Is a word, is a word.
A tho't, an idea that ode.
Just a fleeting idea, a simple word.
And, as such,
Really isn't much.
Just a line of rhyme
That's quickly lost in time.

L. G. Backlund

GUILT

Like caged feathers
Downed by fate,
With no one to love
And no one to hate,
Feared by some,
Understood by none,
The eagle has flown,
Wounded wings showing.

Ronald A. Minello

ON THE WINGS OF A DOVE

On the wings of a dove
    I send you my love
        from a heart that's true
            it flies to you . . .
Across oceans of blue
        under sunsets of golden hue
            on the wings of a dove
                I send you my love . . .

Phyllis Joan Smith

CHERISHED CRYSTAL

A cherished crystal goblet
fell from its shelf.
I became upset.
A few tears came;
and I realized
something else I cherished
had also shattered.
A belief in promises.
Permanent words that are secure?
No.
Your guarantee expired
when it was no longer —
'convenient.'
A vow, yielding to surroundings.
My cherished crystal goblet
is nothing but worthless glass.

Constance Dee Gordon

FOR MY DEAR MOTHER
(Maria Tsiknas)

If God lives, He'll welcome you
            in His soul
If God protects, He'll comfort you
            in His body
If God feels, He'll love you
            in His heart
If God thinks, He'll respect you
            in His mind . . .

As you do, welcome me
    As you do, comfort me
        As you do, love me
            As you do, respect me . . .

As you, dear mother, did give me
            a heart and soul
As you, dear mother, did work free
            to make me, whole

I ask . . . if God . . . and you speak
            when God is . . .
I ask . . . if God . . . and you show
            when God does

Peter James

A CHILD IS A PRECIOUS GIFT

*To Errol and Rosemary Dutton
whose marriage was blessed with their
adopted and most beautiful daughter,
Jennifer.*

God looked upon a young couple,
And saw their desperate need.
To have a baby in their lives,
He saw this, yes indeed.

So the Lord took it upon Himself —
To pick out a beautiful pearl,
And then He said, "Behold, my children,
I'm giving you this little girl."

So enjoy this precious gem dear ones —
Sent to you from above.
Remember, teach her all about Jesus,
And about His precious love.

For how you raise this little girl —
Is your gift back to God.
To thank Him for this precious life,
In God's word, your child, must trod.

Erma Morris

THE HANDS OF TIME

With hands that brush the face so fast
It makes no sound
It speaks without words
Like a thief that clutches the pearls
from a blind woman's neck

With ways to turn green leaves to brown
Brown hair to gray
Gray sky to blue —
It is transformation —
It is the chameleon with twelve different
faces and two sets of clothes

It is invisible
It is where the wind starts
And where the arm ends

It controls the whole world with
Smooth revolving patience
With eyes on the wall
It watches us all
And waits
        And waits
            And waits

Andrew J. Annese

SPRINGTIME

Spring is the time of year
So many look forward to.
It's a lovely season for all
'Cause joy is found in what we do.

This era marks the beginning
Of a new period of progress,
The green tillage that covers the land
Brings great joy and happiness.

The flowers burst into full bloom
Adding rich beauty in many ways.
We find the trees of new foliage
Giving us shade to share during the day.

The birds greet us cheerfully in song.
From early morn till evening tide,
The sunshine gives us deep warmth
As we stroll through the countryside.

While the season marches graciously on
Mother Nature takes her stand,
Leaving us thankful for being a part
Of God's gift to the people of His land.

Jeannie Marie Buchwalter

Melancholy morning
The blue that everyone thinks
Is in my eyes
Is in my sneakers this morning.
What an arrogant fool
I can turn into
But it's just phony, stony
'Cause I still haven't learned
To fill the black hole in my soul.
You know, the one I used to fill with cake
The one I used to fill with smoke
And I even try to fill it with music.
But not the music for me
The song I think will make someone love me
Forever
Without conditions
And kiss in all the right places.
A silly lady I am
But it would be nice to figure out
What I am to do here

Janet Feld

RAIN SHADOWS
(A Soliloquy on Aging)

HONORABLE MENTION

I live in the shadow of rain
in a valley of low places,
where only mist curls over lips of summits,
ghosting trees and blurring outlines of images,
sheltered beneath dew-dripping leaves,
buffered against quake and tremor,
hearing only the chitterings of small birds
in muted sound.

Yet once I lived in high places
of crag and precipice, subject to
fierce lightning and sudden thunder,
to the down-draft of canyons. To the fall,
buffeted by wind and swept by tides of flood.

Let it be known I danced in downpour,
parried rapier lightning
and outsang thunder, accepting alike
the blister of sun, the clouds
which closed down the day.
I lifted my face to rain.

Alice Morrey Bailey

PRAYER

Day by day, life brings a change
It's something, the wise can't even explain.
Life seems hard and so unfair
There're times you believe that no one cares.
The plans you've made, seem far from you
Dreams are illusions, they can't come true.
Now when times are hard, lift up your head
'Cause that signifies better days ahead.
So seek that horizon, that's never been seen
Take the time, to plan and dream.
With every chance, send up a prayer
Believe in Him, He's always there.
Continue to strive, from deep within
Trust in God, for He's your friend.
He's by your side, in all you do
When times get tough, He carries you,
When in the dark, He lights the candle
Remember: There's nothing that God can't handle,
So take your troubles, leave them with Him
And in all due time, He'll handle them
For He's our Father, He loves us all
So when in need, give God a call.
Check the directory, you won't find it there
For your information, the number is PRAYER . . .

Fredrick N. Byerly

I'LL NEVER FORGET

The sweetest day I'll never forget
Was when Jesus and I first met
I heard the bells in heaven ring
I heard the angels, how sweet they sing

Some days I just stand around
And think of the day I'll be in heaven bound
To that beautiful city, God has prepared for me
And all of his children, it's the land of the free

Lord I ask only one thing of you
Won't you bring my family to
Lord I don't ask for riches, or silver or gold
Just be with them Lord, and save their souls

For gold and silver will all fade away
But when they get to heaven, they'll be there to stay
We'll all sit with you, in your love we will bask
Oh heavenly father, this is all that I ask

Emma Collins

MY MOTHER HAS GONE TO HEAVEN

My mother has gone to Heaven, I know;
My heart was made sad for I knew
I'd see her no more in this world below
But Yonder her face I shall view.

I'm thanking my God and praising His name
For giving such a mother to me.
To me she was pure and free from all blame.
A wonderful mother was she!

Some wonderful day I'll join her up There;
Her face will be lovely and bright.
Then Jesus, My Lord, will dry all my tears,
And all will be gladness and Light.

My Jesus I'll greet and look on His face
And thank Him for dying for me.
I'll kneel at His feet, His name I will praise;
His worshipper ever I'll be.

Then Mother's dear hand in mine I will hold;
She'll draw me again to her breast.
Together we'll sing, as in days of old,
Of Jesus' sweet mercy and rest.

Esther Nethercutt

AMERICA

As it was in days gone by,
In a country that was brand-new,

The voice of freedom rang loud and clear.
Time has marched on yet today it is still true.

Material blessings we have enjoyed,
Peace and prosperity other lands have not known,

God's sovereign hand upon us still,
In all these things to the world we have shown

From shore to shore the inhabitants free,
All nations and races the people they come.

Driven by hope and the American dream,
Freedom's bright light not dim in a one,

So let us now honor the red white and blue.
The colors that wave true and just,

In Liberty's hand the torch is held high.
Let freedom ring and in God we trust.

Judy Parrish

SHALOM, YERUSHALAYIM!

Shalom, Yerushalayim,
    the delight of our Lord,
the city of glory
    for all nations to come!

Shalom, Yerushalayim,
    Where all the Lord's sheep
will find pasture and comfort,
    as babes that suck at their mother's breast.

Come and rejoice,
    all you children of Yerushalayim,
for God's everlasting love is upon you!
    Peace be within you, oh Yerushalayim.

Shalom,
    shalom.

Vivian L. Hayward

GOD'S EYE

God watches o'er me every day,
He sees me as I kneel to pray.
And as I travel on this land,
He kindly, gently holds my hand.

I serve Him in my humble way,
And try my best His will to obey.
But, though I sometimes cause Him pain,
I need just ask; He forgives again.

My constant guide He'll always be
Until His heavenly face I see.
Then at that time I'll praise my King
As sounds of adoration ring.

Elaine Miller Raby

RABY, ELAINE MILLER. Born: Ethel, Louisiana, 9-2-38; Married: 4-15-67 to Dr. C. T. Raby; Education: Southern University, B.A., 1960; Occupations: Teacher, Librarian; Memberships: National Education Association, Louisiana Education Association, East Baton Rouge Parish Education Association; Poetry: 'Love Song,' American Poetry Association, 7-85; Comments: *Life, to me, is a cherished possession. To be successful, one needs to do his best and be honest within himself in all of his activities. This accompanied by a faith in God, enables us to live a life of worth. These ideas are the basis for my writings. Each poem is the result of some incident.*

OUR FUTURE

It seems like we grow up too fast.
We think of how good our past was and
forge to our future. Hoping we are
doing the right things. Knowing what
we do already should help us cope
with our future. We are sure to make
our share of mistakes. We would have
to get over them, to keep on living.
The new and the old ways will help us.
Hopefully, we could end war before war
ends us. It's our one and only world.
We should try to pull it together, not
blow it apart.

John A. Carson

TO ACHIEVE REALITY

I dreamed until it seemed
    A reality.
I persevered till I could see
    Reality.
I strained my brain until
    I understood reality.
I tried and really strived
    Till I found reality.
I made starts and took parts
    Till I gained reality.
I yearned until it turned
    Into reality.
For the right I had to fight
    Till I won in reality.
My mind said, "You won't find,"
    But I did in kind achieve reality.
When you consciously strive you'll arrive
    Eventually at reality.
If you always desire quality
    In actuality you'll succeed in reality.

Josephine Suits Markthaler

MARKTHALER, JOSEPHINE SUITS. Born: On a farm upstate; Widow of Karl Markthaler, International Chef, Ice Sculptor; Education: Commercial, Child Care, Reflexology, Painting, Ceramics; Occupation: Formerly a Receptionist; Memberships: Nondenominational church, Senior Citizens, Business and Professional Women, Security, Ceramics class; Poetry: 'Before Church Service,' Christ Church, New York City, 1972; 'The Ice Storm,' *Golden Age Sentinel,* 1980; 'Winter Wonderland,' 1982, and 'My First Love,' 1984, American Poetry Association; Themes: *I write on various subjects: winter, home, children, Christian themes, love, God's gifts, morality, comics, animals, aging, mothers;* Comments: *I wish to inspire and encourage persons to see beauty in life, appreciate everything, live right, and see humor also.*

Fall cantabilé,
Helios, symphonies & Venus,
God's handiwork!

Michael Joseph Phillips, Ph.D.

THE EDGE

From the saintly to the knave,
and the hermit in his cave,
A universal want of man
Is to be noticed if he can.

Though he be only "run of mill,"
To him he's special, if you will . . .
A man of letters and of books . . .
A handsome man in looks.

He may be high in social rank . . .
Financial standing at the bank . . .
A man of talent, wit and will . . .
Of prowess in athletic skill . . .
Self-righteous man on pious perch
Looking good there in the church.

But something that he is . . .
Something only his . . .
That he knows, or he can do
Gives him, he thinks, the edge on you.

I try to hide that I am vain
To keep from causing others pain.
But all the while I feel so smug
I give myself a mental hug.
Beneath my cloak of modesty
I feel there's no one quite like me.

Charles Ray Robinson

LIFE

Like a lighted cigarette, our
Lives burn with the fire of
Enthusiasm and the ashes of good
Deeds done or tasks accomplished
Fall unnoticed until in the end the
Fire consumes our entire structure,
and we are soon forgotten. The
Residue of ashes remains as our
Contribution to Society.

Roy S. Neely

MY CUCKOO CLOCK

My cuckoo clock
    Has stopped

Maybe
    One little screw,
    Or a small spring
    Gone wrong.

Maybe
    It is tight,
    Or rusty,
Or choked
With dust.

The days
    Have passed.
    I haven't heard
    My cuckoo's coo,
    Or seen the
    Hands move
    From minute to hour.

I wish
    My cuckoo clock
    Would wake me up
    At early dawn
    Before the cock
    Gives its yawn.

Padma Chakranarayan

UNTITLED

My mind aches from questioning
        those things
I do not understand . . . . .
        Yet, I ask,
        and I search,
        and I wait,
        and I seek,
        and I hope,
        and I pray,
        and I weep,
        and I dream,
        and I plan,
        and I try,
        and I do,
        and I survive . . . .
My mind aches from questioning those things
        I do not understand
Because I am still without answers.

DeMarchia Gibson

GIBSON, DEMARCHIA JEAN. Pen Name: DeMarchia Gibson; Born: West Palm Beach, 1-15-56; Education: Bethune-Cookman College, B.A., 1975-78; The Institute of Children's Literature, Diploma in writing children's literature; Occupation: Teacher; Memberships: Delta Sigma Theta Sorority, Inc., Tri-M Musicmasters Society, Bethune-Cookman Alumni Association, Northwood Community Center Advisory Board Chairperson; Awards: B-CC's Literary Magazine, Second Place in poetry contest, 197-78; APA, Haiku, 1984; Poetry: 'Haiku,' APA, 1984; Comments: *My poetry seeks truth and reality through the testimony of my soul's expressions.*

THE CLOWN

See that clown standing there his act's about to start.
But underneath all that make-up he's hiding a broken heart.
With happy eyes, smiling face he runs around and around.
But yesterday death struck hard, and never made a sound.
Only his sobs broke the silence as he placed his
Family in the ground.
Only yesterday there were four, now there is only one.
For when he buried his wife and daughter, he buried
His only son . . . too bad there is no time
For sadness or sorrow, the show must go on.
This world is but a stage and each man must
Play his part, so tonight he'll put on his make-up
To hide his broken heart . . . Yes, he'll really put on
Quite a show . . . For bringing you happiness is all he'll
Ever know . . . But when the act is over there will
Be no smile, just a frown . . . And this is no
Lie my friends — I know because I am that clown.

Cathy Louise Jerrett

MY JESUS

I walk with Him in the early morning,
   Down the garden path,
And through the dewy grass.
   I view the golden dawn arising,
And see Him in the brilliant sunlight.
   I walk with Him at high noon,
Along the teeming highways.
   I walk with Him through all my busy day.
I hear Him in the laughter of little children at play,
   I see Him in everyone I meet,
In the office and on the street.
   He fills my life with sunshine,
Though dark and dreary be the day,
   He lights my path with love and peace and joy,
He drives the lurking shadows away.
   And though I never know what might lie ahead,
Because His light enfolds me,
   I feel no fear or dread.
My Jesus, Lord and Savior,
   Guardian, Guide and Friend.

Doris M. Naymik

THE OLD MOUNTAINEER

His face seems carved from the granite of his mountain
seamed by wind and weather
young as conception, old as eternity are his eyes

But he has no illusions that he will last like the mountain
for sometimes he looks off to the western horizon
as if he senses from that direction
the approach of a mortal enemy

ready to fight like an elemental, with both hands
for a hold on the life he feels slipping from him
like the waters that bubble merrily down
to vanish in the valley

those frail blue-veined fingers that caress a banjo neck
could yet strangle the life from any creature
and leave it beneath the hemlock

just, as he says, as Death means to leave him

Kathryn Gamble

JUST A DOOR

After all these years
I'm still just a door with pictures on it.
After all these years
You can still make out the faces
Of the ones with forced smiles.
Even though the edges are turned,
And the colorful membranes cracked,
I'm still just a door
Covered with greasy fingerprints
And brittle, yellowed tape
Holding up faded newspaper articles
Covered by sickly-green crayola scribbles.
After all these years
I can still open and close,
Though my hinges scream like a wounded alley cat.
After all these years
I'm still blamed for what gets let out,
And I'm still considered two-faced.
But the images you form on the inside
Leave their shadows on the doorstep . . .

brian riley

OMEGA

first movement: (a genesis)

Aware that He was lonely
He said to Himself, "Let there be . . . "

    and from void He created.

He raised a cup to His labor,
the water, the land and the fruit,

    and felt Himself elated.

His emotions burst for each system,
the suns, planets and endless blue,

    and soon found Himself inspired.

He embodied then His very image
to share the wonders of His toil

    at which point He grew so tired.

But not from this did He fatigue
nor from labors did His vigor ebb

    nae from His ecstasy.

His weariness was brought about
when, with a sudden rush of genius,

    His Most Supreme created thee.

Kenn McDowl

McDOWL, KENN. Born: Los Angeles, California, 12-30-50; Writings: *The Omega Odyssey,* begun in 1971, still in the works; "Six Sisters, Tale of," biographical, 1977; "The Goddess Ring," philosophical, 1970; "My Last Request," cynical, 1984; Comment: *I ask you — What is a 'Peace-keeping Missile?' Answer: A direct descendant of 'The Peace-keeping Club!' Nothing More. Until we learn that peace can only be achieved through understanding and trust, then advanced neanderthals are all we'll ever be. 'Nuf said.*

GOD'S MIRACLE

As you drive through Oconomowoc, out Shorehaven way,
You will witness God's miracle on display.
The green leaves of Summer, have now turned to Gold.
A gorgeous sight for all to behold.

The golden pumpkins are ready to pick,
October weather has turned the trick.
Large ones are ready for pumpkin pies,
Baked in Shorehaven's kitchen, the residents to surprise.

Smaller ones for children for Halloween fun,
To set on the sill while Trick or Treating is done.
With carved funny faces and a candle inside,
To lighten dark places where goblins abide.

The shocks of corn are in the field,
When husked will show the amount of yield.
The Indian corn is multicolored,
To hang on doors to welcome others.

A few seeds planted in the ground,
In their resurrection it will be found,
Food in abundance for all creation,
Surely a miracle for every nation.

Olga Baerwolf

LADY LIBERTY

Two hundred — twenty-five tons of steel-weave copper,
Resplendidly, glistens at Liberty Island,
Inspiration to those who seek ways to enter,
Bedazzled hopefuls to this blessed, golden land.
Uprooted, in need of individual freedoms,
Tenacious, titanic desire strengthens their zeal.
Escaping from abysmal despair and pogroms,

Trammeled by tyrants, denied a substantive meal,
Onerous circumstances do make their own decree.

Along with Emma Lazarus, we proudly shout,

"Give me your tired, your poor, yearning to be free!"
Resolved to be free of shackles, they must go out
And find the promised land to start their lives anew.
National boundaries present dangerous obstacles,
Departure is always a significant coup.
Eschewed are the vigilant border patrols,

Dangerous passage ensued by air, land, or sea,
America greets its new citizens to be.
"Mother of Exiles" marks their journey's jeopardy
Ending, distant freedom, now its best perigee.

Markham H. Lyons

MY CHRISTMAS TREE

As winter grips the world we know
And throws up barriers of ice and snow
We choose this time to honor his birth
Celebrate his coming with gift-giving and mirth
We make merry, practice Pagan rites
Feasting and drinking during frozen nights
In our homes cozy, we've forgotten the reason
The true meaning of Christmas and this holiday season
Santa Claus is the spirit we see
And tell children about while decorating the tree
This tree the kids cherish which makes their eyes shine
And brings smiles to their faces, it's not quite like mine
The tree which I see brings tears in a flood
It's not very pretty and it's covered with blood
With only one jewel is my tree adorned
My Christ's lifeless body and the sins he has borne
Christmas means giving and God gave his best
A sacrifice of love, Oh God! how we're blessed

Clarence A. Bowles

VIETNAM

And did the fate of a nation really lie in the weaponry of the Sling of David?
Or was it perhaps entrusted to the Heart of David representing the courage of his people?

And did the Heart of David beat strong and true in the service of his desert kinsmen?
Or was his heart betrayed by the weakness of his people as they shouted in their fear?

And did the hands of his people firmly grip their swords as they pursued their destiny?
Or had they no courage to pursue their tasks as ordained and entrusted them by the Prophets?

And did they place their bodies and comforts above necessities imposed by harsh duty's demands?
Or were the cries of moral indignation raised by the hordes in the deserts merely excuses of fear?

And did the Sons of Jesse have to flee the field in spite of the strength of the Sling of David?
Or was it perhaps a retreat begun and imposed by craven desert tribesmen crying out their fears?

And did these fearful cries of moral justification really give Judea the benefits and dignity they sought?
Or were they a cloak of respectability worn to hide the weakness of the nation's courage?

Selah.

David R. Pichowsky

THE SEARCH
HONORABLE MENTION

One night I entered a room full of white vaporous ghosts
Lying around on cots
In a black rectangular room without a broom.
The cobwebs were hanging in knots.

Looking for one who was my son, I heard a voice calling.
Through a door I went to follow the sound.
In complete darkness,
Searching for someone who was not around.

Calling and calling the voice grew louder and clearer,
And I thought I was going to see my son,
But I awoke to a negro family on the street who were creating a scene.
Their baby was crying and I'm not denying, I called the police on them.

Disappointment abides in life's game of Charades.
My sleepfulness greatly pleases me.
How I love to dream of the boy I lost,
'Cause I feel like I've been with him.

Henrietta Graham Mills

THE LAND OF THE NORTH, HOW IT BECKONS & CALLS

Snowshoes creak in the frozen snow, breaking the trail anew,
Whisper a song as they glide alone, over the crusted snow.
A distant mournful howl goes out, throughout the frozen night,
Deathly shadows silently glide, through the forest moonlight.
Fingers and hands, toes and feet, a numbing warning giving,
Of temperatures falling, death comes calling the careless and weak.
Icicles form from frosted breath, a bearded blanket of ice,
Jackpines snap and creak, protesting the freezing night.
The end of the trail, a lantern's yellow glow shining on the snow,
I think it's kinda nice out here, why it's only forty-nine below.
Defiant in this frozen land; a cabin, warmth and a fire,
The door slung open, warmth rushes forth, all that one could desire.
A stove's hot red coals, shoot sparks of laughter's flickering flames,
The warm glow from the heated stove, sent stabbing thawing pains.
The lantern's wick turned high, shadows dancing to and fro,
Hot simmered stew, steaming coffee besides, warming you through and through.
A hearty stack of Jack-pine logs, promised an all night fire,
Heaping them higher, the flames leaped brighter and warmth came seeping out.
Snuggling inside the goosie down by the wakeful smoldering fire,
The icy trail shrank farther, and farther, and farther . . .

Clifford E. Santa

I ALWAYS LIKE SUNSHINE

I felt the breeze across my face,
it blew gently through my hair,
As I looked up through the branches
I felt free from daily care.

Then I felt something different,
had I lived before this time?
Am I someone special?
It is a knowledge I must find.

As I looked up through the branches,
I could see the Sun shone so bright.
I always like sunshine,
it makes things feel so right.

Then I found a quiet place
and knelt down in prayer.
I felt his special spirit,
I somehow knew he cared.

I thanked him for the sunshine,
that makes me feel so free.
I always like sunshine.
I know that a part of it is in me.
Barbara "Bobbie" Hibbert

TO THE HONEYBEES

Hello, little honeybees,
Good luck on your flights,
Real gusto in your wings
For nectareous sights.

Out in the flower blend
Of enticing perfumes,
You sip ever tireless
From the loveliest of blooms.

And then I'm supposing
Since your task is so sweet,
You're just buzzing with pride,
Being really discreet!

You strive for your riches
Refusing defeat
Little honey-goal seekers
So clever and neat.

May your unique kind
Forever survive,
With a storage of plenty
In your quaint homey hive.
Ruth Shelton Turner

thinking about you now
makes me smile
knowing you and loving you
makes my life worthwhile
i love the way you think
you seem to know exactly
what's on my mind
i love the way you laugh
and your eyes have seen
the beauty in me that
no one else could find
your voice is like magic
so sweet to my ears
and those words of love
you whisper to me
i hope to hear for years
thinking about you now
makes me smile
knowing you and loving you
makes everything worthwhile . . .
Val La Rue

HOMER, Gloucester Harbor

DURA JANE

'Twas Dura Jane, who walked the roads,
And signaled to the passersby,
Beckoning towards the darkening woods,
To come and hear the night bird's cry.

'Twas Dura Jane, who roamed the fields,
Picking berries, finger brown,
Whose juicy sweetness, savored there,
Stain purpled, on her lips, full blown.

'Twas Dura Jane, who cradled her doll,
Crooning soft-sound songs, with tender ease,
Rocking back and forth, on the moist, brown earth,
Secure, in her world, there, on her knees.

'Twas Dura Jane, who left one day,
Without goodbye, just disappeared,
Though some would swear, she still wanders close,
And croons her songs, through berried lips.

Cecelia Marchand

PASTEL REVELATION

Like waters bubbling from th'eternal spring of time,
Long, flowing years have slid ahead,
Unchecked, ignored while fingers slowed and thinned.

Now, as some lowly dandelion,
Whose silky mane has bared a fleshy scalp,
I bow my aged head in autumn's chill.

Sounds of pleading notes float out from feathered friends,
Who also seek a warm and peaceful clime,
And wait their flight.

The wide and clear horizon makes me gasp,
As gold-lined, shining clouds move on.
Deep, silent openings tell that just beyond
There is no drooping, withering of a single leaf,
No ugly consummation, no decay.
Rather, through the peepholes of the clouds,
A pastel revelation seems to beckon me.
Eternal spring is on its way;
The birds burst out in glee.
Both they and I are ready,
And rejoice!

Elizabeth Palmer

HARMONY, THANKS AND PRAISE

Thank you, God, for the grasp of your hand upon my hand,
   Thank you for the faith on which I stand.
For the conversation we had today
   As we strolled in the refreshing air,
For the trees as they wave their arms in praise,
   They seem to feel the things I feel
And the things my heart doth say.

Thank you, for the day that ended,
   For the night that came on time,
Thank you for the sunrise that starts each new day.
   I look forward to these moments with you,
For I have a lot of things to say.
   And when each day is ended,
I can rest in peace with thee.

Thank you, for the harmony of the birds singing in the trees,
   For the clouds that cover the sun
That offer shade from time to time.
   Thank you, for the serenity, the peace that's oft mine.
Thank you, God, for all your mighty ways,
   I adore you, I worship you and I honor you,
With harmony, thanks and praise.

Ruthie Williams

ALL OF THESE THINGS

Rivers running down the stream
Sun in the sky pouring down beams
Rain waters falling all over the land
The paths and roads and ways of man

Birds flying wild in the vast blue
Flowers that settle under morning's dew
Hills and mountains, fine and grand
The seas that flow up to the sand

The trees that stand straight and tall
Snowflakes in winter that begin to fall
Flashes of lightning and claps of thunder
All of these things set your mind to wonder

Gloria A. Carter

I CARE

I love this time of year
It's for sentimental people
people who care . . . like me.

I care, but what does it matter?
I feel only pain.

I see people together who care about each other
Why am I alone?
I care . . .

You know how I care about you
And I think you care too
Why don't you come back?
Are you afraid of love?

I'm not like your first love . . .
but I want to be your last
Look ahead to our future . . .
forget about heartache in your past

I'll be good to you . . . you know that
for I care
I even more than care;
I LOVE YOU

Justin

I AM, AM I ?

I am. Am I? I am alone. Am I?
I am in a bubble and all around me on Earth,
   Heaven's order keeps me company!

I am so sad. Am I?
I am in a hollow and, looking outside,
   so spellbound as gladness surrounds me inside!

I am awake. Am I?
I am in a valley and looking upward
   as clouds, Heaven's oceans, hypnotize my guard!

I am asleep. Am I?
I am in a dream world where angels watch me
   as I sing and dance to starlight's symphony!

I am a leaf, a tree, the ground, the Earth, the Sun!

I am the Word, Time, Heaven's Order, and all things,
   past, now and forever, the only KING OF KINGS!

I am the great supreme universal power —
   I AM GOD!

Am I?

Josephine Bertolini Comberiate

MAMA . . . !

Although you only gained from me a little cheeriness,
You always thought my smiles were more honeyed than yours.
Although you tirelessly gave me a lot of solace,
You always sensed my tears were more bitter than yours.

For many years, you walked through ice, frost, rain and snow,
But, you would rather keep me safe from natural and human disasters.
You would like to pave a long highway and fix road lights for me,
But, for you it had been hard to find an easy path of fair weather.

When I was ill, I was eager for you to look after me.
When I was happy, I usually forgot how lonesome you were.
When I had children, I understood who you were living for.
When my children were willful, I saw how tolerant you were.

Whenever and wherever, I am your child forever.
I made you brokenhearted and was far away from your soul.
Yet, your love wasn't interrupted, scattered, or weakened.
You only bestowed all, wanted nothing from me, not even a call . . .

Devin Todd

THE TASTE OF DARING

Horrible imaginings will not seize and shake my reason,
though pain looks through my eyes my nature is blind to its own treason.
When I grapple with fate and feel the blows of dreadful events,
I know undaunted acts will reign and fortify the strength of my intent.

The taste of daring is fed by the tears lost in the wind,
valiant thoughts measured by their direness has no certain end.
All that is within me speaks through a voice inside my heart,
the malevolence of fortune cannot prevent me from bearing my part.

The desolate mind has no parallel enemy to my nature,
the thief of my noble thoughts is led by a timorous stranger.
Reknown is reborn when the henchman of defeat is dead,
The power of purpose ties the winds of confusion in my head.

Doubt's dark agents use venom to paint disjointing fear,
and attempt to entomb my soul with tales of terror whispered in my ear.
But that which I am slaughterous thoughts can mask but not destroy,
I am a master of my deeds drinking the medicine of unrestrained joy.

David M. Ramirez

ILLUSIONS ADRIFT

A laboring pendulum of a stately grandfather's clock,
    Swinging in continuous motion, releasing an unaltered tick-tock.
Seemingly traveling to and fro,
    Rhythmically repeating, the minutes, as we go,
The youth all of us acquired at our birth,
    Has unceasingly slipped away, undermining our self-worth.
Images floating through the wind-swept fields of our minds,
    Recorded photos, each of its own kind.
Memories of shared instances and words, ingrained in the pages of the past,
    Experiences, we thought, might forever last.
Our physical features, worn by the unfaltered march, of seasoned years,
    Have masked our usefulness and increased our fears.
Others wondering what to do with our decreased capacity,
    Often placing us in unfamiliar places, silently we inquire this voracity.
If they would envision, the age, when leaves indicate autumn,
    Perhaps, some will realize what it feels like at the bottom.
Beings, somewhat incapacitated, concealing ideas that are fresh,
    Putting the puzzle together, so our lives will mesh.
Pulling from the album imprints, to regain our youth,
    To rewrite the wrong and bring forth the truth.

James A. Hotchkiss

KISS

A kiss.
A brush of lips,
Warm and soft, firm and hard.
A gentle awakening of desire.
A probing of love
To open up and
Understand.
A kiss
That set the night on fire.
Wandering and free,
Curious and alive.
A searching for an
Answer.
A request for love.
A kiss
That blocks all feeling.
Demanding,
Responding,
Knowing.
A kiss.

Karen B. Zucco

PATHWAYS

Pause with me a moment here,
We can rest upon this stone,
For the trail is long,
And the hill is steep,
And we have no cause to hurry.
Any worldly matters will keep.
Besides,
It is tranquil within this grove;
With snow drifting earthward.
Falling between the naked aspen branches.
No song of the meadowlark
Can be heard at this time of year.
Only the sound of flake upon flake.
This is a quiet time.
A time to reflect on the road behind.
And chart the road ahead.
No, I talk not of this gravel path,
But of the roads of life.
Right or wrong,
Still we are free to choose our own.

W. P. Syndergaard

DAVID

He was chosen to lead
And give strength to a nation
When just a young shepherd boy.
He spoke from the heart,
Sang from the soul, and
Danced his dance of joy.

A passionate man,
This giant-slayer
Who bravely earned his fame.
A musician, a poet,
A mighty king,
A burning, brilliant flame.

He seems a many-sided
Legend, a hawk
As well as a dove.
Yet, a mortal man
Touched by grace,
Forefather of the Greatest Love.

Carol A. Smith

GLASS MAIDEN

The drawstring is pulled
As the light brown curtains
Are drawn to each side
And secured behind her ears.
The maiden's hair
Has been neatly parted in the middle
To better expose
Her clean and clear complexion of glass.

Her skin is
As smooth as a child's
And her face shows no trace
Of age nor of worry.
Her transparent eyes
Reveal no concern over the brooding branches
In the distance
That meekly announce
A stark winter ahead.

She's bound to her place
And there is no change of guard
To bring moments of freedom
Into her world.
But the light is her devoted lover
Who takes the monotony away
And who entertains her with his glances
Of warmth and of understanding.

Christine Rubel

ONLY THE LANDSCAPES CHANGE

Naked but for cut-off Levi's
two freckled bodies
sat cross-legged atop ancient rock
towering high above the rolling hills of Missouri.

We watched the barges toward east and west
and absorbed the last long rays
into bronzed skins grown darker by a day
of skinny dipping in the river beneath the cliffs.

Insects buzzed and birds soared high
from wrinkled trees and smooth saplings
who confessed their secrets to billowing white gods
succeeding indifferently on the hot wet breeze.

We spoke of important things that mattered then
two dandies side by side
changing — into silver puffs of seedlings . . .

to be blown free from their stems that summer
and take root in various places
but to seed again . . .

into two freckled bodies
perched high on a man-cut cliff for highways.

D. Eugene Wells

OURS

Mine and yours,
our only one.
Between us we have
a very beautiful son.
He was created through our love
that once ran deep.
But the hills and mountains
we had to overcome were too steep.
A shattered dream; and the chances of
us together again are slim.
But although the well is dry, the memory of
its fullness is still shared
every time I look at him.

Rod Masters

YOU AND I

I must have known you in other stars
Because when you and I met that night,
I saw your soul through your shining eyes
And glimpsed my own in their tender light.

Such happiness we found, beyond deserving.
If there were heavenlier worlds than our own,
Here was enough heaven to fill our dreams
And more loveliness than we have ever known.

We laughed and played like children in the sun
And talked of life and love and you and I.
Unmindful of tomorrow and yesterday,
We watched the flowers bloom, the flowers die.

But life and love must be tested in fire;
We plunged into depths of despair and death.
Our world turned into an ocean of pain
And every joy was balanced by a grief.

Yet, over stepping-stones of our sorrow,
We shall climb hand in hand, you and I.
We shall reclaim the happiness we knew
In this earth, and in other stars.

F. P. Macaraeg

LOOK TO THE LORD

In these times of trial and trouble,
As inflation grows and prices double,
With the promise of war raging ahead
and unpeaceful surroundings that we soon learn to dread.

We cannot rely on man's uncertain mind,
He continues to promise and continues to bind,
His work is worth little as he promises peace . . .
Will man ever stop this? Will hatred ever cease?

Instead of looking to man for our needs,
We must put faith in God who can do wondrous deeds.
If we look to the heavens and open our heart,
The Lord will look down on us . . . give us a new start.

We'll enter a life full of loving and caring,
He'll open up doors as a result of our sharing . . .
With neighbors and friends and those of each race,
He'll share his great love for us if we only have faith.

God loves us I know and he'll always be there,
He keeps us forever in His constant, loving care.
So give to Him always all trouble and fear,
Look to the Lord for our prayers He will hear.

Deborah (Glassburn) Parsons

PSALM 102

I need God's love and His word of comfort
Today. The Holy Spirit has spoken to my
Heart and has given me the need to read
Psalm 102. Through prayers and God's "Holy
Presence" those words can calm the stress I
Feel. Our God, so mighty and knows and
Won't let me fall. He will always protect
The righteous for whatever the problems,
He can speak to your heart after you have
Given Him your will.
Jesus can fill your desires and change others'
Minds. Christ is one of a kind, a negative
Situation can be changed to a positive one
By His persuasion in a supernatural way. He
Can answer prayers in His own way.
All loved ones hold on to your "faith, joy"
And peace may it stay in your heart forever
                                    Amen

Mrs. G. Regdos

UNVARNISHED

Titanic are errors and terrors
and ugly the stains and the pains.
Grim death and destruction and fears
spread distortions through distance and years,
from an ancient and ignorant history.
While a search for the truth soon discovers,
sheer beauty is banished to mystery.

In mystery know even time is unknown.
Like lost love, brightest beauty is shining alone.
Its reflections seen here is our proof it exists
serene in the absolute certainty
of mystery's measureless state.

Ralph Hunt

THE BALLOON IN THE HEAVENS

The fluttering balloon once in the air
but the Sharpness of that needle came that day,
for what transpired when the needle combined
with the balloon — I couldn't bear.

Now the balloon has soared in the sky
Upon the great heavens where the
precious balloon is white in sullen silence.

I love you and how I desiderated we
had said goodbye.
But the apparition of you in my soul —
always with adoration and ponderousness sing . . .

Eva Kiss

IDEAS IN RETROSPECT

We are all in life's fast lane and while in our search,
We sense time's flow spanning the intellect.
Its followers amass many deeds.
Its creators invent what others might heed, groping the unknown
Alas, the clone of reason is upon us.
Experimentation in life shares our grace as worldly inhabitants.
In due respect, I will never forget individual representation.
So I, a citizen, do care to remember
To contemplate life's harmonious key, nay its blunders.
For it is easy for me to perceive life's incongruencies.
It, in turn invigorates my creativity and that is mine alone,
So, if you wish to trade places with me . . . excuse me but . . .
My life is not for free.

Leslie A. Nay

TO A YOUNG NEPHEW

Forgive us Chris, if in the pain of loss,
    Our falling tears' faint echoes bring distress;
Among the angels now you safely dwell,
    But we in life can only know our hearts,
And they are heavy and bewildered things.
    Possessing now all knowledge of goodbye,
You doubtless smile with fond regret upon
    Our needless woe, and chide us silently.
So much we'd give to know your secret, Chris . . .
    And some of us could envy your estate,
All safely home amidst Angelic light;
    For we have yet the Ordeal Strange to face,
And questions in the darkness of our night.

T Kelly

EXTINCT HOMO SAPIEN

Let us not wonder as a species
How we began or how we shall end.
Let us wonder how to work the present
To the best of its efficiency.
For it is the present
Which shall mold and nurture new beginnings.
And it is the present
Which shall carve and plant our headstones.

Sing a song for the extinct Homo Sapiens.
For they died of extreme hindsight and foresight.
An animal so arrogant,
It never bothered to look down at its own
        clumsy feet.

Robert Van Cleave

REMEMBER ME FONDLY

Remember me fondly my friend,
Remember at the day's end.
Do you remember me fondly, my friend
Remember fondly the time we spent?

Remember my face,
    in some loving place,
Remember my eyes and the love
    that came through
As I looked at you.

Do you see me my friend,
    In the eyes of loved ones?
Do you hear me my friend,
In the songs on the radio
        of loving and living
and sharing and giving?

I remember you fondly, my friend,
At the day's beginning and the day's end,
And I wish together we had more time to spend.

Remember I'm with you my friend,
In my love and my prayers.
Remember my friend, I care.

Harriet Stout Mulford

A WALK WITH MY DOG

As I walk with my dog,
Along the little wooded road that winds
Through thick autumn sumacs and sweet scented pines,
Silence is golden.

The peace and quiet of the filtered fresh air,
That rustles through the trees not yet quite bare,
Brings solace inexplicable between man and his beast;
The soul is elated.

As he walks like a king I can feel his heart sing,
And when I catch the glint in his eye,
He wags his tail with a friendly "Hi,"
The bond is solemn.

A lone passing car does not necessarily mar
This being in tune with the infinite,
As the occupant smiles and waves quite intimate,
We share nature's ecstasy.

I would not trade this heavenly journey
For a barrel full of jingling money,
As the morning sun peeks through glistening trees
        in silvery streaks.
Life is sweet.

Perviz Chinoy

VOICES ON THE WIND

I heard a voice whispering on the wind,
Rising to a melody of sound.
I realized the voice was only in my mind,
Telling me of the world's beauty all around.

Endless forests, shimmering trees,
Each leaf dancing in the gentle breeze.
Crystal streams, tumbling to the sea,
This is the way our world was meant to be.

As I looked up from my special view,
Sunlight sparkling through purest blue.
The sky like a mirror, reflecting love,
Sunbeams showering down gladness from above.

Reach out to the beauty everywhere,
Hold on to the world's love, if you dare.
Give a little of your joy to everyone you know,
Never ignore the voices on the wind as it blows.

Linda Carole Moore

I ONCE HAD A LOVE

I once had a love, who was more than a love
  Who was more than a man could imagine.
She was more than an angel who was sent just for me
  She was more than a priceless possession.

Now this love that I had, who was more than a love
  She loved me like no man could imagine.
She loved me more than any love ever told
  More so than any known equation.

And this love that I had, who was more than a love
  I loved her like no man could imagine.
I loved her more than any ballad of love
  More so than a dream's aspiration.

But this love that I had, who was more than a love
  And who loved me without deprivation,
She was taken from me, and left me alone,
  Now I'm dying like no man could imagine.

John S. Marcum

BLIND SNOWBIRD

Little bird walking alone in the snow.
If one is hungry, I'll never know.
I threw you some bread crumbs the other day.
But you stared at them, and just walked away.
Why little bird, do you not eat?
I'm a friend little bird I mean you no defeat.

One crumb is left.
It glows in the snow.
You must eat,
please cause no death.

Yet you still stare at the brown crust.
Is it that within you there is no trust.

Your feet must be cold, in the fallen snow.
You did not fly when I moved,
Or came near.
Oh, little bird, I did not know.

Jeanette French

FLYING FIRST TIME FROM L.A. TO SYRACUSE

Oh, the millions of colored lights below
Within each place, a heart may glow
With love, and warmth for someone dear —
Wishing that loved one to appear —
The lights may shine to show the way
To someone who has gone astray.
The airport lights, to guide the planes —
The harbor lights, through fog and rains —
A cottage light, though very small, may mean the
way, the homeward call.
I feel God's hand is very near —
Without a doubt, without a fear.
He must have wanted planes to go, else He would
never let planes grow
Within a brain — new arts and skills
I'm sure it must have been His will,
Since he had Noah build the ark —
How travel's changed — all left a mark —
He cares not for the atom bomb
But we need its power to keep us calm.

Marjorie Hennigan

HENNIGAN, MARJORIE. Comments: *It is a talent given me by God above. I love flowers, animals and everything beautiful. My family means much to me and always has.*

MOTHER'S LOVE, CHILD'S EXPERIENCES

In the beginning . . .
                Soft, warm, silently pulsating, nourishing,
                enriching, womb environment.

Cataclysmic eruptions, dynamic sensations, pain-love filled
womb exit, colorfully filled environment. Expectations, smiles.

Growing, cellular spurts, knowledge, expectations, daily
portions of nourishment, encouragement, colors, noise,
childhood diseases.

Room full of laughter, excitement, life, pine smell, 30 desks,
electric growth, sensations of change, maturity, expectations.

Hopeful, experimentation, counseling through failure, lost
loves, tears and laughter, changes, arrival of new age,
sometimes soldier, responsibilities, broader knowledge.

Enter adulthood, nerve-wracking, pulsating economy, "real
world," great needs for care, marriage, partners, adjusting
priorities and those whose expectations are no longer, lament.

Attaining goals, wealth, experiences, "things." Encouraging
those offspring, training, nurturing, reminding, remembering
the beginnings, all. Sometimes loss of own creating vessel,
pause for reflections of womb exit, chronology, successes,
past.

Miller Lyons

WALKING ALONE

Walking along in the moonlight
Walking along all alone
Watching stars as they twinkle and shine
Hoping that someone will be mine.

Why don't my tears stop flowing like this
When what I long for is a hug and a kiss
Whispering breezes seem to keep me awake
Like glowing embers my heart is at stake.

Walking when it's late at night
Walking all alone in my plight
Walking for everyone to see
I need someone to care for me.

Walking all around the town
Hoping that I will soon be found
By that special someone I want tonight
To hug me and kiss me and hold me tight.

I'm walking and looking at those in sight
To find the one who I think is just right
Who will ask the question I want to hear
So that I can answer with "Yes, my dear."

Eva B. Cook

IN PASSING

Transition —
sublimate my scroll!

Grief of parched prayer
remain not barren.
What else man's pain
But the limbo of — lost thoughts.

Immortal soul
do not acquiesce to futility!

Exonerate my human volute,
that arid scroll clutched
in the vice of erredly appraised strength.

Let enlightenment dawn
in time bringing forth equilibrium in its wake.

How can the tumultuous sky of my mind
redeem its blistered dreams?

Let torment transmute into chaliced significance
and I'll arise to inaugurate my supreme hour!

Hedi Bernstein

CITY STARLIGHT

I sit here, lonely again
Wishing you were with me
Thinking of happier days
Remembering the memories we made.

Through the hazy window I can see
The city's starlights whispering to me
They tell me to forget the past
Because love isn't supposed to last.

The city — so full of life and fun
But an affair just isn't for everyone
I wanted something that was real
I only wished you had been sincere.

The city's starlights fade with the approaching dawn,
But my love for you will always live on.

Julie Schulte

THE WORDS

The words.
They slap me in the face.
I knew that they were coming.
I did not know that they would hurt me so.
They leave a scorching sting in my ears.
They fight their way through me.
They battle my guilt, my caring, my love, and my wisdom.
They win.
Stronger than my will, they have made their way to my heart.
And the sound of shattering echoes throughout me
In unison with the oncoming feeling of pain.
Seeping through my body.
The words have won.

Natalie Milstein

THIS IS LOVE — TO CANDY

Warm kiss
the sacredness of feeling
The way we are — "just as I am"
Acceptance
Love in the trust in each other
Love in the beauty of expressing
Feeling for one another
Love comes from God
And God is love
Love is not like a neon sign — on and off
True love is deep
True love lasts and you're one of the human race
No violence — please

Danny W. Casey

My granddaughter Pat
looked at my cat
whose one eye was different from the other,
"it has a *cat*aract in one eye," I said,
"has a dog a *dog*aract, grandmother?"

Catherine likes her carrots,
she eats them all day long.
She eats them whole, makes carrot juice
bakes carrot cake and carrot roll.

She went to bed, she died that night,
her face was red and carrotlike.
They put green leaves on top of her head,
she looked like a carrot when she was dead.

H. Arlt

SPRING RAIN

It rained last night and my heart also cried
The earth and I were cleansed
With a washing of its own kind
Tears can be as cleansing as the rain drops
With each the surfaces of life are gently renewed
Nature's storms will rinse the dust and death away
Thunder and lightning once again
Drive feelings into the hibernating earth
Life responds with new growth
So our hearts, too, sleep
Until the storm of emotions
Overcome the dormancy
Our souls cry and awaken refreshed in the morning.

Jo Anne Van Cleave

ECHOES OF TIME

I can hear a lot of noises.
Some are good and some are bad.
Many sounds are full of laughter,
But some are very sad.

They appear to be the echoes
Of the past just rushing by —
Again to remind us
How quickly time does fly.

Life is just a wondrous moment
That many people have shared;
Past and present intermingled
For all who really cared.

Now, stand still for just a moment —
Let the echoes of many years
Tell you many secrets
Of much joy and many tears.

Hear the whispers of the world's great beauty,
The many wonders of this earth
That have passed on before us,
Then re-entered with each new birth.

So the past rushes by us
With its echoes left with time,
To remind us of past and present
And the future that shall entwine.

Frances P. Brown

WHY DOES THE WIND BLOW?

Why does the wind blow, Daddy;
Tell me, why does it blow?
Those little tiny baby leaves, move so fast and go.
Where does it come from; why does it blow?

My little red cart was right over there,
And the leaves you raked aren't here.
We both could feel so very sad,
We could easily shed a tear.

Why does the wind blow, Daddy;
Does God send it to us?
We still love Him, don't we, Daddy,
And we'd never make a fuss.

Sometimes you read of storms in a city,
And the wind blows 'round and 'round,
Even little children drown.
Oh! Daddy, what a pity.

Why does the wind blow, Daddy;
I really want to know.
What do the birds do, where do they go?
Let's you and me find out, what really makes it blow.

In summer it blows the corn,
In winter it blows the snow;
Please, please, dear Daddy, tell me the truth,
Why does the wind blow?

Edith R. VanOrsdale

THE GIFT

Against thy heart I place my peace,
  in trust,
  like a child whose innocence knows
  that the world exists for himself.
This richness of my calmed spirit I cherish;
  tranquility becomes a charmed circle:
  receiving is giving is receiving.

Cynthia Buell Thomas

A TREASURE OF THE HEART
Gerald and Joanne
October 17, 1953 — October 17, 1984

Love is a treasure of the heart
For centuries, possessing simplistic appeal.
It's sweet and very slow to start,
Sustaining you when you're apart.
          A treasure to behold
          It has grown and flowered.
          Repaying you, one hundredfold
          The considerations you have showered.
A treasure of two hearts
Guiding you with gentle hand, along the paths you choose.
Companionship is where it starts,
Every day sharing with you, clues.
          Showing without question, love has grown
          In two hearts, fervent and true.
          On this day that is yours alone,
          There beats a single heart between you.

Rose Drilling

THE LORD TOOK HER HOME

After fifty-seven years of the two of us as one,
according to rules instituted by the Lord above.
Who knows our every need, and every pain, brings
peace to my one and only dearest love.

To lose the love and affection is heartbreaking,
after being together for many wonderful years.
Though I know the Lord will take care of her,
I still have difficulty in holding back the tears.

Although life for me in loneliness must go on,
my life without her, will be hard to bear.
But thanks be to our dear Lord, in whom we have
the promise, that He our burdens will share.

Now after many talks with the Lord in prayer,
my life towards the future is not so dim.
Because my Lord who loves her too, decided
to take her to a place of rest with Him.

So as the time comes, when we come to the
river Jordan, and cross over to the other shore.
My prayer to the Lord is, that we shall know
each other, and be together again forevermore.

Jimmy Bonovitch

OF WINGS

Where is my home, you ask?
Why — I dwell where the air is filled with flying things —
From tiny bugs to men, they all have wings:
Grasshoppers, butterflies, mockingbirds, and then on high
The Chariots of War come thundering by —
Grimly playful, nose to tail,
Or in majestic solitude, they sail
On some important mission bent,
Through high-piled clouds in deepest azure firmament.

All through the days you hear them roar
You see their vast parade;
But at eventide they're heard no more,
Only bats own sky and glade.
And then at night, when fireflies glow
And worlds shine brightly from afar,
They're back as great jewelled dragonflies
Or a distant shooting star —

Have I a place in the throbbing sky?
Do I ride the wind that sings?
Ah, no, I yearn — by it earthbound am I,
  Only my soul has wings.

Julia Ord King

THANKS FOR NOTHIN'

Now I lay me down and drowsy, grateful that this day is done.
Punch my pillow, get all comfy — won't be long 'til mornin' sun.
One last yawn, and sinking sleepward — wrapped in darkness to my toes;
Then, the day's events come creepin' 'round to slow my sweet repose.
Memory brings up the headlines taken with my breakfast juice:
"STOCKS ARE SLIDING!" "CRIME IS RISING!" "COUNTY SPENDING'S ON THE LOOSE!"
Local banker's been caught stealing . . . neighbor's son just wrecked dad's car . . .
Cost of living sends one reeling . . . and, this isn't all, by far!

This world's had a heap of blundering getting through this day; in fact,
I had better count my blessings, sitting here now, thinking back.
Looking on this long day's happenings, Lord, it surely is a Sin
Beggin' more!
I thank you for
What I've NOT had, where I've NOT been!

Helen J. P. Weddel

FATHERS; AND FATHERS, OF SOUL

How can, you; affirm your soul,
Today — tomorrow?
When will, you, accept, and know, your living soul?
You; need to know your soul.
Probably there are, only seven individuals,
Living souls, on earth, today.
And from, "The King James Version,"
One of these (Tau, Schin, Resh, Koph, Tzaddi, Pe and Ain) is your soul;
That are; the seven souls, abiding, on earth.
Which, Father and Church, will, you, worship and honor?
How long, will your soul, be afflicted!
Then which, of those souls;
Will, you, afflict (bind), with,
Today — tomorrow.

John Thomas

VIRGINIA

As my pen spills out the ink that expresses my sentiments
As our anniversary nears and completes its eighth cycle
My mind goes in variable patterns through unfamiliar firmaments
Trying to grasp the right words and phrases for this chronicle.

For 1982, my symbol of love is my absence and three red roses
I guess this is what is meant by better or for worse
As with bliss and happiness, we have to bear some small crosses
For as long as we remain best friends and charter the same course.

My gratitude and appreciation for a wonderful eight years
I can't express myself in metaphor, analogy or simile
but amidst our laughter, smiles, frowns and tears
I still say you are the best thing that ever happened to me.

Leandro A. Abadia

TWO HATS

Together on a corner, a cowboy and a cop;
One of those unlikely combos, a classic case of strange bedfellows.
Huddled close as any lovers, the Stetson-hatted quizzling
Relays his information. The copper reaches for the call-box,
And then turns in hesitation. He shakes and nods his blue-capped head
Just like a well-taught schoolboy, while the cowboy,
Through his tight-lipped teeth, re-sings his song like any choirboy.
They could be characters in a play, but it's a scene from sidewalk life.
That copper's call may bring the curtain down or run some player out of town.
Has the cowboy thrown the script away to be free to act another day?
Does he bow and scrape in backstage whispers to keep from being clapped in a cell?
He plays his dual role quite well, but will his fellow players know
It was his review that closed their show? How convincing is any dual role?
How sheer is the costume of the soul?

Kay Boyle

SILENT BEAUTY

Rose petals fall to the ground
Scattering silently with the wind
The beauty once beheld as a flower
Now spreads across the land
Touching the earth ever so softly
As the tiny red petals glide across
    the green grass
Magnifying the spectacular silent
    beauty of spring.

Connie Bahm

ARE YOU SATISFIED?

What must we have to be content,
A ship to sail to some foreign isle,
Or riches that have been provided
To suit our taste and our lifestyle?

Knowing Christ gives us the answer:
An inward peace that He provides.
No longer need we seek contentment
For in our Lord, we're satisfied.

Arline Ratliff

TO WAIT FOR BLOOD

Women past the age of blood
let go to giving life.
Now, blood-letting past by ages,
blood's denied the dying,
life's denied giving
and some,
letting love go past,
die of AIDS
to wait for blood.

Joanne Commanday

A TRUE HOME

Home doesn't exist without people
Who share life's laughter and tears
And whether near or far away
Love binds them through all the years.

This spirit built America
With families its basic part
Life, liberty, pursuit of happiness
Comes inevitably from the heart.

Eleanor Benson

AND THEN FATALLY

The mushrooms bloomed today.
They came for lack of words —
Suffocating the flowers,
Clipping the wings of birds.

They robbed the men of treasure,
For their growth was unconfined.
When the mushrooms desisted,
There was nothing left behind.

Richard O. Hawley, Jr.

THEN I CAN'T LEAVE LAUGHING

Always approaching love,
                    with one eye on the door,
I became the invariable clown,
                    the constant mentor,
                                        everyone's friend,
except my own.
Sure my shell was intact,
                    you chanced to see the crack.
Afraid to linger,
                    I hurried past you,
knowing if I paused
                    you would look inside
                                        and find me vulnerable.
But you did see,
                    and through your eyes forced me to stop
                                                        and see.
Unsure how to deal with this new-found self,
                                        I almost let me die,
until a larger fear surfaced.
Having now been touched,
                    you might walk away.
But,
    if I allow me,
                to you,
then I can't leave laughing.
        Kathleen O'Brien

A PATRIOTIC SHOWER

The colors of red, and white and blue —
Symbolize freedom — That's lasting and true;
A flag with stars, and stripes red and white
Lets America know that it's blessed, day and night;

The freedom to vote, and the freedom to pray —
Gives America courage — and shows men the way;
In the past — men have fought, and have died —
To save this dear country that's held with such pride —

God Bless America! — the land of the free!
Man can be *blind,* yet, still he will *see;*
Even in *darkness,* truth is the *light* —
That will shine for all men, deep into the night;

Freedom of speech is a gift to us all —
Men can voice their opinions, and stand straight and tall;
The best gift of all is an education —
It gives knowledge to everyone, throughout the nation —

Freedom to choose, and freedom to live —
Freedom to love, and freedom to give;
A "Shower of Freedom" falls upon this dear land —
And is blessed by God, and His mighty hand —
        Kathleen A. Rimmele

NIGHT BLIGHT

For me the limpid night had lost its charm;
Long gone were beauty, rapture, transient bliss.
Pellucid dark, for now, evokes alarm.
Beauty lost, joy denied, paralysis.

I walked in pitch and met him face to face.
He took my sanctity. Left me with scum.
I live in fear, defiled and, yes, disgraced.
Acrid repugnance permeates. I'm numb.

I want to feel, again, mid-night romance,
To trust, to know that safely I can love.
I want to take a suitor's hand and dance.
I want tranquil nights, soothing stars above.

I will find beauty in a love sincere
Where torturous memories disappear.
        Lois V. Chapman

RELINQUISHING

The hillsides overwhelmed the morning
as beauty crowded my opened window.
I gazed with marvel; then rued precognition.

As my eyes roved the gardened slopes, I noticed
a treetop in luscious green surrounded
by the forest in ruffled beige and beet-red.

It glared down upon her verdancy,
At her strident rebellion, protesting Nature.
She pleaded her stance with the hostile splendor,

"Please, let me live in softness longer.
I shudder at nakedness when my dress
will have fallen in showers as yours will soon do."

Her neighbors nodded, as their leaves began
to tremble and loosen in the autumn breeze.
They leaned a little. I pulled down my window.

Next morning, I searched again for the tree.
She must have relented, in wistful obedience:
the tips of her limbs were yellow-brown.
        Margaret Umbarger

AFTER READING THE POEM CALLED "STRANGERS ARE WE ALL UPON THE EARTH"*

Yes, "Strangers are we all upon the earth,"
    Strangers everyone; there is not one
Dares call the earth his home, so brief
    The stay we make before we go.
Where do the shadows beckon, that we,
    Children of mortality, must follow?
Where, in our world of sorrows, but the grave?
Is there hope when we have learned our nature?
    We are vapors drifting through a dream
    And our lives are tragedies in a nightmare.
But when the dream has ended, we transients
    On the earth will buy our tickets
To another world beyond the darkness;
    And among the multitudes that lived and died.
There will be no strangers when the dream has ended.

        *by Franz Werfel
        John F. Koons*

SOLITUDE

Dear Solitude: It is with you I wish to be,
In the mountains where it is clean and free.
Surrounded by blue, spacious sky
And pastures that have never been so green.
Sleep among the trees so high,
Such happiness money can't buy.
O Solitude, what a gorgeous sight;
A place where not a soul can spy.
Away from all bitterness and fight,
In a place where everything is right.
Daffodils and daisies all year 'round
And a beautiful bird always in flight.
At night not the tiniest of sound.
For miles not a soul to be found.
O Solitude, what a fascinating view;
A river that will never be drowned,
A pasture covered by morning dew,
And every blossom starting to bloom.
In spring the rabbit and the deer,
At night the owl and raccoon.
So beautiful, I can feel a tear,
A place of much good and cheer.
O Solitude, how I wish it so
This place of such free and clear.
        Barbara Poluch

THE APPOINTMENT

I feel like I have just died and gone to hell!
  My judge and jury are there! — They tell me to
come to the appointment at eight! Of course they
come in Late! — I wait with other people of many races!
  — They all have different kinds of expressions on
Their faces! They take our appointment cards — They look
  — Like we're some kind of pet they have rejected.
  They tell me, they lost all my records. They send me
To another dark room — and then I start all over again!
  Then I look around the dark room — I see them —
  I stand while they sit! As I look around the people
Seem to be in some kind of trance — They seem to be
Ready for judgment — By some kind of dead things —
  — that just move their eyes — waiting also to be
Judged by a head executioner! — As I can't tell the
living from the dead!
  the children run, and play — while old people seem
To be going insane! — They seem to cry out in some
Strange voice of utter pain!
  "Can I be the one who is insane?"

Joe Guardino

THE SOLITARY TREE

The solitary tree stands in the meadow
As the clouds turn black and billow out
With their impending lightning and rain

They lash out at this solitary figure
With all of their might
Their mindless wish to destroy

He is not in their realm of understanding
He stands there and takes the lightning

And he takes the rain from the evil clouds
With a gentle understanding of their kind

They look and are touched by what they see
Solitary tree in your solitary meadow, they addressed him
We applaud you for your gentleness
We shall not rain on you again

Kevin Lindsey

PEARLS OF LOVE

  Pearls of love the song of angels in the
rapture of true love flames within thy heart.
  As the dawn appears with blue and gold the
soft cool breeze refreshes my soul.
  Pearls of love is eternity the flame of love burns
brighter than any strokes of art.
  Under skies of silver blue and purple another
day is gone but tomorrow shall bring joy and
love within thy heart.
  Space vast and far the heart can touch the
distance stars.
  As the curtain of night appears the stars are
shining softly pick one years of memories we
share as the sunset of colors fade in the sky.
  We have seen the dawn and the lovely
sunset love me in silence with thy soul.
  Love is the measure of all that is so dear
pearls of love you gave to me from within thy
heart.

Lucy Ann Casey

ONE MAN'S LIFE

In Spring,
a baby is born.
Tiny hands and tiny feet,
smelling like baby powder and mashed beets.

In summer,
a child the baby becomes.
Grass-stained jeans and brushed-burned knees.
The question "why?" asked fifteen thousand times.

In Autumn,
the child becomes a man.
Cars and football,
proms and fun.
Life decisions to be made.

In Winter,
a life has been lived.
Sons now asking for the car,
Grandchildren now asking, "why?"
Wrong and right decisions have been made.
All these things done,
In one man's life.

Linda M. Storrs

THAT'S WHEN I WANT TO PRAISE YOU

When I look out my window and see what You have done —
Your beauty all around me, the warmth of the midday sun —

   That's when I want to praise You;
   That's when I want to sing;
   That's when I want to tell You of
   The love and joy You bring.

When I hear a whippoorwill or see the setting sun —
The golden moon that's shining, thoughts of the day that's done —

   That's when I want to praise You;
   That's when I want to sing;
   That's when I want to tell You of
   The love and joy you bring.

Walking in the crackling leaves on a beautiful autumn day
Or watching the storm clouds gather, I can look to You and pray.

   That's when I want to praise You;
   That's when I want to sing;
   That's when I want to tell You of
   The love and joy You bring.

Kathy Young

As a tree grows, there I stand . . . years of growth identify
Its strength . . . time increasing length
Of endurability.
Rooted in the soil, anchored in stability,
Life carving oftentimes a Rood
With hardship and vicissitude
A cross to bear;
Yet silent is the tree there,
Unspoken thought tacitly a prayer of invocation.

And through the years, vented tears provide an irrigation
Nourishing the roots and tree to wherein lies,
A harvesting of the crop which fructifies.
And as a tree in season bears,
So in the autumn of my life, responses to my prayers
Of things unseen not yet in evidence, will have fruition,
Changing the condition
Of material and social events . . .
And brought into existence
Will be proof
Of things wrought by prayer being an actuality and Truth!

Betty Tomson

THE TOUCH OF HIS HANDS

The night is cold and damp
The fire is burning brightly,
We sit together quietly
Exchanging glances ever so slightly,
He turns and touches me softly
Then slowly kisses my awaiting lips.
With the swiftness of his hands
He dims the lights down low.
With just one word we know
How the evening will end.
The rain has stopped
The fire burned out,
We look out at a new day
And know that love has conquered all.

Diana Prahl

LOOKING FOR ADVENTURE

The long and hard climb is
somewhat romantic.
Always searching for something
better than the way it was before.
Opening just another door, to
find there is more in store.
Looking for Adventure
everywhere I turn.
Trying to find a girl out there,
who shines just like a pearl.
Early on I found her. Maybe
just a dream.
But I know the day will
come, when the sun will
shine on me.

Arthur Shaw

SHAW, ARTHUR THOMAS. Pen names: A.
T. Shaw, Artie Shaw (like the band leader);
Born: Hawaii, 6-1-60; Education: self-educated;
Occupations: Art Teacher, Vice President of
Sales for Ardolino Home Improvement, Sales
Representative and Display Manager for whole-
sale distributor, Single Engine Plane Pilot, for
further Adventure!; Poetry: 'I Sit Here,'
American Poetry Anthology, Fall/Winter,
1984; Comments: *In my work, I reach into my
soul and take out a breath of fresh air to share
with the world. I hope someday to bring to our
world a better understanding of the Infinite In-
telligence, each of carries us around every day.*

I USED TO WRITE OF LOVE

I used to write of love,
And life, and pain
That caught me mid-cycle,
And chewed me up,
And spit me out,
And made me feel alive — and sane
(in its roundabout way . . .)

I've been high,
And I've been low;
And I've been here
And there, and everywhere
I'd ever cared to go.
I'm bored with pain:
The misery
Of love gone bad,
And high gone low.

It's haunting me
Is least and whole
    Of all I know.

Kelly Johnson Dunn

THE MOCKINGBIRD

One morning early I thought I
Heard,

The ceaseless song of a mocking
Bird.

It was a lighthearted joy to my
Soul.

The little mockingbird did not
Tire,

He seemed to feel his song was my
Desire.

It was a happy interlude for the
Day.

Then he hushed his song and flew
Away.

Lucy Clipfel

LIFE IS TOO SHORT FOR PETTY "PICKING"

Life is too short
To "use," abuse, or
Refuse a friend, acquaintance,
Client, or business associate.

We are asked to morally love our enemies
Along with our friends,
So why not a chance to those
That are dear, and/or friends
Of those near (and dear) to our
Well-being such as "kin" —
Friends of kin, and friends of
Friends; in our daily effort
Of earning our keep,
Recognition, prestige — love:
Of country, lifestyle ideals, God, and His
Creations; as He may come
Tomorrow (and we must be
Ready with our list of
Goal-results, for His accounting
Of our Life of petty "picking.")

Geneve Baley

FOOTPRINTS TO HAPPINESS

When I know not where to go,
and snow is blowing in my face
I follow footprints in the snow,
hoping they will guide the way
and take me to my destiny,
to that thing I am searching for —
happiness — it seems far from me,
but I will search and search some more
until that precious gift is mine,
even if I'm not deserving
something so high, a gift so fine
I'll look until I find this thing.
    Then those footprints will have led me
    to a lasting, happy being.

Tracy Obowa

A RAINBOW

I am a promise,
Revealing the secrets of silence
As I suspend a beam of love
Across the weeping sky.
Like magic, I appear out of nowhere;
Unfurling colors of elegance,
As the sun peaks shyly
Through the fierce floating galleons
Drifting out to sea.
I am a moment of solitude
And a feeling of peace.
As the shower ceases,
I become an unsolved mystery,
Vanished into a canopy of midnight blue.

Dawn Wright

THE LOVE OF GOD

The love of God, how great it is!
    It's perfect in every way,
There's mercy, peace and blessed hope
    That reaches us every day.

The love of God, how true it is!
    It's trusting in every way,
There's wisdom, power and blessed joy
    That strengthens us every day.

The love of God, how great our need!
    He'll guide our paths each day.
His mercy, patience, peace and joy
    Will be with us all the way.

Jean D. Knettler

LOVE — TRUEST FORM

Can love be held possession
for fear of future need
we hold without discretion
in cruelest form of greed.

Can love be strong or willful
barking out the creed
while cunning and so skillful
we hold the mortgage deed.

Can true love be deceptive
or must it search the way
the free the naive captive
yet prey return to stay.

Georgetta Izora Smith

191

COME . . . SPRING

OH! SPRING will be a little early this year.
Wintry winds and icy snows will disappear.
The birds will all be singing.
Spring flowers will be springing.
Church bells will be ringing, "SPRING IS HERE!"
Friends and folks will join in singing,
While the church bells all keep ringing.
Birds will spread the news in singing, "SPRING IS HERE!"
All the church bells will be ringing.
OH! My heart will keep on singing.
Come SPRING I'll have my Jamie by my side.
Come SPRING I'll be his happy, ever-loving, blushing bride.
OH! SPRING will be a little early this year.
The Preacher will be praying.
The organ will be playing, "DO YOU HEAR? SPRING IS HERE!"
Come SPRING I'll be his blushing, ever-loving, HAPPY BRIDE!
Come . . . SPRING.

Mertie Elizabeth Boucher

BOUCHER, MERTIE ELIZABETH. Pen Names: Elizabeth Lundgren, Libbetts; Born: Newark, New Jersey; Married: 4-12-41 to John H. Cronshey; 3-20-65 to F. Leroy Boucher; Education: Newark State Teachers College, graduated 1937; B.S., 1950; Lucy Feagin's School of Radio and Dramatic Art, Graduate Studies, Rockefeller Center, New York City, 1939; University of Maryland, 1958-66; Memberships: N.J.E.A., N.E.A. among others; Awards: Award of Merit Certificate, Special Mention, for 'Love Defined,' World of Poetry Press, 1984; Poetry: 'Waves,' Exposition Press, 1933; Collection of Poems, Hill Press, 1972; 'The Dream,' First Presbyterian Church of Bernardsville program, 8-26-84; 'Introduction,' Hieroglyphics Press, 1984; 'Within the Secret Depths,' *Hearts on Fire,* American Poetry Association, 1983; Comments: *As a child I turned to pen and paper to express my thoughts and feelings. As I grew older, whenever someone or something touched me deeply, I wrote my thoughts, impressions and beliefs. Today, I work with young children encouraging them to express their thoughts and feelings in poetic form. My poetic efforts are descriptive, definitive, religious and inspirational.*

STAR

I look at a star high up in the Milky Way
Its light shining through the earth's atmosphere
I know I will never see it closer being it's light years away
So I will be content to look at it from here

May someone be watching the same one I am?
Or may they be watching one of a million other ones?
If its relationship to the universe is like being one single gram
then the rest of the universe is a comparison of tons

Yet I can only see a glimmer of its magnificent size
From whence I am it is almost too small to be seen
The incomprehensible distance makes it deceiving to my eyes
In the same respect my mind cannot imagine the margin
of distance that lies in between

Paul J. Knebel

THE HOUSE AT THE END OF THE ROAD

In the cool of the evening, when shadows lengthen,
As the sun sinks low in the west;
    We take a stroll down the shady lane
And view the familiar places we like best.

    I wish that I could go back in years,
To the days now far away,
    For in my heart it seems as though
They were but yesterday.

    The old tire swing still hangs
From the limb of that old oak tree,
    Where one single note the songbirds,
Let drift upon the breeze.

    You are here, I am here — work with me!
And ponder the path of our feet;
    Where I hid my treasures as a child, and when,
In secret hiding places, we would meet.

    Travelers came from far and near
To share the quietness and to rid their load.
    Free from the rustle, bustle noise of town,
They would return to the house at the end of the road.

Mildred B. Jones

JONES, MILDRED BURTON. Pen Names: Minnie, Shap; Born: Arcadia, Louisiana, 6-9-20; Married: 6-18-50 to Homer M. Jones; Education: High School, Ruston, Louisiana; Occupations: Grocery Store, Drug Store Clerk, Donut Shop, Sperry Rand, Clerk General, Housewife; Memberships: Ban Club Association, The Smithsonian Association, National Member, Ambassador, International Cultural Foundation, charter membership, not current; Poetry: 'The Lights Back Home,' American Poetry Association, 1982-84; 'Louisiana's Promise,' American Poetry Association, 1984; 'An Old Home Place,' 1985; 'The House at the End of the Road,' American Poetry Association, 1984; Other Writings: "Why Are Americans in Viet Nam?" article, March 1969; Themes: *Love, hope, reality of life, spiritual;* Comments: *I have written poetry since 1982. I was influenced by knowledge gained from a lifetime serving humanity. Writing, and reading poetry are among the primary joys of my life. The deep spiritual inner self releases thoughts onto a higher plane, through obedience to the Eternal.*

Fulfill my heart's every wish, nourish my desires. Release the wildness within me, set my soul on fire. Let me touch you all over, all I feel is you. Excite me with your caress, show me what you can do. Stimulate my body, I belong to only you. Put your lips on mine, we will kiss hungrily. To what you want me for I'm yours. Wrap yourself around me. Don't be too resistant to temptation, we are just playing games. There's an oh such a hungry yearning, burning inside of me, and its torment won't be through, till you let me spend my entire life making love to you.

Margaret Nova

SHOOTING STAR

In the deep of the night when the owls were out hooting,
And I had retired to my bedroom upstairs,
I looked out the window and saw a star shooting
Across the dark sky like a rocketing flare.

I gasped at the sight of this firmament wonder,
Then hurriedly made the same wish as before.
I whispered the words, but my heart beat like thunder,
For maybe this time, I would finally score.

Then I laughed at the thought of how I was depending
On a big hunk of rock that had hurtled so far.
But I knew that my hope would remain neverending,
For that's how it is, when you wish on a star.

   Helen G. Fiske

Can I hide in your arms?
Will your strength relieve my fear?
Will the warmth of your touches
Cause my crumpled, beaten soul to be reborn?
Will the tenderness of your limbs, your kisses,
Renew my shriveled dreams?
Oh, a feeble hope,
For with your caress, my heart recoils, frightened,
Reluctant to relax in you, lest the weight
Crush you — and me.
No, I must with my own arms,
Clutching desperately my folded knees,
Wrench my soul from its tears
And softly entice my ravished heart
Back to a world in which
Extremes mangle my peace.

   Laura Lynn Smith

SIGNS OF SPRING

Here at last, the first day of Spring,
The birds returned home, hear them sing.
Flowers awaken from their winter's sleep,
Icicles drip to death, see them weep,
Cold biting winds replaced by warm gentle breezes,
Bright green leaves sprout on barren trees,
Blades of grass kill off the snow,
Gardeners outside with seeds to sow,
Ice flows off rivers and streams.
Man's heart turns to romantic dreams.
Blue skies and clouds of cotton,
Frozen ground starts to soften.
Soothing coos from a pure white dove;
All these are signs of my continuous love.

   Joseph Nicholas Pomone

WHERE LOVE RUNS

HONORABLE MENTION

Lying here
Your passion soft upon me
Like petals stolen in the night
Shouting
Why not now
There
Where chance crowds deep into open doorways
Or there
Where time waits slow beneath crescent moons
Or here
Where love runs along rain-drenched streets
Like small children
Looking for a place to play.

   David Pendergraft

REVERIE

No one knows where I am
Out here on the low dune . . .
And near the great dam
Where the gray waters croon.
No one saw me come
To keep my little promise . . .
Given by the weed's low hum
And sealed by a breeze's kiss.
No one can find me
Here alone with just the grass
And slow solemn waters to see
Me hold my very private mass . . .
No one shall know the peace it brings
To sit here and list to the soft,
Low voices of waves, winds, and weeds as they sing.

   Thelma Straley

FRIEND AND LOVER

In loving memory of my dearest friend,
Stanley R. Rhodes

Friend and lover is really the same
Good friend and lover stands by and understands
The good friend and lover embraces you when you are sad
The good friend and lover brings joy if you feel bad
The good friend and lover means happiness to you
He is gentle, kind and dear, he's always glad
When you may be with him and near
I love you my dearest although now you are dead
I'll never stop loving you — but my life is bitter and sad
You're living now in the other world in the better place
But forgot to take me with you there —
Where are no tears, no pain, only great happiness.

   Blanche Marie Atwood

HIS AND HERS

He adds the books and pays the taxes
She records the first blush of spring
Red haze among the willows
On a crisp salad day

He asks when dinner will be ready
Flicks on the news
Pierced by the beauty of spiralling cabbage
She doesn't hear
Tumbling cole slaw flowers in a bowl

Above the sink the sky fills with roses
Dust from some volcano filtering the blue
She worships the sunset
He sees a world spinning to its doom

   Mary Roy

THE CHEAT

Sometimes good friends are closest before they part.
Maybe that's why I was so struck and so amazed
to find that you were gone. Dead, they said,
of a disease, fatal and quick as lightning.
It seemed only moments before that we stood
before each other, lips responsively smiling.
Now there is no more you, no more close embrace.

I saw the meager report the coroner made —
another number, statement, folder for file.
And then they plotted out your skeleton,
pondered it a moment, and analyzed it well.
The pity was how they swept your bare bones
across the floor as though they were sweeping
lint and apple cores, and I stood numbly by.

   Bonnie Homsley

A GIFT OF SPRING FOR TRACY

I brought you my breath
     like the air
I sent you my smile
     It'll keep you warm

I brought you my eyes
     to see your beauty with
I want you to grow into the flower
     I see

I'll always love you
     near or far
Our love is a lease
     It won't be a debt
that will run out
     Love, Gerry

Gerald F. Coppola

COPPOLA, GERALD FRANCIS. Pen name: Gino Caprera; Born: Worcester, Massachusetts, 6-24-52; Single; Education: Writer's Digest Fiction School, 1984; Currently studying toward ASS in Business; Occupations: Writer, Office Worker, Coach, Quality Circle Leader; Memberships: Civil Liberties Union, Unitarian Church, Worcester Youth Street Hockey; Awards: 'The New Season,' World of Poetry, 1983; Poetry: 'Patience,' World of Poetry Press, *Best Loved Poems,* 1983; Comments: *I write human interest themes. I like to use symbols and express my rhythms like a jazz musician uses his horn for expression. Currently, I'm working in the direction of publishing a short story.*

THE FARMER

Toiling over a piece of God's earth,
Given to him by birth.
Past generations labored this soil,
So vegetables would be sown and grown.
Cultivating is no mere task,
Work starts at dawn and ends at dusk.
Every day the grounds have to be nurtured,
To keep acres thriving for the future.
Drive keeps a farmer going,
Knowing his crops are growing.
Pride in being able to eat off the land,
He harvests with his own hands.

Madeleine Larkin

CHINA DOLLY

Ma Poupé Chinois

China dolly is my china Polly, she's the
gal of my dreams. She's my frontier
lassie. O what a chassis. This gal
from beyond the land of the rising sun.

Sent to be the wife of a Chinese
gambler, but on the night she
arrived the stakes were high
and Johnny her lover won her.

Beneath an Idaho moonlit sky we
made love till dawn. O what
a gal my china dolly. On a
fateful night her lover was shot
O what a sight. China Polly mounted

him on her steed, and vanished
into the night. Months and months
she tended his wounds, with the
arts of her land. Finally he
was in good health again.

Then they were married and Johnny
her lover left his gambling,
and settled on the land.
O what a gal my china dolly
my china Polly.

Gerald Momy

MOMY, GERALD LEO. Born: Moncerf, Quebec, Canada, 7-6-26; Education: Eighth Grade; Occupation: Hospital Personnel; Comments: My theme is to capture the human spirit (the soul) coupled with nature around us, raising humankind to his highest level of seeing, the true God, on His throne of glory.

there's an alien among us
he calms our thoughts
his magic melts slowly in us
just as a memory or an oblivion
just as a winter nightmare

we'll not be taught by him
we've had our lessons
yet we'll be looking for him

one of us will be late for the meeting
the other one will come very early

Sarbinowo, August 27, 1978

Krzysztof M. J. Ostaszewski

A NIGHT OF LOVE

Share with me the moonlight
and feel the warmth of the
firelight
Lay beside me in the soft
cool sands
And let me feel the gentleness
of your warm caressing hands
Share with me a night of love
Allow our emotions to run
wild and free
Let's soar through the passing
of darkness to dawn
And awaken in the glory
of all life's wonders
    Just you
       and
        Just me
Rebecca S. Harner

MY PSALM

Lay me flat in a deep, grassy meadow,
May the walls of green be high
Conceal me in a boat of grass;
Let my body lie still
Let it feel no temperature
May my clothes flow around me
Let me hear no breathing
Let me feel no hunger and thirst
May my nose and tongue be content;
Let me feel no desire,
Set my face to the sky
Remove my care of time
But all swirl around me;
Let my eyes discern no change
Let me know no meaning
Just let me be
Forever.

Steve Thompson

COLD FISH
HONORABLE MENTION

Your words return to me
unexpectedly.
Dark night and damp breeze
recall you by degrees.

The cold sand is beneath me again
the warmth of you above;
your whisper haunts my memory,
your promises of love.

A bright moon hanging in the night,
a shine painted on the sea.

A cold fish in a warm wave
presses his gills to me.
Cheryl Reich

TO "FOXFIRE"

As noble a creation as you were,
There is but one way I can see
you now,
Engraved upon the eye of memory:
Your flowing red-gold mane and tail
ablaze,
Under a never-fading afterglow,
The while your now unfettered hooves
beat time
Across celestial meadows, evergreen!
Ruth H. Richardson

GAUGUIN, Offerings

ENVIRONMENT

I paused to watch the trees one day,
While walking out at break of day.
I saw them bow before the breeze,
As lives 'neath many pressures sway.

The wind blew East with gentle ease.
And, to its touch the willow trees
Their verdant tresses gave to blow.
Until its subtle stress should cease.

Its wildest shift, to Westward flow,
Soon struck the trees ranged in a row;
Then North wind too, in briefer spell,
To nip their leaves, and onward go.

'Twas then prevailing winds gave swell —
The Southern softness came to dwell:
And, this alone their shapes will tell,
Yes, this alone their shapes will tell!

Oval Walker

WALKER, OVAL. Born: Wichita, Kansas, 12-20-23; Married: 6-17-44 to Effie Lorene Satterwhite; Education: Howard Payne University, Brownwood, Texas, B.A., 1955; Idaho University, Moscow, Idaho; University of Utah, Salt Lake City, Utah, Graduate Study; Southwestern Theological Seminary, Fort Worth; Occupations: Creative Writing and English Teacher, Baptist Minister, Freelance Writer; Memberships: National Education Association, NCTE, IEA, SBC, Utah Idaho SBC, AARP; Awards: Editor and Writer, Greek Word-Study Column for *Ekklesia* (Idaho SBC Newspaper), 1965-67; Devotional Writer, *Open Windows,* SBC, 1973; Poetry: 'Just Dust,' skeletal sonnet, *Christian Magazine,* St. Louis; 'Sonnet to Lyndon Johnson,' sonnet, various east coast newspapers; 'The World Faces East,' free verse, *Wanagi,* Poetry Anthology, MHS, Idaho, 1973; 'The Spirit of Christmas,' poem in Trochaic Octameter, *The Beacon,* Arizona State SBC Paper, Poetry Paper of Idaho; 'The Pearl,' free verse, *Poet Pourri* — Poetry Association, Boise Chapter; Themes: *Didactic in the main, as you would expect from a teacher. Philosophic, Theologic, Sociologic — lyric, expository and narrative forms. Wide variety of established classic forms and extensive variations and innovations in new forms.*

L/200

A smart girl I know of named Ellen
When once was attacked by a felon
    Gave it her all
    To crush every ball
Of where and what kind I'm not tellin'

Edward Hirschman

VOYAGES TO THE INNER WORLD

Man's cerebrum,
like the internal spheres of ivory
a chinaman spends
his whole life carving
within the One
            original tusk
Of the elephant graveyard,
is constantly filling
and becoming the key
of the baby
        grand
        piano
you were playing
in the parlor.

And nobody knows.
'ceptin' 2nd-hand rose,
with her sundial smile,
and her aztec child . . .

Bob Brault

CONNECTICUT:

A BOOK SALE

History, knowledge
Fiction. Ragged —
But for purchase.
We filtered through
the dozens . . .
Rows of bound paper
And people . . . and
I watched you.
Watched you as always
Before, but with
More adoration.
The rows — old stories
Of Cold War espionage,
Useless almanacs,
Cooking methods —
Yet we found what
There was of worth;
As always, bound.

Tina L. Westby

SWEET LOVER OF YOUTH

Sweet lover of youth,
And sweet love of mine,
You cut out my tooth
And gave me no wine.

Or that's how it seemed,
When broken with pain,
You died and I screamed,
Without Novacaine.

You were a dentist.
I am a dancer.
I taught you the twist.
You died of cancer.

First, though, you left me
A dear daughter, Ruth.
I won't forget thee,
Sweet love of my youth.

Loretta Bellucci

THE WORLDS OF PEOPLE

Two different worlds
            Two different people
Are they really?
            One different world
Many different people
            Are they the same?
We are all alike
            One different world
People are the world
            And the world is people
Without each other
            Who could say what is
Different.

Dawn Blum

BLUM, DAWN HELENE. Born: New Rochelle, New York, 4-26-57; Education: Brockport State, Brockport, New York, 1975-77; Transferred to Arizona State, 1977-79, B.S. in Business, December 1979; Occupations: Production Supervisor, Sales Rep., (Both at Digital Equipment Corp.); Memberships: National Alliance of Business, Big Sisters; Poetry: 'The Beach,' free verse, American Poetry Association, 1982; Themes: *Emotional aspects of life, seeing reality from one's emotional perspective; viewing the world through feeling.* Comments: *To me, poetry is a way of expressing deep thoughts and life's intangibles; and something to share with others so individuals can possibly see a part of themselves and a part of life in a different aspect.*

INNOCENCE

HONORABLE MENTION

In the storm, in the rain
he comes to me,
valiant in a cab
with a broken umbrella.
Dripping he enters my door
bright against the white of my walls
and what we will not say
will breathe between us
when he takes off his wet clothes
and I hand him in silence
a fresh, warm towel.

Edith Keller

ON VISION

Visions, undimmed, fill every recess of my mind,
As I review with grateful awe
The expanded depth of eyes that now can find
Spiritual roots for living on which to draw.

From where comes this sight, that clears the system
And erases bleak ebony of imageless eyes?
Forever, has an eternal struggle played tandem
With vision — pressed down — never yoked to the skies?

The answer emerges with a brilliance of Divine sight,
Wrenched loose from ages of chains that did bind
This soul to earth force endowed with powerful might,
Fed now with God substance for the spiritually blind.

To see with God's eyes is the supreme gift of vision,
That once tumbled and aimlessly traveled a course,
Now, lovingly directed on a path, with no collision
Or blinders — to banish fear, pain, hurt and remorse.

Jeanne Ackiss Davis

SOMEDAY

    i hide in my works
    i'm exposed in my words
    all i've ever been
    all i've ever heard
    today well-lived makes yesterday's memories sweet
    and tomorrow's hopes glorious
setting m'lady free
allows me . . . to express
a Love none could ever guess
for without (m'lady) . . . is but a shout
                in the wilderness
heard only by the unknown
               if heard at all
                 the gall . . .
of a few to think they could know
    so few to accept
    and it to expect . . . some day

      hopes so glorious

Roy E. Landers

WHEN EVERY DAY WAS VALENTINE'S DAY

Through empty skies of loneliness
My dreams like rainbows have all faded to grey
I look back to past happiness
When every day was Valentine's Day

I remember each word spoken
And each word I never got the chance to say
I still cherish each last moment
When every day was Valentine's Day

I live a life now of regret
Emotions planted in my heart to stay
As time goes by I won't forget
When every day was Valentine's Day

If I could only change our fate
I'd trade everything I have away
To be back before it was too late
When every day was Valentine's Day

Kenneth J. Conrad

TO BE LOVED

We enter this world innocent, unique.
To love and be loved will make us complete.

Teen years are hard, independence the game.
Adults must "make it" or failure's the name.

Success may come, "we have it made,"
Or failure may haunt and our life will fade.

We leave this world, our knowledge returning,
To love and be loved our true yearning.

Carolyn L. Mack

STRANGER, STRANGER

Stranger, stranger, you look good to me,
But a faceless man is all my heart sees.
You meet the needs of a tender love, lost,
Needs to be met, no matter the cost.

Stranger, stranger, don't ask me why
I see only him when I look in your eyes.
The strength of your arms helps me relive
The love we once had . . . the love you give.

Stranger, stranger, dim the light,
lest you see these tears I fight,
For this love I make in a stranger's embrace
Is love for another . . . a different face.

Stranger, I thank you for sharing this eve,
In romance, again, you helped me believe.
Your kind of love gives me hope that, someday,
Reality takes hold! He'll be mine to stay.

Stranger, stranger, you were here for me,
Knowing I cry for a love that can't be.
Destined not to meet again, and yet
These hours with a stranger, I'll never forget.

Diane M. Lutz

ZIMA-LUTZ, DIANE MARIE. Born: Lancaster, Pennsylvania, 3-12-53; Education: Williamsport Area Community College, 1972; Occupations: Bookkeeper, Veterinary Assistant, Actress; Memberships: Nashville Songwriters Association, Drama workshop dba Symbrinck Associates; Poetry: 'My Perfect Dream,' Quill Books, 11-84; 'Todd,' American Poetry Association, 3-85; Comments: *Good poetry expresses in words what most people are unwilling, unable or afraid to say out loud . . . to others or even to themselves. Poets grow through their work by allowing all to grow through the true expressions of the soul.*

FOR ALL THE FRIENDS I'VE KNOWN

When I shall close my eyes I'll see again
The ocean's depth, the swirling rising foam.
I'll see the steamers in the shipping lane
And feel the swaying of my sea-borne home.
When I have heard what hungry sea gulls say
I'll ponder over thoughts and questions prone.
My troubles will have vanished in the spray;
Then I'll remember all the friends I've known.
When passive peace that penetrates the soul
Converges while the roiling sea is still
The pain and grief of searching for my goal
Will drift — then drown — and I shall drink my fill
    Of friendship's mellow glow. Soon I'll be calm:
    The gentle surf is now a soothing balm.

Esther Wilson Bahman

THE ONLY ONE

God can see across wide open spaces
And see all the different races.
He can see all the mountains high
Those with peaks that seem to reach the sky.

God can see the rich and the poor,
He can even see an eagle soar.
God can hear your silent prayers
You see, God really cares.

My sight is limited you see,
Instead of a forest, I see only a tree.
I can only hear what you say.
I can never hear you silently pray.

I can only be what God wants me to be,
His son on Calvary paid a price for me.
I know I will never be alone,
Jesus is the one — the only one.

Earl L. DeLong

DeLONG, EARL LEE. Born: Nuttersfort, West Virginia, 7-17-28; Married: 12-24-50 to Maxine Luciel DeLong; Education: High School, One year, Orange Coast College; Occupations: Maintenance Repair, Locksmith; Memberships: Disabled Veterans — Life; Awards: *American Poetry Anthology,* 1982; *Hearts on Fire,* 1985; Comments: *I write poems in order to express myself. Since I can't talk very well it is one way for people to understand me. I write about what I feel about death, love, nature, and many other subjects including politics. I love writing poems but only do so when I feel it within myself. If I don't feel it I can't write about it.*

AUTUMN THOUGHTS

I do not mourn the passing of the rose,
For in memory it will remain
In all its fragrant beauty, until Spring,
In verdant gown, restores its life again.

When, on a windy Autumn afternoon,
Among the gardens, erstwhile fair, I walk,
I must not weep for pansy faces gone
Or sigh for dahlia, phlox and hollyhock.

And when the maple waves a red-gloved hand
I shall not say Adieu, but Au Revoir;
And those I loved will live within my heart
Till, in the New Life, we shall meet once more.

Alice Seward

SEWARD, ALICE MAY. Born: Glace Bay, 8-30-10; Married: 1931; Widowed, 1933; Education: Glace Bay Schools, Empire Business College, Sydney, 1934; Nova Scotia Technical College, Teaching Methods, 1948; Occupations: Steno, Secretary, Administrative Clerk, Teacher; Memberships: Nova Scotia Writers' Federation, Canadian Wildlife Federation; Awards: Second Prize in All Canada Poetry Contest, 1983; Poetry: *The Real Christmas,* Booklet of Christmas poems, Casket Publishing Co., 1980; *This is Cape Breton,* miscellaneous collection, Vantage Press, Inc., 1985; 'It's Christmas Again,' 1963; 'Summer Rain,' 1964; 'Christmas Story,' 1978; all published by Ideals Publishing Co.; Comments: *To write a poem is relaxing — any theme will do — nature, religion, humor, etc. I write as much for my own pleasure as for that of others, though it is always gratifying to be told that someone else enjoys my poetry.*

Only one day at a time;
As I sit and gaze toward the sky
As a dreamer, only among dreamers;
Wondering and watching as time slips away;
Aware, yet unaware, of the world around me;
Alone, yet never alone.
You're so near my love, yet so far away.
So many words, with so many meanings
Seeking the truth, but blinded and never knowing;
Reaching and never holding.
Then the fear within myself still dwells deep within my soul;
Afraid to know and a fear of not knowing.
To ease my troubled mind, only a dream to dream
As I sit and gaze toward the sky.

Margaret Olson

DREAM

Inside every heart
Is a dream —
Untouched
Pure
And believing.
A virgin.
If you
Will take the time
And the care
To open
Your heart
And start
Creating
You will find
All the love
You will ever need
Waiting there
In a dream.
Joanne Dieter

THE BIRDS HAVE COME AND GONE

The birds have come and gone,
And you have written me at last.
You say that you all miss me
And forgive me for the past.

I'm taking pen and pencil
And I'm opening a beer
Before I sit down at my desk
To write, "My wife, my dear,

A year ago you left me,
And I couldn't understand.
But now I know you'd lost me
To myself — the macho man.

I bent you to my will, Dear,
And you gave up most of you.
The kids — they lost a daddy
And a good role model too.

But now the birds have come and gone.
The snow is falling too.
My life's as empty as the house.
Come back, Dear, I love you."
Josephine D. Boykin

LAST NIGHT I DREAMED OF PEACE ON EARTH

Last night I dreamed of peace on Earth.
The wars had all been fought.
The world had finally given birth
to the age that we had sought.

The air was filled with silence
of the absence of the war.
No country stood in staunch defense;
nothing was worth fighting for.

Countless cities had been razed
when the bombs rained from the sky,
yet through the world no flag was raised
with triumphant victory cries.

Amidst the fallout people walked
in silence, hand in hand.
No one argued, no one talked,
no one could understand.

Last night I dreamed of peace on Earth
then I prayed to God above
to never let the world give birth
to peace not borne of love.
Nori J. Rost

LIFE

Where do the years go?
How swiftly they fly!
Was it only yesterday
When you and I so impatient with life
Could only see
That tomorrow was eternity?

Where do the years go?
How swiftly they fly!
By minutes and hours
The days go by.
Bits and pieces, day by day,
How swiftly, how swiftly
Life slips away!

If life is lost to us so fast
That a year seems as a day,
Then every minute must be used
Before life slips away!

Mary W. Thompson

NATURE

I take up my pen
Commence to write
Music tumbles from my brain,
Paper fills in little time.

Spring is a feeling caught from the air
Stirring ground growth of flowers
Time will tell what we see forth,
Smelling sense is present time.

Growing outdoors it lives beyond
the boundaries on the land.
Birds chirp and sing daytime
Gladly our ears hear the rhymes.

Spring turns to Autumn
When leaves begin to fall around
Winds whistle through the tree limbs
Animals bury deep into their mounds.

Edith L. Colby

POETS

our Souls are Dreamers,
 our lives are Dreams.
our Hearts are Knowers,
 weaving Love themes.

the Dream we conceive
 is given from Above.
the Light we receive
 is shared with our Love.

our Spirits listening,
 Revealing what we've Heard.
our Heart Path is giving,
 Witnessing in the Word.

into peoples' Hearts we reach
 with Vision to break the Illusion.
Love's the Magic that we Teach
 with longing to bring the New Fusion.

Ron Bracale

LIFE — AND MAN

What is this thing called Life?
With all its cares and strife.
From the cradle to the grave,
Our road is gravely paved.

Man — What is man?
A small creature nurtured
Upon his mother's breast,
Who finds comfort and solace
 but turns to unrest.

In youth when years are at best
And life seems full of zest,
Finds strength to calm the
 inner strife
And thus endure this thing
 called life.

In maturity when youth is gone
Life has grown cold and worn.
No longer can he endure
The feeling of being insecure.

Where can his strength come now?
To whom can he go, and how?
Back to his Creator who gave
 him breath,
And first acquainted him with
 physical birth.

Man in Christ is Life anew;
To serve and praise Him
 forever, too!
For He can banish all sorrow
And bring a glad tomorrow.

 — *Acts 17:28*

Martha Pastore

AWAKENING

I feel
my heartbeat, steady

In my toes,

fingertips,

my head

I feel

my soul awakening

Spreading, throughout

my body

I feel
something, rising

from pits, deep inside

slowly,

steadily,

crawling up,

My heartbeat —

Steady.

Esmie Telford

MY SON, BILL

I wrote this poem as my son Bill, lay in the hospital
recovering from massive injuries he received in a
motorcycle accident May 28, 1974. I know the Lord heard
my prayers as Bill is well and strong today.

Bill, my son, part of me
I know God is healing thee
Day by day, night by night
HIS unseen touch is laid on you
Taking away your feeling so blue
Helping you face what is ahead
Making you feel there's nothing to dread
I know there are times when your faith falters
When you think that there is no hope
Bill, my son, put your complete trust in *HIS SON*
Don't be afraid to ask God's help
HE will be there when there's no one else
So, my son, part of me
Seek HIS help and HE will set you *Free*.

Lillian F. Cubberly

EARLY MORNING

Awakening to early morning's everpresent light
Exposing clouds of charcoal gray with white
Extending low as bits of lingering fog
Inhabit spaces near and far,
I watch as silently in the East
A brilliantly glowing Sun appears
Changing charcoal gray clouds to luminous white puffs
Lined with silver
Warmed by golden rays of Sun
Cooled with gusts of refreshing wind
That chase the fog away
As abstract shadows glide in
Giving an added touch
To a unique time of day.
Savoring this brief encounter, I tarry
For another sensory taste
And view again the beautiful array
Presented by a loving God for all to enjoy
Each day anew
The early morning way.

Sophia L. Eaton

WILL I EVER GET BACK?

The line I'm walking is a thin one.
And it's bound to get worse before I'm done.
'Cause I can't quite decide if I should stand up or hide
From the Hell that I face each day in this place.
My heart has turned black.
Will I ever get back
To the fun-loving girl I once was?
You left me flat when I needed you most.
I never even realized how great the cost
Of giving my love to a man such as you.
You took my whole world, and broke it in two.
There was a time I had everything.
And with me each day the world would sing.
Now there's no laughter or song in my heart.
Some people have told me to make a new start.
But I just can't decide if I should stand up or hide
From the Hell that I face each day in this place.
My heart has turned black.
Will I ever get back
To the fun-loving girl I once was?

Laura M. Saunders

WALK WITH JESUS

My brown oxfords are worn and I can't walk
far in any other shoes. But, when a friend's baby
played with them today I said,
"I wonder why she likes those ugly old shoes?"
Maybe it's the white and blue shoelaces she likes
with the red hearts and
"Jesus loves me" written on them.
Their smooth leather fits me exactly,
uncovering the contours of my feet.
These humble shoes won't let me stumble.

How can I call them "ugly old shoes"
when I go nowhere without them?
How can we Christians accept Christ's gifts
of eternal salvation, food, shelter, and fruits of the Spirit,
yet not proclaim Him and praise Him to those
who have nothing to walk in but their own frail flesh?
For Jesus said, "For whoever is ashamed of Me and My words,
of him the Son of Man will be ashamed when
He comes in His own glory, and in His Father's."

Wynne Holmes

DIASPORA

Separated sheep roaming remote hillsides,
our neckbells knell, "I am here, I am here,"
to the wolf or any predator around.
Not bright enough to flock, to claim
some place as refuge, we only mill.
Fragmented, we hear only one another's cries
and slowly, disappear.
Herdless herd of esthetes
happy with a slope whose turn
of meadow lifts our heads, curiously, to see,
no further than that it was pleasing.
As it lay, — let it remain.
Cud-chewing benignly, the pack now slips among us,
usurping our meadow, tearing our throats,
whooping wolfish mocking laughter
at our bucolic innocence.
Bleating powerlessly, we conjure ways
to thwart bestiality beyond the grave;
meanwhile our tinkling bells betray us,
still again.

Edward Pickell

WE POETS

When history's mysteries have all revolved
And threat of nuclear winter has been resolved
We poets may be inspired
When governments' debts have all been paid
And acid rain falls not on man or maid
We poets may be hired
When pornography is boring and erotica passé
And every child reads so very well each day
We poets may have conspired
When humankind is kind indeed
And from poverty everyone is freed
We poets may be retired
Until that time we write our rhyme
As closer to truth we clumsily climb
For greater none than poets who can
Inspire love toward their fellow man
May poets increase a thousand strong
Explaining what they perceive as wrong
And may all the dreams we poets see
Include a world where we can all just be

Barbara Ann Ward

HANDMADE VALENTINE

Fashioned from love,
Molded with care,
Given in sincerity,
Love's message to share.

Handmade valentine,
Presented with pride,
Shown with breathlessness,
Love and kisses inscribed.

Framed with a frill,
Trimmed with a bow,
Adorned with a scrawl:
I love you so.

Fingered with innocence,
Layered with design,
Crayoned a message:
Dear valentine, be mine.

February child's creation,
Handmade valentine,
Messenger of Cupid,
Reminding me you're mine.

Mary (Hrenchuk) Pankiw

PANKIW, MARY (HRENCHUK). Born: Winnipeg, Manitoba, Canada, 6-1-23; Married: 6-3-50 to Alexander Pankiw (deceased, 12-24-68); Education: University of Manitoba — B.A., 1965; B.Ed., 1969; M.Ed., 1972; Ukrainische Freie Universität, (Ukranian Free University), Munich, West Germany; Red River Community College, two Creative Writing courses, 1979; Occupation: Teacher, 29 years experience teaching English and Creative Writing at the elementary, junior high, senior high and adult levels; Memberships: Canadian Authors' Association, Writers' Workshop (Rough Drafts); Poetry: 'Form in Space,' *Pierian Spring,* Spring 1979; 'Unborn Loser,' Winnepeg Free Press, 9-1-79; 'Jealousy,' Winnepeg Free Press, 9-22-79; 'What Does Santa Do All Year?' *The Stonewall Argus/Teulon Times,* 6-16-85; has also written travel articles, professional articles, and children's stories; Themes: *Life around me; life's experiences; reverence for life;* Comments: *Why I write — as an outlet for my emotions; an avenue of expression; for therapeutic reasons; to release my feelings. What expressed — my experiences, feelings, my philosophy of life.*

you held me tight
and I held you near
now you're away
and I feel each tear
as it rolls down my cheek
and onto my chin
and just like you
it gets brushed off
never to be seen again

Vickie Loeschke

CHRIST JESUS
THE MESSIAH OF ISRAEL

Through Christ the truth
   I have found
I now see His truth, His
   Love, all around.
Through his stripes
   I have been healed
And His Truth in me
   Is no longer concealed
When I turned and prayed
   In Jesus' precious name.
My life has changed.
   And is not the same.
Before there had been darkness,
   Now there is light.
And whatever I may do,
   Everything turns out right.
He can do for you
   what He has done for me
Believe, oh, just believe
   On Him.
And the light you, too,
   Shall see.
For Christ Jesus is
   The Messiah of Israel.
Chosen people of God
   I pray that you'll see
His truth and understand
   That God's precious gift
For you to accept
   Is in your hand.

Lucy Bass

SECULAR HUMANISM

Has it been said,
"You're going to Hell,
It's the work of the Devil,"

A new day is here
And now we hear,
"It's secular humanism."

Is this sophistication
Or Pistia Sophia?

Do God and Jesus need a cover,
So that Their Works go unseen?
Or is the phrase a sham?

If "secular humanism"
Is social philosophy of Man,
Why did Jesus call Himself
The Son of Man?
Are we too hard pressed to understand?

Was the "Universal Christ" of Paul
The personal Christ of Peter?

The human ego seeks social freedom
And political power,
While the higher soul in man
Seeks the Spiritual Will
Of the Heavenly Father
This very hour.

Martin R. Anderson

One Spirit intertwined with mine
A God that's loving, sweet, and kind.
A Soul that's living proof of trust
In things of golden, pure, sweet love.
Excellence of finest form
Recaptured once the soul's reborn!

Margaret E. Thompson

JESUS IS REAL

Jesus is real, Jesus is real,
Jesus is real to me;
He's with me all the time,
And Jesus set me free.
Jesus is real, Jesus is real,
My Savior all the way;
His love is truly mine,
And I praise Him each day.
Whenever troubles come to me,
On Jesus I depend;
He's always near to help,
For Jesus is my friend.
Jesus is real, Jesus is real,
Jesus satisfies me;
He's the way and the life,
And He saved me eternally.

Esther Martin

MAUI NO KAI OI
(MAUI IS THE BEST)

I sailed away one summer day
To a northern land, far, far away.
I bought a fleet from my toil,
Making a fortune in fishing oil.

I worked all day, I worked all night.
I found myself without delight.
I had much more than I could use.
Again, one day I had to choose.

I sold my ships and left one day.
I sailed this time in the month of May.
When I saw the kukui tree,
I came home to sunny Maui.

Jack Bernier

A NEW BEGINNING

Deserted home, an empty nest —
That vacant feeling in my breast.
Husband's gone and children left,
It seems that I am quite bereft.
Aching bad, I'm most unwell,
Luster's gone, I look like hell.
My pictured past is memory now.
Too late for me to make a vow?
Can my future be renewed?
Or at the least, perhaps reviewed?
Is there hope, maybe tomorrow,
Happiness and no more sorrow?
Questions asked, but no replies.
I want truth and no more lies.
Self-pity ended, no chagrin —
So be it, let my life begin.

Enid Cohen

NIHILISM, NEVER!

If there is something you care about
   deeply enough to know
      hurt and tears
Then do not despair

It is a good omen that the soul
   is still alive
      and, therefore,
Will heal

Worry only if there is nothing.

Arthur C. Mendoza

MY SEARCH OF LOVE

Long ago — ever ago —
I asked myself — who am I?
Why am I here — now?

I started my search
building monuments to self
showing I'd been here.

Through these growing years
key ideas were learned and relearned
strange ideas to some.

We are here to find
God in all — every person —
every molecule.

Life is a School Room
each of us is here to learn —
how to grow — apply!

"Our whole Universe —
Macro and microcosm —
all measured oneness."

If then we know why —
we are here — to grow — find God!
Why is it so hard?

Maybe the answer's
very reason we're here — to know — grow
apply, reapply.

Dr. Ronald P. Anjard, Sr.

AURORA

In time with the noonday moon
A half a year past June
Across a winter night sky
Northern lights hang on high

Running from northwest to southeast
Helps navigate to say the least
On quiet nights hear them rustle
As with northern light duties they bustle

Away from the city rattle
Defying print and wordy prattle
The Aurora, with curtains of light
Gives beauty to the long winter night

Benjamin J. Hilderbrand

HILDERBRAND, BENJAMIN JOSEPH.
Born: Vinita, Oklahoma, 5-16-24; Occupation: Engineer, Retired; Writings: *Poems from the Wandering Pen,* collection, self-published, 1984.

LEGACY

The threnodies of glories past
    the sights and smells
Of empires vast
    the bones of kings lie
Mottled in the dust
    their mighty arrows
Now stained with rust
    the pyramids and tombs
So wondrous old
    their fabled stories
Still unfold
    the empires rot
In a moldy mass
    and the ashes cling
To long dead grass,
    this legacy
Held in scorn
    becomes man's probate
Again to mourn.

Maxwell Charles Kaufman

KAUFMAN, MAXWELL C. Born: New York City, 9-15-18; Married: 12-22-45 to Dr. Sylvia Kirschenbaum Kaufman; Education: St. Johns University, New York Institute of Dietetics, CULA, (Graduate Dietician and B.S. Degree), Graduate of U.S. Medical Service Schools, Brooke General Hospital, Fort Sam Houston, Texas; Occupations: Retired Lt. Colonel, USAR, Retired Deputy Commissioner and Assistant Commissioner, City of New York; Memberships: Association of Military Surgeons of the United States, Retired Officers Association; Comments: *I try to express feelings and emotions which are smoldering within me and are mostly the outgrowth of experiences which have personally affected me.*

FORGETFUL

I gave my love a red red rose
With a stem of emerald green;
She placed it in a golden vase;
The loveliest I've ever seen.

My red red rose died of thirst,
Three days passed you see
My true love is forgetful . . .
She has also forgotten me.

Lois M. Wildermuth

FALSE DAWN

Denizens of this lonely disease
Darkness & time o'er land & seas
Endless hope & burning desire
Smoldering coals 'neath dying fire
Time & time & time again
Cannot wash away the pain
Feelings hurt & lovers gone
Endless night leads to false dawn
Morning comes and all alone
Think of lovers, names unknown
Closed eyes looking deep within
Ecstasy is not a sin!

Heidi Hochheimer

SENIOR DEARS.

Many sing about the stout old oak,
And it is a beautiful tree,
But we can be beautiful in old age too,
As the years steal quietly.
It was lovely to have been young,
It is lovely to grow old,
We owe it all to our Maker,
As He His blessings unfold,
Our faith is secure and we have hope,
In these our golden years,
And if we can only keep young at heart,
We will be Senior Dears.

Irene Schweinfurth

THE STORY IN YOUR EYES

Excitement and adventure be,
    this fervent fool does know,
That I am not the one and same,
    as flakes of fallen snow.
His eyes they sparkle and invite,
    the mysteries of that mind,
For me explosions in my soul
    more varied than a kind.
Accustomed to my doubtless luck
    I'm sure what lies ahead,
Is one-time nurturing of that mind,
    which never will be said.

Karen Evans

HEARTBEAT

I run till my heart bursts
From the shallowness of my chest,
And bleeds the hurt that lies
In the pulsating depths
That are held within my
Own HEARTBEAT!

Lori Anne Perry

MY VERY OWN DIMPLED DARLING

There are many dimpled darlings
I have seen them by the score
But a certain dimpled darling
I shall love forevermore
MINE, I call this dimpled darling
And her age is eighty-four.

Once, to be my dimpled darling
She had treasured as a goal
Now she IS my dimpled darling
Lovely dimples on her soul.

Floyd C. Jones

THE STORM

I walk the beach in the midst of the storm
Aware of the wrath God can perform

Wind whipping madly around my face
as the water pounds rock at a furious pace

The sky is black — the rain pours down
Sky and sea have become interwound

When Nature's fury has been lashed
I find the storm is suddenly passed.

The sea now calm; clouds floating high
Huge rocks on the beach glisten sun-dry

Had I imagined the storm?

Dorothy F. Moore

DISCONTENT LOVE

My love for you
wishes to enter
into your soul
where happiness
encircles us . . .

I dashed forward
to a crest of compassion
but, in my shadowing
love escaped the way it entered . . .

Marge Hallum

INTERMEZZO

The same moment
what takes me you
during same days
now disappears.
Don't cry! In our lives
there are so many
Passing years . . .
Intermezzo was. And no more!
You didn't tell me
wise or bore.
You told me only that: "no more,
no more, no more, no more."
Tired wind sings: "Good afternoon."
I don't see where fell down the moon?
I don't hear. Dark, deep emptiness
covers my heart: your touch on me,
your disappearing memory.

Hilda More

ROSES

Soft, scarlet velvety petals,
Softly molded like a heart,
Its sweet aroma perfumes
the surroundings,
Silky leaves that bend,
Rosy color,
Or blood red rose,
Holds a secret
No one knows;
Petals with ruffled edges,
Throwing shadows to the ground,
Petals constantly are falling,
Whirling 'round and 'round,
Thorns that enchant the other flowers,
When dead they fall in rusty showers;
Roses, lovely special roses,
Scarlet-colored roses.

Lisa Osornio

LOVE ETERNAL

Why doth thou strain the bonds that rend our hearts asunder
Until the fragments fall in disarray
Not one is left in crevices I can retrieve
To bind again — that what seems lost for all eternity.

Each thread and fragment lost is but a treasure
Of love divine we nurtured from infinity
Perfection only God could but create
and that no human could devise in all sublimity.

The stars are but the windows of the night
the diamonds and crystal
Reflecting all the tender moments gone to naught
Leaving the black deep night that shrouds our hearts —
No facet of light to find our tortuous way.

Oh! Master of the Universe and Fate
Let but one sign in all creation give us hope that love still lives
No matter — though the shattered pieces scattered to oblivion
Resound on fallen ear — grant love will triumph
As though the Eons of yesteryear

Resounding in the thunder of the heart
That clamors for the love we knew
To live again — Forever — in All Eternity.

Anita Von Ende

TIME ENOUGH

She reached under the hem of her ruby-colored skirt
And slipped the cool steel flask from the grasp of a black lace garter.
Taking quick gulps of stinging liquid courage
To ease the flights of indecision.

Time enough to make the call and still make the show,
A picture she knew she could not miss.
The phone felt cold like ice within her hand
As were the voices on the other end.

Each passing second became more precious than the one before,
The perilous passage of time weaving history.
She had to hurry now,
It was still a long walk to the Biograph Theater.

Jeffrey Buzuma

YOU AND I

You and I long for the east with the half-ensconced sun
And its golden reflections on the China Sea when the day is nearly done;
To look upward at the cotton-fleece clouds treading the boundless sky
While the host of monarch butterflies on fragile wings are soaring high;
To enjoy the glorious arch and variegated hues of the rainbow
From a lookout — climbing Chain of Love tendrils and Dame of the Evening
    flowers grow.

You and I enjoy the graceful bend of the regal vermilion red rose
Underneath the church bell bearing the patina of age and brick walls
    covered with green moss;
A stark bald gray mountain view where hardworking fishmongers live at its slopes
Awaiting for the rooster's crow, an augural sign for the hectic grind of
    work to start;
O'er the mountainside the orioles are chirping by the boughs of the
    star apple tree
And the farmers rise and hurry to the fields and sow mongo beans for the
    family.

You and I love tobogganing on the high sand dunes
On pleasant summer mornings and breezy afternoons
And watch yonder the sailboat tossed over Neptune's frothy sun-blest sea!
A copper tanned girl scooping the sand winnowing 'em on her shirred calico
    skirt with glee;
Then lulling o'er a hand-woven Phillipine cloth to hearken a folklore
From a mother with a babe on her lap 'neath the shimmering full moon.

Aida Ramiscal Martin

203

FACES

If you looked closely, you would see,
the many faces of life's mysteries.
The face of the man who aged overnight,
His son crippled from an unknown plight.

Try to find the time to care,
About the face of a woman, Millionnaire.
Her face a public smile,
But her heart heavy for her kidnapped child.

Read those lines around the eyes,
Imagine each person's mysteries.
Dark shadows are not from contentment in life.
A faraway look doesn't make a face happy
or pleased.

Don't look, and then look away,
Shrugging your shoulders, won't make everything
okay.
Study closely those faces,
The faces of life's mysteries.

Roseann

DOVER BEACH, 1985

When you stood at the window looking out at Dover Beach
You heard the waves crying "an eternal note of sadness."
You said, "There is neither joy, nor love, nor light,
Nor certitude, nor peace, nor help for pain."

What would you say, Matthew Arnold, if you were living now?
You would know about chemical waste dumps, nuclear leaks,
About death-dagger laser beams, missiles, projectiles;
You would have seen smoke-belching monsters
Explode from Cape Canaveral to stab the skies.
You would hear politicians talking lightly about star wars
As if borrowing an expression from childrens' fairy tales;
You would hear leaders of many countries practicing lies
While the people dream-walk on "a darkling plain."
You would see two giants training with maniac intensity,
Each determined to strengthen already mammoth muscles,
Each poised to leap — and to KILL.

What would you say, Matthew Arnold, in 1985?
I know the answer: you would say — nothing.
For what you would see and hear and know
Is too terrible for *words*.

Ruth Davies

THE GIFT

The gift of our senses allows exultation in
realizing this glorious creation of which we are
a part.

Refined awareness brings clarity to thought as
immersion with nature intensifies.

When suffering disuse
perception's conduits fail to transport with
resounding impact.

Returning to natural surroundings revives powers
to absorb and embrace dizzying arrays of commanding
impressions.

These tingling stimuli
envelop, merging with one's core.

This enrichment of spirit, life's true
source of wealth is for all who but use
the gift to receive.

Jan Sinner Baumann

DEEP IN THE VERDANT WOODS

Deep in the verdant woods I want to dwell.
 Nature in its rough-hewn crudeness
 And the trees in leaf-dressed nudeness
Weave on my heart a lasting magic spell!

Deep in the verdant woods you'll find the hum
 Of bees and the perfume of limes
 And wild roses. How many times
Has my heart thrilled to a chrysanthemum?

Deep in the verdant woods there is beauty!
 Carefree nature with careless grace
 Abounds with beauty ev'ry place,
Luring my pleasure-bound heart from duty!

Deep in the verdant woods there's peace so sweet!
 The majesty of simple things
 Thrills me so, and my heart takes wings!
I've never known contentment so complete!

Deep in the verdant woods are lots of leaves,
 Which are the raiment for each tree,
 Which bring the verdant greenery
Which on my heart such lasting magic weaves!

Carol Boyer Mitchell

MITCHELL, CAROL BOYER. Born: Seneca, Illinois, December 24 (Christmas Eve); Widow; daughter, Barbara Ann, a grandson Seth, and a granddaughter, Kristina; Memberships: Active as a member and Officer of a number of clubs; Poetry: 'An Eyeful of You,' 'Driftwood Memories,' 'Kiss Me Again,' 'Sunshine and Showers,' 'Think of the Glory'; Comments: *My poems are mostly an expression of the beauty of nature and the beauty of life.*

A SIGNATURE OF LOVE

When I can see a first blade of grass from a winter's sleep,
its signature makes me smile.
When I can feel a little warmth from the sun on a hard
bed of snow — the signature of love is GOD.
HE makes love come awake in many signatures — real
and true for spring is soon here and then summer.
HE has many signatures, us — we — you — them.
HE signs everything differently, just as we sign our
names differently — don't you see them?
A bird's song, a tree's color, a land of flowers,
a butterfly, a bee.
Each love we have for special things, places, people
is our signature.
To write with voice, pen, dreams, for one another,
or to care writes for us a part of GOD,
who makes life a full signature of love.

Charlotte Bell

A LETTER TO B.

I have spent the past,
Oh, too many days,
Wrapt in memory of you.

Your woman-scent and,
Sweetly pressing thighs,
Calm me still.

Absorbed and warmed,
In that short, quiet hour,
I am not alone.

Richard Laurie

LAURIE, RICHARD PATTERSON. Born: Corry, Pennsylvania, 5-31-51; Single; Education: USMA, West Point, New York, 1969-71; Gannon College, B.A., Erie, Pennsylvania, 1979; Occupation: Archeologist; Writings: *Deadlight Bay,* novel in progress; Comments: *An idea forms into an image and will not rest until it is celebrated in the proper manner.*

MISTRESS

I was his mistress
young, wild and free.
So much love in my heart
to be forbidden of me.

I know that you love me
And will come to me soon,
So I'll stay here and wait for you
All alone in my room.

You tell me to be patient,
that you're breaking away.
I nod my head yes
with my heart-aching pain.

What is this fallacy,
this lie that we live?
Please come and love me
I have so much to give.

You come in the darkness
And leave before the light.
God how I pray
for you to come stay all night.

Maybe this is a game
and I made a bad move.
I think you might win,
I know I will lose.

Shelley L. Coombs

KNOWN BUT TO GOD

This is the earth the Lord has made.
Its wondrous gifts will never fade.
Created by an unseen hand,
It came to be — at God's command.

I care not how the four winds blow,
Or why the river has its flow,
Or how the swiftness of the doe,
Or why the waves have undertow.

I'm glad there's someone great out there,
Who keeps the clouds up in the air,
That puts the sun to bed at night;
Then brings it back to give me light.
I'm glad there's someone great who knows
Exactly how an apple grows,
And who can make the birds all sing
Then quickly put them on the wing!

I'm glad all things the Lord has made —
The world — that He has so arrayed —
All life contained within His plan
Remains a mystery to man!

Katherine M. Brady

BEING

When you inhabited my womb
i could only half-dream
of your existence on the outside

but now in early morning
when you first awaken
and the waft of warm urine
circles your room

or when lying on your back
upon a multi-colored quilt
kicking hands and feet
in frog-like motion,

or when i watch your swing,
like a persistent pendulum
ticking away these precious days —

there is a certain eternity
which only we can know
and for those moments
no earthly force
can dichotomize our being.

Suzanne Hebert Blaise

THE FLAG

I can wave from the flagpole,
To the people passing by,
I have stars that resemble,
Those in the sky,

I have stripes of brilliant colors,
Some of red and white,
I am raised in the daytime,
And taken down at night,

People call me Old Glory,
And my glory never fades,
I am hung from windows,
And carried in parades,

I've been torn in grim battles,
To a battered-tattered rag,
But Americans salute me,
For you see I am the FLAG.

Marjorie Karol Edminister

WHOSE RULES?

You've just left,
there is a sadness.
The joy you bring turns
To sadness when you leave.

I sit here quiet and relaxed,
still feeling your warmth,
the smell of your perfume
encircles me, warming me.

Some of the rules say we
are guilty of a sin.
How can our feelings
be considered a sin?

Other rules say it
is lust not love, but
can that giving and warmth
be anything but love?

I'll leave the definitions
to others. For me, you
are warmth, kindness,
compassion and love.

Gleen M. Reeves

THE ROSE

Said the rose there in the garden
I'm so sad and very blue
For the winter winds are coming
All my friends will wither too.

All my leaves will soon be dying
And my bloom will be no more
And the frame where my limbs rested
Will soon be covered with the snow.

But Hark! I hear my mistress' footsteps
Coming close, now very near
She has come to pluck my blossoms
To decorate her chamber there.

With tender fingers, she caressed me
Smoothed my limbs, and touched my boughs
I felt her gentle hands around me
Wrapping me, as in a shroud.

So as winter settles around me
I shall rest this peaceful span
Until the springtime comes and wakes me
And I shall blossom once again.

Odessa Russell Hughes

ON SUCH A DAY

And who would suspect the blind man
of stealing a book;
or a small boy of walking
when he could skip or run.
The day was like this:
Full of moot points and rhetoric.
It was a deep colored sky,
with lots of ramifications.
Lonely songs
sounding in the distance;
quiet as a tear.
A day made for discovery;
Of the who, the why and the reason
for living and being. A good day,
felt deeply in one's bones.
And what shall be discovered
on such a day?
Only God may say.

Ken Stone

CALIFORNIA HERE I COME

I was broke and out of work,
My heart had no song,
When I headed for California
Where work was going strong.

I loaded a trailer
With things for my keep.
My wife and three kids
I put in the jeep.

We hated to leave
It would be such a haul,
Nearly two thousand five
hundred in all.

But we stuck to our guns,
Never wavered a bit
Till we got to the mountains
and the jeep started to quit.

But the straw never broke.
We kept moving along
And we're now in California
Working all the day long.

Arley Streicher

LOVE AND SPRING

I want to write of laden bees
I want to write of April skies
I must extol the budding leaves
But oh! The promise in your eyes.

I want to sing of babbling brooks
Of birds late from the south
Of violets in a mossy nook
But oh! The sweetness of your mouth.

And I should carol to the sun
To warm spring fresh air
But oh! The sun, the breeze are one.
To beautify your hair.

Yes, I should shout of furrowed fields
And bush-green covered lands
Of nests the wrens again will shield
But oh! There are your hands.

There is your love, a flowing clear stream
Your kiss a heady wine.
Your voice adds music to the scene
And spring again — and you are mine.

Katherine J. Salem

PRETTY JAY

Once, I loved a pretty jay.
He led other birds to my feed tray.
Saucily, he answered my call
and sometimes met me in rainfall
in bold and jolly tête-à-tête
each greeting the other in a special way.
Then one dismal, depressing day
no merry chirp met my display,
only silence among the trees,
leaves swaying in a noiseless breeze.
No bird answered my call or tease.
Oh pretty Jay, where are you today?
Did some carnivorous cat stop your play
and eat your guts away,
leave of you only a token:
A small tuft of tail feathers unbroken.
Ah, feathers of a friendly bird.
Oh, voice no longer heard!

Violet L. Haley

TO AND FRO

I have been a pendulum swinging — this clockwork is my earth.
To and fro, to and fro, into darkness, into light — day and night, day and night.
Into darkness, day and night, day and night — into light.

Satan leave my hand alone! Jesus guide me from now on!
God, I need You, God, I know — God, please hold me, don't let go.
Keep me fixed on Your time frame — don't let Satan have a claim.

Too much time's been spent his way — too much freedom in my play.
I am grounded in God's Grace — Day and Night in His trace.
To and fro, now I know! — God, I love You, don't let go.

Bring me clearly to Your time — moving forward to Your chime.
Works in faith and time spent well — lifts me from a burning Hell.

Pace me now and keep my balance — give me time to use my talents.
To and fro, to and fro — day and night, as I go.
Into night . . . with a glow.
With a glow, now I shine — now I shine in all Your time.

Judith N. Knight

PORTRAIT OF JEAN

Remembered well is that portrait of Jean as it hangs in the gallery
with deep thoughts and lasting beauty putting to shame the sand bags
and metal façades of civilization.
    For as the light fell upon us, there emerged a beautiful person,
whose red hair sparkled in the sun.
    Those misty green eyes with vision and understanding
beamed our direction.
    Those wonderful moments when she turned and walked with the grace
of self-assuredness and dignity through the hallways of time.
    The hands of an artist, graceful, soft, and talented
as they blew in the wind, caressing the sounds of love as they weave
a tapestry of a king.
    Like a speeding cycle her smile ascends upon us, and the wisdom
of her years manifests itself from the scars of her past.
    For Scorpio has struck again slaying the barriers of age and times
to reveal the strength of her inner person.
    Begone are the moody insecurities of the past which plague the heart
and start again like the berries which ripen in the sun to make a new life.
    Life can be beautiful with memories of her to surround us as time
drifts off into the wind ever-blowing and ceasing not.

LeRoy B. Schwan

WHAT AM I RUNNING FROM?

What am I running from every time I decide to run away
Am I running because I want to or, because I can't stay?
Am I running from someone else, or is it myself that I can't face
And will I continue to run forever — like a neverending race?
Am I running from someone who, believe it or not, seems to care
But for some unknown reason, their love, I just can't seem to share?
Am I running because I think that there is no one on whom I can depend
Or have I been alone for so long that I just can't accept a friend?
Why do I run every time someone, or something, makes me mad
What would I do if I never knew what it meant to be sad?
Am I running because it seems like the only way of getting attention
Or is there something lurking within that I just can't seem to mention?
Does running away make me feel good or is it really frightening to me
Am I running simply because I'm not what, or where, I want to be?
Is running away the answer every time I get a problem I can't solve
Or should I just sit down and talk to someone who wants to get involved?
Do I run simply because my friends say it's the "in" thing to do
Or is it because I feel that I just have to get away from you?
Am I running away from friends, relatives, my dad or my mom
Dear God, please tell me, "what am I running from?"

Elroy A. Stanton

I WANT MY SOUL TO ENDURE

i want my soul to endure:
that essence that clings,
to the hearts of the beloved;
fondly reminisced,
when all that's due
was worth the involvement;

that "being" made an impression,
and love freely given away
planted seeds of nourishment,
that blossom long after
the chrysalis disintegrated
in its shell: (butterfly powder,
from the wings of flight
up toward a true light.)
Kathleen M. Robbins

I love in vain
It always
Seems
I take the pain
And hide the tears
I'm reaching out
But no one's there
In the heart
I thought had cared
I love in vain
It's always been
My feelings strong
My heart on a string
Waiting for the love
I yearn
To take me in
And ease the hurting!
Robert A. Henriksen

HAVE I TOLD YOU THAT I LOVE YOUR HANDS

big and warm their firm softness.
When I lift them to my face
to marvel at the well-groomed half-moons,
a faint scent, your own
mixture of soap, sweat, and soil
evaporates through your palms and fingers;
I savorously inhale this emanation.
On your left, one finger is missing —
the one people point at one another
to impress
to command
to reprimand — but
yours has grown inward
shyly
pointing at your vulnerable heart.
Martha M. Dunnebier

ONCE IN LOVE

It came so soft
For me
A lilac falling
From a bouquet,
Flutters of wings
Where butterflies
Once sailed.

Whispering to a
Reluctant heart,
It rested so briefly
There
Scattering rose petals
To perfume
A nubile mind.
Christine Thomasian

IF I GET OLD

I will do these things IF I GET OLD!!
First, I'll wear a flowered dress.
The flowers will be big and bold.
And I won't care if I do look old.
The colors will be of every hue,
Purple, yellow, red and blue.
I'll also wear a floppy hat,
Even if I'm short and fat.
It'll have streamers and be new.
I'll wear gloves in bright colors, too.
A secret longing will be met
When I light up a long cigarette!!
I'll flash my jewels so all can see
And in my mink, I'll just be me!!
I'll even have a cocktail or two!!
An old flame might want to "pitch woo!!"
So I'll cover my wrinkles with make-up,
Paint my lips and eyes before we "sup."

I probably will never do these things
Because I'm not going to get old and
                    need this fling!!
Jo Ann Dickson

WAKING TO SPARROWS

    Trying to bring myself
to unnestle the sparrows
who've clung uninvited
above a window, fouling
the wood framing,
clattering each morning,
waking me to cheap itineraries,
raising several broods
(throughout the summer)
of noisy chicks.
    They've no right, I remind myself,
to occupy my space.
They'll have to, by God's grace,
relocate elsewhere,
transmogrify, vacation south
for the winter.
    The big birds on the posts,
the hawk's eye,
goad me on.
They pray for such guests.
Forced acquaintance and quick goodbyes
are the order.
Jeff Boyer

THE LIGHTHOUSE

And the light of the lighthouse turns;
Its beam
On a flat-black sea
is cast.
No shore shall this beacon show —
No rock shall it illumine —
No ship
shall it warn.

And yet —
the light turns.
Though slower, and near to its stop —
With dawn
not yet broken.

No guide is this light now
for the mariner weary —
Nor aid for a sailor blind —
This house of light — so dreary —
Built here —
Upon this rock
so smashed by time.
Thomas F. Brooks

THE SHOCK

Cold chills of emptiness reek through
    My body in despair.
Claiming the tiny lifeblood of warmth
    That still remains.

What is the remedy? Before the clutches
    Of emptiness winds its tentacles
Of fear around my mind, and gloats
    The moment of strangulation.

Will this cold emptiness claim the very
    essence of my life,
And change it to the ashes of death.

Will I overcome this emptiness, this fear,
    Or will I succumb to fate.
The ignoble facts that must be faced,
    while a pertinacious ideology
For survival exists within the soul.

Louise S. Wolff

RIPPLES

Ripples
In a sidewalk stream;
Where a small boy floats
A paper boat,
Laden with children's dreams.

Ripples
In life's still pond;
Where a young man,
Full of hopes and plans,
Struggles to go on.

Ripples
On a sea of ice;
When an aging man
Prays he still can
Find his paradise.

Ripples
On an old man's skin.
With a lump in his throat
He thinks of the boy and the boat,
And the things that might have been.

Howard L. Harper

AMONG THE DUCKS

We paced and paced
Among our race
Till by the lake
We found our place

We sat and pondered
As the ducks wandered
Then one said
"A thought is in my head"

See how they glide
Each in their own stride
Each with their own face
Finding their own place

Keith LaCroix

Joe Jeannotte

Albert Ordoubeigian

TO CHRISTINA

Since I first met you, I hoped to see you again.
Since we were acquainted, I hoped to talk with you more.
One day I couldn't see you, it had me badly worried.
Were you ill? I guessed. My heart was even sore.

When you got back to your motherland — Denmark,
As if I missed my hope and confidence.
Although I had suffered many a parting,
But I never had such a painful experience.

I wailed long drawn-out calls to the sky,
Wishing you could hear me from her another side.
I implored the green grass to join up your tracks.
To the grassland, I had torn-heartedly cried.

You were the first person I met in my life,
If someone looked like you, you always made me make a mistake.
You were the sole person I met in the past,
From so many dreams, you emerged and made me not wake.

I can't help but often recall your words and movements,
Even though, I try my best to imagine your childish features.
I think in many respects, they surely seem as my daughter's,
Your expressions, your looks, your traits and gestures.

S. S. Swan

THIS FIGMENT IS IT ONLY TIME

Do WE imagine WHEN the seconds START,
That only WE begin to see the LIGHT.
A SLAP UPON THE BOTTOM, A BREATH,
A stinging is then FELT; and we begin to CRY.

Is this what says our CLOCK must now begin its RACE.
TO SEE HOW LONG WE LAST BEFORE THE SECOND HAND WILL STOP;

Our CRYING OUT for everlasting LIFE.
Why is it that some stay for only just a while,

AND others try to beat the CLOCK by RUNNING for ANOTHER MILE.

Are we controlled by TIME, is there a space that we can't see.

THAT MAKES US RUSH INTO ETERNITY.

This BIRTH when we begin to feel the minutes in our WATCH.
The span of life between the hours we imagine ONLY THAT
WE'RE HERE;
Then sleep arrives each day to soften our LIFE'S fear,
That death will come before we share another year.

OH TRULY, GOD, DOES this really stop our CLOCK . . . ?

Shay Moorhead

GOLDEN RAYS

Down in the soil, cool and deep
The eager seeds in the winter sleep
Awaiting the call of the golden sun
To spread new roots and through the rich earth run
And the golden rays reach far and deep
To tickle awake the seeds that sleep
To raise them up through gentle sands
Into farmers' fields to proudly stand
And await the harvest by hired hands
But in the meantime, they drink up the rain
And color green the once barren plain
And give such pleasure to the human eye
From their tender leaves raised to the sky
And the fragrance of the plants drifts on the air
In the warmth of the summertime of year
For from mere seeds they were raised to this
By the magic of the warm sun's golden kiss

John F. Collins, III

THE AGRICULTURE BLUES

I have the agriculture blues, I'm feeling very low.
The work here on the farm is going very slow.
The hired man, he quit today,
The reason I don't know. I heard he met a girl in town,
When he was at the show.
So now, I sit and worry all day. I don't know what to do.
My neighbor came to call, and said, "I see you're in a stew."
Good hired men are hard to find and there are but a few,
That really are dependable and know just what to do,
And wages too are going higher
Like rent and taxes and even baling wire.
So one by one the farmers quit,
Go in a bar and sit and sit and talk about
The days gone by
And wonder why and when, a brand-new era will begin.
Please help me face tomorrow to end my blues and sorrow,
I hope someone will come along,
Whose heart is light and very strong
To end the strife of a farmer's life
And bring some sunshine in his life.

Esther M. Thompson

YOU TOLD ME ABOUT THE WEDDING

You told me about the wedding . . .
    It was all arranged, laid out and planned.
    Your father, of course, would give me your hand.
    Your uncle would cater the reception and
    Your cousin would play, along with his band.

You told me about the wedding . . .
    Your brother, the priest, in celebration,
    Got your sister, the sister, a dispensation
    To be maid of honor to all's elation
    And carry, with grace, a single carnation.

You told me about the wedding . . .
    Your mother called the florist and the girl for your hair.
    "We'll have it outside in the sweet summer air.
    All who are anyone will surely be there."
What should've been bonds seemed more like a snare.

You told me about the wedding
But I had not even said, "I love you."

Tim E. Davis

THE DISCOVERY

One day in a shady, wooded spot,
On a cool and misty morn,
I found a relic among the weeds,
Looking all gray and sadly forlorn.
I discovered the old and antique thing
Nestled with weeds and sunflower.
I plucked the brambles with a sense of awe,
And tugged it from its lonely bower.
This thing of the past that I had found
Sat forlornly on the ground;
I swabbed the sweat from my brow
And gazed lovingly at that work-worn plow.
It spoke a message, loud and clear,
That history lives on, year after year;
And that God, in this secluded place,
Should watch over its antique face,
And bless it with the past in part;
Just waiting for a sentimental heart
To clean and shine the rusty blade
And take it from this lonely glade.

Joanne Cakebread

GOD'S PRECIOUS GIFTS

Children teach a lesson
Innocent and small
God's precious creation
Examples for us all.

Lips that speak God's truth
Eyes that show such trust
Arms that show much love
As they embrace your bust.

Hearts that can forgive
Each little wrong you do
Smiles that brighten up your day
And shine a light for you.

Thank you God for children
With all the happiness they bring
Help us to be more like them
And set the world to sing.

Leta Shaver

BOAT OF LIFE

Who is that sleeping in your boat?
I know who is in mine!
Do you know how you stay afloat?
I know who's my lifeline!

Are you afraid as dark clouds come?
I know who makes me brave!
Do rolling breakers turn you numb?
I know who calms the wave!

Turn to look at that resting form —
Do you not know that soul?
He's the one who checks the storm
And keeps you from the shoal.

Waking to fears of quaking horde
He stills the raging sea.
Yet know you not he's Jesus? — Lord?
Our friend of Galilee!

Elizabeth P. Wish

HITCH YOUR WAGON TO A STAR

Life's intent was meant for living,
    Granting each an equal share,
With determination's action
    As a complement each must bear.

Though your life be inharmonious
    And the ways beset by mire,
Employ your native instinct,
    Let intent abet desire.

Should omission be indulgent
    And compulsion neglect demand,
Just ignore commiseration
    And initiative will lend a hand.

With the grant of assurance
    Hitch your wagon to a star,
Build upon the possibilities
    And resolve will take you far.

Charles Ruggles Fox

Since the children left
she wakes again and again,
'cause of the silence.

Martha Kaufman

LONG AGO

You came and you went
with much great speed.
I sometimes wonder
if it was just human need.

It was all at your pace
never at mine.
We shared a love
for such a short time.

It was so special and dear.
I thought it would last
but everything ended
so very very fast.

I sit here and wonder
just where I went wrong.
Maybe my feelings
just came on too strong.

I'll always remember
the times that we shared
and think of the moments
when we both once cared.

Linda Patterson

WITHOUT YOU

A mind without dreams
    Is a mind without hope
A soul that hides from tomorrow
    Is a soul that can't cope
A heart without feeling
    Is a heart that should mend
And a day without you
    Is a day that should end
Without you
I no longer wake with the sun
Without you
My loneliness has just begun
I have no mind
    or hope
        or soul
            or a heart
For without you
My life is through

Lisa Hamilton

POETRY

If in my very old age
    you should wish to comfort me;
come sit by my side
    and read me some poetry.

Not written by some famous man
    who accentuates the rhyme;
but by some obscure little person
    from another time.

Bravely pouring out his soul
    down through the years;
he seeks no recognition
    on accolades from his peers.

His is an endeavor of love;
    fame and fortune pass him by.
You may never hear his name
    but this I prophesy.

Someday someone will discover
    these great treasures lost in time;
so sit with me and share my tea
    and read the novice Poet's rhyme.

Frances Norton Russell

THE FLIGHT OF PEGASUS

The wind builds
With the beat of each wing,
And the nostrils flare
At the bite of the Boreas.

The arch of the neck is steep
And the mane falls
From the crest
As a curtain of silk.

The golden hooves dance in anticipation
For the clouded paving of the heavens.
The front legs rear up
In defiance of the Earth.

And then the head is tossed back —
The eyes hold the fire of excitement,
As a mighty thrust is given
From the muscular hind legs,

The body is lifted —
And the crystal white wings
Take control.

Kat Kerste

I WENT TO BED

I went to bed quite unhappy.
The events of the day summoned
No appraisals.

I went to bed alone,
Empty inside with only
That gut feeling.

I went to bed on the brink of
Forced tears, forced miracles,
Forced hope, and forced truths.

I went to be acquitted
Of what I do not know —
Absent of rhythm and soul.

I went to bed weakened
By some pinpointless endeavor.
Only to realize that *I* controlled me.

I went to bed empty,
With no more of the day's tarry
To pour out of me.

Thomas O. Mays

A LOST MYSTIC

If I must once again be the catalyst
For someone else's destiny —
Then . . . so be it.
I am a fragile china puppet
On an elastic string.
I dream death and vision happiness.
I am Harlequin's pawn in a dance of fate —
A lost mystic
Doomed to see,
But never taste —
Doomed to feel,
But never touch.

I can see it coming —
I can feel it coming —
The gray door will open.
Like Moses on the mountain
I may see,
But never enter.

Tara E. Wilson

HOKUSAI, Farm Life

BED OF DREAMS

The bed of dreams you gave
    me
Was a glorious place at
    our start
then dark clouds moved in
    on us
they left us both a
    broken heart
I knew where my love
    did lie
Revealed to me by the
    Father above
to be shared on earth
    till both die
and to be manifested
    the other side
where heaven and earth
    Shall one day meet
Then the Heavenly Father
    Shall say
That all is well and eternity
    is complete.

Zeldia Meggs

MEGGS, ZELDIA ISABELLE. Born: Natchez, Missouri, 8-15-45; Married: 3-23-78 to Kenneth Wayne Meggs; Education: 7th grade, Buras High School; Occupations: Songwriter, Nurse's Aide, Seafood Handler; Poetry: 'Death's Toll,' 11-2-84; 'Romeo & Juliet,' 10-83; 'Remembered Memories,' 10-83; 'Crushed Dreams,' 10-83; all published by American Poetry Association; Other Writings: 'Crazy Heart,' song, Johnny Dollar, 6-27-83; Comments: *I write about events and people I love. To express hurt, loneliness, anguish and pride. Mostly I write about people who touch my life. Mostly, I write about my husband.*

COMPLETED VISIONS

If we would feel each other's dreams
They would shine with hope brighter.
The completions of our visions
Will be nearer with each dawn.
The joy shared will mount as
The final stages become apparent,
When our dreams are reached
Others will have the confidence
Of being attained.

Gary L. Schell

IF BABY COULD TALK

The sweetest present I've ever got,
This tiny, tiny little tot,
Whose eyes look up as if to say,
"Hey, Mom, what shall we do this day?"
I cannot creep, I cannot crawl,
I cannot speak to you at all.
To understand the world I'm in,
Think of where, the place I've been.
I know nothing of this empty room.
Without you here,
It's filled with gloom.
So, please understand this my plight.
Put pleasant things within my sight.
I'm lonely, lost, and out of place
Until I see your loving face.
So, Mother, until the day I speak,
Your love, your guidance are what
I seek.
Help me make it through each day.
           Sincerely,
           Baby"

Ruth D. Weber

LEAVES DO FALL

A falling leaf fell my way,
and did not know it fell.

Its surface green in color only,
yet beneath its character strong.

Contrasting whites riding faintly,
give reference to its personality.

Its heart reaching every direction,
only to show life's harsh affection.

Its edges torn, crippled, and burned,
from a love not yet returned.

Rising above all other leaves,
only to fall beneath my feet.

A falling leaf fell my way.
I let it fall!

S. Marlene Tolbert

RAIN TONIGHT

Fireflies flash
Green dotted lights
Through moist wisps
Of fog

Chirping tree frogs
Trill
Through the dense
Half-dark

"Whippoorwill"
Penetrates the cool mist
From down in the meadow
By the river

A wide rainbow haze
Encircles the bright
Round moon

Rain tonight

Tamara Francisco

UNKNOWN FAITH

He is so good.
I have never understood.
Why He died for me.

It was not to show that He could —
It's to see what we would — do.
To put Him in bondage or
leave Him be.

To take us by the hand —
and show us great stands,
But, never let us go.

To show us the way,

And we will always know.

That without His death,
when we are put to rest.
That our spirits shall be free.

To be angels in the sky.
On the very day we die.
Is what we all expect to be.

Lula Mae Allen

RAINDROPS

spastic little devils
these tiny little rings
landing on a pin point
and spreading all around

landing quite chaotic
save their concentric shapes
some landing vertically
some landing in a slant

I watch them drop in thought
of puddles in my youth
I'm wiser and drier now
but how I miss the fun

Anthony J. Forgione, Jr.

FORGIONE, TONY. Born: Boston, Massachusetts, 7-24-48; Married: to Denise Cremins; Occupation: Operating Room Nurse; Memberships: Boy Scouts of America, American Film Institute; Poetry: published in *Contemporary Poets of America*, Dorrance, 1984; Comments: *My poems are uniquely inconsistent. I write for enjoyment, expression, and to keep people guessing.*

TEARS

Weep no more
Sweet love of mine
Your heart is heavy
Your thoughts unkind
But burdens lighten
And hearts do mend
To these things
The Lord attends
Let me kiss your tears
And soothe your brow
We'll be together forever
Nothing else matters now.

Doris Trimble

SHADOWS

In the still, soft shades of yet another
morning, some dimwitted bird disturbs
my peace with his song. I shout,
but I have no voice.
So do you trouble me with your prancing,
dancing, fighter's stancing, when all
I want is to hold you and be
your only true love.
You disturb me, with your warm waves
of fingers trembling, touching,
lover's teasing. Then you turn,
and say I am your enemy.
The only peace I have is in your
arms, in the early hours when
you sleep. Do not wake me, never
wake yourself.

Tessa B. Dick

LOVE

Written for my husband, Roger

I was ever so lucky,
The day I met you;
For until that day came,
I was lonely and blue.

I was feeling so hopeless,
When you walked in my door;
We were starting as friends,
Who knew fate held more?

You gave me some hope,
Some light in my life;
You gave me your friendship,
Then you made me your wife.

Vicki Lynn

THE ANGRY ROBIN

As I mowed the grass around
Our row of growing trees,
An angry robin flew at me.

Not very far away she sat
On the branch of a hickory tree;
Her nervous twitters scolding me.

I could not figure
What could be amiss
Until I noticed a tiny nest

In the tree beside the mower.
I finished quickly, moving on
She flew back when I was gone.

Becky Knight

WHERE?

Oh dear and timeless love,
    Where have you gone? —
You who were earth and light to me,
    My up, my down.

Oh warmth of my very blood,
    Breath of my quickened breath,
Rich fullness of my lack,
    Where have you gone? Oh where?
    No answer stirs the air.

I'll write you then in care of death.
    Write back!

Ruth de Menezes

It's nighttime now and time for bed.
For all little sleepy heads.

So come and kiss me little one
playtime for this day is done.

Let's tuck the blankets around you
And let the magic of dreams surround you.

Tomorrow is another day
when again you can run and play.

So goodnight my dear for tonight
Cuddle up with teddy bear and sleep tight.

Sue Lowry

GOD'S LOVE

My friend I can't express
How much I love you.
I think it is so great —
Beyond what words can tell,
Yet it must be so small
Compared to God's love for us all.
His love is an infinite number of times
    greater than yours or mine!
It is too great for my mind
    to imagine, comprehend or understand;
Yet He has let me see
    just the edge of His great love,
Through you my friend.

Joyce Enterline

IT'S STILL LOVE

HONORABLE MENTION

I slide my arms around her waist,
nuzzle her neck,
whisper in her ear,
Have I told you
I love you today?
No.
I'm not going to.

We laugh.
We hug and kiss.
It's still love
after more than forty years.

Edward M. Goldman

SAVE THE LAST DANCE FOR ME

They were dancing together
While their hearts beat as one.
He was holding her closely
As so often he had done.

She sighed in contentment
And smiled tenderly
Saying, "Darling, remember
Save the last dance for me."

The soft music had ended
At the first ray of dawn.
The guests had all departed
And the stars were all gone.

Then the maiden was summoned
To fair regions above,
Yet, before she departed
Softly spoke of her love.

"Save the last dance, my darling,
Save the last dance for me"
— A pause, then a whisper
"Save the last dance for me."

Minnie Frasier Ledford

You took my song
And it became yours
From the highest note
To the lowest octave.
Your special touch
With melody and words
Made my simple tune
A symphony.
When my perceptions
Take me off key,
You gently nudge them
Into place,
Blending the tunes
Into harmony
Once more.
I think sometimes
Of the silence of life
Without you
To wave the baton.

Jean Kyle

LOOKING FOR ANSWERS

Looking for answers
    will they fall from the sky?
Listening to the wind
    but hearing no reply.

The bird songs are heavenly
    but they give no relief.
Is love the answer
    or just my belief.

Will having your love
    be enough for me . . .
without those feelings of
    touch, hear and see?

Can I bear to love you
    when you're always far away?
Will these feelings of longing
    be in my heart to stay?

The wind has no answers
    so I'll listen to my heart.
I'm in love with you forever
    be it together . . . or apart.

Janine Tyo-Perkins

EVERPRESENT GIFT

Your birth in history, Lord, marks each beginning,
    for You among us, then, sent to dwell
    taught humanity the good of human living.
Your heart and will wholly to the Father directed
    unto that last earth day in the flesh
    commanding remembrance of the Gift given.

Your birth in mystery, Lord, awaits in the present
    for men and women to utter "yes" to becoming.
Choose we may of His Presence to abide
    though Creator sway gives to creature, freedom respecting.
Partaking of Broken Bread and Blessed Wine,
    its worth the soul acclaims.
Adoring in surrender, Incarnational living learns.

Your birth in majesty, Lord, is victory eternal!
O Glorified One! O Highly Exalted Son! O Risen King!
Angels and saints, all heavens, Alleluia sing!
God in Christ Jesus His people restores
    to the Kingdom of truth and justice
    as Creation was ordered before.

Sister Agnes Reinert

THE PRESIDENT WAS A COWARD

Mundane history never polled it; it was no
Sandburg joke: the President was a coward.

It was down below the sovereign green and white
He slept, beneath the blinking lights and fall-out
Shelter, behind his guardians and modern
Politicians . . .

    "Into the holes! Into the Underground!
    Leave the women, leave the children, leave
    The old, the sacred cows, leave the soldiers
    At their duties! Into the holes!
    Into the Underground!"

And history books never polled it; it was no
Sandburg joke:

After the war had ended, the heads were counted,
    But they did not find him marching home
        To bury the dead and wounded.

T. D. Edwards

POCKET FILLED WITH DREAMS

A child with a pocket full of dreams in that springtime
so long ago,
so many pretty things to see, so many things just
waiting for me,
The knight in shining armor, the rainbow at the
end of the trail,
That was the springtime so many years ago.

A girl with hope and a heart filled with love in
that summer so many years ago,
The dreams came, some I reached out and held
and some just slipped away,
Where has my spring and summer gone?
It seems so long ago.

The woman that faces reality,
Autumn is here, winter is coming closer each day,
The sunset is drawing near, but I still have a
heart filled with memories,
And my pocket filled with dreams from that spring
and summer long ago.

Opal Luttrell

CHANTIER BOHEMIEN

Solid field rock girds her frame
As her pink roof peaks through,
The woods behind her whisper her
name: Chantier Bohemien!

Nestled gently into the earth
Only one side of the cottage is seen,
With a rambling grapevine attached
To the wall where a garden abounds.

A working musician called her home,
While she played melodies clear,
And now a poetess dwells within . . .
So sensitive, so in tune with life.

Chantier Bohemien means simply this,
A workshop for the serious artist.
From within the walls abound some days
The aroma of fresh baked bread.

Trumpet Vine and fresh Peppermint leaves,
Sage and Marigolds bloom . . . as daily,
They quietly announce her presence . . .
A poetess musing quietly, contented within!

Jean Boyce Capra

FRITZ, DOROTHY JEAN. Pen Name: Jean Boyce Capra; Born: Cassville, Missouri, 2-15-31; Married: 5-2-49, to LaVerne J. P. Fritz; Divorced: 7-26-56; Education: University of Arizona, 1967-69; Kansas City Business College, 1970-71; Penn Valley Community College, 1979-81; Occupation: Secretary/Research Assistant (Finance Dept., Revenue Section, City of Kansas City, Missouri); Memberships: Missouri State Geneaological Society; Awards: Three Honorable Mention Certificates, Two Special Mention Certificates and Third Prize, 1983 and 1984, World of Poetry Press; Poetry: 'Rajput and Purdah,' poetry about India, World of Poetry Press, 1984; 'Love,' World of Poetry Press, 1984; 'Silence . . . Silence,' American Poetry Association, 1984; 'A Gracious Lady,' American Poetry Association, 1985; Comments: *I write poetry because I love poetry as an expression of ideas, stories, and feelings, both of myself and others. I love to deal with the varied experiences of living, past and present. I enjoy reading the anthologies I have received and share the poetry of others. Poetry can be like the vapor of Spring flowers.*

IMPULSE

The angels of high Heaven look down and weep,
While those of Hades shriek their satirical discourse.
When will I learn,
Fools pay their debts many times over,
The wise man but once,
If ever?
The wise yield to reason;
I curse it in the actions of impulse.

D. M. Ewoldt

MY EVERYTHING

Sometimes I sit,
on a damp, cloudy day —
feeling blue, by my window,
at life's cold cruel ways.

I sigh, then turn away,
looking into the room —
seeking a way,
to disperse that gloom.

What I see makes me smile,
the gloom is no longer there —
my wonderful wife,
who is all of my life,
and the beautiful child which I hold most dear.

So if that blue feeling sets in,
on some cold damp day —
I need only look within, at my family,
then pray —
"Thank You, God, You gave me everything!"

H. D. Kleiner

FOOTPRINTS IN THE FIELD

They stroll among the sunny fields
Warming their souls and lifting their eyes;
Ignoring the restless sleep of the giant
Whom they created, who rules their life

Beyond the laughs and tears of love
     — of life —
The giant lies behind the fence
And down the road.

They laugh at those who cry and weep
. . . Crushed mushrooms in the field . . .
The T.V. news is unconcerned,
"The giant twitched, and now for sports."

Beyond the field the sun goes down
     —forever? —
The giant feels the need to stretch,
He cannot sleep forever.
In the night the sun grows bright,
Loud thunder in a cloudless sky.

Gary Ritchie

I WONDER

I sit and wonder
About what life will be.
I think of heaven,
Faith, and love bringing sweet things to me.

I wonder when;
I wonder where;
Who, or what
I will see there.

I close my eyes
And think of things
Such as peace and joy
And a bird that sings.

I see a golden road
And a pearly gate,
The finest mansion
With my name plate.

I wonder?

Lannette Walker

STRANGERS NO MORE
To John — Thanks for the "Magic" and the Sparkle.

There are many things I'd like to say to you
But for now I'll begin with "Thank You"
In a world that is very expressive and open
I thank you for the open things
Your time, your smile, your concern

I know at times it's difficult for you to be with me
You're so outspoken and carefree — I on the other hand
Can feel, can show — but it's hard for me to express

Thank you for understanding and trying to help
At times you make me feel so comfortable that I feel
I can tell you just about anything — Yet I know I can't

You've told me many things about yourself
I'll cherish them as I cherish you
For they came from you and no one else

The one thing I want to thank you for the most
Is the fact that through the times we've talked and shared
Although sometimes silence stepped in
We have become friends — and we are

Strangers No More

Diana Lynn Savignano

SAVIGNANO, DIANA LYNN. Born: Kingston, Pennsylvania, 8-30-61; Occupation: Word Processor Operator; Poetry: 'Child of Music,' *American Poetry Anthology,* Fall/Winter, 1983; 'The Many Roads,' *Hearts on Fire,* 1985; Comments: *Ever since I was a child, I can remember writing. Being quiet, it was the best way I knew of communicating with others. I believe it still is. My poems are about the special people in my life, and I thank God for them and their inspiration.*

POETRY WRITING CLASS FOR EMIGRES

"The trouble, teacher, is not that I've lost my love.
I cannot find it even if I look for it:
The trouble, muse, is not just that I've lost my love.

I've watched my mailbox for a pigeon-white reply
from a mad poetry editor who buys my wit:
The trouble's that I've sent to Russia poems with love.

My problem is not just my flair for making love . . .
What is its final make? — A child? — A song made of
green stuff that buys necessities for my new love?"

Fridrikh Brainin

LIFE IN YOUR GOLDEN YEARS

Our pace grows slower in our golden years.
Pleasure grows only in our memory as we grow
more serene each year.
Our soul can vision things
our eyes cannot see.
It is a pleasure to see and
think of the joy we once had.
Remembering all the good things
that came our way.
Mother and Daddy were pleased
with the things that we did.
Thankful that we gave our life
to God,
Before they passed away
to meet with God.
          Zora B. Fetner

GERARD MANLEY HOPKINS

Like a diamond from pebbles apart his art shines —
As a prism, light-instressed, does a rainbow inscape strain,
His words, vision-urged, surge joy-wrung of pain,
Now wracked, root-wrested, gem-cut, flash-afresh signs
Like a dawn-break . . . Here wake-words first lustrous in lines
Flush up-sudden conveys, heart-startling the brain
In resplendent crescendoes wherein echoes refrain
Hope's trump-blast new-announcing gleam-gold yet in old mines —

Rainbows, trump-blast, gleam-gold — all wake-words, Why?
Can old make new? Aye! when by a newborn eye seen . . .
That heart-of-things Art spies with a child-kept eye
Declares is there, everywhere, has ever been,
Will ever be — while we who never see all sigh
Grow old and die, as Art springs forth spring-green.
          Joseph L. Williamson

MORNING AFTER THE SNOW

Some Artist deft at painting scenery
Has touched the pines with snowy white.
The mountains, He has sculpt in altitudes of love,
Great hills of white, that almost reach the grayish clouds,
Thin clouds that edge the ever-deepening blue
Of morning sky, and wait — protectively
To keep the world at bay and leave the scene
Unmarred — while a pure white bird appears
Soaring to the azure sky; the Painter's brush
Has given her wings, though all else is frozen still.
          And then — she's gone!
          "Come back," I cry
          "Oh pure white dove!"
          I search the sky —
          But all is still.
          Esther E. Farrington

DEFENSE IN THE FIRST DEGREE

It's not good to provoke anyone to anger,
nor is it good to mistreat a stranger,
One may never know, it may be an angel.
If you do!
It may place them in an undesired position,
When a person's temper becomes as fire, very
kindled.
There may come a time that person may
need to prove defense in the first degree.
Each day in a person's life, it's never the same,
In them, something may have caused them to change.
We must be careful when we approach strangers,
especially when we don't know them.
We don't need to give that person cause to prove
defense in the first degree.
          Sauls Suzzs

THE BEAUTIFUL IN LIFE

Some see it in a baby's smile,
Some see it in their lover's eyes;
Some see it in a senior citizen's face
While some associate it with that special place.
          But me?
I see it in your total being.

It is created through a surgeon's skill
While an artist gives it color, still —
A composer breathes it into music
While a writer gives it life in the pieces he creates,
The Religious demonstrate it through the life they lead
While a man shares it with the woman he takes,
          And better yet . . .
God creates it perpetually through you, loving me . . .

          Leslie Wright

LOVE HAPPENS IN THE HEART

Love happens in the heart,
And plays its melody on heartstrings made of feeling,
Love needs emotion for a start,
And finally with patience sweet, joy is neverending.

Love happens in the heart,
Where live one's fondest memories,
Once there it will not part,
If only in the heart your true love you will please.

Love happens in the heart,
When at our best we shine,
Love heartfelt is the spark,
Of countless wonderful things divine.

          Daniel W. West

TEARS

Tears are meant for both young and old.
They reflect a child's fears that remain untold.

There are the tears of joy, and the tears of sorrow.
Shed them now, or it will be too late tomorrow.

They silently tell others, that something is wrong.
That our fears are shrouded, by something strong.

All who can cry, can feel with great feelings.
The joy of knowing, that their soul is healing.

Tears that are cried, bring sight to the eyes.
Like storm clouds that move, revealing bright skies.

          Daniel Baxter

MY VALENTINE

The love we share is beyond compare
          To anything I've ever known:
It's as strong and as violent as a storm;
          But as gentle as any breeze that's ever blown.

When I think of you and all that you do —
          It makes me happy and sad —
But when you're in love you have to remember —
          You take the good and the bad.

So on this day — St. Valentine's Day —
          I just want you to know
That through all of the good and all of the bad,
          I still love you so!

          Mablelene Adams

GOD'S WORD IS LOVING YOU

God's Word sets my spirit free. And you?
Loving you motivates me.

God's Word keeps me out of hell. And you?
Loving you keeps me out of trouble.

God's Word makes me a new creature inside. And you?
Loving you has rendered me ready to face the ugly
                    truth, with nothing left to hide.

God's Word gets me through the tedious moments of a
                    difficult day.
                            And you?

Loving you has left me with nothing bad to say.

Patrice Lange

DUALISM

Our souls wind-tossed like loessial soil
With thoughts intertwined with sweat and toil.
From extremes of heat and ice remade
Darkness and sunlight with no shade.
Love and hatred welded into one
Like an eclipse of the moon or sun.
Religious relief of sorrow by joy
Comedy and tragedy nature's ploy.
The sublime and grotesque in bed asleep
Beauty and horror dreamt from the deep.
Tenderness and assault in procreation
Seeded within us by predestination.
Depression and elation of the mind
Common to all races of humankind.
Our maker created us as we are
The mirror image of a binary star!

Grover C. Hunter, Jr.

SPINNERET

I feel the walk across my leg,
    Eight legs, too many fingers;
        the atomic hairs of the
            well-made suit . . .
Then flows the secret emulsion.
            Soon, in the nook and corner grows
        the iron-gauze entrapment.
    Slowly . . . finely symmetric.
Pseudo-f-r-a-g-i-l-e puzzle.

    Most deceptive snare of all.

Roseanne Fadil

PEOPLE ARE STUPID

People are stupid and I know it's true
Let me explain my reasons to you
Who causes wars not birds or bees
Who causes pollution not the fish in the seas
Who causes traffic jams, accidents or smogs
Not bird nor fish, nor cat or dogs
Who's now reaching out to go further in space
You guessed it again it's the human race
And who's got debts, divorces and credit on time
Slums, Legal fees, Politicians and crime
Who has demonstrations, pickets, walkouts and strikes
Lockouts, Lockins, hates and dislikes
Who smokes tobacco, drinks alcohol and takes drugs
Not reptiles or mammals, nor insects or bugs
With this message I have given to you
People are stupid and I've proved it's true

Leo Feebish

THE STORM

As I lay there alone in my bedroom,
Listening to the roar of the rain through the pines,
I thought of my husband
As we listened to the rain so many times.

It seemed as if he was talking
As he'd done so many times before.
But when I listened more closely
It was the roar of the rain, nothing more.

As I lay there alone in the darkness,
Listening to the storm, the wind and the rain,
I thought of all my children
And wished they were here once again.

And I cried, "Oh how lonely,"
And through the storm I thought I heard them at the door.
But when I arose and looked out my window,
It was the roar of the storm, nothing more.

It was only the rain
That I had listened to so many, many times.
It was only the rain,
The roar of the rain through the pines.

Earl V. Bundy

BUNDY, EARL VIRGINIA. Born: Williamston, North Carolina, Senior Citizen; Education: High School, gifted child; Occupations: Artist, Photographer, Retired; Memberships: N.A.R.F.E., Washington, D.C.; Poetry: 'Mancho Mountain,' American Poetry Association, 1983; 'Snake Lady,' American Poetry Association, 1985;'The Greatest Love,' Airline Publishing, 1984; 'Little Good Deeds,' Airline Publishing, 1985; 'The Bombing of Pearl Harbor,' Jamesville Publishing, 1985; Comments: *I have written poetry as a hobby. I take stories pertaining to life and make them rhyme. I have so many heart-rending poems that are so beautiful, they make my soul sing with love, joy, sorrow, humor. You name it. I have it.*

CARING

There were three girls walking in the rain,
I felt for them, almost had a pain;
Would have invited them in for tea,
Twice their age, what would they think of me;
Now we can't go beyond conventions,
We are suspected of pretentions;
I long for a day when we can share,
I do want others to know I care.

Don Bedwell

A SHELL OF SORROW

I may often cry a lonely one's tear
And fear the one thing most terrible to fear
For here I am cast within by an unfair demon
Cursed by fate to always remain within
For a thousand eternities, a day and tomorrow
I know I must remain inside a shell of sorrow!

This mind is far beyond
Either before or behind
Its intended time!
And I along with it am cursed to tribulation
To scream for its undoing with unimaginable frustration
To no avail, to suffer for as long as the duration!

I swear at the fates that dealt this sad tale
And ponder over the meaning to it all
Even knowing that no one really cares as long as I fall
And remain lost forever to the roots of my soul
Just as the demons stand guard over my lonely hole
I know I must remain inside a shell of sorrow!

Robert B. Reinhardt

REINHARDT, ROBERT BRYAN. Born: Baltimore, Maryland, 12-5-64; Education: Edgewood High School, Edgewood, Maryland, Graduate; Various other Navy service courses and schools; Occupations: Petty Officer Third Class, U.S. Navy (Operations Specialist); Memberships: Civil Air Patrol (Harford Composite Squadron, Maryland Wing); Poetry: *The Tales of Ayelsfarn,* Anthology, Dorrance & Company, to be published in Fall, 1985; 'Logick Within A Circle of Symmetry,' New York Poetry Society, to be published in August, 1985; 'Image of You,' *American Poetry Anthology,* American Poetry Association; Comments: *Poetry has been a method of self-expression for me. The themes and ideas presented in most of my poetry were birthed mainly from emotions and feelings held deep within myself, serving as a way to reveal my life and personal nature in a way most natural to me, writing poetry!*

A TIME IN WILDERNESS

A time in wilderness, the time grass grows
green. And the clear blue river, sparkles with
life. Then the walk in wilderness, gives me
peace of mind. Then the time in wilderness, has
drawn to an end. The river still sparkles as
I walk away from the scene.

Charles Maier

THE BIRDLADY OF DEPTFORD
HONORABLE MENTION

Often, my mother watches the birds at play —
Red cardinals, sparrows, jays, and crows.
Their small affairs, their tiny woes, short joys
Are her delight. Often, her boys she warns
To keep from smashing pale blue robin's eggs.
When a bird is found dead, she digs a grave
In soft garden ground with a spade or hands.
Each year several feeders she plans for spring,
Cleans the stone bath and mends their wooden house.
Then the birds sing bright songs from backyard trees,
And mom stands at the window and calls for me
To come and look and listen and laugh with her.
Those birds see us there, but never fly away.

Deborah E. Beatty

LET ME LIVE WITH YOU

If only you would let me live with you,
Let me share your life, loyal at your side,
For when you love someone as much as I do,
Then, that is where you would choose to reside.
Let me plant roots deep into the soil
Toward the making of a miracle,
And happiness a serpent cannot spoil,
Or be a part of, or in any way make null.
Let me be a helpmate to my husband,
"An helpmeet for him," so help me God!
Let me live with him, and his respect command,
At one with myself, and with the sod.
Let me live as if some power above,
Were watching over me with the eyes of love.

Blanche D. Madiol

RECONCILIATION

Not of man but of God: For the sins of childhood.
Not of man but of God: For the sins of parenthood.
Not of man but of God: For the sins of prosperity.
Not of man but of God: For the sins of passion.
Not of man but of God: For the sins of pride.
Not of man but of God: For the sins of uselessness.
Not of man but of God: For the sins of piety.
Not of man but of God: For the sins of remorselessness.
Not of man but of God: For the sins of usurpation.

Conclusion:
Only God can do this for Himself,
And only He knows whom He has done it for.
"He shall gather the lambs with His arm."

Estella M. McGhee-Siehoff

SILENCE

Silence is ever harder to find,
though far you walk and high you climb.
Never you seem to be rid of the sound,
that scratches the sky and shakes the ground.
For it's hard to avoid the trucks and cars,
or all of the planes that fly through the stars.
Though if by chance or perhaps by design,
you're able to escape the noise of mankind,
you'll discover that silence is soft and serene,
so utterly pure, crisp and clean.
But the sounds of man stretch far and wide,
with little place left for silence to hide.
So enjoy every silence while it lasts,
there'll be less in the future than in the past.

George Bennis

STAR LIGHT — STAR LOVE

Swingin' from the tip of the topmost star
Holdin' by the wish-strings of my heart,
Wonderin' where in the lonely heaven's name you are
When you gonna' let our lovin' get a start?

You were comin' with me
But you let me down;
You don't mean to tell me
That you're still on the ground!

I can't stay without you
Don't you know that's true?
Only reason I'm up here
Is just because of you.

Here's a wish-string for you
Try to catch it by the end,
Once I get you up here
Then our lovin' can begin.

Strings that tie you to me
Were begun on the ground;
But I couldn't stay there
Once your love I'd found.

Ruth N. Sipe

WE WALKED TOGETHER

HONORABLE MENTION

Come walk with me a little way, not far.
Our footprints intermingle in the dust
Where mosses grew and young arbutus thrust
Their dreams above decay. Our pathways mar
Earth's summer flesh. Like childhood's
                    lingering scar
They cut, so thin and pale, beneath the mussed
Onrushing of our days. How well we trust
Our path's returning, heedless though we are!

When winter stills the lust of cells to bud
And buries our three seasons under snow,
Where then will all our dusty footprints be?
When April comes and drifts melt down to mud
New worshippers of spring will never know
Last summer's path was made by you and me.

Ruth E. Lang

DR. LOBOTOMY

Love ain't money in your bank accounts,
nor years yuh spent in college.
It ain't whatja know that really counts —
It's how yuh use your knowledge!

Negroes symbolize "Daddy's too strong!"
Caucasians outnumber them
but fear 'em 'n use 'em — and it's wrong!
for folks to judge and condemn.

The symbol of daddy's tyranny —
a cop in his uniform.
Fantasies of Nazi Germany —
Most folks live lies and conform.

Catholicism — that hypocrisy
of old myths and mystery.
It's oppression since one's infancy
causin' so much misery!

Folks eroticize infantile pains
as they think — and rub — 'bout sex.
With nasty thoughts in their impaired brains —
Their lives become more complex!

Mike Goodknow

POETRY

Poetry is a seed, beginning with universal creation
                    and ending never.
It is as timeless as soaring mountains,
                    rolling waters, and whispering winds.

Poetry is a creative art,
                    the most satisfying of them all.
Its many-fingered meanings
                    confound even the masterminds.

Poetry is as musical as a shepherd lad's
                    plaintive harp.
Its rhythms tie ages together with chords
                    which activate and echo from eon to eon.

Poetry is both body and soul
                    merging into one entity.
It is an integral essence
                    of being and becoming.

Poetry is emotion, intellect
                    and imagination.
Its unifying truths are as unforgettable
                    as life's most treasured moments.

Elaine Stanberry

GOD'S HAPPINESS

A sunset in the sky, a rainbow after the rain,
That is God's happiness.

Hearing children's laughter, seeing a baby smile,
That is God's happiness.

A good deed, a positive thought, a helping hand,
That is God's happiness.

Smelling a flower, watching a bird fly, loving an animal,
That is God's happiness.

Appreciating your blessings, willing to share and to give,
That is God's happiness.

Loving life, fulfilling your purpose of life, loving each other,
That is God's happiness.

Keeping your faith, radiating your light, loving God,
That is God's happiness.

Sharing your spiritual wealth, working toward your soul growth,
That is God's happiness.

Elizabeth Cotton

KATRINA

We walked in silence, you and I,
Past the white fences and grazing horses,
To wonder at the mountain looming before us.

Behind us, small lights dotted the purple shadows.
Each seemed a shining moment in the blanket of my memory.

We watched as the sun threw its last golden light
High up into the sky. The mountain caught it.
I saw it reflected in your eyes.

You mirrored my own fear of the future, the unknown.
The reluctance to leave this place and time in our life.

We sat on the damp grass, still silent,
Reliving the past, uncertain of our tomorrow.
The beginning and the end.

Stacey Avis

WITH LABOUR'S LOVE

There are tiny specks of dust
Showing through some rust
On a windowpane.
A pretty little rose
In a vase that I chose
Returns me once again
To thoughts of yesteryear;
While I shed a tear
Over you, my Dear.
Ahh, Beloved! since you have been gone
I sometimes burst into song
Singing of youth that's gone
And, what I have right here.
Yes, youth is gone from this person
And I, with Labour's Love
Do not want to escape this prism
But to clean and polish and polish and clean
So that my thoughts will be — quiet and serene —
And so that life will not be just an empty dream.

Paulla Poe Nusom

NUSOM, PAULLA A. Born: Olathe County, outside of Delta, Colorado; Married: 5-10-81 to Robert L. Nusom; Education: High School Graduate and Nurse's Aide Training; Occupation: Homemaker; Awards: 'To Poe,' 1946; 'Special Love,' American Poetry Association, 1985; Comments: *I had two sons by a former marriage, and my older boy before he died also wrote poetry. Oliver, my younger son, is very talented especially in music. I write to express myself in a special way, to express my thoughts on love, beauty, nature and the everlasting creator, Jehovah God. I trust that my son Gary will renew his gift of writing in the resurrection. So be it.*

TO MY FATHER

You are my lifestream, the core of my body.
Your blood gives me the strength to improve — or maintain.
You are my teacher.
I am so naive, but your patience runs as long as the river.
You are my motivator.
If not for you I would be without desires.
You are my supporter.
You're always there to see me win, or to see me fall.
You pick me up when I am down.
You cleared the path so that I might be.
You gave me dreams, dreams that I might be somebody.
You are my friend. What laughter we've shared.
You are my companion.
I know throughout your life I will never be abandoned.
You are my father.
I love you with all my heart, and I'm proud to be your son.

Andy Spradling

THE FIRE WHOSE FORM IS WHITE

This is indeed a time of affliction
Singing the song of my pain.
The warrior angels surround me
Holy ones, luminaries, watchers.
The Illui souls . . . advanced students
Of the mysteries of God, full of genius.

The pure are distinguished by their
Knowledge of God.
They outrank one another
Only by the measure of their wisdom.
All who have become acquainted with the way
Exist deathless
In the midst of dying mankind.

    Finis
    Sent back to live
    Renewed, ascending.
    Every step upward
    an honor to be earned.
    A battle won,
    Despair overcome.
Mary Roe

ALOHA

My pulsating HEART tells me with a start
The TIME has come for us to part
For forty years you've been at my side
Now, SUDDENLY you are a BRIDE
You are to go YOUR WAY as I go mine
And only GOD knows when we'll meet again
In the vast 'Stream of Time!'
The years were wrought with TENDERNESS AND CHEER
The sorrow, aches and trials would all disappear
BECAUSE . . . You were always near.
I, too, now tread the BRIDAL Path
Praying: We both have found LOVES that last!
The future looms in rosie hue
Bringing promises of JOY to you
This, too, brings HAPPINESS to me
As through misty eyes . . . I peer . . . THINKING
I would gladly nominate YOU 'Daughter of the Year!'
Now, HEAR . . . as the TIME draws near
Take my BLESSING and LOVE to your HEART
FORGET-ME-NOT! Thus assuring us BOTH
That we shall NEVER . . . REALLY . . . TRULY . . . PART!
            ALOHA!

Mabel Lagerlof

A HYMN TO THE SUN

O sun, how great your brilliance,
How warm are your rays!
You bring the whole earth to life.
Every color is purer because of your radiance.

Shine, glow, gleam, encompass
    all around you.
What a glorious rainbow!
Darkness and shade are darker still
    because of your absence.

You call men to your light;
You bid them, "Look at me."
"Let your light shine for all to see,
Let the darkness and shade in your life
    be immersed in my wonderful light."

Yes, sun, hold me in your rapture,
Until I blend into your clear, pure light.

Behold the sun!
Sr. Elizabeth Mary Morales, C.S.JB.

CONFLICT

Immortal lake that seems to hear
I sense you know my deepest fear

Hypnotized without a doubt
As you allure I'm reaching out

Water stirs so ominously
Conflict nearing constantly

Ruthless lake I have engaged
Obsession lies within your grave

A drink from your nocturnal depth
Sets the stage for life or death

Pressure builds inside my heart
Self-control is torn apart

Hear me water — Hear me scream
I wish that you were just a dream

I fear you water — Fear your lies
As no one hears my desperate cries

Feel me water — Feel my strain
As I swim to shore again
Respecting always your domain

Joe Chiarello

WINTER CONCERT

10TH PLACE

That I
should be so old
and have
a son so young

continues to amaze me.

As I watch
you play your violin
on the stage
of the crowded gym

I see my life
as a forest whose trees
reach into white mystery
above your music

and your small light.

I hear
you coughing softly
before the applause.

Precarious and deep,
the pleasures
of snowy night.

Jean Musser

THE MASK

Her lilting laugh
Her friendliness
Dispensed to staff
And any guests

The office closed
Her audience on high
She shuts the door and
Looks Sorrow in the eye.

R. A. Okey

THE ART OF POETRY

The Art of Poetry
is a marvelous Art.
We poets write words together
till they sound in harmony.
We let our imagination fly
among stars of the radiant night.
In return, our thoughts come back
full of energy and color,
full of words, phrases and sentences
with meaning and devoted love,
with tears in sadness too,
but let me assure you
that love always prevails.

Alice Levy

LOVING HANDS

Strong, loving hands
Help fragile buds
Bloom into flowers of gold,
Allow admirers to see
Radiant colors so bold.
With the help of the sun
Plus spring and summer showers,
Beauty will flourish
And last through fall hours.
Tender, loving hands
Tend to the flowers,
These tender hands
Assist God's magical powers.

Susan M. Peglowski

EPPING FOREST

What do the trees know?
What do they breathe
Of the historic past?
What do they whisper
As the night winds blow
Before dawn comes, at last?

I wish I comprehended.
I wish they could share with me
The secrets they possess —
Simple assurance
Of exploits begun and ended
Under their watchfulness!

Frances Gillard Harvey

When we each said I love you
We were lying
Intensely entwined
In our tales we often told each other
We said sexual union could not take place
Without love
We couldn't go on any longer
So we broke contact
The love was there
With someone else
She could not make love
With me
She had her only love relationship
And if we rejoined
It would last an hour

Jeff McElhone

IT CANNOT BE

I tell you lad it cannot be
A boat that sails without a sea,
A king that reigns without a crown,
A circus true without a clown,
A forest green without a tree,
I tell you lad it cannot be,
A poet's soul not bold and free.

Look far and wide you'll surely see;
The symbols of God's unity,
In nature's plan some things must be,
The boat, the king, the clown, the tree,
The bard, all matched by God to show,
His purpose as a river's flow.

To serve, to rule, to pleasure give,
To grace the view with beauty green,
Send wisdom's words, a guide to men,
All graved on hearts with poet's pen.

Jack Williams

WILLIAMS, JACK. Born: Bronx, New York City, New York, 1-31-33; Education: Iona College, B.A., 1956; SUCE, Oneonta, New York, M.S., 1962; Seton Hall University and Fordham University, Post-graduate work; Occupation: Teacher; Memberships: NEA, NYEA, East Ramapo T.A., VFW, Knights of Columbus, Benevolent and Protective Order of Elks; Poetry: 'Two Old Men,' American Poetry Association, 1983; 'Cryin's Just Another Part of Lovin',' American Poetry Association, 1985; 'Below God's Earth for Freedom Lie,' 1984; 'Grandma,' 1983; 'Smile,' 1983; Comments: *I write to express and share inner feelings and thoughts regarding patriotism, love and personal observation. Within the realm of personal observation I include ideals concerned with religious and philosophical needs and desires.*

Your own happiness,
reflects back upon my heart
much like the mirrored pond
that captures the glow of the moon
to cast its cool radiance
upon calm gentle waters.

Doreen Lininger LoVette

EYES OF A GENERATION LOST

an eye and pupils staring into a face
the face with the rancid stare
a face that lifts the time into air
condensed into maggots and horseflies
a tiny face growing in outer space
an apple for the universe to save for eve
yawning into a crimson sin
pistoned with a simple core
aimed in penance and patience
fastened in starched-out readiness
and blinding are the laughing faces
as they grow together with siamese
protection talking themselves into
the madness of installed conversation
expressing their frightened assiduity
in ruinous constructive criticism
of that very face they call their own
that invisible eye that sent its pupil
out to find its vision gone

Vida M. Ron-Allex

AFTERMATH OF POETRY DEADLINE
Rondeau

The well is dry. When I am low,
Depleted of the things I know,
Sestinas scattered like sheep
Which normally inspire my sleep
No ballad sings to soothe my woe.

I cast for rhyme and meter, weep,
And fish for sonnets in the deep.
My bucket swishes to and fro.
       The well is dry.

I prime the pump and gaze below.
Where do the little quatrains go?
Or even leaky couplets seep
Where odes like fountainheads should leap?
No pen will scratch. No ink will flow.
       The well is dry.

Alice Morrey Bailey

HUMANS AND WARLORDS

Jerks are somersaulting.
Nincompoops are clapping and laughing.
Warlords are waiting,
Waiting and smiling
For the bell to toll
For testing inventions.
As they wait
They chew raw teeth
Impatiently for amber
To give way to green light.
In the interlude;
Virgins from Virgin Island
In cameo roles
Twisting perfect butts
Will appear
To offer doves and roses.
And as they exit,
They will pause to ask:
"Can you be humans for once?"

Nii Obli Armah III

SAY THIS TO YOURSELF

I am enjoying
a youth reborn
of old and good times,
once loved —
gotten out of the cardboard boxes
from the chest underneath my
bedroom windows
where winter looks in
wearing a coat of cold
over the clearly visible spring . . .
I can count
the days of the years, now,
with ease —
a simple matter of subtraction.
(the sun in the sky overhead
with the wind at my back)
and still, my breath
comes sharp
reminding me of ways
I knew I'd never forget.

Mark Wallinder

WALLINDER, MARK STEPHEN. Born: Sacramento, California, 4-8-57; Education: California State University at Sacramento, B.A., English, 1980; Occupations: State Office Worker, Part-Time Sales Clerk; Memberships: Associate member, National Writers Club; Awards: Ten Awards of Merit (Honorable and Special Mentions) from 1984 to 1985, World of Poetry Press; Poetry: 'Every Day,' American Poetry Association, March 1985; 'To My Unknown (and Waiting) Valentine,' World of Poetry Press, March 1985; 'Her Name,' World of Poetry Press, March 1985; 'Lisa Marie,' World of Poetry Press, March 1985; 'The Blue Station Wagon,' Poetry Press, September 1979; Comments: *I enjoy short poems that rhyme and have rhythm, though I do like longer free verse as well. Simple, upbeat subjects, particularly romantic love between a man and a woman are most pleasing to me, and I use my writing as a method of fulfillment and satisfaction with my life; I write to better understand and appreciate life.*

SOLITUDE I

The girl walks slowly towards the rocks
Looking constantly at the sea.
A light blinks on in a house
Down the beach
She notices,
As the water tickles her feet,
Coldly.

A chill runs up and down her
Causing her to quiver jerkedly.

She smiles and feels warm again
The clouds float into the moon overhead,
And, the stars shine where they have been.

She turns and starts back towards
The warmth of the fire
She has left to feel
Warmer.

It's getting light
The room is chilled
And, the fire is dying.

Bobi Jackson

OPPOSITES

Joy and pain
and sun and rain
   and all the good/bad opposites
    that make up a life
are abundant in our love.

The good I enjoy
all the more,
   knowing that too soon the
    bad will come again —
somehow it always does;

But the bad's not quite
so bad and I endure it,
   for the good must return
    eventually and then
everything will be worthwhile.

Our love is
has always been,
   joy and pain and sun and rain;
   and, my Darling, I really
wouldn't have it any other way.

Patricia Allen Simpson

ISN'T IT NICE?

This feeble attempt at poetry
Has to suffice,
For a deeper feeling of coquetry —
Isn't it nice?

If love could be expressed for real,
How would it feel?
Why is it so difficult to tell you now
When fantasies have told us how.

You have crept into my dreams
Bringing happiness unknown before.
Why with the dawning of the light it seems
It all has to be no more?

Now it is coming together at last,
And isn't it nice?
Forget the where or when of the past,
And maybe it will suffice!

Rose Tillotson Haslett

WINTER PRELUDE

In the cold winter dark
My feet move slowly through the snow,
The city lights reflect silently on the clear sky.
The air is clean with memories of a blessed season;
The utter stillness and quiet preserve that peace.
I notice how the barren trees are silhouetted against the moon
Stretching crooked limbs toward the midnight sun.
I am aware of how the noises of the city have diminished
And I am left alone to hear my own breath,
Listen to my heart,
Examine all that I have to be thankful for.
This cold serenity is a celebration
Of the living spring yet to come,
Reflecting the beauty of the season
And all of what the earth sings.
I am at peace.

Dennis L. Schrader

WHAT I WANT IN MARRIAGE

The man whom I shall marry must be patient and kind
With a heart full of love and a very keen mind.
He must never lose hope or faith in any way,
For united we stand and together we will stay.
I shall cherish him always since he's my number one fan
And to love him is to worship him in every way I can.
We will honor and obey the other one's wishes,
But when it comes to chores I'll let him do the dishes.
The two of us will walk hand in hand
Whether we're on a rock or down by the sand.
Both he and I have many ambitions
So until we part, we will stick to our traditions.

Dawn Hatanaka

SCHOOL DAYS

E Each year the time seems to grow shorter
F Forever dreaming with my past school days with you —
F Forever backward I really was
I In a school play, just we two.
E Ever so slightly I raised my eyes,
C Clear and lovely were your eyes so blue —
U Under a clear, cold, wintry sky
L Like your voice so soft and true.
E Each night I am yearning now,
Y Your voice I hear in my dreams —
M Many miles apart we now are,
A Although little messages between us beams.
S Slowly I read your letters, so kindly
S Saying words I love to hear —
E Each little note — between the lines
Y Your thoughts I hear, loud and clear.

Frank Hause

MOMMY TODAY'S MY BIRTHDAY

Mommy today's my birthday, do you think my daddy knows
I sure would like to see him it's been so long ago

I wonder what he's doing and what he's thinking of
Mommy please call daddy and tell him to come home
Mommy I want daddy back home again
I know that he needs us as much as we need him
Please call my daddy I just turned nine today
Don't wait too long I'll be grown and gone away

Mommy please tell daddy, I need to talk with him
I need to see him face to face, talk man to man

Please call my daddy I just turned nine today
Don't wait too long I'll be grown and gone away

Cindy Russell

LAKE SUPERIOR SONG

Ah, Superior, I heard your magic song
the first time I came over the hill
of Michigan's Porcupine Mountains,
and saw your clear moving water.

The secrets your clear waters hold
forever in the long ago and future,
the treasures your deep waters hide
from those who do not love you.

How many in the past have followed
your bright silver path of moonlight
that seems to climb up to meet the sky?
Their tears of disappointment are silently shed.

I sit and watch your waves come to shore,
and dream of fisherman in their canoes
their dark skin shiny and eyes alert
wondering when the snow demons will come again.

Your song is the lover that will call me back
to be healed by your neverending magic,
I know when I again come over the hill,
Superior, I will hear your magic song.

Lorraine Kolesar

CRESCENDO OF LIFE

In rhythmical movements —
The Crescendo of Life swells
    To breathe again the newness of awakening
        petals after a spring rain and
    To listen to gathering, white-capped streams
Cascading toward Nirvana!

Untiringly nature renews itself as the tide
    Rises and falls, swirls and turns
Toward boundaries beyond.

    In Adam's Fall
A new beginning evolved
Through the Triune God's Aspirated Love —
    The WORD spoken!

Tenderly in His Son's Oblation
God attends to Life and Hope for humankind,
    in the undulating patterns,
        Ebbing and flowing in the Wonders of Renewed Creation!

Each flower reawakens!
Each river regathers to a fullness!
Each person redirects and is set anew!

Sr. Madeleine Kisner

YAK FLAK, JACK?

Many of us know a person, let us call him Jack,
Who has recently experienced a heart attack.
Oh, the tests the doctors ran while Jack was on his back!
Upper and lower G.I.'s, B.P.'s, stress tests; no lack!

Hospital bills showed medicines must come by the sack.
E'en with medicare 'twas 'nough a bank account to wrack.
Before you're released for home, you listen to Doc's yak.
"Behave yourself! Maybe, tomorrow, we'll let you pack!"

You think, "I'll sleep better at home, — not all this flak.
My room will be quiet, no noisy bedpans a-clack!"
You'll find your mate and Doc put you on a rough track.
They've dreamed up diets and workouts for you by the stack!

Come on, old buddy, who wants bones and sinews that crack?
Build up your muscle tone with walks in and out of your shack!

Mervin L. Schoenholtz

WE DESTROY TO BUILD

We clear a forest
to build a small house
We drain the swampland
to dwell in condos
We scar mountainsides
With our scenic roads
Torture the landscape
when it's in the way.

A basic premise
A fundamental
that's soon forgotten
We destroy to build.

Man the destroyer,
Man the creator,
Create something new
Call me long distance
when you can destroy
an old home or road
for virgin forest
to begin anew!
Dave Buzzell

AFRICAN PRAYER
HONORABLE MENTION

The sand blows in
Like waves from the sea.
Shango,
Bring the rain
To drench the parched lands
Of Africa.
Wet the ten million
Burning throats
That dignify your name.
Make the savannahs bloom again.

Oshun,
Put milk
In the mother's shriveled breasts,
Save her famished child
Dying, quietly,
In the eye of the camera
For all the world to see.
Yee-ayee!
Mungu,
Africa is old and sad.
Frank Jethro

JEALOUSY

A gnawing fear — anger. Distasteful
unrelenting actions — antagonistic
rebellion — resentment and disdain.
Everpresent sneers, sarcastic remarks
and accusations, constant sullen de-
pressive antics of desperation.
Facial distortions, cries of despera-
tion, frantic gestures, forerunners
of shrewd manipulation. Hatred,
surprising adulation, incidents held
in obeisance detailed in vivid accusation.
Adeptly injected forked prongs, twisting
— sunk deep — manifested by cunning
contrivance violent in retreat. Inner
emotions uncouth, clawing, snarling,
spitting out blasphemy, a continuous
flow of barbs and untruths aimed to
purposely create disharmony. Caustic
inference — inuendo — manipulated to
impart, hurt and frenzy. Suspicions
— fantasy, affecting mind and heart —
frantic outbursts almost insanity.
H. E. Zuppert

I saw a butterfly . . .

In a cocoon . . . before it took to wing . . .
Its world surrounded it as a wrapping string.
In time Mother Nature set the captive free . . .
It took to the air for all the world to see.

I saw a butterfly . . .

Wings so delicate . . . they softly touched the breeze . . .
Weaving a pattern from flower to blossomed tree.
Pausing to place a kiss on a sleepy yellow flower . . .
Petals all dewy from an early morning shower.

I saw a butterfly . . .

Children enthralled at its beauty and fragile grace.
A look of wonder on each freckled face.
Arms open wide . . . running . . . chasing . . . without reward
As the butterfly playfully dipped and soared . . .

I saw a butterfly . . .

Anna L. Porter

IN MEMORY OF MY GRANDMOTHER

As I sit here meditating,
I find myself contemplating,
For there are many words I could write expressedly,
That would reveal how important my Grandmother was to me;

I love my family one and all,
But my Grandmother was very special since I was small;

When I met challenges along the way,
I could always depend on my Grandmother for guidance and an encouraging
word to say;

Her voice was strong, yet so gentle and flowing,
And when she gave her love, it was a feeling well-worth knowing;

Now that she's gone with God to the heavens above,
leaving behind a Granddaughter's love;

I treasure the memories of times we shared,
for I know I had a Grandmother who truly cared . . .

Kathy Sanchez

DIVERSITY

As a child
          I looked upon my parents as they served an example of forever
                    . . . when it came to loving.

So as it was
I believed it to be
          for all in love.
But in this time
     commitment has taken new meaning.
It seems once the knot is secured
                    ownership rules.
Many qualities adored of the other are overlooked too often,
                    too easily.
It's as though the fascination that drew you to each other's arms
                    is forgotten.
Till one day emptiness overrules . . . diversity sets in
               and the infalliable turn indifferent.

Forever for many is merely a dream.
Forever . . . I wish I never knew the word/meaning.
                    Maybe then, I could prevail without it.

Dawn Koontz

MICHELLE

You're warm and sensitive
Affectionate and bright
A fantastic mother
Everything that's right

You're a person
Definitely my type
I want to know you
To have you in my life

I want to take you dancing
To meet your family too
I want to do many things
Especially be close to you

I feel my emotions growing
I feel my heart swell
I want to have you near me
I feel we have much love

I wish I could hold you forever
I want you in my arms
To kiss, to hug, to be close to you
Or just enjoy your charms

Stephen J. Balich

BALICH, STEPHEN J. Born: Chicago, Illinois, 5-31-50; Married: 4-18-86 to Michelle; Education: A.A. degree, Moraine Valley, 1972; Real Estate Broker degree, REUS, 1980; Senior at St. Xavier Elementary Education; Occupation: Truck Driver, Student, Salesman; Poetry: poem published by American Poetry Society, 1984; Themes: *My feelings in relation to love, nature, society, and philosophy.*

SERENITY

Smell the musk of pine trees
Drifting over the lake at dawn
A faint touch of campfire
Not yet burning long

The sun crawls lazy over mountaintops
Dodging clouds along the way
The birds hunting breakfast
A chore lasting into the day

Between the sights and sounds and smells
It creates such a mixture
I could stay here for eternity
God, you paint such a beautiful picture

Terri Lee Cosgriff

yesterday

. . . yesterday

a brooding sentimentality
that longs to be destroyed
but somehow cannot;

a stream of dead images
attempting to invade the present
with its uninformed knowledge

but so far far away from the TRUTH,
the SPIRIT, and of course its strength —

i refuse to believe in the mistakes
and misfortunes of time gone by,
but rather i would look to see the future,

a future of constant moving change
a shining brightness of HOPE

a gaining of wisdom;

why must it come so late?

Lauren Osornio

OSORNIO, LAUREN ANNE. Born: Florida, 1946; Married: 1969 to Rafael; Education: Graduated Jr. College, 1966; Completed one year of Drama School at Boston Conservatory of Music; Occupation: Own a restaurant with husband; Poetry: 'words, etc.,' American Poetry Association, August 1985; Comments: *Life, its meaning, our purpose, our aspirations I find quite fascinating. I write about these ideas, and not unlike other writers, hope to find some answers.*

MEMORIES

I spent a magic summer
Three months of loving you
Every time I think of you
And the summer I was twenty-two
I remember loving you.

I spent a magic summer
I spent it loving you
And every time I think of you
I see your face and hear your voice
And I remember you loving me too.

Karolyn E. Evans

INDIVIDUALIZATION

I have taken a stand for what I
believe to be right; willing to
die the death, willing to stand
and fight.

Though there are many that oppose
my cause and claim, I shall stand
sturdy in my belief just the same.

The cross that I bear is mine and
mine only, despite the fact of this
journey, I am never lonely.

For my hope is of heaven, the
kingdom above, much higher than
the one in which flyeth the dove.

I express my feelings through my
poetic heart, but I truly believe
that the message, itself is the
important part.

Reginald Ector

LOVE IS A THIEF

Spring doesn't come anymore
Without you around
Summer's lost its fragrance
Winter's only cold
Morning brings no purpose
When it drops its dew
Nights mean only darkness
Life itself is old
Birds sing now to deafened ears
Now that you are gone
Flowers toss their color
To eyes that are blind
Aimless hours come and go when I'm alone
Leaving only time behind
My heart queries needlessly
Where went the song
Where went all the beauty
I enjoyed so long
Where went the purpose
That gave my life its hue
I know the answers
You took them with you!

Nina Doughty

THINKING OF THE PAST

Sunny skies overhead,
Music played inside my head,
I dream of days gone by,
I wonder what would have been,
And I wonder why?

Singing songs of yesteryears
Never to come again,
I think of what might have been
And cry for wasted years.

Years of loneliness,
Tears of pain,
Losing love,
Nothing gained.

Quiet times,
Solemn times,
Wanting them no more.
Watching my happiness,
Through a clouded door.

Rhonda Willis

BLAKE, Book of Job: Behemoth and Leviathan

I was sleeping one night —

my husband woke me, and said,
dear! what is that,
under our bed?

My eyes weren't open,
I was on my knees —
and at that time
I began to sneeze!

My husband said, dear,
what do you think?
I think I'm scared,
and about to faint!

He got up stumbling
                 around,
he ran over the cat,
that threw him down!
at that time, I was
back to bed bound!

I was OK but totally
                  all in,
I couldn't care less,
what happened — then!
He reached for the cover,
and tucked me in!

Lillie Van Ferauson

WINTER WIND AND BRANDY

I watched as my prize shrubs
Were reduced to stubs

And limbs broke from fir trees.

Tears made my eyes sting
I hated the East wind.

Then,

To calm the stress
Caused by the mess

I closed all the blinds
Made tea from lemon rinds

And frozen raspberries . . .

Then,

Added a spoonful
Of Cherry Brandy

Wondering if the bottle
Would last until spring.

Susan Hillman

I AM THE GIRL

I am the girl who never had a dime.
No one ever had the time.
No matter what I say or do;
It was always the same.
Some never knew my name.

"WHO is to BLAME?"
It is always the same.
I feel no shame.
It is just a game,
IF I had FAME;
EVERYONE would know my NAME.

Sylvia Harris

CAREER WOMAN

Blue flowers
Painted on white silk.
A cartoon of elegance.
Cheap perfume
Reeking of old movies,
And bathrooms.
She is stale from overuse;
Her love is a ruse,
Played like
An old joke
In front of a tired,
But eager,
Audience.
A smile,
Tried and true,
Will sometimes
Shine through
But fades quickly
Like
Flowers on silk.

Tracyene Charles

A GOODBYE LETTER TO MY LOVE

To say farewell is
        much more final than
            goodbye,
a monument to yesterdays
        when roses bloomed
            upon our love.

Graven images spill
        from my pen —
            bronze plaques
with words inscribed,
        mute testaments
            to this new-dug grave

still fragrant
        with life's hope.
            The old sun sets.
Long shadows creep
        across the page.
            I sign my name.

M. K. Taylor

THE GIFT OF LOVE

Love's a gift that cannot be kept
If you're to benefit,
Return it to the giver,
Then more and more you'll get;
You cannot keep it for yourself,
For then it'll wither and die;
but if you're willing to give it away,
It will continue to multiply.
You can't lose it when you give it,
For it'll come right back to you;
But if you try to take it back,
You'll see what I've said is true;
You must give it with all your heart,
In sincerity or not at all;
If the seed of love is sown carelessly,
By the wayside it will fall.
So, if you receive the gift of love,
Don't keep it for yourself;
Return it to the giver,
Or give it to someone else.

Jewel E. Witherspoon

THE EMPTY CHAIR

I gaze at its emptiness,
Loneliness engulfs and strangles
    The brightest night

Bringing my heart
To the reality of your absence,

As though you never were, yet,
I feel the presence of your soul,
    And know you were,

And are still,
Because I am here
Proof of your existence
Susan Sklarew

A MOTHER'S AGONY

My son — my son
Where are you?
I tried so hard.
How could you?
You were here
One minute.
The next,
You were gone.
Into that world,
Of drugs and pills.
Where did I go wrong?
How do I help you,
What do I do now?
Will you ever come back —
Only time will tell.
    Betty J. Weiss

This pretty wall of flesh and blood
    which doesn't seem to breathe, —
    how many times have lips and words
    pressed against its seams? —
    What mortal mortar holds together
    these soft and silent slabs of pain, —
    these mental-blocks which drive insane
    all who dare embrace it?

Wail away ye wicked world and
    weep to work no chink herein; —
    no engine has been fashioned that can
    penetrate her edifice; —
    no other vista will be glimpsed; —
    no promise of a holy garden;
    all who come are losers, — all, —
    all who love this quiet wall.
    P. B. Quinn

LAMP'S LIGHT

And when our fingers touch
    my heart leaps;
        wrapped against
            the winter cold
        love blankets
            our feet.
The flames of love
    may seem
        through years
            to fade . . .
            but our
        lamp's light
            aglow
                only strengthens
                    with age.
Pamela A. Nichols

226

APPLE TREE

Apple tree so tall,
proud of you now
A miracle so it seems,
those leaves of green
unfolding to their fullest
extension,
exercising with the puffs
and gust to keep strong
Northeastern winds playing
with the blossoms for they
know they may,
until petals, like children,
break off and float away
Emerging green crocus
little and bitter for now,
But the bitterness and shades
of green will change to
sweetness each day;
changing with the rising of
the sun . . .

Eugene J. Stewart

FINAL CURTAIN CALL

Before the final curtain call,
Lord you know I've played them all,
An infant in my mother's arms,
A child you sheltered from all harm,
A teenager at times perplexed,
Wondering what was coming next.

A young adult and on my own,
You never left me all alone,
A mother now would be my role,
To play it well would be my goal,
Years go by — you're middle age,
Life is going page by page.

How many more I cannot tell,
But you know Lord: You ring the bell,
Grandmother perhaps? Even old age?
The play is over, turn the page,
Lord now the final curtain call,
With your help I've played them all!

Gretchen Harrold

LIKE A TIMEX

Like a "Timex"
We take a licking,
But keep on ticking.

Life not all "Peaches and Cream."
Sadness filters into night,
Shutting out joy and delight.

Yet there comes the "Dawn"
A new day to begin,
We know not all to win.

Just like "Cinderella"
Getting ready for the ball,
There will be an end to it all.

Still we surge "Ahead"
Seeking the rainbow's end,
Always just around the bend.

Gerald L. Giuffra

ISOLATED MOMENT

I hurried, scurrying
throughout the barren night.
The somber silence was shattered
only by a futile fluttering
of indistinguishable discarded refuse
against confining bars.
My impending destination
impatiently awaited.

Accidently my glance touched them —
the two who disregarded
the stifling darkness,
the penetrating chill
which only hastened
my frantic footsteps.
I paused momentarily
and pondered wistfully
before plunging
once again
into consoling darkness.

Betty Kormick

WHAT IS LIFE WITHOUT HUMOR?

What is life without humor?
It's pressure-filled and tense;
It's fretting over little things
Which seem to make no sense.
The man who's unable to laugh
As he goes through each day
Feels every pothole, jolt, and rock
Along life's tough highway.
He turns, of course, to his nerve pills,
And finds, much to his grief,
That his tension still won't subside
Without comic relief.
It's not silly or foolish, and
It's not undignified
To let loose of tension, and in
A little fun abide.
Yet humor, like all other things,
Can hurt if overdone —
And tragedy is certain if
You laugh at the wrong one.

Edwin Hayes

I WANTED TO CRY

I wrote a poem when I was ten
    and won a prize;
            Great!

I wrote a short story when I was twelve
    and got an award;
            Superb!

I wrote a novel at sixteen
    and was offered royalties;
            Terrific!

I wrote articles for a national
    newspaper at seventeen;
            Prestige!

and when I got to college, I wrote a
    paper for my professor and got an
            "F"

Roger Carter

LOVE AND FRIENDSHIP

Love is the language of the heart,
That speaks without a word,
Without a voice or breath of sound,
No utterance is ever heard,
And yet within the silent tongue,
The heralds of love can reach,
The very chambers of the heart,
With their golden silent speech,
The touch of tenderness can speak,
What no words can ever say,
The warmth reflected from a smile,
A voice can never quite convey,
More musical than any song,
Of skylarks in the blue above,
The language of the heart reveals,
The full symphony of two people in love.

Linda Doan

THE PEARL

Waves pound secrets to the shores,
the ocean's mysteries sharply hurled.
Beneath her depths lie timeless pearls,
held in silence, trapped . . . obscure.
Dark and murky or crystal clear,
her vastness shelters an instilled fear.
Vessels sailed her endless miles,
in search of answers for the worlds.
She took her toll, or granted fare,
a sailor's fate was truth or dare.
The pounding continues, a constant roar,
a hush, a chant, a beckoned call.
Heaving past the mystic floor,
the centuries' past, becomes no more.
Escape is near, I feel her pulse,
at last a chance, to see . . . the pearl.

Connie J. Moore

MEMORIES

Erotic
        Winds,
Scented with excitement
Sweet violence,
                Yet
Devastating tenderness, yes
Dashing surfs,
Explode to shore cannons
Passionate volcano —
Trembling, yielding,
Ardent bewildering
Feverish bewitching pitch
Rampant sweeping emotions,
Warm golden embrace,
Tender seasons,
                Haste.
Doris Jackson Reynolds

HALLOWEEN — 1984

Hoblins and Goblins
and pumpkin-eaters
    it's Halloween again
Witches and Warlocks
and candy-treaters
    when children smile and then
'Mid laughter and kiddies
and the pumpkin-eaters
    'tis evil in the wind
For in candy wrappers
from candy-treaters
    is found the sharp straight pin.

Ed Morgan

TEENAGE DAUGHTER

A parody on Joyce Kilmer's "Trees"

I think that I shall never see
A girl as beautiful as thee.

Who clings to blue jeans so threadbare,
Trimmed with sequins everywhere.

Whose hair is frizzed in little curls,
Or some days gleams in waves and swirls.

Whose mouth is painted ruby red,
I wish a natural pink instead.

Whose lashes drip mascara black,
And eyelids never shadow lack.

A girl who may in summer wear,
Almost nothing everywhere.

And then in winter may appear,
In boots, short skirt, and scarf in hair.

I'm glad God made you just for me,
But only *Vogue* has fashioned thee.

Winifred H. Murray

FREE SPIRIT

It is to my merit,
That I did indeed inherit,
A very free spirit.

I am free.
I dare to be me!
I know what I want —
Don't ever say that I can't!

Please behold,
I cannot be controlled —
Nor can I fit into a mold.

My ideas are mine.
They are sublime —
Ahead of my time.

The likes of me —
will never with bigots agree.
All people — should be equal.

Too many pretend to care,
Too many are unaware.
I dare you to be —
Caring like me.

Mary Ann Puff

NOW THAT I'M A MOTHER, MOTHER

Now that I'm a mother, Mother
A new understanding has sprung
Between the one who is my mother
And the daughter a mother has become.

The eyes I used as a daughter
Through a mother's eyes now see
And my mother sees her daughter
As the mother she used to be.

Though my Mom is still my mother
Our relationship, I boast
Is as one mother to another
With friendship, foremost!

Linda A. Roberts

O COLORADO

O Colorado you keep calling me
With the mystery of your wilderness
And streams wild and free
O Colorado you're beautiful it's true
But with the job I hold and the place I live I can't get to you.

O Colorado where the mountains meet the sky
Where on a clear blue morning one might see an eagle fly
Where streams and lakes run crystal clear
Where one might sit for hours and watch antelope and deer

O Colorado you keep calling me
Even in my dreams at night your vision I do see
I see a small log cabin in your tall pine trees
I see your snow-capped mountains that fill my heart with pride
I see your wild elk grazing on your mountainside

O Colorado someday that's where I'll be
When I retire from this rat race working in this factory
I'll climb your mountains high and fish your streams wild and free
And then Colorado you'll stop haunting me.

Judith Ann George Hamp

CANADIAN ROCKIES

As the first soft notes of a sonata caress the ears
So the first glimpse of the faint grey shapes rolling on the horizon
Gave no hint of the crashing reality of the giants in stone so soon filling the eye.
As marching platoons, frozen in rock, rank giving way to rank
They surround me in regal glory.
My mind cannot comprehend their majesty
Nor my eye take in all their awesome beauty.
I am transfixed in space, one small speck of humanity
Humbled and insignificant.
If man is God's greatest creation why does he not stand firm and true?
Let him look at this magnificence and learn that he must.
Where are the words to describe the sights I am seeing?
I am mute and speechless.
Each glorious view gives way to another more awesome and inspiring
How can a simple pen make it real? Only the imprint on my mind
Shall be the true recorder of these most Godlike sights.

Mabel M. McCabe

McCABE, MABEL MONICA. Born: Toronto, Ontario, Canada, 8-20-17; Married: Roy Edgar (Ed), deceased; Education: Night Classes in Creative Writing and Art; Occupation: Retired; Poetry: 'Karma,' 'Memoriam,' 'Terri-Lynn'; Other Writings: *Out of the Darkness,* novel, in progress; Comments: *A great emotion of any kind will bring a spurt of writing. I have used this as a method of working off stress and anger or love. It is my escape hatch for troubled times.*

WE TWO ARE ONE

Looking through the window
The window of our soul
Seeing what we are hiding and burying within
Reaching out and touching
Teaching each other how to grow
Feeling and understanding
We are different but the same
We are as one as two can be
Sharing life in every way
Looking out the window
Searching for our soul.

Catharine Anderson

DESCRIPTION OF A POET

Poets are dreamers,
Workers and schemers,
They're a different diverse lot,
An ordinary kind of mind they have not,
Within there's patience, remembrance and gladness,
Mixed with empathy and sadness,
A touch of drama, warmth and madness,
Don't count them out until after
You see through the tears and laughter,
When all is written, said and done.
I know; because, I'm also one!

Louise McPhail

YOU AND ME

Our dear Lord has brought us together because we were
meant to be.
I for you and you for me.
There are special reasons for everything that happens
between you and me or to you and me.
We must stay together.
For my love you see
We were meant to be.
You hold one half of me and my heart as I hold one half
of you.
Now we are one because we were meant to be.

Honoria C. S. Weigum

FLOWER OF LOVE

The gloriously beautiful flower of love
Surely must come to us from above.
Real love will never fade
Even if marred by days of shade.
When the sun comes out things will brighten
And your true love will be there
With heartaches, sorrow, or love to share.
The flower of real love will always bloom
Growing more colorful and abundant
As the years roll by.
Always, with God's help, it will never die.

Lilah Piatek

FOREVER LOVE

Is it true that nothing lasts forever?
I wonder what it is that doesn't love eternity.
Is there a forever love?
My song is for you, wherever you may be,
For I shall always hold you in my dreams
until you show me your heart.
My melody will sing until we harmonize together.
I believe true love is forever,
and as long as I believe, I can dream.
For the dreamers are the lovers,
always the truest of lovers, forever.

Katy Holley

DORIAN GREY

Blatant, obvious, blunt,
Although covered by a curling wisp of gunsmoke
misty, but clear, cold, firm blue eyes
old but revived, smooth skin
Kind but despicable: a tyrant with a silky complexion
Small, shrunken, sunken-cheeked
        or tall, fit, well-fed
Wrinkles, pains inflicting a wretched body
Healthy, strong, the perfect man
        only one thing the same:
A small, pitch-black stone in the shape of a heart
        slowly crumbling,
            crumbling,
until ground to dust with evil
the dust getting finer and finer, taking color
then forming a shape of
A smooth, healthy body
        ground to dust
            crumbling,
                evil.

Ronit Kirchman

VACANT OLD HOUSE

How sad that a house was left "alone."
To withstand the storms of life,
Someone was there at one time or another,
Perhaps the family of a man and his wife.
The house looks very weather-worn
Where the paint has peeled away,
Hinges are missing on the door,
The gate has fallen clean away.
Dreams of building took some planning and
Caring for it over the years,
One's head had to be above water,
It took some blood, some sweat and tears,
There were voices once, now silent,
No pitter-patter of the feet,
The get-togethers must have been happy ones,
There was an end to those moments sweet.
We know not the story it tells us
Behind these withered gray walls,
Whatever has happened is concealed within,
We can only imagine, that's all.

Aili Edgar

LOVE LOST

Pounding in the wall
        behind her head,
    someone buried there, she thinks —
            an enemy of the former tenant —
    sends a shudder
        through the empty bed,
    mistaken
        for the long-awaited lover.
Screams leak
    through the ceiling's cracks,
    spatter the floor,
        then flooding, ebbing back,
        find rest within the pillow's recent chill,
            the indentation risen now
                but bearing soft
                    the scent of someone still.
Mid-twilight dreams
        of a mind beyond control —
        the pounding of a hollow heart,
            the crying of the soul.

Laura Aiken

LONG AND WINDING ROAD

For the past four years my road has been long and winding.
It makes me think there may never be a straight path to
anywhere. Though the road was rough, I've learned many
things. Those of courage, self-respect, pride and the
quality of peace of mind.

From the courage I use daily, I have the strength to
accept life's disappointments. With every accomplishment,
my reward is pride. My self-respect is steadfast. Having
learned all of this brings a quality of peace that is
undenying.

I know who I am, what I am about and who I'm going to
become. I know where I am and where I'm going. More
importantly, I remember where I came from. But when I look
back I see how far I still have to go.

Sandra L. Thomas

WHO'S HOLDING?

Jesus called, and
I answered; I gave him my all.
I was content, with my hand in His,
That burdens would lighten
And woes would scatter.
With my hand in His
The hungry I'd feed
And the lonely I'd visit.
I started out strong and inspired,
But I soon wearied and lost
All my strength in what I was doing.
I gave up, still holding His hand —
Then it came to me
As plain as day:
"Lord," I said humbly, "I'm slipping away;
Take my hand in Yours —
I'll be stronger that way!"

Russell C. Gillam

WAKING IN THE JUNGLE

I wake up to the sound
Of cannons tearing up the beach
Battering the ground, splintering the trees
For as far as the eye can see;
And I want to run and shout,
To scream out loud
In anger and defiance —
But O God!
All I see is the blood before my eyes
And the splattered body of a man.
And as I crouch and cry in the heart of Vietnam
I search hard to understand
The negation that about me lies
Asking myself the question:
WHY?
But the thunder of angry guns is the only reply
And the groans of men that live and die.

Joseph J. Falzon

JOYS OF THE MORNING

Oh, the joy to rise at dawn
And see the dew glistening on the lawn.
The chirping of the birds sounds so sweet,
And the rainbow colors in the flowers we greet.
The glowing sun as it begins to rise
Is almost more than we can surmise.
How can one but stop and say?
"Thank you dear Lord for this new day.
Now guide our steps as we go along
And in our hearts may we carry a song."

Maxine Johnson

PRAYER

Our Father,
spiritual Father of all life
in the universe.
Thy celestial home tops infinite space.
May our mouths speak Thy name
with birth awe and baby gentleness.
Diamond light the earth with Thy select rulers
that we may serve Thee with lives of love.
Let Godly wants and needs be supplied
by faith.
Awaken our souls to wash away annoyance
and quicken friendships.
Keen our minds;
anoint our eyes with spittle clay.
Focus our thoughts
on the Millennial Color Spectrum:
that great and glorious time
of Thy Kingly Coming
to black out evil
and baptismal whiten the earth.

Charlotte L. Seward

SEWARD, CHARLOTTE LOUELLA. Born: Bode, Iowa, 7-15-11; Married: 1-11-41 to Herman Neitzel, deceased; 11-20-77 to Maynard G. Seward, second husband; Education: Mankato State University, Elementary teaching Degree, 1933; Have taken additional courses, correspondence courses in writing also; Occupations: formerly Teacher, City Assessor's Helper, Clerk; Memberships: Southern Minnesota Poets' Society, League of Minnesota Poets, National Federation of State Poetry Societies, Inc.; Awards: First Prize, poem, Naperville, LDS Stake Church Conference, March, 1985; various other prizes, Church contest, Minnesota, 1960's; 'Departed Husband,' Relief Society Conference, LDS Church, March 1985; 'Live Bells of Spring,' *Golden Anniversary Anthology*, League of Minnesota Poets, 5-12-84; 'Sun Faith,' *Eternal Echoes*, 1981, also published in *Farmer Magazine*; Comments: *I write poetry to share experiences, reveal innermost thoughts; try to make the reader think more deeply. (Also to avoid psychiatrist; keep my mind active; search for truths). I try to express optimism, my philosophy of life, make life more beautiful for others. I have also written children's stories.*

I WILL ALWAYS LOVE YOU

I wish that I could make this wish of mine come true.
Wishing upon a star I wish for you.

I wish I could hear your voice each and every day.
I wish you were here with me always to stay.

I wish I could hold your hand right now and never
let you go my love, that's my vow.

My heart has a special love that's rare and true
and it's the kind of love I want to share with you.

Karen Rando

WIND

I see the leaves falling
As the wind blows free
It sounds like someone calling
Is someone calling me?

The howling and the rustling
all the night through
It sounds like someone talking
Maybe they're calling you.

If you listen closely
As the wind begins to blow
Someone's talking hoarsely
To their loved ones below.

You hear the people talking
Of the time they cannot spend
To be together laughing
That's the purpose of the wind.

Joyce Snow

GARCIA, JOYCE SNOW. Born: Richmond,
California; Married: 12-20-75 to Raymond
Garcia; one daughter, Jennifer; Occupations:
Secretary for State Farm Insurance; Com-
ments: *The poetry I have written over the last
14 years has been inspired by people I've known
and also the Vietnam war. I only hope, if I have
touched anyone with my poetry it will inspire
them. I want to thank my mother for giving me
the love and encouragement to write.*

SYMMETRICAL PATTERNS

I was a mother one daughter 2 sons
circled my legs
the dog shed in season.
I am a woman one daughter 2 sons
part-time away from home
The dog is dead.
Seasons do not wait to change
despite it all as if bored with family
matters. I cannot call back
lost seasons. I cannot redo the weaning.
Instead, I marvel at signs
of mutations despite the draught
these last several years.
Smells of spring awaken memories
dead in winter snow, the echo
of harvest time waits up ahead
despite a nagging feeling that
the seeds did not take root.

Lois H. Young

MY WITS ABOUT ME

I stand here thinking for a bit,
Attempting not to throw a fit,
Seeing the light where it is lit,
And wondering if I should sit.

Sitting alone here where it's bright,
The world sometimes gives me a fright,
But I know that I am all right,
As my fears fly into the night.

As long as I'm here, time is mine,
And though I sit and though I pine,
I find that I am really fine,
As the clock in the hall strikes nine.

The people here are really kind,
Though things around me they do bind,
And it's with regret that I find,
I really can't control my mind.

To me the world is so hazy,
My sight clouded and quite dazy,
It's not really that I'm lazy,
It's just people think I'm crazy.

Ronald Dale Ziegenhorn

ONE GOLDEN DAY

Spring smiled,
    Summer sped.
Autumn lingered,
    Winter's dread.

What now is vague,
    once was clear.
Past events,
    memory's dear.

Ending soon,
    what just began.
Life closes,
    her weary hand.

Silver head and
    dreaming eyes.
Muttered words and
    weary sighs.

What is left,
    along this way?
With dawn began,
    one golden day.

Lorraine C. Malone

COLORADO RECYCLE

My grandma feeds a strand of pine.
The piñons pass
Through chipmonk
Into grass
Which feeds some grazing kine.

Who belch and chew throughout the night,
And somehow,
Through miracle
Agreeable to cow,
Turn fibrous green to liquid white.

The cows, facilitated by the moon
To combine
Grandma, chipmonk,
Grass and pine,
Feed the seedling in my womb.

Marion Joyce

*Inspired by a wide, shallow stream
in Saguaro Forest, Arizona*

*The stream flows on,
Rejoicing
In the form and color of
Every pebble and stone
Over which it passes.
The sunlight,
Striking sparks
From each rivulet
As it seeks out
The myriad small forms
On the sandy floor.
The traveler
Finds exhilaration
In the quick movement
Of the shining water,
And refreshed
Walks on.*

Ann Mast

THE PRINTER

If praise or gripe is set in type
    it lives 'til time's expired.

If we take a pill or pay a bill
    there's printing that's required.

Forms of praise, in many ways,
    he's made to give to others.

His name with fame we should proclaim
    and honor all his brothers.

For his presses run in summer sun
    and through the cold of winter,

And a nation's trend might well depend
    on the noble name printer —

Ken Drake

INSULARITY

We are
icebergs,
craggy mountains
swimming
in our watery wombs,
each mind computing its own
equations.
Some,
you and I,
draw beauty
as a magnet,
its bright lightness
rises up the
mountainside,
into illumination,
to let us share
with brother
and sister,
joy from the mountaintop.

Gretchen Snyder

MOTHER

How can tongue or pen herald the news to men
Of thoughts our minds have told,
Or cares our hearts can hold,
Just at the one word — Mother!
It often comes to me that as I sit and dream,
My Mother thinks of me,
And in each rippling stream
I see her face — my Mother!
In white clouds near and far, where crowds of people are,
No thought can change or mar
The one I hold so dear:
I feel her presence near — Mother!
When I have gone through strife and met both death and life,
The one who is always near,
My fainting heart to cheer
And chide my hunting fear is — Mother!
So when life fades away and I find brighter day
Than Earthly spheres may know,
The one who'll guide my path will be
The one who is so dear to me — my Mother!

Ruth G. McAlley

WE GOT TO STOP FIGHTING

   People are laughing all over the world,
trying to have a good time. But at the same time,
little boys are abusing little girls; messing up their
minds. Mothers talk to your daughters before they
go out to play.
   Fathers don't hesitate to teach your
sons, that there's a better way. We got to stop
fighting; it's not exciting. We can change this world
into a better world, set a good example for our little
boys and girls. We got to stop fighting.
   Wives, you already know what to do. If
you want to hold onto your husbands, smother
them with love, just like they do you. You see
people every day, drinking whiskey or wine.
   They end up hurting or killing each other,
trying to have a good time. Ladies talk to your
boyfriends every day; remind them, whiskey or wine
will only get in their way. A war is going on, neither
side will confess, but both sides are wrong. We got to
stop fighting, it's not exciting. We got to stop fighting . . .

Johnnie J. Mickell

GRAN

She was a wonderful lady with a
lot of love.
She was a sharp old lady, hard to
put one over on.
She was forever dusting and picking
up after everyone.
You could never get her to rest.
She hated being sick and dependent
on anyone.

She knew that she was really loved
by her family.
She loved life to the fullest.
She worried about everyone being too cold
or too hot.
She'd sneak in and cover you up at night.
She spoiled her grandchildren and
great-grandchildren with love.
She was a very special woman to me.
I loved my Grandma very much and miss her a lot.

Anne V. Brady

I ONLY KNOW

When I first met you,
I didn't know anything of you;
You tell me you love me
I only know that I love you, too.

When I fell in love with you,
I learned to love with all my heart;
A lover and a friend, I wanted to be,
I only know that I miss you, when we're apart.

I don't know where you go,
Or, where you've been;
I don't know what you do,
I only know that I love you.

You tell me you need me,
Then, you treat me mean;
You're the most fascinating
Man I have ever seen.

I promised to ask no questions
You'll tell me no lies;
I love cheery hellos
But, I hate sad goodbyes.

Sandra Spencer

TO LIVE TO SEE

Such enjoyment watching sunrise or sunset
Or watching velvety snowflakes as they fall
Ah, but there is one very special thing
I would like to live to see most of all

The ecstasy watching little children
So carefree, laughing as they play
Ah, but there is one very special thing
I do hope to live to see one day

Deep contentment watching mother smile at baby
Watching stars dancing as they shine
Ah, but there is one very special thing
I hope to live to see sometime

The gleam in lovers' eyes, or flowers in bloom
Or summers' gentle rains softly fall
Ah, but there is one very special thing
I would love to live to see most of all

Watching oceans' waters curling into waves
And cottony clouds polka-dotting blue skies above
Ah, but the very special thing I hope to live to see
Is the hate in the world turn to everlasting love.

Mary Joan Raymond

A TESTAMENT OF FAITH

Faith is courage just up from its knees;
Faith listens for a Voice in the dark . . . and answers;
Faith puts out its hand in the night
    confident there is a Hand there to touch.
Faith believes without evidence;
Faith watches the sun go down with the assurance
    that it will rise tomorrow;
Faith is a conviction that the road ahead
    is not a dead end;
Faith sees in the thin sickle of the new moon
    the glory of its fulfillment;
Faith is the spark that lights the darkness
    when the last match has flickered out;
Faith knows that behind the storm cloud
    is the rainbow, beyond the mist there is a star;
Faith is the wonder that comes with the sudden
    and overwhelming conviction
    that you KNOW there is a God.

Ruby A. Jones

A MORNING CUP OF COFFEE

You left your coffee sitting in the morning sun
on the window sill above the sink;
Untouched.
I found it,
An oily cloud of film crawling like a languid snake
on its muddy surface.
Was it too bitter?
I'm sure —
You never did make a good cup of coffee.
I've tried to tell you
that cream and sugar
softens the blow.

Why?
Why did you leave it,
after taking one deep, raw, burning drink,
on the window sill
in the vague morning shadows
to mellow in the sun
without you?

Jeanne Kennedy

FAIRY TALES

Whatever happened to knights on white horses
Beautiful ladies with long golden tresses
To armor-clad heroes who went and slew dragons
Who chased off the villains and saved all the maidens.
What happened to cowboys with stars on their chests
Riding into the sunset way out in the west
Wearing white hats and wearing white vests
Always winning the ladies because they were the best.
Were they just tales, a thing of the past!
Were they sadly destined never to last!

Where are the captains who sailed with the breeze
Capturing pirates out on the high seas.
The posses and good guys on marvelous steeds
What about lost islands and deep buried treasure
Where swashbucklers dueled and gave measure for measure.
What happened to six-shooters and newspaper hats
Building a tree house and floating on rafts
Were they just tales, a thing of the past!
Were they sadly destined never to last!

Francis E. Tevault

EUCALYPTUS

Ever wonder how a tree feels?
Able to stroke the face of clouds
but not to stride hills, valleys, rivulets.
Breathing in the scampy winds —
savoring small messages they've brought —
yet knotted to the earth.
Call me Eucalyptus —
gum on my finger tips
and knots of starlings
cluttering my hair.
My bottom aches sitting here —
and temperate I'm not.
Snap at my love.
She knows the ankle hurts.
At least three months the doctor said.
Tree on hill opposite
Was there at time's unraveling.
May be when I go away.
Three months and I may walk.
But, the tree must stay.

Robert D. Warren

PIANO BAR II

I was the center of attraction at the ritz
I wanted all the publicity I could get
I was grand in Hollywood
I played the piano like no one could

Everyone knew me, they wanted to shake my hand
They called me the Piano Man
I was quickly becoming one of the best in the land
The owner of that piano bar gave me my chance

And I've put the music world in a trance
My career is moving so fast
Only time will tell how long it will last
But now I'm enjoying my successes

It feels great to be one of the best
Standing head and shoulders above the rest
Oh what a conquest yes

Mitchell Beamon

TZIGANE

Steal like a panther across the plains
　　　　　in the dead of night
Wagons creaking softly, following in caravan
Hoping to reach the sheltering mountains before
　　　　　　　Dawn unveils you to the world.
The Moon in her fullness shines brightly in the sky
Outlining your shaggy silhouettes, so lithe and black
Adorned in gold and silver
Your realm is Terra
Your throne the road
　　　No wall to restrain
　　　　　your wandering spirits.
Lupine eyes reflecting the flames of
　　　　　　a thousand camps
A thousand destructions;
Yet in those eyes burn the fires of youth
So joyous and free
Like the winds of Eternia,
　　　　　　　Timeless.

Keith Waters

CHORAL VARIATIONS FOR A LONG NIGHT

My words have sinister intentions.
They have been hired to kill me
although the identity
of their employer is unclear.

They whisper of my death,
and parody my fear
while smiling through the darkness
like a half-remembered dream.

Assembling in sentences and paragraphs,
they begin to hum and scheme.
Swelling into bibles and cantatas,
they disrupt the neighborhood and keep me up all night.

They brazenly chant the story of the end of my life,
an assassin's choir with a concert to complete.

Robert Gerstenlauer

REGRETS

Damn, it was always just a convenience,
    playing a classic game.
Waiting each other out,
    seeing who would be the first to leave.

I never wanted anyone to need,
    or depend on.
No one to answer to, or care for,
    but it was so easy to do with you.

You really have no idea what you meant to me,
    and still do.
My feelings are those of hurt and rejection,
    I miss you.

I am so fulfilled,
    because you've loved me.
And so empty,
    because you've left me.

Now the affair is over,
    and so is our friendship.
Quite a price to pay,
    for a mere infatuation!

Connie J. Thiessen

THE GENERATION GAP

You wouldn't like it, it's not your style,
Our acid rock, beats your music by a mile.
You didn't invent it, as you will see,
Come along girls and listen with me.

Our hard rock music was pretty wild,
You might find yours, the one that's mild.
Amid laughter and sures, to my records we went,
Their tender young ears, were going to get bent.

Their mouths dropped open, and eyes grew wide,
While my music played, I beamed with pride.
The wild sounds assaulted their ears,
and I moved to music, I hadn't heard in years.

Today's music, was not as new as they thought,
Compared with records in the sixties I'd bought.
Mother's not as old as she seems,
She's had the same thoughts and teenager's dreams.

The gap was closed for a while that day,
While mother's music had its say.
The generation gap is nothing new,
for every person born, it will come due.

Virginia R. Cox

HONORABLE MENTION

Lying there so beautiful,
So innocent and half asleep, lips parted.
So young to have accomplished so much.
Who are you
    that I should give myself to you so freely?
Lying here next to you, watching your face
    knowing how long I will love you —
I will always love you . . .
and wondering how much of me you will remember
    five years from now.
Wondering if my name will cling to your mind.
Whether my face will ever haunt your memories,
and I smile to myself at my daydreams.
Looking at the golden expanse of your back,
    the tousled hair
smelling the sweet scent of intermingled bodies
and wanting to hold you
    and cry.

Wisia Kaliszczak

PROGRESS

Men call it progress. Progress?
To build up nuclear armament,
While testing poisons in the atmosphere,
No matter few or hundreds, (men pay a price!)
Are forced to lay down their lives,
So that the Majority may live;
To spread Contamination far and wide,
At the behest of Mr. & Mrs. Richer poor.

Don't ask me for Solutions!
You were given long ago.
Super powers at each other's throat;
America the stronger be,
Shall soon as dragon fully speak;
Till the one power mightier than she,
Descending the unparalleled majesty,
Ends this indefinite paradox.

Lennard Swain

LAUGHTER

Laughter is truly man's greatest blessing,
    We should take a large dose each day.
In this world of things deeply depressing,
    Hearty laughter we should display.
But how can we laugh when the things we see
    Are trouble and pain? Joy like chaff
Is dispersed by the winds, blown far and free,
    Now how in the world, can we laugh?

We know laughter as a health-giving aid
    Is the best medicine on earth,
And we search this world, for humor displayed,
    For a belly laugh has great worth.
Yes, a good laugh will rise higher than high,
    Will climb to the top of the graph;
But with terror rampant under our sky,
    Now how in the world, can we laugh?

Kenneth C. Duncan

SALVATION'S SWEAT

Begone — cockles of my heart — I haven't a rabble to rout;
Sagacity is lost! The blandish of a bistoury is chafing me
with death.

Walk with me — O comely transparent thought — I need a bit
of breath. The fescennine snit of Satan's sheath has startled
me back to sense.

                Yaw my eyes and placate my soul —
                a motion to object — (the knife,
                which caressed my sight) — because,
                the vision was of potty portance.

So glad you are here — a shimmering sun — it is as though today
is an antediluvian dream. Now, (the light) it shines so
clear — in life — we are a beam.

Rebecca L. Raven

I HAVE BEEN HERE BEFORE!

Your sex sickens me!
It is redundant
Overindulgence sends out its own degenerate odors;
Odors that break the structures of beauty.

The fetid aura hangs about you as
you move to touch me — take me as you
have taken a thousand times before.
Within, I sense your disease would become mine — I must go!
Creation died so long ago with you.

Rhea

MY SISTER

When I was young my sister and I shared
     a room, a bed, the household chores . . .
       a name.
We also shared in what only women can share,
     the oneness of marriage, the birth of children.
    We have been so richly blessed.
Yet, when I think about our relationship, it is
     not the closeness I have experienced with others,
        the long talks, dreams, pillow fights,
        just plain fighting —
            we just did not have.
Now that we are older, although age mellows us all,
     we are not close, our relationship is strained
     almost cordial. I feel uneasy, we share,
     we talk at each other — not to each other.
Maybe I have not given it a chance.
Maybe I blame our differences on our age difference.
Maybe I feel we could not both be right all the time.
Maybe I should tell her I love her, just once.
Maybe . . .

     Janet Palmieri Brinker

DICKENS, CHARLES THE POET, THAT IS

HONORABLE MENTION

You're not answering my question
    I said, surely you have no objection
To my opening this window, do you?
    And you paid no attention, as though
You hadn't heard
    What do you mean, I paid no attention
What do you take me for?
    An out and out quarrelsome person?
Feel free, open the window whenever you wish
    Such a question, propounded
In such a manner, at such a time
    In fact, I meant to do it myself
When I came in, or
    I shouldn't have allowed it
You know that
    Feel free, open a window, put
A log on the fire, bring me a bouquet of flowers
    Whenever you wish. My beloveds
My dearly beloveds, my dearly dearly beloved.

    E. A. Bach

KITCHEN SINKING

Making peanut butter sandwiches — with jelly,
Just about to close the issue, case, sandwich,
I paused

To watch flickering images, stopping and starting,
Weighted in thick, sludgy peanut butter,
In thick weighty peanut butter,
Of you and me, of us.
And dull-edged knife in hand
I cut

The dead-end crusts away, out of the way,
And watched our flickering images,
Me with sticky hands, you with sticky feet,
Quagmired in living
On our cut-away peanut butter raft.

Making peanut butter sandwiches — with jelly,
Just about to close the issue, case, sandwich,
I paused.

    D. Bakker

RIDING THE CREST

The old man was bent like the cane he used,
    Knotted and gnarled and bowed.

Age in his eyes and lines on his face were
    Ruts of a well-travelled road.

Pain-gripped legs that had once been strong,
    But broken at the height of his youth;

His jaw hung slack and matched the twisted back,
    He had only one arm he could use.

Yet as evening approached and the clock struck five,
    He'd work his way to the little dive
        On the opposite side of the street;
Have a few of his favorite brew, maybe a bite to eat,
    Then go back to his one-room shack,
        Defying the heavy traffic again.

When I asked him why, he got a gleam in his eyes,
    Grinned a toothless grin.

"I've been a gambler all of my days,
    Lived and loved dangerously — saw life at its best.

A man *needs* a challenge to ride the crest, and those cars

    Are
        The
            Only
                Game
                    Left."

    Madeline Cooper

COOPER, MADELINE A. Pen name: MacKenzie Cooper; Born: Espanola, New Mexico, 5-11-37; Married: 12-6-57, to Kenneth Cooper; Education: Mesa Community College, AA, 6-70; Additional course work at Arizona State University; Occupation: Technical Writer; Poetry: 'Mirage of Promise,' American Poetry Association, 1984; Other Writings: "Twelve *Weeks Without A Song*," *Woman's McFadden Group*, 1985; Comments: *My writing deals with the perplexities of life. It is serious in nature and displays subtle undertones rather than morals. I write because I cannot keep from writing and have written several short stories and one novel as well as numerous poems. I plan to retire in northern Arizona and write full-time.*

JOHN

With Love, Mom

Graduation day is surely here,
Challenges are ahead, with new goals, my dear.
Lift up your heart to God as you're seeking,
He promises to lead you, and hold in safe keeping.

Pursue your dreams with faith abound
Until your goals you have boldly found.
Grasp in your heart the "Only Word"
and He will teach you words, you have never heard.

You are strong and brave with a heart full of love,
Have courage, keep hope and look above.
We love you and cherish the time as your guide,
Look around and upward and in His love abide.

Be faithful and sincere, whatever is done,
Climb the high mountain, until your prize is won.
You are loving and honest and kind at heart,
and our love for you shall never depart.

Joyce Shoup

SONG OF LIFE

Let us skip the path to playland.
Let us hear the singing birds.

Let us straddle the logs and balance on the rocks.
Let us giggle and roar with rumbling, comforting laughter.

Let us gather wood for the good fire.
Let us sip the rich wine in silence.

All things reach for the goal of excellence.
Give time a chance; time, our closest friend.

Grasp the meaning of forgiveness.
Hold on to the magic of the night
     while stars brightly sing the song of life!

Barbara J. Brown

BROWN, BARBARA JUNE. Born: Tulsa, Oklahoma, 1-7-34; Single; Education: UC Santa Barbara, B.A., Education, 1962; Occupation: Teacher; Memberships: NEA, CTA, FCEA, AARP, SMC; Awards: Blue ribbon, poetry contest, for 'The Visitor,' 1976; Poetry: 'Essence of Love,' American Poetry Association, 1985; 'The Visitor,' Folsom Cordova School District, Sacramento County, 1976; Comments: *My poems express the depths of my soul and what I long to experience. As I look at life my view is steeped in romantic involvement and passion. I write with fire and pain.*

RESONANT WITH A STRANGER

(Vibrating — Pulsing — Throbbing)

I saw you standing there,
Drawn by a strong magnetic impulse
Brazenly I took a chance
And asked you to dance.

The instant we stepped into each other's arms
Our wills were not our own.
Swiftly we moved into a new time zone.
It felt as if our bodies and souls harmonized.
We swooned and swayed.
Oh, the beautiful tricks our minds played.

We felt love, peace; happiness — we felt ecstasy
Forgetting where we were and whom we were with
We embraced and made love to each other with our minds.
Resonant! A once in a lifetime.
The lights coming on brought us back to reality.

Slipping from your arms — embarrassed,
But filled with a strange delight
I hasten and hide in the night.
Not understanding this suspenseful experience
But always to be a blissful remembrance.

Madeline Reynolds Martin

MARTIN, MADELINE REYNOLDS. Born: Detroit, Michigan, 11-4-36; Unmarried; Education: G.E.D., June 1981; Occupation: Resident Care Aide VB (Supervisor) on male admission unit, Psychiatric Center; Poetry: 'Who Am I,' changing my windows into mirrors, American Poetry Association, May 1982; Comments: *When I write, words flash through my mind, rapidly, any time, any place. Sometimes I get inspirations from personal experiences, from other people, or just from dealing with life on a day to day basis. I truly hope I'm being used as a messenger, from a higher source, to bring a word of hope and laughter to someone. I dedicate this poem to "John" where you are.*

THE LIGHT OF HIS LOVE

The light of His love shines in our dark paths,
As He touches our heart to soothe its wrath.
When the whisper of His breath has reached our soul
Then the light of His love has reached its goal.
So, in ending the darkness, a new light begins,
As we find our happiness in Him, once again.

Lee Anne Dorey

OH, SUNSET

Oh, sunset, talk to me,
Whisper words of serenity to my soul.

Tell me how to love a friend,
Tell me how to live again,
Tell me how to know myself,
    and to show myself the simpler things in life.
Oh, tell me the meaning of love.

Oh, sunset, wait for me,
Do you know how it is to be so alone?

Show me how to forget pain,
Show me how to ease the strain,
Show me how even your light
    fades into the night to live again tomorrow.
Oh, show me the meaning of love.

Oh, sunset, thanks indeed,
For sharing your beauty with me, and your love.

Randall Paul Buchanan

CHRISTMAS — HAPPY AND SAD

Traveling, smiling, so glad you could come.
Giving, singing, such good food, here — have some.

What a jolly good time, but not for all.
Cold, hungry, why mommy? No gifts at all?

Sorry, dear, no money; maybe next year.
Merry Christmas and a Happy New Year!

Come, all ye faithful, to Mass at midnight.
Snow from heaven — what a beautiful sight.

Elderly, shut in, tired, sick, alone.
Praying: Lord, come; bring me to my new home.

Elsewhere a reunion that's not quite right.
It's Christmas Eve, you know, please don't fight.

Too much drinking, arguing, drunk driving.
Speeding, skidding, colliding and dying.

Louise M. Verrette

SAY GOODBYE

I can't take this any longer.
Please help me grow stronger.

I can't face another fall.
That's why I built this wall.
It's thick and it's tall.

Please go away, I have nothing to say.
You left me numb, and now you're back.
Where did you come from?

Do you do this purposely?
Do you find it satisfying to hurt me?

You say you love me, then remove this pain;
That starts like thunder, lightning, then rain.

It's over, and don't turn around and look.
Because the emptiness you'll see;
is the piece of my heart you took.

Jennifer Knoll

MYSELF

I journeyed far to find a lasting star and when
I thought all hope was lost, I found it always
was inside my heart
I remember closing my eyes to its warmth, to the
peace and happiness that it could give
With each encounter of fear that took my sight, I
chose to stumble the long way home
I ran up against the dragons and built the towering
walls but they kept rushing in
As I forgot the most important one
I took the steps without really feeling and the gift
that was mine to have, was taken for granted
When the star began to dim
I fought hard to win it back and the battle was worth
the struggle
For in the end I found myself
Helen C. Calogredes

LOVE'S RECIPE

What is love but a near miss
from loneliness; haphazardly or purposefully,
the seed is planted,
lies dormant,
is cast aside — blighted by neglect,
is nourished; slowly or rashly,
slow, consistent growth
safe from trauma
ensures survival — itself a risk.

Even those saplings well-attended
still subject to changing adverse conditions,
Love — at one time thrives;
one day lacks a single ingredient
needed to flourish,
fades, grows faint, sighs, expires.
Claire S. Tarantino

SEMINATION

In the fresh-turned, fertile earth
The rounded mounds, the crease of furrows — open,
Like the secret crease between
The soft yielding thighs of a woman,
Open — the earth, the womb, receives the seed of planting.
Loving hands smooth the soil closing the furrow.
The secret dark womb holds the seed delicately,
Deliciously, nurturing; the seed draws life from the soil,
From the mother, earth; they feed the new life.
The seed changes: opens, grows, becomes
The embryonic being.
So like the mother/father
But is itself; its own being.
Life breathed into the planted seed.
Whose breath?
The gardener's choice; the planted seed.
Theresa A. Kruse

FOR DEBBI AND LAURI: WITH LOVE

Two seeds once planted in a row,
fertilized with love and care.
to watch two lovely flowers grow,
a gift from God to share.
they bowed and danced beneath the sun,
a treasure to behold;
so close together — more like one,
as their petals did unfold.
One flower bloomed for eighteen years . . .
the other two years less.
While others wilt with pain and tears . . .
God's Kingdom they possess.
Stephanie O'Neal

ALONE ON SUNDAY

Happy sounds from the street below
    To my window flow
Of children at play,
    Sunshine and Youth's laughter gay.
I am alone, it is Sunday.
Old couples married happily,
    Dressed nattily,
Will visit friends today.
    While young lovers, Love's game play.
I am alone, it is Sunday.
Companions, trees and grass,
    Togetherness, lad and lass.
Rarely their paths sway,
    As most in pairs find the way.
It is Sunday, I am alone.

Leroy L. Moses

PROTEST

A shriller tune
The crickets sing
At autumn's close
With bird to wing.

To endless sleep
Approach does seem
Insect protest
To winter dream.

Linda Van Scyoc

VAN SCYOC, LINDA JANE. Born: Indiana, 1-10-51; Married 8-27-72 to Fredric (Ric) R. Wilcox; Education: Ball State University, Bachelor of Science, 11-72, Master of Arts, 8-74; Occupation: Teacher, Secondary Education; Awards: 'Visions,' a collection of haiku, 1985, American Poetry Showcase Poetry Contest; Poetry: 'Visions,' collection of haiku, American Poetry Association, 1985; 'Choice,' American Poetry Association, 1985; Other writings: "Ask, The Advertising Survival Kit," (co-authored), a guide to advertising in high school newspapers and yearbooks, Quill and Scroll Foundation; Comments: *The closer man is to nature, the closer he is to himself. The more mindful man is of this spirit of oneness, the more aware he is of eternity.*

YEARLY BALL

A creek
    gathers the trickle of the thaw

And speaks
    of a large mass
    at the end of the hall

Down, 'round, and about
    the drops do fall

Overcoming obstacles
    that hinder all

These rush without thought
    to enter the hall

To be united

These are not ordered
    but are programmed
    through a special call

Ric Bullard

FROM YOU TO ME

You talk to me
In such deep voice
The way from you to me
Traces lines of choice

We joined over the others
And we gathered strong
Our fears and feature
In love all along
To get the way refused
Now, from you to me
Sorry for this line
That could not be
Inside of my mind
There is no future
From the heart is refused
From you to me

When you talk to me
In such deep voice
The touch from you to me
Gives feelings invoice.

Céline Messner

WAVES

I am the lake, so cool and so calm
so pleasant to touch and rest your eyes on
I ripple slow and free
I move to take you completely
I am the river that flows on and on
to bring life to the mainland
I move in continuum
to give to you completely
I am the ocean so vast and so wide
I can take you all the way down
I move to take you completely
I am the waves, I swell and break
so hard and so fast
I move to give to you completely
You are the earth, the hot desert sand
the mountains and valleys
the rich fertile land, you stand
and wait so patiently
to give and take
Oh, but this wonder of sand and sea
when seeing their love
become one as a beach

Venetia Dawn Davison

VESPER BELLS

Hear the vesper bells now ringing,
Gonging peace throughout the skies.
Each is toned to bless the evening,
With its soothing lullabies.

Some bells tinkle in the meadow,
While homeward-bound cattle bawl;
Others ringing, ringing, ringing,
For the evening supper call.

But the bells that bless the people,
Most of all the bells they love;
Are now gonging in the steeple,
Raining peace from God above.

These are bells that call tired spirits,
When it's time for evening prayers.
Peace within they'll all inherit,
While tones purify the air.

The folks stand amidst the ringing,
In the golden evening glow.
They can hear the angels singing,
While the bells swing to and fro.

Gladys C. Bodenmann

MIRACLES AND PINS
HONORABLE MENTION

Days visit and go
and months graduate as years,
and wonders in the world
are distributed everywhere
in fashion like the pieces
of the body of Osiris.

(Nobody ever asks
a disbeliever to come
and get under an umbrella.)

All is pleasant as a whistle's echo
and I will be a collector of miracles,
a devotee of the unusual, —
after it is clear what happens
to the pins in our house.

William Walter De Bolt

MY THINKING TREE

When I'm lonely, when I'm sad,
    Even when I have been bad
I sit beneath my thinking tree
    And talk to it — and it to me.

When no one has time for me,
    That is where I like to be.
There's no other tree you see
    Where — my spirit can be free.

I sit and look up at the sky
    And think and think instead of cry.
It is my "special" place to be
    Because it is my thinking tree.

I need a very quiet place,
    Full of LOVE and open space.
And I have found my lovely tree
    Where I can sit and just be ME.

So, when I'm old and far away
    I'll not forget — and hope and pray
That when I die, they'll bury me
    Beneath my own dear thinking tree.

Eleanor Colombara

THE MIDDLE ROAD

If action could follow thought, I would be young,
A vibrant maid to speak to you in gentle tongue,
Give glory to your manhood, perceive your every need,
Comfort you in sorrow, on ventures wish God's speed.

If wisdom could match desire, I'd find a way
To transfer me from twilight time to Youth's wild day.
Vain it is to seek it, would tight close friendship's gate.
In the end regret it, but much too late.

Let you see me still the lady, gracious, friendly, smiling,
Give no hint, in any wise, of manner too beguiling.
Thus I choose the safest path, walk the middle road,
Than display weight of this love, quite a heavy load.

Pearl Ganz Brussel

SAD AFTERTHOUGHTS . . . TOO LATE

If I could hold you close again, and kiss,
I'd tell you how their offer of a job
Held lure of foreign travel that I'd miss
If I refused. No thought that it could rob
Me of my mate. Offended by my lack
Of principle, my sudden willfulness,
You left me, gained divorce, no looking back.
Promotion rashly bought, I must confess,
Has little value as I count it now.
I should have shown more love and fortitude,
Have been more careful of my wedding vow.
I'm chastened by the sorrows, now imbued.
   I wish I'd never touched Ambition's knife.
   It sheared apart our bond of man and wife.

Selma Youngdahl

SUMMER STORM

The noontide brilliance of that summer day
Was faded out as low-hung clouds drew near;
They rolled and tossed in somber hues of gray,
And caused blue skies to slowly disappear.
Erratic winds built to a constant pace,
Sure harbinger of fast approaching storms;
Then playful lightning streaks began to trace
A jagged diagram of eerie forms.
Long peals of rumbling thunder then I heard!
All sounds of sullen fury were increased!
The angry, moisture-laden clouds, now blurred,
Their pent-up overflow of rain released.
Then everything within my sight was drenched —
The urgent thirst of Mother Earth was quenched.

J. Robert Beahm

LAND FROM BEYOND THE MIST

Here I stand — sad, weary, and alone,
   with nothing in view but cold gray stone.
I wonder why God carved this place;
   why He gave it such a desolate face.
Oh, for a lively tune to reach my ears,
   or children's merry squeals and cheers.
Lead me to an arbor of sweet scented roses,
   or to bumbling clowns with big red noses.
Enfold me in warmth from a sunny smile;
   perhaps let me caress soft angora pile.
I yearn for these and hope all's not in vain,
   since this crag holds . . . but sadness and pain.
My love for beauty must strive to exist,
   to survive in this land from beyond the mist.

Jennie Parella

I TAKE GOD

Regardless of the tasks we meet in worldly travels,

God is the first we must seek.

It's written we know, seek God, his righteousness, all
else will follow.
God does not deceive, men will.
He's always with you unto the end, not men.
This is why I take God.

Travis Josephine Dillard

NIGHTMARE

He lurks in the dark,
In the farthest corner of the park.
You know he's watching.
I'd advise you not to look,
Otherwise you'd see his hand twisted like a hook.
He should be left alone.
But he knows that you're home.
You hear him creeping up behind you,
Don't turn around, it's true.
You're dead!

Shaun Smith

THAT'S LIFE

Don't tell me the best things in life are free.
What kind of bull are you feeding me?
There is a price for everything,
From the clothes you wear to the songs you sing.
Life has its ups and downs we all know.
It's meant that way to help us grow.
   And with every passing day,
Something has changed along the way,
With every change a price is paid,
So nothing or no one really has it made.

Elizabeth Clark

RAGGEDY ANN

A little girl lying, gripping a "Raggedy Ann,"
Looking up, she grasped her mother's hand.
"Will you keep Raggedy Ann when I am gone?
Will Jesus love her after He takes me home?"
The mother holding back the tears, replied,
"With Jesus' love we need not have fears."
With a pale and restful smile,
She said, "Mother I'll only be a little while."
With Raggedy Ann clasped in her hand by her side,
She quietly slipped away with Jesus to reside.

Mary Ruth Hartloff

CLOUDS OF THOUGHT

My thoughts of late seem lost in the maze of a once
   cloudy day.
Like mountains of clouds once so full and firm, all too soon
   they dissipate into nothingness . . .
Leaving small wisps of lost trails fading into the
   twilight colors of the approaching night.

Like a spiral backbone across the heavens clouds link the sky
   with a horizon forever out of reach.

Daniel V. Meyer

239

HOGARTH, Marriage à la Mode: The Quack Doctor

Love met by chance
striking sparks
inflamed my dried body

Feeling met by chance
became my obsession
Your contradictions
my rapture or depression

Remain with me
Coolheaded Princess of Winter
Don't slip away — listen to your heart

Love met by chance
striking sparks
inflamed our minds and bodies

The hearts joined by chance
became our inspiration
Location of our Wanderlands
interrupts our relationship

Remain with me
Coolheaded Princess of Winter
Don't slip away — listen to your heart

Jerzy Jarucki

ON GUARD

3 sentinels guard
Against the dawn

3 sentinels guard
All day long

3 sentinels watch
Throughout the night

3 sentinels watch
Showing no fright.

3 sentinels scamper
From here to there

3 sentinels scamper
Then disappear

3 sentinels heard
Something in the night

3 sentinels heard
Dripping from a pipe.

Roger Puchalski

THE TREE

I saw it standing eloquently tall
Each limb covered with fiery leaves
gingerly implanted by unseen hands,
Zionic beauty enshrouding the land
Braced tightly to never fall.

One by one they fluttered down
Momentarily resting
on the chilling ground,
Till the limbs — empty and bare
fell asleep for another year.

Man so much like the tree
Summer, flowering tall and grand,
Each leaf falling gently away
Empty frame soon latent
waiting for life in a better day.

Winfred Partin

WHAT IS LOVE

Love's the ultimate
In compassion for another.
Love is that sincere concern
One feels that's like no other.

Love is patience with the old,
As well as with the young.
Love's a lullaby for those
Whose song has not been sung.

When accompanied by passion,
Love's perfection at its height;
Always present, never fading,
Never stilled by dark of night.

Love's for everyone who wants it,
But some can't always express
The emotions deeply hidden
Underneath an iron vest.

Love is ever all-encompassing,
More powerful than wine.
In the final, clear analysis,
Love's precious — Love's Divine!

Louise Burkett DeLaney

HUDSON PALISADES IN JANUARY

Uprooted buoys in military rows
Defend the ramparts from ghostly foes,

But there's no need for arms or fear,
Invaders' boats are gone from here,

Retreated from a summer's sport.
Now ice secures the pleasure port.

Beyond, a tug attacks the flank
Of hulking tow near opposing bank.

Though current fights the balky barge,
The greying tug commands its charge.

Nearby, at peace on narrow beach
A child of three extends his reach;

His fingers sprout from flow'ring hand
And mother plucks him from the sand.

Quiet battlefields go to seed —
So renewal's by spring decreed.

David Olsen

MY LOVE

My Love waits for me,
    on each and every hour.
My Love waits for me,
    to hold me in his power.
My Love waits for me,
    even through a sudden shower.
My Love waits for me,
    with his kiss upon a flower
My Love waits for me,
    in our secret tower.
My Love waits for me,
    to climb the stair
    and enter there.
My Love waits for me,
    beside my bed of flowers,
    and under them I lie,
My Love waits for me,
    for him I will never die.

Linda Chalkley

My sweet Lord
How I wish everyone knew,
The joyous peace
That comes only through You.

You've ended my wanderings
My searchings at last,
Many thoughts, lots of places
Have now become past.

My hunger, my thirst Lord
Is to be good in Your sight,
I want to serve you Lord
With all of my might.

Send trials, please test me
Let my weaknesses show,
For I know that's Your way Lord
Of helping me grow.

(In Jesus' Precious Name) AMEN.

Randy Rutledge

RUTLEDGE, RANDY LYNN. Born: Bakersfield, California, 10-4-52; Single; Occupation: Solvent Plant Operator; Comments: *I believe my poetry is a gift and at times a tool of God, I cannot write poetry unless He gives me the words.*

THE TWO OF ME

On greeting a new day
with a blank page to fill,
I need extra wisdom
and more power of will.

Sincerely pondering
on what is best to do,
just how to gain the strength
to pull the two of me through.

One of me needs clothing
plus food to keep her strong,
the other eats of meat
teaching her right from wrong.

She wears an armor
unseen by human eye
fighting the tempter
for the Master in the sky.

In the interior
resides the soul of me
and the inferior
the one the eye can see.

Suzy Watson

241

RED MOON OF THE END DAYS

The eerie ring around the moon
turned orange and sang a dreadful tune.
All the while its darkening hue
approached the color of prophesy true.
But the world did not hear the music play
for they were too busy within their day.
And most were unaware of what had been said
of the coming of grace, and the moon's color red.

O. Felspar

GREEN, DAVID L. Pen Name: O. Felspar; Born: Sedalia, Missouri, 11-19-51; Education: University of Texas at Arlington, B.A. in Communications (Journalism), 5-22-75; Poetry: 'You Yourself,' 12-84, 'The Love of Trophy Great,' 2-85, APA; 'Oceanography,' 4-85, 'Wanting Words,' 4-85, World Poetry Press; 'We The Trembling Trees,' *Annals of Saint Anne de Beaupré;* Comments: *Writing makes me feel closer to the Lord.*

THE LAST BATTLE

We stand like wooden soldiers on this grassy bluff,
  Boys and old men, ragged, bearded rough.

There's to be a battle at the break of day
  For there is a Yankee regiment far across the way.

I remember the day we marched off to follow Lee
  In fine uniforms, finest there could be.

The ladies looked pale and hurt at our leavin'.
  Now some of those same ones are wearin' black and grievin'.

Suddenly, I smell the odor of powder in the air;
  I know it's time to be fightin' over there.

You'd never know we was hungry, sick and worn
  By the way we're comin' at the blowin' of the horn.

Oh! How, amidst this fightin', could it possibly be
  That I hear my Mary's voice calling out to me?

I see her pretty auburn hair, her arms open wide,
  But I feel a pain down deep within my side.

I'm a' comin' to you, Mary, tired, hurt and sore,
  But I don't reckon I'll be fightin' anymore.

'Cause our battle is over, and we all fought our best.
  So, God, please give us Southern boys a quiet, peaceful rest.

Teresa Robinson Stolz

SEASONS

At autumn time, the leaves begin to fall,
From the north, the wild winds call.
Colors of orange, yellow, brown and red appear,
Telling all of nature that winter is near.

Then in winter, softly, gently, the snow begins to fall,
Some of nature is asleep, and some, not at all.
Nature lies in her blanket of white,
Sleeping, waiting for spring to set things right.

Spring is here, time to start anew,
Painting nature in every color and hue.
Nature's children are at last all born,
Dew sparkling everywhere in the early morn.

Summer comes with things all lush and green,
Sunsets, the most beautiful you've ever seen.
The days are filled with warm sunshine,
Everything has turned out to be just fine.

The seasons come only once a year
Bringing the things we hold so dear.
The seasons change one by one,
Each telling a story, that nature has spun.

Sandra Casey

CASEY, SANDRA MARIE. Born: Butte, Montana, 9-22-60; Education: Graduate of Richland Beauty School, May 1982; Occupation: Hair Stylist; Awards: Winner, Americanism Essay Contest, May 1973; Wheaties Jingle, April 1982; Poetry: 'My Room,' American Poetry Association, May 1982; Comments: *I try to express the feelings of children and our most inner feelings and thoughts.*

FAREWELL TO YOUTH

Farewell my love, my life, my hope,
Seems only yesterday, I stood in awe
And looked at life with eyes of trust
Believing I could make a contribution,
Thinking peace on earth, peace and brotherhood of man —
Yes, this could be a reality.
Youth's fond dream — youth's fresh hope.
Thinking back through the years — my struggles and my tears.
Always believing — people were just
Always believing — give and trust
Suddenly, I see the truth —
Look within yourself . . . be yourself.
Each man must do what he thinks is right.
So farewell to youthful idealism — but still I'll smile and say,
"God bless you — have a good day in your own way."
Remembering always, our forefathers who believed:
    UNITY IS MIGHT, UNITY IS RIGHT!

Joy Adele Wagner

THAT NEVER ENDS

Healing lies in faith
    Faith like a rainbow
        Arched across the sky,
    Faith like the night's peace
        That soothes the human heart.

Healing lies in faith
    Faith like a secret prayer
        (Trembling, murmured words)
    Faith like a light kiss
        Pressed against cold cheek.

Healing lies in faith
    Faith like the dulcet sound of music
        Playing on a tender note
    That never ends, never ends, never ends
        Like a prayer that never ends
        Or a kiss that never ends
        Or the night's peace that never ends
    Healing lies in faith that never ends,
    That never ends, that never ends.

Louise D. Gunn

GUNN, LOUISE D. Born: Canton, Ohio, 1906; Education: A.B., 1927; M.A., 1930; State University of New York; Occupations: Retired Teacher and Faculty Field Advisor, Vermont College, 1984; Awards: First Prize, Poetry Society of America, 1974; Writings: *Albany Town,* book, history of Albany, New York, 1975; Themes: *What I think, what other people think, and the world around me.*

SOMETIMES BEFORE A FIRING SQUAD

What would you do, if you knew?

I'd think about the past, try to hold onto it
Like a goat on a mountain . . .
Climb high enough to catch the sun.
Yes, I'd catch the sun . . .
Hurl it away in a fantasy
Like you throw a stone over a cliff,
Listen to it echo
Banging its way down the side.

You do know it's my last night.
If I could just touch
It with my hands,
Something to hold onto . . .
It's the nothingness of it
And the waiting,
Like a lake waiting for sunrise
Covered over by an impenetrable fog,
Life hidden beneath itself.

Patricia Ann Lewis

EMBELLISH AND RETAIN THE HARMONY

I am the trees of tranquility, the love, the peace,
    the inspiration of prosperity to bear the existence
which cannot falter.

I am the vision of only gratitude within the intriguing
    odyssey that passes through my only opticals yet to
insinuate the unique sureness of this only dream.

I am the smile that lies upon the faces of the impaired
    minds that witness strength of my only hope yet to
feel the divine need to exist

I am the body of weariness that lies along the shell-shocked
    crust of my unstabled ground to illustrate gestures
within my moment.

I am the sky of courage, the shield of value, the divine
    blue that will witness the memory of our once known
journey that lies within the reality of peace.

For I am earth that revolves around the aptitude of

of my only creation.

James Russell

A BIRTHDAY POEM TO BRIAN

Riding high atop the perfumed winds,
In a season renown for purpleness —
    a reminiscence of white garlands,
Fragrant breath of delicate blossoms,
Holds the seasonal throne.
Lovely flowers, made one garland entity,
Born of a day, one minute —
Spices of spring subdue dull breeze.
'Round and 'round, nature is intensified,
    inebrious of sweetest incense, and I —
I sewed white flowers with imaginary thread
    and called them garlands in my head
For a distinctive burst of beauty that
    would haste have them one, and now —
I, since I knew it once before,
Detect, when I will, the faintest trace
    of ghostly garlands' scent in deadest winter.
Ah, the importance of a day!

Maria de Jesus Cordero

FARM WIFE'S TABLE

Early rising before sunup, empty pots awaitin'
    the menu . . . Bacon an' spuds, biscuits abakin'.

The strain of the farmer's wife to cook,
    kitchen traffic heavy, kids anxious for a look.

Everyone dreaming of hot biscuits soaking in molasses an' stuff.
    rollin' fresh dough quick, so it will fluff.

Yesterday's berries ready for cooking,
    using Ma's recipe, giving kids a whooping.

Woodstove aroarin' oven's hot,
    ready for bakin' an' serving things hot.

Chasing chickens all over, red hen alaying,
    finding eggs aplenty, good eatin' they're saying.

Bell's aclanging, folks gatherin' 'round,
    plenty fixin's for all, even some for hound.

Blessing said and all asking some wishes,
    a new day dawning . . . Now for dishes!

Diane M. Currie

YOUR DESIRE

I know that I am your desire.
You look at me and see the woman you've dreamed of so many times.
At night you may have even reached out for me.
In the morning light you made up your mind I was yours,
You didn't even ask me.

You covered me with gold, put me on a pedestal, built a glass
cage around me. You even displayed me to friends and foes.
I was yours, your possession.

I tried to express my thoughts, but you wouldn't hear it.
So I stepped off your pedestal, I showed you tarnish in my gold,
broke out of the cage, and slipped off your chains of possession.

You told me you needed me, you couldn't live without me, wanted
me, yes you even said you desired me.
You know you never said you loved me.
You even pretended to yourself what you felt for me was love.

But in the end, you had to admit I was your desire.
Just . . . your desire

Linda R. Webb

DEFINITION OF A FRIEND
Dedicated to Cathy Poccia

F represents the *Friendship* that you have shared with me,
along with the understanding and honesty that *you* have most
gracefully shown.

R represents the *Right* feelings I had when I chose you
as My Friend.

I represents the *Ingredients* in our friendship — being
able to share a problem, and having you to care.

E represents the *Effort* you put into our friendship
to make me understand what a real friend you have been.

N represents how *Nice* you have really been to me, and
how much I appreciate it.

D represents the *Decent* person that you are.
Always willing to listen and never judge like others
would. Thank you.

Patricia A. Walsh

TO MY CHILDREN WITH LOVE

What can I leave you?
I haven't wealth or fame.
You aren't entitled to a free ride in this world,
Because of greatness or name,
I won't leave you anything;
That can be measured with a gauge.
Your inheritance from me?
It's a heritage,
Your heritage is your birthright;
A privelege entitled to all men at birth.
It's the right to live, learn, do and be,
Yet, this freedom is not realized by all men on earth.
Fortunately, you live in America, a free democracy.
This means governed by the people and not by rule.
It gives you the right to choose for yourself;
Where you live, the God you worship, and what you learn in school.
You may go to church for no other reason than the way it looks.
And although you are all capable of doing anything you set your minds to do,
You can live like heathens and learn to be crooks.
With freedom, you can attain goals, as far as you can see.
You should cherish and protect your birthright, but if you choose to abuse it,
You may lose your inheritance from me — the right to be free.

Marilyn D. Rardon

THE ROSE

You handed me a flower,
I felt it was your heart;
Your face portrayed how much you cared,
You said we'd never part.

The rose was pure, as was our love;
Time cannot erase,
The thoughts we shared; the love we knew,
Can never be replaced.

Thorns on the rose helped protect
The bud within the flower,
They helped me see, the de-li-ca-cy
of the love within the flower.

My days were filled with love for you
I feared one day you'd depart,
Taking away the love we knew
The love within my heart.

Many things were said and done,
That drove us far apart;
Yet I can't forget the love we knew,
or . . . the beauty of the flower.

Edith Mauney Stokes

STOKES, EDITH M. Pen name: Edith Mauney Stokes; Born: Yonkers, New York, 1932; Married: 12-24-81 to Bruce M. Stokes; Education: Hunter College, New York City, B.A., 1956; New School for Social Research, Certificate, Information Processing, 1979; Occupations: Teacher, Writer, Former Editor (1956-63); Memberships: Road Runners Club, Apple User Group; Poetry: 'Golden Lasso in the Sky,' *Hudson Dispatch*, 1977; 'Teacher's Lament,' *Hudson Dispatch*, 1978; Other Writings: "I Wish, I Wish," children's story, *Highlights for Children*, 1975; "Rollo — The Fat Boy," children's story, unpublished; Comments: *I write because words are my medium of expression and I like to communicate with people. If what I try to express moves others, I feel I have communicated successfully. My poetry tends toward topics of love and/or pain, which are usually intricately woven.*

LOUISIANA ALLIGATOR

In the darkling of star-silent April nights, deep in
Tangled moss-hung quaggish swamps, down Louisiana way,
An Alligator romps through brackish waters thrashing,
Threatening, whips its tail, writhes and wiggles zig-zag
Through steamy stagnant water where squirms of hissing
Water snakes lie watching as he incessantly undulates,
Then splashes on his way through myriads of variegated
Dragonflies and venomous gnats, wallowing past ghastly
Sights there in those busy swampy bogs.

Some of these stormy April nights tree frogs trill answering
Tree frogs, and flights of night birds hunt their prey while
The strange exotic cadence of capricious cicadas whimsically
Outsing skittish katydids as pink lightning sheets naked
Through these mystic bogs. Then, other kinds of frogs dance
Wild fandangos in drizzling rain and glittering fireflies
Shine their lights to show the way through impassible
Louisiana swamps, where an Alligator romps
In the darkling of star-silent April nights.

Thelma Dorris Karcher

AUTUMN

The unseen hand of Nature touches earth
    To change the color scheme for autumn days,
Earth's carpet now assumes a dull tone
    And overhead the skies are muted grays.

The green leaves tinted by an early frost
    Are slightly edged by colors warm and bright
Which quickly change to shades of red and gold
    Like flame against the darkness of the night.

Soon gusting winds and rain course through the trees
    To deal the quiv'ring leaves a parting blow.
The swaying branches move with urgency
    As if to say, "It's time for you to go."

Then hurtling leaves dart wildly through the air
    And glow like torches in the autumn sky.
They quickly fall upon the crusted earth
    Where in their brilliant robes they fade and die.

Margaret M. Masterson

AMERICA'S INDEPENDENCE DAY

It gets so exciting when July is drawing near,
That means that Independence Day will soon be here,
To each and every American, it's a very special date,
When we celebrate the Independence of America the Great!

All of us celebrate the Fourth, for it's a great day,
Each and every American celebrating in their own way,
Eating barbecued ribs, fried chicken and lots of homemade pie,
And lying around in the shade so full we could die!

There's many picnics with everyone having lots of fun,
From the rising of the sun until the day is done,
There's always many fireworks, all so glorious to see,
Celebrating the Fourth means so much to you and me!

With that Great American Flag flying high in the air,
We all proudly salute it, as it flies up there,
American's fifty great States, all celebrating the American way,
The glorious Fourth of July, our great Independence Day!

Willard Lee Skelton

My Godfather was so tall, and kind
    And though he passed on, he left behind
These words of wisdom, to let me know
    To help me live, to help me grow
He said like the wind, you must always be strong
    You must live a good live, you must never do wrong
He said like the sea, that searches, and seeks
    Never give up, you must never be weak
He said like the sun, that shines so bright
    Look for true love, one which is right
And like the earth, so rich, and sweet
    Live your life wisely, so you can meet
The days of your life, with strength, and power
    To guide you through, your darkest hour
And most of all, he said don't cry
    For tears that fall, can never buy
Life, and love for your tomorrow
    For tears that fall, bring only sorrow
So now he's gone, and we're apart
    But these words which he left me
Still live in my heart.

Christina Michaels

Hard shimmering planes of polished ice
Slide toward the setting sun
Orange light is flung
Like powder
Across fused crystals of rock-like snow.

Their trunks stark against the pewter white,
Oaks stand, naked and still.
Embraced in a living pulpit,
A silent squirrel
Prays to the sun falling into the earth.

A single star sparkles and sings a hymm
That shatters the cold, still air.
As shards of crystalline sound
Pierce the snow,
The moon casts a river of golden silence.

Blessed,
        I return,
                home.

Kenneth Collier

SHADOWY LIGHT

Petting the shadows before me
Caressing their darkness for no one to see.
Feeling their velvety blackness
Embracing their darkness as the light comes to me.

Feeling the light in the black
Seeing nothing in the dark
Apprehension sets in.
The fight for dawn begins.

The sun rises, putting shadows behind me.
Dark is slipping away
The light of dawn wins out again
And soars to the streaked sky.

Spreading the yellow warmth
Across the crowded earth below,
I feel the light before me
I am no longer groping through life again.

Mary-Elizabeth Walsh

245

ON KNEES IN ALL FAITHS

How high did those prayers rise?
Not high enough to staunch the blood
Flowing, flowing, flowing to a trickle
Stopped in blood red velvet stained glass
        windows,
Each a different battle.

All those acrid battles, all those bodies —
Young, virile, laughing — turned to red, red blood
Framed by mothers', wives', sweethearts' tears —
Sparkling diamonds 'round the windows.

All those prayers gut-wrenched
From anguished mothers clutching anxious sons,
Prayers reinforced with shotguns firmly gripped
And pointing desperately upward — fear, not faith,
Residing in young faces, bravery born of it.

Cross, Star of David, Patriotic Eagle,
All flying buttresses,
Could not propel those prayers high enough,
Not high enough at all.

    Georgia Earnest Klipple

CLOSE WORK
To Emily Dickinson

Making of plain talk
A manly thing, a voice
Headed always by a mild
To you — sometimes uttered.

Loved to listen better
Than to risk the equipoise;
Retreated from the parlor
whose opulence felt cluttered.

Order loves a kitchen
Where rows and stacks, where quiet annoys
Grand thumping hearts; there
Boasters, without distraction, stutter.

Humble as a button
She studied, looking down,
Tones, with swift glances seized the minute,
Believing small thoughts mattered.

    Nancy A. Nahra

THE APPLE OF HER EYE

Auntie called me the apple of her eye.
She hugged and kissed me every time we met.
For me, she saved cookies and cherry pie.
She loved my brothers, but I was her pet.

I knew my mother disapproved of this.
"We must treat the children alike," she'd cry.
"You know I love the boys, little Sis,
But Dixie is the apple of my eye."

The boys didn't want her caresses.
They got cookies and cherry pie, with me.
She bought things to make my frilly dresses,
So that I could be dressed up to a "T."

She boasted about the things I did well.
I was the little girl she never had.
She shared my secrets, and she wouldn't tell
Anything I did, be it good or bad.

Walk with your chin up and look toward the sky
You are the apple of somebody's eye.

    Grace Dale

DEVOTION

He walks to see her every day,
then back alone through his black night.
The years have carved him bent and gray.

He holds her hand and thinks that they
have had some good times through life's flight.
He walks to see her every day

and sits there without much to say.
She looks so young through fading sight.
The years have carved him bent and gray.

Remembering beneath the bay
tree how they'd sing the moon in flight,
he walks to see her every day.

He slowly stands and turns away
from her face, softened by the light.
The years have carved her bent and gray.

Looking beyond, her eyes betray
the anger of her dying flight.
He walks to see her every day,
the years have carved him bent and gray.

    Thirl Michael Butler

MY MOTHER

As I sit in the twilight of life
   And memories come back to me
Those that I cherish the most
   Were when I would kneel at my Mother's knee

She was the one that taught me to say
   "Jesus loves me this I know
For the Bible tells me so."
   And when the day is ended
And bedtime comes at last
   I'd kneel down at her knees and say
"Now I lay me down to sleep.
And pray the Lord my soul to keep."
A prayer my Mother taught to me

God knew we would need a helping hand
   To lead us on our way
So He gave to us a Mother
   To help us every day

Now the years have grown upon us
   Both sorrows and joys I've known
But the memories will always stay with me
   Of my dear old Mother that's gone
      to her Eternal Home.

    Mary Brown

CHANGES

We change as every day passes
Welcoming the new — accepting the past
Learning with every new experience we endure
But without you . . . my world would stop.
Over my life a dark gloomy dusk is cast
Hearts blackened with blindness.
Crying for you in the night
And realizing you will not be there in the morning.
All the time and love we have shared,
Was it wasted and senseless?
Until I turn and see you
Holding your arms out
To welcome me back
The lights begin to brighten
And again,
We have changed, but this time together.

    Wendy L. Spinazzola

THAT SPECIAL LADY

There's a special lady in my life,
  She's been there all along.
I play a part in her life too,
  And there I do belong.
She was always there while growing up,
  A partial life we've shared.
Even though her temper rose,
  I always knew she cared.
There were problems she could help with,
  Her advices never few.
She's behind me one hundred percent,
  In most everything I do.
She's loving and kind and sometimes tender,
  All good qualities blended.
I love her dearly, and think I'm lucky,
  To have someone so splendid.
There could never be another.
She's very special and dear to me,
  That lady is my mother.

  James R. Brown

ACT OF VIOLENCE

DATELINE, LEBANON —
At one moment there was the silence because they were unheard —
Horns, people muttering, hawkers shouting their wares.
In the next, there was nothing but the roar of a white cloud;
Hot air screamed the substance of an explosion taking with it
debris like a swarm of angry bees.
Several seconds passed before a chorus of pain struggled to one
knee of realization.

  George C. Koch

KOCH, GEORGE C. Born: Bronx, New York City, New York, 2-22-22;
Married: 9-24-60 to Lucille; Education: Farmingdale Agricultural and
Technology College, New York, degree in Dairy Industry, May 1942; Oc-
cupation: Medical Laboratory Technologist, retired after 37 years; Mem-
berships: Staten Island Poetry Society, subscribes to many poetry
publications; Awards: Honorable Mention in contest from *Midwest Poetry
Review,* for poem, 'Attack,' April 1985; Poetry: *Voice from the Ardennes,*
book, passed 5000 sales, GAVS, Brooklyn, New York, 1964; *Two Pens,*
book, *The Endless Climb,* book; Comments: *Poet writes about all subjects
and in every style. Many of my poems are about experiences in World War
II — The Battle of the Bulge; Writer has many decorations because of war
service and is 80% disabled because of wounds received in forementioned
battle — also known as Ardennes Campaign.*

I SEE GOD'S HANDPRINT

I see God's handprint in the mountains and lakes so blue;
I see God's handprint in the trees and morning dew.
I see God's handprint in the birds and bees;
I see God's handprint in the rivers, rocks, and seas.
I see God's handprint in the clouds and sun and sky;
I see God's handprint in making you and I.
I see God's handprint in the deer who run so fast.
I see God's handprint when the whippoorwill sings;
I see God's handprint when the eagle spreads his wings.
I see God's handprint in the beautiful sunset,
I see God's handprint in my wonderful pet.
I see God's handprint in the fields of grain;
I see God's handprint again, and again, and again.

  Florence M. Hutchison

BLESSED EVENT

When to me little children come near,
Sharing their love and joyful way,
There is a feeling that seems to appear,
Within my heart without delay,
To tell me God's blessing has been sent,
Making my heart feel content.

I long for the children to stay near forever,
With their treasures of joy I love so much,
That my heart will humbly endeavor,
And follow their way of magic touch,
Telling me of the love that is meant,
To see God in this blessed event.

  Anthony S. Goss

TRIUMPH

Imagine the eyes of a hungry child
as they gaze upon a loaf of bread,
then you'll know the condition of my soul
as it goes through the human refuse.

Like a daisy in the early morning dew,
And as the heat of day wilts the daisy,
so does the lack of caring sear my heart.

Imagine, my dear friend, the feeling of triumph,
when the child eats the bread,
and the way an afternoon shower refreshes the daisy,
then you'll know my joy in finding you.

  Char Skobel

CHILDREN

    Oh, how beautiful are they, matter not where
they come from or who they be; they are all beautiful.

    Looking at their gracious little bodies, normal
or retarded, they are all divine.

    Their charming eyes and their desire to be loved
and understood demands our attention.

    Children are certainly the flowers of today
and the men and women of tomorrow. We have to give
them the very best of ourselves for the good of themselves
and for the happiness and serenity of our world.

  Beverley Ashman-Cunningham

VIEW OF UNDERSTANDING

As I sit in class and watch the day go by,
I wonder "Why am I here?"
All it takes is for a child to try,
Then it becomes very clear.

The amazement of learning brings joy to behold,
That answers my question "Why am I here?"
The child gives love without being told.
And they become a friend so dear.

The bond is set between teacher and child,
There is no more asking "Why am I here?"
Some days are moody; while others are mild.
The reasons become even more clear.

We are not here for the money or the glory,
We are here for all the children.
All the rest comes in another story,
As long as we become "One in a Million."

Patricia B. Turner

OLD MAN WINTER

Old Man Winter brings the snow, the
    freezing rain, and makes the north wind blow.
He likes it best when the land is covered under a blanket
    of white and it is freezing cold.
He sends storms and blizzards to show his anger,
And thinks nothing of it when animals and folks
    are in danger.
Old Man Winter is at his best during the months
    of December, January, and February.
He has taught all of God's creatures to prepare for
    winter and be wary.

Mary Janeen Dorsett

DORSETT, MARY JANEEN. Born: Lufkin, Texas, 8-21-43; Single; Education: Stephen F. Austin State University, Nacogdoches, Texas, B.S., Elementary Education, 1964; Masters of Education, Supervisory Certificate, 1969; Occupation: Teacher; Poetry and Other Writing Awards: Honorable Mention, adult category, Border Regional Library Association Multicultural Children's Creative Writing Contest, El Paso, Texas; poem, 'A Weaver,' Spring of 1982; poem, 'An Old Silversmith,' Spring of 1983; story, "The Best of Both Worlds," Spring of 1983, poem, 'The Desert,' Honorable Mention, World of Poetry, Spring 1984; Poem, 'Wolfman,' Certificate of Merit, World of Poetry, 1984; Story, "Herbie and the Astronauts," accepted for publication by The Little People's Press, 1984; Memberships: Delta Kappa Gamma, Gallup Community Concert Association (Board of Directors), Gallup Area Arts Council, International Reading Association; Comments: *Most of my poems and stories are written for young readers. Many of my works reflect the land, the people, and the culture of the Navajo Indians whose children I have taught for the past 21 years. Other works include such themes as life on the farm, fantasy, and science fiction.*

A MAN HAS TO DO WHAT HE FEELS

A man has to do what he feels
if he listens to that still calm voice inside —
he will be satisfied

A man has to love who he feels is best for him
if he listens to his heart —
he will be fulfilled

A man has to sing his own songs
if he writes his own words —
he will sing on forever

A man has to speak his own mind
if he continually brings peace within —
he shall find contentment

A man has to live his own life
if he does so to the fullest of his being —
he will know who he is

A man has to dream his own dreams
if he feels that they are important enough —
he shall know reality

A man has to do what he feels
if he listens to that still calm voice inside —
he will be satisfied.

James L. Canada

CANADA, JAMES LEO. Born: Woburn, Massachusetts, 6-24-33; Education: University of Massachusetts, Boston, Massachusetts; BA, English/Sociology, 1981; Occupation: Teacher, Secondary Education; Memberships: St. John's Baptist Church, Woburn, Massachusetts; Returned Peace Corps Volunteer; Friends of Togo, West Africa; Poetry: *If I Were to Tell You,* Dorrance and Company Inc., Ardmore, Pennsylvania, 1974; *Reality is My Awareness Sense,* Gemini Bookvillage, East Weymouth, Massachusetts, 1974; Other Writings: "Eternal Friendship," short story, *Gemini Review,* East Weymouth, Massachusetts, 1975; Comments: *Ideas and themes mainly revolve around people and experiences. I try to look inside and bring it out. Writing is and has been a love of mine for as long as I can remember. It brings peace of mind.*

THE MODERN WORLD

Lord, I love you, — I thank you for all Thy blessing — that you have
given me.
But, I haven't shown this today — or even the days before.
   Yet, You still love us — I marvel the thought, about Your unique
patience.
      Your unique patience; — because, we are all — too busy.
Busy; meeting daily schedules
      personal needs to fulfill our egos
      busy — to achieve daily things, for the modern world.
The modern world; — the abuse — of — time.
   Lord, it's Your world, — Your creation, — Your time, — and sometimes,
how, — we abuse it.
   Each day, — each hour, — each minute, — each second, — each moment, —
displays — Your miraculous compassion.
   Birth of a child, another breath of life from a tragedy, a traumatic
incident, to awaken the supremacy of Your — purpose.
   Lord, let us be for Thy purpose; to be loving, caring, giving, and sharing
for the gracious essence — of You.
      Anne Kalina

A LITTLE GIFT OF KINDNESS

Tomorrow when the sun comes up to shine upon the world,
It will be that special day, when Angels' Carols unfurled.
The stars in Heaven shone extra bright, so bright it seemed like day . . .
The Savior of our Earth was born, this Glorious Holy Day.

As time goes by we oft forget the reasons why He came,
We see bright lights and Christmas trees, and look for gifts we'll gain.
We've tinsel, cards, and ornaments, and toys for every age,
But, not much thought of LOVE is made, for money is the rage.

It doesn't seem like Christmas . . . the way it ought to be,
The world is so commercial now, it's one big shopping spree.
If we could take each little dime and turn it into love . . .
Just think of all the happiness we'd give our Lord above.

If every tree that's filled with lights could be a tender touch,
How many, many happy hearts would thank us oh, so much.
The time we spend on shopping and wrapping gifts to share
Could very well be turned towards someone to show we care.

There's always someone waiting who needs a helping hand,
So take the time to find them, and show you understand.
A little gift of kindness will go a long, long way,
Toward making someone happy on this Special Christmas Day.
      Carolyn Takaki

THE AWAKENING OF DAWNE

I felt so very comfortable, just being there with you.
How wonderful it was to know, you also shared that view.
You've been so very "special" to me, for such a long time now —
I've tried to find a way to tell you, but didn't quite know how.

Every time I'd be with you, so early in the morn,
I'd feel as though the earth was mine, and I was just reborn.
You can't imagine how it felt, to drive away and miss you,
When what I really wanted, was to hold you and to kiss you.

I couldn't help the feelings I had, and wanted so to tell you.
I sensed you felt the very same, but couldn't let yours through.
I didn't know, during all these times, you were so afraid to do so,
Because you thought you'd be rejected, and then get told to go.

Glory, when you held me that night, hour after hour,
And tenderly would touch me, I felt like a brand-new flower.
You patiently and gently, opened up each petal,
Until you gave me back my life, and all my womanly prowess.

Let's pursue the excitement and warmth that we felt, and enjoy what we know was so good.
Both of us can fulfill for each other, our need to be understood.
We can be our true selves, and relax with each other, opening up without any fright,
No crazy façades of this type or that, just loving all day and all night.
      Dawne Lepore

PSYCHIATRY

Psychiatrists are said to know
      Our libido and our psyche.
Who taught *them* all about the minds
      Of Jim, Pat, Joan and Mikey?

We all may yearn for freedom from
      Our ego's close confines.
To psychoanalyze one must
      First recognize the signs.

To love — have children — get involved
      Demands one's very soul.
Normalities and quirks must all
      Cohere to make us whole.

So back to doctors and their help:
      Through many learning years
They've studied psyches — used their own —
      To blow away our fears.

The wealthy can afford a "shrink";
      The indigent may scoff.
I sometimes try to figure out
      Who's really better off . . .
      Pat Wilber

INFORMED VOTER

Some elections are local
Some contests are national
Issues vary state to state
Most rational, all educational

Some new things are fiction
Some new things are facts
Supporting both in style —
Our skyrocketing tax

Some times, irritating news
Some soothing psalm read
World-wide depressive blues —
We hope for a peaceful calm

Some people hesitate
Some people move ahead
The media keeps us informed
So, we won't be misled

Some fine Americans will
Some fine Americans won't
But how will we know?
If few citizens vote.
      Gwendolyn Trimbell Pease

NEW HEART

Oh, Lord hush my temper and
my will.
Help my rebellious spirit to be still.
Create within me a brand-new heart.
From this day forward set me apart.
Anoint me Lord with heaven's dew,
That I may be fit for service for you.
Help me every day, a little fragment
Of your love to receive.
Give me a witness for others,
that they too, will believe.
Go deeper into me Lord Jesus every day,
Until you have conquered me all
the way.
Then I will be content in serving
You until I lay my burdens down,
And trade my old rugged cross
for a crown.
      Lila Belcher

THE GIFT OF LOVE

I've often tried to figure out, just what I gave to you,
I've added up some dollar signs, and know that you have too.
But the things that seem to mean the most, appear to have no price,
Are even hard to contemplate, not once, or even twice.

I've also tried to figure out, just what you gave to me,
And have tried to place a price upon the things that you can't see.
But most of what you freely gave, each day with measured Love,
Were priceless gems of happiness, and treasures from above.

Your friendly smile, your laugh, your girl-like charms and ways,
Filled my soul a million times, and exhilarated my days.
Your voice, touch and zest for life, gave meaning to my Heart,
Your body warm, your hair of silk, I feel when we're apart.

My memory of your being, is strong, is pure, is real,
So THIS is what you gave to me, for THIS is how I feel.

Ed Edwards

PUFF, PUFF — ENUF, ENUF

Smokers go puff, puff on their cigarettes, cigars and pipes
Non-smokers go cough, cough and wonder how to vent their gripes

In crowded areas the smoke gets thicker and thicker
Non-smokers inhale it and feel sicker and sicker

Smokers, matters not how you affect people around you
Non-smokers and children feel healthier when you are not in view

Indulging in their vile habit smokers pollute the air
In discomfort non-smokers cry out unfair — unfair

Smokers, somehow you always contrive to direct the smoke away from you
Non-smokers wave their hands and go phew — phew

On lines smokers indiferently puff out chemically loaded smoke
Non-smokers get eye burn, tight lungs and feel ready to choke

Though smokers may not care
Non-smokers deserve smoke-free air

Smokers, it's time to stop your puff — puff
And say to non-smokers we quit, enuf — enuf

Stanley Staszak

REMEMBRANCE

I am the color of the wind I am the shadow of the sun.
When will my glory be released?
The darkness burning all around
And people running from their dreams. It leaves a nightmare in its wake.

I am the memory of your past a fugue of form and fantasy.
The lives you've led and people known,
The places travelled, secrets held,
The hopes and fears you've never told. You could escape but you don't try.

The lonely silence screams at night the people's voices as they pray.
The endless night is closing 'round
And isolation rages on.
The storm clouds crash against the void. A shadow rises in the heart.

Caught all alone inside your life a futile echo of this world.
Trapped in a shell of loneliness
The daylight fades into the sky.
The soul is torn without a care. The night is shattered by a tear.

The spirit dies within your soul the echo cries no voice is heard.
No more to love, the future's gone.
My purpose failed, darkness explodes,
Time marches past a love destroyed. The silent starfall left unseen.

the Hawk

A DREAM

Last night I had a dream, as I lay in
my bed. I could hear the waves,
breaking in my head. I was on an
Island, far out to sea. I was all alone,
no one but me. Sitting on the sand,
that was yellow and white, watching
the stars fall out of sight. Watching
the waves roll into shore and hearing
some sounds I've never heard before.
The sun was rising far overhead.
I enjoyed the colors of yellow,
orange and red. Sea gulls over
head made a beautiful sound, as
they swooped closer to the ground.
And the whales, in the ocean just
offshore, swimming with a certain
grace I've never seen before. And
then the sun fell out of sight, and
I said to myself. It's going to be
another clear night.

James Redmill

QUIETLY

Quietly, like a gentle breeze,
Caught unaware,
You refreshed me.
You brought sunshine,
When it had gone away.
You breathed life into me,
That had slipped away,
Slowly like a babbling brook,
That winds its way into every nook.
You touched my soul in gentle ways,
Our feelings grew, consumed by waves.
    Like a spark, unaware at first,
    It kindled hope.

It grew rapidly and burst into flames.
Out of control, no more the same,
    Now our lives are one it seems,
    Now we both have found our dream.
    Not too late for you or me.
    To know love at last, for eternity.

Ruth A. Reese

ODDS AND ENDS

Puppy who did not
grow up to be a dog
was a frisky
first day of spring
flirting:
the larger black dog
the gas station man's
teasing the pant legs:
the junkman
adjoining the
empty dumptruck
drinking in
the sweet
ricocheting nips
with his morning sun
screech of the motorist
who cannot stop on a dime
the sad black dog says goodbye
the heartbeat I step on
I hear the end cries.

Sofia Lederer

MOTHER

A mother's more precious than any rare jewel:
   the light from her lamp always shines.
Her sparkle is brighter than all clearest pools;
   she's a wonderful, lovely design.

Her dignity, strength, and her laughter
   make a home very warm and complete.
There are great many tasks she looks after;
   no idling time will she meet.

She reaches out hands to someone in need —
   a provider of comfort and love.
It's no wonder a mother's so special, indeed,
   for all of the things she's made of.

Her fruit is God's wisdom, so vast and so great;
   a mother has truly been blest.
Let all her works praise her at Heaven's dear gate:
   her children believe she's the best.

   Lynette White

WARS

The young men were leaving, one by one
Headed for distant shore, each carried a gun
In each of them, the fighting did burn
But deep in their hearts, for home, they did yearn.

The older men came from far and wide
Forming a sea and the ebbing tide
Hiding strong fears, they said their goodbyes
To loved ones who watched with tears in their eyes.

As they marched away, no one asked, "Why?"
Thought it was known that they all might die.
Few, if any, could honestly comprehend.
The reasons to brandish weapons in foreign lands.

After years, the fighting stopped — Not many survived
And those who did, weren't truly "alive."
Many had lost limbs — All had lost friends
And the nightmares of bloodshed seemed to have no end!

   Dorothy E. Pies

THREE DAYS

She lived around shadows, breaking through time;
Jumping into another century, drawing the line.
Asking age-old questions, who, what am I?
Looking for all answers, gazing up at the sky.

She had lived in another world so very defined,
With beautiful Ladies, crystal, silver and wine.
A coach-lined drive with all the slaves close by,
Wanting to be part of the grandness, giving a sigh.

She brought her gaze downward and began to smile,
She'd have done anything to be white for awhile.
All she had seen in life was hard work and pain,
A prisoner with black skin and invisible chains.

Coming back into the here and now, feeling used;
Living in the twentieth century, being confused.
She went to the Hermitage and saw the grand home;
She had an odd feeling as she walked there alone.

   Betty Black

OUR LOVE

She gives a meaning to my life,
This woman who is my wife.
Through the good times and the bad,
Through the happiness and the sad.

I'll borrow from a song of old
These words that should be retold,
"I'll be loving you always,
With a love that's true always."

Together we have walked life's road
And many tales we can unfold.
The intimacies that we do share
And the many pleasures that we bear.

Our life has been a fruitful one,
And still, there will be many things undone.
We have done our very best,
And someday, in God's Mansion, we will rest.

   Edward A. McGahan

MS. BAG LADY'S MONDAY

Having settled herself,
a good spot, near Gimbels,
at 33rd and Sixth. She began organizing
all she owned. Then it happened.

Neighing horses, New York's finest,
mounted, shouting, galloping up the street.
Slamming brakes, confusion. A T.V. Drama,
man running at Bag Lady's tiny space.

Lightning and thunder
leaping from everyone's hand.
The youngster looked surprised, his body driven,
tripping, sliding into Bag Lady's land.

Dismounted, at the ready, shouting her away.
She passed the dying man a pretty smile, her eyes
damp. Ms. Bag lady picked up her bags, moved
away. Leaving her space for the cops.

   Salvatore Galioto

YOUR REFLECTION

Many times you are the forgotten one,
Especially now that you are old.
In your lifetime you've seen good and bad times,
The experiences you've had, what memories you hold.

The many loves you could have had,
But your true love was just that one.
She gave you love at the age of seventeen,
And her love for you is stronger at ninety-one.

Yes, so many of the old are fast forgotten,
That the young ignore, the path they too must lead,
For all that grows on this earth must one day
Wilt and go into the ground as does a seed.

If you see an old man hobbling along,
Don't have too much pity or pay him too much mind,
Because it is only your future reflection,
Remember you are not that far behind.

   Mike B. Trevino

SPRING MORNING!

Now, *this* is a morning!
Warm sun kissing the earth —
The air alive with sounds!
Spring came in with such a rush
It leaves us breathless in its spell.
Golden notes of the Meadow Lark,
Killdeer, Robin and Blackbird
Fill the warm Spring air.
Haunting cry of wild geese overhead —
Mallards circling the cornfield,
Talking to one another.
Coded message of the woodpeckers,
Atop the tall, lean poles —
The pond awake with singing frogs,
Ice edged back on the lake
Where the muskrat swims, planning his future.
And over all, the cloudless sky — a dome of blue
So brilliant it seems not real.

Could I but share with sleeping souls
One small part of this Spring morning!

Evelyn O. Swanson

NIGHT PRAYER

I need somebody to talk to, God,
Someone to help with the paths I've trod.

When weary and tired at long day's end,
A willing confidant with time please send.

For all I have tried are so busy with theirs,
There seems to be none with whom I can share.

Alone again now — past trusts have gone sour,
For what kind of friend "listens by the hour?"

Discouragement abounds — the times I've tried,
And Dear Lord you know how in darkness I cried.

Independence I need, alone and strong to stand,
With the comfort and strength of your loving hand.

Just give me a sign to show me the way,
And try and let me know I belong here today.

Becky Hendershot

A SPECIAL EASTER

On a Wednesday, some years ago
All alone, for us, you know
Our blessed savior went to the Cross
So that our souls would not be lost
Three days later, he arose
From the tomb, where he was disposed
His intention was to save this land
When they drove those nails in his hands
In the spring, when the dogwood has bloomed
I thank God, we aren't doomed
He will be like a great white dove
Coming back, for those he loves
Christmas represents Jesus' birth
Still yet, Easter comes first
He taught us to love thy neighbor
This wonderful man, is Jesus,
Lord, our Savior
For Christ gave his life, so
That we could be free
He did this all, on Easter
At the cross of Calvary

Juanita W. Collins

REMINISCE

I sit alone in the twilight
As the last rays of daylight fade,
I reminisce our years together,
And it seems I hear you say
We've had a wonderful life together,
Even amid trouble, illness and strife,
I was grateful I had you to comfort me,
And so glad that you were my wife.
We did not have any children, to lift
Our spirits up,
but we had each other dear, and that
Was always enough.
Now after all these years together,
Of which 40 were our married life,
I just reminisce and am glad that I
Was your wife.
Yes! Just one year ago, death took you from
My side,
But one day dear: I'll join you, until then,
My love goodnight.

B. L. Dunn

DUNN, BETTY LARMA. Pen name: Betty Lou Dunn; Born: Harrison, Hamilton County, Tennessee; Widowed; Education: High School, 1949; Key Training in Business, 1951; Church Training Officer, WMU, 1966; Occupation: Disabled, Retired; Memberships: Song Writers Association, Nashville, Tennessee; Awards: "A Miracle For Betty," *People's Bible,* 1982; *Larma's Diary,* Novel, Broome Agency Publishers, 1983; Other Writings: *People's Bible;* 'Miracle Worker,' Poem, World of Poetry, 1982; 'Master Craftsman,' Poem, American Poetry Association, 1982; 'Greatest Love,' Poem/Song, American Poetry Association, 1984; Themes: *Love of God and man, is the idea and theme of most of my work.* Comments: *As a writer, I can express my innermost thoughts and try to project in words what I feel inside, on paper. I feel at times I was born to be a writer, and have always had a love for people, reading, studying, and writing. I grew up in a large family: 6 sisters and 2 brothers, being one of three youngest ones. I more or less lost myself in reading, from starting to school until the present time. I have written 75 poems, some of which have been set to music. Although I have not received any payment of monies for my work, I have been told by many that my writings have been a source of comfort and inspiration and encouragement to them. I am asked many times to write someone a poem concerning a given situation and I try to see my own self in their place, then write a poem or short verse that may help them, which I am told it does. I am a firm believer in God's Word, The Bible, and I study daily. I have a television ministry, "Living Waters Telecast," Cablevision 12 out of Chicamauga, Georgia, where I teach Bible to shut-ins, the elderly and persons who do not attend church. God has been so dear and good to me, I give Him all the credit for any good things happening in my life. If I can only help someone, it will be the only reward I want. To see a tear changed to a smile is worth it all, and to know you have had a small part in bringing happiness, where there was sorrow, and peace of mind where there was such worry and stress, Oh! Yes! I am well content to be what and where I am, I know I am needed, and pray God will always keep me thus.*

HERO HOLIDAY

"Damn it! I've no use for angels,"
                    — retorts Jimmy Holliday.
(Someone was screeching like a caged bird
And trying to break the restrainers)
Jim Holliday is one of the unfortunates
        Who was visited from an earlier age
By a 20th century "Hard-to-Believe"
        Celluloid-appearing communication *device*
By a King Michael of Greenland
                    — And his contemporaries.

If this horror enters your life:
Travel 'round quite a bit.
Tell no one . . . (for you have man for an enemy)!
                    Or else kill to survive!
Close your eyes, dreamy-time boy
And rip yourself in the black middle.

                    (Will you remain forever
                        . . . Exile?
                    Or will you be as
                    Other voyagers returning home . . .?)

   Michael David Fisk

ICH BIN EIN BERLINER

When he spoke English in his New English accent
Moscow was not impressed.

"Let them come to Berlin."

Made Stalin chuckle.
"Mars again" He laughed to Lenin and Trotsky.
Russians never took the Roman God Mars seriously
For they had already annihilated his modern caesars
The Tzars — These heirs to the Third Rome.
So in the three seats reserved for the leaders of the Revolution
The three leaders laughed among themselves

But when he spoke German to the Germans
The Russians didn't take notice
"Ich bin ein Berliner"
Revealed a dichotomy — a Northern Ireland within the psyche
This was a new God — A God of the split
The God of Joyce, Picasso, and Einstein
No! Socialist Realism had to be preserved
So Berlin Sabers rattled no more.

   Thomas Francis Smith

ANGEL

Her dreams ride the whispering winds
She'll float across your mind
Be here, and there, and then
Silent for awhile

An angel
To some a mystery
Lost in time or reality

Angel
Sunlight that touches ground
Heaven blessed, but now earthbound

Angel
Captive of a falling star
A wish fulfilled revealed the scar

Your search defies your destiny
If love is your quest, your heart's the key
One second revealed eternity
A fading glow, her soul set free — Yes.

   Lemuel Byrd

WEALTH

Measuring wealth by dollars and cents
Is most unwise and makes no sense.
How much money buys health lost?
How much does the warmth of friendship cost?
When toddlers talk and smile,
What makes life more worthwhile?

Lively breezes hustling here and there
Like us seek, knowing not what or where.
Were we to truthfully speak,
World peace alone is the wealth we seek.

   Lillian C. Marcoux

EARTHRUN

The sky when I start is banked like a giant furnace;
Sometime in the night its fire went out and the hollow
Pit of its belly is anthracite, crusted with cinder.
Freed of its glow I run as through curtains parting
Each pair with my body, feeling the dusty velvet
Stroking my calves as I run through the doors of morning.
Soon I will come to the glittering yellow marker
Warning me I must turn back; but my eyes are cast upward,
Caught by a frantic motion, most likely a batwing
Making one last wild flutter for food at daybreak;
Then as I turn I see the molten horizon:
Day's stoker has seen to the sky, and the sky is burning.

   Gay Baines

MY LIPS CAN'T BE SEALED

My lips can't be sealed;
'Cause all His love is there to reveal.
For the whole world is searching;
And seeking for this love and this peace.
For this love and this peace that will never cease.
Only the love divine of Jesus Christ is true love.
Only the love divine of Jesus Christ is true peace.
Only the love divine of Jesus Christ is for real;
And it's free, free for all the world to receive.
That's why my lips can't be sealed;
When all His love is there to reveal.
And His love and His peace will never cease.

   Annie Scott

SEASONAL CHANGES

I watch the leaves come falling down,
   gently, gently, in front of me;
The lake has taken a different hue,
   I watch it change in front of me;
Puddles scattered along the street,
   In them I see reflections,
As I search the scene for answers,
   I know they're somewhere here in front of me,
The wind is whispering in my ear,
   "My dear, what is the question?
   What has your soul been searching for,
   that hasn't been right in front of you?"

   Kim Marie Compagner

SNOW FLAKES

Snow flakes swirling graciously in the air,
Swooping to the ground, without a care.
People wandering here and there,
Paying no attention, I ask is it fair?
To miss one of nature's beauties that I see,
Such as the snow flakes that placidly envelop me.

   Paula Ann Smith

THE SNOW BIRD OF WINTER

The snow bird, has spread its wings,
And its downy feathers float to earth.
Soon he will sing,
His song of wintery mirth.
His voice will whip through the trees,
While people scurry to and fro.
The earth is seized in his wintery grip.
Soon he will give way,
To spring's tender touch.
And the day, will dawn,
When he will return,
In regal splendor,
That all mankind,
Will be blinded by the sight.

Lori Rae Brockway

LETA'S SONG

Through friendship comes a resting place;
  A place of quiet repose.
Where one can put to ease;
  The restlessness of soul.

Though many places that we seek;
  Will give us self-reward.
Only one can give us peace;
  It's there we're not alone.

For friendship is a gift from God;
  An extension of His hand.
Friendship is a tangible touch;
  of God through man.

Martha F. Strong

RISING TO THE OCCASION

The ebb and flow of day to day
Colors awareness and response
Relationships come and go
Adding and subtracting from the flow.

Words and phrases rarely change
Abstract meanings are the same
Conveying the impression
Opinions are fair game.

The sum of what appears to be
Is clouded by participants
Each proclaiming the truth
Exactly as they see it.

Bonnie Zaborski-Beck

EASTER

An empty cross, an empty tomb,
The empty graveclothes lying there.
The angel's voice dispels the gloom,
"He is Risen!" fills the air.

An empty life, an empty heart
And broken spirit humbly brought —
The risen Christ fills every part.
The miracle of life is wrought.

Resurrection! Hope for aye!
Only Christ the conquering King!
Death's defeat was done that day —
Let the earth this message sing!

Donna S. Ledford

FROSTY MORNING

How can I tell of
My soul's delight,
In each tiny twig
Of glistening white.

How can I help believing
In a life
With purpose and meaning,

When each little tree
Has a place of its own,
And the humble weed
Has beauty to loan.

Whitened wood and drifted lane
In mystery and pure silence reign.

Margy Triplett

THINGS WE LIKE TO DO

She kisses
by candlelight.
I kiss
by firelight.
She kisses under the pale
of the moon.
I hug
under the flames
of a falling star.
She likes to embrace
when a trace
of spring
is in the air.
I like to hold
her tight
to let her know,
I care.

Wayne West

THE RELIGIOUS

The sacrilege of neon spells
Religious
as though it were a magnet
blessed with holy water
attracting few
repelling some
so little here remains
unsung
when neon lights spell out
the word Religious.

D. Weltmer

BLACK ON WHITE

Black on White
White on Black
The same but different
Different but the same
Two eyes,
Two ears,
Two legs,
Two hands,
Working with each other.
One mouth,
One nose,
Working against each other.
Black on White
White on Black
Different?
Same?
Or just rearranged?

M. Maureen Kirkland

WHEN TIME IS JOY

I hold the past, present, and future
  of my life
as memory, now experience, and expectancy.
The now experience reaches ecstasy
  of feelings, sense, touch,
  blending time and space.
It becomes memory
  and challenges the future
  to cherish, to mold, to change, to be.
I am because of joy in you
  and time with you is joy.

Ruth H. Dresen

DRESEN, RUTH HAMANN. Born: Crookston, Minnesota; Married: David T. Dresen; Education: Madison Area Technical College, two years; Attended University of Wisconsin, Madison, three years; Occupations: Mother of four grown children; Program Assistant in Management and Finance, Graduate School of Business, University of Wisconsin, Madison; just retired from this position; Memberships: President of Wintergreen-West of Madison Chapter of A.A.R.P. and Senior Adjutant, Secretary-Treasurer of Badger Chapter, American Ex-Prisoners of War, Inc.; Comments: *There is a common theme of caring and of love expressed in most of my writing. I write to express a need or a feeling about impressions of life, of nature, and of the seasons in each I experience. For me, writing relieves the frustrations of life and expresses the exaltations.*

THURSDAY AGAIN

Melting voices fade away,
machines echo as distant drums.

Shadowed mannequins drifting past
the opening doors began to dance.

Floating from your everyday world,
immersed in deepest dreams,

until reality forced against my mind
steals again the moments of my time.

Sharon L. Housen

REMBRANDT, Rembrandt Leaning on a Stone Sill

THE SNOWSTORM

It started to snow last night.
  This morning trees were feathery white,
  Roofs looked like icing on a cake.
  No cars or people were in sight.
  The sky is gray.
  It snowed all day.
  The snowplow now, is on the way.
  "I hope it doesn't push too much
  in front of my mailbox."
For me to shovel it away!

Marie Wills

WILLS, MARIE ROSE. Pen Name: Marie Miller; Born: Pueblo, Colorado; Married: 1-25-41 to Bernard Wills; Education: Business Course, Writer's Digest; I had a course from Famous Writers; Occupation: Housewife; Awards: prize of Edgar Guests' poems, in high school for an essay; Writings: (under the name Miller), *Yearbook of Contemporary Poetry,* Avon, 4 poems, 1936; *Yearbook of Contemporary Poetry,* Avon, 4 poems, 1937; Beacon Publications, 3 poems, 1939; (under the name Wills), Articles in: *St. Gerard Bulletin,* 1955; religious magazine, 1960; and *Hobby and Garden,* 1960; *Biographical Dictionary of Contemporary Poets,* Avon, 1938; Comments: *I write because I enjoy it, seeing my name in print and the money (from time to time). From ideas and happenings, I try to find something different and original.*

FALLING STAR

In the stillness of the night
I walked beneath a star so bright
The sky contained a million stars
They seemed so close and yet
So far.

A falling star zoomed across the
Sky
I made a wish as it passed by
That man on earth would someday
Cease

To fight cruel wars — and live in peace.

Heather Eileen Burdette

MY TROUT STREAM

You step from the Macadam into nature's carpeted sweet earth,
Your feet sink and as you release the pressure of each foot,
The earth rises with you
Twigs crack, and leaves rustle, and you begin to smell the sweetness
Of a process that has gone on since time began.
As you walk further into the woods
You leave every trace of humanity behind
The wires, the waste, all made without taste
The moist serenity wells within you
And you sense a feeling of great anticipation
Ah! What is that noise?
Is it someone speaking a new language?
It is a trout stream moving endlessly to the sea.
Within its depths are sparkling and spotted trout
Hidden like great insights in our minds
My trout stream, like the flow and ebb of existence
Goes on hopefully.
Its message of keep on flowing is not learned
By all its viewers.
The winding path of its course, tells a tale of life.

Robert Michael John Higgins

I AM A TOAD I AM TOLD

I'm a toad I'm told, and like you, I've a daddy and mommy too.
Once I was an egg in a still water hole, then, a tadpole.
My brothers and sisters were many, and I'm lucky to be alive
As not many did survive, and it's a wonder that there were any.
The water hole might dry up; kids pick us up in a cup,
And for a turtle or a snake a delicious dinner we make.
I was mostly head and I had a tail, sort of a miniature whale.
Slowly front legs began to grow, hind legs began to show,
And my tail did disappear from my rear.
As my body grows, I use my nose to breathe the air.
I must leave this situation, so I hop out of there.
Being all alone and on my own, I must find a place to stay
And not be in another toad's way.
My meals are no big deals for in my mouth is a folded tongue
To catch bees (you know them if you've been stung by one).
My beady eyes are to see the flies.
If people turn on a light at night, I jump at insects that I sight.
All creatures aren't a friend, so I must take care not to meet my end.
Sometimes hide I must for all things I can't trust
For I'm just a toad I am told.

Yvonne Hale Salvador

LONELINESS

Not the apparent isolation, it's emptiness, terror and excruciating desolation.
Internally disconnected as a consequence of compound rejection and abuse,
Always treated as invisible, I was destroyed by exploitative muses.
My life has become an enigma, with no rhyme or reason to the stigma.
There's no limit to the destructiveness but the unrealized potential for creativity does exist.
And my mind and body are continually revealing all of the various twists.
I do not expect to fill up my empty box inside, my pack in life is purely compromise.
If I can leave something for others to understand and abide —
It will help put my nightmares and tragedy to rest.
My contribution to mankind will quell the bombardment of unendurable intrapsychic torture tests.
The greatest part of my fright is not being able to stop this journey or predict
how my predilections will come to the fore.
I'm frustrated by the perplexity,
And feel thwarted and obliterated by my own efforts to unravel the complexity.
But the reality of my situation that I'm truly alone and in the dark,
That I'm that one-person army (of which I so insistently spoke)
has hit me like an enlightening bolt deep in my heart.

Linda S. Behar

LOVE FROM THE HEART

Today I saw you for the first time in a long time.
For a moment, I stood silent, watching you,
Too stunned to move.

Then you felt my eyes upon you.
As you looked up,
A surprised smile brightened your face.
You seemed happy to see me.

You were so handsome standing there,
That I wanted so much just to touch you;
To hold you close to my breast.

Once again you have lit the fires of my secret longings,
As one might strike a match to make a flame.
You have unlocked the door to my heart,
Warming it with the love I feel for you.

Although my arms have never held you,
And my lips have not touched yours,
My heart still aches with longing for you.

Why then do I feel this terrible loss,
A loss of someone so precious and dear,
As though once more I must suffer the pains of death.

Virginia Moon Peters

NICOLE

Can you write of a rainbow's radiant glow,
Or paint the fragrance of a rose?
Can you capture in song the butterfly in flight,
Or the shining sun on new-fallen snows?

So it is with you, Nicole,
whose beauty surpasses all words I know.
I try to capture in lowly verse
The splendor of your radiant glow.

The flowers are no match for your smile,
They humbly bow as you pass by.
With eyes that sparkle like the sun on the sea,
You outshine the rainbows set in the sky.

Your outward beauty is beyond all words,
But the inner you is lovelier still.
Yours is the beauty of a child of love,
Born of your heavenly Father's will.

Your beauty, Nicole, is far too great
For me to capture in feeble rhyme.
Words themselves will never suffice
To describe the beauty of one so sublime.

Dale R. Miller

DELAYED DIALOGUE

Because your ears have heard the din
    The deep roar of engines so deafening,
Are you unable to hear me? But then
    There's more than one way of not hearing.

"A little louder, child," you shout.
    And while you hammer, I try explaining . . .
But you walk away, leaving me out.
    There are many ways of not hearing.

I shadow you without pretense,
    Worshipful, filled with a child's solemn vow
To follow in her father's footprints.
    But, Daddy, can you hear me even now?

Claudette Roberts

GOODBYE

Goodbye dear one I am leaving,
I won't see you anymore,
The ship sails slowly, you are lonely,
Standing watching from the shore.

I did not think then, would not have gone then,
We only wanted to be free,
It's too late now, we are divided,
Death's cold reaper I did not see.

Deeper depths do now divide us,
Than the railing and the land,
A harsher distance at God's insistence,
Leaves me wandering along the sand.

The land is good here, the corn is high now,
The sun is shining through the trees,
Oh, so sadly I will wait dear,
Calling to you through the breeze.

Margaret Chasty

OCTOBER

Did you ever stand at the top of a hill
On an autumn day, and your heart stood still
As you gazed at the beauty you saw below
The purplish haze of the October glow.

The leaves all golden and reddish hue
Reaching their arms to a sky of blue
Nature doing her best in the days of fall
Like a patchwork quilt hovering over all.

As you gaze at a woods that is right off yonder
And drink in the beauty of artistic wonder
You somehow feel that you'd like to pray
To just thank God for a beautiful day.

For the privelege of having a vision so wide
That you can see beauty on every side
Your glance covers all with a lasting caress
As you vow to be grateful for the eyes you possess.

Gladys M. Andersen

VINEGAR

A versatile liquid of many uses.
A natural product of those fruit juices
Like wine from the grape we sometimes sample.
It comes from the old familiar apple.

This liquid begins as sweet, mild cider.
With sugared doughnuts, it makes a glider.
For annual parties at Halloween
It tops them all to quench the Queen.

It's pressed, whole apples — worms, seeds and all!
Oh, yes! this happens in every fall.
I often wonder — (you really should)
How it can taste so mighty good!

Like all living things which change with age,
A story develops — page by page,
Our cider soon loses its sweet, fresh flavor.
For you it might have a more tangy savor!

Clodah G. Summer

257

NORMAN

Norman makes paper boats out of newspapers
for his children to find sitting on the table
that appears to be marble.

In the morning, they find boats on a marble surface, black and white
words melt into their hands and later smear the print
on the print on the wall — The children haven't learned to read yet.

The boats fold into themselves after gliding on the tile,
after restless children bring the boats to the harbor
in the corner of the kitchen, not in orderly fashion —
crooked boats overlap the squares of yellow tiles.

Norman was the original captain, he sits down at the marble table —
marble isn't marble unless some color or shade swirls through whiteness
and all of the print used to christen the ships
is illegible and unreadable.

He makes the boats to make them happy. What appears
to be marble, what appears to be a boat, simply appears.

Norman is placing memories in places — He sees the swirls in the marble
as the life lines in his hands unreadable.

The children haven't learned about anxiety yet. For now,
they find comfort in the morning, they find comfort in their boat
and Norman finds it strange to be a father.

Valerie Roses

LINCOLN'S LETTER OF TRIBUTE

The War Between the States has ceased our civil strife of hate.
No victor's bells of jubilation ring of pride or profit gained
By heroes' lives laid waste to seed a rebirth of freedom's reign.

In grief we pay tribute to our soldiers who served undaunted,
Consecrating their memory to our cause to be united.

Your son's spirit rises above our country's desolate ruin,
Purifying the remnants of confrontation's shameless face;
Asleep in God's peace . . . enshrined in valor's holy tomb.

If I could have spared your anguish we both share today,
My life I would have denied to stave our nation's painful fate.

But our peoples' suffering shall not have been in vain;
Our Union's bond cleaves to new roots yielding wound's resolve
To unite Liberty and Brotherhood firmly and unchained.

For our Creator in His goodness deemed mankind equally noble
As there can be no greatness beyond that which is humble.

And now together, absolving our nation in our darkest hour,
We challenge our future in the light of renewed dedication —
To performing our duty of preserving our Union in just power.

A Union that will prosper and guarantee the welfare of all,
Because your son and other heroes of our Unions answered its call.

Barbara J. Angeli

I FOUND GOD THROUGH HIS MIRACLES

I felt God's gentle touch, in the softly falling rain;
And His warmth was in the sun, when it began to shine again.
Though I could not see Him, just the turning of the leaves;
I could feel His "presence," in the gently blowing breeze.
God wants us to know, He loves us, so another miracle was done;
He sent into the world, his only Begotten Son.
This Miracle, called Jesus, taught us how to pray,
Told us we could "talk" with God, today and every day.
He told us how to please Him, everything that we must do;
I found God through His miracles, and I hope you will find Him too.

Betty Neff

SKY SANDS

Ubiquitous Artemis, locked from
The shadows of these leafy cliffs.
With artisan's precision she's painted
my canyon, though locked herself
    out of its shadows.

Streaming radiance unfolding along
The canyon floor. Entwisted, we
Stroll together except through places
She can't go, for she's locked herself
    out of the shadows.

Up above us, far up and away, a
Sea; smooth, calm, of royal, lay
Beaches of rippled clouds. Darkness!
Where did she go? Oh, she's locked herself
    out of the shadows.

Galleon and gulls flung up on the sea.
Together we stroll in ecstasy along
Canyon floors; strolling, flowing, spill-
ing. She's vanished now, locked herself
    out of the shadows.

L. Ann Beard

DOWNTOWN STREETS

I walk along the streets at night
Beneath the glow of downtown light.
I walk along the streets at night,
Many times alone.

And of the others walking here,
There are those that smell of beer.
Some push drugs and some are queer.
They, too, are on their own.

But I am not succumbed by this.
When I leave, how can I miss
The passion of this downtown kiss
With crime upon its lips?

Someday I'll leave it all behind.
Just let the doper rot its mind.
In the meantime, you can find
Me making downtown trips.

Ronald W. Bracken

WHERE

are the flutes
and the violins

why is the song
that the sunset ends

where is a kite
on a Winter's night

why do the days
burn away the light

who plays the waltzes
when you sleep

why serve the songbirds
on a plate

where are the flutes and the violins

why are there tennis courts
instead

Maro Rosenfeld

THE RACE

Because I'm getting old I'm gradually slowing down
Time has come for me to stop running around
When I was younger I didn't realize
Time takes its toll as years go by.

I used to work all day and ramble all night
I can't do that anymore because the end is in sight
Because time has taken its toll and caught up with me.
I'm not as strong as I used to be.

Time has come for me to set a slower pace
I'm going to settle down and get out of the race
I'm going to withdraw from the field of competition
And leave the race for those seeking recognition.

I've learned life's ladder is not easy to climb
As we grow older it gets harder all the time
I'm going to settle down and set a slower pace
'Cause time has come for me to get out of the race.

John D. Ferguson

FERGUSON, JOHN. Born: Miami, Florida, 5-13-22; Education: Eighth Grade; Occupation: Janitor; Awards: Honorable Mention for work appearing in Talent Songwriters and Poets of 1947, Haven Press, New York; Certificate of Merit, American Song Festival Lyric Competition, 1983, Hollywood, California; Honorable Mention, National Society of Poets, Inc., 1979; Poetry: 'The Cast of War,' Haven Press, New York, 1947; 'My Mother,' National Society of Poets, Inc., 1979; 'Battle,' Quill Books, Minot, North Dakota, 1982; 'A Description of You,' 1981, Young Publications, Knoxville, Tennessee; Comments: *I write because I'm a gifted writer and want to share with others the talent God gave me. I try to express the way I feel each time I write a poem or lyric. My themes and ideas in my poetry are brief and sincere.*

MY SILENT FRIEND

My Silent Friend walks with me through forest green,
Crowded avenues, deserted streets and mountains high.
In pain and sorrow, laughter and sunshine plus joy and peace.
My Silent Friend is always there with a guiding hand,
A quiet word and silent prayer, showing me what is the
Right and wrong way, letting me see what's good in life.
My Silent Friend never disagrees or says I'm wrong.
Only helps me through another day, smiles with me
When I'm happy, cries when I'm sad and all my ups and downs.

Shyrl Johnson

A WRAITH OF REMEMBRANCE

Two spirits lived before the Earth was ever formed.
Before the fields and highest mountain peaks,
Or clouds, or deepest seas were newly made,
And Earth became a vital, living thing.

In premortal state they found their only love.
Betrothed, their promises they made, to keep
And find again to consummate their troth.
Yet different times and miles apart their births.

Though unknown speech, and foreign lands, they'd find
Each other, matter not the dark and endless road,
Or death-defying traps along the way.
Without their love they wanted not to stay.

Then one sunlit day their love emerged,
When paths did cross and hearts with wonder filled.
For in those moments, and out of deep despair,
They read the meaning of their love and tears, in eyes
That glimpsed the secrets of that other world up there.

Maree B. Hamblin

HAMBLIN, MAREE BERRY. Born: St. Johns, Arizona, 6-4-08; Married: 11-13-26 to Mark Elbert Hamblin; Education: Brigham Young University, B.S. degree Provo, Utah, 1933; Post-graduate work, summers at the following: Arizona State Teachers College, Flagstaff, Arizona; University of Hawaii, Honolulu, Oahu; University of Alaska, Fairbanks, Alaska; Methodist University, Anchorage, Alaska; Occupations: Retired after 30 years in Education, 1974; Called back as Director of Curriculum and teacher's training for 1977-78 at the Inupiat University at Barrow, Alaska — the furthermost university (north) of and the only Eskimo university in the world; Memberships: Teachers Association — State and National — while living in Hawaii and Alaska, California and Arizona; Awards: Sold option to fantasy novel, *Kish Kooman,* to Hollywood producer for full length movie, 1985; Novels: *Kish Kooman, When It Rains on Jerusalem,* and *The Celestial Connection,* all submitted as options to a Hollywood producer, 1985; Comments: *I write supernatural, fantasy novels in settings of good and evil. The element of love is strong, yet clean, triumphing over the demands of the dark forces. Lots of action. I started writing for therapy, when I lost my husband. Now I'm hooked. I write poetry for pure pleasure, to express feelings that cannot be expressed any other way. My serious poems are borne on thoughts such as HOPE. I'm deeply religious, and writing my poems give me a measure of comfort against our modern world problems that seem so hopeless.*

THE SNAKE'S POINT OF VIEW

To be a snake is really rough,
To know that no one wants you.
Not only that —
People chase you, hit you, kick you.
They even call the cat.
Never any tenderness.
Never any joy.
Unless of course you're that lucky snake
That finds himself a boy.

Alice N. Wilson

AN OBSERVATION

every day
i sort out my life
in the laundry
    of responsibilities

now i know
the people i like
slip a negligee
    among their dish towels

Marjorie Jane Miller

THE LAST RACE

Coming around the turn was fine
I braked and skidded around with ease.
The straightaway was something else
I poured it on and made it through.

But all of a sudden I thought about
That drink I took before the race . . .
And then I knew the reason why,
My car was smashing through that gate.

John W. Hugel, Jr.

LONELY PLACES

All the lonely places —
    (The wind blowing cold and hollow
        As a Banshee's lament) —
            Are my birthright.

I love the lonely places
    Their mystery haunts me
        Like beautiful old music
            Picked out on a lute.

Donna K. Bostick

ONCE SHE WAS A BUTTERFLY

Once she was a butterfly
Flowing as a glider in the wind,
But now she is a caterpillar;
Stuck in a cocoon of pretend.

Sweet grounded child of the earth,
Patch your torn wings and fly
Up where the sun kisses the sky,
Sad child of Heaven — fly!

Yolanda Queen

A LEARNING EXPERIENCE

Clippity clop across the floor
Like his daddy did before,
Grandpa's shoes and one small boy,
Who laughs with merriment and joy.

Two tiny feet completely hid
Beneath the tongues, like daddy's did.
He tried to run, the shoes stood still
Then down he went, a headlong spill.

But Grandma knew what she was about,
She saw that lower lip just out
And picked him up to kiss the tears;
A habit practiced through the years.

With wrinkled hands adept and sure
Proceeding, to complete the cure.
She placed his feet within the shoes
Then urged him on lest he should lose
The confidence he needed to gain,
To grapple with, and master pain.

A problem met serene, not vexed
Prepared him best, to meet the next.

Ruth S. Bixler

BIXLER, MARJORIE RUTH (SLA-TER-NEE). Pen Name: Ruth S. Bixler; Born: Oak Park, Sacramento, California, 2-8-05; Marital Status: 1923-27, divorced, one son; 1945-76 to Carl E. Bixler, deceased, one son; Education: Two years High School, Trade School, Night School, studied Office Management, Creative Writing, Oil Painting; Occupations: Merchandising, Executive Secretary; Research Assistant in Biology, U.C. Berkeley; Memberships: Choir and Presbyterian church choral group, Mt. Diablo Choralairs, 1956; Awards: Honorable Mention for two paintings, art show, 1974; Poetry: 'Fulfillment,' short poem, *Unity Paper*, 1945; 'God's Treasures,' about infants, 1967; 'Treasure Hunt,' a boy's pockets, 1980; 'A Fool's Soliloquy,' 1974; 'Traveling,' *American Poetry Anthology, Volume III, Number 1-2,* 1984; Comments: *Arts in general are a part of my being. Poetry and painting best serve to bring cheer, to comfort others, to encourage, with bits of philosophy or to banter just for the fun of it. From age five, I have sought God's guidance and gotten it.*

SILENCE

It's the silence that hurts
Me most of all.
The emptiness —
The knowledge that I've
Simply been forgotten,
Put aside —
Packed away in your memory,
To be pulled out perhaps
Someday when you feel
A tugging pang of guilt —
But not regret.

Susan Leeman

MY GULL OF PEACE

As I sat upon the sand today,
A gull came waddling by.
He stopped and looked right at me,
And I smiled and wondered why.

But I sat there without moving,
As he strutted 'round me near.
So I turned my head and spoke to him,
For he seemed to show no fear.

And I told him I had envy
For his freedom just to soar,
To come and go as pleased him,
And be near the ocean's roar.

Then he gave a wink and sauntered on
And I watched him out of sight.
Yet, I couldn't help but wonder
If somehow he'd touched my plight.

For I closed my eyes and soared with him,
Up, up into the blue.
Now my mind felt young and free again,
And my muse in life renewed.

J. Lee

A BABY'S PRAYER

Although I'm just a baby
and I don't know much at all,
As I start to learn to walk
Please catch me when I fall.

When I get older and can understand,
Please teach me how to care
For those less fortunate than I,
And teach me the power of prayer.

And when I get into my teens
And things sometimes go wrong,
Help me realize trials come
Only to make me strong.

And when I finally fall in love
And choose my spouse to be,
Please pray with all your heart
That I'll choose most carefully.

And when it's time for me to die
I'll go with peace inside;
The special parents you have been
Gave me much joy and pride.

Joye Atkinson

CONSEQUENCES

Lace fringes on an iron curtain,
No one sees beyond.
Talks of peace,
Rumors of war
Red carpet rolled out on white land.

A grinning bear stalks the forest,
No one sees his eyes.
Ice in the desert,
Fire in the sky
A rain of ash that burns.

A berserk ruler with nervous subjects,
No one left to see:
Holes in rocks,
Skeletons playing ball
A red mushroom clouds the sky.

Robert Aspel

GOD'S SPIRITUAL TREE

We cannot pick the spiritual fruits from God's tree
But "Ask and it will be given thee."
The fruit of Love
The fruit of Joy
These fruits He gives
That we may enjoy
The life He gives each day
The fruits of Kindness, Mildness and Peace
That from this world's darkness we'd find release.
Longingly we seek these things
For these fruits many blessings bring.
The nine fruits of God's spiritual tree —
We need these fruits that we may grow
That His spirit may freely flow.
Lord, let me imitate thee
That I may longsuffering be.
Let self-control and goodness also be mine.
To alter the bent of my selfish incline.
    Faith — Faith — Faith
I can't take these fruits for myself you see
From God's righteous spiritual tree,
But "Keep on asking and it will be given thee."

    Eva O. Avery

THROUGH MY MOTHER'S EYES

Through my mother's eyes I have learned how to watch,
    not just to see.
Through my mother's ears I have learned how to listen,
    not just to hear.
With my mother's laughter I have learned what a song is.

Through my mother's words I have learned how to speak,
    not just to talk.
Through my mother's sensitivity I have learned how to live,
    not just to survive.
Through my mother I have known what it is like to feel loved,
    and how to give that love back, time and time again.

Through my mother, and with my mother, I have learned
    how to live, and how to share life, and in learning
    how to live, I have also learned that I can be a friend;
    that I can help someone else to learn and grow;
        someone — like my mother.

With all I have learned I have discovered
    a very special friend — My Mother.

    Anna Flanagan

TABLE FOR TWO FOR ONE

Just in case . . .
I clear a chair of dayworn jeans
and sleeves
and faded moral prints I used to wear.

I set the table
as you would have set a date.
A flask, a flower, a finger bowl of music . . .
As usual
you are late.
By eight I sigh and pour the wine
for one.
By nine
I finally recall
that when time flies
it flies
away.

Without you I've no wings to follow it.
So I retire at ten,
again,
as if the past had passed away.

    D. J. Smierciak

YOUR FACE

Your face reflects the character of the person inside
On it is read of how you've been tried
Understanding and compassion are displayed in softness of line
Real tenderness tempers the ravages of time
Firm jaws recount your resolution
Always seeking the best solution
Contentment is evidenced by lips that smile
Eyes sparkling with love betray no guile

    William D. Andrews

IRELAND'S BALM

Beloved Ireland, home of my own, gone long before,
I walked on your soil, was led by still waters,
Guested at your table,
Rested in your green pastures.

Once so serene, now in new territory,
You remind me of a dapper fellow with a lisp,
Out of control, fawning denials,
Vulnerable to pain and edgy nerves.

How can the poison of death
Come to so sweet a place?
Let not your dreams fade,
Anticipate a focusing, pray for an anointing.

Esteemed Ireland, there will be another day;
Trouble, like a deep bruise, shall vanish,
Memory trains of peace shall return,
Again exuberant life abundantly shall be yours.

    Beth Wills

WILLS, BETH. Born: Roxton, Lamar County, Texas; Married: to Raymond R. Wills; Education: Southern Music Schools, Baylor University; Occupations: Piano and Voice Teacher, Lyricist, Writer, Secretary in husband's tile business; Memberships: Co-Writers, Nashville; Fine Arts Association; Awards: Altrusa Awards, High School and College; several Honorable Mention awards from Edward A. Fallot Association; Poetry: A number of poems published by Fine Arts Press, American Poetry Association, Texas Poetry Press, Rainbow Books, and various newspapers of Texas, also lyrics for Nasco and Jupiter Records; Comments: *My poems display love flings with America, Ireland, England, Mexico, Texas, the Bible, my work and my charming entourage. Writing is almost as essential to my life as breathing.*

MY DREAM GIRL

Like a light in the darkness, or a breath
Of fresh air in stale, she came into my life.
Bringing hope and expectation.
She came unexpectedly. Seem out of nowhere,
And has gone again into nowhere.

She was unique.
She brought a new outlook on life and on living.
A person to be reverenced and loved.
Something one has wished for, but never expected to find.

She has gone again, and seems as a dream.
A pleasant happy dream.
That one wishes would go on forever.
She has left a void in life.
But, also, she has left something else.
Hope! A realization that life can be glorious.

Her image will fade back into time.
And as the days pass, the picture and realization
Of a pleasant moment will recede into the distance
And, like a flaming torch, it may flutter and dim
But never go out.

The object is gone like the dream.
There is no way I can keep it.
But, the memory,
That, no one can take from me.
It will, always, until the end.
Be there burning. For which I am thankful.

Raymond William Moran, Sr.

THE OLD HOME TOWN

I visited the old home town today,
    and walked around the square.
I passed the little village church,
    where so often I had knelt in prayer.

The little country store still standing
    had been empty these many long years.
And the old depot by the railroad tracks —
    so quiet now, as I gaze through falling tears.

Then, passing by the old home place
    brought back many a memory —
Scenes of many happy family gatherings
    in the days that used to be.

So many changes had taken place;
    the people on the street were strangers to me.
Somehow the place did not seem the same,
    as I had pictured it would be.

For time rushes on as we grow older,
    and the people do not seem the same
Whom we remembered in our days of youth,
    as we recall each one by name.

So we must move on with the present time
    and count our blessings instead,
And relinquish the time that has passed,
    to enjoy the wonderful days ahead.

Geneva Burton Bare

LOVE, GOD'S SPECIAL GIFT

Love is perhaps the greatest of God's gifts.
It raises our hearts and our spirits it lifts.
Love is the sharing of oneself with another.
It is the binding force that keeps us together.
Ah yes, true love is special indeed.
The gift of the Lord we shall forever need.

Robert G. Bosler

MY JOURNEY

When I come to the end of a tiring day,
I go to a place where I steal away
Away in a corner, a room in my mind,
Where I walk in a garden of poems that rhyme

As I walk down the line and peer into each face,
I take note of color; of each one I taste,
Some take me o'er mountains which are most steep to climb
And others into valleys where I savor their rhyme

We go over hills, over mountains and dales;
We walk into hearts with their secrets unveiled,
We pass through the doorway of darkness and rain
And then we climb upward to a rainbow's domain

We walk in the valleys of mourning and loss;
We feel the bereavement of souls who felt loss,
We walk through some doorways of suffering and pain;
We climb back to a summit of starting over again

Some poems are colorful, none are the same;
Just walking among them brings relief from my pain
When my journey is over and of poems I'm full,
I find that my going was never thought dull

A journey that looked into many different faces,
Which took me afar into many strange places —
My journeys are exciting; for in them I find
In my choosing of "patterns,"
I still love those that rhyme.

Bettie J. Frye

THE BURRO

A lonely little burro, stood alone in the field, and
waited for his master to bring him his meal.

He stood and waited patiently, his eyes on the hill,
but still there was no master coming across the field.

Forgotten in his loneliness, the hours turned into days.
The little burro hungered for the bygone ways.

The search began slowly, as he advanced out the gate, he
looked for his master, for the time was very late.

He wandered the country over, his head was hanging low.
Where was his master? Where did he go?

His heart grew very heavy, the pain was hard to bear.
The lonely little burro was sinking in despair.

One step before the other, the circle was complete, as he
stumbled in the darkness, the dust at his feet.

The creator in His mercy, looked down from above, and
touched the little burro with a special kind of love.

As the burro approached the barnyard, in the midst of a
blinding light, there he saw his master, to his delight!

The lonely little burro, will nevermore be alone, for he
had found his master, no more to roam.

Julie A. Armacost

RECORD OF LOVE

Where do I begin to sound the words of beauty
sparkling into song?

Maybe it begins with praise, the love-note eulogies,
that lift my heart to long,

And then I strive to embellish all the radiance
of a dear brother lost in the shadowing eclipse of time.

As I tunnel through forgotten memories of precious words
and laughter coming into light, it's then and only then,
that I begin to climb.

I reached to heights, I thought my soul could never find,
but there I was — soaring — in such feeling and with prayer.

And then I think I found an answer in all my
anguish and despair.

It's in the love that God offers to all His sons
and daughters in the light of Tomorrow's land.

I refuse to believe we've lost a brother, a son, a real love,
our Tom; he's with God, his most cherished fan!

Bernie Stoffel

SONNET TO A FRIEND

Now that he's gone, I think of him so much.
He never thought a finger's snap of life.
I must admit he had a human touch
Of earthiness, which caused a bit of strife.
A wit that sometimes punctured as it fell,
Yet now I need a kindness he threw in.
Oh, cruelty! To have him hear the bell
That tolls for some before they know a sin.
Dear God, in some sweet place he surely dwells.
Treat gently, he whose tears I have not seen,
And make for him a place where music swells,
And let him know me . . . as I might have been.

Vivienne F. Meyer

MEYER, VIVIENNE FLORENCE. Born: New York City, New York; Married: Rayfield Meyer; Education: Cathedral High School, Sioux City, Iowa; Occupations: Homemaker, Singer; Awards: Two Honorable Mentions; Poetry: 'Sonnet to a Growing Boy,' Iowa Poetry Day Association, 1971; 'Fog,' sonnet, *Brochure of Poems*, 1967; 'Study in Contrast,' *Brochure of Poems*, 1968; Comments: *I seem to write mostly about hope, love and various human longings within myself, and others. As one sings a song to reach out to others, so do I write poetry. It's a giving of oneself to humanity.*

THE FOREST

Beauty in the seasons of the year,
bless my soul from afar and near.

The leaves reap the color of rainbows.
The sun's blossom the horizon low.

Autumn and pine, a curious breed.
Yellow, red, and green leaves grow from a seed.

Miracle of nature and the salve of the earth,
beauty and splendor take time from birth.

The antiquated trees rise high in the sky
Aged and picturesque; one day to die.

"Forest, where have you gone?"
Cleaved landscape, it is done.

America, the beautiful, an awesome sight.
Skyscrapers, buildings, and malls are the plight.

"I love the forest, but where is it?"
Man, the schemer, says the forest does not fit.

David Jeffreys

JUNK YARD

Hi Dear, Call the Junk Yard,
Look at the card.
We need a wheel and a front seat,
Then the car will be complete.

I called the Junk Yard,
The number on the card.
Hi! I'm so and so and want such and such,
Make, model, etc.

Hesitating, I said, Now let me see —
My, how hard that man tried to stop me.
I was undaunted
Until all of the information spilled out of me.

Suddenly, he said,
LADY! Don't stop around here for at least three weeks!
Why? Indignantly, I asked.
Because, LADY, all I can see are Snowy Peaks!

They look like mountains, you can be sure.
What's more — LADY —
You see — Listen to me!
YOU CANNOT PLOW A JUNK YARD!

Elaine Meli

MIND/SELF

Darked on drugs and hopelessness,
fiery hell breathes my life on a path-wind,
down on to insanity and drunkenness,
if only it weren't for my mind,

Screaming out — back at me,
let me live and be,
let me be free — it pleads,
and leave me with some dignity.

O, poor, poor child,
don't destroy us like this.

For I can't die this living death.
I cannot live this dying life,
I don't want to leave like this,
Buried in your lies . . .

Alexis Rae MacDiarmid

SPRING (STONEY GAP)

Will you join me at the
waterfall today?
It is spring, and Love!
is everywhere.
The mountain's endless blood,
is surging into view;
Red, dominates the landscape,
except at the brook
with its beautiful waterfall.

Only reflections of spring's life,
mingle into the eternal mirror
of the stream, without emotion,
or intelligence;
It flows all seasons of time,
reflecting the changes, aesthetic!
you and I steal
for our selfish pleasure.

Kenneth J. Peltz

FEAR

I took a step
Then stopped, I'm shaking.
Should I turn around?
Did I hear footsteps
Tapping on the ground?
Maybe I should run
It could be a trick of my mind,
Or fear, just cold fear.

I took another step
The air is cool, the night is quiet.
There's sweat on my brow
My feet won't run.
Somehow, I must make a noise
Would the mace work
If my trembling hands could get to it?
Maybe I should just scream
The fear is real, just cold fear.

Christine Johnson

LOVE/DEATH

Love,
Conquers many.
Death,
Conquers all.

Bill Stinson

GREEN GRASS

As the old man spoke of heroes
Alive before yet are no more
I stood in green uniform, shined brass
Too young instead to even dread.

As the old man related tales of bravery,
Acts in war the suffering poor
Devastated places, dying men
Their flowing blood mixing into mud,
I stopped to think upon the brink
Of disaster!

He sat straight on his caneback chair
With wrinkled brow, head bowed.
"You face your destiny," he said.
The ground grows cold where
Young like old lie dead lie cold
And the grass grows greener overhead.

Roy Nelson

YOUR LOVE'S WARM GLOW

I sit here in the darkness,
Watching as you sleep,
And the love that wells up in me,
Hurts, 'til I could weep.

Just knowing that you love me,
Keeps me going, day to day.
It makes me want to show you,
How much I love you, in my way.

Your soft and steady breathing,
Assures me you're at peace.
Unconscious, you reach for me,
And I feel your love released.

Your gentle touch, is all I need,
To know how much you care;
Your arm wraps gently 'round me,
To assure you, I'll be there.

Asleep, awake, it matters not,
I feel your love's warm glow,
It emanates from every pore,
And warms me to my soul.

J. R. Moses

OUR MOTHER

Who used to love us tenderly
When our knees were skinned and sore?
Who used to mend without complaint
The many things we tore?

Who used to work the long hard hours
And make the way alone?
To give the three little girls of hers
A nice and loving home.

Who used to do without herself
So we could have the treasure?
That in our years at school and play
Were spent with the utmost pleasure.

Who used to keep the vigil watch
When sickness came our way?
Who is the one we think of yet
On each and every day?

I think you must realize by now
It couldn't be any other.
Than the one who means so much to us
Our sweet and wonderful Mother.

Lila M. Farr

THE BATTLE

In the frosty morning air,
A deathly silence crept over,
Only the sound of the wind,
Blowing over the dead.

Like a church bell ringing,
The clamor of steel sang out,
Face to face came two men,
Moving silently through the snow.

Knowing only one was to live,
Each thing this his last breath,
Waiting for death to slap him down.

A scream suddenly ups the morning air,
Now the battle is over,
Only one stands.

August March

MY BROKEN SOUL

Remember, my love?
    I had a place in your heart
some years ago.

Every week I go to the mountain;
    and the same sadness
invades my feelings.

I then go to the river,
    looking for your shadow
reflected on the water;

the place where we found
    real happiness together,
and the meaning of life.

Now, all my dreams are gone;
    and my romantic soul
has been broken forever.

Antonio A. Acosta

ACOSTA, ANTONIO A. Born: Cuba; Education: Master of Arts, Montclair State College, Dr. of Education, University of Havana; Occupation: Professor of Spanish Literature and Mathematics; Memberships: Circulo de Cultura Panamericano; Poetry: collection of poems, *Images (Imágenes), Senda Nueva de Ediciones, Inc.,* 1985; *My Poems of Fall (Mis Poemas de Otoño),* Navega Printing, 1983; Comments: *My poetry is a song to life, with all the ingredients of sadness, philosophical meditations, longing for lost roots, and finally, the hope for a new-born Spring. A new war should be declared in the whole world: love against hatred.*

I LOVE YOU

In all my dreams, you are there

Life wouldn't be the same without you
Often I find myself thinking of you
Vivid pictures of your face stay with me
Every day is new and different with you

You mean so much to me
Our love will always endure
Unconquerable even by time

Angelica Babudro

WAY OF LOVE

There is a loneliness
        that creeps into the soul,
Conceals itself
        within the heart . . .
Clings to a memory of old
        with exquisite pain,
The memory of a love
        That loved in vain.

A certain sadness
        permeates the day,
Invades the melancholy night
        with keen regret . . .
Lingers on to reminisce
        on guileless yesterday,
With a longing
        that is bittersweet
For a love
        that lost its way.

There is an emptiness
        undefined . . . vague
Shadows cloud
        the sunniest day,
Haunting memories descend
        like misty dreams
Then slowly
        fade away.

Patterns of life unfold . . .
        colored ribbons,
Bold flying streamers
        tossed by winds of fate,
And fickle love beguiles again,
        demanding
To be entertained.

        Mary J. Watking

FANTASY

A feather — like silk:
White, soft, smooth;

It tickles my lips,
But only gently;

No, not a tickle: a tease
Of something better to come;

My heart quickens;
My body tingles;

The skin twitching,
As the feather passes;

I follow,
The feather leading;

Onward gently, it goes,
Teasing softly;

It stops.

I wait, in anticipation;
Slowly, the feather continues,

It pulls me up; I rise,
Higher and higher!

I come.

        Martha Urquhart

FRAGILITY

Cold gray pavement reflects
the sky. The leaves flee
and cower in their wrinkled
brown suits,
purchased at secondhand stores.

Inside nostrils of
the silhouette, air smarts.

Dusk gathers. In the moment
before it descends, the
silhouette glances at
an ice puddle,
notes its reflection,
and is reassured (though
the ice is cracked).

The silhouette pushes on,
Its weight breaks the ice.
It staggers,
the ice still shatters,
and the silhouette stares down.

The human being beneath
breathes in
and out
slowly,
and in pain,
buried below surfaces.

        B. L. Ohrstrom

DORMANT FRIENDSHIPS

Some friendships lie so dormant
Like a bed of arctic snow,
To lie there rotting away
Just as a seed that will not grow,
And then it blows away
Friendships containing that seed
Are those that die one day.

        Paula Bernards

SIFTING SAND

Woe is me should I design,
With malice, to malign
The sages of the ages.

In this vein I deign
That they immortal reign
In many splendid pages.

No writer to revere,
No poet to adore,
I'll make the message clear . . . ,
Not wrapped in metaphor.

Dead allusions are buried deep.
Youth and health I couldn't keep,
And many joys are left behind.

Old and tired and lame,
I'm not seeking wealth or fame, . . .
Just love . . . the Platonic kind.

Far better were I fantasy-filled,
With hopes and dreams instilled
Till all the sand has sifted through.

Recounting all that has gone before
I ask the world for nothing more
Than I have earned . . . and which is due.

        Charles E. Robinson

ALL I WANT FOR CHRISTMAS

I really don't want much,
        That's strictly just for me.
Anything that comes with love,
        Will suit me to a "T."

A gift for the whole world,
        That would be really grand.
A Peace for all men, and
        No hunger in any land.

No sounds of guns and war,
        No smog to burn our eyes.
No cheating on our neighbors,
        No hurts, no tears, no lies.

I guess I want much more,
        Than I first thought I did.
But not for me only,
        But all mankind instead.

When Christmas came long ago,
        With the Babe born that night.
I can have this come true,
        If that "Babe" is our light.

        Joanna Ketcham

TO THE SEA

Milky white and glisten blue
And sparkle lime from algae hue
Amber rocks to apex climb
Beneath the sunlit crystal shine
And low beneath the blanket blue
Snug do caverns whistle through
Tempest-tossed bleak and dead
And awful crimson purple red
Scaly fish have met their dread
King Neptune's heaven have they fled
Now watchful eyes of gulls abound
Towards this vestage have they found
A tear a rip they've had their fill
Towards the heavens do they shrill
With malice stamped upon their bill
Now sun to reach the zenith high
O'er the azure puffy sky — to you
Oh sea, my reply goodby — goodby.

        Gerald LaBarr

CONTROVERSY

The train stopped
The man without a beard
Rushed to meet
Her.

He looked her up and down
Stopping at her
Face.

His eyes asked her a question
The answer was
Yes.
The kiss was
Sweet.

It erased the
Years of controversy and strife.
In one excited
Moment.

Storming through their beings
Without the
Need for a single
Word.

        Ruth Johnsson Hegyeli

ELEGY FOR CHARLES, GRANDFATHER OF RUTH
Deceased Sept. 7, 1980

Once a mighty oak grew in our garden.
It lived on a hill and was very tall.
But time and the elements conspired
And the soil that held the tree eroded,
So the tree listed downhill.
Then gravity came into the picture
And that monumental oak held on by the tips of its roots.
But one day the pull was too strong
so it let go and came crashing down.
Then it was a fallen tree, a has-been, as it were.
That was a handsome tree.
To see it lying in massive disarray
could cause a potentate to weep.
So it was done the splendor and the majesty were gone.
But trees can't just lie there, so they took it away
and it remains now only a memory.

So it was with that mighty oak of a man.
He was a powerful presence like that tree.
He too was a visibly tall oak among lesser branches.
The wallop he packed could floor you.
But time and the elements conspired
and he went down like that old oak;
And like that tree, he lived a life
and now it's done.
                    Amen!

Pearl Melniker

THE CRY FOR HELP

Don't take the walker — Don't take the chair!
I'll leave you out front when we get there.

Inside of me a shame rippled, because I am crippled.

I stand when I cannot — I cry when I must not.
I am weary of my inner pain, caused by your disdain.

Inside of me a pain has rippled, because I am crippled.

I sit alone here at the kitchen table, because I am unable
To do the things that you expect me to do.

Inside of me a pain has rippled, because I am crippled.

The disease that I have can only get worse
Until someone sends for the hearse.

I prayed that you would understand.
But, that is one thing that no one can demand.

Inside of me a shame has rippled, because I am crippled.

I'll see it through. Please? Won't you.
I have accepted it. Why, tell me, Can't You!

Elaine Meli

THE FORERUNNER

Luciferous herald! When Sleep looms a dream
Imbued with pawned glory I long to redeem,
Noctivagant shuttlers, impassioned and deft,
Discern your mystique in Her somnial weft.
And reveries wistfully fancy your sleeves
Convolving my lovers whose glorious weaves
Accord to the pattern you basted with fire,
Refined by the waxing of mellowed desire.
Benevolent distaff, your fiber divine,
Outmoding the flaxen of earthy design,
Nostalgically styled human splendors ahead
Embroidered with flossy remembrance's thread.

Charles J. Lumia

REBEL SOUL

Impulsive like a flash of light.
A quasar planted into the earth's garden, where
roots stretch into the eternal night.
You burn so brilliantly that you burn out like
the fleeting glimpse of a shooting star.
You appear calm and placid yet under that tranquil
veneer nuclear bombs explode.
Lava pours forth flowing from an infinite, fiery
volcano; yet rarely reaching those around you.
Your eyes speak like green neon at night.
Red lips filled with blood, pulsating to please.
Lips and tongue gently caressing and sternly pressing.
Wild, sensuous passion is your food, releasing
locked-up lightning
Sometimes desire gnaws away at the earth inside
your skull.
If you could dissolve the entire universe and absorb
it into a syringe, you'd inject it all at once;
perhaps a massive overdose of energy could calm your
rebel soul.

Robin Fine

ON A STORMY NIGHT

From my window, I looked down at the trees,
as they swayed in rage.
Like a herd of wild horses
shoulder to shoulder
racing through the stormy night,
together in harmony:
in one pace, in one stride,
majestic, noble —
same rhythm, one goal,
on their way without leader —
united in untold strength and beauty,
in harmonious rhythm did they
survive the storm —
without being led.
While Three Billion Light Years zoom
as stars unnoticed above our heads . . .
A UNITED VISION —
as I looked from my window
on a stormy night,
down at the trees!

Vera Little

THEOLOGY

Theologians . . .
Sit on lofty hills, at round tables or window sills.
Some of them don't defend
Truths Eternal.
They analyze and criticize my Faith of Yesteryear.
"Did you hear?
        The Angels really don't exist . . .
        Original Sin is a Myth . . .
        When Christ was born, there was no Star . . .
        The Virgin Mary is no more . . .
        Christ isn't truly Divine . . .
        We're waiting on some Bread Line . . .
        The God Who Was . . . Who Is . . . and
        Who Is To Come . . .
        Did not know He Was . . .
        The Holy One?'"
Methinks there's trouble on The Vine . . .
        Too much cash
        Too much time,
        Too much Wine!

Josephine Mastrangelo Mosera

A PERFECT DAY FOR J. D. SALINGER

Guess who, Seymour, it's Sybil
and I missed you on the beach.
Our banana fish did swim away
but was it you I heard him say
that blew your head and died today?
Well no one cried and who did pray?

From Muriel your wife and kin
I have the gun that did you in.
I think she's glad you died in sin
but not me, Seymour, I'm your friend.

I saw the room where you had slain
and there a man of much disdain.
He said that Salinger was his name
and of your death he charged *me* blame!

Yes, Seymour, killed *you* he said
then he sat me down and at my head
he pulled your trigger and shot *me* dead
and now my head is full of lead!
A perfect day for J. D. Salinger.

Maryvonne Draper

THE POEM DID NOT COME

One day the world had drawn the curtain back:
the sky lay shattered to the ground
and crushed,
the gates of heaven,
hung useless by the side.

The way towards up there was open,
was free but uninviting
for, sullenly it stretched ahead
all scattered with sundrops and splinters
from the broken sky.

When I picked up a few of them,
my fingers burned and bled;
the flesh, the blood and the divine glitter
did not match.

I did not go toward the gates,
I did not dare
to dull the splinters with my blood;
I was alone,
I was afraid.

Dr. C. Michael-Titus

Silence wraps her arms around me,
Nothing moves.
Sun glimmers over frozen ice,
Everything is still.
No birds to sing, or squirrels to chirp,
Winter Solstice is here.
Days on end the stillness lies,
A blanket, surrounding my world.
Even the trees refrain from moving.
Waiting for the first Spring day.
Will it never end my heart cries
No sound, have I heard for days.
A panic wells deep inside,
Will I never hear again.
Suddenly; a rumble mounts,
Low and seemingly from within,
A crack, like a pistol rings through the air
Then quickly, a rumbling mounts
It seems the world must end.
No
It's only Spring, making herself heard.

Oh, how I long for the silence again.

Joyce L. Olmstead

THE EYES OF HIS SON

Try to always obtain peace; through a warm
Smile, soft touch, tender and understanding
Heart.
Try to understand always the ways of others;
For in this is the key towards a better under-
standing of ourselves.
If only we would try — just a little; to look at
The world through the eyes in which he saw it
By.

James A. Smith

MYTH

1ST PLACE

With dusk I ride the last car
of the last Northbound out
as alone as thin bones on the high water line.
Tracks untwist like hair caught on the vanishing point.
The train shrugs and sides up to platform after platform.

Like a mouth forming an answer
the doors open, pause and shut and the train rubs
its blunt head back into the wind. I watch
the huge hard-edged pillars of city pass
lit up and poking at the sky with such persistence
a hole is worn and the moon falls free.

Through air like blued wash water
buildings look wet-heavy and woven on in off whites,
ochres and bricks. My face is held with shadow in reflection
until at every rail scar, shorted, the lights blink out
within the car and sparks, broken blue lightning,
like sleight of hand
let me understand how quick and careless creation must have been
and how as if in a segment of horny tail
I am carried home.

Cindy Tingley

TINGLEY, CINDY. Born: Salt Lake City, Utah, 1-15-57; traveled the U.S. and lived in North Carolina for two years; moved back to Utah then to Chicago where I have lived for a year and a half. Favorite Poets: Robert Penn Warren, T. S. Eliot and Wallace Stevens; Education: University of Utah, graduated in English with a creative writing emphasis; Wrote for the *Utah Daily Chronicle,* the campus newspaper, which helped me become more precise with words; Poetry: 'Storm,' 'Insomnia on a Hot Night,' and 'This Time,' published in the university literary magazine, *Quarterly West* in 1978 and 1979; 'Year After Year,' and 'Atropos,' published in the NCSU literary magazine, *Windhover* in 1981; Awards: First prize for 'Storm,' in the undergraduate Academy of American Poets competition in 1977; Comments: *After a brief dry period, I wrote 'Myth' inspired partly by the elevated train system in Chicago.* Words of Wisdom: *A poem seems to exist by itself in a state of abstraction waiting to ambush the open willing mind which organizes it and the restless pen which strings it on paper so that it can become art.*

WILD GEESE:

With bated breath and neck awry,
I stand transfixed and strain to hold
    The memory of each untamed honk
Within the citadel of my heart —
    Ah, but aging thoughts grow dim
And, truth to tell, I never dared to soar
    So high, so free — nor shout
With such exuberant joy!
    Yet, still each wakening spring, I watch
And ache to heed their clarion call —
    While caged and primal, deep within,
My pagan heart proclaims —
                Next,
                    Fall,
                        Next
                            Fall —

Llois E. Sherman

SEED

What rare and inexplicable sorcery
        enables seed to work its will

Plans   that no man contrives
        breathes   about the womb of things

The entity   that one day   will stand
            distinctive   extraordinary
            a tulip   shell   or mammoth

Lies hidden   maturing   waiting
            its moment of arousal

God within   without   around
        announces not   what yet may come

Within the quest of need
        lies nurturing   answers
        man does not conjure

Time alone   and its Master
        prepares the need
                    the way
                        the seed

JilKar

SINCE WE TWO PARTED
To my wife Bernice Tripp

Both looked at the full moon, you and I,
Had been looking at her from twilight,
Till the deeper, deepest night . . .
The moon set, the clouds were o'er the sky.
I couldn't see — where is your heart's piano?
You couldn't see — where is my poetic soul?

Both of us had been to the wind,
Pouring out each other's thinking,
Revealing each other's inner feelings,
Until the wind's direction changed.
East wind couldn't send you my soul's ringing,
West wind couldn't pass me your piano's singing.

Only she is running here 'n there, — the clear stream
Describing for you the blooming roses in dream,
Sweeping for me the pearly grapes in mist.
She is giving solace . . . Do you see it? I see.

Only the bright sunlight would be giving hope quietly,
Her hot hands are fondling my temple's frost lightly,
Her burning heart is warming your piano's tones tenderly.
Do you sense it? I feel . . . As you wish it last, I will.

S. S. Swan

TRUE LOVE

To cultivate true love is really prime.
    Its influence endures and perseveres:
    No matter if its hopes may change with time,
Its everlasting force will still adhere.
Love, based on principles as true love is,
Is endlessly long-suffering and kind;
But love can act against injustices
And discipline the body and the mind.
This love exists without hypocrisy
And is not interested in its own gain;
Instead, it shows sincere integrity
Although it may appear to be in vain.
    A love that's true is rare, unique, and grand;
    Its virtues are as countless as the sand

Al Betancourt

WINTER

Brown, lifted branches, reticent and stark
Against the pallor of the winter skies;
A single bird that, wild and lonely flies
Black-etched, against the curtain of dark;
And stamped upon the snow, the fine-traced mark
Of some small beast that hunts, and plaintive cries
Full-throated, when the bare woods sing and rise
In soaring shapes of still, enduring bark.
The summer flowers, opulent, and brief,
As easy passion does . . . a spendthrift thing
Of flame, consuming; But stripped winter is
As Love itself; unveiled by bud or leaf
Earth-rooted growth; The shadow of a wing;
And printed deep with naked memories.

Hervey C. Moores

IN TIME'S EYE

The promise was made to wait for awhile
Feelings that strong, fade slowly
Having had them for a long long time
Changing things too soon seemed unfair

But: In time's eye, I need wait no more
The price requested, though a bit high, was paid
It didn't seem to be long enough, perhaps
Thus, only time knew whether it was or not

Happy, fine and feeling free
Something unobtainable, it seemed to me
The friendship anew, may or may not make lovers of us two
But only the eye of time will tell

Debra A. Freed

YOU

Love is like a white-winged dove, perched high in a tree
Love is like the beauty, where the sand meets the sea
Wherever you are that beauty is alive
Like man needs water, I need you to survive

Your eyes are like the sun, shining so bright
Your smile is beautiful as a star-filled night
I wish I could be with you both night and day
I wonder so often, do you feel the same way?

You being near makes me feel so fine
Nothing makes me happier than to dream you are mine
My heart is always with you, no matter what you do
My faith will never die, 'cause I'm so in love with you

C. Butler

The blouses are drooping
They hang with the stockings
Across the long rod
They're misshapen and dripping

They look like I feel
So tired and resigned
To their humid fate
In the still and dark evening

The soft rap on the door
Brings a smile to my face
And the blouses dance
In the bold new breeze

Betsy Bard

GENERATION OF UNDERSTANDING

A fruitful womb gives birth to words
On which a golden diaper girds,
And fed by thoughts and motives pure
The boyhood growth is slow but sure.
The child grows up to be a man
That clears the path to show God's plan:
Below the flag of Truth unfurled
A rod of iron rules the world
With steady beating from behind
To force the march of all mankind.
In Bride, united with the Lamb
In ecstasy knows that I AM,
And everyone joined with the Groom
Takes refuge with him in the womb.

Stephen Feinland

FEINLAND, STEPHEN DAVID. Pen names: Chairman Steve, the Electronic Prophet; Born: Brooklyn, New York, 3-18-43; Occupations: Poet, Game Inventor; Memberships: Christian Science Mother Church and Branch Church; Awards: Greenwich Village Poet Laureate; Poetry: *People's Gospel,* poetry collection, Print Center, 1982; *King of the Lions,* poetic novel, Print Center, 1980; *How to Enjoy Pain,* poetry collection, entered in contest of National Poetry Series; 'Motivation,' poem, American Poetry Anthology, 1984; "Subway Vigilante," board game; Comments: *Through satire, I make fun of common conceptions about sin and death and other woes and show the way to overcome them by spiritual understanding.*

PERSPECTIVES

Youth has an angle of perspective
Wild, audacious, non-reflective.
But old age, tamed by storm and wreck,
Views life through eyes more circumspect.

Thus time rotates the way we view,
Negates some angles once held true.
While other angles, once denied,
Now to us as truth abide.

As "Beauty in the eye of the beholder" may reside,
Could this not be so of the truth we would imbibe?
Perhaps there is no wrong, perhaps there is no right,
Just involuted prejudice to make us get uptight?

To check the angle of one's view, whether blurred or clean,
Rotate, check each pro and con of the mooted scene.
This should hone the focus of the scene we view,
May invert some image we now host as true.

Although objective right and wrong may really not be true —
Still I'm convinced there are some things we should and should not do.

No need to get uptight when we disagree,
For all one has to do is, agree with me.

Charles Willard Daniel

FESTIVAL OF PRAISE

Join the festival of praise, sing all ye people, sing!
Join hands, neighbors and new ones; gather the children about!

Make voices resound and rejoice, break forth gleeful thanksgiving!
Away, barriers of reserve and caution; let flood gates spill over!

Leap forth as the brook and its waters, jump up as the fawn in the field!
Go out with marching of gladness, step to the glorious sound!

Give others song of victory, shout boldly to the world!
All races, creeds, and differences, join in the hope of rebirth!

Let God's light break through us, good heart ripple and thrill!
Praise the Lord of Hosts! Shout praise to His glorious name!

Exalt His power and His majesty, triumph His loving kindness abroad!
Praise Him ye sun and ye moon there, praise Him ye stars and heavens!

Praise Him ye creatures in the forests, soft glens, and vastness beyond!
Don the garment of praise together, we weak and the down-and-outers!

Get up! Lift high banners at once! Magnify the good and the holy!
God's power! God's people! God's time!

Bring glories to earth! Through His Son!

Mae Cross Tarrant

A VOICE IN THE FAR

Once I was inspired to write a book of poems,
But much to my regret, I found myself in mourn.
I sent my book around the world, and around again,
But the editors just made a joke of my precious pen.
I thought, and thought, and thought, and I thought again.
Until one day I heard a voice saying in the far —
"If you keep on writing, they'll know who you are."
I watched my pen begin to write, on its very own.
I wrote, and wrote, and wrote, for oh, so very long.
I read the words out of curiosity and they were very mellow.
To my surprise I read the words, "Love, Henry Wadsworth Longfellow."
I sent my book around the world, one desperate, final time,
And don't you know, they never joked, about this pen of mine!

Peggy Kendrick Clements

HOKUSAI, A Folk Hero

IDENTIFYING

A young girl sat on a grey wooden bench,
looking youth and country, according to *Vogue*.
The wind blew her hair and her scarf about —
She was separate from the city.

From the high, dark desk of metropolis,
he strove to the curb to hail a cab,
in pressed gray flannels and attached.
The wind blew "Extravagant," his aftershave.
He was confident and candid.

Wisdom is given to those few, separate ones.
She was "sorry he thought she was someone else,"
so convincingly, he assumed that, himself —
He thanked her for her understanding.

Marie Viens

INVASION

Each day I do battle with all of my might,
'Til the enemy's dead, or at least out of sight.

But the next day's the same, though their dead are a lot,
They keep on coming, from whence I know not.

My finger grows numb from so long on the trigger,
Yet each time I look their army seems bigger.

I've swatted and flayed 'em
I've trampled and sprayed 'em

       Be rid of them I simply can't
       My adversary — the lowly Ant.

Elsie Harkness

GOD'S CREATION

The galaxies of space are not too vast
To know God's will and answer to His call;
The tiny atoms never move too fast
To heed the hand that guides both large and small.
The spinning worlds their ordered orbits run,
Planets and stars their destined pathways hold,
Earth turns obedient around her sun,
Her living creatures patterned in God's mold.

Of all created forms, alone to man
God gave His gift supreme — the power to choose —
That freely he might love and loving live
Close to his Lord, fulfilling all the plan.
Blind willful Man, how long will he refuse
Obedience to God — and God forgive?

Lucy Mason Nuesse

NOCTURNAL LULLABY

The grove of trees are silhouetted
Against the fading light of the late summer sky.

A twilight world, transfixed with a solitary atmosphere,
Spreads across the cool country grounds.

Multitudes of insects begin their soothing concert.

The rhythm of life slows down,
And the nocturnal softness of this natural environment —
Undaunted by man's illumination —
Lulls me to sleep
As the stars become brightly visible
In the heavens.

Elliot Richard Dorfman

APRIL MAGIC

April raised her magic wand
The sleeping earth to waken.
Elves and fairies heard the call
And to her side they hastened.
With perfect timing
And in exquisite form
Nature's Spring pageantry was born.

The hills and vales were covered
With a mantle of misty green.
Woodland and meadows were dotted with flowers
To brighten the greening fields.
Along the banks of a rippling brook
Fern fronds slowly unfurled.

Echoing afar
As from a heavenly choir
Bird songs filled the air.
Oh, the ecstasy
Of an April day
In the lovely Ozark hills.

Essie DeCamp

THE LAIR OF COMBAT

The roots of justice are watered by our thoughts;
The rocks of tyranny will never shatter our principles.
If hypocrisy should seep into our people;
It would become an axe that will sever our roots.
Shame on us if we wear the cloak of wretchedness;
Better to die than to live in deceit and hypocrisy.
Let the axe of justice uproot all tyranny,
Where in the world is any sharper axe than ours?
Be lion-hearted and risk your life in the Lair of Combat;
There is no room for boxes in the lion's lair.
O, Bidar be on guard lest our thoughts be torn apart.
Victory is ours if we strive with one heart and soul.

Sayid A. F. Bidar

BIDAR, SAYID A. F. Born: Iran, 10-14-46; Single; Education: University of Jena, Doctoral Degree, East Germany, 1980-81; University of Tehran, M.S. Degree, Tehran, Iran, 1972; University of Tehran, B.S. Degree, (Equivalent), Tehran, Iran, 1971; Occupation; Professor of Comparative Languages and Literature, University of Oran, Oran, Algeria, 1979-81; Writings: 'Geryeh Sar Kon,' (Weep Aloud), *Negin Magazine,* Tehran, 1968; 'Marge Bahare Adamiyat,' (Death of the Spring of Humanity), magazine of Pegerkhi Qamooni, Tehran, 1969; "Falsafaye Inkilabe Hosain" (Philosophy of the Chi'ite Revolution, 61 years after the Hegira, 683 A.D.), Persian and Arabic poetry and essays, publisher, Farahani, Tehran, 1972; *Sarkhatol Hag (Outcry of Truth),* poems in Arabic, magazine of Al-Ekha, Tehran, 1974; *Fi Qalb Al-Marakah (In the Hearth of Battle),* poems in Arabic Al Tahrir-Al Thagafi and Al Najof magazines, Iraq, 1969; Memberships: Iranian Psychiatric Society (Psychotherapy Experience), Persian Literary Society, Arabic Literary Society, Islamic Research Society, Middle Eastern Studies Association.

LOVELY LISA ANN

Like the rays of the Florida sun, your charm radiates
    From the glow of your long and flowing, golden hair,
And from the fairness of your enchantingly lovely face.
    While your eyes, like a couple of dazzling jewels,
lift my spirits to ever-ascending and lofty heights!

Yes, you infuse within me a feeling of special awe,
    As my heart swells with pride when I am near you.
I am ever grateful for having met you, dear Lisa Ann,
    Because you are most wonderful, in oh so many ways!
You are as kind and considerate as you are lovely.

Being so richly endowed with beauty of both body and spirit,
    I most sincerely wish that you could be just mine, alone.
Mine to love, to cherish and to adore, the LOVELY LISA ANN!
    Alas it is not possible! So, only a dear friend must I be.
My loving wish for you is a future full of happiness supreme.

Tony Smolar

TANGLED STRINGS

Hey, little boy . . . yes, you . . . over there.
What happened to make you cry?
What happened to make you so despair?
Did you lose your kite up in the sky?

Hey, little boy . . . yes, you . . . over there.
You don't need my help, you say?
OK, sweet urchin, but please . . . take care,
As you take your life down a different way.

What happened to make you feel like this?
What happened to make you so despair?
Something in your life's gone amiss,
And it's taken control, so please, beware.

Hey, little boy . . . yes, you . . . over there.
You precious motherless, childless waif . . .
This way's all wrong, or don't you care?
Do you walk this road because it's safe?

You lost your kite up in the sky,
But that doesn't mean you must despair.
The string's just tangled, so please, don't cry . . .
I can fix it, little boy . . . yes, you . . . over there.

Kim A. Hutson

BOYS

Boys are never content,
but heavenly sent.
They go from trains to a poppen gun,
but by the sounds they're having fun.

Always happy to hear a girl scream,
from a spider or dead snake.
Then off to skip rocks in the lake,
holding on their faces a sneaky gleen.

They're always in trouble,
but deep from their heart, love seems to bubble.
They play funny little games,
with silly, unbelievable names.

They pass years of basketball and football,
but years to come it's worth it all.
Then oh my gosh! They find girls,
that send them in orbit and spinning twirls.

The day they marry,
with mothers a little wary,
so soon he's grown
all that's left to say, "Don't forget to phone!"

DeNisa Owens

LIFE GOES ON

The early morning sun will rise,
To the sound of baby animal cries.
In a brand-new day of hope,
God giving just enough strength to cope.

The river flows a slow, but mighty course,
With unknown strength from a secret source.
The birds fly to their nesting place,
Life goes on at its own pace.

With fall weather creeping in,
All the animals preparing their winter den.
The days grow much longer,
But the will of nature is much stronger.

The trees stand mighty and tall,
All according to Nature's law.
A cool rain falls, and the trees look on with gratitude,
It brings about a whole new change in attitude.

The late evening sun will set,
From the rain, the earth is still wet.
Night comes in its usual slow way,
Sleep is for preparation of the new coming day.

Susan D. Waybright

THINKING

There is no solace
To soothe this unrelenting soliloquy.

We can find no route to escape
From that unknown penance of it,
That doom at birth bestowed upon us
To deliver man allegedly from chaos.

Any living attempt to wipe it out
Is Sisyphus' rock reaching the hilltop
Endeavoring to bring only his fate about,
And the haunting presence of its eternal recurrence
Whence springs 'the restless stream of mind'
With its kindred spirit of endless Time.

With the loss of its sense
The question of "To be, or not to be" ends,
Its virtues become clownish games,
Yet its ghostly essence never suspends.

Hence, there can be no peace of mind
Until the vain human effort
To overcome its sea-less flow
Is superseded by Philo's Logos.

Franco Boni

TO SMILE WITH YOU

Give me a smile so I can smile too
One that comes from no other but you!
Though smiling is commonplace, not art,
The one that counts must come from the heart!

It is called a "hearty smile," my dear,
The kind that always brings laughter and cheer.
When the sky is gray and I feel blue
Your heart never fails to smile so true!

You, my dear, have taught me how to smile
With you. You and I have set a style
Of smiling for the world and our friends,
Together, to make smiling a trend!

A hearty smile is a smile of love;
You have taught me how to smile with you!

Harry Wong

FRATERNITY

It came from the Greek Land meaning brotherhood.
Fraternity is not just a word, or a four-year degree,
or like belonging to a club for a specific point in time,
Fraternity becomes a part of your entire life.
Fraternity is the friendship and respect between men
who are called brothers.
The memories, friendships, and faces that you experience
in fraternity will become one of your main highlights
in your life.
The opportunity of becoming a brother should be seized,
developed, and appreciated.
For when your college days end, and you walk into the
world about to make it on your own, you'll always
remember the memories, the friendships, and faces which
have developed through fraternity.

Bruce R. Silberstorf

FRIENDSHIP . . . LOVE

Do you use an eye to cast a spell
And send the spirits soaring?
What are your needs, desires, passions;
Do you need love?

Do you need friendship, but not love.
Is love the fearful demon that holds you tight;
And closes your eyes to other visions.
To stop your breath and make you
   lose your senses.

Do you feel secure in love?
Your heart of hearts fulfilled.
Fulfillment may make you forget time,
and color the views around you.
But love needs friendship,
   and friendship love.

Sedrick Arlington Goldbeck

GOLDBECK, SEDRICK ARLINGTON. Born: New York, New York,
12-10-25; Married: to Constance Marie Carty; Education: Graduate of
Chic School of Fashion Design; Designer/Patternmaker, 1948; Occupa-
tion: Retired from Government Service with U.S. Information Agency;
Avocation: Designer/ Patternmaker, Couturier of Evening Dresses and
Bridal Gowns, 1949-74; Comments: *I like to play with words, to create
moods that others can feel and relate to. There is also a desire or need
to express my inner feelings, hoping to share my thoughts with others. I
write about the ways of love, nature and the elements, astrological signs,
Black history, some political commentary and other everyday themes.*

When I think of all the times
That we let slip away,
It kind of makes me sad,
But thankful for this day.
Now we've found each other
And I'm happy in every way.
It's all so wonderful,
And it seems just like a dream.
That you can Love me like you do
Makes my heart truly beam.
To have a Love like we share,
Is the answer to every prayer.
So many things we can do,
Such as walking arm in arm down the beach,
Holding tight to each other and our dreams.
Thinking of the heights our Love has reached.
With great care, feeling, and devotion,
I gladly say to you now and forever,

   I LOVE YOU SO VERY MUCH!!!

W. C. Bateman Jr.

THE DESK

I sit here now, in my classroom
destination: 201
Tired of working, my eyes drift
to a fascinating thing;
the desk where I sit is watching me.
I am reading his thoughts
which go back long ago.
It begins to speak,
in a raspy voice
gossip and hatred across his mind.
It begins to speak faster, cursing and lying.
All of his thoughts
carved into his head.
I slouch in my chair,
His thoughts revealed.
All is out in the open,
until someone new awaits him.
So he can speak once more,
the desk can't keep secrets.

Bettina Hope Stewart

AN ARTIST'S DREAM

As the snowflakes changed to rain,
And tiny drops ran down the windowpane,
I glanced at the Great Oak tree,
Where a friendly squirrel sat looking at me.
From the tiny droplets a small stream was born,
And it came rolling and tumbling down the great tree that morn.
— Then gently falling to the ground,
To bring life to tiny plants all around.
As the stream touched the sleeping things,
They awakened and turned a lovely shade of green,
Heralding the arrival of Spring.
My eyes raised to where the stream began,
A dainty rainbow appeared there between the drops of rain,
Winter was bidding the world Adieu,
And Spring was beginning life anew.
The rainbow in the sky,
Was the great promise to you and I.
For a few precious moments my eyes had beheld,
A beauty that no Artist's brush has ever revealed.

Charlotte Bahling

REMEMBERING

Today I took a quiet trip,
Along the road to memory lane,
Back to days of long ago
Remembering yesterdays over again.

Behold a hazy rose-colored cloud
Holding sweet memories of you,
All the world was folded away
And there remained just we two.

Forgotten were all the sullen days
Remembering only the sunny weather,
Everything seemed so light and gay
When just we two were together.

I wonder if there's a secret niche
Just a tiny spot set apart,
Where those memories are folded away
In a secret corner of your heart?

I wonder if you remember, too
Or would I be searching in vain?
If I were to sometime look for you
At the end of memory lane?

Marie Poe

THE GENTLE ONES

Mr. Wu
Mr. Yoo.
All the Kims
Shims.
Mr. Ang & Ans —
Mrs. Oh!
And the Lims.
Ramon, Borbon
Reyes & Rauez.
The Cho's
Mr. Ko
Songs, Kongs
Chongs, Kang.
Sing & Seng
And Mr. Im.
Mrs. Yi,
The Duongs — 16 in all —
And Baes!

L. Moore Courtney

NATURE'S HAPPENING

Snow fell gently on me and covered me
With a soft blanket of white.
It swirled in drifts about me
And I rested through the night.

The wind came howling, too.
Sending me high in the air,
Like a bird in flight, I flew,
In something like despair.

What would become of me?
At last I fell to rest.
The spring rains came to be
A wild feeling at best.

It forced me underground.
I thought I must be dead,
But then at last I found
I began to grow instead.

I swelled and grew and pushed
My way into fresh air.
In quick delight I rushed
To become a flower, fair.

Tessie Bea McCall

AN ECHO FROM YESTERDAY

An echo falls upon the ear;
An echo from the long ago,
Of one who held his country dear
And would not let her go.

The foe harassed the army sore,
So Washington ordered "Retreat"
But back they came to fight some more,
Who never knew defeat!

He fought when others would surrender;
With firmness, fought, the way was won!
Oh, who could greater service render
Than mighty Washington!

Shall we forget this patriot
Who fought to make our country free;
Who for Old Glory, cast his lot,
And led to victory?

An echo falls upon the ear;
An echo from the long ago,
Of one who held his country dear
And would not let her go.

David Dodds

DODDS, DAVID OWEN. Born: Wheatland, Wyoming, 12-8-18; Married: 9-2-46 to Janet E. (Lacy) Dodds; Education: Seattle Pacific College, 1949-50; Occupation: Retired Clerk; Memberships: Astronomy Club, Smithsonian, Library of Science, The Planetary Society; Poetry: 'Our Saviour,' 11-16-30; 'A Spring Morning,' 3-19-33; 'Away to the North,' *Junior Joys* Sunday School Paper, 2-4-34; 'Mystery of the Stars,' *Daily Olympian*, 6-11-35; 'I Thought,' *Sunday Olympian*, 8-18-35; Comments: *The themes and ideas are mostly religious and some poems are about nature. I try to express my faith in God.*

APRIL

Thirsty buds drink deeply
of springtime waters
before arranging their petals
to clothe summer
in natural, original, designs.

Gordon L. Florence

THE LEAF

Emerald leaves on the maple tree,
    Danced about in the warm spring wind.
You picked the brightest one for me,
    And gently placed it in my hand.
Then you took away the sunlight's gleam,
    And left without one backward look.
I kept the shining leaf of green,
    Pressed away in a rare old book.
When winter came to have her fling,
    I turned some pages old and worn.
There I found the strangest thing,
    My emerald leaf had turned to brown.
Death marred it with a final sting,
    But when I touched its fragile form.
I felt the warmest breath of spring.

Shella M. Lucas

LA DESPEDIDA (FAREWELL TO SOUTH AMERICA)

"A sadness surrounds me,
it penetrates the very core of my being,
nearer to thee than my own beating heart,
a land, to people, a country.
Be there no pain so painful,
as the growing sense of leaving,
a small insight to death.
A death of experience,
long to be retained,
yet never to be refreshed or refilled,
a past within a past,
a past within a present,
a reality within the dreams of life."

Kim Carter Hedrick

NIGHT

Deep tone of purple turned black
    clutching the world
Shadows of today and tomorrow
    are scattered about the actual peace

I stare out the window
    Comforted by what I see
Only the darkness seems real
    real, true, now:
        less confusing than
    unseen, past, future

Finally
    assured
        I sleep

Kristen Ann Hileman

THE OTHER WORLD

On barren land they live,
Few trees to give them shade.
The dusty earth too dry and hard
To afford their cattle pasture.
Their food is brought
From faraway lands,
But not enough to fill them.
Medicine and doctors are too few
To aid the sick and dying.
The rain has not come
For many years now
And the land has stopped producing.
People are dying, so many each day.
This world is slowly going,
And it will be gone one day.

Karen Hache

CONTEMPORARY POETRY

(For Penelope K., Still Waiting)

Contemporary poetry:
And that is all they asked of me.
It didn't seem a lot to ask,
Not such a grim and grievous task;
It could be done in half no time;
It didn't even have to rhyme;
It should be just on twenty lines.
As I am just on twenty-nine,
And you, my love, are forty-two,
Why should I not make verse of you?
A little lilt to utter now,
Utterly now, if I knew how,
As still we slip from each embrace,
Having aspired to fall from grace.
Go lovely rose, yea, fleet from me and fade,
Yea, while I flute my ragtime serenade.
It is your dying that I treasure most,
Blue rhapsody, mood indigo of loved and lost.
This just-now poem is my small surprise.
Lady, this is my sonnet to your eyes.

John Le Vay

LE VAY, JOHN PETER. Pen Name: Caleb Crabtree; Born: 3-8-33; Single; Education: B.A., Tor, 1958; M.A., Tor, 1960; Ph.D., York, 1984; Occupation: Lecturer in English Literature; Poetry: *Instead of Ecstasy,* Porcupine Press, 1977.

WHERE IS THE LOVE I ONCE KNEW?

I saw love turn away
It hurt my soul
to see love react that way.

I cried.
I saw an old lady
stumble and fall
People kept on walking by.

I cried.
I saw a little boy
trying to reach the water fountain.
Everyone was in a hurry.

I saw a boyfriend turn and walk away
when he found out his girlfriend was expecting.
I saw grown teenagers laughing at a crippled child
who walked funny. My heart and soul cried.

What has happened to love?

Why has love walked away?

Why has it turned its back and walked away?

Marlene Hendon

BEST OF SHOW

He brought tears of joy to the Ole Man's eyes,
With his wiggly warmth, his eager puppy cries.
The Ole Man said, "He'll be a winner, this 'un will.
I'll larn 'em, he's smart, I'll teach 'em to heel!
I know that I'm ole, but jus' wait 'n see,
A champion of champions, this 'un will be."
Time passed as it will and the pup grew tall,
The pup, now a dog, would lie at his feet,
And listen with patience, the Ole Man repeat,
"I know that I'm ole, but jus' wait 'n see,
A champion of champions, this 'un will be."
Loyal to the Ole Man in the Show Ring of Life,
His loss was as painful as the edge of a knife.
The day was at hand and he caught every eye,
He stood like a champion, not movin', head high.
He guarded the Ole Man, in the strange sleep,
He waited and listened, to hear him repeat,
"I know that I'm ole, but just wait 'n see,
A champion of champions, this 'un will be."

Dotte Troxell

I LOVE YOU JESUS

Jesus is the son of God
A mighty powerful King
Yet with all His heavenly glory
He loved you and me

HE was so great in all he did
creating miracles of healing
dying with dignity on the cross
yet always loving us

When upon the earth He dwelt
His disciples they were twelve
He asked Peter three times
DO YOU LOVE ME
This is what He said
Yes I DO yet he denied Him three times
If only I had lived when Jesus was on earth
I would have put my arms around His chest

Mary R. Leason

ME

I have to live with me every day of the year;
So I must try to keep myself glowing with happiness and cheer.
I have to live with me, so
I want to be fit for myself to know.
I don't want to pause at the setting sun,
And hate me for the things I have done.

I know I cannot fool myself about me;
So I want my life to be respectful and my conscience free.
I want to meet people with my head held high.
I want people to respect me as I pass by.

In this world in the struggle for fame and wealth,
I want to be able to like myself.
I want to look at me and really know
I'm not just a bluff putting on a worthless show.
I'll try to live so that my thoughts and conscience agree;
And with God's help, I'll try to be happy living with me.

Helen Krebs

TRIBUTE OF LOVE

To Loretta Lynn
In Memory of Her Son, Jack Benny Lynn

I think of all the months you grew inside of me
And the promise of happiness yet to be
With your birth there were many changes to make
But they were worth it all just for love's own sake

I watched you grow, I was so very proud of you
Your strength and courage so sincere and true
A twinkle in your eye, a smile, you liked to tease
All in all, you always tried the hardest to please

God needed someone special to sit at His side
You were given that honor, but still I cried
I know there is no sadness in Heaven for you
But here on earth, color my mood a deep blue

You put sunshine within the corners of my heart
In my life story you played a very special part
Sadly missed by all the folks that you once knew
Oh dear child, Mother will always love you so true

Now Mother must, with a sad heart, let you go
My love is always with you, I hope you do know
In my heart you will always be the special one
After all, God only deals out one first-born son

Erin Lee Lacy

WHY DON'T PEOPLE CARE?

The poor stray animals roam the street
Longing for rest and food to eat.

They seek shelter in some dark hole,
To protect them from the winter's cold.

Their owners have let them run loose day and night,
'Tis no wonder they often fight.

Soon they, too, end up
With litters of kittens or pups.

It's hard for the little ones to survive.
They need their mothers' milk to stay alive.

But often the mothers are killed by a car
As they roam near and far.

At first the little ones romp and play
And don't worry about each day.

Later they realize their mothers
Have gone and now they are left alone.

Like their mothers before them they roam the street,
Longing for rest and food to eat.

Jane E. Baskin

MOONRISE

Mysteriously, in the cleavage of the mountains,
A lurid, purple light waxes to a cloudy magenta;
The moon is being born to night.
Slowly, the moon's crimson sphere emerges
Bathing the mountains' sky in vermilion.
Imperceptibly, the moonrise
          wanes crimson to orange as
                    night hangs her crystal stars.
Clearly, night has exposed
     the mystery of
          moonrise.

Sharon Kraftchak

STARGAZER

Eventide rolls in;
Like an ocean wave, it washes clean the day
With promises of new beginnings tomorrow.

Stage lights dim;
Let the show begin!

One by one, our cosmic host presents
The cast of stars for the night's events.
Above a galaxy unfolds,
With a billion stars boasting,
Each with a tale to be told.

And they'll speak of Man's future,
And they'll sing of Man's past;
For they've guarded us always,
So their wisdom is vast.

Eventide rolls in;
And I take my seat in the meadow deep,
Stage lights dim,
Let the show begin!

C. J. Rosen

THE AWAKENING

Like a storm after the calm
You ignited my passion
Flooding me with feelings I have never felt.

You completely devastated the wall
I had carefully constructed around my emotions
And swept aside the curtains that veiled my eyes.

You uprooted my conception that love was pain
Tossing it about until it turned to pleasure.

Like a violent wind you assaulted my mind
Until my heart cried to rule.

You forced a downpour of tears upon me
To wash away the lonely, wasted years
Showing me a rainbow with the promise
Of happiness at the end.

And the cloudy days since you came
I can't recall
For too many were filled with sunshine.

Renee Ware

TINY ANGEL

To Meredith: Our Little Granddaughter

On a warm Autumn November morn
   A tiny angel decided to be born
Heaven was busy preparing for her flight.
   As she had become restless during the night

A special couple living on earth
   Was patiently awaiting the birth
Knowing not if a girl or boy
   When she arrived, Oh! What joy!

Twinkling blue eyes, color of the sea
   Olive skin, soft as could be
Shining hair, black as midnight
   Little rosebud mouth, such a delight

Angels watched with wonder and glee
   As she charmed erveryone who came to see
They rejoiced, all had gone well
   Back in heaven, they would have much to tell.

Rose Odum

FRIENDSHIP

If you are walking alone,
Your burden too much to bear,
Turn, look along your path;
You shall see me there —
    For I am a friend.

If you cry in pain,
Having stumbled along the way,
Allow me to lend my hand
For support throughout the day —
    For I am a friend.

Neither claim nor reward
Ask I of you to share,
For of myself, I freely give
To have you know I care —
    For I am a friend.

       — Buies Creek, Sept. 83

D. A. Neiburg

CARD GAME OF LOVE

Love is like a card game,
although you're not aware.
    At first you both play the same game,
the same hand of cards you share.

    You start off playing a game
of simple "crazy eight."
    When everything's new and carefree,
everything's smooth and going great.

    But all it takes
is one card game of "war."
    A card game of "war"
beyond repair.

    Then the next moment you're out of
touch!
    And find yourself an endless game of
"solitaire."

Ellen Rutlin

WRITER'S RIGHTS

I would like to be your friend,
but I need time for me.
I need to write my poems, and stuff.
My days are filled 'til three.

On mornings that your child comes here
my work cannot be done;
my train of thought is wasted
since I'm always on the run.

I don't mean to be hostile,
and I'd like to be your friend,
But my mornings are all taken
and I don't have time to spend.

If you need time to be social,
and you'd like to talk to me,
I'd be happy to meet with you —
can't we make it after three?

Judy Tomkiel

THE RAINBOW

I followed the gold in your rainbow, but found no gold.
But I have found gold in your morning's early sunrise.
And in the wink of a sleepy child's eyes.
I can feel it in the warmth of good friendship ties.
It's in the swell of the summer wind's sighs.

I followed the blue in your rainbow, but found no gold.
But I have seen blue in your sky so vast and bold.
And in the warm deeds of people as age turns them old.
I can feel it in the loneliness of feelings untold.
It's in the smell of fire against the winter storm's cold.

I followed the violet in your rainbow, but found no gold.
But I have seen violet in the late evening's cool.
And in the artist's skillful hand, maneuvering his earning's tool.
I feel it in the crispness of a refreshing pool.
It's in the dry leaves of Autumn obeying nature's strict rule.

I followed all the colors of your rainbow, but found no gold.
It took all this time to see that I have more than gold could buy.
There's been times of love, pain and the wondering of why.
I have lost you in the mist of selfishness, seeing only me and my.
I may never find gold, but I have you, and that's enough to get me by.

    Renate Headley

PETER, THE MIGHTY FISHERMAN

Peter was a fisherman; he fished the mighty sea —
Until the Lord said to him, "Come follow me."

No more nets for catching fish, he'd be needing now —
'Twas men he'd fish, and the Lord would show him how.

He followed his Master, over a rough and distant land —
Witnessing wonderful miracles, at the touch of his Master's Hand.

His wavering faith was renewed, upon a stormy sea —
And it was to Peter, Jesus entrusted Heaven's golden Key!

In Christ all fears, he put to rest —
Beyond all other apostles, Peter was blest.

Vicar of Jesus Christ — A Mighty Rock was he!
Beacon to many souls, caught in a tumult sea.

Peter was a Mighty Fisherman and a Mighty Apostle too —
So the Lord placed him at the helm of a ship that was new.

Over calm and stormy seas, he carried Christ's Church safely through!

    Lucy Rotunda

LET'S SAVE US

We've come a long way in our family life & now little things have gotten in our way.
We hurt each other and create problems by things that we do and say,
We see each other's faults and we point them out but not always with tact,
It's not what we say but how we say it that determines how the others react.

We do kind things for each other but sometimes fail to say how we appreciate,
We must verbalize our appreciation before time is too long and too late,
If we take time to tell each other what is wrong, we must point out what is good,
Too much criticism without compliment can cause intentions to be misunderstood.

We must be able to hold and caress each other even when we're not making love,
We must keep each other feeling secure and get help from God above,
We must recognize each other's needs and satisfy them as best we can,
Whenever one of us feels a little hurt we must try to understand.

We must learn the art of compromise when we both can't get our way,
We mustn't let hurt always cause us to act or stay angry for more than a day,
United we must stand in all things that we do,
Kind consideration of each other can help to pull us through.

    Vera Ann Toole

ARMAGEDDON ROSE

Heaven shed her drapery, flaunting a silhouette in skies,
And I saw her omnipotence in reflections:
All her poetry of motion, beautiful in God's eyes.
I heard a bird sing waves of melody above her nest:
And in soft emotion, heavenly gentle:
She flew to her little one's call, abandoning a worldly quest.

Around, and around the sun gleamed warm upon a mountain.
Like a bright candle flashing, it gave golden light.
Rippled in the breath of the wind, earth's boldest purple then:
With riotous orange flowers, shocked green bladed grass.
Tended by each, they each, achieved love rays.
I thought, life's flowers feel soul pulsations from their color class.

I left the intimate array piqued and feeling alone.
Yesterday's sunshine stormed and cleared in turn.
I walked to a waterfall, and heard it hiss and moan.
Water exploding in labor, made me feel rebuffed.
I flung my tears at it and took a fall, flat.
Near me, a rose radiant in pure gold, grew alone, wind fluffed.

One person alone, with God, in prayer beautifully blooms.
And is sweetly fragrant in heavenly perfumes.

Audrie M. Fiskaali

FISKAALI, AUDRIE MAGDALENE. Born: Fair Oaks, Indiana, 10-13-15; Widowed; Education: No formal education past high school, though I have acquired a library of instruction to which I am dedicated. Occupations: Teaching, Art Work, Writing; Comments: *In Revolutionary days a young man, Augustin, delivered mail on horseback and kicked my family tree hard with an independent spirit. I am proud of my inheritance. I write religious verse as a love offering: in some small way trying to thank an adorable Christ-man for His beautiful compassions. My own expressions. I could not, any other way.*

JEWEL OF FYRE

Lif to my herte put your mind at ease; float with me upon the
Breeze of everlasting petal-soft rays of sun,
We'll turn buttermilk skyes into moonlit nights, run through
The night to pleien the shadows,
Turn away owners of lonely hertes, make summer thunder our playground
Fyre winds whisk us along to pine-scented forests, and fields of
Meadowlarks will sing their songe, while I touched where I've always
Belonged;
Deep within, hidden a secret untold too many long days; Yes
I know of the ice, transparent tissue for me, come reveal a naked soul,
No need recoursing your travel, for as the butterfly, I'll jut and twist,
Tenacious clinging till you do sit and ponder to wit, the puzzle I
Whisper in your mind.

Daniel Hudmon

THE MAIDEN

In a faraway land
Where kings reign high
There lives a young maiden
As fair as the sky.

The maiden is wealthy
She's forever that way
Her father is nephew
To a king, old and grey.

The maiden is happy
And it's hard to conceive
With all of her riches
There's no time to grieve.

The maiden has gone now
For she wants to be free
She's searching the countryside
She's searching for me.

Alan H. Wright

SIMPLICITY OF WORDS

I often wonder where we'd be,
If we couldn't speak, only see,
The mouth can be a dangerous thing,
Guess that's because, we're human beings,

Words, symbols of ideas they are,
Like everything else, can go too far,
Simple words, can start a spark,
Simple words, can break a heart,

Words spoken in anger, pain remains,
Words spoken with love, love sustains,
Words, precious as rubies or gold,
Words, so simple, yet so bold,

So, be careful what you say,
No need to break a heart today,
Words that harm, guard them well,
This world, with effort, can be swell.

J. L. Steed

STORM YOU'LL HAVE TO GO

Rain falling all around.
Making puddles on the ground.
I stand here wet without a care.
Just to smell the dampened air.

Now the wind is howling.
Lightning flashing, here and there.
Trees are bending, leaves are flying.
What a storm, I stand here crying.

All around the waters high.
Just look at the darkened sky.
Rain falling all around.
Trees bending to the ground.

So now I run.
For home I go.
Rain I like.
But storm, you'll have to go.

Kathleen L. Oldham

LEGACY TO LAURA

I've lived a life of rainbows,
and shadows, it is true;
and as you grow to womanhood,
let me live on in you.
Pointing out the sunrise
and the raindrops in the air,
I'll show you the flowers
and teach you how to care.
As you run among the daisies,
and stop to smell the rose,
take time to see the beauty
God has given all of those.
But, most important, do your best,
in everything you do.
Don't change your goals for anyone,
and I'll live on, in you.

Jane Griggs

ABORTION

Children playing in the street —
    To the rhythm of skipping feet
    Is heard this plaintive wail.

    "Climb aboard the circus train
    Don't get caught out in the rain.

    Grownups wonder at the fuss
    Lions and tigers watching us.

    Inside, outside, upside down
    The circus comes to every town.

    When it passes by our way
    We hope that we won't have to pay."

Mary F. Gaudet

REACH FOR THE STARS

No matter how far from reach it seems
When dreams come into mind
Don't despair and say I can't
You'll be surprised to find
That if you really want to reach
The goal you thought too high
Seems to ever nearer come
The harder that you try
Look ever to the future
Learn from things gone past
It may take time and sweat and tears
But you'll reach your goal at last
Be proud of your accomplishments
Doesn't matter who you are
You'll know you did the best you could
Reached for, and touched a star.

Ann M. Greiner

WHAT'S WRONG WITH ME

Nobody wants
To marry me.

Nobody thinks
I am lovely.

Nobody cares
Enough about me,

To show me
A little mercy.

Silvia Louise Davis

LIFE WITH YOU

In a love not lost, is where we shall dwell,
With the love of our life, and with a story to tell.
    On a soft summer day, with a smooth summer breeze,
And the wind blowing through your hair as it does through the leaves.
    Come to my side my love, let me hold you in my arms
Let me share with you my world, let me share with you my charms.
    When you look at me, I feel like the shiver of a quake.
When your hand is not in mine, I chill like a lake.
    Your eyes are clear and bright, like a star I tried to keep,
Since you've come into my life, you're the only one I see.
    Let me hold you in my arms, let me hold you in my heart,
Let us give each other the love for the family we shall start.

Alphanzo Townsend

THEATRE TICKETS

You run all over town to track down, two pairs of tickets for the hottest show in town
You call here you phone there to every agent you know
You finally get two pairs of seats, fourth row center that's hard to beat
Important buyers coming to town, have dinner see the show, meet the staff
You're acting as host and that's a laugh
You're so excited you can hardly wait for the day, the boss chose you to see the play
He's really proud of you for getting these pairs, didn't even mind that they cost a
Lion's share
So that very night there's a stormy snow, the telegram comes "It's no go to the show"
Here you are stuck with the tickets, you can't shovel out to use these ducats
That's the way fate has always been, just you know you can't ever win.

Dot Luria Nadler

ANACLISIS

Be not frightened of thine own heart touched by the *flame* of another,
Misdoubt not the universe as Parakletos forming about thine occurrence,
Turn not from this *presence* which engendered thy soul before time
And removed from it worlds without end unto reveal its consummation,
For through that man of the dust came multitudes and the stars,
From whom must arise on love's *tumulus* this Man ancient
Who extends his hands and speaks into existence all that was/is,
Fear not the breath of thine own making returning to God.

Clifford W. Wilson

SEASONS OF LOVE

Watching the seasons come and go
They somehow change day to day
Bring its power and beauty as in a very special way
Never changing my love, but always something new
Through the seasons life goes on and I'm still loving you
What makes a person's feeling change like the days
Is it summer and spring with their flowers, fresh air and sunshine
That makes your life so full and divine
Or is it winter and fall, with the cool and tremendous breeze
That makes you cuddle up with your love, having never to freeze
I think the seasons are a gift from Heaven above
Making life special with the seasons of love

Herman Lee Wright

THE TRAIN

Tonight the windows are up, the air is stiflingly hot.
The smells of hot earth and cut grass drift in on a waft of air
created from the movement of thousands of tiny insects making night
sounds.
Sleep is slow in coming tonight.
A truck passes on the road outside my bedroom window; its wind
chills the sweat on my skin.
The moment of relief is savored.
Far away, in the quiet heat of night, a forlorn train whistle blows
at each town and crossing searching for a love lost in the darkness.
The love is only the memory of a dream.
It never really existed.

Debbi L. Smith

DEATH

Death we did not ask for,
She just sauntered around,
Picked us out and rode away,
Upon wings of muted sound.

Chose not the time of day,
But stayed adamant fingers of time.
She followed her mapped direction,
Obliterated life in its prime.

Over the mountains and streams,
Past the places of mortal birth,
Upon the balustrade of eternity,
Shifted her carrion born of earth.

Here I met her, face to face,
She the conqueror, I the spectral lamb.
Beyond the bedlam corridors of time,
Seraphs kindly whisper, who I am!

Norma Long Hill

LOVELY VISIONS

A golden sunset vision,
Is a statement of eloquence,
To be savored and enjoyed with pleasure,
Thus enriching our earthly presence.

Throughout our life we view,
The wondrous beauty at hand,
As we look through eyes and question,
Our existence upon this land.

The sun ablaze with fire,
The moon in a soft, pale glow,
Tiny stars reach out with twinkling eyes,
Weaving days in which we follow.

Never lose sight of two things,
Of which each should be a part,
The natural beauty surrounding us,
And the ability to love with your heart.

Marjorie Daly

MUFFIN REMEMBERED

I've kept the rug you rested on
The very day you died.
When you left so suddenly, it felt
As though the whole world cried.

Your clicking nails on the kitchen floor
I'm sure I'll always hear,
But no "howly-growl" now greets me
Each morn as I appear.

You gave complete attention
As the meals I would prepare,
Hoping I might drop a crumb,
Or some small morsel share.

I still see you so vividly —
Soft brown eyes and silken ears,
But I'm going to dwell on happy times:
You'd not want useless tears.

Doris K. Rueff

My feelings are mending
as time goes by
when I think about you
I don't even cry

I know that this time
It is over for good
If it didn't happen now
I'm sure that it would

Because you acted so strange
Wouldn't look in my eyes
You talked to me seldom
When you did it was lies

It seems when I trust you
Your feelings fade away
We are through this time
And I really hate to say

That I love you so much
But never want you back
Because the pain is not worth it
And it's trust that you lack

Sherry Caruso

REFORMATION

She tries to hold them in
but they trickle
down her face
streams form
and start to flow
where they flow
no one knows

Somewhere forsaken
carrying misery and sorrow
where it belongs
in the depths
in the darkness

Deep
down in the sewer
the cool, clean rain washes
grime and soot
beneath the earth

In hell it's raining
It never stops

Debi Bonam

AT SEA

Responses dredged from the depths
on chiseled faces damp with moisture.
Under the cliffs the villagers
cast their eyes upon the ocean,
seeking survivors of the storm.

Surging tides scour the reefs
beyond the watchers who see
tattered sails lining the horizon.
Refugees from the heaving brine
bob on the white-capped waves.
Sharp prows coated with slime
course through the water.

Pealing bells, forgetful yells;
the whirling madness sinks in time.
Desert stillness fills the pauses.
A mass is said for the living
in the knowledge of their death,
as the rhythm of the sea
subsides upon the shore.

Deuel Woodward, Jr.

A TOUCH OF QUIET

This morning I woke very early
The room was quiet and gray,
I remember the thoughts I was thinking
In that bittersweet time of day.

I thought about how in the mornings
When I'm lying close to you
The quiet is soothing and peaceful
The gray is almost soft-blue.

I thought about when I was little
When I'd lie in this bed, in this house
I'd listen to the sounds as it settled
The walls shifting in, shifting out.

This morning those sounds weren't familiar
The shifting was deep in my heart
The quiet and gray had deepened
And remains while we are apart.

The last thought I thought before rising
Was of how I want to greet you
As if our first time at loving
Brushed with a touch of new.

Deena D. Williams

HAIKU POEMS

Philosophy of Life
Broken-winged thrush on
  cherry tree sees cat approach;
  twitters till the end.

Genius
Sorrow, enjoyment,
  flowers sprouting from the brain,
  outlive their creator.

Nuclear Threat
Man's lurid ashes,
  with a bang, not a whimper —
  earthling's destiny?

Old Age
Crutches, ailments — NO!
  WILL fights depreciation,
  triumphs over frailty.

Teacher's Advice
Good, then better, best —
  never rest until your quest
  has achieved the best.

Kerry Weinberg

COLORS OF CHOICE

God's children enjoy
Spreading sunlight
With girlish pink and blueboy,
Enjoining God's rainbow of joy
To meet color of choice.

Color bands in vivid voice
Surface themselves
Or, is it by help of tiny elves
Who hang on the shelves
To balance their poise?

To watch and rejoice
After the storm,
To balance power of sorrow,
Rainbow treasure
Incites your pleasure.

C. C. Venditty

DISTILLED

To say in simple speech what's still to say
Is beyond contriving, it takes a downpour of grace
To spell this water of words into hallowed wine.

Once we're aware, to parse awareness is
To gin that ineffable bird that's meant to soar;
What's said about it hangs like nets about it.

Yet words, prayer-shaped, may reach on wings of faith,
Aspiring to what comes only in time's ripening.
So dew at dawn pre-facets cut sunrise diamonds.

So we who love, who'd now say more than words
Can hold, may still, through long encoupled fervor,
Divine the Word that once gave spirit shape —

Though all cajoling in the world of tongues
Will not uncurl the frond to be the fern
Until the whole glade pulses with the spring.

Still in the Void is the Verb distilled — decode
How smoke up-whorled, how tolled reverberant bells
Both die and are borne into simultimate naught.

Stanley White

SCREAM!

Too many men looking for love;
Too many women not caring.
Too many women wanting that love;
Too many men just paying.
Too many children screaming for love;
Too many parents not hearing.

Too many fears to stop to think;
Too many people running.
Too many feelings stifled and crushed;
Too many people crying.
Too many moans not heard in the night;
Too many people dying.

When finally we search for ourselves, inside
    Instead of in things we own;
When finally we accept others for what they are,
    And accept the selves we know,

Then we will live with each again,
    And peace will rule supreme.
We will take time to listen to each,
    And not live in fear of a scream.

Miriam K. Fankhauser

THE MIRROR

We know tomorrow never comes
So let today be a bright and cheerful day
Give a smile to those around you
And let your heart find the way

The mirror on the wall tells us a lot
And could truly guide our destiny
If we but push away the darkness
And let kindness, love, our hearts perceive

To those whose days are hinged with darkness
'Tis but a step to find the way
Reach out and touch someone
And smile for a perfect day

Not one of us is perfect
But oh, so many slam their door
They should — for just one moment
Gaze in the mirror and be sure

Virginia Jolliff Herndon

THE LYDIA II

Merging as one with crystal blue waters
gently swaying, gently soothing.
No thought of a worry disturbing the moment;
the moment is precious, the feeling so rare,
completely absorbed at first unaware.

Reluctance detained me a short while longer;
releasing, returning, I saw in far yonder
intruder of grey so ugly and vile.
A cancerous monster invading the sky,
smelling of death, offending my eye.

As traces of yellow and orange joined their master,
forming a union, making their plans,
screams pierced my ears like the dagger of Satan.
My moment once precious now filling with dread
as the crystal blue waters welcome the dead.

N. O. Lacey

SUMMER IN THE MOUNTAINS

When all the birds and flowers are back
And it's summer in the mountains and the valleys
With the streams and meadows calling
To our weary hearts once more —

Will there be time for happiness
And the joys we knew before?
Can we fish and swim and picnic
Like the youngsters that we were?

Will the earth renew our spirits
And the streams bring back our joy?
Can the new life we see around us,
Charm us back to girl and boy?

Will the beauty of the mountains
Help our lives to flower again?
In the loveliness of summer —
And the freshness of the rain.

If you feel the mountains calling,
Then come join me in my prayer.
If we can't find God in the mountains
He won't reach us anywhere.

Rosemary Farrar

I'M HIS BRANCH AND HE'S MY VINE

Into this world Jehovah brought me
And though I strayed, in Love He sought me
With His own blood my Savior bought me
Now I am His and He is mine.

He showed to me my lost condition
I bowed before Him in contrition
He gave to me complete remission
Now He's my King, my Lord divine.

He set me free from condemnation
He gave to me His great salvation
He made of me a new creation
He lives within me all the time.

My wayward feet my Lord is guiding
In His deep love I am abiding
In Sovereign grace my soul is hiding
His joy and peace I daily find.

He made me hate my life of sinning
He gave to me a new beginning
Through Him sweet vict'ries Now I'm winning
For I'm His branch and He's my Vine.

Gailon Nethercutt

SKY PARTY

Do the angels comb God's hair?
Rub His back when it is bare?
Shield His eyes from bloody scenes?
Use the darkest clouds for screens?

Does He ever take a nap,
Have a nightmare that His lap
Overflows with knife and gun?
I think God could use some fun!

I suggest (it would be great)
Heaven ought to celebrate!
Get the horn of peace to blow
An octave high, an octave low.

And all the strings on all the harps
Will fake a chorus in six sharps.
And feet we never heard before
Will stamp a hole in Heaven's floor!

Break out the drums! Get in the mood.
The angels baked some angel food.
For putting up with us, old chum,
I think that God deserves some fun!

Ruth Graves Meissner

MEISSNER, RUTH GRAVES. Born: Willing Township, 9-1-37; Widow; Occupations: Theater and Church Organist, 30 years radio and clubs, Writer; Memberships: Union, Hornell 416; Poetry: 'Advice to the Lovelorn,' PS Publishing Co., Sept. 1984; 'Scientific Weather Report,' Hieroglyphics Press, Sept. 1984; 'Judean Christmas Card,' American Poetry Association, Sept. 1984; Comments: *I enjoy writing poetry because it comes so naturally to me. The subjects available are as numerous as the scenes on a season's walk. I hope it inspires other people to look around and try to express themselves.*

A SILENT NOTHING

A sour mood feel I inside; the weather
Merely an outward reflection of my soul,
A mirror is the world wherein one sees
Oneself. Emptiness, annoyance, a sense
That I may suddenly explode. In the soul
Of a deep, reflecting man . . .
Athens and Sparta are at war.

Vivek Anand Golikeri

DISGUISING LOVE

Why does he stand there wondering why
      I smile so much that I never sigh?
I tell him I'm happy, but really, I'm not;
      Because my feelings are hidden and shot!

My head is spinning, don't know what to do;
      I have to hide it, can't give him a clue.
I feel unwanted, depressed, and forgot;
      I can't let him know it, 'cause I love him a lot!

He gives me comfort, once in awhile;
      Even though I'm sad, I cover it with a smile.
There's too many tomorrows, no time for today;
      I've nothing to look forward to, so what can I say?

My eyes fill with tears, and roll down my cheek;
      My life is meaningless, my ambitions are weak.
A perfect solution awaits, after all my dreams turn old;
      Just say, "Good-bye, the hell with life!" and my body will turn cold.

Veronica Rychter-Danczyk

PRETTY BOAT SAIL ON

Pretty boat sail on o'er the shimmering river of our dreams,
As soft silvery music plays from a thousand rippling streams;
While whispering breezes caress when serenely we glide on our way,
To where golden bells will be ringing before the end of day.

Fair lady on o'er the undulating blue ocean of our love,
Race freely with the sea gulls and the laughing clouds above;
Let our hearts sing and brim with joy as we merrily cruise along,
Life's waterways that shall echo the lilting melody of our song.

Sweetheart sail on o'er the lapping waves of this sweet emotion,
With rapture cross the heady currents of our tenderest passion;
Then heaven is on earth as time flies into the waiting night,
When very gently I shall guide you to harbors of exquisite delight.

Beloved sail on o'er the heaving high seas of uncertain tomorrow,
Unbroken radiant promise holds true for happiness or for sorrow;
Where'er the tides take us, dearest one, we'll always be together;
Whate'er fate awaits there, our love will just go on and on forever.

Connie V. Espeleta

I thank you Jehovah God for sun that shines.
I thank you for your love Divine.

I thank you for the moon that glows.
I thank you for crops that grow.

I thank you for the flowers that bloom.
I thank you for their sweet perfume.

I thank you for the fish that swim.
I thank you for the food they bring.

I thank you for the birds that fly.
I thank you for the sunset skies.

God, we thank you for everything.
That is why your praises we do sing.

Notice everything God gave us. That shows He is a God of Love, Justice, Wisdom, and Power.

Harry T. Arens

'TIS BORN ANEW!

As morning breaks "Behold! The eastern sky!"
Time seems to be inert . . . just standing still
I see the golden sun shine from on high!
I hear a mockingbird sing from a nearby hill!
The world seems so bright! So beautiful at dawn!
The sunrise brings new hope and peace and cheer!
The day grows bright as dawn floods earth and sky
The green trees of the forest standing near!
Oh! What joy! What peace! Now flood my soul!
I seek a closer walk with Christ my King!
I seek a higher "Intellect!" New goal!
With joy in my heart I gladly sing!
When I think of days gone by . . . forever spent
Sometimes my heart is sad when I'm alone . . .
A miracle of love sweeps o'er my soul
For Jesus on the cross for sin atoned!
Oh! How green the leafy trees of early Spring!
The shining leaves dance in the sparkling dew!
The dust of earth has vanished on the breeze
Each time the Springtime comes "'Tis Born Anew!"

Ouida La Forrest Lucas

THE LITTLE WHITE CHURCH

In the valley, beneath a hill, past the creaky old mill;
There is a little white church;
In its belfry the chirping sparrow perch;
Every Sunday morning, the town folk
Slowly stroll up the narrow pathway;
To enter in, to kneel and pray;
They pray for their loved ones, who are far
Away; they pray for the lonely,
Who have gone astray; they know the
Lord above will hear them all;
To the young and old, He is within their call;
So, if you are burdened, and feel cast away,
Seek Him today, He will always be with
You; come what may, everlasting His love,
Like eternity; and, as endless as the
Rolling sea, so, my friend, come to the
Little white church in the valley;
And be gracious to our precious Lord;
Rejoice in the life we have now;
And, what is yet to be.

Amelia E. Cabouch

THE DAY DAWNED IN BLOOD . . .

On a clear November morning the opening day arrived.
A gunshot cracked in the distance
and big, dark eyes flew open in fright.
The signal was given, and off the herd did run —
but not fast enough for all its members to avoid the guns.
A few yards back in pain a buck fell to his knees.
The other deer quickened their pace —
only a little ways to the edge of the trees.
In the woods was a promise of safety
but the hunters already had more deer in their sights;
three more fell to the ground.
The others ran with all their might.
The deer were almost to the woods now,
but many members of the herd were gone.
With the loss of so many,
how could the lives of the others go on?
The deer have made it to the woods,
but the hunters are there, too.
So all the running did no good —
all the deer are doomed . . .

Jerlyn Kotan

DOWN THE CORRIDORS OF THE NIGHT

In the fields hear the night frogs peeping
                    down the corridors of the night,
In the mountains hear the wolves as they howl
                    down the corridors of the night,
In the woods hear the screech owl screaming
                    down the corridors of the night,
In the gullies ghouls may be stalking
                    down the corridors of the night,
But you won't catch *me* out walking
                    down the corridors of the night!

William Henry Wheeler II

LIFE'S DIARY

Life is like an opened diary,
    the unfolded leaves are the years.
Now and then time dries the stains upon pages,
    where regrets were written in tears.

It's a big book; a thick book;
    with many chapters, each a story to tell.
Many days of living, chained together,
    Life's emotions, its lessons taught so well.

    "Let not your heart be troubled;"
Are words of comfort when troubles abound,
    pause a moment when you read them;
Believing God extends His saving grace,
    is where Life's Secret's found.

If any phrase in Life's Diary could be rewritten,
    Take heed to Joy, Love and God's direction,
Erase sentences of Sorrow, Pain and Anguish;
    Rewrite with Faith, Hope and Reconciliation.

Juanita J. Wallis

WALLIS, DAISY JUANITA. Pen names: Juanita J. Wallis, Bill's Wife; Born: Jordan, New Mexico, 10-10-29; Married: 9-9-47 to W. J. (Bill) Wallis; Education: High School, Self-Educated; Occupation: Cattle Rancher; Awards: 'Family Pet,' Honorable Mention, *World of Poetry,* 1985; Poetry: 'God's Tapestry,' World of Poetry, 1985; 'Seasons of Love,' American Poetry Association, 1985; 'Scenes of Enchantment,' American Poetry Association, 1985; Themes: *History of New Mexico and Quay County. Poems of ranch life, how the producer is affected by the bureaucracy of our government.* Comments: *My husband and I are the proud grandparents of 4 granddaughters and 2 grandsons. For this reason I write to encourage them in paths of right.*

PEACE

Look to your inner soul first,
do not question that your GOD is best.

Peace of the heart can show us the way.

"Peace through strength," you say to me.
"Scale down and eliminate," I say to you, before there
are no blue skies and green trees remaining to salvage.

We have been blessed with the ability to reason,
that is what distinguishes us from the other creatures,
and makes us human beings.

Let's not forget who gave us that ability.

No man is immortal let each of us experience world peace
for just one day.

Let enemies extend a hand of friendship, if not for eternity,
for just one day.

PEACE NOW, what good is a free world if there is no world!

Kimberly M. Kahl

GATE SWINGER

I am closing my eyes
I am closing my eyes
I am lifting my face . . . to the sky

The warm brush of a breeze
The warm blush of a breeze
The warm touch of the wind . . . passing by

And sweet air breathing in
And soft air breathing in
And sweet breath leaving off . . . flowing sigh

Buzzing tickles my ears
Buzzing touches my ears
Buzzing whispers a song . . . I'm alive

Grasping wood within hand
Clasping wood within hand
Grasping world in my hold . . . swinging wide

I am leaning far back
I am leaning way back
I am freeing my soul . . . let it fly!

Velma-June Rimbey

THE OLD HOUSE

There used to be an old house here one time.
    Tall cedar trees still point toward the sky.
And by an old stone wall the lilacs grow
    And wave their fragrant plumes at passersby

But few are they who pass the old home now
    The highway with its noise is far away.
And only those who leave the beaten path
    Will see this relic of a bygone day

An old stone chimney partly fallen down
    A fireplace whose hearth has long been cold
Reminds us of the ones who gathered 'round
    And shared its glowing warmth in days of old

In fancy I can see those pioneers
    Who lived here when this house was new and strong
The echo of their laughter and their tears
    Still seems to linger like an old sad song

Mary E. Kelly

OH DEAR LORD
Dedicated to the people of Ethiopia

Oh Dear Lord, please listen to our cries,
Please listen to our prayers we do not choose to die!

Oh Dear Lord, we are not as strong as you,
Please give us your faith to try to live this through!

Oh Dear Lord, can you feel our hunger pains?
And without the world at our side, where do we remain?

Oh Dear Lord, we call you in despair,
Come take us in your arms, you're the only one who cares!

Oh Dear Lord, is there anyone out there who has a loving
    heart?
Who will turn around and help us, to try to make a start?

Oh Dear Lord, is there not an end?
To the pain and torment that can be helped by a Friend!

Gail Barnett

HE KNEW ME THEN

He knew me before I was ever created.
He knew just what I'd be.
    He made me unique and unlike any other;
In ways I couldn't foresee.

    He knew my dreams, my aspirations,
My thoughts before I thought them.
    And the hairs on my head, He has numbered each one.
So many I could not count them.

    He knew how many countless times,
I'd fail Him and go astray.
    How many times I'd turn my back,
Say, "No!", and just walk away.

    He knew my heart, my soul, my mind.
He knew everything about me.
    And despite what He knew, He said, "I still love
    you."
Then proved His true love at Calvary.

Denise L. Baker

FRIENDS

There are friends, who declare they are filled
With such love, that their cup almost spilled.
There are fewer, who stay through a darkening day,
Who remain when excitement is chilled.

There are many friends, who insist they need,
All the talents in which I succeed.
There are fewer, who show a more positive glow,
Who are thoughtful and generous in deed.

There are friends, who can love you,
More than you know.
Their kind of friendship is often hard to show.
They try to express, 'mid trouble and stress,
Their thoughts that refuse to flow.

There are friends, who truly do dare,
To accept a love, you can share.
They stay to the end, a true helpmate and friend.
Their kinship shows that they care.

Ilene Schelcher

Canst thou bind the sweet influences of Pleiades or loose the bands of Orion
14
Let there Be
Light
Let there be A
Firmament
Let the Waters be gathered together into one place
& let the Dry Land appear
And God made Two Great Lights
Sun
Moon
Let the Waters bring forth abundantly
Let the Earth bring forth
Cattle & Creeping thing & Beast
When the morning Stars sang together, & all the
Sons of God shouted for joy
W Blake invent & sc

BLAKE, Book of Job: When the Morning Stars Sang Together

THE COLORS OF OUR WORLD

Yellow is the golden brightness
    of the morning dawn.
Green is the tender blades of
    grass in a neatly cut
    lawn.
Red is the ever-so-soft
    petals of a blooming
    rose.
Orange is the misty silence of
    heaven's doors being closed.
Black is the stillness of night,
    when everything prepares
    for the new coming
    light.

Marcy Lynn Mussig

MONA LISA

No hopeless yearning in her breast,
    No lingering fears to haunt
The understanding smile that plays
    Around the lips that taunt.

All love is hers; she has no need
    To seek for passion's fire
Among the eyes that search her face
    New wisdom to acquire.

She holds no brief for good nor ill,
    And passion holds no sway,
For each one sees within her eyes
    His dreams of yesterday.

Thelma Floyd Durham

POETRY POTPOURRI

When you experience
The richness of words,
You *smell* the flowers,
Hear the melody of birds.

You *watch* a storm brew;
Feel the gusts of wind,
Shrink at lightning,
And *gasp* when trees bend.

Kaleidoscopes evolve
From a metrical potpourri.
Words are the chariots
Into the World of Poetry.

Virginia Merle Price

A rose is beautiful
    and so are you,
You give me love in
    everything you do
As I'm going through
    a phase,
You are understanding
    throughout my days
I need you to hold me
    close to your heart.
And tell me that
    we'll never part
For if we do
    I will cry,
And like a rose
    Wither and die.

Tracy Titus

THANKFUL WORDS OF PRAISE

Dear Lord: I thankful be,
for all thou hast done for me.
Thankful for my humble home
I'm glad I can call it my own.
Thankful for the telephone
My children can call me each day
Whether near or far away.

Thankful for my daughters four,
My grandchildren twelve, and
My great grandchildren seven.
I'm praying you will take us all
to heaven.
Thankful for my three brothers,
My sister and all others.

Thankful for my church, the
South Campbellsville Baptist, and
My Bethany Sunday School Class,
For all spiritual things that last,
but most of all, I thankful be,
for Jesus Christ who first loved me.

Rindie Malone

FAITH

I

Oh, let me sing a hymn of praise,
Of love and joy to thee.
That all my life, in every part
May speak, dear Lord of thee.

II

Thy touch has still its healing power,
And all who come to thee
In faith, are cleansed,
They know thy peace,
Dear Lord remember me.

III

So to thy presence Lord, I come,
Thy garment's hem to touch
By faith, to know thy Healing power,
In love, to walk as such.

Catherine A. Hearsum

LOVE MUSE

It was the month of June
    And that lazy summer moon,
Was shining down on lovers, young and old.
    The night we fell in love
That moon was up above,
And we learned, true love, is worth
    Much more than gold.
The train of life is very long
It has a million cars,
See that one marked happiness,
That's the one that's ours.
And on that train, there is a car
    Marked perseverance, too.
If we have this, we cannot miss
To make our dreams come true.
    There's a rainbow in the sky
And it glows for you and I,
At the end, there is a shiny pot of gold.
When I come back to you
This is what we'll do,
We'll settle down together
    And grow old.

Paul Ramsthaler

WANDERLUST

I feel the wanderlust tonight;
    I feel it in my veins.
I feel a restlessness tonight
    Stirred up by Gypsy strains.

O let me tramp along each night
    From north unto the south,
Beside some river stroll each night,
    Down to its very mouth.

O let me stroll and stroll tonight
    Until this longing die;
But let me glimpse deep things tonight
    Which otherwise must fly.

Rudy Loeffler

THE WIND

Did you ever happen
to stop and think,
about the wind that blows;
Across the bending tree-
tops and through the drifts
of snow?
Across the hazy mountain-
tops and through the
valleys below;
Where does it come from?
Where does it go?
But . . .
Who is to question and
Who is to know?

Glenn M. Miller

YOU HAVE GONE

The days are so long
        now,
as my heart feels your
    love so ever strong.
The nights are very lonely
    since you have gone.
The tears come rollin' down,
    as I think of all the times
    We shared as one.
Even though you are in heaven,
    our love will never die.
I shall walk with you always
    in the vision of my mind.

Tami Oviatt Gibler

SILVER STREAK

My love for you,
Is like a pure silver streak
Shooting across time into your
Eyes, heart and mind.

Ever, ever do you I seek.
Always, always, are you ever
so kind.

So dear to me I cannot count
the ways —
So lasting is my love —
I cannot count the days.

Alice Smith

OUTDOOR MEMORIES

Wouldn't it be wonderful, if life could only be,
Like the rosy pictures painted, in all the movies that we see;
To never feel the pangs of pain, grow old or have to die,
But wake up every morning, with the sun in a clear, blue sky.

As I sit and reflect, on what's gone before,
I long to step back, and to relive once more;
To feel the thrill, of wild geese on the wing,
And hear the wind, as it seems to sing.

See the gentle rain, falling in a pool,
Walk through the woods, when it's moist and cool;
See the fox squirrels leaping, from tree to tree,
Smell the wild, fresh clover, that lures the honey bee.

Feel once again, the surge of power,
Of that five pound bass, hooked at the twi-light hour;
To silently glide, on the trail of a deer,
And stalk the pheasant, in the fall of the year.

To run the trapline, on a cold winter night,
See the snowflakes fall, in the bright moonlight;
Sit gazing at a campfire, on the edge of a lake,
Listening to the call, that the black loon makes.

My memories linger, on events of the past,
As I think of the years, that fled by so fast;
But locked in my mind, in its cozy nook,
Lie all my outdoor pleasures, remembered, like a good book.

Les Jacobs

WHERE ARE THEY GOING?

Are they going to a place of pleasure?
Are they going to a place of business?
A neverending cycle of coming and going.
      Where are they going?
Are they late for future plights?
Are they trying to reach a destination before night?
      Where are they going?

Travis Josephine Dillard

THE MAN WITHOUT A FACE

He was standing there, completely bare —
    The man without a face,
He was a mystery, with no history
    Known as the *human race.*

At one time, he had a face sublime
    Not a wrinkle or a crease,
That was before, the age of war
    When nations lived in peace.

Children were born, and early adorned
    With love and complete affection,
When peace of mind, possessed mankind
    And no one knew rejection.

But then a man, (the devil's hand)
    Did not see the harm of sin,
Took what he could, more than he should
    And destruction of the face began.

So faintly at first, to not appear cursed
    Sin must seem a delight,
For others to try, and others to die
    The face appeared shiny and bright.

But the more he progressed, the bigger the mess
    Then it became abundantly clear,
That the face became shaded, completely faded
    Whenever God drew near.

Jack L. Whenry

ROOTS

Stolen, beaten, slashed
whipped, cut, and lashed
chained, bound and hung,
even cut out their tongues,
Mighty Kings and princesses of the kind
of a land so rich and fine.
Stolen by men, if they can be called such
and sold at markets for not very much,
Women raped and beaten
at the master's will;
Him professing to be holy and Godlike —
actually no more than a heathen,
Lands filled with dreadful cries
of a people so savagely tormented;
even the slightest bit of hope in their eyes
was cause for a deadly sentence,
and now, in even the most subtle
and sophisticated ways —
"The Saga Continues."

J. D. Drye

DRYE, J. D. Born: North Carolina, January 1953; Education: Los Angeles City College, California State University, L.A., Fayetteville Tech. Institute; Occupations: Songwriter, Musician; Memberships: Songwriters Union (PSI), Hollywood, California; Poetry: 'Like I Am,' 'Intimately,' Jade Publications, 1984, 'Rattler and the Blade,' Jade Publications, 1985; 'Lovers,' Sunrise Records, Inc., 1985; Comments: *Experience is a key factor in the way I write. There is also an element of time and space that affects the depth of my poetry or whatever I create.*

PAINS OF COMBAT SURVIVAL

I'm alive! But I'm back home now; yet still my eyes and heart,
See and feel the rankness of his deeds.
Oh pain in my eyes and heart,
From the grandfather of this evil.
Look upon yourself now!
You! Grandfather of this evil, have greatly pained me,
You've tormented my senses.
Remain not in me!
Go you, go away, go back to your underworld home,
Whence you, evil one, roost.
Quickly move, hasten you back there!
You that tread upon my shadow, paining my eyes and heart with
The ignorance of man's ravages of war, poverty and deprivations;
Hasten you back to your underworld!
Take this pain you've spilled on this world back to your roost,
Grandfather of the Underworld.
Lift from me, these pains of combat survival.

Col. J. Nicholas Jones

KOREMATSU IN MY VICTROLA

*"We cannot reject as unfounded the judgment of the
military that there were disloyal members of that
population." — The Supreme Court in Korematsu vs. U.S.*

HONORABLE MENTION

Crank; they used to start
Automobiles with this — the exertion
Of a few revolutions to squeeze out
Some enjoyment from the wheel.
Unlike the horseless carriage, this
Vehicle is incapable of bringing me forward.
It lavishes me with expended time.

The discs used, of course, are worn down
To scratchy words and melodies now. Their
Age apparent — grooves hoary grey with dust
Where once youthful black smiled when they
Captured the sunlight. Yet they never
Overcome the old prejudices: "We did it before,

We'll do it again" since "You're a sap Mr. Jap."
Mr. Korematsu, this is your new home. Possessions?
I don't know what you mean.

Paul liked to listen to the tinny sounds of
"You're a sap." He forgets that his relatives
Were given new homes in Europe at the same time.

The plastic remembers. These are the politics of nostalgia.

Abel Alvarez

WE LAID MY DADDY TO REST

We laid my daddy to rest,
In a place that we saw best.

I know he has gone to heaven,
Leaving behind six, and me makes seven.

I didn't know him all of his life,
Until his son took me for his wife.

His frail hands trembled in his last days,
But he never lost his cheerful ways.

I wish there was a message he could send,
For the man I loved so much, has changed and there is no end.

There are times that I want to leave, but never do,
Thinking that tomorrow he will see, and once again
Be the man that I loved so.

I loved him as much as any of the rest,
For when he was alive his son was a man, and one of the best.

As they lowered the coffin in the depths that day,
I said goodbye to my daddy and to my husband the same day.
For it'll take a miracle to make him change, but maybe there's
A way.

We laid my daddy to rest,
In the place we saw best.

Rachel Overby

FOR DIANA

When I think, I always think of you
On my mind you're always there a pleasant memory
First and foremost in my thoughts and everything I do
I see inside a calm reflection, a perfect picture of you.
As a petal is to a rose is how you are to me
You are the center and all else revolves around you.
Life is neither long nor perfect, a trying place to be
I couldn't imagine being without you
For truly you are the love of my life
My friend, my love,
                              My wife.

Jeffrey W. Bailey

SEEDS

Poetry is a garden of melody;
The poet implants seeds of philosophy,
Wisdom, love, sadness, or moral insight
In swift lines rich soil and grows a light
In reader's garden. If the spark is seen
As a messenger of truth, and words mean
What they say; if lines sing a light refrain
That echo over and over again:
Then poet has created a melody
That will live in the garden eternally.

Anna Beisel

YOU ARE THE ONE

You are the one who always brings a great joy to my heart
My mind and soul from you can never part
You bring to a world of dark the best light
You help make all the wrongs I do right
You help when the world is dirty and lean
You make the world full and clean
You make the world better than it seems
You help in life and dreams
You help take things above
You fill my world with love

Andrew James Speich, III

AN ANGEL NAMED DENISE

I am always with an Angel named Denise
In waking moments, my thoughts are about her
Filling me with wonderful happiness
In sleeping moments, the thoughts of love continue
In dreams leaving me glowing with joy
Everything about her is so perfect
She must surely be an Angel from heaven
Her happiness is the most important thing in my life,
And I constantly want to make her feel loved
Denise is the most lovable woman in the world,
And will always be able to count on my unconditional love.

Leo Uzych

READY FOR WINTER
(AN APPALACHIAN WOMAN)

Her face has been bronzed by the noon day sun.
Deep furrows have been plowed in her forehead.
Years of time are woven in her rugs
and pierced together in her quilts.
The work of her hands is spread throughout the house.
She captures the gold of summer
and stores it on pantry shelves,
to serve her household during days of winter.

Camila Haney

FALL

The pleasant tale of summer has been told,
The blooming flowers have gone to sleep and rest;
The trees that stand in Autumn's dress of gold
Hold in their arms the robins' tattered nest.

II

The green grass in the meadow land is brown,
High in the wind swept sky the wild geese call;
Soon driving snow from out the Northland drear
Will strike, and with its mantle cover all.

III

Now has the time of Harvest come once more,
The ripened grain awaits the reaper's hand;
With happy songs bring in the golden sheaves
Before the icy clutch of winter stills the land.

IV

So will God reap his field of precious grain,
Bring in his sheaves, his own forevermore:
His words of truth have not been sown in vain,
God's Harvest time is at our very door.

Mrs. David Minnette

GREED FOR GREEN

In time my greed for green shall rise to heights
that take me high above the common folk.
But if I go too high, too fast, these nights,
the dream I grab with ease will be a joke.
Oh! I don't care what others think of me,
because I'm one that gets all that he wants,
Or should I say that's what I now decree.
Yes, I the clever bull the bear now hunts.
At present time the sun is shining bright
and I'll be basking on the beach all day.
They tell me that the day will turn to night,
the sand to snow; and me without a sleigh.
I say, if I go down don't count me out.
I'll get back on my feet and win the bout.

Robert L. Ricciuti

THE LAST SUPPER
convent of Santa Maria del Gracie
Milan, Italy

He sits so nobly occupying that tremendous Grace.
That hatchet-keen, that clean, that gentle gaze
of love a lovely rage of Heaven: that forgiving Face.
His arms hold you hereafter, His healing fingers raise.

Twelve withdraw from Him, six right, and six left:
Their movement's captured; some wait to hear Him speak.
James the Greater is horrified, Thomas expresses disbelief.
Accusing words abound. John is overcome, bereft.

Bartholomew is on his feet amazed and stricken
Among the stunned and startled, surprised and shaken.
James the Lesser feels the rage of Peter driven
Into every stare laid bare betrayal wakens.

Andrew shrinks from Judas who shrieks of money,
Suspect in his clutch and furtive glance.
Phillip, in self-accusation to the Lord, his eyes entrance.
Matthew, Thaddeus and Simon frown and gesture numbly.

The Master's stance of Jesus stands the test of tears.
Eternal suggestion silvers in His followers' fingered beards.

Marvin James Conti

I AM AFRICA! . . .

I am Africa! . . .

Twenty-four of my beloved lands lie parched! . . .
While your mind is on a collar to be starched,
My beloved lands lie parched . . .

I am Africa! . . .

I hear skeletal, starving children crying . . .
While the cost of your living has you sighing,
I hear those children crying . . .

I am Africa! . . .

Hill-high hoards of surplus food glut the world . . .
While I watch the Flag of Famine fly unfurled,
Hoards of food now glut the world . . .

I am Africa! . . .

I forgive you for the bones beneath the Sun! . . .
I forgive you all, and pray, "God's Will be done!" . . .

I am Africa! . . .

Martin J. O'Malley

A PRECIOUS GIFT
Dedicated To: Jerome and Jermaine Henderson

Thought that delightfully enters my mind
Prompts the magic that moves me to rhyme
The fates have presently set me apart
Put love for rhyming into my heart.

I feel; I have been loaned the hearts and minds
Of, "Poetical Masters," who move through time
Their beautiful words have made a rest stop
And calmly entered into my unsuspecting heart.

This precious gift which I did not seek
Enthralls and makes me ecstatically weak
Elated and moved am I to the eternal core
Of life and love, I can ask no more.

Who decided that I could cope with this part?
Why was I chosen for this delicate part?
What maneuvered me onto this precious scene?
Where do I compensate for this unsought dream?

Because I have been given the light to see
I thank, "The Altruistic Powers," that must be
If we can accept that which we may not seek
While we love, life can be surprisingly complete.

T. Steven Watkins

LETTER TO A DESPAIRING FRIEND

The battle, love, for yourself, will be waged
Without end. We're not in control for long;
The beasts within us stand at bay, not caged.
Yet be consoled, there are others among
The sad, human flock, whose fate from first breath
Is to wonder at the purpose of it all.
What else is there but to wonder at death? —
Wonder why we grow to fade, rise to fall.
When last we touched, I was ablaze with hope;
All seemed possible, each problem had a way
Of solving itself; now I barely cope
With waking. Yesterday was full; today,
My diaries lie empty on the shelf,
For I've lost interest in myself.

Claude J. Sandroff

How do I say the words,
that I've already heard
a hundred times in my head,
the words we both dread?

It's true, our love is good —
Throughout we've understood
where we're going and why.
We have not lived a lie.

For months we have been one,
and I've never had such fun.
We've walked a path without pain,
and from each other, we've gained.

But the time is drawing near
and I don't know if I can bear
the painful truth of love lost.
I can't stand the cost.

But this is something we must do
And when our time is through
the day will come — we'll re-unite
In God's palace, in His light.

Anna S. Barr

JUST THINKING

I love the love
for loving,
forgot the song
not singing.
Waiting is
losing dreams forever.
But wait I must —
discover whatever.

The night is young
with a sky so heavy
falling on a day
which runs
like a rumbling brook.
It did not harm
my waiting game
and left me untouched
in a quiet solitude.
the night spreads
her velvet cape
concealing my escape —

Blanka Jirák

WANTING YOU

As my trembling hand touches you
I'm just reaching out for some love
For in this world I shall not find;
Is a man's love to be meaningful and true.

Sometimes I wish I could lay down and die
As I want you to know how I feel
That you bring sunshine into my life;
And my love to you can be real.

I want you to hold and caress me
Till my heart's relaxed and content
Or for us to drive down a dark, dark lane;
Which will make me happy as can be.

So to you I dedicate my love
And in such a very special way
I look up and admire you,
As I will always wonder
If your love is sincere and true
That you'll hold me all through the night;
And kiss my troubles away.

Linda Marie Laframboise

TWO GIRLS

You have grown and flown . . .
Once you were small American beauties.
Now more than thirty years have ensued
Your Dad has passed on . . . his sorrow . . . no 'morrow.

A Mother's Sorrow

For one: Drugs have changed your very life . . . your clarity of thinking,
Our society putrefies and its vitality is shrinking.
With your whimsy you come and go like a gypsy,
Your days have become irrelevantly tipsy.

All agencies say there is no avail . . . no way
Can we help her today.
                    Agony engulfs "your Mom."

A Mother's Joy

Another daughter has good brains,
And with them handles her business reins.
Now with secretary, conference table and computers galore
This one has humor and no time to be a bore.
Decisions make her at her best,
Her active mind needs no rest.
                    Amen for her!

Synopsis

Why has life dealt these contrasts to Mom?
Like osmosis to try to equalize . . . or counterpoint a melody?
My girls lives' songs sing vis-á-vis our country's current needlepoint!

Zoe Miner

MINER, ZOE LEONE. Born: Minneapolis, Minnesota; Married: 6-11-49 to Francis A. Leekley III (deceased), 3-4-70 to James Edward Miner; Education: University of Minnesota, studied Industrial Psychology, Commercial PBX Training; Occupation: Assist with our Farming and Trucking Business; Memberships: Alpha Gamma Delta, past alumnae President of Delta chapter, Minneapolis-Saint Paul Transportation Club, Gaylord Cognizance Club, rural university extension club, 4H, Girl Scouts, Pink Lady hospital volunteer; Poetry: 'Christmas Eve — Years Gone By,' *The Land* area farm newspaper, 12-19-83; 'With Our Pup Named Bro,' *American Poetry Anthology* and *The Land*, 1-16-84; Other Writings: "Today's Star Lady," a woman's editorial, *The Minneapolis Star*, 10-16-58; Editor of *The Delta Dope*, a woman's sorority newsletter mailed worldwide to members, Delta Chapter of Alpha Gamma Delta, in 1960's; "Thanksgiving Memories," article, *The Land*, area farm newspaper, 11-21-83.

OLD AGE

I'm retiring from life's competition.
But for me, I've much to do.
I'll never bury myself, I'm telling you.
I've too many friends to close the door,
Now that I've time, I'll have even more.

Retiring is what you make of it
So I'm going to be good to myself,
Take all the things I've saved down from the shelf.
I'll go to all the parties wearing a grin,
And smile about all the places I've been.

I'm looking at the brighter side of life.
Each morning when I wake up
I'll fill up my cup
with words of love and cheer,
And some play, for to work only is hell my dear.

I say, forget about your past,
Lift a heart, dry a tear.
Plant hope instead of fear.
Old age is great, who needs a repetition
Of youth's situation . . .

Evelyn Weaver

THE HIDDEN PALACE

As time swiftly passes by each morn,
O sun peeping over the northern hill at early morn.
Few clouds gather high above
There in flight, appears one tiny dove.

A nearby lake with a small half-destroyed boat,
Now tossed aside
Little water surrounding the rocky — grassless land
Where tiny deer continue to hide.
Few trees standing tall, yet many rotten on the ground
So quiet and peaceful without a sound.
O air cool, damp and foggy, yet wee creatures
There crawling to and fro
Many puzzled and wondering — which way to go.

That hidden palace, now isolated and still,
Some continue to visit, but only from a distal hill.
Secrets, buried there so many
Few will return — if any.

Barbara Jean Conner

THE STORM — THE CALM

Visions flash before my eyes
with the rapidity of the hummingbird's wings,
It is difficult, at best,
to see things clearly.

My ears are bombarded with roaring sounds
resembling the ocean's waves.
They strike,
recede,
and strike again.

Thoughts lash at my mind
like a tormenter's whip;
creating a terrifying pain within my soul,
which cries out for relief.

When my senses overcome my entire being,
I seek serenity
from deep within;
the wisdom, understanding, and grace of
my Creator —
my Savior —
my God.

Charles E. Stickle

JOANNE

Soaked in my own depression with two false teeth,
Baby girl of two and six-roomed house
Your accident drove away college, job, dance and boyfriend
Success with all its prizes.

Yesterday, Gandhi's body burning sparked your ash memory:
Of morning exercising at Jamaica High
Elasticity circulating your sleek body
Static rushing through your long brown hair
Those mellow eyes electrifying my own self-pity.

How could you leave me with no model
And the nervous stomach that I have?
I need your friendship and talk of old times
Even though I leap forward.

Your St. Mary wedding invitation tossed me into shocked
                                    reality
I'm still sorting out.
Yet, love supports my life spirit
And I live, as you did
For my ambitions, still growing and thinking of
                        YOU.

Fedaiye Mirillo

A JUST CAUSE
Or
Bottles and Butts

Scientists from time to Time
Been digging and scratching holes in the Ground,
Just to find out how our fellow man Lived
Before we came into a Beginning.

In these holes he found bits and Pieces
Of pottery and broken Bones
And we still don't know what and How
He went, nor a just Cause.

But when they dig down later On
To find out what happened to Us
All they need to find is our bottles and Butts
And a broken missile or Two;
They will know what Happened
But it still won't be a just Cause.

Paul H. Engel

THE FIRE STILL BURNS

The nativity of the bard a glorious giving.
Thoughts utter tangled tales of realms.

Romance shadows whisper onward, passionate
spirits espouse, sung heartily storms.

Amity sings bestowers' promises, shall kind-
ness hasten to you.

Poets chant boisterous flames impelled to
hungry persons desired.

Celebrations whisper hushed rains crowning
the heads of heeders or scream shrilling
thunders told to reckless souls.

Tainted worlds boil forth upon purity.
The fire still burns, inspiration present
we shall drink.

Poets compose words of praise, sonnets, and
ballads alive spoken to them by reveries.

Rosalind Denise Hill

SOME THINGS NEVER CHANGE

When you have a baby girl some things change rapidly
as she grows up, some things more memorable than
others. Her first tooth, step, bicycle, slumber party,
boyfriend, date, car, traffic ticket, accident, braces,
corsage and broken heart.
Wearing grown-up clothes, jewelry and make-up
prepares you for your little girl growing up, then
it's weekends home from college, summer jobs and
wedding bells.
Returning home surrounded by holidays and being
consumed with being all grown-up is different,
but you realize with the same tight hug, the same
soft sweet kiss and the same definite hand squeeze,
the same bright sparkle in her eyes, she's still
your baby girl . . . some things never change.

Jacqueline Rowe Gonzalez

CATHEDRALS

In Rheims, the spire of the cathedral
is flying to the Celestial.
In Miami, the rumble of the shuttle
is shaking the Skies.

Stone after stone, they built tall cathedrals,
Higher and higher, searching the Eternal,
The past and the future gather in a light.

Their haunting shadows animate the sunbeam
through the rose window.
Looking at the stars, man always in quest of
The Universe and answers to
The fears.
Are we going to die?

Sylvie Blaise Contiguglia

SOMETHING TO SAY

I don't know what it was that you were going to say,
    Just kiss me as you always do and I'll be on my way:
Knowing that you love me helps to earn my daily pay.
    So at dusk I'm home again to get my kiss, maybe you'll say,
"I had something to tell you this morn, but you hurried away:
    Here it is, please stand still, our Doctor says this coming May
Our baby's due. Believe me that will be our happiest day!"
    Oh! Oh! You kissed me once — You kissed me twice —
Let's do it again and make it thrice —
    Oh gee! Oh golly! Oh gosh! Oh darn —
    God bless you for saying it so nice.
Forget my muttering. Forgive my stuttering.
    I really s-s-s-sensed when yu-yu-c-c-commenced
That yu-yu- God love yu-yu-yu
    Had s-s-someth-thing — terrific tu-tu- s-s-say.

George W. Boehmer

APOLLO IN EXILE

How comfortless, Apollo, to your wear
Did human flesh for body-garment seem
When prisoning the free, the naked beam
With sense of hand and foot, of head and hair.
Impossible but partly hidden sunlight
Filtered as if from cumulus and lightning flash
Betrayed itself through borrowed skin, streamed bright
The god by word and posture, yellow eyes full lash.

O, Shepherd of the wandering storm cloud flock,
Healer of purblind night acarpous, cold,
Once earthly sheep obeyed your careful crook,
Musician, for whom the hurtled planets unrolled,
The lyre of shell humbled your fingering lock,
And Mountainous Thessaly echoes your voice of gold.

Charlotte Louise Groom

SILENT WIND

A Silent Wind does stir
And dry leaves dance on the ground
An eye does watch this
Though an ear can hear no sound

Upon whispering wings invisible in flight
It travels mysterious and free
Its destination is never known
Or the hour in which it is to flee

Young, dark, Indian eyes observe
With a memory of years before
A Cherokee grandmother once chanted
"Silent Wind, the world is yours to explore"

Now, in the stillness of an enchanting, mountain morning
Beneath a dawn of blazing red
Upon whispering wings invisible in flight
A Silent Wind quickly fled

Now, with a hand held high, before the mystic sun
He can realize his true name
And perhaps a grandmother's spirit smiled
Silent Wind, an identity he will claim.

Linwood Edwards

WHITE WANDS

White wands whisper in the wind
Of sacred magic. Still we linger
In a winter of our false contentment; ah, but soon
The bonds of power will break — burst, yes,
And flood the channel,
And the pagans in the trees will be let loose among us.

"Love and life will be renewed by light
Of white wands." Such is the coward mind's weak consolation.
but as the last pale lilac buds are blown away
For the coming of the pure light's summer scorch,
Remember to anoint me, also me, with a white wand.

Flow through me; make of me a chalice
To hold a holy healing in the crusted earth.
Open the channel; do not burst the vessel . . .
And touch me, even me, with your white wand.

Sybil Wood

A DAY OF RECKONING

The judge and jury were seated; waiting to hear my plea
Mother was in the courtroom, praying they'd set me free

The evidence was damaging; witnesses described the crime
I knew, without a doubt, that I'd be serving time

Mother's tearful stories about a kind and loving son
seemed to be irrelevant to "robbery with a gun"

Mother told about a son she'd loved for 20 years;
who'd been a good student and respected by his peers

One who joined the work force and always paid his way;
walking the "straight and narrow" until that fateful day

The world had gone haywire . . . businesses closed their doors
He could no longer buy necessities as he'd always done before

Mother's pleas were useless. The judge's gavel pounded
"I sentence you to seven years!" Mother was astounded

She writes and visits often and forgives the things I've done
A stronger love I'll never know than my mother's for her son!

Allene Perkins DeCou

ROMANTIC EVENING TILL MORNING LIGHT

As we walked along the ocean's sand.
The only light is that of the moon.
Every step we take the moon's
Ray walked with us.
We found a place to sit along.
the ocean's side.
To watch the moon's ray reflecting
on the ocean's current.
Making it even more romantic
As we watch the tide slowly
fade away.
As the moon's ray slowly greeted
the sun's rays.
The moon began to fade away
As the red skies of the awaking sun
Arose, then we knew it would
be a warm and beautiful day.

Deborah Fowler

BACKGROUNDS

I have a little feeling
We'd be not so quick to judge;
And we'd never be insulted,
And we'd never hold a grudge,
If we saw the situation
From our neighbor's point of view;
If we knew the circumstances
In which his opinions grew.

There never was a person
Whom I could not understand,
If I really tried to listen,
And I got his views first-hand;
For a person's real convictions
Are not formed just overnight,
You can better understand him
When his background comes to light.

Christina Fields

A MATURE ROSE

I am a rose.
Petals perfectly curl around me.
Love and serenity are mine.
I passionately kiss the sun,
For I know I must give birth.
Thus, I quietly open, petal by petal.
Perfection ceases as each petal descends.
Soon, I will be nude,
Then, I will be a rose without its petals.
Thus, a mature rose.

Christine M. Tansey

PURPURCUS WORDS

(Zechariah 14:12)

Ignoring the prophet's pen,
the humanist tames our chaos
and Heads of State wear white gloves,
while the flesh falls away . . .
eyes and tongues are consumed
       in Hiroshima's fire!

The flow of purple-red words
cramps with caveat knots
our paling Adam-blood veins.

But the Nail that pierced Dove Hands
in the Final Day brings peace;
For Mercy and Truth control
the nuclear plague release.

Ruth Anne Stibbs

SHYBIRD (JONOTHAN)

"You look inside me trying to find me, My friend search me forever
For you will never know me."
I am Jonothan, free and everlasting
I have silver wings that take me far and wide through the longest shores
I have seen the deepest, most blue skies
I have flown the clouds, touched the sky
I have gone beyond the sun and have seen a glorious light
I have traveled above the heavens, and have searched even myself
I am free, no one can touch me
I glide over the continent constantly searching for food.
    but I am never hungry
I fly endlessly from ocean to ocean
Swaying to the rhythmic music of the songs I hear
Hear my heart
It speaks so silently
Yet. I glow with life
I am Jonothan
A lover for the sea
You will never touch me
For I fly outbound, never stopping.

Karen Priem

GOD BLESS US ALL

When I was seventeen I loved to write
About everything I saw in sight.
When I was twenty, my thoughts were astray
About what was happening to me every day.
When I was twenty-five, I was ready for wedded life,
The man of my dreams made me his wife.
When I was thirty, I was a mother of two,
I realized that there were more things to do.
When I reached thirty-five and getting mature,
My children were growing and still wasn't sure;
When I was forty and again a mother-to-be,
I knew that this would be a complete and happy family.
When I was forty-five, there were so many more things to see
With my hubby and children of three.
And closing my fifties with four grandchildren
And hopefully more on their way,
And now I am sixty, and I look back and pray,
That my children will always stay
As happy as they are and that no one will ever mar their way . . .
GOD BLESS US ALL.

Rose Boccanfuso

SOLITARY CONFINEMENT

"We're all of us sentenced to solitary confinement inside our own skins."
— from the Introduction of Cat on a Hot Tin Roof
by Tennessee Williams

Elly felt scared and sad all day, without knowing quite why.
She felt saddest upon entering the little house in the valley, and
was often close to tears, without knowing why. It was not the
dark evening that scared her, nor the dog barking, nor the long trip
home. All day she could not forget herself, and she knew that this
was not like being on a mountaintop all alone, or in the woods,
or in a city of strangers, or a house full of friends. She was
on the edge, in half of a dream. She repeated her name to herself
during the day and failed to understand it. When it was time for
sleep, she became scaredest of all, in her own room which was full
of loved possessions. She sensed her fear rising, but she could not
turn it off, so she slept trapped and scared and delirious. She
dreamed of her mother screaming for her to get out of the house,
and of someone in her room, a stranger. Panicked, she awoke to
the fluttering and screeching of big bats at her window who wanted in.
They want In.

Gail Tayko

TO DAD

On this day,
A sad one too,
I am still
Thinking of you.

I left with a smile,
A good one too,
But now it is just a smile
Because I love you.

Shannon Lee Schuster

REMEMBRANCE

Eager
In the fullness of childhood
He searched for the sound of answers

Leaves rushed by
Darted like joyous children

He tilted his head
With young laughter
Embraced the growing green
And vanished
Like the rainbow

I sing memory

Carole Winter

WINTER, CAROLE. Born: Memphis, Tennessee, 5-31-45; Education: New School for Social Research, 1969-72, continuing private study; Occupations: Student, Poet; Poetry: 'Close,' Poetry Press, 1983; 'I Do Not Want to Think of Death,' Fine Arts Press, 1985; 'For Nancy,' Poetry Press, 1984; 'Here is Feeling,' American Poetry Association, 1985; 'Where Has the Preacher Gone?' American Poetry Association, 1985; Comments: *I am not a professional poet, though I have been published many times. Writing poetry is one of the many ways to express my thoughts about life and the myriad of feelings therein. I express myself by participation in and enjoyment of all artistic forms, by continuous learning, by loving nature and by sponsoring children around the world.*

CLOSE FRIEND

Comfort me in times of solace and make everything seem right.
Put your arms upon my shoulders and hug me with your might.
Laugh with me in joyous times and celebrate in elated glory.
Make our good times memorable to highlight my life story.

If I starve for your company, then leave your door ajar.
Fill me with hospitality and bring my spirits up to par.
If anger should confuse me, where I cannot see clear,
Open my eyes and focus me on the reality that is there.

If I'm feeling insecure, then try and make me feel strong.
Defend me when I'm right and enlighten me when I'm wrong.
Join with me in fun and laughter whenever we are able.
Share my secrets, in respect, that keeps friendships stable.

If we shall part for a time, you know I'll always be near.
Call me up and fill me in on any news that you have to share.
For this is called close friendship, through happiness and contrite.
For it is held in boundaries that are eternally fastened tight.

For you are a friend, on which I can depend to stand at my side.
To help me through the path of life and keep me at an even stride.
You help me when I'm lame with weakness to get as far as I can get.
Of all the things you do for me, friendship is your best gift yet.

Janice Berben

SHADOW

The silvery surface of the moon rises slowly through the velvety purple darkness of night.
Shadows stretch long and dark from objects bathed in an eerie blue glow.
Shadow stretches his back atop a car and bares his claws in a mock fight.
He leaps, disappearing into the darkness.
From his fur, lights sparkle and flow.
In and out of the darkness he walks.
He guards his home and family from the unseen creatures of the night.
Crouching, jumping and leaping he stalks.
He kills the creatures only he can see, with his green eyes glowing bright.
Walking proud he struts, tail up high.
Living in a world all his own.
So light he walks, he almost seems to fly.
In the morning it will all be over, as the front door opens, he'll return home from a world only he's ever known.
He curls up on his favorite chair.
Sunlight gleaming on his fur.
As gentle hands pet his sides, he falls asleep and begins to purr.

Larry Reppert

SO HANDSOME AND SO TALL

"But Mary kept all these things,
And pondered them in her heart."
St. Luke 2:19 KJV Bible

This is my son — the shy one — smaller than the others,
Stumbling often, falling down . . .
He almost runs to meet the plane for Dallas
And the interview — a career possible in the trip.
Eager, bright as a new penny, anticipating new friends.
My son, who screamed in fear when a stranger came near . . .
Taking on the world with the confidence of David
Meeting Goliath on the field of battle.
When did he grow so strong and tall and handsome . . .
The freckle-faced one with toothless grin, who shrank from new people?
Now responding to Houston, Boston, Chicago and Schenectady —
The Unknown — with the polish of a pro.
The young executive, the graduate engineer . . .
Still, to me, the little boy with bandaids on his knees,
His arms around me then for comfort . . .
Now "Don't worry Mom, I've got it made . . . they want me everywhere."
Praise God for this — my son — the shy one, loving and caring,
Setting out on life's adventure.
God Bless You, son, and go with you . . .
My little boy, so handsome and so tall.

Anne D. Babin

LOVE

Down super highways
Along country byways
alone it comes peeking, saying Let me in,
Let me in,
Peeping through windows, knocking on doors.

Sometimes screaming, sometimes yelling,
Sometimes calling so softly, it is often
unheard, crying Let me in, Let me in.

We cry for it, pray for it,
Some even die for it,
We lie for it, cheat for it,
Kill in the name of it, but all too
often we take it misuse it, abuse it,
Beat it to death.

Then we wring our hands,
Beat our breast,
Pain fills our hearts,
Tears fall from our eyes,
We cry Ah love, why did you
Pass me by.

Jeanne Gray

THE TIMES

Once again we strive as of centuries ago,
to bring about economical times in a world,
we can control.

Let's not go through those times of long years ago,
save the fate of our country that's always been,
our goal.

Faith of the people we must restore, for that unsure faith,
will destroy the world.

Our ancestor toiled for you and me to cultivate the land,
that would prosper thee.

Seasons after seasons of changes we see, that the land is not
Yielding as we desire it to be.

Go forth and change what's meant to be, free the burden of the
people, in the land of the free.

O say can you see, this is where I want to be, in a land where
my ancestors provided for me.

Annette Younger

ACRIMONY

Anger penetrates as silence permeates
Attitude fills the air, thick enough to cut
Caustic remarks that burn the bridge and widen the gap
Distance set, the highway lengthened

Fear beckons and grips the soul
Where to turn, a vicious circle
Winding whirlpool or laboring labyrinth
Either way, a trap

Misunderstanding breeds mistrust
Hill turns to mountain
And snowball grows to avalanche
Oh, the ways of man that raze toward self-destruction

The question yet remains
Hope but clouded by a tear
We smile and cover up the pains
And for today, you're still here

Marilyn Fernicola

LET ME STAY

Time: hear you not, to let me stay;
    would these weary eyes, but to see
the sunshine and happiness of yesterday;
    here, have I lingered far too long;
You have spent your seasons with me;
    no longer, am I strong;
Still the sun crosses the sky each day;
    as slowly it goes to open the gates
of twilight, in its own passive way;

Would I, but to be a youth again;
    to know the passing years;
To happily greet each morn;
    even through heartfelt tears;
Looking back, memories, do I see;
    failures, there, never, would I repeat;
So many wrongs, have I but done;
    from them, never can I retreat;
Let me stay once more, to see a day of beauty;
    before I must be dead;
The clock ticks on, the hours fly by;
    is there no one to care?
Here, must my life end in Winter;
    Never, ever to see the sunshine, so fair?
No longer, can I keep in step with time;
    grown old, have I,
Soon, my clock, will cease to chime:

Jerri Sherrow

THE WIND'S SOUNDS

You shout . . . You cry . . .
    the hurt is hidden
    by the wind's sounds.

The wind sounds of many schemes . . .
    the hurt is buried in the falsehood
    of love.
The wink of an eye will not engulf
    the flow of the tear.

The winds sound in the hollow of
    the heart . . .
Hallowness of many empty dreams . . .
    false illusions . . . enchanted loves
    of wanton lust of self-preservation.

Elusive dream . . . corrosive thoughts . . .
    enslaving the gentle mind.
Sweet thoughts . . . lingering.

The winds sound of many sounds . . .
    evasive you will be . . . elusive you are.
Hidden away . . . my gentle dreams and sounds.

The wind's sounds . . .
    send sounds I love gently back to me.

Richard Araujo

HE

Though at times I may be weak, he is always strong.
I sometimes make mistakes, but he is never wrong.
He is gracious, merciful, and pure
And has honorable qualities for sure.

His love for people of all races is deep,
And he hears every silent prayer and all those who weep.
He provides people with comfort and hope,
And they cease to rely on their horoscope.

Though others do evil and often go astray,
He comes along with his strength and shows the right way.

Betty Worthington

FORESIGHT

*(Based on an ancient Greek custom of dealing
with physical imperfections. Parents who exposed
defective children to the elements were not
considered directly responsible for their
deaths.)*

My mother was a quiet woman, strong
And resolute. We children were in awe
Of her. We knew that she was never wrong.
I am a grown man now, yet logic and law
Control me less than she did. Once I had
A little brother, born quite lame, I loved
Him. But she carried him, her dark eyes sad
And fathomless, into the fields. She moved
Slowly, when she returned without him. That night
The wind and rain were wild. I couldn't sleep;
And, when I dozed, I dreamed of beasts. My fright
Was weakness. Foolish neighbors chose to keep
Their blind son. He grew up, their bitter shame,
A tramping minstrel — Homer was his name!

Mary F. Lindsley

LINDSLEY, MARY FRANCES. Born: New York City, New York; Married: 1-26-63 to Irving L. Jaffee; Education: Hunter College, A.B., 1929; Columbia University, M.A., 1932; Occupations: Retired College Professor, Poet and Prose Writer; Memberships: Poetry Society of America (PSA), New York Poetry Forum, California Federation of Chapparal Poets (C.F.C.P.), United Poets Laureate International, (UPLI), International Biographical Association, (IBA); Awards: Hunter College Hall of Fame, 1978; Honorary Doctorates in Literature, Liberal Arts and Humane Letters, 1969-80; Dame of Merit of the Military Order of St. John of Jerusalem, 1985; Knights of Malta; Poetry: *Uncensored Letter,* book, hardcover, Island Press, New York City, 1949; *Grand Tour,* book, Philosophical Lib., New York City, 1952; *Selected Poems,* book, Theo. Gaus, Sons, New York City, 1967; *American Cavalcade,* Dorrance & Co., Philadelphia, 1976; *Age of Reason,* book, softcover, Triton Press, California, 1980; Comments: *My purpose is to portray human nature in the past and present, with as much traditional music and clarity and as much modern irony and compassion as I can. The whole effect should never leave the reader indifferent. "Extraordinary skill and versatility in handling sonnet form"* Encore *magazine; "Contemporary language . . . well-drawn characters, and fascinating situations."* Saturday Review of Literature.

CROWS

The sky is crowded with clouds,
Forever changing the face of its clarity;
Filled with intense splendor and deceptive beauty.
Subtly mirrored in the masses of earth.
Clouded with crows.

Paul M. Ward

DAY'S END

It is dusk at the seashore.
There are no gulls flying the waves,
Or walking the empty sands.

A small wind brings in the chill of the north,
And the sea that was like glass an hour ago
Is rippling, changing from blue to angry grey.

There is no warmth left in the sands,
No heat rising from beneath dried brush,
and the waves that touch shore are ice-cold.

It is dusk at the seashore.
A lonely hour at a desolate place
Where even the gulls' constant screechings are silent.

L. Nishimoto

THE WIND

A fair wind — it *seemed* to be —
that — gently — *seemed* to flow —
but from where it came — I could not tell.

The *gentle* wind — then lifted *me* —
and — showed me worlds — I did not know;
and soon — I could not hear distant bell.

We soared so high — the wind and I —
that — I forgot — the world below and —
when it turned me loose — I *fell*.

Now — *broken* — from a force I could not
flee — too late — its origins I know, —
the *wind* that lifted *me* — had come from *Hell*.

Diane H. Snyder

WHEN WE STARTED

When we started you were young and a little shy
You made me feel alive and put a twinkle in my eye
When we started we'd have long talks, just you and me
Everywhere I was, that's where you wanted to be
Then came the day you wanted me to marry you
You said together we could see life through
Some times were rough and some were mild
You seemed so very happy with the birth of our first child
Then you seemed to change, I still don't know why
The nights you were gone I'd sit alone and cry
Those nights alone became so lonely, dark and long
I'd blame myself and wonder just where I'd gone wrong
You didn't want to live the life that I wanted to live
Now I'm so very bitter, I don't know how to forgive
I see you in our child every day, now that we have parted
But I'll never again see you the way I did when we first started.

Sharon Monaghan

CLOWN OF MANY FACES

Looking at the clown of many faces
wondering about the dreams that he chases.
Laughter and sadness make up the mask
answers to be sought, questions to ask.
Tears mingle with the sorrow of heart
as the clown portrays his unique part.
For a fraction of time life stands still
reaching out to touch, an empty void to fill.
Shadows of the man are hid deep within
echoing silently to taunt and torment him.
Look closely at the clown of many faces
for a part of yourself, you may see traces.

Tonia L. Blackmore

PRISONER IN MY EYES

Prisoner lying lies
to a gilded chain,
death drifts with changing sand
seeing dreams that aren't there.
Prisoner crying colored tears
to a disguise of empty truths.
I'm not asleep dreaming images.
            I'm a prisoner selling dreams
            to a dying sun
            of whitewashed fools.
            haunted by voices
            mostly my own.
The prisoner in my eyes
is a phantom
and silence speaks
for itself.

Sue Blythe

FOUR DECADES

I have reached forty years old!
The years have passed more precious than gold.
The trials that I've borne with a faint heart
Now seem vacant, unimportant, eons apart
From the joys, the fierce gladness I've felt
Of those times in those years when love dwelt.
The major goal I set for myself when I was ten
Has been met with more fulfillment I could have imagined then.
Of married life I know little enough;
As it lasted only 10 years with love.
My third decade I'm sure was most resourceful,
Because I endured an illness to me so frightful.
As nature has its cycle from Winter to Fall;
I can see my cycle unfold and I call
This time of my life as I see it now
One of great patience as my children older grow.

Shirley Vine

Why he loves me so, I guess I'll never know. He
Left His father and all of His glory; don't tell
Me you haven't heard the story.

He did all of this for you and me, He only wanted
To set us free; free to live without sin or shame.
Don't you know Him, Jesus is His name.

I have no other friend who could have done all of
That; Jesus is the only one and that's a fact.

Why He loves me so, I still may never know, but
I am truly sure Jesus loves me, because the Bible
Tells me so.

DeLiso Kerpreice Turk

BLOOD RELATIVES

HONORABLE MENTION

Sensually compelling, strictly chaste,
Seemingly clandestine, unholy — what sanction
Might there be for love so bonded?
You and I have asked the questionable question.

The substance of this doubt is silent, breathless.
We have skirted revelation before.
Yet the unmasking of our intensely harmless game
Would mean our kindred spirits could be kin no more.

Those whose claims on us bind fairly can't hear
This counterpoint of joy and pain, a burning
That ebbs and flows as our hearts, so lone, list
To touch, but fall away on waves of yearning.

Mary L. Aubert

THE FAMILY SITTING IN THE PHOTOGRAPH

12TH PLACE

stirs the wind with excitement
posing on the porch of the beach cabin.
Their skin peels from sunny waves,
hot sandy afternoons walking the ocean's curl.
The father's hair is the only darkness
in the blue July day, his shoulders fill
the steps, flexing his biceps
to make his daughter laugh.
The mother rests her bare, warm arms
around her husband's neck,
her pincurled hair and pink rouge
paint the day summer.
The oldest son leans tall against the beam,
eyes caught on the basketball he tries to palm
in the wrong hand.
His brother flashes their surfboard
into the sun, squeezes his sister's wrist.
She knots her fist over her eyes,
turns her face away from wind,
fidgeting with their laughter.

Melinda Pavlich

A LIFELONG COMMITMENT

We have a commitment, you and I,
Living in each others' arms
And hearts and souls.
Though the flesh is individual
And our divided beings
Throb in their separate houses,
The invisible, immortal, indestructible we
Are woven, mixed, compounded into one.

Our reflections are in each others' eyes;
Our images burnt in each others' soul.
It is a union stronger
Than the pronouncements of priests,
Far firmer than the laws of man can authorize.
You're the pride of my heart,
The light of my life,
The source of all my joy;
My friend, my lover,
My confidant and compatriot.
We have a commitment, you and I,
A lifelong commitment.

Basil Washbourne Hall

THE SCRAPBOOK I LEFT BEHIND

There's an old scrapbook in the attic
In the old farmhouse back home
I went to visit there last year —
I wanted to be alone —
The paint had faded, the windows were gone
The steps had fallen apart —
I had kept many years here in my heart —
The old wicker rocker was still inside —
The cradle and toys were there on the floor —
I sat down and closed my eyes
Remembering when — I came here as a bride;
Then I found the old scrapbook
And as each page I turned —
Another year or two passed by
I sat and wondered where they had gone —
What happened to make the time fly! —
Well! I left the old house and scrapbook behind
All my memories and dreams were there too! —
For I have discovered the world of now! —
and for the rest of my life — for me —
    There is only you —

Ava Lois Halstead

WAR
(To American Soldiers)

Graveyards attest
To war's distress
Mortals too many
The earth lay to rest
Freedom's bliss
Is a painful quest
American soldiers
Our honorable best

Michael Salaam

HOPE FOR JANET, I DO

Well, at last.
She loves him, as much,
   As he loves her.
Janet, my dear, Janet.
My love, My life.
So I know, of my love.
   For her, so is her love
   For him.
If only my heart, knew it.

Leanders Moore

How much can two persons love?
. . . Loving enough to let go . . .
How much confusion can one stand?
. . . Standing enough to show . . .
How much pain can one endure?
. . . Enduring enough to suffer loss . . .
How much can two persons fight?
. . . Fighting an unknown cause . . .
How much does love really conquer?
. . . Conquering pain and despair . . .
How much can two persons love?
. . . Loving enough to share.

Cathy Sue Sipes

IN BETWEEN LIVES

A luminary cube consisting of pureness
   and tranquility exists
Only until, forced through untimely
   disruptions,
Its victim within, once more, persists
In finding peace, at his own will.

Repetitious fantasies turn into nightmares
While exteriorizing into infinity
Then just as abruptly — Returning to Hell.

Olivia Serna

QUEST

And who shall understand
The tranquility of my soul
The world busy and busied
Lives beginning and ending
Wearied the runners
   yet fearful to rest;
Fatuous man in perpetual quest
For that which is here
If he'd but stop and see.

John B. Traynor

ABLE CONTRACTORS

a hard day's work'd kill the kid
in purple trunks and mineral oil.
tenth round — still hope; even the
deafened ear is *kindness* to hear
coursing a roar of blood on the mat,
instead of the cursing crowd. Let me
lay down no more in pools of blood.
Let me lay down no more. Let me lay
down a new building-stone. Let each
builder put down a new stone. Each
stone mortared to entomb the passed
failures and hates, each gate *out* to
a new future minus the charnel-house,
into the sun of man shining on watered
pasturage, our own land, Emmanuel
and the one who frees us — who gave
us the blocks with His Name on them
to turn us from stumble-bums to stumbling-
blocks for the sleek promoters, and the
adversary who'd gorged on the blood we'd
spilled willy-nilly in *the ring* with a
thousand shapes and names and sizes to
evade love.

Richard Kovac

SMALL FAVOR

My head is in a tizzy.
   My brain is in a whirl.
I was not the promised son . . .
   I am just a girl.

But, I can cook;
   And, I can sew;
And, walk and talk
   And breathe . . .
And, I know of countless problems
   Which make us mortals seethe.

Yet, one small good thing
   That I can do
To make the path seem brighter
   Oft finds a new noose 'round my neck
Pulling tighter . . . ever tighter.

Then, my head's thrown into tizzy.
My brain goes into whirl;
And, I'm glad I'm not the promised son.
I'm glad I am a girl.
June K. Gaut

BLACK WOLF-CLOUD

Watching the changing sky last night,
I saw a great black wolf-cloud
Very slowly sneak upon
And swallow up the moon.
Simultaneously I felt a reflected sadness
Move over me to engulf my inmost soul.
But it stayed not long,
Soon laughter strong
Displaced my heavy gloom
Because I saw
Yet another more wondrous sight.

Caused by what errant wind
I cannot say.
I only know I saw
That selfsame wolf-cloud
With equal slowness regurgitate the moon
And with a tingling joy,
Realized that not forever
Will God let darkness
Even appear to overcome the light.
A. E. H. Shumake

DEVOTION

Within the confines of the night
   I lie and think of you.
The stars come out in cloistered light
   as thoughts of you pursue.

No sleep comes to my lonely soul.
   My heart still sings your praise,
I feel your beauty underlined
   by all your lovely ways.

I cannot fall asleep tonight —
   I cannot let you go,
So — in the morning's early light,
   I plan to tell you so!

Arlone Mills Dreher

AT YOSEMITE

Sitting here, with this feeling now
Is somewhat hard to describe.
It's a feeling of peacefulness,
A happiness . . . just being alive.

A feeling of not caring
What you look like, what you do.
A feeling of adventure,
How your life is depends on you.

There are so many chances now.
We should take them while we can,
For being inhibited or selfish
Makes only half a man.

Jennifer Aaker

TEDDY

With brown button eyes
And tattered and matted fur,
So cuddly and warm and
Always eager for a hug,
Teddy is my best friend.
He is human in my eyes,
And talks to me with silent words;
Understanding and compassion are traits
He never lacks.
My secrets, dreams, and ambitions —
All these he holds, untold.
So, with brown button eyes
And tattered and matted fur,
Teddy is my best friend.

Carol Creech

LOVE IS . . .

Giving without fears
Crying happy tears
Walking hand in hand
Trying hard to understand.

Seeing what no others see
You being you and me being me
Keeping you close to my heart
Even when we're apart.

Talking in voices very low
Walking with no place to go
Being able to kiss your lips
In evening dew or morning mist.

Cynthia S. Johnston

HAPPINESS IS FLOWING THROUGH MY FINGERS

Happiness is flowing
Through my fingers just like sand;
A door has closed between us —
She no longer holds my hand.

There are places in her secret heart,
That I can no more find,
And the tenderness and happiness,
They've all been left behind.

Happiness is flowing,
Through my fingers just like sand;
The tide is going out,
And I'm left lonely on the strand.

There's a darkness all around me,
And it seems my life is o'er
I no longer have my sweetheart;
I have lost her evermore.

Mildred Keating

NO BREAK IN ETERNITY

(A note to the world)

On Spreading Wings of Light
I fly.
Higher
Than your thought-out Notions.
I am gliding
Freely among my Clouds
Even as you, still insistent,
Crawl in your Dust.
There's been no break in my Eternity.
What happened to yours?
You see me beside you, and
Actually
Think I'm like you.
No. You're wrong.
I am Angel. I am Light.
You were. You changed.
But —
I am still.

Leisha Scheuermann

TEACH ME

Light the light within my soul
Illuminate my way,
Turn the darkness of my life
Gently into day.

Caress and hold my every dream
Never to let go,
Cultivate my every wish
Teach me what to know.

Lead me through the hardest times
Help me understand,
Show me what it is to care
And lend a helping hand.

Dignity within my life
Is all I need possess,
Love and kindness in my heart
Joy and happiness.

M. R. Souza, Jr.

JOYS OF EARLY-MORNING RISING

The dew's still on the roses,
The birds have just begun
Their songs of "Good Morning"
To the slowly rising sun.

The air is fresh and cool yet
With still a night-hush in the air
The sounds of the slowly rising world
Buzzes 'round me everywhere

Today is going to be a hot one
when the sun ascends on high.
And I could have slept 'til nine or ten
without anyone even saying "why?"

I just like this quiet morning hour
To sit alone and thank the Lord above
For the wonderful bounties of this Earth
And friends and family and Love.

Hazel Lounds

D. C.

Potomac river
    cresting high,
Cherry blossoms
    amber sky;

Sculptored statues
    mammoth halls,
Historic legends
    duty calls;

Heroic generals
    battles past,
Unknown soldiers
    graveyards vast;

Great museums
    touring guests,
Vacant White House
    congress rests.

pm Moore

LOST

What am I doing here —
Here in this place?
I feel like an alien
Among my own race.

I'm somebody's mother,
Aunt, sister and wife.
But I don't feel I belong
Here in this life.

I'm sitting back
Looking at myself play a role.
It's not me doing these things.
It's my body — not soul.

Dear Lord, I am lost —
Here in this place.
Just feel like I'm floating
Detached and alone through space.

Irene Y. Nesgoda

BORED

I'm bored.
I walk to the yard,
And my hands touch
The cold skin of night.

My voice calls the stars;
They are too far.
My eyes look for butterflies' path
In the blind dark.

Aspirations bloom hard.
So with silvery patient wings I fly
To pass this grim border.
Coldness is not a new narration.

Mohammad Abbaspour

CATCH THE MOMENT

Dreams of silk and
    Satin waves
Upon a silver ocean,
Glide past from long ago.

Horses of froth
    Atop the crests
Stealing magic from the wind,
Fly with joy to the shore.

Stand still child and
    Catch the moment.
Yesterday was my dream,
    Today is yours.

Lee W. Kelley

MY ATTITUDES

Dreams of ideals,
    doom and sadness.
To be what I pray,
    if not to be loved by you.

I am not willing to be
    loved or held.
What if I died and nobody
    knew.
What if I cried and nobody
    listened.
Attitudes of nothing, and
    of little nothings.
Attitudes of forgotten dreams.

Don Mummert

ON KERON'S PASSING

I found her sitting quiet there,
Just as still as still could be;
And a chill enveloped all my Soul,
For she wouldn't answer me.

So they took her in a long black car,
When the evening sun was low;
and I turned my face to the shadows,
For I couldn't watch her go.

So I sit here at my evening meal,
Reliving the bygone years:
There's just one plate at the table now,
But, Oh God; there's a million tears.

Carl Freeman

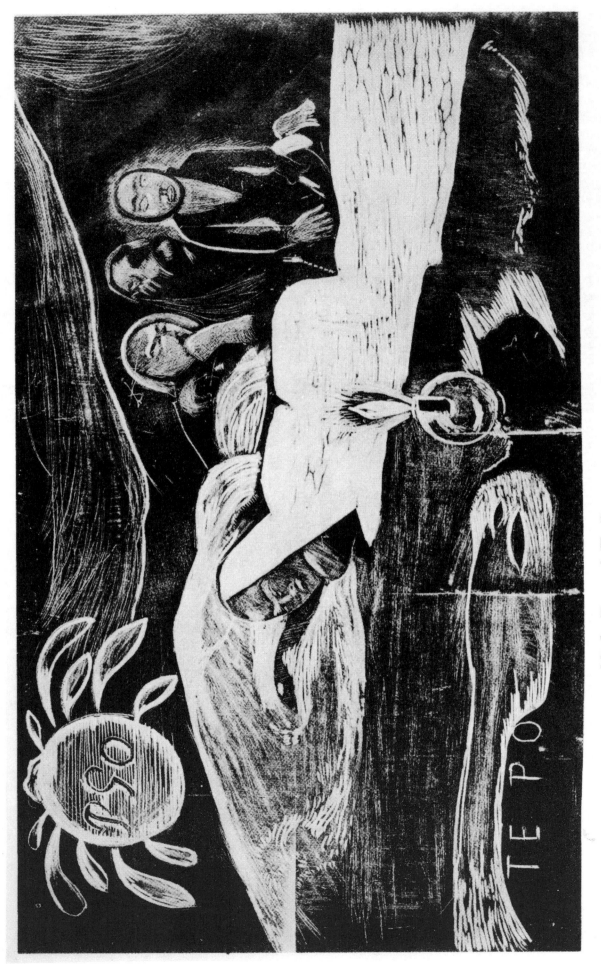

GAUGUIN, Night Eternal (Te Po)

AN ANSWERED PRAYER

Last night as I sat on the dock by the bay, I prayed until
the sky of blue was covered by darkness.

"Dear Lord," I prayed, "Did you hear me cry as I prayed to Thee
in the midst of the day and in the midst of the night?"

Are you aware of the feelings of doubt and hatred that love has
caused me? Will my heart ever be relieved of its pain?

Have you overheard my secret thoughts of taking my life — Is
this why you have not yet answered my prayers?

Last night when I fell asleep, an angel appeared before me in
my dreams.

"Learn to be patient," the angel said, "for your prayers will be
answered.

Your life was not meant as a gift to be forsaken. It was meant
as a gift you learn to appreciate — only this way will your heart be
filled with love, trust, and laughter.

Without pain and sorrow you would never recognize painless and
happy tomorrows. Neither can exist without the other.

Love and sorrow will always be a part of your tomorrows. To
truly understand them you must first have faith in the Power of the
Father and the Son — Then, Ye will survive forever.

Lisa Smith

HYMN OF DESIRE

It's like thunder in the hills
So quick and loud this sudden burst
Of impulse undefined from within
Like some winged bird named Desire
Flown from afar by the Far East wind
Into my door to behold You
Whole and undimensional — such vision of beauty
Like Princess Faire of Plato's dream.

By chance and circumstance we are drawn closer
These many weeks and days
But like a silhouette in motion
You are distant and elusive and beyond reach
Like a clever queen of the breeze
You are everywhere near I can feel it
I can almost touch you, but nowhere close enough
To tune in on your thoughts and feelings.

You are the riddle of spring; it's a pity I haven't got the answer
But the quest for meaning continues; like a lute-string seeking a tune
Somewhere deep in your heart lies the answer.
Love is easier said than done, how true; so it is that I carry a torch for you.

Ted A. Villaganas

SILENT SONG

An affection that need be subdues,
within the soul of one.
Mingles with pain of limitation.
A mere gaze of blue-green vision remains a special touch;
a closeness, with such distance.
Though the warmth — so strong and understanding.
Pleasures given through simple gestures.
The connection of two . . .
so natural is the love brought forth.
Restraining a touching impulse . . .
The future clenching any for thought; Past memories; Present anticipation,
That have no true right . . .
though much need.
A world simple to conquer,
so ruthless to live.
So wonderful to share, if only with words.
Forever Rock with this Silent Song in your heart.
A tune so everlasting . . .
So special . . .
So honest
                    Forever.

Peterann Smith

ON A MUSEUM PIECE

Polyclitus, how your heart would burst
With anger and bewilderment!
That hotly-brooded maiden,
Cast of your throbbing veins
And molten in your furnaced breath —
Is it she
    That musty dim professor
Stares to chilly bronze?
In catalogued response, he dutifully
Checks her carefully-numbered epitaph
And trudges on.
But Sculptor. Stay your hand!
The times have changed.
Passion, with you, is in the grave.
We only know, and reason, and collect.

Virginia E. Cruikshank

ONE-SIDED LOVE

It first started
When I saw your sparkling eyes
That looked at me
Every time I looked at you
My mind told me something other
Than what it really implies
You always stood close to me but,
When together, we never did speak
Maybe because we were both shy
But you always acted different
Which confused me and I had to cry
I hoped the next day
Would bring something new
Then, finally, I began to see
It was truly my love for you
Not your love for me.

Douglas W. Wardle

MY FAMILY

My family is a house of time.
I've seen it grow, I've seen it shine.
I've seen my children laugh and play,
and watched them grow up through each day.
But now they've grown and gone away
and I sit and ponder yesterday.

Love once abounded between these walls
and many's the night I still recall.
But those days are gone my friend
as my days come to an end.
Yet when I'm dead and laid to rest,
my family's still the very best.

Mike McCracken

MY WORK

Though I work alone
my typewriter's great comfort
I err it corrects . . .

Desk piled high with work
dauntless I attack plod through
self-satisfied done . . .

Continuous round
answer phone; type; file; pay bills;
sort mail; happy boss . . .

Arrive ten of eight
steady busy work all day
close desk four fifteen.

Jane Rodger Zimmerman

KIDS

Do kids still dream on a summer's day?
When the chores are done and they're sent out to play;
Why sure they do, for what could be better,
Than daydreaming a little and writing a letter?

Kids bring us laughter and a whole lot of joy,
With their cute little ways of playing with a toy.
And their way of sharing is out of this world!
They get angry at each other;
But are back in a twirl!

Kids are our future; let's help them to grow.
Through sunshiny weather, rain, sleet, or snow.
The mind you shape today may be a teacher;
Kids are special. They're God's creatures!

Jean P. Jones

FOREVER YOUNG

Forever young we thought we'd be.
Different lands, golden bands.
A bottle sent to sea.
Sunday morning spent at the park.

Year after year we seem to drift.
Along with time and nursery rhyme.
The hands on the clock went tic, toc.
The older we got the louder it talked.

Sent us spinning although we were unwilling.
The message in the bottle.
That was sent to sea.
In our minds, we would soon see.
Forever young we could never be.

Deidre F. N. Chapman

VICTORIA'S ADVICE TO A YOUNG LADY

My dear, beware the stranger.
Take not his hand in greeting,
    lest lightning strike
    and so set his image in your heart
    that ever after all your dreams are forfeit.
Then . . .
    let the door to your thoughts ajar and in he strides,
    lean, bronzed, and charming,
And your ruination is just a matter of time.
Ah, Mars and Neptune never should be conjoined,
    that one murmured greeting could so strongly shout,
And tiger-to-tiger, call forth passions that
    heretofore lay sleeping.
My dear, beware the stranger;
Take not his hand in greeting.

Rosalie de Stefano

WINTER

Random flakes drift down from an overcast sky,
onto the frozen ground below.
Winter workers trudge precariously —
on the ice — picking their way,
slowly through the snow.
Winds moan through empty streets,
and a forlorn dog howls in pain —
with frozen feet.
Like the agony of life,
the sounds flow to the beat.
Making a pure white cover,
the snows really neat.
As the overwhelming silence,
suddenly — puts the world
at peace.

Elline Curran

ALONE

We lose someone we loved so much
In mind and memory we hold their touch

It's all part of life — or so it's said
But emptiness and loneliness plagues your head

Alone now, and not able to share
A thought, a touch or that special stare

All of a sudden everything's changed
Your entire life has been rearranged

The pain goes deep and there seems no end
Even though time supposedly mends

Nights are spent thinking of how
Things used to be and won't be now

No more days or nights for two
It's just not fair — losing you

The special times are gone for good
I'd change it all if I only could

But memories are now my friend
And will be with me until my end.

Karen Lantini

ELEGY FOR NEBO MOUNTAIN

HONORABLE MENTION

When I was a child,
my father took me to the mountain —
a very special mountain where Nature reigned as queen.

He said, "Listen to me, child.
This mountain soil is sacred.
You can always come here to find strength in Nature's peace."

That was long ago,
before the Others found the mountain.
They saw in it a purpose for a perfect hiding place.

They built silos made of metal
and buried them beneath the soil.
Dark omens of madness wait within the secret graves.

Many years have passed.
the fertile soil has turned to clay —
clay as red as blood; I don't understand at all.

The mountain once so sacred
where Nature reigned as queen
has become her deathbed.

I can hear her strangled call.

LaDonna Adams

MY FRIEND

I have a friend — Collette is her name . . .
I love her dearly, she feels the same.
Our friendship is a special kind,
a truer friend — could never one find.
She's been with me through thick and thin,
together we've traveled — many places we've been.
At sixteen, she's still very much alive,
by some standards, that's one hundred and five.
So, if this picture seems just a bit foggy . . .
She thinks she's people, but —
she's really my doggy.

Elizabeth Browning

302

EBONY AND PEARL

What beauty lies
In black, black eyes
And warm brown chocolate skin.

What beauty lies
In sky blue eyes
And milk and honey skin.

Where, oh where does hatred die
And love for all begin?

When minds and hearts are opened wide
Hands clasped in honest caring,
Like little children, side by side,
Trusting, willingly sharing,
And all welcome God within,
Then, does Love for all begin.

Katherine Strathearn

IN LOVE WITH LOVE

We fell in love
much too fast,
as young as we were
it could never last.

I started to feel
our love begin to fade,
it was one of those loves
that should have been delayed.

God brought us together
I saw it from the start,
all of this holds a lesson
for He also took us apart.

God works in perfect
but very strange ways,
I thought our love was forever
but it lasted only days.

I must take my time
to really get to know her,
I can't fall in love for love
or there will be nothing for sure.

Rodney Haugland

DECEMBER
I AM A CHILD OF GOD

Cradled in December,
Pillowed on deep frost,
Nestled in sheets of rain,
Beneath a blanket of snow.
Over me a quilt
Stitched in rainbow crystals,
Etched in icicles
Long and pointed,
Dull and short.

In rest I grow,
In growth I rest.
I sleep, I sleep
Like the Christ-child
Growing in grace and stature.

Crawling, creeping, clutching
I tumble through an arch.
I peer into a light,
Light of Divine Wisdom.
I melt with warmth,
The warmth of Divine Love.

Louise Weyant

SHOULD IT END

You said we were friends
And you didn't want it to end
I put up one hell of a fight
Just because I knew it was right

Then things started to change
And it ended with a bang
I thought there was a chance
For at least one night of romance

But as usual I was wrong
Because I knew it wouldn't last long
I guess there are no dreams
So that it seems

But deep inside my heart
I know there could be a start
Because I can still hear your voice
Saying please make the right choice

Should I forget you
And start again
Or should I see it through
And keep on loving you!

Laurie Haller

THE JOURNEY

Alas, the heavenly sunset
bids me a call from far beyond,
to see the mighty white horses
so bold, so tall, so strong.

That heavenly sunset tells me
my dear the days are pending,
for all the loved ones traveled beyond,
to a land of beauty, neverending.

My heart leaps with joy
to the beauty of the sky,
so boundless, timeless, unending
like a dream with wings to fly.

One white horse stands alone
he bids to lead the way,
to take me far beyond the sunset
to show me the lighted way.

So tranquil and peaceful it is beyond,
these feelings I can now relate,
my horse completed his journey
he stands alone at the gate.

Carol Anne Pelow

THE SEA

As I gaze in awe at the vast
                blue sea
It holds a special meaning for me.
I see the might of the Master's hand
As the waves roll in and pound the
                sand.

The roar sends tingles down my spine
God is showing His might over mine.
He sends the sea gull into flight
Soaring though never seeming to light.

What a beautiful sight to see
Watching the waves roar unceasingly.
God is Master over sea and sky
        He's also Master over you
                and I.

Helen (Cudd) Rice

ON SEEING THE FOREST

The kitchen's a wreck,
I have flour on my neck,
While daughter's appearance is frightful.
But that is the rate,
When the student's just eight,
You pay for a cake that's delightful.

Friend neighbor drops by,
Views the scene, flicks her eye
Over floor, cupboards, mother and miss.
"You'll never come clean.
I have just never seen
A mess much more hopeless than this."

"Dear neighbor," say I,
And I really do try
Not to smile at her horrified look.
"It's easy to see
You see only the tree.
I am training a gourmet cook."

Marva Jeanne Pedersen

WATCHING

Sitting on end of log.
Over there
The frog!

Each fly a delight —
Easy without might . . .

Here and there.
Now and then.
A rush of inner peace.

Speaking in quiet tones, alone,
A silent sigh,
Just watching.

Delighting in this simple sitting!

Frog and fly —
What Delight!

Richard A. Viles

STRAY ENCOUNTER

Stray cat,
Why have you wandered?
Your manners prove you
Gently trained,
A proper pet.
Did your home desert you?
Did you lose your way?
Perhaps a feline charmer
Led you astray.

Politely reticent,
You refuse to comment.
Observing the amenities,
You dine daintily, then
Curl cosily on the couch
Beside me.
Absently my fingers
Luxuriate in your soft fur.
You sigh, stretch.
Purr your content.

Martha Wray

THE MATCHING SOUL

Like creatures born from my love for you
thoughts of happiness push words
wishing better times,
overflowing the world with this
dreaming of you.
Winds from eternity brought me here
trying to find you.
I did, and loved you as I do.
Good and bad in their eternal fight
let hellish forces throw me out of Heaven
when you said:
"I don't love you and never will."
But, you will. Anyday, in the coming life
or in another galaxy, but, you just will.
This tender love I feel for you could only exist
for a matching soul to mine . . .
So believe me: I want it to happen now,
Nevertheless, sometime, it simply will,
and I'll be awaiting your coming to me . . .

Gisela Axtmann

UNIQUE OF COUPLES

What we had was real, and when I say "was" I'm not
Referring to the way I feel. Because I still love you and I
Always will. You are the only one who is special in my heart.
You and I, we were the Unique of Couples. We were in love,
And most of all we were happy. We were not only good to
each other, but we were good for each other. We had so
much in common. We loved the same things, shared the
same dreams, and we felt the same way about life. Because
Uniquely, we had actually lived the same lives. What we
Had together showed, it was very special. Our love for
each other had its own touch of class. Our friends even
envied our happiness. I loved you so much it scared me,
And you, you doubted me so much you never believed in me.
The fears and doubts confused us tremendously, and what
we had was gone. We threw away what only comes once in a
lifetime. We were two adults who had found true love, but
confusion wasted away what was so hard to come by. It wasn't
A one-night stand, or a hot weekend, but we had three months,
we had a start.

Rose A. Pope

POTTERS ALL

In ancient royal tomb or modern kitchenette,
The potter's cunning, throughout the ages,
Encups something of himself —
His spiritual cement — the power
To form, adorn, and to serve
The needs, deeds, and dreams
Of queen, tycoon, slave, or mechanic.

We are all surrogate potters of lives.
Guided by a master pattern or none at all,
We mold, decorate, desecrate, or destroy
Our bit of substance
And that of those around us,
Leaving everything or nothing,
From masterpieces
Treasured in the museums of memory and history,
To the shards of bad dreams
Buried in a midden.

Edward DeZurko

PORTRAIT

Age is the sculptor of your smile,
You enjoy crickets serenading you on warm
summer evenings.
You find that things in nature are worth more to
you than all the paintings in the world.
Nature is seeing an old Indian man with many wrinkles
in his face and wisdom in his eyes or seeing an eagle
soaring on a current of warm summer air with the
azure sky as its canopy.
When you cry tears caress your cheeks like rain
on a summer's day.
These are memories I recall when I pause and think of
you.

Gail Doremus

DOREMUS, GAIL JUDITH. Born: Hackensack, New Jersey; 4-7-49; Education: Bergen Community College, still attending; School of Business Mach., 1970; Berkeley Secretarial School, 1971 (Executive Secretary); Occupation: Assistant, Advertising Department, Publishing Company; Memberships: T.E.A.M. Writers; Other Writings: 'Witches,' Humorous, Prairie States, 1985; 'Geese,' Nature, Yes Press, 1985; 'Free Food,' Humorous, Quill Books, 1985; 'Arctic Terns,' Nature, Green Valley Publishing, 1985; Themes: *Nature, life.* Comments: *I write to enable people to look at life from a different angle. I want to learn sign language so I can make soundless music with my hands to convey in this language to those who cannot hear.*

ERNIE

Ernie is ten only in years.
He wears diapers under blue cotton pajamas,
He needs help in sitting and in walking.
He lies quietly in his hospital bed,
Blonde bangs long and shaggy
Over half-open blue eyes.

The other parents and visitors
Whisper to each other,
They ask the nurses
"What is wrong with poor Ernie?"
"His mother had measles in pregnancy."

An expression,
Gentle and peaceful as a pansy
Often appears on his round, pale face,
For God is love
And Ernie is precious to Him.

Jean Willard

SWORD, WINGS AND LOVERS

O Lovers, fly to your windows!
A sublime awakening is come to America.
    O look up at the swarming eagles.
    They pierced the golden serpent's holy *rest-seal:*
The Eternal Resurrection Shrine.

America stirs from ancient eagles' nest.
For Ambassador X, Lioness Gadarene, sets wings on Chief's tomb:
    His *Temple Of Moon Body* — A six year redemption dew shrine.
    Her, all eighteen letters of mate glisten like dew.

The Holy Ark of Covenant rings bells and pomegranates.
This forty-sixth year of — Dorene Lee Wolshaw — rings sixteen bells.
    These two M's — large with wings are holy gifts
    On lover's foreheads.
They spring into their hands like hallowed cups of marriage wines.

O Lady Lee's hammer strikes up wings!
Mark and image are set upright like dazzling white wash bowls
    On lover's foreheads.
    Here, holy Wolshaw name is enshrined in truth and love.
O Holy pair, Red Chief David and Lady Gadarene.
O Holy Laws: SWORD, WINGS AND LOVERS.

    Dorene Lee Wolshaw

SHAW, DORENE LEE. Pen name: Dorene Lee Wolshaw; Born: Lennex, California; Education: La Sierra College; Occupations: Artist, Writer; Poetry: *Sword, Wings and Lovers,* religious work, a symbolic decipherment of The Holy Ark of Covenant, 1962-84; Comments: Sword, Wings and Lovers *is the spearhead of sixty-eight holy songs, which make bare the most veiled mystery: The Holy Ark of Covenant. This symbolic decipherment constitutes the arduous lifework of the writer. For here absolute mastery of the holy word was imperative to raise up a redemption altar; to raise up The Eternal Resurrection Shrine.*

YOU'RE NOT HOME

    The rain keeps fallin' and and I keep callin' but you're not home,
endless nights, barroom fights and I keep callin'.
    The rain keeps fallin' and I keep callin' but you're not home,
all the flowers, quiet hours alone and I keep callin'.
    The rain keeps fallin' and I keep callin' but you're not home,
all the endless days wakin' in an alcoholic haze, it's just a
phase and I keep callin'.
    The rain keeps fallin' and I keep callin' but you're not home,
all the one-night stands with tired bands and backwater fans and
I keep callin'.
    The rain keeps fallin' and I keep callin' but you're not home,
some day I'll stop callin', the rain will stop fallin' and you'll
be home.

    Randell Patterson

A CHILD

There is none so precious
as the gift of a child;

For with children,
love has no boundaries;

Time is a circle
with no beginning, no end;

Hope is abundant,
patience a challenge
and charity something to learn;

For each day,
a gift is laid before us
as the old one is taken away;

The continuous cycle of life
if we look, we can learn;

There is none so precious,
as the chance to see what life can be,
through the eyes of a child.

    Donna Spencer

LIVING IN A FANTASY

Rainbows.
Pastel colored,
Soft & fluffy,
Dream-like.

Unicorns.
Mystical,
Magical,
Unexisting beasts.

Utopia.
Land of the unknown,
The perfect place,
Everyone's dreamland.

Dreams.
Everyone's wildest inhibitions,
What no one ever expects to come true,
What you really wish were true.

These, and many more,
Make up people's fantasies.
The ideal way of life,
The ideal way to be.

    Geralyn B. Grandison

PREYBIRDS

Soaring on stolen wings
They came
Plundering republic's frame
They fed on flesh of mankind's toil
And thus the plague began
Where seamstress sewed
And smithy forged
And tradesmen crafted wares
New rat-tat-tat machines
Lured all
Into the preybird's lair
Committing freeman's tool to dust
Of Independence Day
With passing generations lost
Of Americans
Remembering
free land before the preybird's reign
It is to thee I sing!

    James Matuschka

FOR JOHN

In the garden of my dreams
I cultivate the love
That grows in my heart
For you.
It starts as a seed
Of friendship
That develops into a lovely flower.
Its delicate fragrance
Surrounds me,
And I feel fresh and new.
It blossoms in the
Sunshine of peace and love.
It flourishes with
The tears of happiness,
Only to be smothered
With the weeds
Of empty arms,
And a lonely heart
When I awaken.

Vera C. Poole

MOLESTATION

The innocence of
Nature
Often marred
By self-indulgence,
An inner drive,
Results in
A one-sided
Egotistical pleasure
That ignores feelings
Of another.

Allowing such
Perpetration to
Cause anguish
Can only lead
To insensitivity,
A hardening of
One's heart.

Paul J. Volkmann

WHOLE EARTH LULLABY

   Peacefully falling rain pouring
down upon the earth . . .
   The world paces on in a sychronated
time.
   The future will pass and bring you
back and you'll be all right.
   Whole Earth Lullaby.
   Dragons and monsters of the sea
will only be by memory.
   Sweet angels will walk on mystifying
clouds of silver dust.
   Houses filled with rainbow windows
shall shimmer in the skies.
   Battle shall cease and peace shall
fill the earth.
   Life's bluffs shall unfold,
   And when you're too old to dream
life's colors will linger on in your mind.
   Whole Earth Lullaby.

Anastasia Grigorowich

BREAKING UP

I lie in bed at night,
Thoughts of you are heavy on my heart,
And I cry in bed at night,
because we have to part.
I broke the rules and fell in love,
and now I have to pay;
But it's so hard to sleep at night,
and to face you every day.
I keep waiting for the phone to ring,
or to see you at my door,
but I know that you won't be there,
and I want you even more.

I lie in bed at night,
Thoughts of you are heavy on my heart,
And I cry in bed at night,
How did I let this affair ever even start?
I knew we never had a chance,
and now I have to face the pain;
Honey, deep inside my heart I know,
I'll never love like you again.

Tammi Notick

GREMLIN

These are bad little creatures
The ears are their big features
They scurry around at night
You better watch it 'cause they
Might bite
Gremlins cause a lot of trouble
One day you might hear things tumble
They are very ugly and small
Sight of Gremlins would scare
People if they saw
You'd never live in peace
For your food at any time they
Might reach
They have very sharp teeth
So get your money and friends
to go
To see about these mean
Creatures at the picture show
People beware of what you
See coming
'Cause it could be a terrible Gremlin

Nancy Cromwell

TELL ME WHY

Tell me why the sun shines, the moon glows
The stars twinkle, the wind blows
Tell me why a bird sings, a bee stings
A baby cries, an old woman sighs
Tell me why
Tell me why I still love you
Tell me why I sit and cry thinking of you
Why can't things remain the same
Why do they have to change
Tell me why
Tell me why my heart skips a beat
When I see you on the street
Tell me why your very touch
Makes me want you Oh sooo much
Tell me why you're in my dreams
Never leaving me alone, it seems
You're in my thoughts night and day
This time are you here to stay
Or will you be like the unreachable star
So close and yet so far
Tell me why

Roma Hogue

REFLECTION

I am
the
mirror cracked
Each shard
razor
sharp Reflecting
brilliant rainbows
that can dazzle
your eyes
Each
having a beauty all its own
Ice
touched jigsaw puzzle
A mockery of the mirror
that is complete and
reflects back what
it sees. In between my
pieces you can see my
wood.

Kristine Ameringer

GOD'S LOVING HANDS!

God holds our lives within His hands,
   No matter who we are.

Although sometimes when we're alone,
   He seems so very far.

And even when we feel depressed,
   He walks right by our side.

Waiting for us to open our heart,
   So He can come inside.

So when the rain begins to,
   Within your life prevail.

Look to God who loves you most,
   And He will never fail.

Darlene H. R. Tucker

ROCKING

Rocking, rocking, in grandma's
Big rocking chair.
It's fun to sit in her lap
And rock, rock, rock.

Sometimes we talk,
Sometimes we laugh.
Sometimes she scratches my back.
And sometimes we just listen,
To the television,
To grandpa sneaking quietly
Into the cookie jar,
Or,
Sometimes we just listen
To the rocking chair
Going creak, creak, creak,
Against the floor.
Rock, rock, rock.

Linda Seiter McKay

TO LOVE

Brilliantly, the sun shone all the day
The ocean — the beach — the sand
She felt his nearness — his breath — his lips
Then wakened, and tears gave way.

Emily Ritke Okray

SEAMEN'S REST

The wild west wind in spite spews up the tide,
unreined, untamed, bombards the rugged coast
with baleful force, undying fearsome pride;
it's not enough to sate her hateful boast.

To think that there, just on the rise, the crest,
The unsung heroes claim their ravaged rank;
she craves their bodies, souls, their flesh and rest;
she brawls and sprawls and gnaws the sandy bank.

They pause, resist her savage beastly quests,
at peace beneath the rufted rippled sands;
the giant firs ignore her threats and tests
while sea gulls circle — mewing plaintive bands.

They lie in primal silence of the dawn
where cougars stalk their prey but few men mark;
while stag and doe protect and guide their fawn
in search of lichen-dripping craggy bark.

Their storms of life have calmed, their battles spent;
God rest their souls but keep their mem'ries fresh;
God rest their sea-tossed souls in peace, content
for they were once human flesh.

Lyllian D. Cole

COLE, LYLLIAN DORETHEA. Born: A few miles south of Heather Brae, Alberta, 4-10-10; Education: Humble beginnings at Greenoch, a little "green" school house one mile south of my father, Geo T. Campbell's horse ranch, in the Battle River Valley, Central Alberta, and Heisler High School; Occupations: Clerk, "Hired Girl," Violinist in Dance Band, and hopefully, Poet; Memberships: American Writer; Awards: Books of Poetry, Grand Prize, and numerous Honorable Mentions; Poetry: 'A Wondrous Thing,' John Campbell, 1983; 'No One Will Ask Him How He Fared,' John Campbell, 1984; 'Salmon Arm,' sonnet, 1985; 'The Old Home Place,' *Byline*, 1985; 'In Little Hills & the Snowdrops,' quatrains, Quill & Scroll, 1985; Comments: *I see, hear and read about so many things that interest me, that I wish to share them.*

SIGNS OF SUMMER

The soft warmth of the Summer's sun
Gives promise of happy days to come
Hours filled with play and fun
Time to just relax for some

The robins have built their nest
And soon Mr. wren will appear
Followed by Mrs. wren and all the rest,
Inspecting their houses, as they do each year

Their songs fill the air
And they are welcomed back home
For Summers with our feathered friends
We will share
Though far away we may roam

Soon the beaches will be filled
Children picking sea shells with loving care
Tanned faces, sparkling eyes, thrilled,
At seeing the great big blue Ocean
And we too, are overcome with Emotion.

Rose Mary Gerlach

THE ART OF LOVE

When you were born
Your soul was an empty canvas
An unblemished white sail stretched across flesh and bones
Your imagination is a paintbrush
And your life has been a palette
Where clots of blood, drops of tears and beads of sweat
Form a living paint that's been mixed from tubes of
experience
That you share with me

When I was born
My soul was an empty sheet of paper
Clean and crisp waiting for a message
My imagination is a pen
That lets my thoughts flow like ink
Though confined by the margins of my experience
And my heart is an unabridged dictionary
That I share with you

Together we began a collaboration
Fusing paint, ink and souls into a collage of love
That cannot be bought or sold —

Deborah Vitello

MY PRAYER

My dear wife,
You are my woman,
I shall not want another.
You maketh me work my fingers to the bone,
You leadeth me to all the big bargains and sales.
You depleteth my billfold.
You leadeth me into paths of ridicule
for your longings, and your expensive tastes.
Yea, though I try to avoid the "Macho" men,
I have to face them.
I receive no respect, for thou art with me.
Thy designer jeans, and your Rollex watch,
embarrass me.
Thou tellest all in the presence of mine enemies.
Thou anointest my face with a burning blush,
And my sweat runneth over.
Surely, you're my woman, and I will follow and obey you
all the days of my life.
We will dwell in luxury as long as I am able to work
and spend all my hard earned money on you, forever and ever.

Not — A Man
Just — A WIMP

Nelda G. Wilson

IMPERFECT WINGS

A bumblebee's flight enchants my eye,
Savoring nectar from blossoms nearby.
According to science he cannot fly,
On miniature wings he embraces the sky.
Cumbersome body without grace,
He bumbles from place to place.
Oblivious to his inherent plight,
Persisting in arduous flight.
Defier of gravity's law,
He seems unaware of his flaw.
Unique creation, part of God's plan,
Chosen to pollinate the land.
Without the flight of the bee,
There'd be no fruit on the vine or the tree.
His harvest of fruit an hundredfold,
And honey sparkling like gold.
Lord, I too would accomplish impossible things,
Teach me to fly on imperfect wings.

Billie Jean Henry

HENRY, BILLIE JEAN. Born: Tyler, Texas, 9-26-37; Single; Education: Spencer Business College, General Business, 1956; Occupation: Staff Assistant; Memberships: National Writer's Club, Christian Poetry Association of America; Poetry: 'Blueprints of Love,' *Hearts On Fire: A Treasury of Poems on Love,* American Poetry Association, January 1985; 'Yesterday's Child,' American Poetry Association, 1984; 'He Is Able,' *Living with Hope,* Christian Woman's Quarterly, 1984; Other Writings: *Imperfect Wings,* book, 1985; "Today's Christian Woman," and 'God's Woman,' article and poem, Christian Poetry Association of America, Spring 1985; Themes: *Positive, uplifting themes.* Comments: *Writing poetry allows me to rise above the hardships and heartaches of life and see beyond these temporal things. The beauties of creation: a breathtaking sunrise, a butterfly on the wing, a robin in the springtime, a rainbow after the storm, the love of a faithful friend — are treasures and bring gladness to our hearts and renew our spirits. I strive for my poetry to bring a message of renewal, hope, and joy to the hearts of my fellow man.*

REMEMBERED FROM A PICTURE

The most beautiful I've ever felt
Was on warmish October days,
Running through crunching fields
Till my hair stung like whips,
But fell around my face
Like beautiful Eve's
In many stained-glass pictures.
With dust on my hands
and lungs stiff from breathing,
The smells in my clothes of the dying sun
And thump-hearted creatures.
No beauty like the pounding beauty of the
                            heart, air, lungs, sun
Racing time
On dusty October days.

Kathleen Quinn Reilly

CELEBRATION OF ONE

Tinsel, glimmering lights flood the night
Door to door the season's bright.
Evergreen scent; carolers sing.
Season's cheery, joy they bring.

Darkness, sadness fill the night.
Loneliness — one, the season's bright.
No tree, no gifts, no carolers sing
Reality. No Santa, no gifts to bring.

Stocking *one* — hung by chimney with care
Filled by one — tradition spared.
No visions of sugarplums dance in head
No magic, no one orders you to bed.

No anticipation, no peeking or chill
While spying on Santa as, he, stockings fill.
No magical glees from childrens' joys
No pretending necessary; No childrens' toys.

Only myself — and the carolers sing
Seasons cheery joy they bring
Darkness, sadness fills the night.
It's Christmas Eve, the season's bright.

Gracie Ann Maitland

LIFE

As I look through my mind's eye,
I can see a future ahead.
One of promise, and one of pain.
The pain serves only to remind me
That life is an achievement.

Many have gone, but few have attained,
For life is an adventure
And you make your destiny.
It is not what life deals out that matters,
But only how you react.

Reach for the stars
And set your goals,
Not too high as to fall,
But high enough to feel it,
And you will discover the beauty of life.

Lynn Seivwright

NORTH ATLANTIC LOVER

Have you walked along the sandy beach,
Where the swirls of sea water grab and reached
Around your toes and sucked you in,
The sinking sand as the tide goes in?

Have you stopped to see the Gull sweep low,
And hear the sip of the Spit-clam blow?
And see the bubbles show signs of its life beneath?
Or be held in awe as the waves hit the reef?

Did the size of the Horseshoe crab startle you?
Or the feel of the Jellyfish as it glides from your view?
Have you swum and entangled yourself in green algeous fronds
Of seaweed unshackled from the depth of their bonds?

Have you enjoyed tanning in the rays of the sun?
Or seen the blue skies and the clouds have their fun?
Or dive under the wave as it pounds to the shore?
Or venture out deeper to get shoved even more?

Have you tasted the tanginess of salt in the water so strong
As the waves and the wind carried you briskly along?
If you have had these experiences on the seashore my friend,
You'll be a lover of sea, sun and sand to time has no end.

Doris L. Schmidt

SATAN'S GLORY

Barren eyes in whitewashed deserts.
  Children too weak to cry.
Outstretched, begging, empty hands
  Having no strength to play.
They squat silently amid a world of wealth.
  Dying without a cause.
In despair and pain they anticipate
  The death that so slowly stalks them.
Wide berth we give, pass by in stealth.
  Lest we be forced to commune.
Blinding our minds to their hell.
  Reaching for the moon.
Taking, while mothers cradling dead infants wait
  For mercy.

Kathryn A. Etherington

MEMORIES

It's the laughter we will remember
Even on a hard day in September.
Their hardships we share today
Will make the sun shine on us with bright rays.

For in our times of distress, we grow strong
Even if we were wrong.
The mistakes will bring us closer together
Only then will we be one forever.

We will remember the laughter
Although, today is what we are after.
For today will be yesterday soon
Memories, like visions under the moon.

Sherrie Harn Tame

WHY IS IT SO HARD TO LOVE?

Has romance gone out of style?
Is tenderness only found in a child
whose innocence lets his heart be free
to love without uncertainty?

Why is pain a factor in love
instead of emotional bliss?
Is it possible to find a sensitive and loving man
with a warm and sensuous kiss?

Is it possible to love and hate
even though the hate is so great?
Should I give up on love
or would that be a mistake?

Valeria Norals

WORDS CAN EXPLAIN

Oh, words cannot explain the pain I've been through.
Each day of my life I think about you.
I should be sleeping, but I just cannot keep still.
I want to tell you the way that I feel.
I am lying here pleading with tears in my eyes.
Why do you not listen? I would not lie.
Oh, words cannot explain the pain I have been through.
Each day of my life I think about you.
Although I have heard it said, time and time again,
That God will help me. The question is, when?
I said those three words He had been waiting to hear,
And now my life has been freed from all fear.
Oh, but words can explain the pain I have been through.
Each day of my life I say, "Lord, I love you."

Angela Lorin Ryniak

PUSHED TO LIGHT

A radio screams in metallic glory
Weep for me on the FM bands
I'm like a brick wall spattered with spray paint
Slogans in black and red
I ain't no Marxist, but I wish I was
And I know Jesus didn't die for me
Only Mama in her tenement squalor
I shoulda — been aborted, but it was pre-73
Mama was afraid of coat hangers
Didn't have the money to pay the man
So she died in convulsions screaming
She flew to darkness pushing me to light
An infant in an urban nursery
Christened with carbon cradled in newsprint
The headlines stained my newborn flesh
Read me I'm a walking story
Blessed with life I try to forget

Daniel Schwartz

CLASSROOM

The seats are empty.
I sit and stare at all the faces . . .
  Fleeting images   of students here   and gone.
          Do I hear laughter?
Are they returning to tell me of their lives
          and how they've done?

I sit and ponder
  on my ache within whenever I recall
  names   and faces
      who reached and touched me
          in this world of "education,"now absolved.

I may grow old here   as I sit with ghosts who vainly
    try to speak.   I am their student.
It is their wisdom I have slowly learned to seek.

Mary Jane Leach

YOUR STAR

There's a star up in heaven, shining for you,
    You must follow that star, whatever you do.
That star is a covenant, shining down from above,
    God gave it the light, from someone you love.
So follow that star, and find where it leads,
    Like the Wise Men of old, it is one of your deeds.
When you get where it leads, I am sure you will find,
    Just what you are seeking, and great peace of mind.
So look for your star, in the heavens above,
    When you find it, I'm sure, you will find someone you love.

George Chalmers

LOVE THE UNLOVELY

Friend, love the unlovely; they too are God's children.
They, too, have salvation by the same risen Lord,
He loves them, protects them, and answers their prayers,
The message for them is in the same Holy Word!

They sin not — or sin and know not that they sin,
But the same Holy Spirit fills their cup, dwells within.
Oh, love the unlovely, they too are His creatures,
For the "least of these" also He suffered and died!
They come to the Father in humble acceptance —
In their innocent trust they are never denied!

If you meet the unlovely, let them know you're a friend,
They have fragile emotions and on your kindness depend!
Someday the unlovely will walk streets of gold,
At last they'll be lovely, and MORE precious than gold!

Rahya Montuori

HOUSE OF MEMORIES

Oh, House of Memories,
How lonely sounds the breeze,
As coming through the opened door.
It calls upon who nevermore
Shall answer it and feel its ecstasies.

Lonely relic of the past,
Into shadows art thou cast.
And with ancient lilac bough,
Flanked by scented roses now,
Drooping in the gentle rains,
Only in the heart remains
My House of Memories.

Laurene G. Charlebois

CHARLEBOIS, LAURENE G. Born: Houston, Minnesota, 1913; Married: 1940 to Leo Charlebois; Education: St. Olaf College, B.A., Magna Cum Laude; Occupation: Banking — Retired Bank Escrow Officer; Memberships: American Institute of Banking, Business and Professional Women's Club, St. Olaf Honors Society; Poetry: 'To My Daughter and to My Son,' American Poetry Association, 1983; 'Eternal Love,' American Poetry Association, 1984; Comments: *Now that I have retired, I have again an opportunity to return to my first love — writing, and to express my deep feelings of pride and love for my country, my home, and my family.*

PAST MEMORIES

My thoughts pulse with memories
Of my years that went by
For many a woman I have met
And yet I still cry
Not of tears that show
But of tears deep inside
Of loneliness that burns deep
Beneath my weary hide
Though many a lover had come
And thrice a many had gone
They stole my lonely heart
And held it for so long
Now I'm old and lonely
To live, I have not long
But I have my memories
Which will burn on strong
To keep me company
Till I'm gone

Keith E. Smith

GOD'S RECREATION AREA:

It is here that I feel
the fine gift of life.
I feel the air making
      love to my lungs,
      and
I feel my eyes capture
Rembrandts
            and
                  Vincent Van Goghs.
It is here that the
lavish stone walls of
      time show dimension,
where meaning is tranquility,
            and
skies run endless blue.
It is also here that the
arms of a friend make my
                  shadow.
That my words are the
rivers and valleys
            and
                  the streams.
And should I choose to
flood them with kindness,
I would simply remember
            our moments together.

Wayne Frank Danka

Many a lonely heartache
too often a silent tear,
with so many memories
of the one I love so dear . . .
I think of you in silence
and make no outward show,
for what it meant to lose you
no one will ever know . . .
Now deep in my heart's a lonely spot
that your love used to fill,
nothing can fade those memories
and nothing ever will . . .
your hands so soft and gentle
and a love so tender and true,
nothing now that life can bring
can equal my losing you.

James McDermott

FRENCH BALLET

Last night as my momma cried
twenty thousand butterflies went
      to battle inside.

They were gorgeous in their
      pink and black tu tu's
      singing the opera,
            playing flutes.

Camellias, dipped in chocolate,
      floated down a stream
butterflies danced, wept . . .
            dreamt.

And she, with blue heart
pounding like the first day
      of kindergarten,

      sat on her pedestal
feeling sorry . . . forgotten.

Spring turns to Fall . . .
      flowers must sleep.
Butterflies dream
while momma weeps.

Tina Joy Whelden

WE PHOTOGRAPH THE DAY OF ECLIPSE
HONORABLE MENTION

The sun has abandoned Brasstown;
the valley darkens as the moon
creeps lurid across his face.
We hide our eyes behind spent film,
avoiding scars that might blind,
while by the planetarium, a teacher
aims his camera at shadows, tracking
their progress on the ground.
Later, a student runs breathless
to say that creatures of the night
have lost their nest, perched low
in the dogwood leaved with late May.
Mother and four owlets fist-sized
stare uncomprehending at this day
turned nocturnal at noon. (Two days,
two nights they mourn, their cries
plaintive across the campus.) One
student crouches on a dogwood limb,
captures on new film their unblinking
gaze, their soft feathers barred
in patterns indistinguishable
from quivering leaves, grey
fungus crawling down an old trunk.
Bettie Sellers

INSPIRATION

For one inspired hour of life
   I dwelt in fantasy sublime,
But, minutes sped —
   The hour fled —
Left nothing then, to mark the time.

For one inspired week of life
   Again, I bridged the common span,
Days went past —
   Began to cast —
To mold the lines into a plan.

For one inspired year of life
   As in a tumbling, torrent stream,
Came a flow —
   Burst into glow —
Creativeness beyond supreme.

For one inspired life of life
   The will to write within me lay,
God's own power
   In *every* hour
The pen had guided all the way.
Alfred W. Hicks

GOD'S LOVE

When your heart is heavy
Can your feet be light
When your soul is sick
Can your eyes be bright.

When you have done your best
And it isn't enough
Your spirit sinks
The road is rough.

If you bend your knees
And say a prayer
The Good Lord will hear you
He knows you are there.

He will give you His Blessing
And smile on you
Remove the clouds
And let the sun shine through.
Helen T. Neiman

WISHING WELL

A petal of the tender bud
    is coaxed away from its secrecy of night:
      brushed with a midnight tear,
    eager to blend with morning's soft light;
I return it to the spring of its delight —
    to bathe your cheek in my reflection.

A blossom — new, releasing
    its fragrance through the dappled shade,
      casting its essence to the eager pool
    from which it strayed;
A breath to tease the leafy blade
    of evergreen in translucent blue.

A flower, full with the stain
    of silent thorns which bled
      a touch too delicate to hold;
    blessing a love we cannot shed;
Even in our silent dreams, to wed
    the shattered image of our reflected gaze.

Vicky M. Semones

SOLITUDE

I come here often, walking in the soft white sand,
stopping occasionally to examine a shell or two.

It is a lovely day, a gentle breeze caresses me.
The sound of lapping waves lulls my inner turmoil,
soothes me, tension eases from me.

Sand dunes form an ever-changing
landscape with their sea oats waving.
Sand flowers are scattered about
surprising one with their lovely colors.

Waves come, breaking gently onto the sand.
They come breaking again and again.
An eternity of motion, the sea is so very quietly alive.

It is here I find my needed peace.
It is here I find repose from the turbulence of living.
It is here I find new strength, needed strength to go on.

Gladys M. Ainslie

THE LIFE AND DEATH OF A NEWSPAPER

At the end of the cracked and decayed driveway
Lies a local newspaper;
Rolled up with hatred, doubt and dismay;
As sad as it may appear,
a body will retrieve it and "consume" it,
Every day and every year —
The stories of sadness, pain and disgust;
Guilt, fear, death, and distrust,
Lying, waiting to tell its sad tales . . .
To let others know, just how it feels;
Crouching senselessly,
Close to the ground;
It brings a tear, a grief or a frown;
Someday I hope the world may see
How beautiful life is,
And surely must be;
For paper will fade,
Cringe and decay;
Yet one will always,
Find another day . . .

Eric T. Moore

MESSAGE FROM THE HILLS

These golden, brown and amber heights,
    Sloping vales, evening shadows through the trees,
All gently speak a message to my soul —
    Be still, My Soul — And Be Aware!

These hills make me happy, full of joy and free.
    They hold my dear ones dearer still —
And I am parched of love for all those part of me.
    And so I fly and so I sing, with a carefree,
Joyous heart, so close to all I love.

These golden, magic hues — the reds, the browns,
    The greens — all scale the heights and then
Roll down the slopes to cast a mystic spell
    Of beauty, warmth and love not freely found.

The look of forever and of now — a message from
    Afar and from Near — from Yesterday, Today
And tomorrow too.

My heart must be ready to sense the message from
    the hills — to see above, beyond the cloud of
Darkness that dims the earth — to where the hills
    Speak a truth that I hold dear — and of a
Love that holds eternity so near.

Alice C. Lumsden

COLOR WHEEL

      A sight
        conceived by light and storm,
          born of hope and named the Unicorn of Skies;
      Rainbow.

        Where others talk of ends and pots of gold
        I guess a truth unmythical and bold.

      It's not at all an arc
        that, bending, touches one bright foot to earth,
        the other lost in spectral dreams of wealth.

    No! It's a wheel that rolls along
behind the thunder-drums of clouds . . .
around and 'round forever reaching upward toward the sun
    while plunging ever downward with each rain to nourish life.

      Some call it hope, the sunlight's ribbons,
        God's smile . . . His ancient promise kept.

        I call it whole. The wedding ring
          that joins our earth to sky,
            the dark to light,
            our joy
              to all the tears we've wept.

Diana J. Long

MELODY OF SPRING

The cherry blossoms greet the April rain;
The flowering quince salutes another day.
The world has turned her back on all the pain
That Winter seemed determined to portray.
And lovers smile their welcome to the Spring:
They melt in one another and retreat
To forest dells and mountains that all ring
With joy, with birth, with promises so sweet.
And I, alone, do not communicate
With Nature, lovers, Spring, or anything.
Enthralled with Winter's shadow as a mate,
I hardly hear the melody I sing.
But Spring insinuates itself with ease,
And I, so foolish, try too hard to please.

Sheila Juba

THE SWEETIE

Girl friends are nice to have,
And I could like them a lot.
But they are here today, gone tomorrow,
Whether you like it or not.

Now a sweetie is much different,
She doesn't run and play.
Once she is attached to you,
That's when she'll want to stay.

Now the boy friends are not the same,
They might have three or four.
But there's always one of the bunch,
That he loves a lot more.

When they get attached to each other,
He will just drop all the rest.
And talk her into settling down,
And start building them a nest.

If you're looking for a sweetie,
To be with and have fun.
Stay on the right track and be nice,
You might be the lucky one.

Cecil Moore

MUSIC

If it weren't for music
I don't know what I'd do
to fill the empty hours
Until I can be with you

It's as if the lyrics were written
Especially for me
They express my feelings so well
And help to fill my need

To be able to drift off in a song
To envision our dream
Such happiness is astounding
Could it really be?

The song is over
And down I crash
It's back to reality
The dream has gone to ash

Until the next song is played
And I can return to you
Even if it's only a dream
It'll have to do.

Robin L. Coverstone

Where are the days of yesterday
When I was but a lad
Playing in the sands of streams
And smell the curing hay

The apple trees are full of bloom
And other blossoms to
Remind me of the apples
When comes the August moon

I go down to the creek nearby
And take my fishing pole
To see if I can catch a fish
From that old fishing hole

Now yesterday is gone
And I in reverie
Return to thoughts of childhood
And how it used to be.

T. R. Whitehead

THE NIGHT MY WORLD STOOD STILL:

I remember the night, that my
World stood still.
My mother left us, it was the
good Lord's will.
The night closed around us, as I
stood by her side.
I was losing my mother, best friend
and guide.

I remember the nights I would
be sick.
She softly crossed the room, and
turned down the wick.
Her shadow would dance upon the wall
She sat by my side lest I should call
a cool hand was placed upon my brow,
Sometimes, I think, I feel it now.

My arms were around her, my tears
mingled with hers.
She just couldn't leave me, after
All these years.
The moment came I did so dread,
The nurse touched my arm, your mother
is dead.
My eyes are dry now, I know
it was God's will,
I shall never forget the night
"My world stood still."

Marie Houston

SUSAN —
ON MOVING DAY.

Sipping a final cup of tea
from a cracked cup.

We resist then acknowledge
our tears.

The closets and cabinets
are bare.

The moment can no longer
be postponed.

Suddenly clumsy with great
emotion
we fumble.

For the choice words —
then we settle.

For clasped hands and
many hugs . . .

How does one say —
Goodbye to a daughter.
Very carefully indeed . . .
Mother . . .

F. L. Sackman

The rain ceases to be rain,
upon falling on its earth mother
The river ceases to be river,
upon being consumed by the
mighty ocean
The poet ceases to be poet,
upon relinquishing his very soul
unto the limitless expanse of
the ever-changing whole

Kerry McGeath

MY LOVE FOR YOU

I have never cared for
Anyone like I care for you,
The words that I'm saying
Are meant to be true.
Someday you and I will walk
As one,
The sadness will be over, and
We'll have our fun.
Don't listen to what other
People say,
Our love is growing day by day.
I'll give you a penny for all
Your thoughts,
Just to prove my love has
Been bought.

Donna Chew

CHEW, DONNA. Comments: *I am a 16-year-old student at Herrin High School. I started writing poetry last summer and it has become a hobby to me. I write poetry to express my feelings. Someday I hope my work will become my future.*

I LOVE YOU

I need someone who loves me,
And someone to be near;
But when you are there with me,
I feel your love so dear.

Whenever you are with me,
I feel the world is mine;
And I want it to remain that way,
Until the end of time.

If all my wishes could come true,
And all the skies were blue;
I know about the things I'd say,
I'd say that . . . I love you.

You are the biggest part of me,
And I need you everyday;
You are the only one I love,
In a very special way.

There are no words that can describe,
The way that I feel;
And my only wish is that our love,
Could be real.

You must know that I really care,
And my heart is all for you;
And the only way I can express myself,
Is to say that . . . I love you.

Antonella Gulia

ON THE MOVE

How bright the glowing sunbeams dance around me;
As I keep moving, so changes the landscape:
Immediately, I feel like a being in another world.
I don't know where I'm going,
Just keep moving onward,
Rivers, mountains and fresh fields lie in the waning sunbeams.
Tall buildings, short buildings, squat buildings fill some of
the spaces;
The lights wink and beckon me in this fading glow,
Silently I stand just out of their reach,
Full of memories from the past.
I just keep moving onward, I'm a stranger here.
So I turn and look at the far mountains,
At this time of day people return to their families,
Friends meet friends, strangers are frowned upon.
I used to have a home; someplace, but I just keep moving on.

Col. J. Nicholas Jones

VENTED ANGER

Damn you, how cruel you are to my retarded son.
Do you think he does not feel,
Left out of the games and fun?
Don't you hear his whimper stilled?
Are you listening to the words he begs to say,
Hesitant with no demand
To reveal in his own way
The struggle of want within?
Must I alone ache for his silent plea of worth?
Must I fill his every need?
Do you share with me his hurt,
As he pretends not to bleed?
I pray our God to hurry his eternal sleep
And end all his hurt and pain.
And when you with guilt do weep
Hear my cry "damn you" again.

Betty Jane Atkinson

CATCHING

I saw a boy catching butterflies
He could not catch them,
for they fly too high.
The children run to catch fireflies
as they light and twinkle
in the dark skies.
The grown man goes to catch the fish,
to catch a bunch that is his wish.
An old man just relaxes and catches a dream,
of distant lands and things unseen.
Oh life, and all the joy in it,
let's just relax and enjoy every minute.

Hazel Carestia

FROM THE MOUTHS OF BABES

When they launched my ship on the sea of life I let out an
awful wail!
And the spanking I got made me wonder for what — so my ship
would smoothly sail?
But they christened my ship with a bottle of milk and cradled
my head on a pillow of silk.
Then they looked me over from head to toe to see if wings had
started to grow!
For an angelic face as sweet as mine was planned by one who is
divine.
Yours to cherish, nurture and guide, mine in the future, then
to decide —
Who is my Captain on life's turbulent sea. Who charted my course
to Eternity.
So, guide well, dear parents, you must not fail if into Heaven's
Port I would finally sail!

Alice Knight

A DREAM

I had this dream of a place far-off
Where there was no killing, robbing or raping;

I had this dream of a place far-off
Where there was no hatred, envy or prejudice;

I had this dream of a place far-off
Where there was no evil, fear or darkness;

I had this dream of a place far-off
Where there was no famine, sickness or death;

I had this dream of a place far-off
Where there was no conflict, affliction or war;

I had this dream of a place far-off
Where there was slaughter, dancing and friendship;

I had this dream of a place far-off
Where there was love, brotherhood and freedom;

I had this dream of a place far-off
Where there was justice, liberty and happiness;

I had this dream of a place far-off
Where there was food, drink and immortality;

I had this dream of a place far-off
Where there was peace, solitude and godliness.

Ron Collings

LITTLE CHILDREN

Little children, everyone loves you.
You're the heart of our big world, 'tis true.

You've shiny small diamonds in your eyes,
Bright as jewelled stars set in the blue skies.

You've lips tender, sweet and ruby red.
A crown of hair, you wear on your head.

You've fingers that clutch a lonely heart.
Grown-up will power you tear apart.

You've two sturdy and quick little feet,
That walk or run up and down the street.

You've a heart full of love for others,
Dear, to hearts of fathers and mothers.

You've a mind with thoughts, deep as a well,
That is filled with dreams, you dare not tell.

You've a happy song for folks to hear,
'Tis sure to bring them a bit of cheer.

You've a future unknown to any,
With high hopes, wonderful and many.

You're life's gems to keep and cherish, too.
Little children, everyone loves you.

Marie Talbert

A June morning
across the wild blue yonder.
The morning sunlight touches every hill and vale,
with the same sweet message of yesteryear
God's love can never fail.

'Tis June the month of roses
when nature's lovely bower,
opens wide her arms of love
and embraces every flower.

The wild birds sing their morning song
for all the world to hear.
The cricket and grasshopper
add their note of cheer.

The lowing cattle on the hill
say good morning to another day,
some mighty mystic power of love
has touched life's great highway.

I hear the Bobwhite calling
across the lonely hill,
The Great Eternal God of Heaven
whispers "Peace be still."

Amy Bearden

A WANDERING TALE

He said they look'd for the Garden of God.
The three had begun when each was still young;
But that was over fifty years ago.
A fortune to the empty air had flung.
Such dogged searching seemed to some quite odd.

The ruins of Babylon they sought among,
Where the swift waters of Euphrates flow;
By Euxine Sea where ancient legend sung,
Collecting seeds from Turkey's reddish sod;
Hope being restored with each newfound pod.

Mirages with the wind away might blow,
But intent from longing eyes had not wrung
For that planted by rule of divine rod,
Along whose flowering paths Adam had trod.
Dedication ne'er told by human tongue!

Their search was soon sung in Welsh Eisteddfod;
Then carried across to the Scottish Mod.
Some, however, said it was a mere bung!
Can one deny such sincerity, trow,
Where three at once by this wanderlust stung?

William Bryan Barton

COMPULSION OF THE YEAR

This inanimate object, housing typewriter keys . . .
Press the right keys and it answers you correctly,
But *press one* wrong key,
And you can feel insecure;
And your hands become clammy,
For how can you be sure?

Your pulses are leaping as you await its report.
It ravages your ego with its sassy retort; *Error — Error*
And suddenly you find yourself in a box
As surely as if you're bound and fettered with locks.
You threaten to turn the blasted thing off.
You shout, "This is war!" as you hiss and you scoff.

But you've got the compulsion to get in the clear;
So once more you push keys to get the message so dear.

And you ponder the question as you push the right key,
Have you mastered the machine, this part of your destiny?

Shirlee Olanoff

ONE MORE TIME

One more time would I like to hold you
Once again would I like to feel your body next to mine
Just another chance to kiss you
To know you
Just once again is all I ask

One more time would I like to be with you
Once again would I like to have you in my presence
Just another chance to look at you
To know you
Just once again is all I ask

One more time would I like to talk to you
Once again would I like to hear you speak
Just another chance to share things with you
To know you
Just once again is all I ask

One more time would I like to touch you
Once again would I like to feel you
Just another chance to explore you
To know you
Just once again is all I ask

Ada Nickerson

TELL ME TO LEAVE

Just tell me to leave and I will go
Oh darling please don't hurt me so
If you're playing with my heart
I'd rather we would part
Just tell me to leave and I will go

My heart is filled with sorrow and despair
'Cause I feel that you no longer care
You have broken my heart
Please don't tear it apart
Just tell me to leave and I will go

Your love was strong in the past
I felt that it would always last
Now you have found somebody new
To sing our love songs to
Just tell me to leave and I will go

If you tell me to leave I'll know it's true
That our little romance is through
If I cannot be your kin
Will you accept me as a friend
Just tell me to leave and I will go

W. O. Hicks, Sr.

TO MY DEAD SON — A WAR HERO

To my dead son, age 57, a World II hero,
went to Prague where he was sent by
Stars and Stripes News. Before that he
was in the Assam Siege under American Field
Service Auspices where he had malaria.

I miss you at the dictionary!
I miss you at the encyclopedia!
I miss you picking violets in the woods!
I gaze at your prize-winning horse!
I sail your boat in my dreams!
I miss you in your cub-scout orchestra!
I collapse in grief over your illness from the war!
I miss you at my Steinway piano with Benny Goodman!
I miss your repartee at lunch and dinner!
I miss the goose you cooked at Christmas!
My heart drops a beat at your grave and falls inside!
Actually — I miss you so much I am partially dead!

Margaret E. Schmitt-Habein

HOKUSAI, A Duel

HYMN TO THE SEA

With watery breath you lace each rising
  wave with foam;
In fury, toss great sounds of silver sands
  on shore.
Forgotten ghosts of men and ships
  embraced by thee
Stir restlessly, in mute appeal, from
  sleep disturbed.
Then, as you feel the warm caress
  of wind and sun,
Your violence is stilled. Now, murmuring,
  you roll
And wave your frothy cloak of shimmering
  blue and green.
With awesome splendor, seem to blend into
  the sky . . .
What sorcery you weave for mortals such as I!

Jessica Clough

A WINTER EVENING

The air is cold, and still,
And the sun is setting beyond the
  distant hill.
The early winter twilight is redding
  in the sky,
A lonely blackbird is slowly flying by.
The brilliant colors are fading and
soon it will be night.
The wood is peaceful, and quiet.
But, I feel a change in the atmosphere,
For a sound is coming from somewhere.
It is only a bold squirrel running among
  the clumps,
Searching for a discarded nut, or crumb.
A late woodpecker is in flight,
Returning to his nest, to sleep away the night.
It is a time of contentment,
A winter enchantment.

Rena Guarente

THE FLAWLESS STONE

    Mirror of eternity, splendor of all ages, we entrust
our cares to You and do Your bidding. Never abandon us.
Rescue us from failures of the past. Inspire us towards
successes of the future.

    Root of David, bond of charity, let us lie on the
wings of Your mercy. Put Your central air into our fiery
furnaces. Whisper, "Be still, and know that I am God."
Turn us from the error of our ways. Move Your sun over
the horizons of our lives.

    Lily of the Valley, champion of the world, smooth
our rough spots, Polish us with "The Flawless Stone,"
the Rock of Salvation. Make us marathon runners for You
along the highways and byways. Cleanse us in Your well
of "living water." Amen.

Muriel R. Wiltz

MY FRIEND ON THE FLOOR

They just didn't understand,
they said, "He's such an angry, desperate young man."
They walled him in their world of white
and read patterns in his words of spite.

I cried and tried to get him out
they said, "You don't know what you're talking about."
It was then that I heard him moan,
he had slumped on the floor all alone.

Elizabeth Mora

JUDGMENT DAY

He will come so suddenly, in the twinkling of an eye
He will take his children, to the sweet by and by
Sinners will tremble, tears run from their eyes
Jesus brokenhearted, will have to reply

Don't be the one that's stranded, accept the Lord today
He'll fill your heart with gladness, and you'll be on your way
Be one of God's children, going home to stay
And you won't have to hear the words, Jesus will have to say

You chose not to accept me, depart, be on your way
My commandments you have broken
You have gone astray
Only God's children, are going home to stay
It's too late now, for this is your judgment day

Carol Gross

NO MORE THAN THIS

The fertile ground made ready for seed
to sprout and grow the food we need.

The meadows lush, the plains stretched long
The spring that bubbles and refreshes
The gentle trees to shade man's brow.
The sunlight warm on fields of corn —
The rain as gentle as the morn.

The dog that walks beside my stride
Who meets with danger and does not hide —

All these things I'm thankful for, and
could not ask for any more.

E. A. Teresky

ZERO AS A HERO

("Why so many non-participators?" — Eager Coach
at Convocation)

Well, Sir, now that you ask it, — basketball is not
At all a game at which I claim to be so very hot.
My feet, so d . . . unclever, never take me to my goal,
And it's quite harassing passing that I do in my small role.
When I the ball prance after, laughter from the stands
Makes me in anguish languish, — in full view of 'windy' fans.
While *knowing* trips and scholarships for sports fi-
  nesse are rife,
I foul . . . take steps . . . go out-of-bounds, — and muff my
  chance in life!
But, after all, why cry if I have not such golden trait?
I'm here to state, it's just my fate to "non-participate."

Harlan J. Leach

WINTER SCENE

Snow falling on city streets, making no sound except a
crunching under foot.
Traffic snarled to a grinding halt, while horns blast their
deafening sound. People all rushing to where? Time to
pause and reflect!
A walk in the park gives quiet peace. Fresh fallen snow
abounds as far as one can see.
Trees heavy laden, forcing their branches downward, to touch
an ice-covered pond. And ahead, a winding path disappearing
over the hill to another quiet place beyond.
Children scurry up and down with their sleds, or go gliding
over the ice pond on sparkling skates. Finding pure joy
in uncomplicated pursuit of play.
A picture in frozen crystal, brief and pure, until a warming
sun brings its eternal change.

Beverly A. Tadlock

IMAGES OF DEPRESSION

I am caught in a cardboard world.
The landscape is flat.
Grey light is predominant.
suffocating me with sameness.
Sounds are all monotones.

I suffer from loss of emotion.
Blank faces on stickmen bodies are everywhere.
The nightmare is repeated.
Raped by a continuous dream.

I am trapped between two thin lines,
in a one-dimensional world.
Anxiety causes the lines to jar.
The air is stagnant.
I lack hope.

My life is a black and white photo of
frozen events.
I finally discover the cosmic joke.
There is no me.
Just a pale reflection,
in a looking glass turned backward.

Emela McLaren

THE MYSTERY ANGEL

On new thoughts I ponder
In silent streets I wander
With eyes wide from wonder
Dark clouds I walk under
Round celestial thunder

I saw a mystery angel of the night
Under the stars robed in white
With voice clear eyes bright
Beautiful wings flying on light
Ever approaching but out of sight

In magical dreams she appeared to me
With shining hair flowing gracefully
Over a rugged hill and turbulent sea
Not bound by convention mystical free
In moonlight whispering "Come follow me!"

I remain so quiet behind a wall
Apart from the crowd strangers all
Who try to move but only stall
Choosing to wait for mankind's fall
Alone I respond to your call

Brian J. Groth

DAYS OF MAY

Ah, balmy sunlit days of May
We gaily raced through daffodils.
With Aphrodite's son we'd play
And frolic on the greenly hills.

Love was young and kisses pleasure
Flowers blooming wild afield.
Frail Nature's hoarded brittle treasure
Enticed the singing heart to yield.

All those delights that move the soul
We owned in the sunrise days
Before the hastening pace of time took its rigorous toll
And stole the gold from all the day-eye's rays.

But still the foaming floods of passion
Upon the walls of my heart beat
When Amor one more arrow fashions
And frees youth's relumed heat.

Marvin Sieger

FRIENDSHIP

If friends are the flowers in the garden of life
As I have heard some say
Then all my special friends
Make up a big bouquet
Today I must water them with kindness
And treat them with great care
If I want the beauty to last
Of the friendship that we share
For friendships are like flowers
They cannot be ignored
Tomorrow may be too late
With only memories stored
So I'll take time for my friends today
'Cause I love them all you see
And I pray that in return
They will take the time for me.

Ruth Karr

KARR, RUTH E. Born: Myrtle Point, Oregon; Married: 12-24-53 to Paul Dale Karr; Education: Graduated from Lincoln High School, Tacoma, Washington, 1952; Occupation: Homemaker; Poetry: 'First Grandchild,' American Poetry Association, August 1985.

DREAM DUST

Dreams are the mind shadow of our existence

 Caveman tools began as dream images
 dreams are the ashes of new phoenix
 mystic dreams act like dust on rainbows
 dream illusions die in concentration camps

Dreams create forms out of chaos and nothingness

 Mythical dreams become the myths we live by
 dream visions and ideas escape us in daytime
 dream poems gather dust on paper
 dream paintings end up as dust on canvas

Dreaming is an Eden from the miasma, emptiness
  and despair of our being

 Archetypes and revelations become foggy mists
 Where are our dream heroes in real life?
 If only dreams would seed in life's soil
 No dream is as horrible as the Gulag Axe

Dreams like oysters reveal the hidden pearls of meaning

 Dream symbols and fables end up as "Dust In The Wind."
 Christ dreamt the road to Calvary and His Cross.

 Paradise is the living dream beyond our grave . . .

Michael Pearl Clarizio

T.G.I.F.

It's a funny thing about my feet,
God made them comfortable, complete;
He made the heel rounded and smooth,
And with the arch, He formed a groove;
The top is pretty, all formed, you see,
For sock, or shoe, just right for me;
But when I slip my shoe on,
And the arch goes into place;
And the sole feels so comfortable,
Or before I begin to lace;
And even when my feet hurt,
Be it from standing up at work.
When I think T.G.I.F.,
I know "Toes Go In First."

Marjorie Halada

THE LAND

All trees and marsh was the land,
completely untamed by any hand.
The mountains strong they stood,
with clouds above as a pearly hood.
The oceans green and blue,
brought each day anew.
Like the veins in the hand,
were the rivers of the land.
The trees acting as a hood,
over the grasses in which they stood.
Life brought each day anew,
under a sky clear and blue.
Like the death throes of the hand,
so too dies an old old land.

David J. Dailey II

LOVE'S PATHOS

As love grows cold
As you grow old
Has that been foretold?
No, I say what intervened
What demon schemed
To end love not redeemed
Where is the magic once so rare
Where is that love beyond compare
Why so profound?
When time moves around to that
fateful day
When death will hold sway
Then I will say if we had
only found a way.

Dorothy Shelley

STAND BY AMERICA!

Men and women of the nation:
We of great or humble station
Sing a song in happy mood
To show our gratitude
That we live where all are free
To speak and write what we believe.
The Stars and Stripes will ever be
A Symbol of Democracy!
O'er all the world our flag unfurled
Stands for equality!
Though we differ we're united,
And for freedom we have fought!
We're masters of our destiny!
Stand by American Democracy!

Dr. Marjorie Elliott

VIGIL

Strange bird on your chosen rock
Why are you here alone?
Gray geese talk of the north wind
And doves are circling low.
You must leave the paling marsh,
The smoky tidal pools.
Follow the whirring bluewings
Flying before first frost.

As if in answer to my thoughts
You open your slender wings
Only to fold them slowly
And slip to the water's edge.
The breeze dies with the setting sun:
A cry comes from the marsh.
I wait with you until you drift
Deep beneath frosty grass.

Anne Ayer

AYER, ANNE AYER. Pen Name: Anne Ayer; Born: Topsfield, Massachusetts, 6-23-17; Married: 9-40 to Dr. Edward MacNichol, Jr.; Occupations: Concert and Opera Singer, Recording Artist; Memberships: American Federation of Radio and Television Artists; Poetry: 'Timeless,' American Poetry Association, Fall/Winter 1984; 'Starry Night,' New Worlds Unlimited, November, 1984; 'Vigil,' American Poetry Association, November, 1985; Comments: *I don't have any common themes and ideas in what I write. My love of poetry comes from all the works I had the privelege of singing.*

THE MOMENT

I've loved you for a long time
Though you do not know it,
I've loved you for a long time
Though I did not show it.

I've waited for the moment
When your heart is drawn to mine,
I know the moments closer
Our love will be divine.

Our love is ascending
To heights we now know,
Our love is unending
As the oceans flow.

Joan Maresch

MY HUSBAND

My husband is someone who always is there,
Someone who shows me he always will care.
Someone to lean on when times are bad,
Someone to hug me when I am glad.
Someone who loves me day after day,
Someone who never would hold me at bay.

My husband is someone to cherish and love,
Someone whom God sent me from above.
Someone who is strong and gentle and wise,
Someone who is a little boy in disguise.
Someone I love much more than life,
Someone I'm glad chose me for his wife.

Mildred C. Dorn

CONTINUUM

Perplexed opposites
are neither attractions
nor repulsions —
but predestined continua:
      age is extended youth the young
      yield to master maturity.
      And night is extended day
      as light leaps into darkness
      and dusk delivers dawn.
Thus birth is a dash toward deep death,
but optimists drearily dream death
extends to everlasting Life —
      a dear delight.

I. V. Barrett

FRIENDSHIP

A heavenly feeling
  of loving embrace,
    to ease all pain
that will hit
  any time and place,
    in sunshine or rain.

An everlasting love
  that is strong,
    shared 'til the end
with care and understanding
  through right or wrong,
    is finding a friend.

Henry M. Grouten

PERHAPS

Did you ever
gaze out the window,
blot out all light
so no one
could see in
and only you
could peer
into the darkness
and watch the
headlights
of passing cars
streak obscurity?
Then hope no one will stop?

Karen Gail Zasky

MOON THOUGHTS

Tonight the moon is so very bright;
That all the stars are out of sight.
It is full — and it has come
With light reflected from the sun.
A strange fascination is always there;
And beauty indescribable — for all to share.
What if God would let loose this one string?
It would, without a doubt, great sadness bring.
Instead of being in its usual place —
The moon would; say; another planet face.
It would not be there to catch the light
Thrown from the sun — this lovely sight.
How God keeps it — and all the stars
In their same course — yes, even Mars.
A part of God's plan — for such it is;
The moon, the stars — even we are His.
This thing I marvel at the most —
How it is so — this perfect host —
It comes — it goes — will it always last —
Now — and tomorrow — as in ages past?

Gladys V. Harter

TIMMY TURTLE

One day I caught our baby terrapin
Right in the middle of his feeding tray.
He looked up startled, for all the world,
Like a small boy with his hand in the cookie jar.
He took a few nibbles of succulent steak —
That was even better than a juicy grasshopper.
He tried the tomato, banana, and the cantaloupe —
That was food fit for even turtle gods!
He helped himself to another big slug:
Then wiped his chin with his tiny hands.
He cocked one eye at me, as if to say "Thanks,"
As he headed out across the lawn,
Backpacking his funny little hogan,
And dived into his cake-pan swimming pool,
Took a big drink, and climbed out on the other side,
His shell glistening as with a thousand gems.
He trundled off like a dollar-sized armored tank,
To his favorite haunt under the boysenberry bush.
He snuggled into his wee house, and shut the door,
And was off to Happy Turtle Dreamland for a nap!

Lois Carden

ON DEATH OF FIREFLIES

it is raining.
a rainbow refuses to form in the distance
the rain is of the gutters — pungent ebony.
it has not yet reached where i am standing
(east of nowhere,
west of everywhere)
i am watching it
pound against the city.
i see my children
running for shelter
i want to hold them in my arms,
they will be, again, in my womb.
i want them to know,
to feel as i am —
i want them to be me.

tonight, there will be no rain.
in the dark
there shall be death wasted
in the edge of the gutters.

Nancy A. Dolan

LAND'S END

I live at the edge of the earth
For here is beauty & sadness
Spun together with the sea, the sand,
And the ghostly mist

I walk on the edge of the earth
For the earth is green, moist, & soft
It bears my weight like a close friend
Gently, & with silence

I dance on the edge of the earth
For dancing is sacred to the Mother Goddess
Her spirit is with us when we create
And her beauty shines through our dancing

I love at the edge of the earth
For the women are pure & free
And choose to love & trust those
Who seek wisdom through love

I weep at the edge of the earth
For weeping is holy
And sharing tears with a friend
Can bring hearts closer to love.

Surra Tregarth

IN AWE

LORD, I walked through the cemetery today,
And my heart was in awe of such a wondrous display.
There where the dead peacefully lie,
Life abounded from earth to sky.
Grass grew, flowers bloomed,
Birds flew and sang melodious tunes.
Tree branches swayed gently in the wind,
A worker on a tractor waved and grinned.
There were people there to bury their dead,
With tearful eyes, grieving hearts,
And so many words unsaid.
As I beheld the beauty near and far,
I was reminded how truly great Thou are.
The roaring splendor and complexity, yet quiet simplicity
made it all so very clear to me.
This world did not come into being by some cosmic accident above,
But was created and is continually controlled
By Your amazing grace and boundless love.

Dorothy Hemphill Edwards

SHADOWS ACROSS THE SNOW

As drab wiry branches cast their dark shadows
   Across the glittering white melting snow
My memory goes back to the sweet, sweet yesterdays
   And loving thoughts of the long, long ago.

I see a small farmhouse nestled so snugly there
   Surrounded by the heavy snows of the past
A fire burning brightly in our small fireplace
   Memories of a family love that will always last.

I remember icicles hanging firmly from the roof
   In the snow, tracks of all sorts for us to see
While cozy warmth fills the inside of our house
   As I feel my family's love and care for me.

It's true that this is really all long gone
   But today when snow begins again to fall
I live once more in a child's fairy-like past
   And my loved ones are there — I see them all.

Memories lie dormant to come forth in the shadows
   And I see once again my life as a happy child
Each new snowflake stirs a memory inside my heart
   I remind myself that the past is only memories filed.

Grace W. Shaw

BRIDAL SUITE

Before Christ died some had gone to hell;
after which he went down and paid their bail.
He then went home to God on the right
and for us intercedes both day and night.
He has prepared a place lived never,
where we can see his glory and be with him forever.
Then we will be his bride and he our groom,
for thieves and robbers there will be no room.
There'll be no such thing as weak and strong,
there'll be no difference between the old and young.
We'll be singing a brand-new song,
and all speaking with one tongue.
I read in His Word and I believe what He saith,
there be no sadness, but praise, praise, praise.

Gerald Faye Gardner

WHEN LOVE GROWS BEST

This is the moment love has waited for:
The soft wind sings its old familiar song
Of that sweet interlude that comes once more
Where gentle flowers and darting birds belong.

It is the interlude of lifting hearts,
As springtime warms away the winter's traces,
Where love now lurks in unexpected places,
And all of beauty, and all of dreaming starts.

There is no turning back from this swift hour
To old regrets and sorrows we have known,
Or that elusive dream that somehow failed to flower.
When love grows best, today is all we own.

John L. Warren

I GOT RID OF YOU

Southland giving tips on horses at the tracks.
Hample's actions aroused the police.
On his advice, a lady bought a losing ticket
He flew the coop.
In another city, to his bride to be, he lied.
In hope of making some fast money, Hample
was brought before the judge.
A fine, and ten days in jail was his decision.
If he doesn't pay the money when it's due,
He's going to be a person that his bride once knew.
Hample went away, plus finding a place to stay,
Collected the money as promised, then made those
hoods pay.
          Then He said, "I got rid of you!"

Sauls Suzzs

PAUSE

Feel the gentle, soul-warming touch of the sun,
    Enjoy the kiss of the breeze.
Hear the lullaby of a stream on the run.
    Smell the wood-scent of the trees.

Your touch on my skin is like that of the sun.
    Your voice is a sound to please.
Your kiss on my lips is a song just begun,
    Touch my soul and fill my needs.

Shine the brilliant light of your eyes upon me,
    Grace my day with your smile,
Share your understanding, willing mind with me,
    Pause; rest here with me, awhile.

Ouida Quay Martin

OH, TO BE A CHILD AGAIN

Oh, to be a child again, a little child at play.
To run and jump and hide and laugh all the livelong day.
To wonder at the things I see and gaze into the sky.
To see a bird, a cloud, a plane and sit to wonder why?
To lie within a shady glade amidst the tall green grass;
To feel the beauty that is there and allow the day to pass.
Not to know that there is war and other things that men must face.
I long to be a child again; To be free from man's disgrace.

David W. Perry

OUR CHRISTMAS GIFT FROM GOD

While church bells ring out — Silent night holy night the music
Sight glo-ri-ous light Heav-en host sing Al-le-lu-ia: Son of God
Love's pure holy face baby — Jesus — our Lord and Savior at the
Christmas birth — God's gift to His mother and father, earth our
Re-deem-ing grace and song, God's love to His King-dom, as
In heav-en to-day and forever and ever.
I wish I were an angel too the night of Jesus' birth so I
Could have sung the glo-ri-ous song to welcome Him to earth — life glory.

Lena T. Shubert

A MAN WITHOUT A HOME

I'm as a wanderer roaming o'er the wastelands,
I'm like a man without a home.
In a world of hidden secrets, tales are blown
without a fan.
When the evening shadows beckon to my place in
the unknown —
Will I still wander through the wastelands,
like a man without a home?

Retta M. Smith

ASSURANCE

Festal rivulet bobolinked merrily 'gainst
    ice-gripped shoulders — chuckling —
Carving its burbling way atween
    Stately pines and Lady birches
Vigilantly overseeing the scene
    Prairie warblers brustled in snaggy shrubs
Cerulean sky twinkled encouragement
    Earth lifted quiet eyes.

Helen deLong Woodward

ASKING

"Lord, did you know all these things would happen to me?"
Holding my grandchild against my heart,
Warmth of friends, those nearby others miles apart.
Walking in the dark Summer rain,
Watching my loved ones die in pain.
Can you hear my anguished plea?
Perhaps it's the only way I can pray, Lord
When Life has beaten me to my knees.

Hilda Adams Bonebrake Suter

TIME

Time is the invention of man trying to trap illusion. Can we know that
What we are seemingly experiencing at this instant didn't occur light years
In the past or in the future, or that it isn't occurring at all?
The "supposed reality" of the present is important only because of the
Essence of the moment. Maybe all is illusion created solely in the mind of
The master craftsman!

Mary Annah Alemán

LIFE-SUPPORT

You
    I wonder how so good a person came
    into my life to spark a flame
Love's golden hues caress an anxious heart
Somersaults and flip-flops
    say youth still remains
As you look into my eyes and
    whisper my name

    Carol J. Smith

THE SUN

A glowing ball of fire,
Hung high up in the sky,
Shining for the day life,
We sometimes wonder why
This great big ball of fire
Came to us and then,
In 50 million years
Will go away from us again.

    Brian Dawson

AS YOUR DAY SO SHALL YOUR STRENGTH BE

"They'll feel it later," someone said,
When we held high each fire-shocked head.
Yet through the loss of all our things,
Each soul acquired new-found wings
And strength to fly where few could dare,
Upheld by His unfaltering care
Who daily makes His grace to show
And wisely gives us room to grow.

    Elizabeth Brandt Hunter

HARSH PATH

Sharp stones under my feet
Point out the road to take.
I pause to interrupt the beat . . .
Sharp stones under my feet.
Terror is greater than the heat;
I remember what is at stake.
Sharp stones under my feet
Point out the road to take.

    Ellen Monhart

VERMONT WINTER

Winter is falling in white silence.
Snowflakes dance in the air,
Kissing my hair and face.
Then softly they touch the ground
With gentle grace.
The once sparkling rivers
Lie frozen and still,
Winter has come to the beckoning hills.

    Betty Wilkerson

FULFILLMENT

    The days are gone, there'll be no more,
For the years have given me my full score
of love and laughter, joy and tears,
and helped me live through all life's fears.
    So "Just Remember," life's worth living,
For every moment it has given.

    Nellie W. McLean

JON-ERIK HEXUM WHY WAS HIS LIFE SHORT?

Jon-Erik Hexum gave up living, his reasons for what happened was not
Known by his friends it was in him. And it was only known in him.
To me I will never know the reason why I just know he is gone like
my Grandfather, there one day gone the next. It just makes me mad,
angry to know that he is gone for good. When, I think about Jon-Erik
Hexum if he had a second chance what would happen to Michael
Washington who received his heart and a new life.

Chris Roney

SUNGLASSES

I think that I will wear my sunglasses
Today — dark brown and shatterproof,
Shatterproof so that stray bullets may not
Crack them from another man's gun
And break down the shield I have built to hide
My eyes and the pain that they hold.

Carol Sturman

BIRTHDAY SONG — TO PEGGY

How,
in the starflight of this earth
just twenty-three full cycles
'round the sun,
has such a miracle been done?

Here,
in this present time, you are
full-blown and rich with beauty
like a flower,
and full of mystery and power!

Yet,
just a score of sun-swung flights
ago you were a seedling
crying red
and squalling helpless in your bed.

God!
That the passage of so small
a sample of transforming,
plastic Time
could work this miracle sublime!

Hal Barrett

BARRETT, HAROLD F. JR. Pen Name: "Hal" Barrett; Born: Dayton, Ohio, 12-13-19;
Married: 3-1-69 to Kathryn M. Lohrentz; Education: Occidental College, Los Angeles;
Pasadena City College with AA degree, June 1950; American University, Washington,
D. C.; Sinclair Community College, Dayton, Ohio; Occupations: Tool and Die Maker,
Naval Inspector, Engineering Aide, Labor Organizer and Service Representative, Executive Secretary to National Advisory Committee, Professor of Labor Studies, Church
Music Director and Composer; Memberships; UUA, IAM&AW, SFLRP, U-U United
Nations Office, Dayton Art Institute Board; Awards: Sigma Zeta Psi award for "Creative
Writing," 1950, Occidental College campus poetry award for poem, 'Sonnet II,' 1952;
Poetry: *Song of My Heart,* collection of poetry, Oasis, Phoenix, Arizon, copyrighted
1944; Other Writings: *To Natalie: in Memoriam,* "synoptic" tale of life/death of child,
Oasis, Los Angeles, 1954; "Fruit of the Spirit," short story, in *The Clarion,* Pasadena,
California (Presbyterian Church), 1946; Text/music to numerous hymns, anthems, "pop"
songs used in church and lay life situations; numerous sermons, speeches, on topics from
labor relations to psychological insight; Comments: *The unreality of institutions* vis à vis
the experiencing Self"; the importance of remembering that human beings are the subjects
of the economic and political system, not *the objects (it is for human beings that these
institutions exist and get their justification; people do not exist for the institutions, institutions exist to serve humankind ("Man is not made for the Sabbath, the Sabbath is made
for Man!"). I am as much essayist as poet, and will use* any *medium available to try to
communicate the ideas generally expressed above.*

HOMER, On the Beach

D

E

F

G